from the

MODERN REPERTOIRE

Series Three

PLAYS IN THIS VOLUME

Leonce and Lena by Georg Büchner; *A Door Should Be either Open or Shut* by Alfred de Musset; *Thérèse Raquin* by Emile Zola; *The Magistrate* by Arthur W. Pinero; *Anatol* by Arthur Schnitzler; *Dr. Knock* by Jules Romains; *Saint Joan of the Stockyards* by Bertolt Brecht; *Intimate Relations* by Jean Cocteau; *Cecile, or The School for Fathers* by Jean Anouilh; *The Cretan Woman* by Robinson Jeffers.

PLAYS IN SERIES ONE

Fantasio by Alfred de Musset; *Danton's Death* by Georg Büchner; *La Parisienne* by Henry Becque; *Round Dance* by Arthur Schnitzler; *The Snob* by Carl Sternheim; *Sweeney Agonistes* by T. S. Eliot; *The Threepenny Opera* by Bertolt Brecht; *The Love of Don Perlimplin and Belisa in the Garden* by Federico García Lorca; *The Infernal Machine* by Jean Cocteau; *A Full Moon in March* by W. B. Yeats.

PLAYS IN SERIES TWO

Jest, Satire, Irony, and Deeper Significance by Christian Grabbe; *Easy Money* by Alexander Ostrovsky; *The Epidemic* by Octave Mirbeau; *The Marquis of Keith* by Frank Wedekind; *him* by e. e. cummings; *Venus and Adonis* by André Obey; *Electra* by Jean Giraudoux; *The King and the Duke* by Francis Fergusson; *The Dark Tower* by Louis MacNeice; *Galileo* by Bertolt Brecht.

EDITED BY ERIC BENTLEY

From the
MODERN REPERTOIRE
Series Three

INDIANA UNIVERSITY PRESS / BLOOMINGTON

*This collection is dedicated to the
memory of Bertolt Brecht (1898–1956)*

FOREWORD

THE present volume brings the total number of plays From the Modern Repertoire up to thirty. I believe that the ten plays in Series Three are of the same caliber as those in Series One and Series Two. They are certainly as unavailable elsewhere. *The Magistrate*, which, like *Dandy Dick* and unlike *The Second Mrs. Tanqueray*, represents Pinero at his best, has long been out of print in this country; so has the famous Granville-Barker version of *Anatol;* and Jules Romains' famous *Dr. Knock* (also Englished by Granville-Barker). Musset's *A Door Should Be either Open or Shut* and Zola's *Thérèse Raquin*, classics of the French drama, are not only out of print; they needed complete retranslation; and have been retranslated especially for inclusion in this volume. *Saint Joan of the Stockyards, Intimate Relations*, and *Cecile, or The School for Fathers*, outstanding continental plays of more recent date, have never before been published in English; none of the three has yet been performed in America. *The Cretan Woman*, surely one of the finest of American plays, lay hidden in a volume of the author's poems. (One wishes that, for theatre people, a volume of poems were not a hiding place, but it is.) Though successfully produced in Greenwich Village, *The Cretan Woman* has appeared neither in a separate volume nor in any other anthology of drama. Of my own version of *Leonce and Lena*, it would be improper to say more than that it is the first American one to be published.

E. B.
New York City
Winter, 1955–56

ACKNOWLEDGMENTS

PERMISSION to print (or reprint as the case may be) was kindly given by the following:

A Door Should Be either Open or Shut: Jacques Barzun.
Thérèse Raquin: Margery Vosper Ltd.
Anatol: Curtis Brown Ltd.
Dr. Knock: Field Roscoe & Co.
Saint Joan of the Stockyards: Bertolt Brecht and Frank Jones.
Cecile, or The School for Fathers: Dr. Jan Van Loewen.
Intimate Relations: Dr. Jan Van Loewen.
The Cretan Woman: Random House Inc.

I should like to thank all those who have suggested plays for inclusion here, whether or not I finally followed their advice, and I should like to thank the Indiana University Press, particularly its director Mr. Bernard B. Perry, for taking over FROM THE MODERN REPERTOIRE when the University of Denver Press, its original publisher, went out of business. This is the first volume in the series to come out under Indiana auspices but, if Mr. Perry and I have our way, it will not be the last.

E. B.

CONTENTS

Leonce and Lena

A Comedy in Three Acts

by GEORG BÜCHNER

English version by Eric Bentley

ALFIERI: E la Fama?
GOZZI: E la Fame?

ILLUSTRATED BY PETER LARKIN

CHARACTERS

KING PETER *of the Kingdom of Popo*
PRINCE LEONCE, his son
PRINCESS LENA *of the Kingdom of Peepee,*
  betrothed to PRINCE LEONCE
VALERIO
THE GOVERNESS
THE PRIVATE TUTOR
THE MASTER OF CEREMONIES
THE PRESIDENT OF THE COUNCIL OF STATE
THE COURT CHAPLAIN
THE PRESIDENT OF THE DISTRICT BOARD
THE SCHOOLMASTER
ROSETTA
SERVANTS, COUNCILLORS, PEASANTS, ETC.

Note on pronunciation of names: The present version being in English, there is no more reason to say Lena in the German way (*Layna*) than to say Peter in the German way (*Payter*). Full Anglicization is recommended: L*ee*na, L*ee*-unce, Val*ee*rio.

ACT ONE

O that I were a fool!
I am ambitious for a motley coat!
—As You Like It

SCENE 1

LEONCE, *half lying on a bench. His* PRIVATE TUTOR.

LEONCE. Well, what do you want from me, sir? You'd like to prepare me for my calling? I'm afraid I have my hands full already, I've more work than I know how to get through. First I have to spit on this stone three hundred and sixty-five times in a row. Did you ever try it? Go ahead. It is peculiarly entertaining. Then again, you see this handful of sand? *He picks up some sand, throws it in the air, catches it on the back of his hand.*

I throw it in the air. Shall we bet? How many grains on the back of my hand—odd or even number?—What? You don't want to bet? Are you a pagan? Do you believe in God? I usually just bet against myself, and I get along pretty well, but if you could find me someone else to bet against once in a while, you'd certainly be doing me a great favor. Then too, I have to figure out how I can contrive to see the top of my head. If a man could but see the top of his own head! That is one of my ideals, it would set my heart at rest. Then too—yes, then infinitely more too. Am I an idler? Do I have nothing to do? Indeed, it is sad . . .

TUTOR. Very sad, your highness.

LEONCE. . . . it is very sad that the clouds have been moving from west to east for three weeks running. It makes me quite melancholy.

TUTOR. And well it might, your highness.

LEONCE. Why don't you contradict me, man? You have urgent business, haven't you? Sorry to have kept you so long.

The TUTOR *withdraws with a low bow.*

When you bow, dear sir, your legs form a beautiful parenthesis. My congratulations! *Alone, he stretches out on the bench.* The bees sit lazily

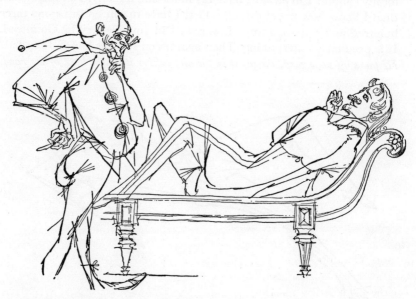

on the flowers, the sunshine lies idly on the ground, a terrible idleness rages!—Idleness is the starting-point of all the vices. What people won't do out of boredom! They study from boredom, they pray from boredom, they fall in love, marry, are fruitful and multiply from boredom, later on they die from boredom, and all this—which is the cream of the jest—without in the least knowing why, though they keep a straight face and think their own thoughts, and what thoughts! These heroes, these geniuses, these blockheads, these saints, these sinners, these heads of families are, one and all, nothing but sophisticated idlers.—Now why must *I* know this? Why me in particular? Why can't

I be important to myself and dress up this poor puppet of a body in a tail coat and put an umbrella in its hand to make sure it's very law-abiding and very useful and very moral. As a jester I'm a fiasco. Then again, why can't I look serious when I make my jokes? This fellow who just left—oh, I envy *him*, I could give him a beating, I envy him so much. If only one could be somebody else for once! Just for a minute!——

VALERIO, *a little drunk, enters.*

How that man runs! If only I knew of anything that could still make *me* run!

VALERIO, *coming right in front of the prince, puts one finger to his nose, and stares at him.* Yes!

LEONCE, *also staring.* Correct!

VALERIO. You take my meaning?

LEONCE. Perfectly.

VALERIO. Then let's change the subject. Meanwhile I shall lie on the greensward and let my nose blossom above the blades of grass and get romantic notions when bees and butterflies light on it—

> As if a nose
> Were a rose!

LEONCE. Don't breathe so hard, my dear fellow, or the bees and butterflies will starve: the flowers are their snuffbox, and you're taking great pinches of the snuff.

VALERIO. Oh sir, how much feeling I have for Nature! The grass, for instance. It's so beautiful, I'd like to be an ox to eat it, and then become a man again to eat the ox that ate the grass.

LEONCE. Unhappy man! You, too, seem to labor under ideals!

VALERIO. [*Do I! For eight days now I have run after the ideal of beef without in reality meeting with a single slice. *He sings.*

> Our hostess has a merry maid
> That sits in her garden night and day
> That sits and sits in her garden
> Till twelve o'clock has chimed away
> And the infantry comes ma-arching.

He sits down on the ground. Look at these ants! Is it not marvelous, children dear, the instinct we find in such tiny creatures? Order! Diligence!

* The passage in brackets, ending on page 7, is relegated to an appendix in the Insel edition, as belonging only to a draft.

—There are but three ways, dear sir, of earning money in a humane manner: finding it, winning it in a lottery, and inheriting it, though, of course, you could steal it if you were smart enough to be able to do so without compunction.

LEONCE. You have managed to grow fairly old on these principles without dying of hunger or on the gallows.

VALERIO, *still staring at him.* Oh yes, sir. And my contention is that whoever earns his living in any other way is a rogue.

LEONCE. For work is a subtle form of suicide, and a suicide is a criminal, and a criminal is a rogue. *Ergo*, whoever works is a rogue.

VALERIO. Correct.—And yet ants are a very useful sort of vermin, though not so useful as they would be if they did no harm at all. Nevertheless, worthy vermin, I cannot deny myself the pleasure of kicking some of you on the behind with my heel, wiping your noses, and cutting your nails.

Enter two policemen.

FIRST. Stop! Where is the fellow?

SECOND. There are two.

FIRST. Take a look if anyone's running away.

SECOND. I think no one is.

FIRST. Then we must question them both.—Gentlemen, we are looking for someone, a subject, an individual, a person, a delinquent, a suspect, a fellow. *To* SECOND. Take a look if anyone's started blushing.

SECOND. No one's started blushing.

FIRST. Then we must try something else.—Where is the warrant, the description, the certificate? SECOND *takes a paper out of his pocket and hands it over.* You check these subjects! I'll do the reading. "A man . . ."

SECOND. *A* man? There are two.

FIRST. Blockhead! "A man walks on two feet, has two arms and, to boot, one mouth, one nose, two eyes, two ears. Special characteristics: a highly dangerous individual."

SECOND. That applies to both. Shall I arrest them both?

FIRST. Two? That's dangerous. There are only two of *us*. I'm going to make a report. It's a case of very criminal complication or very complicated criminality. For if I get myself drunk and lie on my bed, that's no one else's business, it's my affair. But if I have to sell the bed to pay for the drinks, then it *is* someone else's business, but *whose*, you rascal?

SECOND. Well, I wouldn't know.

FIRST. I wouldn't know either, but that's the point.

Exeunt both.

VALERIO. And there are people who don't believe in Providence! Think what you can achieve with a single flea! For if this flea hadn't run across me last night, I wouldn't have carried my bed out in the sun this morning. And if I hadn't carried my bed out in the sun this morning, I'd never have got to the Moon Tavern. And if sun and moon hadn't shone on the bed, I could never have pressed the wine out of the mattress and got drunk on it. And if none of all this had happened, I wouldn't be in your company now, worthy ants, letting you pick my bones bare and leave my skeleton to dry in the sun. No, I'd be cutting myself a slice of meat and drying up a bottle of wine—in the hospital, naturally.

LEONCE. "The course of true love never did run smooth."

VALERIO. The wars were running pretty smooth, and the enemy would have run a bullet through me if I hadn't been so handy at running for cover. But anything to save a life. I ran till I had the galloping consumption, at any rate that's what the doctor thought. But of course I *had* to let consumption consume me if I for my part was to consume good soup, good beef, good bread, good wine, and save the life of a patriot and a soldier.] What a pity one can't jump from a church steeple without breaking one's neck! One can't even eat four pounds of cherries complete with the pits and not get belly-ache! Look, sir, I could sit in a corner and all night long to the end of my days sing:

> Hey! Just look at that fly on the wall
> Fly on the wall
> Fly on the wall

—and so on.

LEONCE. Oh shut up with your song! It could make a fool of a man.

VALERIO. Then a man would be something. A fool! A fool! Who will trade me his folly for my reason?—Ha! I'm Alexander the Great! The sun seems a golden crown on my hair, and just look how my uniform glitters! Generalissimo Grasshopper, let the troops advance! Finance Minister Spider, I need money! Lady-in-Waiting Dragonfly, what is my dear wife Beanstalk a-doing of? My good Court Physician Cantharides, I'm in need of an heir to the throne! And on top of these rare fantasies, one gets good soup, good meat, good bread, a good bed and one's hair cut for nothing—in the madhouse, naturally—while with my reason intact I could at best sell my services to a cherry tree for the promotion of ripeness in order to—well?—in order to?

LEONCE. To make the cherry trees turn red with shame at the holes in your trousers. But, noblest one, your craft, your profession, your trade, your rank, your art?

VALERIO, *with dignity.* Sir, what keeps me so busy is idling. I am very good at doing absolutely nothing. I have an infinite capacity for laziness. My hands were never desecrated by a callus, nor has my brow ever given the earth a drop to drink. In work, I am a virgin. And I would take the trouble to explain these merits of mine to you in greater detail, if indeed the trouble were not too much trouble.

LEONCE, *with comic enthusiasm.* Let me clasp you to my bosom! Are you one of those godlike beings who walk the great highway of this life untroubled, with a clear brow, and who, like the blessèd gods themselves, enter Olympus with gleaming feet and blooming bodies? Come! Come!

VALERIO, *singing as he leaves.*

Hey! Just look at that fly on the wall
Fly on the wall
Fly on the wall

Exeunt both, arm in arm.

SCENE 2

A room. KING PETER *is being dressed by two valets.*

KING PETER, *as the dressing proceeds.* Man must think, and I must think for my subjects; for they don't think, they don't think.—Substance is the thing-in-itself, that's me. *He runs about the room nearly naked.* Is that understood? "In-itself" means "in-itself," do you understand? Then come my attributes, qualifications, affections, and accidental properties. Where is my shirt, where are my trousers? Stop! Pah! Free will's flies are undone! Where is morality? Where are my French cuffs? The categories have been shamelessly confused. Two buttons too many have been buttoned. The snuffbox is in my right-hand pocket. My whole system is ruined!—Ha! What does the button in this handkerchief mean? Fellow, what does the button mean, what did I want to remind myself of?

FIRST VALET. When your majesty deigned to tie this button in your handkerchief you wanted——

KING PETER. Well?

FIRST VALET. To remind yourself of something.

KING PETER. A complicated answer!—Indeed! Well, and what do *you* think?

SECOND VALET. Your majesty wanted to remind yourself of something when you deigned to tie this button in your handkerchief.

KING PETER *runs up and down*. What? What? Human beings get me all mixed up. I am in the utmost confusion. I am at my wit's end.

Enter a servant.

SERVANT. The Council of State is met, your majesty.

KING PETER, *joyfully.* That's it, that's it, of course: I wanted to remind myself of my people!—Come, gentlemen. Walk symmetrically! Isn't it very hot? Then take your handkerchiefs and wipe your faces! I'm always so embarrassed when I'm to speak in public!

Exeunt omnes.

Re-enter KING PETER, *this time with the Council of State.*

KING PETER. Beloved friends, faithful retainers, I wanted to announce and make known—announce and make known—for my son either gets married or he doesn't—*with one finger to his nose*—either, or—you do understand me? There's no third way out. Man must think. *Stands musing for a while.* When I speak my thoughts aloud this way, I don't

know who's speaking, myself or someone else. And this frightens me. *After prolonged musing.* I am I.——What do you think of that, Mr. President?

PRESIDENT, *with slow gravity.* Perhaps it is so, your majesty. But perhaps it is also not so.

WHOLE COUNCIL OF STATE IN CHORUS. Yes! Perhaps it is so! But perhaps it is also not so!

KING PETER, *moved.* My wise men!—Well then, what were we talking about? What was I trying to make a speech about? President, why do you have so short a memory on so solemn an occasion? The meeting is adjourned.

He solemnly withdraws, the whole Council of State following him.

SCENE 3

A richly decorated hall. Candles are burning. LEONCE *with several servants.*

LEONCE. Are all the shutters closed? Light the candles! Away with the day, I want night, deep, ambrosial night! Put the lamps under crystal shades among the oleanders so that they peep dreamily out from under the leaves like eyes from under girlish lashes! Bring the roses closer that the wine may sparkle on their petals like dew-drops! Music! Where are the violins? Where is Rosetta?—Away! All of you, away!

Exeunt servants. LEONCE *stretches out on a couch. Prettily dressed,* ROSETTA *enters. Music from the distance.*

ROSETTA, *approaching with flattering mien.* Leonce!

LEONCE. Rosetta!

ROSETTA. Leonce!

LEONCE. Rosetta!

ROSETTA. Your lips are lazy. From kissing?

LEONCE. From yawning.

ROSETTA. Oh!

LEONCE. Oh, Rosetta, I am faced with the terrible task . . .

ROSETTA. Yes, what?

LEONCE. Of doing nothing . . .

ROSETTA. But loving?

LEONCE. A task indeed!

ROSETTA, *offended.* Leonce!

LEONCE. Or an occupation.

ROSETTA. Or pure idleness.

LEONCE. You are right as always. You're a clever girl. I set great store by your perspicacity.

ROSETTA. You love me then out of sheer boredom?

LEONCE. No. I feel boredom because I love you. But I love my boredom as I love you—the two of you are one. *O dolce far niente!* Your eyes are deep and hidden magic springs, I sit dreaming over them. Your caressing lips lull me to sleep like the rushing of waves. *He embraces her.* Come, dearest boredom, your kisses are a voluptuous yawning, and your steps a pretty hiatus.

ROSETTA. You love me, Leonce?

LEONCE. Why not, indeed?

ROSETTA. Forever?

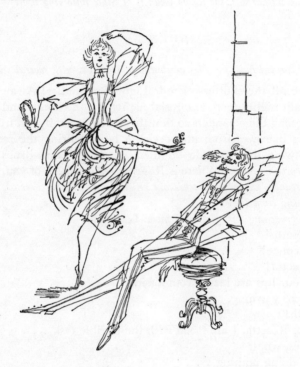

LEONCE. That is a long word: forever. If I love you five thousand years and seven months, will that do? It's a lot less than forever, but at that it's quite a time: we could take our time at loving each other.

ROSETTA. Or time could take our love from us.

LEONCE. Or love our time from us. Dance, Rosetta, dance!

> That time may move with the beat
> Of your small attractive feet.

ROSETTA. My feet would rather be out of time. *She dances and sings.*

> Tired feet of mine, must you dance
> So gaily shod
> When you would rather quiet lie
> Beneath the sod?
>
> Hot cheeks of mine, must you glow
> In the night
> When you would rather be
> Two roses white?
>
> Poor eyes of mine, must you flash
> In torch-lit park
> When you would rather sleep away your pain
> In the dark?

LEONCE, *dreaming away to himself, meanwhile.* Oh, a dying love is more beautiful than a budding one! I am a Roman: at a fine banquet, during the dessert, golden fishes are sporting in colors of death. See the color die in her cheeks, the light in her eyes go out! How gentle the undulation of her limbs, their rising and falling! *Addio, addio,* my love, I will love your dead body. ROSETTA *approaches him again.* Tears, Rosetta? A delicate Epicureanism—to be able to cry! Stand in the sun so the fine drops will crystallize—they'll make splendid diamonds— you can have yourself a necklace made of them.

ROSETTA. Diamonds, yes. They cut into my eyes. Oh, Leonce! *She tries to embrace him.*

LEONCE. Look out! My head! I have buried my love in it. Look in through the windows of my eyes. You see how dead the poor thing is? You see the two white roses on its cheeks, the two red ones on its breast? Don't push me or it will break an arm, and that would be a shame. I have to carry my head very straight on my shoulders, the way the undertaker woman* carries a child's coffin.

ROSETTA, *playfully.* Fool!

LEONCE. Rosetta! ROSETTA *makes a face at him.* Thank God! *He keeps his eyes shut.*

ROSETTA, *scared.* Leonce, look at me!

LEONCE. Not for anything.

ROSETTA. Just one look!

---

* Strictly, the layer-out, but this term is no longer familiar.

LEONCE. Not a one. What are you after? One little thing like that, and my belovèd love would come back to life again. I am happy to have buried it. I retain the impression.

ROSETTA, *going sadly and slowly away, sings in parting*.

> The poorest orphan child am I
> Afraid, all, all alone
> Grief, my darling
> Will you not come with me home?

LEONCE, *alone*. It's a funny thing about love. You lie half-awake in bed for a full year, then one fine morning you wake, drink a glass of water, put your clothes on, pass your hand lightly over your brow, and be-think yourself—bethink yourself.—Heavens, how many women must one have in order to sing the whole scale of love? One woman can hardly manage a single tone. Why is the vapor around our earth a prism breaking the white ray of love into a rainbow?——*He drinks*. In which bottle is the wine I'm to get drunk on today? Can't I even do that any more? I feel as if I were under an air pump. The air is so sharp and thin, I'm freezing—as if I were to go skating in nankeen trousers.—Gentlemen, gentlemen, do *you* know what Caligula and Nero were like? *I* do.—Come on, Leonce, do me a monologue, I'll be a good listener. My life yawns at me like a great white piece of a paper that I should cover all over with writing, and I don't get a word written, not a letter. My head is an empty dance hall—a few faded roses and crumpled ribbons on the floor—burst violins in the corner—the last dancers have taken their masks off and are looking at each other, their eyes are dead tired. I turn myself inside out twenty-four times a day like a glove. Oh, I know myself, I know what I shall think and dream in a quarter of an hour, in a week, in a year. Lord God, what crime have I committed that You make me do my lesson over so often like a schoolboy?—Bravo, Leonce, bravo! *He claps*. It really does me good to call out to myself like this. Hey, Leonce, Leonce!

VALERIO, *from under a table*. Your highness seems to me well on the way to becoming a *bona fide* fool.

LEONCE. Looked at under the light, that's how it seems to me too.

VALERIO. Wait, we must discuss it more thoroughly in a minute. I've only to eat one more piece of meat that I stole from your kitchen and drink one more glass of wine that I stole from your cellar, and I'll be right with you.

LEONCE. How the fellow smacks his lips, he gives me the most idyllic sensations, I could go back to the beginning and start with the simplest things, eat cheese, drink beer, smoke tobacco. Go ahead, but don't grunt so with that snout, don't make such a racket with those tusks!

VALERIO. Are you afraid for your thighs, most worthy Adonis? Don't worry, I'm neither a broombinder nor a schoolmaster, I don't need twigs for my rods.

LEONCE. You leave nothing unpaid for.

VALERIO. I wish the same could be said of my lord.

LEONCE. You mean I owe you a thrashing? Are you so concerned for your upbringing?

VALERIO. Heavens, we are more easily brought *into* the world than brought *up* in the world. If our first condition is foetal, our second is fatal, isn't that sad? If a man—like an oration—is easy to conceive but hard to deliver . . .

LEONCE. O foul conception when *you* were conceived! Find yourself a better mode of *ex*pression or I'll give you an *im*pression of all the *op*pression that I . . .

VALERIO. What about this? "At the time that my mother was rounding the Cape of Good Hope . . ."

LEONCE. And your father was being shipwrecked on Cape Horn . . .

VALERIO. He *did* have a horn, he was a night watchman. But he didn't put that horn to his lips as often as he put the other one on the heads of noble sons' fathers.

LEONCE. Man, your impudence is heavenly: I feel a certain need to come into closer touch with it. I'm in the grip of a passion—to thrash you.

VALERIO. That is a very striking answer.

LEONCE, *making for him.* Yes, I'll do the striking, and you'll be struck!

VALERIO *is running away when* LEONCE *stumbles and falls.* You are a proof that has yet to be proved, for it falls over its own legs, which certainly are unproven. Those are extremely improbable calves and highly problematic thighs.

Enter the Council of State. LEONCE *remains on the floor.*

PRESIDENT. Forgive us, your highness . . .

LEONCE. As I do myself; I forgive myself for good-naturedly listening to you. Won't you take your places, gentlemen? Just sit on the ground and don't be embarrassed, it's the place where you'll take your place for the last time one day, and it yields nothing to anyone, unless it's the gravedigger.

PRESIDENT, *snapping his fingers in his embarrassment.* Would your highness deign . . .

LEONCE. Don't snap your fingers like that unless you want to make a murderer of me!

PRESIDENT, *snapping more and more violently*. Would you graciously take cognizance . . .

LEONCE. Heavens, stick your hands in your pockets! Or sit on them! He's quite beside himself. Pull yourself together!

VALERIO. One should never interrupt children in the act of pissing, they may get a complex.

LEONCE. Take a hold of yourself, man. Think of your family, think of the country! Let the words come out, it's dangerous to hold them in, you could have a stroke!

PRESIDENT *pulls a paper out of his pocket*. Your highness will permit . . .

LEONCE. Then you can read? Well now . . .

PRESIDENT. That the long-awaited arrival of your highness's betrothed, Her Serene Highness Princess Lena of Peepee, is expected to take place tomorrow—such is the message which His Royal Majesty wishes to convey to your highness.

LEONCE. If my bride awaits me, I'll defer to her wishes and let her wait. I saw her last night—in a dream. She had eyes so big my Rosetta's dancing slippers would have made them a fine pair of eyebrows. And, on her cheeks, instead of dimples, she had a number of ditches to drain off the laughter in. I believe in dreams. Do *you* dream, Mr. President, once in a while? Do you have premonitions?

VALERIO. It goes without saying. Always, the night before a roast burns, a capon drops dead, or His Royal Majesty gets the belly-ache.

LEONCE. By the way, did you have something else on the tip of your tongue? Pray say all you wanted to say.

PRESIDENT. On the day of the nuptials, it is the will of the Highest Will in the land to place the highest expression of that Highest Will in the hands of your highness.

LEONCE. Tell the Highest Will in the land that I shall do everything except what I shall leave undone, which will, however, not be as much, in any case, as if it were twice that amount.—Pardon me, gentlemen, if I don't accompany you myself. A passion for sitting down has just come over me, but my benevolence is so great that I can't measure it with my legs. *He spreads his legs out wide.* Will you take my measure, and remind me later what it was? Valerio, you accompany the gentlemen.

VALERIO. On what instrument? And can they sing? Are they a flock of singing birds in disguise?

LEONCE. Man, you are nothing but a bad pun. You have neither father nor mother, you were begotten by the five vowels.

VALERIO. And you, my prince, are a book with no words in it, nothing but dashes. And now, come, gentlemen! Isn't it sad about this word Come? If you want an *in*come, you have to steal, and the only *out*come of life is death: first you come up to the gallows, then you come down to your grave. Of course, an up-and-coming fellow can always give the oncoming, upcoming generation a becoming come-uppance, and all of us will somehow come through if we keep our wits about us and have nothing more to say, like me for instance right now, or you before you even open your mouth. And so, gentlemen, come!

Exeunt Council of State and VALERIO.

LEONCE, *alone.* How mean of me to act up like that before those poor devils! Though, of course, at times a certain enjoyment lurks in a certain meanness.—Hm! Getting married! It is to drink a well dry. O Shandy, old Shandy,* who will make me a present of your clock?——

VALERIO *returns.*

O dear, Valerio, have you heard?

VALERIO. Well, you're to be king. Which is a funny business. One can go driving for the whole day and make people ruin their hats through having to take them off all the time. Out of the cloth of law-abiding people one can cut law-abiding soldiers, just so everything will stay normal. One can make black tail coats and white cravats into servants of the state. And when one dies, shiny buttons turn blue, and the bell-ropes tear like cotton thread with all the tolling. Isn't that entertaining?

LEONCE. Valerio, Valerio! We must do something different. Advise me.

VALERIO. Science! Knowledge! Let us be scientists and philosophers! A priori? Or a posteriori?

LEONCE. A priori—that can be learnt from my father. And, a posteriori, everything starts like an old fairy tale: once upon a time there was.

VALERIO. Then let us be heroes! *He marches up and down, as with trumpet and drum.* Pom-pom-*pah*-plonk!

LEONCE. But heroism gets revolting tight, it catches a fever and has to be taken to hospital, it can't exist without lieutenants and recruits. Be off with your Alexander and Napoleon romanticism!

VALERIO. Then let us be geniuses!

LEONCE. The nightingale of poetry is at it over our heads all day, but the

---

* Tristram Shandy's father did his duty as a husband whenever he wound up his clock—once a month.

best of the stuff goes to the devil before we've pulled out her feathers and dipped them in ink or paint.

VALERIO. Then let us be useful members of human society!

LEONCE. I'd rather hand in my resignation as a human being.

VALERIO. Then let us go to the devil!

LEONCE. Alas, the devil is only there for the sake of contrast—so we'll grasp the idea that there's something to heaven. *Jumping up.* Ah!

Valerio, Valerio, I have it! Don't you feel a gentle breeze from the south? The undulation of a glowing and dark blue ether? Can't you see the light flashing from the sunny, golden ground, from marble columns, marble bodies, from the salt and sacred sea? Great Pan sleeps, and, in the shade, above the deep and rushing waters, bronze statues dream of the old magician Vergil, of tarentella and tambourine, and of mad, deep nights full of masks, torches, and guitars. A *lazzarone,** Valerio, a *lazzarone!* We're going to Italy!

* "One of the homeless idlers of Naples"—*Webster.*

SCENE 4

A garden. PRINCESS LENA *in her bridal clothes. The* GOVERNESS.

LENA. Yes: now! It's here. I thought of nothing the whole time. It drifted by, and now, of a sudden, this day of days looms up before me. I have the garland in my hair—and the bells, the bells! *She leans back and*

closes her eyes. Look, I wish the green grass were growing over my head with the bees murmuring above. Look, I'm all dressed, and the rosemary's in my hair. Isn't there an old song:

> Beneath a headstone I would rest
> Like a baby at its mother's breast?

GOVERNESS. How pale you are, my child, beneath those flashing stones!

LENA. Lord, Lord, I *could* love. Why not? The journey is very lonely, you reach out, hoping someone will take hold of your hand till the under-taker woman* comes and parts the clasped fingers and folds the hands of both of you, each on his separate breast. But why should a nail be driven through two hands that did not seek each other? What has my poor hand done? *She pulls a ring off her finger.* This ring stings me like an adder.

GOVERNESS. But—they say he's a real Don Carlos!

LENA. But—a man . . .

GOVERNESS. Well?

LENA. That one does not love. *She rises.* Pah! I feel ashamed, you see.—Tomorrow I'm to be robbed of all fragrance, all lustre. Am I then no more than the poor and helpless water in a well that, willy-nilly, must give back from its still depths the image of everything that bends over it? Flowers open and close their cups to the morning sun and the evening wind as they please. Is a king's daughter less than a flower?

GOVERNESS, *weeping.* You're a lamb, a lamb to the slaughter, my angel.

LENA. Too true. And the high priest's knife is poised in the air.—God, God, can it be that we have to redeem *ourselves*—with this grief of ours? Can it be that the world is itself a crucified savior, the sun his crown of thorns, and the stars the nails and spear in his feet and side?

GOVERNESS. My child, my child, I cannot bear to see you so. It cannot continue, it's killing you.—Perhaps there is a way. I believe I have an inkling. We shall see. Come! *She leads the* PRINCESS *off.*

* Layer-out, as above.

ACT TWO

How a voice was ringing, ringing
Out within me
In a moment quite extinguishing
My memory.
—ADALBERT VON CHAMISSO

SCENE 1

Open field. A tavern in the background. Enter LEONCE *and* VALERIO, *the latter carrying a bundle.*

VALERIO, *panting.* On my honor, prince, the world *is* a frightfully spacious sort of building.

LEONCE. Not at all, not at all. It's like being in a room full of mirrors, I hardly dare stretch my hands out for fear of hitting them—all the lovely mirrors in fragments on the floor and me staring at the naked walls!

VALERIO. I am lost!

LEONCE. That'll be a loss to no one but the man that finds you.

VALERIO. What I'll do now is place myself in the shadow of my shadow.

LEONCE. You're completely evaporating in the sunshine. You see that lovely cloud? It's equal to at least a fourth part of you. And it's looking down on your coarser constitution rather patronizingly.

VALERIO. To think that if one let that cloud fall on you—drop by drop— it wouldn't harm a hair of your head. A delightful idea, by the way!— We've run through a dozen duchies, half a dozen grand duchies, and a couple of kingdoms, all in the utmost haste, in the course of half a day—and why? Because one is to be king and marry a beautiful princess! And in such a plight, you still live! I don't understand such resignation. I don't see why you haven't taken arsenic, climbed to the top of the church steeple, and put a bullet through your head, just to make a thorough job of it.

LEONCE. Ideals, Valerio, ideals! I have the image and ideal of a female in my head. I must go in quest of it. She is endlessly beautiful and endlessly mindless. Her beauty is as helpless and touching as a newborn infant's. Is the contrast not delightful—eyes both heavenly and dumb, a mouth both divine and moronic, a profile that resembles both a Greek goddess and a sheep's nose, an intellectual death in a body uncontaminated by a single grain of intellect?

VALERIO. Hell, we're at the frontier again! This country is like an onion—nothing but skins. Or Chinese boxes—one inside the other—in the biggest, nothing but boxes, in the smallest, nothing at all. *He throws his bundle to the ground.* Shall this bundle be my tombstone? Look, prince—and now I'm getting philosophical—I give you an image of human life: with aching feet, I drag this bundle through frost and blazing sun because I want to have a clean shirt to wear of an evening, and when evening finally arrives my brow is so deeply furrowed, my cheek so hollow, my eye so dim, I've just enough time left to put that shirt on—and use it as a shroud. Now wouldn't it have been smarter of me to have taken the bundle off the stick and sold it in the first good tavern and got myself drunk and slept in the shade till evening, without the sweat and the corns? And now, prince, I come to the practical application: people today—out of pure modesty—want to put clothes on the inner man too and cover their insides as well as their outsides with coats and trousers. *Both approach the tavern.* Catch a whiff of that, my dear bundle! Oh, the smells of the kitchen, the aromas of the bar! And you, dear old trousers, how you start to thrust your roots into the ground, to put forth leaves, to blossom and bloom! Long, heavy grapes hang down into my mouth, and the must ferments in the winepress! *Exeunt.*

PRINCESS LENA. *The* GOVERNESS.

GOVERNESS. It must be an enchanted day, the sun doesn't set, and it is such an endlessly long time since our flight began.

LENA. Oh no, my dear, the flowers have scarcely wilted that I picked in token of farewell when we left the garden.

GOVERNESS. And where shall we take our rest? Till now we have hit upon nothing. I see no monastery, no hermit, no shepherd.

LENA. I suppose we dreamt it all quite differently behind the garden wall with our books between the myrtles and the oleanders.

GOVERNESS. Oh, the world is revolting! A wandering prince is simply out of the question in such a world!

LENA. The world is wide—endlessly wide and beautiful. I'd like to go on walking forever, day and night. Nothing moves. A glow of red flowers is playing over the meadows, and the distant mountains lie on the earth like resting clouds.

GOVERNESS. Jesus, Mary and Joseph, what will people say? And yet, is it not very tender and feminine? It is a renunciation, it is like the flight of Saint Ottilia.* But we must look for shelter: evening is near.

LENA. Yes, the plants are folding their little leaves together in sleep, and the sunbeams are rocking themselves on blades of grass like tired dragonflies.

SCENE 2

A tavern on a slope by a river. Extensive view. The garden in front of the tavern.
VALERIO, LEONCE.

VALERIO. Well, prince, don't your trousers make a delicious beverage? Don't your boots slip down your throat with the greatest of ease?

* Who fled her father rather than marry any but the Heavenly Bridegroom.

LEONCE. Do you see the old trees, the hedges, the flowers? They all have their history, their secret and charming life-story. Do you see the friendly old faces beneath the grapes at the tavern door? Do you see how they sit holding hands and are afraid because they're so old and the world is still so young? And, oh, Valerio, I am so young, and the world is so old! Sometimes I'm afraid myself, and *about* myself, and could sit in a corner and take pity on myself and weep.

VALERIO *gives him a glass.* Take this bell, this diving bell, and lower yourself into the sea of wine till pearls bubble over your head. *He sniffs it.* What a bouquet! Look! The elves are hovering over its flower-cups, in golden shoes, beating their cymbals!

LEONCE, *jumping up.* Come, Valerio, we must do something, do something! Let us busy ourselves with profound thoughts, and inquire how it is that a chair will stand on three legs and not on two. Come, let us dissect ants and count filaments on flowers! I shall find myself some really princely hobby yet. I'll come across a baby's rattle that only falls out of my hand when I gather wool and pull at the blanket. I still have a certain quota of enthusiasm to use up; but when I've cooked a dish till it's hot enough, I need an endless amount of time to find a spoon to eat it with, and during this time it goes cold.

VALERIO. *Ergo bibamus!* This bottle is no mistress, no theory, it doesn't have labor pains, it doesn't get boring, it's never unfaithful, it is *one* from the first drop to the last. You break the seal, and the dreams that lie slumbering within come sparkling toward you!

LEONCE. Lord, I'd spend half my life giving thanks to God if just one straw were vouchsafed me to ride on like a splendid horse—till the day comes when all I need straw for is to lie dead on.—What a curious evening! Down here everything is still, and up there the clouds change and pass, and the sun keeps coming and going. Look what strange figures are chasing each other up there! Look at the long white shadows with bats' wings and appallingly thin legs! And all so swift and swirling, while down below not a leaf stirs, not a blade of grass. The earth has timorously curled up like a child, while ghosts ride over the cradle.

VALERIO. I don't know what you want, I feel pretty comfortable. The sun looks like an inn sign, and the fiery clouds above it like the inscription: Golden Sun Tavern. The earth and the water below are like a table that wine has been spilt on, and we are on this table like cards that God and the Devil are playing a game with out of boredom— you are a king, and I am a jack, only a queen is missing, a lovely queen

with a big gingerbread heart and a mighty tulip in which her long
nose is sentimentally sunk, and—by God, there she is!

The GOVERNESS *and the* PRINCESS *have come in.*

But it's not a tulip, it's a hunk of tobacco, and it's not a nose, it's a
snout. *To the* GOVERNESS. Why do you hurry so much, worthy lady,
that one sees your late lamented calves right up to your genteel garters?

GOVERNESS, *much enraged, stopping.* Why, honored sir, do you tear your
mouth open so wide that it makes a hole in the view?

VALERIO. So that you, honored madam, won't bump your nose on the

horizon and make it bleed. Such a nose is like the tower of Lebanon that
looketh toward Damascus.

LENA, *to the* GOVERNESS. Is the way so long, my dear?

LEONCE, *dreaming away to himself.* Oh, every way is long. The ticking of
the death-watch beetle within our breasts is slow, every drop of our
blood measures out its time, our life is a creeping fever. To tired feet,
every way is *too* long . . .

LENA, *who listens to him, fearful, musing.* And to tired eyes, every light is
too strong. And to tired lips, every breath is too heavy. *Smiling.* And to
tired ears, every word is one too many. *With the* GOVERNESS, *she goes
into the house.*

LEONCE. Oh, Valerio, I could say what someone said before me:* "Would not this, sir, and a forest of feathers, if the rest of my fortunes turn Turk with me, with two provincial roses on my razed shoes, get me a fellowship in a cry of players, sir?" I spoke the lines quite melancholically, I believe. Thank God I'm beginning to come down with melancholy! The air isn't so cold and bright any more, Heaven glows and sinks down with its arms about me, heavy drops are falling.—Oh, that voice: "Is the way so long?" Many voices are heard in this world, and one can say they talk of other things, but this voice I understood, it rested upon me like the spirit that hovered over the waters before there was light. What fermentation in the depths! Something is growing within me! How that voice pours itself into space—"Is the way so long?" *Exit.*

VALERIO. No. The way to the madhouse isn't as long as all that. It's an easy place to find, and I know the footpaths, trails, and highways that lead there. I see him now taking a broad avenue to it on a winter's day, bitter cold, his hat under his arm, as he walks in the long shadows of the bare trees and fans himself with his handkerchief.—He is a fool! *He follows him.*

SCENE 3

A room. LENA. *The* GOVERNESS.

GOVERNESS. Just don't think about the man.

LENA. He was so old under those yellow locks. Spring on his cheeks, and winter in his heart! That is sad. The tired body can find a pillow anywhere, but when the mind is tired, where shall it rest? An appalling thought comes to me: I believe there are men who are unhappy, incurably so, merely because they exist. *She rises.*

GOVERNESS. Where are you going, my child?

LENA. I want to go down in the garden.

GOVERNESS. But . . .

LENA. "But," dearest mother? I should have been brought up in a pot like a plant, you know that. I need dew and night air, like flowers.— Do you hear the harmonies of the evening? The crickets are singing the day to sleep, and night-violets are lulling it with their scent! I cannot stay indoors. The walls are falling in on me.

* *Hamlet,* Act III, Scene 2.

SCENE 4

The garden. Night and moonlight. LENA *is seen sitting on the lawn.*

VALERIO, *at some distance.* It's a fine thing, Nature. But it would be a finer if there were no mosquitoes, if hotel beds were a little cleaner, and

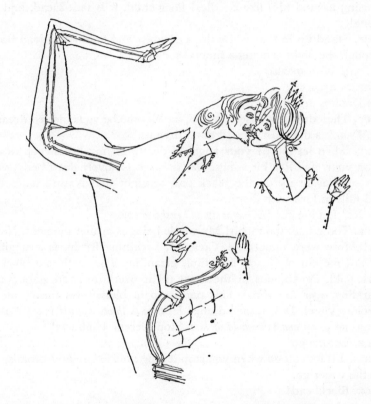

death-watch beetles didn't tick away so in the walls. Inside, men snore. Outside, frogs croak. House crickets chirp inside, field crickets outside.

> There is cause to say alas
> Dear grass.

He lies down on the lawn.
Enter LEONCE.

LEONCE. O night! Balmy as the first night that slowly descended on paradise! *He sees the* PRINCESS *and softly approaches her.*

LENA, *talking away to herself.* The hedge sparrow has twittered in its dream.
—The night sinks into a deeper sleep, its cheek is paler, its breath
calmer. The moon is like a sleeping child whose golden locks have
fallen over his dear little face in his sleep.—Oh, his sleep is death!
Look how the dead little angel rests on his dark pillow with stars
burning around him like candles! Poor child, it is sad! Dead, and so
alone!

LEONCE. Stand up in that white dress of yours and follow the dead body
through the night, singing a funeral song.

LENA. Ah! Who speaks?

LEONCE. A dream.

LENA. Dreams are blessèd.

LEONCE. Then dream yourself blessèd, and let me be your blessèd dream.

LENA. Death is the most blessèd of all dreams.

LEONCE. Then let me be your angel of death, let my lips swoop down
upon your eyes like his wings. *He kisses her.* O lovely dead body, you
rest so charmingly on the black pall of night that Nature hates life
and falls in love with death.

LENA. No! Let me go! *She jumps up and rushes away.*

LEONCE. Too much, too much! My whole being is in that moment. Now,
die! More were impossible. Creation, breathing freely, is struggling
toward me out of Chaos, beautiful, gleaming. The earth is a bowl of
dark gold, light foams in the bowl till it overflows, and stars come
sparkling over the rim.—This one drop of blessedness makes me a
precious vessel. Down, sacred cup! *He tries to throw himself into the river.*

VALERIO *jumps up and takes hold of him.* Stop, Serene Highness!

LEONCE. Let me go!

VALERIO. I'll let you go when you stop letting yourself go and promise to
let the water go.

LEONCE. Blockhead!

VALERIO. Lieutenant's romanticism—hasn't your highness got beyond
that? Drinking your mistress's health, throwing the glass through the
window?

LEONCE. I half-believe you're right.

VALERIO. Take comfort, man. If you aren't to sleep *under* the grass tonight,
sleep *on* it. To try and sleep in bed at the tavern would just be another
attempted suicide: in that place one lies on straw like a dead man and
is bitten by fleas like a live one.

LEONCE. A lot *I* care. *He lies down in the grass.* Man, you have cheated me of the loveliest suicide ever! Never in my life shall I find so exquisite a moment for it again, even the weather is excellent. Now I'm out of the mood already. The fellow has spoiled everything for me with his

yellow waistcoat and sky-blue trousers.—Heaven grant me a disgustingly healthy sleep!

VALERIO. Amen.—Having saved a man's life, I have something to keep me warm tonight—a good conscience!

LEONCE. I hope it works, Valerio.

ACT THREE

SCENE 1

LEONCE, VALERIO.

VALERIO. Getting married? Since when has your highness decided to serve a life sentence?

LEONCE. And do you know, Valerio, that even the least among men is so great that life is much too short to love him? As for a certain kind of people who fancy nothing is so beautiful and holy that they oughtn't to make it still more beautiful and holy, I say: let them have their fun, there is a certain enjoyment in such pleasant arrogance, why shouldn't I let them have it?

VALERIO. Very humane and philobestial. But does she know who you are?

LEONCE. She only knows that she loves me.

VALERIO. And does your highness know who *she* is?

LEONCE. Blockhead! Ask the carnation and the pearly dew their names!

VALERIO. I conclude she is *something*—if the term is not too indelicate and suggestive of police records?—But how can the trick be brought off?— Hmm. Prince, shall I be Minister of State if you and the ineffable Nameless One are this day welded together in holy matrimony in the presence of your father? Your word?

LEONCE. My word.

VALERIO. The poor devil Valerio pays his respects to His Excellency Valerio of Valerianvale, Minister of State.—"What does the fellow want? I do not know him. Get out, you rascal!"

He runs off. LEONCE *follows him.*

SCENE 2

Open space in front of King Peter's castle. PRESIDENT *of the District Board. The* SCHOOLMASTER. PEASANTS *in their Sunday best, holding fir branches.*

DISTRICT PRESIDENT. How are your people holding up, Mr. Schoolmaster?

SCHOOLMASTER. They hold each other up, Mr. District President, and have done this many a day; and so, one may say, for all their little troubles, they hold up well. Of course, in this heat, they couldn't hold themselves up at all, if they didn't have occasional recourse to the bottle. Courage, my men! Stretch your fir branches straight out before you, so everyone will think you're a forest, and your noses are strawberries, and your three-cornered hats are stags' antlers, and your leather pants the moonlight in the trees. And remember: the one that's last has to keep running in front of the one that's first. That way, it will seem that we've raised your number to the second power!

DISTRICT PRESIDENT. And, Schoolmaster: you answer for their sobriety.

SCHOOLMASTER. Of course. I'm so sober, I can barely stand.

DISTRICT PRESIDENT. Now, people, pay attention! In the program it says: "All subjects of the king will of their own free will place themselves along the highway cleanly clothed, well nourished, and with happy faces." Don't you disgrace us!

SCHOOLMASTER. Steady does it, my men! Don't scratch yourselves behind the ears, and don't blow your noses, while the royal couple is driving past. And show you are properly touched, or you'll be improperly touched where you won't like it. And realize what is being done for you: you are being placed where the wind blows straight from the kitchen and for once in your lives you can smell the smell of a roast. Have you remembered your lesson? Huh? *Vi!*

PEASANTS. *Vi!*

SCHOOLMASTER. *Vat!*

PEASANTS. *Vat!*

SCHOOLMASTER. *Vivat!*

PEASANTS. *Vivat!*

SCHOOLMASTER. There, Mr. President, you see: intelligence is on the upgrade! Just think, it's Latin. But we are also presenting this evening a Transparent Ball, in which ingenious use will be made of the holes in our jackets and trousers. And we shall beat cockades onto our heads with our fists.

SCENE 3

Great Hall. Dressed-up ladies and gentlemen, carefully grouped. In the foreground, the MASTER OF CEREMONIES *with a few servants.*

MASTER OF CEREMONIES. It is pathetic. Everything has gone wrong. Every roast has dried up. Congratulations are falling flat. Stand-up collars are all sitting down, and looking like melancholy pigs' ears. The peasant's fingernails and beards have been growing perceptibly. The soldiers' hair is starting to stick up. Among the twelve virgin bridesmaids, there isn't one who wouldn't prefer the horizontal position to the vertical. In those white dresses, they look like worn-out silk rabbits, and the court poet is grunting and snuffling around them like a guinea pig in trouble. The officers are losing their posture, and the ladies-in-waiting stand there like beach shrubbery* at low tide, with the salt crystallizing on their necklaces.

SECOND SERVANT. No one could say they carry too much on their shoulders. And if they aren't openhearted, at least they are open right down to their hearts.

MASTER OF CEREMONIES. Yes, they're like playing cards from the Kingdom

---

* Büchner uses a word ("Gradierbäue") which even in German editions has to be explained in a note.

of Turkey: they show you the Dardanelles and the sea of Marmora. Away, you rascals! To the windows! Here comes his majesty.

Enter KING PETER *and the* COUNCIL OF STATE.

KING PETER. So the princess has disappeared too. Is there still no trace of our beloved son and heir? Have my orders been obeyed? Are the frontiers under observation?

MASTER OF CEREMONIES. Yes, your majesty. The view from this hall allows us to exercise the strictest supervision. *To the* FIRST SERVANT. What did you see?

FIRST SERVANT. A dog looking for his master has been running through the kingdom.

MASTER OF CEREMONIES. How about you?

SECOND SERVANT. There's someone taking a walk on the northern frontier. But it isn't the prince, I'd recognize him.

MASTER OF CEREMONIES. How about you?

THIRD SERVANT. Excuse me—nothing.

MASTER OF CEREMONIES. That is very little. How about you?

FOURTH SERVANT. Also nothing.

MASTER OF CEREMONIES. That is equally little.

KING PETER. But, Council of State, did I not decree that My Royal Majesty would rejoice today and that, today also, the wedding would be celebrated?

PRESIDENT. Yes, your majesty, that was announced. That is protocol.

KING PETER. And, were I not to execute what was decreed, should I not be compromising myself?

PRESIDENT. If it were otherwise possible for your majesty to compromise himself, this would be a case in which he might compromise himself.

KING PETER. Did I not give my royal word?—Yes, I shall at once put my decree into practice: I shall rejoice. *He rubs his hands.* Oh, I am quite extraordinarily merry!

PRESIDENT. And we all share your majesty's feelings insofar as it is possible and proper for subjects to do so.

KING PETER. Oh, I am completely overcome with joy! I'll have red coats made for my chamberlains, I'll make some cadets into lieutenants, I'll permit my subjects to—but, but what about the wedding? Does not the other half of the decree read that the wedding should be celebrated?

PRESIDENT. Yes, your majesty.

KING PETER. Yes, but what if the prince doesn't turn up, and neither does the princess?

PRESIDENT. Yes, if the prince doesn't turn up, and neither does the princess, then—then——

KING PETER. Then? Then?

PRESIDENT. Then, of course, they can't get married.

KING PETER. Stop! Is the conclusion logical? If—then— Correct! But my word, my royal word!

PRESIDENT. Let your majesty take comfort with other majesties! A king's word is a thing—a thing—a thing—that is no thing.

KING PETER, *to the servants.* You still see nothing?

SERVANTS. Nothing, your majesty, not a thing.

KING PETER. And I had decided to rejoice on such a scale! I was going to start precisely on the twelfth stroke of the clock and go on rejoicing for a full twelve hours. I'm going to be quite melancholy.

PRESIDENT. All subjects are earnestly requested to share the feelings of his majesty.

MASTER OF CEREMONIES. Those, however, who have come without their handkerchiefs are strictly forbidden to weep—in the interests of public propriety.

FIRST SERVANT. Stop! I see something! It resembles a protuberance, it looks like a nose, the rest of it hasn't crossed the frontier yet. Now I can see another man. And now two persons of the opposite sex.

MASTER OF CEREMONIES. In which direction?

FIRST SERVANT. They're coming nearer! They're coming to the castle! They're here!

Enter VALERIO, LEONCE, GOVERNESS, PRINCESS, *masked.*

KING PETER. Who are you?

VALERIO. Do I know? *He slowly removes several masks, one after the other.* Is this me? Or this? Or this? Shell the nut! Turn back the leaves! Really, I'm rather afraid I may peel myself completely away!

KING PETER, *nonplussed.* But—but, surely, you must be *something?*

VALERIO. If your majesty commands, yes. But in that case, gentlemen, turn the mirrors to the wall and hide your shiny buttons somewhat and don't look straight at me so I'm forced to see my image in your eyes, or, really, I won't know any more what I actually am.

KING PETER. The man gets me all mixed up! I'm falling into despair, I'm
　in the utmost confusion!
VALERIO. What I actually had in mind was to announce to an honored
　and esteemed company like this the arrival of The Two World-Famous

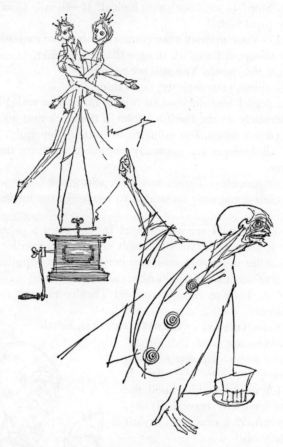

Automata, and to tell you that I am the third of the two, and, at that,
perhaps the most remarkable, if, actually, I had any accurate notion,
myself, who I was, which shouldn't occasion any astonishment, for
not only do I not know what I'm talking about, I don't even know
I don't know what I'm talking about, so the probability is that I've
just been *caused* to talk, and actually it's some system of tubes and
cylinders that's saying all this.
In a barker's voice.

Ladies and gentlemen, you see before you two persons of both the sexes, one little man and one little woman, a gentleman and a lady! It's all mechanism and art, all clock springs and pasteboard! Each of these two persons has a superfine ruby spring in his or her right foot just under the nail of his or her little toe as the case may be. Give it a bit of a push, and the whole mechanism runs a full fifty years. Now, these two persons are so perfectly constructed, you can't tell them from men—from *other* men, I should say—if you didn't know they were just pasteboard. Yes, ladies and gentlemen, you could actually take them for regular members of human society. You can tell they're nobly born: just listen to their Oxford accent. You can tell they're moral: they get up when the clock strikes, have lunch when the clock strikes, and go to bed when the clock strikes; also, they never have indigestion, which proves they have an easy conscience. Oh yes, their moral sense is very highly developed: the lady has no word for underdrawers, and the gentleman would never dream of going upstairs just behind a female or going downstairs just in front of one. They are highly educated: the lady sings all the new operas, and the gentleman wears French cuffs. Take note of this, everyone, they have just come to a very interesting stage, at which stage a new mechanism manifests itself, the mechanism of love. The gentleman has carried the lady's shawl several times. The lady has averted her gaze several times and looked toward heaven. Both have more than once whispered: faith—love—hope. Both look very much as if an understanding had been arrived at. All that's lacking is the one very small word, Amen.

KING PETER, *one finger against his nose.* In effigy, in effigy? President, if you have a man hanged in effigy isn't that just as good as if he received a regulation hanging?

PRESIDENT. Excuse me, your majesty, it is a great deal better, for it gives him no pain, and yet he is hanged.

KING PETER. Now I have it. We'll celebrate the wedding in effigy. *Pointing to* LENA *and* LEONCE. That's the princess, that's the prince.—I shall carry out my decree! I shall rejoice!—Let the bells ring out! Get your congratulations ready! Go to it, Mr. Court Chaplain! *The* COURT CHAPLAIN *steps forward, clears his throat, looks several times toward heaven.*

VALERIO. Begin! Leave thy damnable faces and begin! Now!

COURT CHAPLAIN, *in the utmost confusion.* If we—or—but——

VALERIO. Whereas and in respect of——

COURT CHAPLAIN. For——

VALERIO. It was before the creation of the world——

COURT CHAPLAIN. That——

VALERIO. God was bored——

KING PETER. Make it short, my good man.

COURT CHAPLAIN, *pulling himself together.* If it please Your Highness Prince Leonce of the Kingdom of Popo, and if it please Your Highness Princess Lena of the Kingdom of Peepee, and if it mutually and reciprocally please both of your highnesses mutually and reciprocally to desire to have each other, then, aloud and audibly, say Yes.

LENA *and* LEONCE. Yes!

COURT CHAPLAIN. To which I add Amen.

VALERIO. Well done—terse and to the point. The little man and the little woman are now created, and all the beasts in paradise stand around! LEONCE *takes off his mask.*

ALL. The prince!

KING PETER. The prince! My son! I am lost! I've been deceived! *He makes for the* PRINCESS.Who is this person? I declare the whole thing null and void!

GOVERNESS *removes the* PRINCESS's *mask, in triumph.* The princess!

LEONCE. Lena?

LENA. Leonce?

LEONCE. The flight from paradise? No, Lena, our flight was *to* it.

LENA. I've been deceived.

LEONCE. *I've* been deceived.

LENA. O chance!

LEONCE. O Providence!

VALERIO. I must laugh: it really *was* just chance that your highnesses chanced to meet. Give chance a chance, *I* say. And may you chance to like each other.

GOVERNESS. That I should live to see this sight—at last—a wandering prince! I die in peace.

KING PETER. My children, I am touched, I am quite overcome with emotion. I am the happiest man alive! And herewith I most solemnly place the government in your hands, my son. For my part, I shall forthwith begin to think, quite undisturbed. Leave me these wise men, my son, to support me in my endeavors. *He indicates the* COUNCIL OF STATE. Come, gentlemen, we must think, we must think, quite undisturbed! *He starts to withdraw with the* COUNCIL OF STATE. The man got me all mixed up, I must disentangle myself. *Exit.*

LEONCE, *to all present.* Gentlemen, my good wife and I infinitely deplore the fact that you have had to stand so long today at our disposition.

Your situation is so sad, we would not for anything put your constancy to a further test. Get you home now, but don't forget those speeches, sermons, and verses, for tomorrow we're going to start the festivities all over again in peace and comfort. *Au revoir!*

Exeunt all except LEONCE, LENA, VALERIO, *and the* GOVERNESS.

Well, Lena, have you noticed yet that our pockets are full of toys and dolls? What shall we do with them? Shall we make moustaches for the dolls and hang sabres on them? Or shall we dress them in tail coats and have them conduct miniature* politics and diplomacy with us looking on through a microscope? Or do you long to have a barrel organ with very esthetic mice scurrying around on it, white as milk? Or shall we build a theatre? LENA *leans against him and shakes her head.* I know what you'd like: we'll have all the clocks smashed and all the calendars suppressed, then we'll count the hours and the moons only by the flowers, by blossom and fruit. And then we'll surround our little country with burning lenses, so there'll be no more winter, and in summer the heat will shoot us clear up to Ischia and Capri by a process of distillation. And so we'll spend the whole year among roses and violets, oranges and laurel.

VALERIO. And I'll be Minister of State. And a decree will be issued that whoever gets calluses on his hands shall be placed under surveillance; whoever works himself sick shall be punishable under criminal law; whoever boasts that in the sweat of his brow he will eat bread shall be declared insane and dangerous to human society. And then we can lie in the shade and ask God for macaroni, melons, and figs, for musical throats, classic bodies, and a nice, cosy** religion!

---

* Büchner actually says "infusorial," which explains the microscope. But the word would not be understood in any theatre.

** There are two readings in the German: *commode* and *kommende.* The first has been followed. The second might be rendered: "an up-and-coming religion."

A Door Should Be either Open or Shut

A Proverb in One Act

by ALFRED DE MUSSET

English version by Jacques Barzun

DRAMATIS PERSONAE

The Count
The Marquise

A small drawing room. The MARQUISE, *seated on a sofa near the fireplace, is doing needlepoint.*

THE COUNT, *entering from the right, and bowing.* I don't think I shall ever get over it: I am a born blunderer. I cannot for the life of me get it into my head, once and for all, what your day at home is, and every time I want to see you, it never fails but I come on a Tuesday.

THE MARQUISE. Have you something special to tell me?

THE COUNT. No, but even if I had, I wouldn't be able to; it's pure chance that I find you alone. In less than fifteen minutes there will be a mob of your intimate friends and, I promise you, they will make me take to my heels.

THE MARQUISE. To be sure, today is my day at home. I hardly know why I have one. And yet there's a reason for the fashion. Our mothers used to keep open house; good company wasn't very numerous, even if each circle did include a handful of bores who had to be—borne. But today if one receives at all, one must receive all of Paris—literally the whole thing, town and suburbs. Being at home was like being in the open street. A remedy had to be found and that is why everyone has "a day." It's the only way to see one another as little as possible. When someone says: "I'm at home on Tuesdays," it really means: "Leave me in peace the rest of the time."

THE COUNT. I feel all the more out of place here today because you give me permission to come and see you during the rest of the week.

THE MARQUISE. Make the best of it: do sit down over there. If you feel in the mood, talk; if not, warm yourself by the fire. I don't expect many people today; you can sit and watch my few puppets come and go. But what's the matter, you seem——

THE COUNT. I seem how?

THE MARQUISE. For my reputation's sake, I refuse to tell you.

THE COUNT. All right, I'll confess. Just before I came I did feel rather—that way.

THE MARQUISE. What way? It's my turn to ask.

THE COUNT. Will you be angry if I tell you?

THE MARQUISE. I'm going to a ball tonight and I mean to look well, so I've determined not to be angry even once today.

THE COUNT. Well then, I was a little bored. I don't know what's the matter; it's a fashionable ailment, like your at-homes. I've been miserable since noon. I paid four calls without finding anyone in. I was supposed to dine somewhere and I begged off, for no reason. There is not a single show on tonight. As I came out it was freezing. All I've seen is red noses and purplish cheeks. I don't know what to do with myself and I feel as stupid as a newspaper serial.

THE MARQUISE. I can say the same: I am bored to tears. I haven't any doubt it's the weather we're having.

THE COUNT. True enough, this cold spell is damnable. Winter is a disease. When the empty-headed see the sky clear and the sidewalks dry, when they feel the sharp wind cutting off their ears, they call it a fine frost: One might as well say "a beautiful pneumonia." Much thanks for all such favors.

THE MARQUISE. I agree with you entirely. And yet I think my boredom doesn't come so much from the air outside, cold as it is, as from the air inside—other people's breathings. Perhaps we're getting old. I have begun my thirtieth year. I'm losing the knack of living.

THE COUNT. I've never had the knack. What frightens me is that I'm acquiring it. With the years one either goes mad or conventional. I live in fear of dying like a wise man.

THE MARQUISE. Please ring for a log to put on the fire. That thought of yours gives me a chill.

The sound of a doorbell is heard.

THE COUNT. Don't bother. There's the bell. Your procession will soon be here.

THE MARQUISE. Let's see what the vanguard looks like; do make a point of staying.

THE COUNT. No, it's best that I should go.

THE MARQUISE. Where are you off to?

THE COUNT. I have no idea. *He rises, bows, and opens the door.* Good-bye, dear lady, till Thursday evening.

THE MARQUISE. Why Thursday?

THE COUNT, *standing and holding the doorknob.* Isn't it your night at the Italian Opera? I shall pay you a little call in your box.

THE MARQUISE. I don't want you to: you're too grouchy. Besides, I am taking M. Camus.

THE COUNT. M. Camus, your neighbor in the country?

THE MARQUISE. Yes. He sold me apples and hay with excellent grace. I want to return his courtesy.

THE COUNT. That's just like you! The most boring fellow; they ought to feed him his own produce. And by the way, do you know what people are saying?

THE MARQUISE. No, but nobody has come. Who do you suppose rang?

THE COUNT, *looking out the window.* Nobody. No, a little girl, I think, carrying a box, a—Lord knows what, the laundress perhaps. She's in the courtyard talking to your people.

THE MARQUISE. How elegant of you to call it a Lord-knows-what! It's my bonnet. Well now, what are people saying about me and M. Camus?— And do shut the door; there's a horrible draft.

THE COUNT, *shutting the door.* They say that you're thinking of getting married again, that M. Camus is a millionaire, and that he comes to see you quite often.

THE MARQUISE. Indeed? Is that all? And you tell me this to my face?

THE COUNT. I tell you because others speak of it.

THE MARQUISE. A fine reason. Do I tell you everything that's said about you?

THE COUNT. About me, dear lady? And what can anybody say that can't be repeated?

THE MARQUISE. Obviously everything can be repeated since you inform me that I am about to be announced as Madame Camus. What's said about you is certainly just as serious, for it seems to be unfortunately true.

THE COUNT. Tell me what it is, you almost frighten me.

THE MARQUISE. Another proof that it must be true.

THE COUNT. Explain yourself, I beg you.

THE MARQUISE. Certainly not. It is altogether your affair.

THE COUNT, *returning toward the* MARQUISE *and sitting down.* I beseech you, Marquise. I ask it as a favor. You are the one person in the world whose good opinion matters to me.

THE MARQUISE. One of the persons, you mean.

THE COUNT. No, madam, I said: the *one* person, the one whose regard, feelings——

THE MARQUISE. Heavens! You're going to make a speech.

THE COUNT. Not at all. If you do not see, it's because you will not see.

THE MARQUISE. See what?

THE COUNT. You surely understand.

THE MARQUISE. I understand only what I am told and even then not through and through.

THE COUNT. You are pleased to laugh. But honestly, is it possible that after seeing you nearly every day for a year, finding you as you are, your mind, your charm, your beauty——

THE MARQUISE. Gracious heavens, but it's worse than a speech, it's a declaration you're working up to! You should give warning—is it a declaration or a New Year's greeting?

THE COUNT. What if it were a declaration?

THE MARQUISE. Then I should tell you I don't want one today. I told you I was going to a ball, which exposes me to hearing several this evening. My health won't allow such things both day and night.

THE COUNT. Really, you are most discouraging. I must say I'll be glad when it's your turn to be caught.

THE MARQUISE. So shall I. I assure you there are times when I'd give a great deal to have so much as a tiny vexation. For instance, that's how I felt while my hair was being done, only a while ago. I was sighing in a heart-rending manner, from despair at having nothing on my mind.

THE COUNT. Make fun of me, do. Your turn will come.

THE MARQUISE. Very likely. All men are mortal. But if I act reasonable, is it my fault? I assure you I am not putting up fences.

THE COUNT. You don't want to be made love to?

THE MARQUISE. No, I don't. I'm willing to be good-natured, but love-making is really too stupid. You're a man of sense, tell me, what does it signify—making love to a woman?

THE COUNT. It signifies that the woman is pleasing to you and that it is pleasing to tell her so.

THE MARQUISE. So far so good. But the woman, is it pleasing to her to be pleasing to you? You think I'm pretty, I suppose, and it entertains you to tell me so. Then what? Is it any reason why I should love you? I rather think that if I like someone it isn't because I am pretty. So what does he gain by complimenting me? What a way to make yourself lovable, to take your stand in front of a woman, look her up and down through a lorgnette as if she were a doll in a shopwindow, and then tell her most pleasantly: "Madam, I think that you are charming." Add to this a few insipid phrases, a whirl on the dance floor and a bunch of flowers, and that is what is called paying your addresses to someone. For shame! How can a man of sense develop a taste for such absurdities? It makes me angry just to think of it.

THE COUNT. And yet it's not worth getting upset about.

THE MARQUISE. Yes, it is. You must think a woman's head quite empty of everything but silliness, if you think you can bewitch her with those tricks. Do you really suppose it's a gay life spending one's time in a flood of asininities and never hearing anything but fiddle-faddle? It seems to me if I were a man and I saw a pretty woman, I'd say to myself: "Here is a poor creature who must be fed up with compliments. I'll take pity on her and spare her." And if I meant to please her I'd do her the honor of speaking of other things than her wretched face. But no. It's always: "You are pretty," and: "You are *so* pretty," and:

"So *very* pretty." Good Lord, don't we know that we are? Let me tell you something: you fashionable gentlemen are nothing but confectioners in disguise.

THE COUNT. Very well, dear lady. You are charming, take it or leave it. *The bell rings.* The bell again. Good-bye, I must be off. *He gets up and opens the door.*

THE MARQUISE. Wait a minute. I was going to say . . . I don't remember what . . . Ah, yes. Are you by any chance going by Fossin's on your way?

THE COUNT. Marquise, if I can do something for you, it won't be by chance.

THE MARQUISE. Again a compliment! My, how you annoy me! It's a ring of mine that's broken. I could send it direct but I have to explain, you see . . . *She takes off the ring.* . . . it's here, on the bezel; there was a little projection and you could open it from the side. I hit it on something this morning and the spring won't work.

THE COUNT. Tell me, Marquise, if it's not impertinent: you kept a lock of hair in it?

THE MARQUISE. Perhaps. Why do you laugh?

THE COUNT. I am not laughing in the least.

THE MARQUISE. You are very rude. It was my husband's hair. But no one's coming in. Who do you suppose rang?

THE COUNT, *looking out the window.* Another little girl and another bandbox. Another bonnet, I suppose. By the way, come to think of it, you owe me some information in confidence.

THE MARQUISE. Please close that door, you're freezing me to death.

THE COUNT. I am going. But promise that you'll tell me what you heard about me: promise?

THE MARQUISE. Come to the ball tonight; we can have a nice chat.

THE COUNT. What an idea! A chat in a ballroom! The perfect place for a conversation, with trombone accompaniment and the tinkling of waterglasses! People step on your feet, jostle your elbow, waiters with sticky clothes slip an ice into your back pocket. I ask you whether——

THE MARQUISE. Are you going or staying? I've told you you're making me catch my death of cold. No one has come, why must you leave?

THE COUNT, *shutting the door and sitting down again.* Why, because I feel in such a bad humor that I'm afraid I'll be a nuisance to you. I must really give up coming to see you.

THE MARQUISE. That's forthright anyway. Why must you?

THE COUNT. I don't know, but I get on your nerves. You were telling me so a moment ago. It's understandable. Because I live across the way, worse luck, I can't go out without seeing your window. I stop by, automatically, without knowing what I've come for.

THE MARQUISE. If I said you annoyed me today, that proves it isn't always so. Seriously, I should be very sorry if you stopped coming by. I enjoy seeing you.

THE COUNT. Enjoy? I don't believe it. Do you know what I'll do? I'm going back to Italy.

THE MARQUISE. And what will Miss—er— have to say to that?

THE COUNT. Miss who?

THE MARQUISE. Miss What's-her-name, your protégée. How should I know the name of your ballet dancers?

THE COUNT. So that's the great piece of news you've heard about me?

THE MARQUISE. Just so. Do you deny the facts?

THE COUNT. It's a cock-and-bull story.

THE MARQUISE. Too bad, then, that you were unmistakably seen at the theatre with a certain flowered pink hat, of the kind that blooms only in the Opera House. You belong to the chorus, dear neighbor, and everybody knows it.

THE COUNT. Just as everybody knows you're marrying M. Camus.

THE MARQUISE. You harp on that? Well, why not? M. Camus is a most respectable man, a millionaire several times over. Though he is well on in years, he is just the right age for a husband. I am a widow, he's a bachelor, and he looks quite handsome when he wears gloves.

THE COUNT. And a nightcap: it must suit his face.

THE MARQUISE. Will you please be quiet! Does one speak of such things?

THE COUNT. Why not—to someone who very likely will see them?

THE MARQUISE. No doubt you've learned these pretty manners from the young ladies of the ballet.

THE COUNT, *getting up and taking his hat.* It's better, Marquise, that I should say good-bye. You'd make me say something I'd regret.

THE MARQUISE. What princely delicacy!

THE COUNT. Honestly, you are being cruel on purpose. Isn't it enough that you forbid me to love you without accusing me of loving someone else?

THE MARQUISE. Better and better! The accents of tragedy. When did I ever forbid you to love me?

THE COUNT. You did. I wasn't to speak of it, at least.

THE MARQUISE. All right. I allow it now. Let's hear your eloquence.

THE COUNT. If you meant it——

THE MARQUISE. What does meaning it matter, provided I say it?

THE COUNT. Joking is all very well, but one of us here might be running a risk.

THE MARQUISE. A dangerous risk, sir?

THE COUNT. Possibly, dear lady; though the danger unfortunately threatens only me.

THE MARQUISE. A man who is afraid shouldn't act the hero. Well? You have nothing to say? You threaten: I expose myself, and you do nothing? I expected at the very least to see you fall at my feet like the Cid, or even M. Camus. In your place he would be on his knees already.

THE COUNT. Does it really amuse you a great deal to be forever making fun of us poor devils?

THE MARQUISE. And does it surprise you a great deal that someone should stand up to you?

THE COUNT. Take care! You may be brave, but I was once a guardsman—not so long ago at that, if I may mention it.

THE MARQUISE. Indeed! That's splendid! A declaration from a guardsman must be a remarkable thing. I have never witnessed one. Should I call my maid? She would know how to reply. You'll give us a real performance.

The bell is heard.

THE COUNT. That bell again! Good-bye, Marquise. But I shan't let you off on that account. *He opens the door.*

THE MARQUISE. It still holds for tonight, doesn't it? What *is* that noise?

THE COUNT, *looking out the window.* It's the weather that's just changed. It's raining, hailing in fact, to its heart's content. They're bringing you a third bonnet, and I rather think you'll find a cold wrapped up in it.

THE MARQUISE. But that noise? Is it thunder—in mid-January? Oh! Those almanacs!

THE COUNT. No, it's only a storm, a kind of cloudburst.

THE MARQUISE. It's frightful. Why don't you shut that door: you can't go out in this weather. But what brings it on?

THE COUNT, *shutting the door.* Dear lady, it's the wrath of Heaven, punishing the windowpanes, our umbrellas, the ladies' legs, and the chimney flues.

THE MARQUISE. And my horses are out in it!

THE COUNT. They'll come to no harm—unless something falls on their heads.

THE MARQUISE. Don't you dare make fun of me! I am neat by nature, sir, and hate to have my horses bathed in mud. It's unbelievable: an hour ago the sky was calm and clear.

THE COUNT. At any rate you can be sure that with this hail you won't have a single caller. That's one less at-home.

THE MARQUISE. Not so, since *you* are here. Please put down your hat, it makes me fidgety.

THE COUNT. A compliment, madam? Take care! Since you pretend to hate compliments, one might take yours for the truth.

THE MARQUISE. I have said so and it is true: you give me great pleasure by coming to see me.

THE COUNT, *sitting down again near the* MARQUISE. Then let me love you.

THE MARQUISE. I have said that too: I don't mind at all, not in the least.

THE COUNT. Then let me speak of it.

THE MARQUISE. Guardsman style, of course.

THE COUNT. No, madam. You may be sure that even if I lacked proper feeling I should have sense enough to respect you. But it seems to me that without offending a person he respects, a man has the right——

THE MARQUISE. To wait till the shower is over, you mean? You came in a while ago not knowing quite why—you said so yourself. You were bored, you had nothing to do, you even gave the impression of being cross. If you had found a couple of people here, any two or three around the fire, you would now be talking about literature or railroads, after which you'd go out to dine. So it's because you found me here alone that you think you are compelled—yes, compelled by your honor, to make love to me, that old unbearable love-making— so pointless, ridiculous, repetitious. What have I done to deserve such treatment? Let someone come in now and you will perhaps be witty, entertaining; but I am alone and you have to be as dull as the words of an opera. You go to it at once, and if I paid any attention, you would come out with a declaration, a narrative of your love. Do you know how you men look when you do this? You look like unhappy authors who have been hissed off the stage and who always carry a manuscript around with them, some unacted and unactable tragedy, which they overwhelm you with as soon as they catch you alone for five minutes.

THE COUNT. In short, you tell me you don't dislike me; I tell you I love you; and as far as you're concerned, that is that.

THE MARQUISE. You love me about as much as the King of Spain.

THE COUNT. Now really, that's going too far. You must listen to me for a moment and if you disbelieve——

THE MARQUISE. No, no, and again No! Good God! Don't you suppose I know what you would say? I have a high regard for your acquirements, but just because you have learned a lot, do you imagine I have not done some reading too? Let me tell you something: I once knew a man of sense who picked up in some bookstall a collection of fifty letters, rather well turned, uncommonly good—love letters, of course. Those fifty letters were arranged in a regular order so as to form a kind of miniature novel in which every situation was allowed for. Some made declarations, others were for sulking, for hoping, for moments of pretense when one falls back on "friendship," for quarreling, for despair, for bad humor—even for rainy days like today. I read those letters. In the Preface the author claimed to have made use of them in his own case, and said he never found a woman who could resist beyond Letter 33. Well, I managed to resist the whole collection. I ask you whether I am not a well-read woman and whether it's likely you could teach me something new.

THE COUNT. You are very *blasée*, Marquise.

THE MARQUISE. You call me names, now? I like them better than your sweet nothings: it's less cloying.

THE COUNT. Yes, you certainly are *blasée*.

THE MARQUISE. You are pleased to think so. I'm not *blasée* at all.

THE COUNT. Yes, just like an old Englishwoman with fourteen children.

THE MARQUISE. Just like the feather on my hat. You seem to think it takes a great deal of learning to know you men by heart. But it's the one subject that requires no special study—all one needs is to let you perform. Just think: On the one hand, men who have the strength to refrain from insulting our ears with sugary compliments are extremely rare. On the other hand, it is abundantly clear that in those dreary moments when you strive to please by mustering your falsehoods you are as alike as peas in a pod. Fortunately for us, a merciful providence has kept you from having a very rich vocabulary. As the saying goes, you all know but one song; so that the mere fact of hearing the same remarks, the same words, seeing the same prepared gestures and soft looks—this uniform spectacle with different actors, who may be more or less attractive in themselves but who, in this appalling circumstance, all put on the same look of the conquering hero—saves us by making us laugh or, it may be, by boring us to death. If I had a daughter and I wanted to save her from so-called dangerous approaches, far from forbidding her to listen to what her dancing partners might say, I should merely warn her: "Don't listen to just one, hear them all. Don't shut your book or mark the page; keep it open and let the gentlemen go through their little recitation. If by mischance one of them attracts you, don't fight, just wait: another will come along, indistinguishable from the first, and make you disgusted with both. You are fifteen years old, let us say; well, dear child, it will keep on that way until you are thirty—always the same." Such is my experience, such my wisdom. Do you call that being *blasée?*

THE COUNT. Horribly—if you are telling the truth: I take leave to doubt it. It all sounds so unnatural.

THE MARQUISE. What is it to me whether you believe me or not?

THE COUNT. Better and better! You can't mean it: at your age, you despise love? You see no difference between the words of a man who loves you and those of a bad novel? His looks, gestures, feelings strike you as a "performance"? You pride yourself on telling the truth, and all you find in others is falsehood? Where have you been, Marquise, where did you pick up such ideas?

THE MARQUISE. I have been far and wide, dear neighbor.

THE COUNT. Yes, out with your nurse, no doubt. Women imagine they know everything when they know nothing at all. I ask you, how much experience *can* you have had? As much as the foreigner who saw a red-headed chambermaid at an inn and who wrote in his diary: "All the women in this country have red hair."

THE MARQUISE. I asked you to throw a log on the fire.

THE COUNT, *throwing on the log.* I can understand a prude. She says No, stops her ears, hates love—it is all conceivable. But to deny the *existence* of love is rather silly. You discourage a poor devil by telling him: "I know everything you are going to say." But he has the right to reply: "No doubt, dear lady, you know it all and so do I. I know what one says when one loves, and yet I'm apt to forget it all when I speak to you." Nothing is new under the sun, but it's my turn to say: "What does that prove?"

THE MARQUISE. Very good! My, but you speak well! Except for a few lapses, you sound like a book.

THE COUNT. To be sure, I'm speaking, and I may say that if you are what you pretend to be, I pity you.

THE MARQUISE. Don't mind me: Make yourself at home.

THE COUNT. There's nothing wounding in what I say. If you have the right to attack us, haven't we the right to defend ourselves? When you compare us to unsuccessful authors, what kind of reproach do you think that is? Good Lord, if love is play-acting——

THE MARQUISE. That fire isn't going right, the log is crooked.

THE COUNT, *attending to the fire.* If love is play-acting, the play is as old as the world, and whether hissed or applauded, it is after all what mankind has found that least bad. The roles are trite, I admit, but if they were worthless the world wouldn't know them by heart. And I'm wrong when I say the play is old—old isn't the right word for immortal.

THE MARQUISE. Sir, what you say is sheer poetry.

THE COUNT. No, dear lady. But these commonplaces that bore you, these compliments and declarations and sentimental nonsense are very fine old things—conventional if you like, tiresome, often ridiculous; but they go with something else which is forever young.

THE MARQUISE. You're getting mixed up. What is this thing which is very old and forever young?

THE COUNT. Love.

THE MARQUISE. Sir, what you say is sheer eloquence.

THE COUNT. No, madam. What I mean is this: love is eternally young and the ways of expressing it are and will remain eternally old. The outworn formulas, the repetitions, the bits of old romances that burst forth from the heart heaven knows how, this whole equipment and paraphernalia is like a procession of old courtiers and diplomats cackling outside the king's chamber. They all pass on but the King never dies. Love is dead, long live Love!

THE MARQUISE. Love?

THE COUNT. Love. And even if—.

THE MARQUISE. Please hand me that fire-screen.

THE COUNT. This one?

THE MARQUISE. No, the silk one. Your fire is blinding me now.

THE COUNT, *passing the screen to the* MARQUISE. Even if one only imagines that one loves, isn't it a delightful thing none the less?

THE MARQUISE. But I tell you it is always the same old thing.

THE COUNT. Yet always new, as the poet says. What do you expect—some new invention? Do you want people to make love to you in Sanskrit? This Venus on your mantel clock—she too is always the same—is she any the less beautiful? If you resemble your grandmother, are you any the less pretty?

THE MARQUISE. That's it: the chorus again—"You're so pretty." Please give me that cushion over there.

THE COUNT, *picking up the cushion and holding it in his hand*. That likeness of Venus was made to be beautiful, to be loved and admired, which doesn't bore her in the least. If the beautiful figure found at Melos once had a living model, certainly the great wench had more lovers than she could use and she let herself be loved like the rest, like her cousin Astarte, like Aspasia, like Manon Lescaut.

THE MARQUISE. Sir, what you say is sheer mythology.

THE COUNT, *still holding the cushion*. No, really, madam, I can't tell you how this fashionable indifference, this coldness which rails and cavils, this air of deep experience which reduces everything to naught, pains me in a young woman. You aren't the first in whom I have seen it. It's a disease which is epidemic in drawing rooms. One averts the head, one yawns, one says like you just now that one cannot bear to hear love spoken of. If that's so, why do you wear lace? What is that ornament doing in your hair?

THE MARQUISE. And what is that cushion doing in your hand? I asked you for it to put it under my feet.

THE COUNT. All right, it's at your feet—and so am I, and I'm going to make a declaration—like it or not—old as the hills and flat as your hat; for I am furious with you. *He kneels on the cushion at the* MARQUISE'S *feet.*

THE MARQUISE. Will you do me the favor of getting up?

THE COUNT. No, listen to me a moment.

THE MARQUISE. You won't get up?

THE COUNT. No, no, and again No—to use your own words; I shan't get up unless you listen.

THE MARQUISE. I have the honor of bidding you good-day. *She rises.*

THE COUNT, *still kneeling*. Marquise, in heaven's name, don't be so hard. You will drive me mad.

THE MARQUISE. You'll get over it at the Café.

THE COUNT, *kneeling*. No, on my honor. I speak from the bottom of my heart. I'll confess that when I came here I had no set purpose; I meant to see you only casually—as is proved by my opening this door three times to leave you. The conversation we've just had, your mocking me, your coldness even, have carried me beyond what I should have done. But it isn't today only, from the first day I saw you I loved you, adored you. I'm not exaggerating, it's true: for more than a year I've adored you. All I ever think of is——

THE MARQUISE. Good-bye. *She goes out, leaving the door open.*

THE COUNT, *remaining alone and on his knees, finally gets up*. It is perfectly true that this door is a cold front. *He is about to go through it but sees the* MARQUISE. Ah, Marquise, you are playing with me.

THE MARQUISE, *leaning on the doorjamb*. You have got up?

THE COUNT. Yes, I am going, never to see you again.

THE MARQUISE. Come tonight to the ball; I'll save a waltz for you.

THE COUNT. Never! I shall never see you again. I am in despair, I am done for.

THE MARQUISE. What is the matter?

THE COUNT. I am done for because I love you like a boy. I swear to you on the most sacred——

THE MARQUISE. Good-bye. *She makes ready to leave again.*

THE COUNT. It's my turn to go, madam. Stay, I beg of you. I can tell I am going to suffer horribly!

THE MARQUISE, *in a serious tone*. But really, sir, what do you want with me?

THE COUNT. But dear lady, what I want, what I wish——

THE MARQUISE. What is it? You will end by getting on my nerves, you know. Is it your idea that I should become your mistress and take over a legacy from your pink hats? I warn you that such an idea is to me worse than displeasing, it is revolting.

THE COUNT. You, Marquise, good heavens! If I could, I would lay my whole life and being at your feet—I would put in your hands my name, my property, my honor. How could I confuse you for a single instant, I won't say with the creatures that you only refer to in order to upset me, but with any other woman in the world? How could you suppose me capable of it? Do you give me no credit for judgment? Was I so careless or deranged that you began to doubt my respect for you? A while ago you said you took some pleasure in my company, possibly even felt some degree of friendship—didn't you say?—well, can you imagine that a man thus singled out by you and favored with so precious and tender a privilege, would forget what was due you? Am I then so blind or witless? Make you my mistress—assuredly not, my wife!

THE MARQUISE. Really? Why, if you had said this when you first came in we wouldn't have quarreled. So you want to marry me?

THE COUNT. Of course! I'm dying to! I never dared tell you before, but I've thought of nothing else for a year. I'd give my lifeblood for the merest glimmer of hope——

THE MARQUISE. Hold on a moment: you're a great deal richer than I.

THE COUNT. I don't think so, actually. What difference does it make? Please, please, let's not talk about that: the way you're smiling now makes me tremble with hope and fear. Give me some hint, for mercy's sake, my life is in your hands.

THE MARQUISE. I shall give you two proverbs. The first is: "There's nothing like getting together." Therefore, we shall discuss the matter further.

THE COUNT. Then you're not angry at what I've said?

THE MARQUISE. Of course not. And this is the second proverb: "A door should be either open or shut." Now for the last three quarters of an hour, thanks to you, that door has been neither open nor shut. As a result this room is a perfect icebox. Therefore, again, you are going to give me your arm and take me to dine with my Mother. After which you will go to Fossin's.

THE COUNT. Fossin's, madam: whatever for?

THE MARQUISE. My ring.

THE COUNT. Ah, to be sure. I'd forgotten. What about your ring, dear Marquise?

THE MARQUISE. You call me Marquise, do you? Well, on my ring, precisely, there is a marquise's crown, and since the ring may be used as a seal—what do you think, Count—it might be wise to have the coronet taken off. Now I'll go and put my hat on.

THE COUNT. You make me the happiest of men. How can I—?

THE MARQUISE. Oh, do shut that wretched door! This room will be unlivable.

The COUNT *shuts the door.*

Thérèse Raquin

A Drama in Four Acts

by EMILE ZOLA

English version by Kathleen Boutall

CHARACTERS

LAURENT

CAMILLE

GRIVET

MICHAUD

MADAME RAQUIN

THÉRÈSE RAQUIN

SUZANNE

The scene is a large bedroom, in a byway of the Pont Neuf, which serves at the same time as parlor and dining room. It is lofty, dark and dilapidated, hung with a faded greyish paper, furnished with shabby oddments and cluttered up with cardboard boxes of haberdashery. At the back is a door on the left of which is a sideboard and on the right a wardrobe. On the left wall upstage, on a slant, is an alcove in which can be seen a bed and a window looking out on a blank wall. Below this there is a small door and lower downstage a work table. On the right wall, upstage, is a flight of stairs leading down to the shop. Below this is a fireplace and on the mantelpiece are a columned clock and two bouquets of flowers under glass shades. In the middle of the room is a round table covered with oilcloth. There are two armchairs, one blue, the other green, and occasional chairs.

The setting is the same for the four acts.

ACT ONE

The time is 8 o'clock on a summer evening. Supper is over and the table is still laid. The window is open. The atmosphere is one of peace and of middle-class comfort. CAMILLE *is seated in an armchair to the right, posing for his portrait. He is wearing an evening suit and is stiffly conscious of his best clothes.* LAURENT, *by his easel at the window, is painting. Beside him on a low chair crouches* THÉRÈSE, *her chin in her hand, her thoughts far away.* MADAME RAQUIN *is clearing the table.*

CAMILLE. Does it disturb you if I talk?

LAURENT. Of course not. So long as you keep still.

CAMILLE. I go to sleep after supper if I don't talk. You are lucky to have such good health. It doesn't matter what you eat. I ought not to have had that second helping of the custard—it upset me. I've got such a weak tummy. You're fond of custard, aren't you?

LAURENT. Yes, very. It's good stuff.

CAMILLE. They know what you like here. The custard was made specially for you—although they know it doesn't agree with me. Mama spoils you—doesn't she, Thérèse? Thérèse, doesn't Mama spoil Laurent?

THÉRÈSE, *without moving her head.* Yes.

MME. RAQUIN, *taking up a pile of plates.* Don't take any notice of them, Laurent. It was Camille who first told me that you preferred custard to vanilla and Thérèse who insisted on shaking the sugar over it.

CAMILLE. Mama, you know, you are a humbug.

MME. RAQUIN. Me, a humbug?

CAMILLE, *to* MME. RAQUIN *as she goes out smiling.* Yes, yes, you are. *To* LAURENT. She's fond of you because you come from Vernon like herself. Do you remember the pennies she used to give us when we were children?

LAURENT. Yes, you used to buy heaps of apples.

CAMILLE. And you used to buy little penknives. It was lucky finding each other again in Paris. It was such a relief. I was bored to death. It was so frightfully dull here when I got back from the office. Can you still see?

LAURENT. Not very well, but I want to finish it.

CAMILLE. It's nearly eight o'clock. These summer evenings are so dreadfully long. I wish you had painted me by daylight; it would have looked nicer. You ought to have put in a country scene, instead of that grey background. But there is scarcely time in the mornings to swallow a cup of coffee before I have to go off to the office. I say, it can't be very good for the digestion to sit here after a meal without moving.

LAURENT. I'll let you go in a minute. This is the last sitting.

MME. RAQUIN *enters, takes last things from table and wipes it over.*

CAMILLE. You would have had a much better light by day. We don't get the sun but it shines on the wall opposite and that lights up the room. It was a queer idea of Mama's to take a place in the Pont Neuf Passage. It's so damp. On rainy days you would think it was a cellar.

LAURENT. Oh well, in business one place is as good as another.

CAMILLE. I daresay you're right. They've got the haberdashery shop downstairs to occupy themselves with. But I have nothing to do with that.

LAURENT. The flat is convenient.

CAMILLE. I'm glad you think so. Apart from this room where we eat and sleep there is only Mama's room. You can't count the kitchen. That's only a dark hole like a cupboard. Nothing shuts and you freeze. There's an abominable draught at night from that little door on the staircase. *Points to door.*

MME. RAQUIN, *having finished her clearing away.* Poor dear Camille, you are never satisfied. I did it for the best. It was your own idea to be a clerk in Paris. I would have started business in Vernon again. When you married your cousin Thérèse I had to work again in case you had children.

CAMILLE. Well, I thought we should live in a street where I could see plenty of people passing. I should have sat at the window and watched the carriages. That's fun. But now all I can see from here when I open the window is the blank wall opposite and the fanlight underneath. I prefer our Vernon windows. I could see the Seine flowing by— although that wasn't much fun.

MME. RAQUIN. Well, I offered to go back there.

CAMILLE. Good Lord, no—not now that I've discovered Laurent at the office. After all, I'm only here in the evenings. I don't care if the passage is damp as long as you're happy.

MME. RAQUIN. Now don't bully me any more about this place. It's quite all right.

Shop bell rings.

Shop, Thérèse. THÉRÈSE *does not move.* Aren't you going down? Oh, all right. Just a minute, I'll go.

MME. RAQUIN *goes down to shop.*

CAMILLE. I don't want to upset her but the passage is very unhealthy. What I'm afraid of is an attack of pneumonia which would carry me off. I'm not as strong as the rest of you.

Pause.

I say, can't I relax for a bit? I can't feel my left arm.

LAURENT. If you like. I've practically finished.

CAMILLE. I'm sorry, but I can't stand it any longer. I must walk about for a bit. *He walks up and down the stage and finally comes to where* THÉRÈSE *is sitting.* I've never been able to understand how it is my wife can sit still for hours on end without moving a finger. I should be pins and needles all over. It irritates me to see a person forever mooning. Laurent, doesn't it annoy you to feel her like that there beside you? Now then, Thérèse, wake up! Are you enjoying yourself?

THÉRÈSE, *without moving.* Yes.

CAMILLE. Well, I hope you're happy, sitting there like a stuck pig. When her father, Captain Degans, left her with Mama her great big staring dark eyes used to frighten me. He was a captain, you know, but a dreadful man. Died in Africa, never came back to Vernon again. That's right, isn't it, Thérèse?

THÉRÈSE, *without moving.* Yes.

CAMILLE. She's lost her tongue. Poor thing! *Kisses her.* Never mind, you're a good girl. We've never had a quarrel since Mama got us married. *To* THÉRÈSE. You're not cross with me?

THÉRÈSE. No.

LAURENT, *tapping* CAMILLE *on the shoulder with his maulstick.* Now then, Camille. I'm only asking you for ten minutes more. CAMILLE *sits.* Turn your head to the left. CAMILLE *looks left.* That's it!—now don't move.

CAMILLE, *after a pause.* Any news of your Father?

LAURENT. No, he's forgotten me. Besides, I never write to him.

CAMILLE. It's queer, all the same—father and son. It wouldn't do for me.

LAURENT. Papa Laurent had his own ideas. He wanted me to be a lawyer to act for him in his everlasting lawsuits with his neighbors. As soon as he found out that I was spending the money for my fees on running about the studios he cut off supplies. There's not much fun in being a lawyer.

CAMILLE. But it is a good position. You have got to have brains and it is well paid.

LAURENT. I met a man who was at college with me and who is an artist. So I studied painting too.

CAMILLE. You ought to have stuck to it. You could probably have got a decoration by now.

LAURENT. I couldn't. I was starving. So I chucked it and looked for a job.

CAMILLE. Well, at any rate, you still know how to paint.

LAURENT. I'm nothing wonderful. I liked painting because it was fun and not too much like hard work. But at first what I regretted when I started going to the office was that devil of a studio. I had a divan there and I used to sleep all the afternoon on it. I've had some gay nuptial nights there, I can tell you.

CAMILLE. Do you mean you had affairs with the models?

LAURENT. Of course. There was a magnificent blonde . . .

THÉRÈSE *rises slowly and goes down to the shop.*

We have shocked your wife.

CAMILLE. If she was listening. She hasn't much brain, poor girl, but she looks after me marvelously when I'm ill. Mama has taught her to make my camomile tea.

LAURENT. I don't think she likes me very much.

CAMILLE. Well, you know, these women . . . I say, haven't you finished?

LAURENT. Yes, you can get up now.

CAMILLE, *rises, and goes to portrait.* Quite, quite finished?

LAURENT. It only has to be framed.

CAMILLE. Oh yes—it's a great success, isn't it? Yes, of course it is. *Goes to door and shouts over staircase to shop.* Mama, Thérèse, come and look. Laurent has finished the picture.

MME. RAQUIN *and* THÉRÈSE *enter from staircase.*

MME. RAQUIN. What, he's finished?

CAMILLE, *holding portrait.* Yes, come and look.

MME. RAQUIN, *looking at portrait.* Ah—yes. It's like. Especially the mouth. The mouth is strikingly like. Don't you think so, Thérèse? Now, clear away those things for Laurent. *To* LAURENT. You have finished, haven't you?

THÉRÈSE, *without turning to look at it.* Yes. *Crosses to window, leans against the window frame, her head pressed against the frame, her thoughts far away.*

CAMILLE. And my dress suit—my wedding suit. I've only worn it four times. The cloth of the collar looks absolutely real.

MME. RAQUIN. And so does the arm of the chair.

CAMILLE. H'm, amazing. It looks like real wood. It's my own armchair too. We brought it from Vernon. No one uses it except me. *Pointing to the other armchair.* Mama's is blue.

MME. RAQUIN, *to* LAURENT, *who has put away his easel and painting materials.* Why have you put that dark bit under the left eye?

LAURENT. It's the shadow.

CAMILLE, *putting portrait on easel which is leaning against the wall between the alcove and the window.* It would probably have been nicer without the shadow, but never mind, I look distinguished—as though I were going to a party.

MME. RAQUIN. Laurent, dear, how can I thank you! And you won't even let Camille pay for the paints.

LAURENT. But it is I who should thank him for sitting.

CAMILLE. No, we can't let it go at that. I'm going out to get a bottle of something. Dash it all, we'll christen the picture.

LAURENT. Oh, all right, if you want to. I'm going out to get the frame. *Gets coat and hat.* Today's Thursday and Monsieur Grivet and the Michaud couple must see the portrait in its proper place. *He goes out.* CAMILLE *takes off his jacket, changes his tie, puts on his overcoat which his Mother gives him and starts to follow* LAURENT.

CAMILLE, *turning back.* What shall I get?

MME. RAQUIN. It must be something he likes. He's such a dear boy. He's like one of the family now.

CAMILLE. Yes, he's like a brother. What about anisette?

MME. RAQUIN. Do you think he likes anisette? Some really good wine might be better, with some cakes.

CAMILLE, *to* THÉRÈSE. You're not saying anything, Thérèse. Do you remember if he likes Malaga?

THÉRÈSE. No, but I do know that he likes anything. He eats and drinks like a wolf.

MME. RAQUIN. My dear child—how can you——

CAMILLE. That's right, Mama, you scold her. She can't bear him. He has noticed it. He told me so. It's not very nice. *To* THÉRÈSE. I'm not going to let you spoil my friendships. What have you got against him?

THÉRÈSE. Nothing. He is always here. He has all his meals here. You give him the best of everything. It's Laurent here, Laurent there—it drives me wild! He's not very amusing and he's greedy and lazy.

MME. RAQUIN. Now, now, Thérèse, Laurent is not very happy. He lives in a garret and they feed him very poorly at that little café of his. I'm quite glad for him to have a good dinner here and to warm himself at the fire. He makes himself at home and has a smoke, that's what I like to see. Poor boy, he's all alone in the world.

THÉRÈSE. Oh, all right, just as you like. Pet and coddle him. It is nothing to me.

CAMILLE. Mama, I've got an idea. I'm going to get a bottle of champagne; it'll be splendid.

MME. RAQUIN. Yes, a bottle of champagne will do as payment for the picture. Don't forget the cakes.

CAMILLE. It's not half-past eight yet. Our visitors won't be here until nine o'clock. They'll have a nice surprise when they see champagne. *He goes out.*

MME. RAQUIN, *to* THÉRÈSE. You'll light the lamp, won't you? *Going out.* I'm going down to the shop.

THÉRÈSE, *left alone, stands still for a moment, then looking round she takes a deep breath. Coming downstage she gives a gesture of weariness and boredom. Then, hearing* LAURENT *coming in from the little door, she smiles and thrills with sudden joy. During this scene the light becomes dim as night falls.*

LAURENT. Thérèse.

THÉRÈSE. Laurent, my darling! My love—I felt you would come. *Taking his hands, she leads him downstage.* It's eight days since I've seen you. I waited for you every afternoon. I hoped you'd manage to get away from your office. If you hadn't come I should have done something desperate. Tell me, why did you stay away for eight whole days? I can't stand it any longer. Shaking hands before the others this evening —so cold—like strangers.

LAURENT. I'll explain everything.

THÉRÈSE. You're frightened. You baby. We're quite safe here. *Raises her voice and moves a pace or two.* Who would believe that you and I are in love? No one would ever come and look for us here—in this room.

LAURENT, *pulling her to him and taking her in his arms.* Now, now, don't be silly. No, of course I'm not afraid to come here.

THÉRÈSE. Then you're afraid of me. Now, own up. You're afraid that I love you too much—afraid that I shall be a nuisance.

LAURENT. Why do you doubt me? Don't you know that I can't sleep because of you? It's driving me out of my mind—and I never took women seriously before. You have wakened something in the very depths of my being, Thérèse. I'm someone I never knew existed. And it frightens me because it isn't natural to love anyone as I love you— I'm terrified that it's going to take us out of our depth.

THÉRÈSE. Nothing can ever spoil our happiness; the sun will always shine for us.

LAURENT, *suddenly breaking away.* Did you hear someone on the stairs?

THÉRÈSE. It's only the damp. It makes the stairs creak. Let our love be without fear and without remorse. If you knew what my life has been like. As a child I grew up in the stuffy air of a sickroom.

LAURENT. Poor Thérèse.

THÉRÈSE. Oh, I was unhappy. I used to crouch over the fire making his everlasting concoctions. If I moved, his mother used to scold me. You see, Camille must not be wakened. I used to stutter and stammer and I moved about like a shaky old woman. I was so clumsy that Camille used to make fun of me. But I was strong and sturdy when I was little and I used to clench my fists and I'd have liked to smash up everything. They told me my Mother was the daughter of an African chief. It must have been true. I was always dreaming of running away—of escaping and running barefoot in the dust. I would have begged like a gypsy. You see, I felt I would rather starve than stay and be kept by them.

Her voice has gradually become louder, and LAURENT *crosses the stage to listen.*

LAURENT. Not so loud. You'll have your Aunt coming up.

THÉRÈSE. Let her come. I don't know why I agreed to marry Camille. It was all settled for me. My Aunt waited until we were old enough. I was twelve when she said to me: "You will love your poor little cousin and take care of him." She wanted a nurse for him, someone to make his camomile tea. He was such a puny little thing. Over and over again she had to fight to save his life and she brought me up to be his servant. I never stood up for myself; they made a coward of me. I felt sorry for him. On our wedding night instead of going into my own bedroom on the left of the stairs I went into Camille's room on the right. And that was all! But you—you—oh Laurent!

LAURENT. You love me? *Takes her in his arms and leads her gently to chair by table.*

THÉRÈSE. I love you. I love you. I have loved you since that day when Camille brought you into the shop. Do you remember—the day when you two met again in the office? I don't know how it happened. I'm proud and I'm passionate. I don't know what sort of love it was. It seemed more like hate. The sight of you drove me mad. The moment you came in my nerves were strained to breaking-point—and yet I longed for the pain and used to wait for your coming. When you were painting I was nailed there on that stool at your feet and yet I longed to get away—hating myself . . .

LAURENT. I adore you. *Kneeling before her.*

THÉRÈSE. And our only amusement is our Thursday evenings. Always that silly old Grivet and Michaud. But you know all about them with their eternal dominoes. They've driven me almost mad. Thursday after Thursday the same boring jokes. But now, I'm the lucky one and I've got my revenge. When we are sitting round the table after our meal and having our friendly gossip I shall be taking a wicked delight in remembering my secret happiness. While you are all playing dominoes, there I'll be, doing my embroidery as usual—not saying a word. And in the midst of all this humdrum, I'll be counting over my precious memories and feeling again the ecstasy.

LAURENT, *listening at staircase door.* I tell you, you are talking too loudly; we'll be caught—you'll see, your Aunt will come up. Where is my hat?

THÉRÈSE, *rising.* Yes, you're right. I think you'd better go. What about tomorrow? You will come, won't you? At two o'clock?

LAURENT. No, don't expect me. It's impossible.

THÉRÈSE. Impossible? Why?

LAURENT. My chief is beginning to notice. He has threatened to sack me if I'm away again.

THÉRÈSE. Then we shan't see one another any more? You're leaving me. So it's come to this—all your caution—What a coward you are!

LAURENT. Listen to me—We can be happy—It's only a matter of taking our chances and being patient. So often I have dreamed of having you to myself for a whole day. Then the day becomes a month—a year—a whole lifetime of happiness. A whole lifetime to ourselves for love—to be together. I'd leave my job and I would start to paint again. You should do just whatever you wanted. We would adore one another for always. You would be happy?

THÉRÈSE, *smiling, her head on his breast.* Happy? Yes—ah, yes.

LAURENT, *in a low voice and backing away from her.* If only you were free——

THÉRÈSE, *in a dream.* We would be married. Nothing to be afraid of. A dream come true.

LAURENT. In these shadows I can only see your eyes—your shining eyes. *Pause.*

They'd drive me mad if I were not wise for the two of us—Now it must be goodbye, Thérèse——

THÉRÈSE. You won't come tomorrow?

LAURENT. Now, you must trust me. If we don't see one another for a little while you must tell yourself that we're working for our happiness. *Kisses her and leaves through the little door.*

THÉRÈSE, *after a pause.* If only I were free.

MME. RAQUIN, *enters.* What's this? No light yet? What a dreamer! The lamp is ready, I'll go and light it. *Goes out through door at back.*

CAMILLE, *enters with bottle of champagne and a bag of cakes.* Wherever are you? Why haven't you got the light?

THÉRÈSE. Your Mother has gone for the lamp.

CAMILLE, *in fright.* Oh, it's you, is it? You frightened me. Why couldn't you speak naturally? You know I don't like practical jokes played on me in the dark.

THÉRÈSE. I'm not joking.

CAMILLE. I could only just see you—looking like a ghost. Games like that are silly. Now if I wake up tonight I shall think that a woman with a white face is walking round my bed to murder me. It's all very well for you to laugh.

THÉRÈSE. I'm not laughing.

MME. RAQUIN, *enters with lamp.* What's the matter now?

CAMILLE. Thérèse is amusing herself by frightening me. It wouldn't have taken much more to make me drop the champagne. That would have been three francs gone.

MME. RAQUIN. You only paid three francs? *Takes bottle.*

CAMILLE. Yes. I went to the Boulevard St. Michel where I'd seen one in a grocer's marked down. It's just as good as one at eight francs. It's a well-known fact that these shopkeepers are a lot of frauds and that it's only the label that's different. Here are the cakes, Mama.

MME. RAQUIN. Give them to me. We'll have everything on the table so that Grivet and Michaud will have a surprise when they come in. Give me a couple of plates, Thérèse. *Puts bottle between two plates of cakes.* THÉRÈSE *goes to worktable and takes up her embroidery.*

CAMILLE. Monsieur Grivet is punctuality personified. As nine strikes, in he will come. Be nice to him, Thérèse, won't you? And you too, Mama. He's only a senior clerk but he can be very useful to me. He's really quite important. The older men in the office swear that in twenty years he's never been a minute late. Laurent is wrong when he says he'll never make his mark.

MME. RAQUIN. Michaud is very punctual, too. When he was superintendent of police at Vernon, he used to come up at eight o'clock every night on the dot, do you remember? We used to congratulate him on it!

CAMILLE. Yes, but he seems to have gone all to pieces since he has retired to Paris with that niece of his. It has upset him. Suzanne leads him by the nose. But it really is nice to have friends to entertain once a week.

It would be too expensive, of course, to do it more often. Oh, I've got a plan I wanted to tell you about before they arrive.

MME. RAQUIN. What is it?

CAMILLE. Well, you know that I promised Thérèse to take her to Saint-Ouen one Sunday before it gets too cold. She won't go out with me in the town although it's much nicer than the country. She says I tire her out and that I don't know how to walk. So I thought it would be a good idea if we went on Sunday to Saint-Ouen and took Laurent with us.

MME. RAQUIN. Very well, children, you go to Saint-Ouen. My legs are too old for me to go with you, but it's an excellent idea. That will quite square you up with Laurent for the portrait.

CAMILLE. Laurent is such fun in the country. Do you remember, Thérèse, when he came with us to Suresnes? The idiot! He's as strong as a horse. He jumps ditches full of water and he throws stones to incredible heights. When we were at Suresnes on the roundabouts, he imitated the galloping postilions and the cracking of the whips and the noise of the spurs. He was so good that a wedding party there laughed until they cried. The bride was positively ill, wasn't she, Thérèse?

THÉRÈSE. He drank enough at dinner to make him funny.

CAMILLE. Oh, you don't understand that people like to enjoy themselves. If I depended on you to make me laugh it would be pretty dreary at Saint-Ouen. Do you know what she does, Mama? She sits on the ground and looks at the water. After all, if I take Laurent he will keep me amused. Where the devil has he gone to get his frame?

Shop bell rings.

Ah, there he is. Monsieur Grivet won't be here for seven minutes yet.

LAURENT. That shop is hopeless. *Sees* CAMILLE *and* MADAME RAQUIN *whispering.* What are you two hatching between you?

CAMILLE. Guess.

LAURENT. You're going to invite me to dinner tomorrow and there will be boiled chicken.

MME. RAQUIN. Greedy!

CAMILLE. Better than that—much better. On Sunday I am taking Thérèse to Saint-Ouen and you are coming with us. Will you?

LAURENT. Indeed I will. *Takes picture from easel and gets hammer from* MME. RAQUIN.

MME. RAQUIN. But you will be careful, won't you? Laurent, I entrust Camille to you. You are so strong and I am happier when I know he is with you.

CAMILLE. Mother gets on my nerves with her everlasting fuss-fuss-fussing. D'you know that I can't go to the end of the street without her imagining something awful has happened? No, I don't like always being treated like a little boy. Now, we'll take a cab to the fortifications and then we'll only have the one fare to pay. Then we'll follow the towpath. The afternoon we'll spend on the island and we'll feed in the evening at a little inn on the riverbank. Well? All right?

LAURENT, *putting canvas in frame.* Splendid, but I can go one better.

CAMILLE. What?

LAURENT, *with a look at* THÉRÈSE. A boat on the river.

MME. RAQUIN. No—no boat. I should be worried.

THÉRÈSE. You don't expect Camille to take any chances on the water. He's too frightened.

CAMILLE. Me frightened?

LAURENT. Of course you are. I forgot you were afraid of the water. When we used to paddle in the Seine at Vernon you used to stay shivering on the bank. All right then—no boat.

CAMILLE. But it's not true. I'm not afraid. We will go boating. See? Heavens, you'll soon be making me out an imbecile. We'll see who is the most frightened of the three of us. It's Thérèse who's afraid.

THÉRÈSE. My poor dear, you're pale at the thought of it.

CAMILLE. That's right. Laugh at me—laugh at me. We'll see. We'll see.

MME. RAQUIN. Camille darling, give up the idea—for my sake.

CAMILLE. Mama, please, don't nag at me. You know it makes me ill.

LAURENT. Well, let your wife decide.

THÉRÈSE. Accidents can happen anywhere.

LAURENT. That's very true. You can slip in the street, or a tile can fall from a roof——

CAMILLE. Besides, you know how I adore the Seine.

LAURENT. Right! We're agreed. We go on the river. You win.

MME. RAQUIN, *to* LAURENT. I can't tell you how much this worries me. Camille is so headstrong. You saw how he behaved.

LAURENT. Don't worry. Don't worry. You needn't be afraid, I shall be there. Ah! Now I'm going to hang the portrait. *Hangs portrait above sideboard.*

CAMILLE. You're sure it's in a good light there.

Shop bell rings and clock strikes nine.

Nine o'clock! Ah, there's Monsieur Grivet.

GRIVET, *enters.* I'm the first. Good evening, ladies and gentlemen.

MME. RAQUIN. Good evening, Monsieur Grivet. Shall I take your umbrella?

Taking umbrella and going to put it in upstage corner by fireplace. Is it raining?

GRIVET. It's threatening. Excuse me, that's not the place for my umbrella. Not that corner, not that corner. *Moves umbrella downstage corner.* You know my little ways. In the other corner. There—thank you——

MME. RAQUIN. Give me your galoshes.

GRIVET. No, no. I'll see to them myself. *Taking off galoshes.* I look after myself. A place for everything and everything in its place. And then there's nothing to worry about. *Puts galoshes beside umbrella.*

CAMILLE. And what's your news, Monsieur Grivet?

GRIVET. Well, I left the office at four-thirty. I had dinner at six o'clock at the little Orleans restaurant. At seven o'clock I read my paper at the Café Saturnin and as today is Thursday, instead of going back to bed at nine o'clock as I usually do, I came here. *Thinking.* Yes, I think that's all.

LAURENT. Did you see anything interesting on the way, Monsieur Grivet?

GRIVET. Oh yes, how stupid of me. There was an enormous crowd in the rue St. André-des-Arts. I had to walk on the other side of the road to get by and it put me out. You know I go to the office along the left-hand pavement and come back along the other side.

MME. RAQUIN. The right-hand one.

GRIVET. No. On the left. You see, I walk along the pavement like this—— *Walking with left hand extended to indicate left hand pavement, turns and comes back, still with left hand extended, indicating opposite side of road.* and I come back on the other side in the evening. That makes it the left hand side, you see. I always keep to the left, just like the trains, you see. Then I know where I am.

LAURENT. But what was everybody doing on the pavement?

GRIVET. I don't know. How should I?

MME. RAQUIN. An accident of some kind, I expect.

GRIVET. Yes, of course, it must have been an accident. I never thought of that. You know, that's relieved my mind, your saying it was an accident. *Sits in front of table.*

MME. RAQUIN. Ah, here is Monsieur Michaud.

Enter MICHAUD *and* SUZANNE. SUZANNE *takes off shawl and hat and goes to speak to* THÉRÈSE *at worktable.* MICHAUD *shakes hands all round.*

MICHAUD. I think I'm late. *To* MONSIEUR GRIVET, *who has his watch in his hand.* I know, six minutes past nine. It's the child's fault. *Indicating* SUZANNE. We had to stop and look in every shopwindow. *Puts his stick in same corner as* GRIVET'S *umbrella.*

GRIVET. Please forgive me, that's the place for my umbrella. You know I don't like that. I have left the other corner for your stick.

MICHAUD. Well, well, don't let's worry about it.

CAMILLE, *in an undertone to* LAURENT. I say, I think Grivet is annoyed because there is champagne. He's looked at the bottle three times, but hasn't said a word. I'm amazed he didn't show more surprise at it.

MICHAUD, *seeing champagne*. My word! Do you want to send us home rolling? Cakes and champagne!

GRIVET. What! Champagne! I've only tasted it four times in my life.

MICHAUD. What's the festive occasion?

MME. RAQUIN. We are celebrating Camille's portrait. Laurent finished it this evening. *Holds lamp to show portrait.* Look!

All join her except THÉRÈSE *at work table, and* LAURENT *who is leaning against mantelpiece.*

CAMILLE. It's a striking likeness, isn't it? I look as if I'm off to a party.

MICHAUD. Yes, yes.

MME. RAQUIN. It's only just done. You can smell the paint.

GRIVET. Yes. I noticed a smell. That's the advantage of a photograph. It doesn't smell.

CAMILLE. Yes, but when it's dry . . .

GRIVET. Ah yes—when the paint's dry . . . It'll dry all right. There's a shop in the rue de la Harpe which took five days to dry.

MME. RAQUIN. Well, Monsieur Michaud, you like it?

MICHAUD. Very good, very good.

They all turn back and MME. RAQUIN *puts lamp on table.*

CAMILLE. Now, Mama, what about some tea? We will have the champagne after the dominoes.

GRIVET, *sitting*. Quarter past nine. We shall have time for the conqueror.

MME. RAQUIN. I won't keep you five minutes. You stay here, Thérèse, as you don't feel well.

SUZANNE. Well, I'm bursting with health, Madame Raquin, I'll come and help you. I like being useful in the house.

They go out through door at back.

CAMILLE. And what's your news, Monsieur Michaud?

MICHAUD. On nothing. Just taking Suzanne into the Luxembourg to do her needlework. Oh, but of course, if you want news, there's the tragedy in the rue St. André-des-Arts.

CAMILLE. Tragedy, what tragedy? Monsieur Grivet said he saw a lot of people there.

MICHAUD. It's been crowded ever since this morning. *To* GRIVET. They were all looking up, weren't they?

GRIVET. I couldn't tell you. I had to cross over. So it was an accident then? *Puts on a skullcap and draws cuffs over his sleeves, taking them from his pocket.*

MICHAUD. Yes, at the Hôtel Bourgogne. They found a woman's body cut in four pieces in a trunk—in a trunk belonging to a guest who has disappeared.

GRIVET. You don't say. In four pieces? How can you cut up a woman's body into four pieces?

CAMILLE. How horrible!

GRIVET. And *I* passed the place. I remember now they were looking up in the air. Did they see anything up there?

MICHAUD. The crowd thought they could see the window of the room where the trunk was discovered. As a matter of fact they were wrong. *The* room looks on to the courtyard.

LAURENT. Have they got the murderer?

MICHAUD. No. One of my old colleagues who has the case in hand said they were completely in the dark.

GRIVET *tosses his head and laughs.*

It's going to be a bit difficult to see that justice is done.

LAURENT. Have they established the identity of the victim?

MICHAUD. No. The body was naked and the head missing.

GRIVET. The head missing? I suppose someone has mislaid it.

CAMILLE. Don't! It gives me the creeps—your woman in four pieces.

GRIVET. Oh, but you can afford to take it lightly when you're in no danger yourself. When Monsieur Michaud was superintendent of police he had some very funny stories. Do you remember the one about the gendarme who was buried and they found his fingers in a box of carrots? He told us that one last autumn. It was a good one, I thought. We know we're quite safe here; this is a God-fearing house. I shouldn't say the same thing about some places. If I were going through a dark wood with Monsieur Michaud—well——

LAURENT. Monsieur Michaud, do you think a lot of crimes go unpunished?

MICHAUD. Yes, worse luck. Disappearances, lingering deaths, stranglings, fatal falls—not a cry heard, not a drop of blood seen. The law is there but it has no clues. There's more than one murderer walking about in broad daylight.

GRIVET, *laughing loudly.* I can't help laughing. And they're not arrested?

MICHAUD. My dear Monsieur Grivet, if they are not arrested, it's because there are no clues.

CAMILLE. Then is there something wrong with the police?

MICHAUD. Oh, the police are all right, but they can't do the impossible. Let me tell you again that there are some very lucky murderers living on the fat of the land who are both loved and respected. Don't wag your head, Monsieur Grivet.

GRIVET. Wag my head? I will wag my head. You leave me alone.

MICHAUD. It's quite possible that some acquaintance of yours is a murderer and that you shake hands with him every day.

GRIVET. Oh, I say, don't say that. You mustn't say that because you know quite well it isn't true. If I liked, I could tell you a story . . .

MICHAUD. Go on then. Tell it.

GRIVET. Very well, I will. It's the story of the thieving magpie.

MICHAUD *shrugs his shoulders.*

Perhaps you know it. You know everything. Some time ago there was a servant who was thrown into prison because he'd stolen a silver spoon. A couple of months later, the spoon was found in a magpie's nest when they were cutting down a tree—a poplar tree it was. The magpie was the thief. The servant was set at liberty. You see, the culprit is always punished!

MICHAUD, *sneering.* Did they put the magpie in prison?

GRIVET, *annoyed.* Magpie in prison! Magpie in prison? Michaud, you're an idiot.

CAMILLE. No, that isn't what Monsieur Grivet meant. You're getting him all mixed up.

GRIVET. The police are no good, that's all. It's all wrong.

CAMILLE. Laurent, what do you think? Is it possible for a man to kill anyone and to get away with it?

LAURENT, *goes slowly to where* THÉRÈSE *is sitting.* Don't you see that Monsieur Michaud is pulling your leg? He's trying to frighten you with his stories. How can he know what he confesses no one knows? And if there are such clever people about, well, good luck to them. I'm sure your wife isn't so gullible. What do you say, Thérèse?

THÉRÈSE. What no one knows, doesn't exist.

CAMILLE. Let's change the subject, for goodness sake and talk of something else.

GRIVET. I quite agree. Let's talk about something else.

CAMILLE. We haven't brought up the chairs from the shop. Will someone come and help me carry them up? *Goes down to shop.*

GRIVET, *gets up grumbling.* That's what he calls talking about something else—going to fetch chairs.

MICHAUD. Are you coming, Monsieur Grivet?

GRIVET. After you! Magpie in prison! Magpie in prison . . . As if you could see such a thing! For a retired police superintendent you've made a bit of a fool of yourself, Monsieur Michaud.

They both go down to shop.

LAURENT, *in an undertone, taking* THÉRÈSE's *hands.* Swear you'll do as I say.

THÉRÈSE. I'm yours, all of me. You can make of me what you please——

CAMILLE, *from below.* Now then, Laurent, you lazybones. Why couldn't you come down and fetch your chair instead of leaving it to these two gentlemen?

LAURENT, *answering* CAMILLE. I stayed behind to make love to your wife. *To* THÉRÈSE. Keep hoping. We will be happy together yet.

CAMILLE, *from below.* Oh, that! I give you leave to do that. Be nice to her.

LAURENT, *to* THÉRÈSE. And remember what you said. What no one knows doesn't exist. *Noise on stairs.* Careful!

They separate quickly; THÉRÈSE *resumes her sulky attitude at the worktable.* LAURENT *moves away. The others return each with a chair, laughing heartily.*

CAMILLE, *to* LAURENT. You old humbug. All that nonsense because you didn't want the trouble of going downstairs.

GRIVET. Ah, here's the tea.

Enter MME. RAQUIN *and* SUZANNE *with tea.*

MME. RAQUIN, *as* GRIVET *takes out his watch.* Yes, I know, I've been longer than I said. Now sit down, all of you, and we'll make up for lost time. GRIVET *sits in front of table with* LAURENT *behind him.* MME. RAQUIN's *chair is R. and* MICHAUD *sits behind her.* CAMILLE *is in the middle at the back in his armchair.* THÉRÈSE *is at her worktable.* SUZANNE *goes to join her when the tea has been served.*

CAMILLE. Well, here I am, in my chair. Give me the dominoes, Mama.

GRIVET, *beaming.* Now isn't this delightful! Every Thursday, when I wake up, I say to myself, "Aha! Tonight I'm going to play dominoes at the Raquins'!" You know, you can't imagine . . .

SUZANNE, *interrupting.* Sugar, Monsieur Grivet?

GRIVET. Thank you, my dear. That's very nice of you. Two lumps— may I? *Beginning again.* You know, you can't imagine . . .

CAMILLE, *interrupting.* Thérèse, aren't you coming?

MME. RAQUIN, *giving him the box of dominoes.* Leave her alone. You know she doesn't feel well. She doesn't care for dominoes. And if anyone comes to the shop she'll go down to see to them.

CAMILLE. It's infuriating to have to look at someone who isn't enjoying the fun when everyone else is having a good time. *To* MME. RAQUIN. Now, Mama, aren't you going to sit down?

MME. RAQUIN, *sitting.* Yes, yes, I'm sitting down now.

CAMILLE. Well then, is everyone all right?

MICHAUD. That we are. And tonight I'm going to wipe the floor with you. Madame Raquin, your tea is a trifle stronger than it was last Thursday. Oh, but Monsieur Grivet was saying something.

GRIVET. I was saying something? No, I don't think so.

MICHAUD. Yes, you began to say something.

GRIVET. To say something? I think you're mistaken.

MICHAUD. No, I'm not. He did, didn't he, Madame Raquin? He said "You know, you can't imagine . . ."

GRIVET. "You know, you can't imagine . . ." No, I don't remember it! If this is one of your jokes, Monsieur Michaud, I don't think it's very funny.

CAMILLE. Everyone all right? Very well, then, let's begin. *Noisily emptying the box of dominoes.*

A pause while the players shuffle and deal.

GRIVET. Now we each take seven. *To* LAURENT, *who is standing at table, looking on.* Monsieur Laurent, you're not playing, you mustn't give any advice. No peeping, you understand, Monsieur Michaud, no peeping. *Pause.* Ah! Double six! It's my first go.

ACT TWO

The time is ten o'clock at night and the lamp is lit. A year has gone by but nothing in the room is changed. There is the same atmosphere of peace and intimacy. MADAME RAQUIN *and* THÉRÈSE *are in deep mourning. At the rise of the curtain* THÉRÈSE, GRIVET, LAURENT, MICHAUD, MME. RAQUIN, *and* SUZANNE *are discovered in the positions they occupied at the end of the previous act.* THÉRÈSE, *remote, with the air of a sick woman, her embroidery on her knees, sits by the worktable.* GRIVET, LAURENT, *and* MICHAUD *are in the chairs in front of the round table. Only Camille's chair is empty. There is a pause while* MME. RAQUIN *and* SUZANNE *serve the tea, repeating exactly their actions of the previous act.*

LAURENT. Now, Madame Raquin, you must not dwell on your grief. Give me the dominoes.

SUZANNE. Sugar, Monsieur Grivet?

GRIVET. Thank you, my dear. That's very nice of you. Two pieces, may I? Sweets from the sweet.

LAURENT, *with box of dominoes*. Ah, here they are. Now, sit down, Madame Raquin.

MME. RAQUIN *sits*.

Is everyone all right?

MICHAUD. That we are! And tonight I'm going to wipe the floor with you. Just a minute while I put some rum in my tea. *Pours rum into his tea.*

LAURENT. All right? *Turns dominoes on to table.* Very well. Let's begin. *The players shuffle and deal.*

GRIVET. With pleasure! Now we each take seven. No peeping, Monsieur Michaud, d'you hear, no peeping.

Pause. No. Today it is not my first go.

MME. RAQUIN, *bursting into tears*. I can't do it. I can't—I can't!

LAURENT *and* MICHAUD *rise and* SUZANNE *bends over* MME. RAQUIN's *armchair*. When I see you all round this table, just as we used to be, I remember and it breaks my heart. Poor Camille used to sit there.

MICHAUD. Come now, Madame Raquin, you must be sensible.

MME. RAQUIN. Please forgive me. I can't help it. You remember how he loved to play dominoes. He always turned them out of the box himself, exactly as Laurent did just now. He used to scold me when I didn't sit down soon enough. I was afraid to cross him. It made him ill. We had such happy evenings. And now, look, his chair is empty.

MICHAUD. Dear lady, you must pull yourself together or you will make yourself really ill.

SUZANNE, *embracing* MME. RAQUIN. Please, please don't cry. It hurts us so much to see you like this.

MME. RAQUIN, *still crying*. Yes, you're right. I must be brave.

GRIVET, *pushing dominoes away*. Well, I suppose we'd better not play then. It's a great pity that it affects you like this. Your tears won't bring him back.

MICHAUD. We are all of us mortal.

MME. RAQUIN. Alas, yes.

GRIVET. We came here to play dominoes because we hoped to distract your mind from your sorrow.

MICHAUD. You must try and forget, dear Madame.

GRIVET. He's quite right. Come now, we must cheer up. We'll play the best out of three, shall we?

LAURENT. No—in a minute. Let Madame Raquin have a little time to get calm. We all of us grieve for dear Camille.

SUZANNE. Do you hear, Madame dear? We all grieve for him. Our hearts ache for you. *Sits down by* MME. RAQUIN's *knees*.

MME. RAQUIN. You are all so kind. Please don't be cross with me for spoiling the game.

MICHAUD. We're not cross with you. But it's a year now since it happened, and you ought to be able to think about it more calmly.

MME. RAQUIN. I haven't counted the days. I cry because the tears just come. Please forgive me. All the time, I can see my poor child drifting down the rough waters of the Seine. And I see him when he was little—when I used to put him to bed between two blankets. It was such an awful death—he must have suffered so. I had a terrible presentiment. I begged him to give up the idea of going on the water but he wanted to show he wasn't afraid. If you only knew how I looked after him when he was a baby. For three whole weeks when he had typhoid I held him on my knees without ever going to bed.

MICHAUD. But you still have your niece. You still have Thérèse. You mustn't distress her and you mustn't distress the generous man who saved her. It will always be a grief to him that he wasn't able to drag Camille to the bank too. It is selfish of you to nurse your grief. You are upsetting Laurent.

LAURENT. These memories are so painful.

MICHAUD. You did what you could. Now—the boat capsized when it crashed into a stake, didn't it?—one of those stakes they use for fixing the eel nets, wasn't it?

LAURENT. Yes, that's what I thought. The jolt threw us all three into the water.

MICHAUD. Then when you were in the water you managed to get hold of Thérèse.

LAURENT. I was rowing and she was beside me. All I had to do was to grab her dress. Then I dived in after Camille but he had disappeared. He was at the front of the canoe; he was trailing his hands in the water. He was making jokes about the soup being cold . . .

MICHAUD. You mustn't stir up these memories; they're upsetting. You behaved like a hero—you went in three times.

GRIVET. I quite agree. There was a magnificent article in my paper about it the next day. They said that Monsieur Laurent deserved a medal. It just gave me the creeps when I read how the three people fell into the river while their dinner was waiting for them in the restaurant. And then there was another article a week later, after they had found poor Monsieur Camille's body. *To* MICHAUD. You remember . . . it was Monsieur Laurent who fetched you to go with him to identify the body.

MME. RAQUIN *breaks into fresh sobs.*

MICHAUD, *to* GRIVET. Really, Monsieur Grivet, do hold your tongue. Madame was just calming down and then you start raking up all these details . . .

GRIVET, *in a low voice, sulkily.* I'm sorry, but you began it. As we're not playing dominoes we must say something.

MICHAUD, *slightly louder.* You've talked about that newspaper article of yours hundreds of times. It's in bad taste, you know. Now she's off again.

GRIVET, *rising and shouting.* It was you who began it.

MICHAUD, *also shouting.* Damn it all, it was you!

GRIVET, *shouting.* All right, call me a fool!

MME. RAQUIN. Now, now, you two, don't quarrel.

They retire muttering and grumbling.

I am going to be sensible. I won't cry any more. I like to talk about my loss. It comforts me and it reminds me too of what I owe to all of you. Laurent, dear, give me your hand. You aren't angry?

LAURENT. Yes, with myself, because I couldn't bring both of them back to you.

MME. RAQUIN. You're my child and I love you. I pray for you every night because you tried to save my boy. I ask God to watch over you. Camille is in Heaven. He'll hear me and you will owe your happiness to him. Every time you find some joy in life, say to yourself that it's because I've prayed for you and Camille has heard my prayers.

LAURENT. Dear Madame.

MICHAUD. Hear, hear!

MME. RAQUIN. *To* SUZANNE. And now, dear, go and sit down again. Look— I'm smiling—for you.

SUZANNE. Thank you, dear, dear Madame. *Kisses* MME. RAQUIN *as she rises.*

MME. RAQUIN, *returning to place at table.* Now, come along. Whose turn is it?

GRIVET. You really want to play? Good!

GRIVET, LAURENT *and* MICHAUD *sit down.*

Whose turn is it?

MICHAUD. Mine. *Plays domino.*

SUZANNE, *goes across to* THÉRÈSE. Thérèse, darling. Would you like me to tell you about the Blue Prince?

THÉRÈSE. The Blue Prince?

SUZANNE, *taking a stool and sitting by* THÉRÈSE. It's quite a story. I shall whisper it—There's no need for Uncle to know anything about it. He's a young man. He wears a blue coat and has a fair moustache which suits him marvelously.

THÉRÈSE. Take care. Your Uncle is listening.

SUZANNE *half rises and glances at the players.*

MICHAUD, *angrily to* GRIVET. But you passed five a minute ago and now you are putting down five all over the place.

GRIVET. I passed five? You'll excuse me but you're making a mistake.

MICHAUD *protests and then the game continues.*

SUZANNE, *sitting down again and speaking in a low voice.* There's no need to worry about Uncle when he's playing dominoes. Now this young man used to come to the Luxembourg every day. Uncle always sits under the third tree on the left along the terrace, you know . . . near the newspaper kiosk. The Blue Prince used to sit under the fourth tree and read. Every time he turned the page he used to smile at me.

THÉRÈSE. Is that all?

SUZANNE. Yes. That's all that happened in the Luxembourg. Oh, but no, I was forgetting. One day he saved me from a hoop. A little girl was bowling it full tilt at me. He knocked it hard to make it go the other way. That made me smile. I thought of lovers who hurled themselves at the heads of runaway horses. The same idea must have struck him as he began to smile too when he bowed to me.

THÉRÈSE. And that is the end of the story?

SUZANNE. Oh no, that's where it begins. The day before yesterday Uncle went out and left me all alone with Hortense. She's such a boring thing, so to amuse myself I set up the big telescope—you remember the one Uncle had at Vernon? You can see more than five miles through it. From our roof we can see quite a lot of Paris, you know. I was looking in the direction of Saint Sulpice. There are some very fine statues at the foot of the large tower.

MICHAUD, *testily to* GRIVET. Come, come, now, six. Hurry up.

GRIVET. A six . . . a six . . . I know, I know. Heavens alive. I must work it out.

Game continues.

THÉRÈSE. And the Blue Prince?

SUZANNE. Don't be impatient! I saw chimneys—chimneys—scores of them —oceans of them. When I moved the telescope a bit they looked like regiments of soldiers, marching at the double and bumping into one another. The whole telescope was full of them. Suddenly, between two chimney pots—whom do you think I saw? The Blue Prince.

THÉRÈSE. Oh, so he's a chimney sweep then?

SUZANNE. No, no, of course not. He was on the roof, the same as I was. And the funny thing is that he was looking through a telescope too.

I recognized him at once, with his blue suit and his moustache . . .

THÉRÈSE. And where does he live?

SUZANNE. I don't know. I only saw him through the telescope, you see. It was certainly a long way away—very long . . . in the direction of Saint Sulpice. When I looked only with my eyes and not through the telescope, it all looked grey except for the blue of the slate roofs. I very nearly lost him too. The telescope moved and I had to do that awful journey over the chimney pots again. Now I've got a bearing— the weathercock on a house near ours.

THÉRÈSE. Have you seen him again?

SUZANNE. Yes—yesterday—today—every day! Is it wrong of me? If you knew how sweet he looks through the telescope . . . not much taller than this. Like a little china figure. I'm not a bit afraid of him. But I don't know if he's real—or just something one sees through the tele- scope. It's all so far away. When he does this——*Blows a kiss.* I draw back and then I see nothing but grey. So perhaps he never did this—— *Blows kiss.* And then I can't see him there any longer, however hard I stare.

THÉRÈSE. You're very sweet. *Looking at* LAURENT. But keep him in your heart . . . forever as a Dream Prince.

SUZANNE. Oh . . . no! Sh—they've finished their game.

MICHAUD. We've beaten you, Monsieur Grivet.

GRIVET. Yes, sir, you are the better man!

They shuffle the dominoes.

MME. RAQUIN, *pushing her armchair back.* Laurent, as you are up, will you get my basket that I keep my wool in? It should be on the chest of drawers in my room. Take a light.

LAURENT. No, I don't need one. *Goes out through door at back.*

MICHAUD, *to* MME. RAQUIN. You have a real son there. He's so kind.

MME. RAQUIN. Yes, he's very good to us. I give him little jobs to do and in the evening he helps me to shut up shop.

GRIVET. The other day I saw him selling some needles like a shopgirl. He, he, he! A shopgirl with a beard! *Laughs.*

Enter LAURENT *quickly, his eyes full of terror, as if he were being pursued: for a moment he leans against the wardrobe.*

MME. RAQUIN. Why, whatever's the matter?

MICHAUD, *rising.* Are you ill?

GRIVET. Did you bump into something?

LAURENT. It's nothing. It's . . . My eyes are dazzled, that's all! *Pulling himself together slightly.*

MME. RAQUIN. And my workbasket?

LAURENT. The basket. . . . I don't know . . . I didn't get it.

SUZANNE. What! You, a man and afraid?

LAURENT, *trying to laugh*. Afraid? Of what? I just didn't find the basket, that's all.

SUZANNE. Just a minute, I'll find it. And if I meet your ghost I'll bring him down to you. *Exit.*

LAURENT, *almost normal*. I'm sorry. I'm all right now.

GRIVET. It's the blood. You're too healthy!

LAURENT, *shivering*. Yes, the blood.

MICHAUD. You need some cooling medicine.

MME. RAQUIN. As a matter of fact I've noticed you haven't been looking well for some time. I'll make you a tisane.

Enter SUZANNE *with basket.*

Ah, so you found it!

SUZANNE. It was on the chest of drawers. *To* LAURENT. I didn't see your ghost, Monsieur Laurent. I expect I frightened him.

GRIVET. She's a young caution, that child.

Shop bell rings.

SUZANNE. Don't worry, I'll see to it. *Goes downstairs.*

GRIVET. A treasure—a real treasure. *To* MICHAUD. We agree that I have thirty-two and you twenty-eight.

MME. RAQUIN, *after searching in basket which she puts on mantelshelf*. There now! I haven't got the wool I wanted. I shall have to go down to the shop. *She goes downstairs.*

GRIVET, *to* MICHAUD. Well, the game was nearly ruined just now. It's not such fun here as it used to be.

MICHAUD. Can you wonder? When death strikes a house . . . But cheer up! I've discovered a way to get our good old Thursdays back again. *They start a new game.*

THÉRÈSE, *in a low voice, to* LAURENT, *who has come close to her*. You're afraid, aren't you?

LAURENT. Yes. Shall I come to you tonight?

THÉRÈSE. We must be discreet. We mustn't make any mistake.

LAURENT. A whole year we've been discreet—a whole year I have never had you to myself. It would be so easy—I'd come in by the little door. We are free now. We shouldn't be afraid if we were together now in your room.

THÉRÈSE. No, don't let us spoil the future. We need so much happiness. Shall we ever have enough!

LAURENT. You must have faith. There will be peace when we are in each other's arms. We shan't be frightened when we are together. When shall I come?

THÉRÈSE. On our wedding night. It won't be long now—you'll see. Be careful. My Aunt is coming back.

MME. RAQUIN, *enters. To* THÉRÈSE. Thérèse, dear, go down, will you? You are wanted down there.

THÉRÈSE *goes wearily downstairs; they all watch her as she goes.*

MICHAUD. Have you noticed Thérèse—how pale she looks? She can hardly hold up her head.

MME. RAQUIN. Yes. It's the same all day long. Her eyes are sunken and her hands tremble.

LAURENT. Yes, and she has that consumptive color in her cheeks.

MME. RAQUIN. Yes. You noticed that first, Laurent, dear. Now I see it getting worse. It seems I'm to be spared nothing.

MICHAUD. Rubbish! You're upsetting yourself without any reason. It's nerves. She'll get over it.

LAURENT. No. She has been struck to the heart. Those long silences—that sad smile. It's as if she is saying good-bye to us. She will gradually fade away.

GRIVET. My dear man, you're not very comforting. You ought to liven her up a bit instead of piling up the gloom.

MME. RAQUIN. No, he's right. The sickness is in her heart. She doesn't want to be consoled. Every time I try to make her see reason she gets impatient—angry, even. She shuts herself away like a wounded animal.

LAURENT. We shall have to resign ourselves to it.

MME. RAQUIN. That would be the last blow. She is all I have now. I was hoping she would be there at the end to close my eyes. If she went I'd be all alone here, and I'd die in some corner alone. I'm so unhappy. I don't know what's come to this house.

GRIVET, *timidly.* So we're not playing any more?

MICHAUD. Wait a minute now—dash it all. *Rises.* I want to try and find a remedy for all this. At Thérèse's age—good heavens!—one is not inconsolable. Did she cry much on the night of the tragedy at Saint-Ouen?

MME. RAQUIN. No, she doesn't cry easily. It was a kind of dumb grief, as if her mind and body were utterly exhausted. She seemed stupefied. She has become very nervous.

LAURENT, *trembling.* Nervous?

MME. RAQUIN. Yes. One night——*To* LAURENT. I never told you this before—I heard stifled sobbing and of course I came down to her—she didn't recognize me. She was muttering . . .

LAURENT. It was a nightmare . . . Did she say anything? What did she say?

MME. RAQUIN. I couldn't understand. She was calling Camille. She is afraid to come in here any more after dark without a light. In the mornings she is utterly tired out—she drags herself about. It breaks my heart, it does really. I am certain she is leaving us, that she wants to be with that other poor child of mine again.

MICHAUD. Yes, yes. Well, Madame, I have finished my inquiry and now I'll tell you precisely what I think. But first of all, I'd like you all to leave us.

LAURENT. You want to be alone with Madame Raquin?

MICHAUD. Yes.

GRIVET, *rising to go*. Very well, all right. We'll leave you. *Comes back*. You know you owe me two, Monsieur Michaud. Give me a call when you are ready.

LAURENT *and* GRIVET *go out through door at back*.

MICHAUD. Now, Madame, I'm a blunt man.

MME. RAQUIN. If only we could save her! What is your advice?

MICHAUD, *lowering his voice*. Thérèse must be married.

MME. RAQUIN. Married! Oh, but you are cruel! It would be like losing my Camille a second time.

MICHAUD. But I mean it. I face facts. I'm a doctor if you like.

MME. RAQUIN. No, no, it's impossible. You see what a state she's in. She'd hate the idea. She hasn't forgotten my dear boy. It isn't very nice of you to suggest it, Michaud. Camille is still her husband, in her heart. She couldn't marry. It would be sacrilege.

MICHAUD. Big words, Madame. I only know that when a woman is afraid to go to her room at night, it's a husband she needs.

MME. RAQUIN. And how about the stranger we should be bringing into our home? I am old—it would worry me. We might make a bad choice, and that would spoil any chance of peace we have left. No, no! I'd rather die while we still mourn our dear boy. *Sits in armchair*.

MICHAUD. Naturally we'd have to look for a decent man who would be a good husband for Thérèse—and a good son to you . . . someone who would take Camille's place. . . . Laurent.

MME. RAQUIN. Laurent?

MICHAUD. Why, yes! What a splendid pair they'd make. My dear old friend, this is my advice. Get them married.

MME. RAQUIN. Laurent and Thérèse.

MICHAUD. I knew I was going to surprise you! I've been cherishing the plan for some time now. Think it over and trust my long experience. If you decide to see Thérèse marry again—and don't forget it will bring you some happiness in your old age and it will cure her of this sickness that is killing her—well, where could you find a better husband for her than Laurent?

MME. RAQUIN. I looked on them as brother and sister.

MICHAUD. But think of yourself. I want you all to be happy. I want the old days back again. You will have two children to close your eyes.

MME. RAQUIN. You know, you're almost persuading me. You're right, I do need a little comfort. But I am afraid we'd be doing wrong. No, no. Camille would punish us for forgetting him so soon.

MICHAUD. Who said anything about forgetting? Laurent is always talking about him. Dash it all, it will still be a family affair.

MME. RAQUIN. I am old . . . I even find it difficult to move about now. I only ask to die in peace.

MICHAUD. That's right now. I've persuaded you. It's the only way to avoid bringing a stranger into the home. And I hope it won't be long before you're dandling your grandchildren on your knee. Ah, you're smiling. I knew I should make you smile.

MME. RAQUIN. Oh, it's wrong . . . wrong of me to smile. I'm still very troubled about it. But they'll never agree. They've never thought of such a thing.

MICHAUD. Rubbish! We're going to manage this properly. They're too sensible not to see that their marriage is necessary for this household's happiness. That's the line to take . . . the household's happiness. I'll settle with Laurent while we're shutting up the shop together . . . and I'll call Thérèse up to you. We'll announce the engagement this evening.

THÉRÈSE *enters looking utterly dejected.*

MME. RAQUIN. What's the matter, my child? You have not spoken a word the whole evening. Do—do try not to be so unhappy—for the sake of our friends.

THÉRÈSE *gives a vague gesture.*

I know we can't always control our grief . . . Are you feeling ill?

THÉRÈSE. No, I'm just very tired.

MME. RAQUIN. You must tell me if you're not well. If you're ill we must look after you. Is it your heart perhaps—or your chest?

THÉRÈSE. No . . . I don't know . . . there's nothing the matter. It's just that everything in me seems—seems numb.

MME. RAQUIN. My dear, dear, child. It hurts me so much that you're so silent . . . so alone. You are all I have.

THÉRÈSE. You . . . you tell me to forget?

MME. RAQUIN. No, I didn't say that. I couldn't say that. But I've a right to ask these questions. I must not force my grief on you. And it's my duty to try and find out how to console you. Now, answer me frankly.

THÉRÈSE. I'm very tired.

MME. RAQUIN. I want you to answer me. You live too much alone . . . you're moping. It's not natural to grieve forever at your age.

THÉRÈSE. What are you trying to tell me?

MME. RAQUIN. Nothing, dear. I'm only trying to find out what's wrong. I know that it can't be very cheerful, living with a sad old woman. And then this house . . . so dismal and dark. Perhaps you would like. . . .

THÉRÈSE. I don't want anything.

MME. RAQUIN. Now listen, dear. Don't be cross with me, but we've had a sort of idea . . . perhaps it's stupid . . . but we thought of getting you married again.

THÉRÈSE. Married? Me? Oh, never, never. Don't you trust me?

MME. RAQUIN, *very moved.* That's what I told them. I said that you had never forgotten my boy . . . that he was always in your heart. They made me do it. Yes, you know, they're right, my child. The house is too sad. No one comes here. Now, now. It would do no harm to think over what they say.

THÉRÈSE. No.

MME. RAQUIN. Yes, yes. You should marry again. I can't remember what Michaud said to convince me . . . but I agreed with him . . . and I said I would try and persuade you. Now, if you like, I'll call him. He'll know what to say better than I do.

THÉRÈSE. Can't you leave me in peace! No, my heart is dead to all that. Me marry! Heavens above! And who is the man?

MME. RAQUIN. Well, they had a splendid idea—they thought of someone. Michaud is downstairs now—talking to Laurent. . . .

THÉRÈSE. Laurent—so you thought of Laurent! But I don't love him— I don't want to love him!

MME. RAQUIN. But they're right—really they are. I quite agree with them. Laurent is like one of the family . . . you know how kind he is . . . what a help he has been to us. I felt the same as you did when they first suggested it. It didn't seem right somehow. But when I thought it over it seemed to me that you'd be less unfaithful to our beloved's memory if you married his friend . . . the friend who saved your life.

THÉRÈSE. But . . . I'm still mourning for him. I want to go on mourning for him.

MME. RAQUIN. I know, but you must stop. I will and so must you. You see, they want us to be happy. They said it would give me two children —that it would give me comfort and happiness in my last days. I'm being selfish, you see. I want to see you smile. Say you will, dear . . . do it for me.

THÉRÈSE. My only wish has been to please you—you know that.

MME. RAQUIN. Yes, you are a good girl. *Trying to smile.* It will make my last years happy. We will make a new warm life for ourselves. Laurent will love us both. I will share him with you. You will lend him to me sometimes to help a stupid old woman.

THÉRÈSE. My dear, dear Aunt. But all the same, I wish you had left me alone with my heartache.

MME. RAQUIN. That means you will do it?

THÉRÈSE. Yes.

MME. RAQUIN, *very moved.* Thank you, my child. You have made me so happy. *Falls into armchair by table.* Oh, my son, my poor son and I was the first to betray you!

MICHAUD, *enters.* Well, I've persuaded him, but my word! I had a bit of difficulty. He's doing it for your sake. I begged him to do it for you. He's just coming up. He's putting the screws in the shutters. And Thérèse?

MME. RAQUIN. Yes, she agrees.

MICHAUD *goes to* THÉRÈSE *and talks quietly to her.*

SUZANNE, *enters, followed by* GRIVET. No, no, Monsieur Grivet, you're a conceited man. I won't dance with you at the wedding. Now then, tell me the truth. You've never got married in case it interferes with your little ways, eh?

GRIVET. You've hit the nail on the head, my dear.

SUZANNE. What a dreadful man! Now, you understand, not one step do I dance with you at the wedding. *Goes to join* THÉRÈSE *and* MICHAUD.

GRIVET. All these young girls think it's fun to get married. I've tried to do it five times . . . *To* MME. RAQUIN. . . . the last time to a school-teacher. The banns were published and everything went well until she told me she liked coffee in the mornings. *Disgusted.* Coffee! I can't bear coffee. For thirty years I have had chocolate. It would have ruined my whole life. So I broke it off. I was right . . . don't you think so?

MME. RAQUIN, *smiling.* Most certainly.

GRIVET. It's a good thing when people get on together. And Michaud saw at once that Thérèse and Laurent were made for one another.

MME. RAQUIN, *seriously.* You're right, my friend.

GRIVET. You remember the old song——

> "When a well-matched pair is wed
> Happy is the marriage bed."

Looks at watch. Good gracious! A quarter to eleven! *Sits down, puts on his galoshes and takes his umbrella.*

LAURENT, *having just come up from the shop, goes to* MME. RAQUIN. Monsieur Michaud and I have just been talking about your happiness. Your children are longing to make you happy—dear Mother.

MME. RAQUIN, *very moved.* Yes, Laurent dear, call me your Mother.

LAURENT. Thérèse, are you willing to make our Mother happy?

THÉRÈSE. Yes. It is our duty.

MME. RAQUIN. My children. *Takes the hands of both in her own.* Marry her, Laurent. Make her less unhappy and Camille will thank you. You have made me very happy. All that I ask is that Heaven will not punish us for it.

ACT THREE

The time is 3 o'clock in the morning. The fire is glowing and the lamp is lit. The room is decked in white—white bed curtains, and lace-trimmed bedspread, lace antimacassars on the chairbacks. There are flowers everywhere—on the sideboard, on the mantelpiece and on the table.

As the curtain rises THÉRÈSE, MME. RAQUIN *and* SUZANNE *come in through the door at the back. They are dressed in their wedding clothes.* MME. RAQUIN *and* SUZANNE *are not wearing their hats or shawls.* THÉRÈSE *is in grey silk. She goes wearily to sit L.* SUZANNE *remains for a moment at the door for a little tussle with* GRIVET *and* MICHAUD *who are attempting to follow the ladies.*

SUZANNE. No, no, Uncle! Monsieur Grivet—no! You are not coming into the bride's room. It's not proper.

MICHAUD *and* GRIVET *ignore her protests and enter.*

MICHAUD, *in an undertone to* SUZANNE. Keep quiet, it's a joke. *To* GRIVET. Have you got the nettles?

GRIVET. Yes, of course. I've had them all day long—in my jacket pocket. It was beastly uncomfortable in church and in the restaurant. *He goes furtively to the bed.*

MME. RAQUIN. Now then, gentlemen, you can't stay in here, while we are undressing the bride.

MICHAUD. Undressing the bride! What a delightful idea! If you need any help I daresay we could be of use. *Joins* GRIVET.

SUZANNE. I've never seen Uncle so jolly. He was as red as a beetroot by the end of dinner.

MME. RAQUIN. Let them have their little joke; we can forgive it on a wedding night. There was always plenty of fun at Vernon. They couldn't get a wink of sleep all night, the poor bridal couples.

GRIVET, *by the bed.* My word, this bed is comfortable. Monsieur Michaud, just feel it.

MICHAUD. By Jove, there must be three mattresses on it, at least. *In an undertone.* Have you put the nettles in?

GRIVET. Right in the middle.

MICHAUD, *roaring with laughter.* You're a real old comic and no mistake!

GRIVET, *laughing.* We managed it well, didn't we!

MME. RAQUIN, *smiling.* You are keeping the bride waiting, gentlemen.

SUZANNE. Aren't you two ever going—making a nuisance of yourselves!

MICHAUD. All right, all right, we're going.

GRIVET, *to* THÉRÈSE. Good night, Madame—and our congratulations.

THÉRÈSE, *rising and then sitting again.* Thank you both.

GRIVET, *shaking* MME. RAQUIN's *hand as he leaves.* You're not angry with us, are you?

MME. RAQUIN. How could I be angry with old friends and on a wedding night?

Exeunt MICHAUD *and* GRIVET.

SUZANNE, *calling after them.* Now, don't come back. The bridegroom is the only one who has the right to come in—and then only when we let him.

MME. RAQUIN, *to* THÉRÈSE. You must get undressed, Thérèse. It's nearly three o'clock.

THÉRÈSE *is in chair below fireplace,* MME. RAQUIN *on sofa facing fire and* SUZANNE *on hearthrug.*

THÉRÈSE. I'm worn out. The ceremony, then the drive and then that never-ending dinner. Let me be—just for a little, please.

SUZANNE. Yes, it was hot in that restaurant. It gave me a headache, but

I felt better when I was in the cab. *To* MME. RAQUIN. But it's you who ought to feel tired—with your poor legs. You know the doctor said you are not to do too much.

MME. RAQUIN. He said a severe shock might be fatal, that's all. But today I have been calm and happy. Everything went off very well, I think— don't you? Just right.

SUZANNE. The mayor was most mayor-like. When he started to read from his little red book, the bridegroom hung his head. Monsieur Grivet's signature on the register was magnificent.

MME. RAQUIN. The priest was very moving in church.

SUZANNE. Oh, everyone was crying. I kept my eye on Thérèse. She didn't look much like laughing either. But what heaps of people there were on the Boulevards in the afternoon. We went from the Madeleine to the Bastille twice. The people were quite amused at us. Half of the wedding party were asleep by the time we got to that Batignolles restaurant. *Laughs.*

MME. RAQUIN. Thérèse, you ought to get undressed, my child.

THÉRÈSE. In a minute. Go on talking.

SUZANNE. I know—shall I be your lady's maid? Do let me—then you won't tire yourself.

MME. RAQUIN. Give me her hat. *Takes it and puts it in wardrobe.*

SUZANNE. There, you see, there's no need for you to move. Oh, but you'll have to stand up for me to take off your dress.

THÉRÈSE, *standing.* You do bully me, don't you?

MME. RAQUIN. It's late, my child.

SUZANNE, *unhooking dress.* A husband—oh, it must be awful. A friend of mine who got married simply cried and cried—you hardly pull yourself in at all and your waist is quite small. You're right to wear your bodices rather long. Oh dear, that was a pin. It's very firmly fixed. I ought to go and get Monsieur Grivet to help. *Giggles.*

THÉRÈSE. I'm shivering. Hurry up, dear.

SUZANNE. We'll go over by the fire. *They both cross to fire.* Oh, look, there's a stain on the flounce. It's simply lovely, this silk. It would stand alone. But how nervous you are, darling. I can feel you trembling when I touch you—like Thisbe when I tickle her. Thisbe's the cat Uncle gave me. But I'll be careful. I won't tickle you.

THÉRÈSE. I think I—I think it's a cold coming.

SUZANNE. There now—the last hook—I've finished. *Takes off dress and hands it to* MME. RAQUIN. Now I'll do your hair for the night, shall I?

MME. RAQUIN. Yes, that's right. *Goes out with dress through door at back.*

SUZANNE, *after seating* THÉRÈSE *by the fire*. There, now you have a nice rosy face. You were as pale as a ghost.

THÉRÈSE. It's the firelight.

SUZANNE, *behind her, taking down her hair*. Put your head down a bit. What lovely hair you have. Tell me—I want to ask you a question—I'm afraid I'm very inquisitive—You are trembling and it is because your heart is beating so hard—that's it, isn't it?

THÉRÈSE. My heart isn't seventeen years old, like yours, my dear.

SUZANNE. I'm not being a nuisance, am I? All day long I've been thinking that if I were in your place I should be such a silly little stupid. So I decided that I'd watch you and see how you got ready for your wedding night. Then perhaps I wouldn't seem so stupid when my turn comes. You are a little sad—but you are not afraid. I'm so frightened that I should sob my heart out.

THÉRÈSE. Is the Blue Prince so terrible then?

SUZANNE. Oh, don't laugh at me! It suits you to have your hair down. You look like a queen in a picture book—I don't think plaits, do you? I'll just roll it up in your neck.

THÉRÈSE. Just tie it back.

MME. RAQUIN *returns and takes a white dressing gown from the wardrobe.*

SUZANNE. If you promise not to laugh at me, I'll tell you what I should be feeling in your place. I should be happy—oh, happier than I have ever been in my life. And yet, at the same time, I should be terribly frightened. It would be like walking above the clouds—in Heaven— and coming to a strange place—a beautiful place, but terrifying—with the loveliest music and the most exquisite flowers. And in that dazzling light I should go forward, drawn on in spite of myself, by a joy so thrilling that it would seem as if I must die of it. Is that how you feel?

THÉRÈSE, *almost whispering*. Yes. Music—flowers—a great light—all the springtime of youth and love.

SUZANNE. You're still shivering.

THÉRÈSE. I have caught cold. I can't get warm.

MME. RAQUIN, *goes to sit by fire*. I'm going to warm your dressing gown. *Holds the dressing gown to the fire.*

SUZANNE. And while the Blue Prince was waiting—just as Monsieur Laurent is waiting now—I should take a wicked delight in making him impatient. Then, when he was at the door, I shouldn't be able to think any more. I'd want to run away so that he couldn't find me. And then— I don't know—I'm dizzy when I think of it.

MME. RAQUIN, *smiling as she turns the dressing gown.* Then don't think of it. Children think of nothing but dolls, flowers, and husbands.

THÉRÈSE. Life is harsher than that.

SUZANNE, *to* THÉRÈSE. But isn't that how you feel?

THÉRÈSE. Yes. *Quietly.* I could have wished that it was not in winter—and in this room. In Vernon, in May, the acacias are in bloom, and the nights are warm.

SUZANNE. Now your hair is done—Now put on your nice warm dressing gown.

THÉRÈSE *and* MME. RAQUIN *rise.*

MME. RAQUIN, *helping* THÉRÈSE *to put on dressing gown.* It is burning my hands.

SUZANNE. I do hope you're not cold any longer.

THÉRÈSE. No, thank you.

SUZANNE. Oh, how nice you look. You're like a real bride now—all that lace!

MME. RAQUIN. Now we're going to leave you alone, my child.

THÉRÈSE. No, not alone! Wait a moment. I think there's something else . . .

MME. RAQUIN. No, don't say anything. I haven't let myself speak. You must have noticed. I didn't want to upset you. If you knew what an effort it has been! All day my heart has been full and yet I'm happy in spite of it. We must put away the past. You saw how cheerful Michaud was. We must be cheerful too.

THÉRÈSE. Yes. You are right. I'm being stupid. Good night.

MME. RAQUIN. Good night. *Turning back.* Tell me—are you troubled about anything? Is there anything distressing you that you're keeping from me? It's the thought that we've been working for your happiness that has helped me to bear this. Love your husband. He deserves nothing but love and affection from both of us. Love him as you loved . . . No, I won't say that. I don't want to say that. We have done our best and I wish you great happiness, my child, in return for all the comfort you are to me.

SUZANNE. Poor Thérèse—Anyone would think you were leaving her with a pack of wolves in a nasty dark cave. Well, the cave smells very nice. Roses everywhere. Just a lovely nest.

THÉRÈSE. The flowers must have cost a lot. It was very naughty of you.

MME. RAQUIN. I know how much you love the spring. I wanted you to have a bit of it in your room on your wedding night. You can imagine you are in Suzanne's dream—in the clouds—in Heaven. There now, you are smiling. Be happy among your flowers. Good night, my child. *Kisses her.*

SUZANNE. Aren't you going to kiss me too, darling?

THÉRÈSE *kisses her.*

There now you are quite pale again. *Looks round the room as she goes out.* A room like this—all flowers—it's thrilling.

THÉRÈSE *is left alone and she goes slowly back to sit by the fire.* LAURENT, *still in his wedding suit, comes quietly into the room, closes the door and walks with an uneasy air.*

LAURENT. Thérèse, my darling . . .

THÉRÈSE, *pushing him away.* No, not yet—I'm cold.

LAURENT, *after a pause.* At last we're alone, Thérèse, my Thérèse. They've all gone and we're free to love each other. Our life is our own, this is our room and you are mine—my dear wife,—because I've won you— and you wanted me to win you. *Tries to kiss her.*

THÉRÈSE, *pushing him away.* No—presently—I'm shivering with cold.

LAURENT. My poor darling! Give me your feet. I'll warm them in my hands. *Kneels before her and tries to take her feet, but she draws them away.* The time has come at last—do you realize? Think of it! We have been waiting a whole year for today—working for it for a whole year. We have earned it, haven't we? It's worth all we have suffered. We have had to be so careful but now we have got our reward for it all.

THÉRÈSE. Yes, I've thought of it. Don't stay down there. Sit down for a while. Let's just talk for a bit.

LAURENT, *getting up.* Why are you trembling? The door is shut and I am your husband. You didn't tremble when I used to come in the old days—you laughed and you used to talk so loudly that people might have heard us. Now you are talking so quietly, just as if someone is listening on the other side of the wall. Why, now we can talk as loudly as we like, and laugh and make love. No one is going to disturb us, this is our wedding night.

THÉRÈSE, *in terror.* Don't say that—don't say it. You are pale too, Laurent, paler than I am. You are just talking for the sake of saying something. Don't pretend to be brave. Why, we haven't the courage to kiss yet. You're afraid you would look a fool if you didn't kiss me, aren't you! So silly! We're not ordinary married people . . . Sit down . . . let's talk about something.

He goes behind her and leans against the mantelpiece. She changes her tone, speaking in a domestic, detached tone.

The wind has been very high today.

LAURENT. Yes, and very cold too. It went down a bit this afternoon.

THÉRÈSE. Some of the women's dresses on the boulevards . . . oh well . . . It is to be hoped that the apricot trees will be late in flowering this year——

LAURENT. Frost in March is bad for the fruit trees. You remember—in Vernon . . . *He stops and both are silent in thought.*

THÉRÈSE, *quietly.* Vernon . . . I was a little girl . . . *Resumes her domestic, detached tone.* Put a log on the fire. It's quite nice here now. Is it four o'clock yet, do you think?

LAURENT, *looking at clock.* No, not yet. *Goes and sits at other end of room.*

THÉRÈSE. It's extraordinary how long the night is! Are you the same as I am? I don't like being in a cab very much. Driving about for hours is the stupidest thing. It makes me sleepy. And I hate meals in restaurants too.

LAURENT. There's nothing like home cooking.

THÉRÈSE. I wouldn't say that in the country.

LAURENT. No. But there are very good things to eat in the country. Do you remember . . . the little inns by the river . . . ?

THÉRÈSE. Be quiet! Why do you wake those memories? I hear them hammering in your head—I hear them hammering in my own—and then we begin to go over the whole ghastly story again. Don't let's talk any more. We mustn't think any more. Behind all your words I hear other words. While you're talking, I hear what you're thinking. You'd got as far as the accident, hadn't you? Don't talk any more. *Pause.*

LAURENT. Thérèse, say something—please. I can't bear this silence. Talk to me.

THÉRÈSE, *sitting down, her hands pressed to her head.* Shut your eyes. Try to think of nothing.

LAURENT. No. I want to hear the sound of your voice. Say something to me—anything—as you did before—that the weather is bad, the night is long . . .

THÉRÈSE. Even then I think. I can't *not* think. But you're right. Silence is not good and I feel I must go on talking. *Tries to smile and speaks in a gay manner.* The Mairie was freezing this morning. My feet were like ice. But I warmed them over the grating in church. Did you see the grating? It was close to where we knelt down.

LAURENT. Yes. Grivet planted himself on top of it the whole of the service. He looked triumphant, the old devil—He was very funny, wasn't he? *They both try to laugh.*

THÉRÈSE. The church was rather dark; it was the weather. Did you notice the lace on the altar cloth? It must have cost ten francs a meter at least. There's nothing so good in the shop. The smell of the incense made me feel ill—so sweet. At first I thought we were the only people there in that great empty church and I was glad. *Her voice becomes more serious.* Then I heard chanting . . . You must have seen—in a chapel on the other side of the nave . . . ?

LAURENT, *reluctantly.* I thought I saw people with tapers.

THÉRÈSE, *in growing terror.* It was a funeral. When I raised my eyes I saw the black pall with a great white cross. *Rises and recoils.* The coffin passed quite close to us. I saw it. A little narrow shabby coffin, so sordid and miserable. Some poor creature.

She has reached LAURENT *and falls on his shoulder. They are both trembling. Then pulling herself together she speaks in a low and urgent voice.*

When you went to the Morgue, you saw him?

LAURENT. Yes.

THÉRÈSE. Did he look as if he had suffered much?

LAURENT. Horribly.

THÉRÈSE. His eyes were open and he was looking at you, wasn't he?

LAURENT. Yes. He was dreadful—blue and bloated with the water. And he was grinning—the corner of his mouth was twisted.

THÉRÈSE. Grinning, was he? Tell me . . . tell me everything . . . tell me how he. . . . On the nights when I couldn't sleep I could never see him clearly and I must. I must see him.

LAURENT, *loudly and shaking* THÉRÈSE. Be quiet. Wake up, I tell you, wake up. We're both asleep. What was it you were saying to me? If I answered you, I was lying. I saw nothing—nothing—nothing. What fool of a game are we playing, the two of us!

THÉRÈSE. I knew the words would break out of us, in spite of ourselves. Everything has been leading us to it—the apricot trees in flower—the little inns by the river—the miserable coffin. We shall never be able to talk of ordinary things again. He is there, behind all our thoughts.

LAURENT. Kiss me . . .

THÉRÈSE. All the time I knew perfectly well that you were only talking about him—that I was only talking about him. We can't help it. The frightful thing has been going round and round in our minds and now it's out.

LAURENT, *trying to take her in his arms.* Thérèse, kiss me. It will make us sane again. That's why we're married—so that we can find peace in each other's arms. Kiss me and let us forget, my dear, dear wife.

THÉRÈSE, *pushing him away*. Please—no—not yet. Comfort me. Be kind to me. Be as you used to be.

A pause, and then LAURENT, *as if struck by a sudden idea, goes out through door at back.*

THÉRÈSE, *alone*. He has gone—I'm alone—Laurent, don't leave me. I belong to you. He has gone and now I am alone. I think the lamp is going out—If it goes out—if I am left in the dark—I don't want to be alone—I don't want to be in the dark—Why wouldn't I let him kiss me? I don't know what was the matter with me—my lips were like ice—I felt that if he kissed me I should die. Where can he have gone?

There is a knock on the little door.

Oh God—he's come back—the other—he's come back for my wedding night. Can't you hear him! He's knocking on the bed—he's calling from my pillow—Go away—I'm afraid. *She is trembling, her hands over her eyes, then slowly she becomes calmer and smiles.* No, it is not that one, it is my own dear love, my love of the old days. It was a beautiful thought, Laurent darling. Thank you. I remember your signal. *She opens the door to* LAURENT.

They repeat their actions in the corresponding scene in Act I.

You, my dear one. I knew you would come. I was sure of it. I was thinking of you. It is so long since I had you alone—to myself, like this.

LAURENT. Do you remember—I couldn't sleep because of you. And I used to dream when we should be together for always. Tonight, beloved, that dream has come true—You are here—in my arms—for ever.

THÉRÈSE. The sun will always shine for us——

LAURENT. Kiss me, my wife.

THÉRÈSE, *breaking away*. No, no. What's the use of pretending? We're not in love any longer. We have killed love. Don't you know that I can feel you are frozen even in my arms? Let us talk calmly now. We can't go on like this—it wouldn't be decent.

LAURENT. You belong to me and I will keep you. And I'll get rid of those fears of yours. It would be cruel if we didn't love one another any longer—if the happiness we dreamed of were a nightmare. My darling . . . put your arms round me.

THÉRÈSE. No, that's asking for sorrow.

LAURENT. Can't you see how absurd it is—to spend the night like this after all those times when we risked so much. No one will come in.

THÉRÈSE, *in terror*. You have said that before—don't say it again. I beg of you. Perhaps he might come. *Struggling.* Our kisses would draw him here. I'm afraid, I tell you, afraid.

LAURENT *goes to take her in his arms when he catches sight of Camille's portrait which hangs over the sideboard.*

LAURENT, *recoiling in terror and pointing to portrait.* There—there—Camille——

THÉRÈSE, *quickly placing herself behind him.* I told you—I felt something cold behind me—Where can you see him?

LAURENT. There—in the shadows.

THÉRÈSE. Behind the bed?

LAURENT. No—to the right. He's not moving. He's looking at us—all the time looking at us. He's just the same as when I saw him—pale, all covered with mud—and with that crooked smile.

THÉRÈSE, *watching.* But it is his portrait you are looking at.

LAURENT. His portrait?

THÉRÈSE. Yes, the one you painted, don't you remember?

LAURENT. No—I don't know—it is his portrait, you think? I saw the eyes move—wait a minute—they're moving again. His portrait? All right—take it down. He is annoying me, staring at us like that.

THÉRÈSE. No, I dare not.

LAURENT. Please—take it down.

THÉRÈSE. No.

LAURENT. We'll put it face to the wall then we won't be afraid any more and perhaps we will be able to love each other.

THÉRÈSE. Why don't you take it down?

LAURENT. Because his eyes never leave me. I tell you, his eyes are moving— They are following me about—they won't leave me alone . . . *Slowly going nearer.* I shall keep my head down and if I can't see him any longer . . . *He takes down the picture with a gesture of fury.*

The door opens and MME. RAQUIN *appears on the threshold.*

MME. RAQUIN. What is the matter? I heard someone call out.

LAURENT, *unable to take his eyes from the portrait which he is still holding.* It is horrible—There he is—just as he was when we threw him into the river.

MME. RAQUIN. Oh, my God—they killed my child.

THÉRÈSE *in despair gives a scream of terror.* LAURENT *throws the portrait on the bed in fright and recoils before* MME. RAQUIN.

MME. RAQUIN, *muttering.* Murderers—Murderers!

She staggers to the bed and on trying to hold on to the bed curtains she tears them down. A terrifying figure, she leans against the wall, breathing deeply. Her eyes never leave LAURENT *who crosses and stands by* THÉRÈSE.

LAURENT. The doctor warned her—a sudden shock——

MME. RAQUIN, *making a supreme effort she goes towards them.* My boy—my poor child—wretches—wretches!

THÉRÈSE. It's horrible! She is all crooked . . . I'm afraid . . . I don't dare to go and help her . . .

MME. RAQUIN, *overcome, she falls into a chair.* Oh, it's horrible . . . I can't . . . I can't . . .

She loses her power of speech and stiff in her chair she fixes LAURENT *and* THÉRÈSE *with her eyes.*

THÉRÈSE. She is dying.

LAURENT. No, her eyes are alive . . . they are threatening us . . . May God turn her lips and her arms to stone.

ACT FOUR

It is 5 o'clock in the afternoon. Once more the room has taken on its atmosphere of darkness and damp. The curtains are dirty and the whole appearance is one of neglect. There is dust everywhere; dish cloths lie forgotten on chairs and piles of dirty crockery clutter up the furniture. A mattress has been rolled up and thrown behind one of the bed curtains. When the curtain rises THÉRÈSE *and* SUZANNE *are sewing at the worktable.*

THÉRÈSE. You have found out where the Blue Prince lives, at last, then! So it's not true, what people say, that love begets fools.

SUZANNE. I don't know about that but I'm quite bright at times. After a while, you know, it wasn't much fun seeing my Prince from a mile away and looking all the time so—so well-behaved. Between you and me, he was far too well-behaved.

THÉRÈSE. So you like bold, bad lovers!

SUZANNE. I'm not sure. It seems to me that a lover you're not afraid of isn't a proper lover at all. When I saw my Prince over there, against the sky, in the midst of the chimney-pots, I thought I was looking at one of those angels in my prayer-book, with clouds all round their feet. Pretty—but after a time, boring, you know. So, on my birthday I got Uncle to give me a map of Paris.

THÉRÈSE. A map of Paris?

SUZANNE. Yes. Uncle was rather surprised. As soon as I had the map I set very seriously to work. I drew lines with a ruler, then I measured with my compasses, and I added and multiplied. When I thought I had found the Prince's roof, I marked it with a pin. The next day I made Uncle go along the street where the house ought to be.

THÉRÈSE, *laughing*. Dear Suzanne! What a nice little story. *Looks at clock and in a sudden change of tone.* Five o'clock already! Laurent will soon be home.

SUZANNE. Why, what's the matter? You were so happy a second ago.

THÉRÈSE, *recovering herself.* And so you discovered the Blue Prince's house with your map?

SUZANNE. No—I did *not*. *Sits on table.* If you only knew where my map led me! One day it took me to a huge place that made floor polish—another day to a photographer's studio—and another to a school—or a prison, I don't know which. You're not laughing! And yet it's very funny. Aren't you well?

THÉRÈSE. Yes . . . yes . . . I was thinking that my husband would be coming. When you are married you must have this lucky map framed.

SUZANNE, *rising, passing behind* THÉRÈSE. But I told you—it was no use. Weren't you listening? One afternoon I went to the Saint Sulpice flower market. I wanted some nasturtiums for the roof. Whom do you think I saw there? The Blue Prince! . . . loaded with flowers. Pots in his pockets, pots under his arms and pots in his hands. He looked so embarrassed when he caught sight of me. Then he followed me. He didn't know what to do with his pots. He told me they were for his roof. After that he became friendly with Uncle and asked for my hand and now I'm marrying him . . . So there you are! I made paper birds with the map and now I only look at the moon through the telescope. Have you been listening, darling?

THÉRÈSE. Yes, and it's a lovely fairy story. So now you will live happily ever after, surrounded by everything that's gay and beautiful. Dear child, with your bluebird—if you only knew . . . *Looks at clock.* Five o'clock. It is five o'clock, isn't it? I must lay the table.

SUZANNE. I'll help you, I'll just move these things.

THÉRÈSE *rises and* SUZANNE *helps her to lay the table for three people.*

It is heartless of me, I know, to be so cheerful when your happiness has been so spoiled. How is poor Madame Raquin today?

THÉRÈSE. She still can't speak or move but I don't think she suffers at all.

SUZANNE. The doctor did warn her that if she got over-tired . . . Oh, it's a cruel thing, paralysis. It's just as if the poor old darling had been suddenly turned into stone. When she's sitting in her chair, so rigid, her white head so erect and her hands so pale, in her lap, she makes me

think of those terrifying statues of mourning on the tombs in churches.
I don't know why, but it terrifies me. She can't raise her hands, can she?

THÉRÈSE. Her hands and her legs are dead.

SUZANNE. How dreadful! Uncle says that she can't even hear or understand. He thinks it would be a good thing if her mind goes entirely.

THÉRÈSE. He's wrong. She can hear and understand everything. Her mind
is quite clear and her eyes are alive.

SUZANNE. Yes, they seem to have got bigger; they are enormous now.
They are black now and terrible in that dead-looking face. You know,
I'm not a nervous person and yet when I think about her in the night,
it makes me shudder. You know those stories about people who have
been buried alive? I can see her there—in a grave—still alive and not
able to call out because of the great weight of earth pressing on her.
What does she think about all day long? It's terrible to be like that—to
be doing nothing but think and think . . . But you are both so good
to her.

THÉRÈSE. We are only doing our duty.

SUZANNE. And you two are the only ones who understand what she is
saying with her eyes, aren't you? I can't understand her at all. Monsieur
Grivet pretends to know her slightest wishes but his answers are all at
cross-purposes. It's a mercy that she has you both with her. She has
everything possible done for her. Uncle often says that this is a God-
fearing house. There'll be happier days to come, you'll see. Does the
doctor give any hope?

THÉRÈSE. Very little.

SUZANNE. I was here when he came the last time and he said that the
poor darling might recover the use of her limbs and her tongue.

THÉRÈSE. We can't count on it. We dare not count on it.

SUZANNE. You must go on hoping.

They have finished laying the table and come downstage.

SUZANNE. We never see Monsieur Laurent here these days.

THÉRÈSE. Now that he's left the office and started painting again, he
leaves in the morning and often doesn't come back until the evening.
He is working hard and wants to send a large picture to the next Salon.

SUZANNE. He has become very dignified. His laugh is quieter and he looks
so distinguished. You won't be angry with me if I tell you something,
will you? Well, I shouldn't have wanted him as a husband as he used
to be, but now I think he's most attractive. I'll tell you something else
if you promise to keep it secret.

THÉRÈSE. I don't gossip.

SUZANNE. No, you don't. You keep everything to yourself. Well then, yesterday when we were going past your husband's studio in the rue Mazarin, Uncle suddenly thought we would go up. You know how Monsieur Laurent hates being disturbed at his work but all the same he didn't receive us too badly. You'd never guess what he's working at.

THÉRÈSE. A big picture.

SUZANNE. No, the canvas for the big picture is still quite blank. We found him surrounded by small canvases—sketches of faces. There were children's faces and women's faces and old men's faces. Uncle, who is quite a critic, was very taken with them. He says that your husband has become a great painter. It wasn't flattery because he didn't think much of him before. But what surprised me was that all the faces resembled someone. They were like. . . .

THÉRÈSE. Like whom?

SUZANNE. I don't want to hurt you . . . but they were all like poor Monsieur Camille.

THÉRÈSE, *trembling.* No—no—you imagined it.

SUZANNE. But they were. The children's faces, the women's faces, the old men's faces . . . they all had something which reminded me of him— Uncle would have liked them to have more color. They are rather pale and they all had a crooked little smile . . .

LAURENT *is heard at the door.*

SUZANNE. Ah, there's your husband. Don't say anything about it. I expect he's going to give you a surprise with all those heads.

LAURENT. Good evening, Suzanne. Have you both been working hard?

THÉRÈSE. Yes.

LAURENT. I'm worn out. *Falls into chair.*

SUZANNE. Painting must be very tiring—all that standing.

LAURENT. I haven't been painting today. I walked to Saint Cloud and back. It did me good. Is dinner ready, Thérèse?

THÉRÈSE. Yes.

SUZANNE. I'm just going.

THÉRÈSE. Your uncle promised to come and fetch you. You must wait for him. You won't worry us.

SUZANNE. All right. I want some crewel needles—I'll go down to the shop and steal some. *As she starts to go down the shop bell rings.* Ah, a customer! I'll see what she wants. *She goes down.*

LAURENT, *pointing to mattress.* Why didn't you put that mattress away? There's no need for people to know that we use two beds.

THÉRÈSE. You could quite well have put it away yourself this morning. I do as I please.

LAURENT, *roughly*. Now don't start a quarrel. It isn't night yet.

THÉRÈSE. Well, if you amuse yourself away from home and take walks all day long, it's all the same to me. It's peaceful when you're not here but as soon as you come in, all hell opens. Let me at least have my sleep during the day. You know what the nights are like.

LAURENT, *more gently*. Your tongue is even sharper than mine, Thérèse.

THÉRÈSE, *after a pause*. Are you going to fetch her in for her dinner? Michaud is coming. I am always terrified when she is here with them. I have seen a look in her eyes for some time now. You see—she'll find a way to talk. We had better wait until he and Suzanne have gone.

LAURENT. Rubbish. Michaud would like to see his old friend, although I'm not so happy when he goes into her room. But what can she tell him? Why, she can't lift her little finger.

Exit LAURENT *through door at back. Enter* MICHAUD *and* SUZANNE.

MICHAUD. Ah, the table's laid.

THÉRÈSE. That's right, Monsieur Michaud. *She goes to the sideboard from which she takes a cloth, lettuce and a salad bowl. She sits and during the following scene she prepares the lettuce.*

MICHAUD. You people do yourselves pretty well, don't you? These lovers have a devilish good appetite. Put on your hat, Suzanne. *Looks around.* And how is my dear Madame Raquin?

Enter LAURENT *pushing* MME. RAQUIN *in her armchair. Her hair is white; dressed in black she sits stiff and mute.* LAURENT *places her by table.*

Ah, here is the dear lady herself.

SUZANNE, *kissing* MME. RAQUIN. We all love you very much. You must be brave.

MICHAUD. How her eyes shine! She's pleased to see us. *To* MME. RAQUIN. We're old friends, you and I, aren't we? Do you remember, when I was superintendent of police? It was at the time of the Gorge aux Loups murder, I think, when we first met. You must remember—that woman and that man who murdered a van driver. I arrested them myself—in their filthy cottage. They were guillotined at Rouen.

GRIVET, *enters during this speech and catches the end of it*. Ah, that story of the van driver. I know it. You told me—very interesting, I thought. Monsieur Michaud has a nose for crime. Good evening, everybody.

MICHAUD. And what are you doing here at this hour of the day?

GRIVET. I happened to be passing and I thought I'd give myself a treat.

I've come to have a little chat with Madame Raquin. But you were just going to have a meal, I see. Am I disturbing you?

LAURENT. Not at all.

GRIVET. Madame Raquin and I get on so well together. Just one look and I know what she wants.

MICHAUD. Well, perhaps you can tell me what she's trying to say to me. She's staring so hard at me.

GRIVET. Just a minute—I can read her eyes like a book. *Sits beside* MME. RAQUIN, *touches her arm and waits for her to turn her head slowly to him.* There, now—let's have a nice friendly little chat. Is there anything you want to ask Monsieur Michaud? Is there? No, nothing at all— that's just as I thought. *To* MICHAUD. You were flattering yourself! It's me she wants, not you at all. *Turns back to* MME. RAQUIN. Now then, what is it? Ah yes, I understand—you are hungry.

SUZANNE, *leaning over back of armchair.* Would you like us to go, dear?

GRIVET. Yes, of course, she's hungry. And she's asked me to stay for a little game of dominoes, this evening. I'm so sorry, Madame Raquin, but I shan't be able to accept your invitation—you know my little ways. But I promise you I'll come on Thursday.

MICHAUD. She didn't say anything at all to you. You made it up. Now let me try.

LAURENT, *to* THÉRÈSE, *who rises.* You're right. Keep an eye on her. There's a terrible look in her eyes.

He takes the cloth and salad bowl from THÉRÈSE *and puts them on the sideboard.*

MICHAUD. Now, Madame, I'm entirely at your disposal, as always. Why are you looking at me like that? If you could only find some way of letting me know what it is you want.

SUZANNE. You hear what Uncle says. We would do any mortal thing you want.

GRIVET. I've told you what she wants. It's quite plain.

MICHAUD, *insistently.* Can't you make us understand? Look, Laurent. She keeps staring at me so strangely.

LAURENT. I don't see anything strange about her.

SUZANNE. Thérèse, you can always understand her, can't you?

MICHAUD. Yes, you help her—please.

THÉRÈSE. You're making a mistake. She doesn't want anything. She's just the same as usual. *She goes to face* MME. RAQUIN, *but cannot meet her eyes.* That's right, isn't it? You don't want anything, do you? *Recoils at what she sees in* MME. RAQUIN'S *eyes.*

MICHAUD. Ah well! Perhaps Monsieur Grivet is right.

GRIVET. Of course I am. She's hungry and she has invited me for a game of dominoes.

LAURENT. Why don't you stay, Monsieur Grivet? And you too, Monsieur Michaud. We should be pleased.

MICHAUD. No thanks. I'm busy this evening.

THÉRÈSE, *to* LAURENT. For pity's sake . . . don't let them stay——

MICHAUD. Good night to you all. *Starts to go.*

GRIVET. Good night—good night. *Following* MICHAUD.

SUZANNE, *still by* MME. RAQUIN'S *chair.* Look—look—her fingers are moving!

MICHAUD *and* GRIVET *crowd round the chair, giving cries of astonishment.*

THÉRÈSE, *in an undertone to* LAURENT. What an effort she's making—we can't escape now—it's our punishment. *They huddle together.*

MICHAUD, *to* MME. RAQUIN. What's this? Why, you are your old self again. Look at your fingers—they are dancing a jig.

There is a pause while MME. RAQUIN *fixes her glittering eyes on* THÉRÈSE *and* LAURENT.

Look—she has managed to lift her hand and put it on the table.

GRIVET. Oho—we are a real little gadabout, we are. Our hands are going for a long walk.

THÉRÈSE. She's coming back to life—a statue coming to life!

LAURENT. Don't be afraid—hands don't speak.

SUZANNE. It looks as if she is making signs with her fingers.

GRIVET. Yes, what is she doing there on the oilcloth?

MICHAUD. She's writing, can't you see—She has just made a capital T.

THÉRÈSE, *faintly.* Hands do speak, Laurent.

GRIVET. Good Heavens! She's writing. *To* MME. RAQUIN. Now, not too fast—not too fast. I'll try and read. No, no, I didn't get that. Begin again. *Pause.* It's amazing. T. . . . Tea—that's it—She wants some tea.

SUZANNE. No, no. She wrote Thérèse's name.

MICHAUD. Why, Monsieur Grivet, you don't know how to read. *Reading.* "Thérèse and . . ." Go on, Madame Raquin.

LAURENT, *to* THÉRÈSE. A hand from the grave. She shan't finish. I'll nail her hand there before I'll let her finish. *Makes as if to take knife from pocket.*

THÉRÈSE, *holding him back.* Stop—you will ruin everything.

MICHAUD, Why, it's perfectly clear. "Thérèse and Laurent . . ." She's writing your names.

GRIVET. Yes, upon my word, your two names. It's wonderful.

MICHAUD, *watching fingers.* "Thérèse and Laurent have . . ." Well, what have they? Bless their hearts.

GRIVET. Oh, she's stopped. Oh dear, dear, dear!

MICHAUD, *to* MME. RAQUIN. Now finish the sentence—just one more try.

MME. RAQUIN *looks long at* THÉRÈSE *and* LAURENT, *then she slowly turns her head.*

You are looking at each one of us,—yes, we want to know the end of the sentence.

She stays motionless for a moment, savoring the terror of the two murderers, then lets her hand fall into her lap.

MICHAUD. Ah, now your hand has fallen.

SUZANNE, *touching the hand.* It is like a stone in her lap.

The three of them talk excitedly in a group behind the chair.

THÉRÈSE, *in an undertone.* I thought it was the end for us—we're safe now, aren't we? Her hand is not moving.

LAURENT. Pull yourself together—lean on me—I felt I was choking.

GRIVET. I wish she had finished the sentence; it was a pity she didn't.

MICHAUD. Yes, I could follow her easily. I wonder what she wanted to say.

SUZANNE. That Thérèse and Laurent have made her so happy with all their kindness.

MICHAUD. Why, of course! You're much quicker than we are, my dear. "Thérèse and Laurent have made me very happy . . . Thérèse and Laurent have my blessing." That's how the sentence goes, isn't it, Madame? You want to see that justice is done to them, don't you? *To* THÉRÈSE *and* LAURENT. You are two such dear souls. You certainly deserve a fine reward . . . here or hereafter.

LAURENT. You would have done the same.

GRIVET. They have had their reward. Do you know what the people round here call them? They call them a pair of turtledoves.

MICHAUD. And *we* arranged the marriage. Come along now, Monsieur Grivet. We must let them have their dinner now. *To* MME. RAQUIN. These little hands will soon wake up again, and so will the legs. It's a good sign to have been able to move your fingers. You'll soon be well now. Good night, dear Madame.

SUZANNE, *to* MME. RAQUIN. Till tomorrow, darling.

GRIVET, *to* MME. RAQUIN. There now, I said we always get on so well and we're going to play dominoes together on Thursdays, aren't we? And we'll beat Monsieur Michaud, you'll see, we'll beat him. *To* THÉRÈSE *and* LAURENT. Good night, my turtledoves. You know, you are a couple of turtledoves . . .

While MICHAUD, GRIVET *and* SUZANNE *are going down the stairs,* THÉRÈSE *goes out through door at back and returns with a soup tureen.*

During this scene MME. RAQUIN's *face reflects all she is thinking, for she registers anger, horror, cruel gloating, implacable vengeance, and with burning eyes she follows the murderers through all their wrangling and their distress.*

LAURENT. She would have given us away.

THÉRÈSE, *serves* LAURENT *and herself with soup.* Be quiet. Leave her alone.

LAURENT, *sitting back of table.* Do you think she would spare us if she could speak? Michaud and Grivet were smiling rather queerly when they talked about our happiness. They'll find out in the end, you'll see. Grivet went out with his hat on the side of his head, didn't he?

THÉRÈSE, *puts soup tureen before the fire.* Yes, I think so.

LAURENT. And when he went he buttoned up his overcoat and put his hands in his pockets. He used to button up his overcoat like that at the office when he wanted to look important. And the way he said "Good night, my turtledoves!" There's something frightening—sinister —about the idiot.

THÉRÈSE. Be quiet. Don't exaggerate things. Don't drag him into our nightmare.

LAURENT. When he screws up his mouth—you know—in that way that makes him look so stupid, I feel he's laughing at us. I never trust people who pretend to be fools. I tell you, he knows everything.

THÉRÈSE. They're far too simple. Yet it would put an end to it all if they did hand us over. But they'll see nothing. They will go on treading their humdrum, peaceful, self-satisfied way through the horrors of our life. *Sits at table.* Let's talk of something else. What madness is it that makes you always come back to this when she's here with us?

LAURENT. I have no spoon.

THÉRÈSE *fetches one from the sideboard, gives it to him and sits.* Aren't you going to give her anything to eat?

THÉRÈSE. Yes, when I have finished my soup.

LAURENT, *tasting soup.* It's beastly—you have made it too salt. *Pushes it away.* It is just sheer spite. You know I hate salt.

THÉRÈSE. Laurent—please don't start to pick a quarrel. Can't you see I'm tired out? I've had as much as I can bear.

LAURENT. That's right. Make a martyr of yourself. You make my life a torment with your everlasting nagging.

THÉRÈSE. You want us to quarrel, don't you?

LAURENT. I want you to stop talking to me like that.

THÉRÈSE. Oh, do you? *Pushing away her plate.* All right. Just as you like. We won't have any dinner tonight again. We'll tear each other to pieces and she shall hear us. It's our daily treat these days.

LAURENT, *with quiet force*. And who starts it? You watch me—you whip me on the raw and you're not happy until the pain drives me mad.

THÉRÈSE. Well, I didn't say the soup was salt, did I? Any excuse does. You magnify the smallest trifle and fly into a fury. Now, tell me the truth. Be honest. It makes you happy to wrangle the whole evening, doesn't it? To exhaust yourself so that at night you can get a little sleep when you go to bed.

LAURENT. You don't sleep any more than I do.

THÉRÈSE. Oh, you have made life hideous. I dread the night and its terrors. He is there—between us. This room is full of death.

LAURENT. It's your fault.

THÉRÈSE. My fault did you say? Is it my fault that instead of the comfortable life you dreamed of, you've made everything impossible—full of fear and hate?

LAURENT. Yes, it's your fault.

THÉRÈSE. Stop it. I'm not a fool. Do you think I don't know you? You've always been on the lookout for the main chance. When you took me as your mistress it was because it cost you nothing. You dare not deny it. I hate you. Can't you see I hate you?

LAURENT. Which of us is trying to pick the quarrel now?

THÉRÈSE. I hate you. You killed Camille.

LAURENT. Shut your mouth. *Pointing to* MME. RAQUIN. Just now you told me to hold my tongue in front of her. Don't force me to remind you of the facts, to go over the whole story again in front of her.

THÉRÈSE. Let her hear. Let her suffer. Haven't I suffered? The truth is that you killed Camille.

LAURENT. It's a lie. You know it. It's a lie. I may have been the one to throw him into the river but it was you who drove me to murder him.

THÉRÈSE. I?

LAURENT. Yes, you! Don't pretend you don't know. Don't make me drag it from you by force. I want you to confess your guilt, to accept your share. That at least, might be some comfort to me.

THÉRÈSE. But it wasn't I who killed Camille.

LAURENT. But it was you—it was. You were on the bank and I whispered to you "I'm going to throw him in the river." You agreed and got into the boat. You must see that you killed him too.

THÉRÈSE. It isn't true. I was mad. I didn't know what I was doing. I didn't want you to kill him.

LAURENT. Then when I upset the boat in the middle of the river, didn't I warn you? You clung to my neck and let him drown like a dog.

THÉRÈSE. It isn't true. It was you who killed him.

LAURENT. And then in the cab, on the way back, you put your hand in mine . . . I was burning for you . . .

THÉRÈSE. It was you who killed him.

LAURENT. You don't remember—you don't intend to remember. You drove me mad with love here, in this room. You put me against your husband. You wanted to get rid of him. You didn't care for him. He was always ill, you said. Was I like this three years ago? Was I? Was I evil? I was decent. I wouldn't have harmed anyone. I wouldn't have killed a fly.

THÉRÈSE. It was you who killed him.

LAURENT. Twice you've made me act like a wild beast. I was sane and contented—and now see what you have done to me. I tremble at every shadow like a frightened child. My nerves are as bad as yours. I'm not the stuff that murderers are made of. From adultery you led me to murder before I realized what was happening and now, when I look back at what I've done, I'm terrified. I can see, as if in a dream, the arrest, the trial, the guillotine. *Rises.* And you—you shake with terror in the night—you can't help it. You know that if his ghost came, he would strangle you first.

THÉRÈSE. No, no, don't say it. It was you who killed him.

LAURENT. Listen to me. It is cowardly to deny your share in what we did. You want to make my burden heavier, don't you? Well, you have driven me to the end of my tether. I'd sooner make an end of things. I am quite calm, you see. *Takes his hat.* I am going to tell the whole story to the police.

THÉRÈSE, *scornfully.* That's a good idea!

LAURENT. They will arrest both of us. We'll see what the judge thinks about your innocence.

THÉRÈSE. Do you think I'm afraid? I'm more sick and tired of it than you are. If you don't go to the police, I shall.

LAURENT. I don't need you to come with me. I can tell them everything.

THÉRÈSE. No. Whenever we quarrel, as soon as you have run through all your arguments, you make this same threat. Today you're going to mean it. Well, I'm not a coward like you. I'm quite ready to follow you to the scaffold. Let's go. I'm coming too. *Goes with him to the stairs.*

LAURENT. Just as you like. We'll go and see the Inspector together.

He goes downstairs. THÉRÈSE *clings to handrail, motionless, and listening. She begins to tremble with fear.* MADAME RAQUIN *turns her head, a grim smile on her face.*

THÉRÈSE. He has gone down. He's at the bottom now. Will he have the courage to give us up? I don't want it—I'll run after him—I'll take hold of him and bring him back—suppose he shouts it out in the street—suppose he tells the people he meets—Oh God—it was wrong of me to drive him so far. I should have had more sense. *Listening*. He's still in the shop—the bell hasn't rung. What can he be doing? He's coming up—yes, now I can hear him—he's coming up. I knew he was too much of a coward. *Shouting*. Coward! Coward!

LAURENT *returns, sits R. by the work table, collapsing with his head in his hands*.

LAURENT. I can't. I can't.

THÉRÈSE, *jeering as she goes to him*. Well, you're soon back. What did they say to you? Haven't you any blood in your veins? I'm sorry for you. *Passes between* LAURENT *and fire, faces him, her fists planted on the worktable*.

LAURENT, *sitting, speaking almost inaudibly*. I can't . . .

THÉRÈSE. You are weaker than I. You should be supporting me. How do you think we can make ourselves forget?

LAURENT. So you admit you had a share in it?

THÉRÈSE. Oh yes. I'm guilty. More guilty than you, if you like. I ought to have stopped you . . . Camille was a good man.

LAURENT. Don't let's start it all over again—please, I implore you. When you have driven me frantic then you are happy. Don't look at me—don't smile at me. I shall escape when the time comes. *Takes small bottle from his pocket*. This is dreamless sleep—the remission of my sentence. Two drops of prussic acid—and I have no more to worry about.

THÉRÈSE. Poison! I dare you to drink it—you're too much of a coward! Go on, Laurent, drink it—drink a drop of it—just to see——

LAURENT. Be quiet—stop nagging me.

THÉRÈSE. I'm not worried—you won't drink it.

LAURENT. Be quiet!

THÉRÈSE. You don't understand how women feel. Don't you realize that I hate you now that I see your hands are stained with my husband's blood?

LAURENT, *pacing up and down in a frenzy of hallucination*. Will you be quiet! There's a hammering in my head—it is splitting my brain—What devil has got hold of you—talking now of remorse and of your grief for him? I can't get away from him. He did this—he did that—he was good—he was noble. I'm going mad. He is living with us—he sits on my chair—he is next to me at the table—he makes himself at home with us. He has eaten from the plate that I use—he still eats from it. I'm not myself any more—I am Camille. I have his wife and his place at table—I have his bed—I am Camille—Camille—Camille——

THÉRÈSE. That's a nice thing you're doing, painting him in all your pictures.

LAURENT. Ah, so you know that, do you? *Lowering his voice.* It's terrible. My hands don't belong to me any more. I can't paint any more. He is always there—in my hands. These hands, these two hands are not mine. If I don't cut them off, they will betray me. They are his—his. He has robbed me of them.

THÉRÈSE. This is retribution.

LAURENT. Tell me, haven't I got Camille's mouth? Oh, did you hear? That's just how Camille would have said that. Listen. "I have his mouth. I have his mouth." That's it exactly. I speak like him. I laugh like him. He is there all the time, inside my head, hammering at it with his fists.

THÉRÈSE. Retribution.

LAURENT. Go away, woman. You are driving me mad. Go away, or I'll . . . *Forces her to her knees and raises his hand as if to strike.*

THÉRÈSE, *on her knees.* Go on—finish it—kill me as you killed him! Camille never struck me. You are a monster! Go on—kill me as you killed him.

LAURENT, *demented, crosses, and sits by the alcove, his head in his hands. During all this* MME. RAQUIN *has succeeded in pushing a knife off the table and it falls by* THÉRÈSE. *The noise of its falling takes* THÉRÈSE's *attention from* LAURENT *whom she has been watching. Slowly turning her head she lets her eyes travel from the knife to* MME. RAQUIN.

THÉRÈSE. You made it fall. There is a devil from hell in your eyes!—what is it you want to say—you are right—that creature has made my life intolerable. If he were not there all the time to remind me of what I want to forget I'd have nothing to worry about—I could live my life in peace. *Looking at* MME. RAQUIN *as she picks up the knife.* You are looking at the knife, aren't you? Well, I've got it and he shan't torment me any longer. He killed Camille because he was in the way. All right then—he's in my way! *Rises, with the knife in her hand.*

LAURENT, *the bottle of poison in his hand.* Let's forget all this and finish supper, shall we?

THÉRÈSE. Just as you like. *To herself.* I can't wait for the night—This knife burns me——

LAURENT. What's in your mind? Come and sit down—Wait a minute—I'll give you something to drink. *Pours out a glass of water.*

THÉRÈSE, *to herself.* Better to end it all now.

Goes towards him with the knife raised; she sees LAURENT *put poison in the glass and seizes his arm.*

Laurent, what are you putting in that?

LAURENT, *catching sight of the knife.* Why are you holding up your arm?

Pause.

Put down that knife.

THÉRÈSE. After you have put down that bottle.

Looking at each other with hate and dropping the knife and the bottle.

LAURENT, *collapsing into a chair.* Both of us—both of us—the same thought —the same horrible thought . . .

THÉRÈSE, *falling into a chair.* Oh, Laurent, we loved each other so much— and now we have come to this—poison and a knife!

She catches sight of MME. RAQUIN *and then rises with a sudden cry.*

Laurent—look!

LAURENT, *rising and staring in terror at* MME. RAQUIN. She was there—all the time—to watch us die!

THÉRÈSE. But don't you see her lips are moving! She is smiling—oh, it's a horrible smile!

LAURENT. Now she's beginning to tremble.

THÉRÈSE. She's going to speak—I tell you, she's going to speak.

LAURENT. I know how to stop her.

Is about to hurl himself on MME. RAQUIN *when she slowly gets to her feet. He recoils, walks away and then turns.*

MME. RAQUIN, *standing and speaking in a deep hollow voice.* You murdered the child, now you dare to strike the mother.

THÉRÈSE. Have mercy on us. Don't hand us over to the law.

MME. RAQUIN. Hand you over! No! I thought of it at first when my strength began to come back. I began to write your name on that table. But I stopped. Human justice would be too swift, I thought. I want to watch you pay for your crime, here, in this room where you robbed me of my happiness.

THÉRÈSE, *sobbing and falling at* MME. RAQUIN's *feet.* Forgive me—my remorse is choking me—I am a wicked woman. See, I am on my knees to you —I am at your mercy—I beg you to have pity.

MME. RAQUIN, *supporting herself on the table as her voice gradually gains strength.* Pity! Did you have pity on my poor child—the child I worshipped? Don't ask for pity. I have no more pity—you have robbed me of pity.

LAURENT *falls on his knees.*

MME. RAQUIN. No, I shall not save you from yourselves. I am going to watch remorse tearing you like savage beasts. Hand you over? No, I shall not hand you over. You're mine, mine alone, and I'm going to keep you mine.

THÉRÈSE. No, no, it would be intolerable. We will be our own judges and the verdict is "Guilty."

She picks up the bottle, drinks eagerly and falls crashing at MME. RAQUIN's *feet.* LAURENT *snatches the bottle from her and drinks. He falls R. behind the work-table and chairs.*

MME. RAQUIN, *slowly sitting.* Dead! dead!

The Magistrate

A Farce in Three Acts

by ARTHUR W. PINERO

CHARACTERS

MR. POSKET ⎫ *Magistrates of Mulberry Street Police Court*
MR. BULLAMY ⎭

COLONEL LUKYN

CAPTAIN HORACE VALE

CIS FARRINGDON, MRS. POSKET'S *son by her first marriage*

ACHILLE BLOND

ISIDORE

MR. WORMINGTON

INSPECTOR MESSITER ⎫
SERGEANT LUGG ⎬ *Metropolitan Police*
CONSTABLE HARRIS ⎭

WYKE

AGATHA POSKET

CHARLOTTE, *her sister*

BEATIE TOMLINSON

POPHAM

———

ACT ONE   The Family Skeleton
ACT TWO   It Leaves Its Cupboard
ACT THREE It Crumbles

ACT ONE

The scene represents a well-furnished room in the house of MR. POSKET *in Bloomsbury.* BEATIE TOMLINSON, *a pretty, simply dressed little girl of about sixteen, is playing the piano, as* CIS FARRINGDON, *a manly youth wearing an Eton jacket, enters the room.*

CIS. Beatie!

BEATIE. Cis dear! Dinner isn't over, surely?

CIS. Not quite. I had one of my convenient headaches and cleared out. *He takes an apple and some cobnuts from his pocket and gives them to* BEATIE. These are for you, dear, with my love. I sneaked 'em off the sideboard as I came out.

BEATIE. Oh, I mustn't take them!

CIS. Yes, you may—it's my share of dessert. Besides, it's a horrid shame you don't grub with us.

BEATIE. What, a poor little music mistress!

CIS. Yes. They're only going to give you four guineas a quarter. Fancy getting a girl like you for four guineas a quarter—why, an eighth of you is worth more than that! Now peg away at your apple. *Produces a cigarette.*

BEATIE, *munching her apple.* There's company at dinner, isn't there?

CIS. Well, hardly. Aunt Charlotte hasn't arrived yet, so there's only old Bullamy.

BEATIE. Isn't old Bullamy anybody?

CIS. Old Bullamy—well, he's only like the Guv'nor, a police magistrate at the Mulberry Street Police Court.

BEATIE. Oh, does each police court have two magistrates?

CIS, *proudly.* All the best have two.

BEATIE. Don't they quarrel over getting the interesting cases? I should.

CIS. I don't know how they manage—perhaps they toss up who's to hear the big sensations. There's a Mrs. Beldam who is rather a bore sometimes; I know the Guv always lets old Bullamy attend to her. But, as a rule, I fancy they go half and half, in a friendly way. *Lighting cigarette.* For instance—*going over to* BEATIE—if the Guv'nor wants to go to the Derby he lets old Bullamy have the Oaks—and so on, see? *He sits on the floor, comfortably reclining against* BEATIE, *and puffing his cigarette.*

BEATIE. Oh, I say, Cis, won't your Mamma be angry when she finds I haven't gone home?

CIS. Oh, put it onto your pupil. Say I'm very backward.

BEATIE. I think you are extremely forward—in some ways. *Biting apple and speaking with her mouth full.* I do wish I could get you to concentrate your attention on your music lessons. But I wouldn't get you into a scrape!

CIS. No fear of that. Ma is too proud of me.

BEATIE. But there's your stepfather.

CIS. The dear old Guv'nor! Why, he is too good-natured to say "Bo!" to a goose. You know, Beatie, I was at a school in Brighton when Ma got married—when she got married the second time, I mean—and the Guv'nor and I didn't make each other's acquaintance till after the honeymoon.

BEATIE. Oh, fancy your stepfather blindly accepting such a responsibility. *Gives him a cobnut to crack for her.*

CIS. Yes, wasn't the Guv'nor soft! I might have been a very indifferent sort of young fellow for all he knew. *Having cracked the nut with his teeth, returns it to her.*

BEATIE. Thank you, dear.

CIS, *resuming.* Well, when I heard the new dad was a police magistrate, I *was* scared. Said I to myself, "If I don't mind my P's and Q's, the Guv'nor—from force of habit—will fine me all my pocket-money." But it's quite the reverse—he's the mildest, meekest—— *The door opens suddenly.* Look out! Someone coming!

They both jump up, BEATIE *scattering the nuts that are in her lap all over the floor.* CIS *throws his cigarette away in the fireplace and sits at piano, playing a simple exercise very badly.* BEATIE *stands behind him, counting.*

BEATIE. One—and two—and one—and two.

WYKE, *the butler, appears at door, and mysteriously closes it after him.*

WYKE. Ssss! Master Cis! Master Cis!

CIS. Hallo—what is it, Wyke?

WYKE, *producing a decanter from under his coat.* The port wine what you asked for, sir. I couldn't get it away before—the old gentlemen do hug port wine so.

CIS. Got a glass?

WYKE. Yes, sir. *Produces wineglass from his pocket and pours out wine.* What ain't missed ain't mourned, eh, Master Cis?

CIS, *offering wine.* Here you are, Beatie dear.

BEATIE. The idea of such a thing! I couldn't!

CIS. Why not?

BEATIE. If I merely sipped it I shouldn't be able to give you your music lesson properly. Drink it yourself, you dear, thoughtful boy.

CIS. I shan't—it's for you.

BEATIE. I can't drink it!

CIS. You must.

BEATIE. I won't!

CIS. You're disagreeable!

BEATIE. Not half so disagreeable as you are. *They wrangle.*

WYKE, *to himself, watching them.* What a young gentleman it is! and only fourteen! Fourteen—he behaves like forty!

CIS chokes as he is drinking the wine; BEATIE *pats him on the back.*

Why, even Cook has made a 'ash of everything since he's been in the house, and as for Popham——! *Seeing someone approaching.* Look out, Master Cis!

CIS returns to piano, BEATIE *counting as before;* WYKE *pretends to arrange the window curtains, concealing the decanter behind him.*

BEATIE. One and two—and one and two—and one, *etc.*

Enter POPHAM, *a smart-looking maidservant.*

POPHAM. Wyke, where's the port?

WYKE, *vacantly.* Port?

POPHAM. Port wine. Missus is furious.

WYKE. Port?

POPHAM, *pointing to decanter.* Why! There! You're carrying it about with you!

WYKE. Why, so I am! Carrying it about with me! Shows what a sharp eye I keep on the Guv'nor's wines. Carrying it about with me! Missus will be amused. *Goes out.*

POPHAM, *eying CIS and BEATIE.* There's that boy with *her* again! Minx! Her two hours were up long ago. Why doesn't she go home? Master Cis, I've got a message for you.

CIS, *rising from the piano.* For me, Popham?

POPHAM. Yes, sir. *Quietly to him.* The message is from a young lady who up to last Wednesday was all in all to you. Her name is Emma Popham.

CIS, *trying to get away.* Oh, go along, Popham!

POPHAM, *holding his sleeve.* Ah, it wasn't "Go along, Popham," till that music girl came into the house. I will go along, but—cast your eye over this before you sleep to-night. *She takes out of her pocket-handkerchief a piece of printed paper which she hands him between her finger and thumb.* Part of a story in *Bow Bells*, called "Jilted, or, Could Blood Atone?" Wrap it in your handkerchief—it came round the butter.

She goes out; CIS *throws the paper into the grate.*

CIS. Bother the girl! Beatie, she's jealous of you!

BEATIE. A parlourmaid jealous of *me*—and with a bit of a child of fourteen!

CIS. I may be only fourteen, but I feel like a grown-up man! You're only sixteen—there's not much difference—and if you will only wait for me, I'll soon catch you up and be as much a man as you are a woman. Will you wait for me, Beatie?

BEATIE. I can't—I'm getting older every minute!

CIS. Oh, I wish I could borrow five or six years from somebody!

BEATIE. Many a person would be glad to lend them. *Lovingly.* And oh, I wish you could!

CIS, *putting his arm round her.* You do! Why?

BEATIE. Because I—because——

CIS, *listening.* Look out! Here's the Mater!

They run to piano—he resumes playing, and she counting as before.

BEATIE. One and two—and one—and two, *etc.*

Enter AGATHA POSKET, *a handsome, showy woman, of about thirty-six, looking perhaps younger.*

AGATHA. Why, Cis child, at your music again?

CIS. Yes, Ma, always at it. You'll spoil my taste by forcing it, if you're not careful.

AGATHA. We have no right to keep Miss Tomlinson so late.

BEATIE. Oh, thank you, it doesn't matter—I—I—am afraid we're not making—very—great—progress.

CIS, *winking at* BEATIE. Well, if I play that again will you kiss me?

BEATIE, *demurely.* I don't know, I'm sure. *To* AGATHA POSKET. May I promise that, ma'am? *She sits in the window recess.* CIS *joining her, puts his arm round her waist.*

AGATHA. No, certainly not. *To herself, watching them.* If I could only persuade Æneas to dismiss this *protégée* of his and to engage a music master, it would ease my conscience a little. If this girl knew the truth, how indignant she would be! And then there is the injustice to the boy himself, and to my husband's friends, who are always petting and fondling and caressing, what they call, "a fine little man of fourteen!" Fourteen! Oh, what an idiot I have been to conceal my child's real age! *Looking at the clock.* Charlotte is late, I wish she would come. It will be a relief to worry her with my troubles.

POSKET, *talking outside.* We smoke all over the house, Bullamy, all over the house.

AGATHA. I will speak to Æneas about this little girl, at any rate.

Enter MR. POSKET, *a mild gentleman of fifty, smoking a cigarette, followed by*

MR. BULLAMY, *a fat, red-faced man with a bronchial cough and general huskiness.*

POSKET. Smoke anywhere, Bullamy—smoke anywhere.

BULLAMY. Not with my bronchitis, thank ye.

POSKET, *beamingly at* AGATHA. Ah, my darling!

BULLAMY, *producing a small box from his waistcoat pocket.* All I take after dinner is a jujube—sometimes two. *Offering the box.* May I tempt Mrs. Posket?

AGATHA. No, thank you. *Treading on one of the nuts which have been scattered over the room.* How provoking—who brings nuts into the drawing-room!

POSKET. Miss Tomlinson still here? *To* BEATIE. Don't go, don't go. Glad to see Cis so fond of his music. Your sister Charlotte is behind her time, my darling.

AGATHA. Her train is delayed, I suppose.

POSKET. You must stay and see my sister-in-law, Bullamy.

BULLAMY. Pleasure—pleasure!

POSKET. *I* have never met her yet, we will share first impressions. In the interim, will Miss Tomlinson delight us with a little music?

BULLAMY, *bustling up to piano.* If this young lady is going to sing she might like one of my jujubes.

BEATIE *sits at the piano with* CIS *and* BULLAMY *on each side of her.* POSKET *treads on a nut as he walks over to his wife.*

POSKET. Dear me—how come nuts in the drawing-room. *To* AGATHA. Of what is my darling thinking so deeply? *Treads on another nut.* Another! My pet, there are nuts on the drawing-room carpet!

AGATHA, *rousing herself.* Yes, I want to speak to you, Æneas.

POSKET. About the nuts?

AGATHA. No—about Miss Tomlinson—your little *protégée.*

POSKET. Ah, nice little thing.

AGATHA. Very. But not old enough to exert any decided influence over the boy's musical future. Why not engage a master?

POSKET. What, for a mere child?

AGATHA. A mere child—oh!

POSKET. A boy of fourteen!

AGATHA, *to herself.* Fourteen!

POSKET. A boy of fourteen, not yet out of Czerny's exercises.

AGATHA, *to herself.* If we were alone now, I might have the desperation to tell him all!

POSKET. Besides, my darling, you know the interest I take in Miss Tomlinson; she is one of the brightest little spots on my hobby-horse. Like all our servants, like everybody in my employ, she has been brought to my notice through the unhappy medium of the Police Court—over which it is my destiny to preside. Our servant, Wyke, a man with a beautiful nature, is the son of a person I committed for trial for marrying three wives. To this day, Wyke is ignorant as to which of those three wives he is the son of! Cook was once a notorious dipsomaniac, and has even now not entirely freed herself from early influences. Popham is the unclaimed charge of a convicted baby-farmer. Even our milkman came before me as a man who had refused to submit specimens to the analytic inspector. And this poor child, what is she?

AGATHA. Yes, I know.

POSKET. The daughter of a superannuated General who abstracted four silk umbrellas from the Army and Navy Stores—and on a fine day too!

BEATIE *ceases playing.*

BULLAMY. Very good—very good!

POSKET. Thank you—thank you!

BULLAMY, *to* POSKET, *coughing and laughing and popping a jujube into his mouth.* My dear Posket, I really must congratulate you on that boy of yours. Your stepson. A most wonderful lad. So confoundedly advanced too.

POSKET. Yes, isn't he? Eh!

BULLAMY, *confidentially.* While the piano was going on, just now, he told me one of the most humorous stories I ever heard. *Laughing heartily and panting, then taking another jujube.* Ha, ha, bless me, I don't know when I've taken so many jujubes!

POSKET, *to* BULLAMY. My dear Bullamy, my entire marriage is the greatest possible success. A little romantic, too. *Pointing to* AGATHA. Beautiful woman!

BULLAMY. Very, very. I never committed a more stylish elegant creature.

POSKET, *warmly.* Thank you, Bullamy—we met abroad, at Spa, when I was on my holiday.

WYKE *enters with a tea tray, which he hands round.*

BULLAMY. I shall go there next year.

POSKET. She lost her first husband about twelve months ago, in India. He was an army contractor.

BEATIE, *to* CIS *at the piano.* I must go now—there's no excuse for staying any longer.

CIS, *to her, disconsolately.* What the deuce shall I do?

POSKET, *pouring out milk.* Dear me, this milk seems very poor. When he died, she came to England, placed her boy at a school in Brighton, and then moved quietly about from place to place, drinking—— *Sips tea.*

BULLAMY. Drinking?

POSKET. The waters—she's a little dyspeptic.

WYKE *goes out.*

We encountered each other at the *Tours des Fontaines*—by accident I trod upon her dress——

BEATIE. Good night, Cis dear.

CIS. Oh!

POSKET. I apologized. We talked about the weather, we drank out of the same glass, discovered that we both suffered from the same ailment, and the result is complete happiness. *He bends over* AGATHA *gallantly.*

AGATHA. Æneas!

He kisses her; then CIS *kisses* BEATIE, *loudly;* POSKET *and* BULLAMY *both listen, puzzled.*

POSKET. Echo?

BULLAMY. Suppose so!

He kisses the back of his hand experimentally; BEATIE *kisses* CIS.

Yes.

POSKET. Curious. *To* BULLAMY. Romantic story, isn't it?

BEATIE. Good night, Mrs. Posket! I shall be here early tomorrow morning.

AGATHA. I am afraid you are neglecting your other pupils.

BEATIE. Oh, they're not so interesting as Cis— *Correcting herself.* Master Farringdon. Good night.

AGATHA. Good night, dear.

BEATIE *goes out quietly.* AGATHA *joins* CIS.

POSKET, *to* BULLAMY. We were married abroad without consulting friends or relations on either side. That's how it is I have never seen my sister-in-law—Miss Verrinder, who is coming from Shropshire to stay with us—she ought to——

WYKE *enters.*

WYKE. Miss Verrinder has come, ma'am.

POSKET. Here she is.

AGATHA. Charlotte?

CHARLOTTE, *a fine, handsome girl, enters, followed by* POPHAM, *with hand luggage.*

Kissing her. My dear Charley.

WYKE *goes out.*

CHARLOTTE. Aggy darling, aren't I late! There's a fog on the line—you could cut it with a knife. *Seeing* CIS. Is that your boy?

AGATHA. Yes.

CHARLOTTE. Good gracious! What is he doing in an Eton jacket at his age.

AGATHA, *softly to* CHARLOTTE. Hush! don't say a word about my boy's age yet awhile.

CHARLOTTE, *aside.* Oh!

AGATHA, *about to introduce* POSKET. There is my husband.

CHARLOTTE, *mistaking* MR. BULLAMY *for him*. Oh! how could she! *To* BULLAMY, *turning her cheek to him*. I congratulate you—I suppose you ought to kiss me.

AGATHA. No, no!

POSKET. Welcome to my house, Miss Verrinder.

CHARLOTTE. Oh, I beg your pardon. How do you do?

BULLAMY, *to himself*. Mrs. Posket's an interfering woman.

POSKET, *pointing to* BULLAMY. Mr. Bullamy.

    BULLAMY, *aggrieved, bows stiffly*.

AGATHA, *to* CHARLOTTE. Come upstairs, dear; will you have some tea?

CHARLOTTE. No, thank you, pet, but I should like a glass of soda-water.

AGATHA. Soda-water!

CHARLOTTE. Well dear, you can put what you like at the bottom of it.

    AGATHA *and* CHARLOTTE *go out*, POPHAM *following*.

POPHAM *to* CIS. Give me back my *Bow Bells*, when you have read it, you imp. *Goes out*.

CIS. By Jove, Guv, isn't Aunt Charlotte a stunner!

POSKET. Seems a charming woman.

BULLAMY. Posket's got the wrong one, that comes of marrying without first seeing the lady's relations.

CIS. Come along, Guv—let's have a gamble—Mr. Bullamy will join us. *Opens card table, arranges chairs and candles*.

BULLAMY. A gamble?

POSKET. Yes—the boy has taught me a new game called "Fireworks"; his mother isn't aware that we play for money, of course, but we do.

BULLAMY. Ha, ha, ha! Who wins?

POSKET. He does now—but he says I shall win when I know the game better.

BULLAMY. What a boy he is.

POSKET. Isn't he a wonderful lad? And only fourteen, too. I'll tell you something else—perhaps you had better not mention it to his mother.

BULLAMY. No, no, certainly not.

POSKET. He's invested a little money for me.

BULLAMY. What in?

POSKET. Not *in*—*on*—on Sillikin for the St. Leger—Sillikin to win and Butterscotch one, two, three.

BULLAMY. Good Lord!

POSKET. Yes, the dear boy said, "Guv, it isn't fair you should give me all the tips, I'll give you some,"—and he did—he gave me Sillikin and

Butterscotch—he'll manage it for you, if you like; "Plank it down," he calls it.

BULLAMY, *chuckling and choking.* Ha! ha! Ho! ho! *Taking a jujube.* This boy will ruin me in jujubes.

CIS. All ready! Look sharp! Guv, lend me a sov to start with?

POSKET. A sov to start with?

They sit at the table. AGATHA *and* CHARLOTTE *come in.*

We didn't think you would return so soon, my darling.

AGATHA. Go on amusing yourselves I insist, only don't teach my Cis to play cards.

BULLAMY. Ho! ho!

POSKET, *to* BULLAMY. Hush! Hush!

AGATHA, *to* CHARLOTTE. I'm glad of this—we can tell each other our miseries undisturbed. Will you begin?

CHARLOTTE. Well, at last I am engaged to Captain Horace Vale.

AGATHA. Oh! Charley, I'm so glad!

CHARLOTTE. Yes—so is he—he says. He proposed to me at the Hunt Ball—in the passage—Tuesday week.

AGATHA. What did he say?

CHARLOTTE. He said, "By Jove, I love you awfully."

AGATHA. Well—and what did you say?

CHARLOTTE. Oh, I said, "Well, if you're going to be as eloquent as all that, by Jove, I can't stand out." So we settled it in the passage. He bars flirting till after we're married. That's my misery. What's yours, Aggy?

AGATHA. Something awful!

CHARLOTTE. Cheer up, Aggy! What is it?

AGATHA. Well, Charley, you know I lost my poor dear first husband at a very delicate age.

CHARLOTTE. Well, you were five-and-thirty, dear.

AGATHA. Yes, that's what I mean. Five-and-thirty is a very delicate age to find yourself single. You're neither one thing nor the other. You're not exactly a two-year-old, and you don't care to pull a hansom. However, I soon met Mr. Posket at Spa—bless him!

CHARLOTTE. And you nominated yourself for the Matrimonial Stakes. Mr. Farringdon's The Widow, by Bereavement out of Mourning, ten pounds extra.

AGATHA. Yes, Charley—and in less than a month—I went triumphantly over the course. But, Charley dear—I didn't carry the fair weight for age—and that's my trouble.

CHARLOTTE. Oh, dear!

AGATHA. Undervaluing Æneas's love, in a moment of, I hope, not un-
justifiable vanity, I took five years from my total which made me thirty-
one on my wedding morning.

CHARLOTTE. Well, dear, many a misguided woman has done that before
you.

AGATHA. Yes, Charley, but don't you see the consequences? It has thrown
everything out. As I am now thirty-one, instead of thirty-six as I ought
to be, it stands to reason that I couldn't have been married twenty
years ago, which I was. So I have had to fib in proportion.

CHARLOTTE. I see—making your first marriage occur only fifteen years ago.

AGATHA. Exactly.

CHARLOTTE. Well, then, dear, why worry yourself further?

AGATHA. Why, dear, don't you see? If I am only thirty-one now, my boy
couldn't have been born nineteen years ago, which he was—and if he
could, he oughtn't to have been, because, on my own showing, I wasn't
married till four years later. Now you see the result!

CHARLOTTE. Which is, that fine strapping young gentleman over there is
only fourteen.

AGATHA. Precisely. Isn't it awkward! and his moustache is becoming more
and more obvious every day.

CHARLOTTE. What does the boy himself believe?

AGATHA. He believes his mother, of course, as a boy should. As a prudent
woman, I always kept him in ignorance of his age—in case of necessity.
But it is terribly hard on the poor child, because his aims, instincts, and
ambitions are all so horribly in advance of his condition. His food, his
books, his amusements are out of keeping with his palate, his brain,
and his disposition.

CHARLOTTE. Of course.

AGATHA. And with all this suffering—his wretched mother has the re-
morseful consciousness of having shortened her offspring's life.

CHARLOTTE. Oh come, you haven't quite done that.

AGATHA. Yes, I have—because, if he lives to be a hundred, he must be
buried at ninety-five.

CHARLOTTE. That's true.

AGATHA. Then there's another aspect. He's a great favourite with all our
friends—women friends especially. Even his little music mistress and
the girl servants hug and kiss him because he's such an engaging boy,
and I can't stop it. But it's very awful to see these innocent women
fondling a young man of nineteen.

CHARLOTTE. The women don't know it.

AGATHA. But they'd like to know it. They ought to know it! The other day I found my poor boy sitting on Lady Jenkins's lap, and in the presence of Sir George. I have no right to compromise Lady Jenkins in that way. And now, Charley, you see the whirlpool in which I am struggling—if you can throw me a rope, pray do.

CHARLOTTE. What sort of a man is Mr. Posket, Aggy?

AGATHA. The best creature in the world. He's a practical philanthropist.

CHARLOTTE. Um—he's a Police Magistrate too—isn't he?

AGATHA. Yes, but he pays out of his own pocket half the fines he inflicts. That's why he has had a reprimand from the Home Office for inflicting such light penalties. All our servants have graduated at Mulberry Street. Most of the pictures in the dining-room are genuine Constables.

CHARLOTTE. Take my advice—tell him the whole story.

AGATHA. I dare not!

CHARLOTTE. Why?

AGATHA. I should have to take such a back seat for the rest of my married life.

The party at card table break up.

BULLAMY, *grumpily*. No, thank you, not another minute. *To* POSKET. What is the use of talking about revenge, my dear Posket, when I haven't a penny piece left to play with.

POSKET. I'm in the same predicament! Cis will lend us some money, won't you, Cis?

CIS. Rather!

BULLAMY. No, thank ye, that boy is one too many for me. I've never met such a child. Good night, Mrs. Posket. *Treads on a nut.* Confound the nuts!

AGATHA. Going so early?

CIS, *to* POSKET. I hate a bad loser, don't you, Guv?

AGATHA. Show Mr. Bullamy downstairs, Cis.

BULLAMY. Good night, Posket. Oh! I haven't a shilling left for my cabman.

CIS. I'll pay the cab.

BULLAMY. No, thank you! I'll walk. *Opening jujube box.* Bah! Not even a jujube left and on a foggy night, too! Ugh! *Goes out.*

Enter WYKE *with four letters on salver.*

CIS, *to* WYKE. Any for me?

WYKE. One, sir.

CIS, *to himself*. From Achille Blond, lucky the Mater didn't see it. *Goes out.*

WYKE *hands letters to* AGATHA, *who takes two, then to* POSKET, *who takes one.*

AGATHA. This is for you, Charley, already.

WYKE *goes out.*

CHARLOTTE. Spare my blushes, dear—it's from Horace, Captain Vale. The dear wretch knew I was coming to you. Heigho! Will you excuse me?

POSKET. Certainly.

AGATHA. Excuse me, please?

CHARLOTTE. Certainly, my dear.

POSKET. Certainly, my darling. Excuse me, won't you?

CHARLOTTE. Oh, certainly.

AGATHA. Certainly, Æneas.

Simultaneously they all open their letters and lean back and read.

AGATHA, *reading.* Lady Jenkins is not feeling very well.

CHARLOTTE. If Captain Horace Vale stood before me at this moment, I'd slap his face!

AGATHA. Charlotte!

CHARLOTTE, *reading.* "Dear Miss Verrinder, your desperate flirtation with Major Bristow at the Meet on Tuesday last, three days after our engagement, has just come to my knowledge. Your letters and gifts, including the gold-headed hairpin given me at the Hunt Ball, shall be returned tomorrow. By Jove, all is over! Horace Vale." Oh dear!

AGATHA. Oh! Charley, I'm so sorry. However, you can deny it.

CHARLOTTE, *weeping.* That's the worst of it, I can't.

POSKET, *to* AGATHA. My darling, you will be delighted. A note from Colonel Lukyn.

AGATHA. Lukyn—Lukyn? I seem to know the name.

POSKET. An old schoolfellow of mine who went to India many years ago. He has just come home. I met him at the club last night and asked him to name an evening to dine with us. He accepts for tomorrow.

AGATHA. Lukyn, Lukyn?

POSKET. Listen. *Reading.* "It will be especially delightful to me, as I believe I am an old friend of your wife and of her first husband. You may recall me to her recollection by reminding her that I am the Captain Lukyn who stood sponsor to her boy when he was christened at Baroda."

AGATHA, *giving a loud scream.* Oh!

POSKET. My dear!

AGATHA. I've twisted my foot.

POSKET. How *do* nuts come into the drawing-room?

CHARLOTTE, *quietly to* AGATHA. Aggy?

AGATHA, *to* CHARLOTTE. The boy's godfather.

CHARLOTTE. When was the child christened?

AGATHA. A month after he was born. They always are.

POSKET, *reading letter again*. This is *very* pleasant.

AGATHA, *to* POSKET. Let—let me see the letter, I—I—may recognize the handwriting.

POSKET, *handing her the letter*. Certainly, my pet. *To himself*. Awakened memories of Number One. That's the worst of marrying a widow; somebody is always proving her previous convictions.

AGATHA, *to* CHARLOTTE. "No. 19a, Cork Street!" Charley, put on your things and come with me.

CHARLOTTE. Agatha, you're mad!

AGATHA. I'm going to shut this man's mouth before he comes into this house, tomorrow.

CHARLOTTE. Wait *till* he comes.

AGATHA. Yes, till he stalks in here with his "How d'ye do, Posket? Haven't seen your wife since the year sixty-six, by Gad, sir!" Not I! Æneas!

POSKET. My dear.

AGATHA. Lady Jenkins—Adelaide is very ill; she can't put her foot to the ground with neuralgia. *Taking the letter from her pocket and giving it to him*.

POSKET. Bless me!

AGATHA. We have known each other for six long years.

POSKET. Only six weeks, my love.

AGATHA. Weeks are years in close friendship. My place is by her side.

POSKET, *reading the letter*. "Slightly indisposed, caught trifling cold at the Dog Show. Where do you buy your handkerchiefs?" There's nothing about neuralgia or putting her foot to the ground here, my darling.

AGATHA. No, but can't you read between the lines, Æneas? That is the letter of a woman who is not at all well.

POSKET. All right, my darling, if you are bent upon going I will accompany you.

AGATHA. Certainly not, Æneas—Charlotte insists on being my companion; we can keep each other warm in a closed cab.

POSKET. But can't I make a third?

AGATHA. Don't be so forgetful, Æneas—don't you know that in a four-wheeled cab, the fewer knees there are, the better.

AGATHA *and* CHARLOTTE *go out.* CIS *comes in hurriedly.*

CIS. What's the matter, Guv?

POSKET. Your mother and Miss Verrinder are going out.

CIS. Out of their minds? It's a horrid night.

POSKET. Yes, but Lady Jenkins is ill.

CIS. Oh! Is Ma mentioned in the will?

POSKET. Good gracious, what a boy! No, Cis, your mother is merely going to sit by Lady Jenkins's bedside, to hold her hand, and to tell her where one goes to—to buy pocket-handkerchiefs.

CIS. By Jove! The Mater can't be home again till half-past twelve or one o'clock.

POSKET. Much later if Lady Jenkins's condition is alarming.

CIS. Hurray! *He takes watch out of* POSKET'S *pocket*. Just half-past ten. Greenwich mean, eh, Guv? *He puts the watch to his ear, pulling* POSKET *toward him by the chain.*

POSKET. What an extraordinary lad!

CIS, *returning watch*. Thanks. They have to get from here to Campden Hill and back again. I'll tell Wyke to get them the worst horse on the rank.

POSKET. My dear child!

CIS. Three-quarters of an hour's journey from here at least. Twice three-quarters, one hour and a half. An hour with Lady Jenkins—when women get together you know, Guv, they do talk—that's two hours and a half. Good. Guv, will you come with me?

POSKET. Go with you! Where?

CIS. Hôtel des Princes, Meek Street. A sharp hansom does it in ten minutes.

POSKET. Meek Street, Hôtel des Princes! Child, do you know what you're talking about?

CIS. Rather. Look here, Guv, honour bright—no blab if I show you a letter.

POSKET. I won't promise anything.

CIS. You won't! Do you know, Guv, you are doing a very unwise thing to check the confidence of a lad like me?

POSKET. Cis, my boy!

CIS. Can you calculate the inestimable benefit it is to a youngster, to have someone always at his elbow, someone older, wiser and better off than himself?

POSKET. Of course, Cis, of course, I *want* you to make a companion of me.

CIS. Then how the deuce can I do that if you won't come with me to Meek Street?

POSKET. Yes, but deceiving your mother!

CIS. *Deceiving* the Mater would be to tell her a crammer—a thing, I hope, we're both of us much above.

POSKET. Good boy, good boy.

CIS. *Concealing* the fact that we're going to have a bit of supper at the Hôtel des Princes, is doing my mother a great kindness, because it would upset her considerably to know of the circumstances. You've been wrong, Guv, but we won't say anything more about that. Read the letter. *Gives* POSKET *the letter.*

POSKET, *reading in a dazed sort of way.* "Hôtel des Princes, Meek Street, W. Dear Sir,—Unless you drop in and settle your arrears, I really cannot keep your room for you any longer. Yours obediently, Achille Blond. Cecil Farringdon, Esq." Good heavens! You have a room at the Hôtel des Princes!

CIS. A room! It's little better than a coop.

POSKET. You don't occupy it?

CIS. But my friends do. When I was at Brighton I was in with the best set—hope I always shall be. I left Brighton—nice hole I was in. You see, Guv, I didn't want my friends to make free with your house.

POSKET. Oh, didn't you?

CIS. So I took a room at the Hôtel des Princes—when I want to put a man up he goes there. You see, Guv, it's *you* I've been considering more than myself.

POSKET. But you are a mere child.

CIS. A fellow is just as old as he feels. I feel no end of a man. Hush, they're coming down! I'm off to tell Wyke about the rickety four-wheeler.

POSKET. Cis, Cis! Your mother will discover I have been out.

CIS. Oh, I forgot, you're married, aren't you?

POSKET. Married!

CIS. Say you are going to the Club.

POSKET. But that's not the truth, sir!

CIS. Yes, it is. We'll pop in at the Club on our way, and you can give me a bitters. *Goes out.*

POSKET. Good gracious, what a boy! Hôtel des Princes, Meek Street! What shall I do? Tell his mother? Why, it would turn her hair grey. If I could only get a quiet word with this Mr. Achille Blond, I could put a stop to everything. That is my best course, not to lose a moment in rescuing the child from his boyish indiscretion. Yes, I must go with Cis to Meek Street.

Enter AGATHA *and* CHARLOTTE, *elegantly dressed.*

AGATHA. Have you sent for a cab, Æneas?

POSKET. Cis is looking after that.

AGATHA. Poor Cis! How late we keep him up.

CIS, *coming in.* Wyke has gone for a cab, Ma dear.

AGATHA. Thank you, Cis darling.

CIS. If you'll excuse me I'll go to my room. I've another bad headache coming on.

AGATHA, *kissing him*. Run along, my boy.

CIS. Good night, Ma. Good night, Aunt Charlotte.

CHARLOTTE. Good night, Cis.

AGATHA, *to herself*. I wish the cab would come.

AGATHA and CHARLOTTE *look out of the window*.

CIS, *at the door*. Ahem! Good night, Guv.

POSKET. You've told a story; two, sir! You said you were going up to your room.

CIS. So I am—to dress.

POSKET. You said you had a bad headache coming on.

CIS. So I have, Guv. I always get a bad headache at the Hôtel des Princes. *Goes out*.

POSKET. Oh, what a boy!

AGATHA, *to herself*. When will that cab come?

POSKET. Ahem! My pet, the idea has struck me, that as you are going out, it would not be a bad notion for me to pop into my Club.

AGATHA. The Club! You were there last night.

POSKET. I know, my darling. Many men look in at their Clubs every night.

AGATHA. A nice example for Cis, truly! I particularly desire that you should remain at home to-night, Æneas.

POSKET, *to himself*. Oh, dear me!

CHARLOTTE, *to* AGATHA. Why not let him go to the Club, Agatha?

AGATHA. He might meet Colonel Lukyn there.

CHARLOTTE. If Colonel Lukyn is there we shan't find him in Cork Street!

AGATHA. Then we follow him to the Club.

CHARLOTTE. Ladies never call at a Club.

AGATHA. Such things have been known.

WYKE *enters*.

WYKE, *grinning behind his hand*. The cab is coming, ma'am.

AGATHA. Coming? Why didn't you bring it with you?

WYKE. I walked quicker than the cab, ma'am. It's a good horse, slow, but very certain.

AGATHA. We will come down.

WYKE, *to himself*. Just what the horse has done. *To* AGATHA. Yes, ma'am. *Goes out*.

AGATHA. Good night, Æneas.

POSKET, *nervously*. I wish you would allow me to go to the Club, my pet.

AGATHA. Æneas, I am surprised at your obstinacy. It is so very different from my first husband.

POSKET. Really, Agatha, I am shocked. I presume the late Mr. Farringdon occasionally used his Clubs?

AGATHA. Yes, every day.

POSKET. Ah!

AGATHA. Indian clubs. Indian clubs are good for the liver. London clubs are not. Good night!

POSKET. I'll see you to your cab, Agatha.

AGATHA. No, thank you.

POSKET. Upon my word!

CHARLOTTE, *to* AGATHA. Why not?

AGATHA. He would want to give the direction to the cabman!

CHARLOTTE. The first tiff. *To* POSKET. Good night, Mr. Posket.

POSKET. Good night, Miss Verrinder.

AGATHA, *to* POSKET. Have you any message for Lady Jenkins?

POSKET. Confound Lady Jenkins!

AGATHA. I will deliver your message in the presence of Sir George, who, I may remind you, is the permanent Secretary at the Home Office.

AGATHA *and* CHARLOTTE *go out;* POSKET *paces up and down excitedly.*

POSKET. Gurrh! I'm not to go to the Club! I set a bad example to Cis! Ha, ha! I am different from her first husband. Yes, I am—I'm alive for one thing. I—I—I—I—I'm dashed if I don't go out with the boy.

CIS, *putting his head in at the door.* Coast clear, Guv? All right. *Enter* CIS *in fashionable evening dress, carrying* POSKET's *overcoat and hat.* Here are your hat and overcoat.

POSKET. Where on earth did you get that dress suit?

CIS. Mum's the word, Guv. Brighton tailor—six months' credit. He promised to send in the bill to you so the Mater won't know. *Putting* POSKET's *hat on his head.* By Jove, Guv, don't my togs show you up?

POSKET. I won't go, I won't go. I've never met such a boy before.

CIS, *proceeds to help him with overcoat.* Mind your arm, Guv. You've got your hand in a pocket. No, no—that's a tear in the lining. That's it.

POSKET. I forbid you to go out!

CIS. Yes, Guv. And I forbid you to eat any of those deviled oysters we shall get at the Hôtel des Princes. Now you're right!

POSKET. I am not right!

CIS. Oh, I forgot! *He pulls out a handful of loose money.* I found this money in your desk, Guv. You had better take it out with you; you may want it. Here you are—gold, silver and coppers. *He empties the money into* POSKET's *overcoat pocket.* One last precaution and then we're off. *Goes to writing table and writes on a half-sheet of notepaper.*

POSKET. I shall take a turn round the Square, and then come home again! I will not be influenced by a mere child! A man of my responsible position—a Magistrate—supping slyly at the Hôtel des Princes, in Meek Street—it's horrible!

CIS. Now then—we'll creep downstairs quietly so as not to bring Wyke from his pantry. *Giving* POSKET *paper.* You stick that up prominently, while I blow out the candles. CIS *blows out candles on piano.*

POSKET, *reading.* "Your Master and Mr. Cecil Farringdon are going to bed. Don't disturb them." I will not be a party to any written document. This is untrue.

CIS. No, it isn't—we are going to bed when we come home. Make haste, Guv.

POSKET. Oh, what a boy. *Pinning the paper onto the curtain.*

CIS, *turning down the lamp and watching* POSKET. Hallo, Guv! hallo! You're an old hand at this sort of game, are you?

POSKET. How dare you!

CIS, *taking* POSKET's *arm.* Now then, don't breathe.

POSKET, *quite demoralized.* Cis! Cis! Wait a minute—wait a minute.

CIS. Hold up, Guv.

WYKE *enters.*

Oh, bother!

WYKE, *to* POSKET. Going out, sir?

POSKET, *struggling to be articulate.* No—yes—that is—partially—half round the Square, and possibly—er—um—back again. *To* CIS. Oh, you bad boy!

WYKE, *coolly going up to paper on curtains.* Shall I take this down now, sir?

POSKET, *quietly to* CIS. I'm in an awful position! What am I to do?

CIS. Do as I do—tip him.

POSKET. What!

CIS. Tip him.

POSKET. Oh, yes—yes. Where's my money?

CIS *takes two coins out of* POSKET's *pocket and gives them to him without looking at them.*

CIS, *to* POSKET. Give him that.

POSKET. Yes.

CIS. And say— "Wyke, you want a new umbrella—buy a very good one. Your mistress has a latchkey, so go to bed."

POSKET. Wyke.

WYKE. Yes, sir.

POSKET, *giving him money.* Go to bed—buy a very good one. Your mistress has a latchkey—so—so you want a new umbrella!

WYKE. All right, sir. You can depend on me. Are you well muffled up, sir? Mind you take care of him, Master Cis.

CIS, *supporting* POSKET; POSKET *groaning softly.* Capital, Guv, capital. Are you hungry?

POSKET. Hungry! You're a wicked boy. I've told a falsehood.

CIS. No, you haven't, Guv—he really does want a new umbrella.

POSKET. Does he, Cis? Does he? Thank heaven!

They go out.

WYKE, *looking at money.* Here! What, twopence! *Throws coins down in disgust.* I'll tell the Missus.

ACT TWO

The scene is a supper room at the Hôtel des Princes, Meek Street, with two doors— the one leading into an adjoining room, the other into a passage—and a window opening onto a balcony. ISIDORE, *a French waiter, is showing in* CIS *and* MR. POSKET.

CIS. Come on, Guv—come on. How are you, Isidore?

ISIDORE. I beg your pardon—I am quite well, and so are you, zank you.

CIS. I want a pretty little light supper for myself and my friend, Mr. Skinner.

ISIDORE. Mr. Skinner.

POSKET, *to* CIS. Skinner! Is someone else coming?

CIS. No, no. You're Skinner.

POSKET. Oh! *Wanders round the room.*

CIS. Mr. Skinner, of the Stock Exchange. What have you ready?

ISIDORE, *in an undertone to* CIS. I beg your pardon—very good—but Monsieur Blond he say to me, "Isidore, listen to me, if Mr. Farringdon he come here, you say, I beg your pardon, you are a nice gentleman, but will you pay your little account when it is quite convenient, before you leave the house at once."

CIS. Quite so, there's no difficulty about that. What's the bill?

ISIDORE, *gives bill.* I beg your pardon. Eight pounds four shillings.

CIS. Phew! Here go my winnings from old Bullamy and the Guv. *Counting out money.* Two pounds short. *Turning to* POSKET, *who is carefully examining the scratches on the mirrors.* Skinner! Skinner!

POSKET. Visitors evidently scratch their names on the mirrors. Dear me!

Surely this is a spurious title—"Lottie, Dutchess of Fulham!" How very curious!

CIS. Skinner, got any money with you?

POSKET. Yes, Cis, my boy. *Feels for his money.*

CIS. You always keep it in that pocket, Skinner.

POSKET, *taking out money.* Oh, yes.

CIS *takes two sovereigns from* POSKET *and gives the amount of his bill to* ISIDORE, *who goes to sideboard to count out change.*

CIS. No putting the change to bed, Isidore.

POSKET. What's that?

CIS. Putting the change to bed! Isidore will show you. *To* ISIDORE, *who comes to them with the change and the bill on a plate.* Isidore, show Mr. Skinner how you put silver to bed.

ISIDORE. Oh, Mr. Farringdon, I beg your pardon—no, no!

POSKET. It would be most instructive.

ISIDORE. Very good. *Goes to table, upon which he puts plate.* Say I have to give you change sixteen shillings.

POSKET. Certainly.

ISIDORE. Very good. Before I bring it to you I slip a little half-crown under the bill—so. Then I put what is left on the top of the bill, and I say, "I beg your pardon, your change." You take it, you give me two shillings for myself, and all is right.

POSKET, *counting the silver on the bill with the end of his glasses.* Yes, but suppose I count the silver, it is half a crown short!

ISIDORE. Then I say, "I beg your pardon, how dare you say that?" Then I do so. *He pulls the bill from the plate.* Then I say, "The bill is eight pounds four shillings—*handing the plate*—count again."

POSKET. Ah, of course, it's all right now.

ISIDORE. Very good, then you give me five shillings for doubting me. Do it, do it.

POSKET, *in a daze, giving him the five shillings.* Like this?

ISIDORE. Yes, like that. *Slipping the money into his pocket.* I beg your pardon—thank you. *Handing* CIS *the rest of the change.* Your change, Mr. Farringdon.

CIS. Oh, I say, Isidore.

ACHILLE BLOND, *a fat, middle-aged French hotelkeeper, enters with a letter in his hand.*

ISIDORE. Monsieur Blond.

BLOND. Good evening, Mr. Farringdon.

ISIDORE, *quietly to* BLOND. Ze bill is all right.

CIS. Good evening. *Introducing* POSKET. My friend, Mr. Harvey Skinner, of the Stock Exchange.

BLOND. Very pleased to see you. *To* CIS. Are you going to enjoy yourselves?

CIS. Rather.

BLOND. You usually eat in this room, but you don't mind giving it up for tonight—now, do you?

CIS. Oh, Achille.

BLOND. Come, come, to please me. A cab has just brought a letter from an old customer of mine, a gentleman I haven't seen for over twenty years, who wants to sup with a friend in this room tonight. It's quite true. *Giving* CIS *a letter.*

CIS, *reading to himself.* "19a, Cork Street. Dear Blond. Fresh, or rather, stale from India—want to sup with my friend, Captain Vale, tonight, at my old table in my old room. Must do this for Auld Lang Syne. Yours, Alexander Lukyn." *To* BLOND. Oh, let him have it. Where will you put us?

BLOND. You shall have the best room in the house, the one next to this. This room—pah! Come with me. *To* POSKET. Have you known Mr. Farringdon for a long time?

POSKET. No, no. Not very long.

BLOND. Ah, he is a fine fellow—Mr. Farringdon. Now, if you please. You can go through this door. *Wheels sofa away and unlocks the door.*

CIS, *to* POSKET. You'll look better after a glass or two of Pommeroy, Guv.

POSKET. No, no, Cis—now, no champagne.

CIS. No champagne, not for my friend, Harvey Skinner! Come, Guv—dig me in the ribs—like this. *Digging him in the ribs.* Chuck!

POSKET, *shrinking.* Oh, don't!

CIS. And say, Hey! Go on, Guv.

POSKET. I can't—I can't. I don't know what it may mean.

CIS, *digging him in the ribs again.* Go on—ch-uck!

POSKET. What, like this? *Returning the dig.* Ch-uck!

CIS. That's it, that's it. Ha, ha! You are going it, Guv.

POSKET. Am I, Cis? Am I? *Waving his arm.* Hey!

CIS *and* POSKET. Hey!

CIS. Ha, ha! Come on! Serve the supper, Achille.

BLOND. Ah! he is a grand fellow, Mr. Farringdon.

CIS *and* POSKET *go into the other room.*

To ISIDORE. Replace the *canapé.*

There is a sharp knock at the other door. BLOND *follows* CIS *and* POSKET *into the other room, then locks the door on the inside.*

ISIDORE. Come in, please.

COLONEL LUKYN *and* CAPTAIN VALE *enter the room.* LUKYN *is a portly, grey-haired, good-looking military man;* VALE *is pale-faced and heavy-eyed, while his manner is languid and dejected.*

LUKYN. This is the room. Come in, Vale. This is my old supper room—I haven't set foot here for over twenty years. By George, I hope to sup here for another twenty. *Walks round, looking about him.*

VALE, *dejectedly.* Do you? In less than that, unless I am lucky enough to fall in some foreign set-to, I shall be in Kensal Green.

LUKYN, *looking round the room sentimentally.* Twenty years ago! Confound 'em, they've painted it.

VALE. My people have eight shelves in the Catacombs at Kensal Green.

LUKYN. Nonsense, man; nonsense. You're a little low. Waiter, take our coats.

VALE. Don't check me, Lukyn. My shelf is four from the bottom.

LUKYN. You'll forget the number of your shelf before you're half-way through your oysters.

VALE, *shaking his head.* An oyster merely reminds me of my own particular shell.

ISIDORE *begins to remove* VALE'S *coat.*

LUKYN. Ha, ha! Ha, ha!

VALE. Don't, Lukyn, don't. *In an undertone, to* LUKYN. It's very good of you, but, by Jove, my heart is broken. *To* ISIDORE. Mind my flower, Waiter, confound you. *He adjusts flower in his buttonhole.*

ISIDORE. You have ordered supper, sir?

LUKYN. Yes, on the back of my note to Mr. Blond. Serve it at once.

ISIDORE. I beg your pardon, sir, at once. *He goes out.*

LUKYN. So, you've been badly treated by a woman, eh, Vale?

VALE. Shockingly. Between man and man, a Miss Verrinder. Charlotte. *Turning away.* Excuse me, Lukyn. *Produces a folded silk handkerchief, shakes it out, and gently blows his nose.*

LUKYN, *lighting a cigarette.* Certainly—certainly—does you great credit. Pretty woman?

VALE. Oh, lovely! A most magnificent set of teeth. All real, as far as I can ascertain.

LUKYN. No.

VALE. Fact.

LUKYN. Great loss—have a cigarette.

VALE, *taking case from* LUKYN. Cork tips?

LUKYN. Yes. Was she—full grown?

VALE, *lighting his cigarette*. Just perfection. She rides eight-stone fifteen, and I've lost her, Lukyn. Beautiful tobacco.

LUKYN. What finished it?

VALE. She gave a man a pair of worked slippers three days after our engagement.

LUKYN. No.

VALE. Fact. You remember Bristow—Gordon Bristow.

LUKYN. Perfectly. Best fellow in the world.

VALE. He wears them.

LUKYN. Villain! Will you begin with a light wine, or go right on to the champagne?

VALE. By Jove, it's broken my heart, old fellow. I'll go right on to the champagne, please. Lukyn, I shall make you my executor.

LUKYN. Pooh! You'll outlive me. Why don't they bring the supper? My heart has been broken like yours. It was broken first in Ireland in sixty-two. It was broken again in London in sixty-eight, but in eighteen-seventy-seven it was smashed in Calcutta, by a married lady that time.

VALE. A married lady?

LUKYN. Yes, my late wife. Talk about broken hearts, my boy, when you've won your lady, not when you've lost her!

Enter ISIDORE *with a tray of supper things.*

The supper. *To* VALE. Hungry?

VALE, *mournfully*. Very.

BLOND *enters, with an envelope*. Colonel Lukyn.

LUKYN. Ah, Blond, how are you? Not a day older. What have you got there?

BLOND, *to* LUKYN *in an undertone*. Two ladies, Colonel, downstairs in a cab, must see you for a few minutes alone.

LUKYN. Good gracious! Excuse me, Vale. *Takes the envelope from* BLOND *and opens it; reading the enclosed card*. Mrs. Posket—Mrs. Posket! "Mrs. Posket entreats Colonel Lukyn to see her for five minutes upon a matter of urgent necessity, and free from observation." By George! Posket must be ill in bed—I thought he looked seedy last night. *To* BLOND. Of course—of course. Say, "I'll come down."

BLOND. It is raining outside. I had better ask them up.

LUKYN. Do—do. I'll get Captain Vale to step into another room. Be quick. Say I am quite alone.

BLOND. Yes, Colonel. *Hurries out.*

CIS, *in the next room rattling glasses and calling*. Waiter! Waiter! Waiter-r-r! Where the deuce are you?

ISIDORE. Coming sir, coming. I beg your pardon. *Bustles out.*

LUKYN. My dear Vale, I am dreadfully sorry to bother you. Two ladies—one the wife of a very old friend of mine, have followed me here and want half a dozen words with me alone, I am in your hands—how can I manage it?

VALE. My dear fellow, don't mention it. Let me go into another room.

LUKYN. Thank you, very much. You're so hungry too. Where's the waiter? Confound him, he's gone!

VALE. All right. I'll pop in here. *He passes behind sofa and tries the door leading into the other room.*

CIS, *within.* What do you want? Who's there?

VALE. Occupied—never mind—I'll find my way somewhere.

There is a knock; VALE *draws back.*

BLOND, *without.* Colonel, are you alone? The ladies.

LUKYN. One moment. Deuce take it, Vale! The ladies don't want to be seen. By George—I remember. There's a little balcony to that window, step out for a few moments—keep quiet—I shan't detain you—it's nothing important—husband must have had a fit or something.

VALE. Oh, certainly!

LUKYN. Good fellow—here's your hat. *In his haste he fetches his own hat.*

BLOND, *outside, knocking.* Colonel, Colonel!

LUKYN. One moment. *Giving his hat to* VALE. Awfully sorry. You're so hungry too.

VALE puts on the hat, which is much too large for him.

Ah, that's my hat.

VALE. My dear Lukyn—don't mention it. *Opening the window and going out.*

LUKYN, *drawing the curtain over the recess.* Just room for him to stand like a man in a sentry-box. Come in, Blond.

BLOND, *shows in* AGATHA POSKET *and* CHARLOTTE, *both wearing veils.*

AGATHA, *agitated.* Oh, Colonel Lukyn!

LUKYN. Pray compose yourself, pray compose yourself!

AGATHA. What will you think?

LUKYN. That I am perfectly enchanted.

AGATHA. Thank you. *Pointing to* CHARLOTTE. My sister.

LUKYN *and* CHARLOTTE *bow.*

LUKYN. Be seated. Blond? *Softly to him.* Keep the waiter out till I ring—that's all.

The loud pattering of rain is heard.

BLOND. Yes, Colonel.

LUKYN. Good gracious, Blond! What's that?

BLOND. The rain outside. It is cats and dogs.

LUKYN, *horrified*. By George, is it? *To himself, looking towards window*. Poor devil! *To* BLOND. There isn't any method of getting off that balcony, is there?

BLOND. No—unless by getting on to it.

LUKYN. What do you mean?

BLOND. It is not at all safe. Don't use it.

LUKYN stands horrorstricken; BLOND goes out. Heavy rain is heard.

LUKYN, *after some nervous glances at the window, wiping perspiration from his forehead*. I am honoured, Mrs. Posket, by this visit—though for the moment—I can't imagine——

AGATHA. Colonel Lukyn, we drove to Cork Street to your lodgings, and there your servant told us you were supping at the Hôtel des Princes, with a friend. No one will be shown into this room while we are here?

LUKYN. No—we—ah—shall not be disturbed. *To himself*. Good heavens, suppose I never see him alive again.

AGATHA, *sighing wearily*. Ah!

LUKYN. I'm afraid you've come to tell me Posket is ill?

AGATHA, *surprised*. I—no—my husband is at home.

A sharp gust of wind is heard with the rain.

LUKYN. Lord forgive me? I've killed him.

AGATHA, *with horror*. Colonel Lukyn!

LUKYN. Madam!

AGATHA. Indeed, Mr. Posket is at home.

LUKYN, *glancing at window*. Is he? I wish we all were.

AGATHA, *to herself*. Sunstroke evidently. Poor fellow. *To* LUKYN. I assure you my husband is at home, quite well, and by this time sleeping soundly.

CIS and POSKET are heard laughing in the next room.

ISIDORE, *within*. You are two funny gentlemen, I beg your pardon.

AGATHA, *startled*. What is that? *Sits down again*.

LUKYN. In the next room. *Raps at the door*. Hush—hush, hush!

CHARLOTTE. Get it over Aggy and let us go home. I am so awfully hungry.

LUKYN, *peering through curtains*. It is still bearing him. What's his weight? Surely he can't scale over nine stone. Lord, how wet he is!

AGATHA, *turning*. Colonel Lukyn!

LUKYN, *leaving the window sharply*. Madam, command me!

AGATHA. Colonel Lukyn, we knew each other at Baroda twenty years ago.

LUKYN. When I look at you, impossible.

AGATHA. Ah, then you mustn't look at me.

LUKYN. Equally impossible.

CHARLOTTE, *to herself*. Oh, I feel quite out of this.

AGATHA. You were at my little boy's christening?

LUKYN, *absently*. Yes—yes—certainly.

AGATHA. You remember what a fine little fellow he was.

LUKYN, *thoughtfully*. Not a pound over nine stone.

AGATHA. Colonel Lukyn!

LUKYN, *recovering himself*. I beg your pardon, yes—I was at the christening of your boy.

AGATHA, *to herself*. One of the worst cases of sunstroke I have ever known.

LUKYN. I remember the child very well. Has he still got that absurd mug?

AGATHA. Colonel Lukyn!

LUKYN. Madam!

AGATHA. My child is, and always was—perfect.

LUKYN. You misunderstand me! I was his godfather, I gave him a silver cup.

AGATHA. Oh, do excuse me. How did I become acquainted with such a vulgar expression. I don't know where I pick up my slang. It must be through loitering at shop windows. Oh, oh, oh!

LUKYN. Pray compose yourself. I'll leave you for a moment. *Going to the window*.

AGATHA, *to* CHARLOTTE. How shall I begin, Charley?

CHARLOTTE. Make a bold plunge, do! The odour of cooking here, to a hungry woman, is maddening.

VALE *softly opens the window and comes into the recess, but remains concealed by the curtain.*

VALE, *to himself*. This is too bad of Lukyn! I'm wet to the skin and frightfully hungry! Who the deuce are these women?

AGATHA. Colonel Lukyn!

LUKYN. Madam. *Listening*. No crash yet.

AGATHA, *impulsively laying her hand upon his arm*. Friend of twenty years? I will be quite candid with you. You are going to dine with us tomorrow?

LUKYN. Madam, I will repay your candour as it deserves. I am.

AGATHA. My husband knows of your acquaintance with the circumstances of my first marriage. I know what men are. When the women leave the dinner table, men become retrospective. Now tomorrow night, over dessert, I beg you not to give my husband dates.

LUKYN. Eh?

AGATHA. Keep anything like dates from him.

LUKYN. Mustn't eat stone fruit?

AGATHA. No, I mean years, months, days, dates connected with my marriage with Mr. Farringdon.

LUKYN. Dear me, sore subject!

AGATHA. I will be more than candid with you. My present husband having a very short vacation in the discharge of his public duties, wooed me but for three weeks; you, who have in your time courted and married, know the material of which that happy period is made up. The future is all engrossing to the man. The presents—I mean the present, a joyous dream to the woman. But in dealing with my past, I met with more than ordinary difficulties.

LUKYN. Don't see why—late husband died a natural death—wasn't stood on a balcony or anything.

AGATHA. Colonel Lukyn, you know I was six-and-thirty at the time of my recent marriage!

LUKYN. You surprise me!

AGATHA. You know it! Be frank, Lukyn! Am I not six-and-thirty?

LUKYN. You are.

AGATHA. Very well then. In a three weeks' engagement how was it possible for me to deal with the various episodes of six-and-thirty years? The past may be pleasant, golden, beautiful—but one may have too much of a good thing.

LUKYN, *to himself.* I am in that position, now.

AGATHA. The man who was courting me was seeking relaxation from the discharge of multifarious responsibilities. How could I tax an already wearied attention with the recital of the events of thirty-six years.

LUKYN. What did you do?

AGATHA. Out of consideration for the man I loved, I sacrificed five years of happy girlhood—told him I was but one-and-thirty—that I had been married but fifteen years previously—that my boy was only fourteen!

LUKYN. By George, madam, and am I to subscribe to all this?

AGATHA. I only ask you to avoid the question of dates.

LUKYN. But, at a man's dinner table——

AGATHA. You need not spoil a man's dinner. Not only a man's—but a woman's! Lukyn, Lukyn! Promise!

LUKYN. Give me a second to think. *Turning away, discovers* CHARLOTTE *in the act of lifting the covers from the dishes and inspecting the contents.* Ah, deviled oysters!

CHARLOTTE. Oh! *Drops dish cover with a crash, and runs over to the table and speaks to* AGATHA.

LUKYN. Don't go—pray look at 'em again—wish I could persuade you to taste them. What am I to do? Shall I promise? Poor Posket! If I don't promise—she'll cry and won't go home. The oysters are nearly cold and cold, what must he be? *Drawing aside the curtain, and, not seeing* VALE, *he staggers back*. Gone—and without a cry—brave fellow, brave fellow!

AGATHA. Colonel Lukyn.

LUKYN. Decay of stamina in the army—pah! The young 'uns are worthy of our best days.

AGATHA. Colonel Lukyn, will you promise?

LUKYN. Promise? Anything, my dear madam, anything.

AGATHA. Ah, thank you! May I ask you to see us to our cab?

LUKYN. Certainly! Thank heaven, they're going!

AGATHA, *to* CHARLOTTE. It's all right, come along!

CHARLOTTE, *to* AGATHA. Oh, these oysters look so nice.

LUKYN, *to himself*. Stop, in my trouble, I am forgetting even the commonest courtesies to these ladies. *To* AGATHA. You have a long journey before you. I am sure your husband would not forgive me for letting you face such weather unprepared. Let me recommend an oyster or two and a thimbleful of champagne.

AGATHA. No, thank you, Colonel Lukyn.

CHARLOTTE, *to* AGATHA. Say yes. I'm starving.

LUKYN. As you please. *To himself*. I knew they'd refuse. I've done my duty.

CHARLOTTE, *to* AGATHA. I was in the train till seven o'clock. Wait till you're a bona fide traveller—accept.

AGATHA. Ahem! Colonel, the fact is, my poor sister has been travelling all day and is a little exhausted.

LUKYN, *horrified*. You don't mean to say you're going to give me the inestimable pleasure.

CHARLOTTE *looks across at him, nodding and smiling*.

I am delighted.

CHARLOTTE *sits hungrily at table;* LUKYN *fetches a bottle of champagne from the sideboard*.

AGATHA, *to* CHARLOTTE. Charlotte, I am surprised.

CHARLOTTE, *to* AGATHA. Nonsense, the best people come here. Some of them have left their names on the mirrors.

VALE, *behind the curtain*. This is much too bad of Lukyn. What are they doing now?

LUKYN *draws the cork*.

Confound it, they're having my supper.

LUKYN *pours out wine.*

CHARLOTTE. Why doesn't he give me something to eat?

There is a clatter of knives and forks heard from the other room, then a burst of laughter from CIS.

AGATHA, *starting.* Charley, hark! How strange!

CHARLOTTE. Very. This bread is beautiful.

CIS *is heard singing the chorus of a comic song, boisterously.*

AGATHA. Don't you recognize that voice?

CHARLOTTE, *munching.* The only voice I recognize is the voice of hunger.

AGATHA. I am overwrought, I suppose.

LUKYN, *with his head drooping, fetches the dish of oysters from the sideboard.*

VALE, *behind the curtains.* He has taken the oysters. I've seen him do it.

LUKYN. The oysters.

LUKYN *sinks into his chair at the table and leans his head upon his hand; the two women look at each other.*

CHARLOTTE, *to* AGATHA. Anything wrong?

AGATHA. Sunstroke—bad case!

CHARLOTTE. Oh—poor fellow. *She gently lifts the corner of the dish, sniffs, then replaces cover.* No plates.

AGATHA. Ask for them.

CHARLOTTE. You ask.

AGATHA. You're hungry.

CHARLOTTE. You're married. Comes better from you.

VALE, *behind curtains.* This silence is terrible.

AGATHA, *to* LUKYN. Ahem! Ahem!

LUKYN, *looking up suddenly.* Eh?

AGATHA. There are no plates.

LUKYN. No plates? No plates? It's my fault. Pardon me. Where are the plates?

VALE, *still invisible, stretches out his hand through the curtain, takes up the plates and presents them to* LUKYN, *who recoils.*

VALE, *in a whisper.* Here are the plates. Look sharp, Lukyn.

LUKYN. Vale! safe and sound! *He takes the plates, then grasps* VALE's *extended hand.* Bless you, old fellow. I'm myself again. *Going gaily to the table with the plates.* My dear ladies, I blush—I positively blush—I am the worst host in the world.

VALE, *to himself.* By Jove, that's true.

AGATHA. Not at all—not at all.

LUKYN, *helping the ladies.* I'll make amends, by George! You may have

noticed I've been confoundedly out of sorts. That's my temperament—
now up, now down. I've just taken a turn, ha, ha! Oysters. *Handing plate
to* AGATHA.

AGATHA. Thank you.

LUKYN. Ah! I've passed many a happy hour in this room. The present is
not the least happy.

CHARLOTTE, *trying to attract his attention.* Ahem! Ahem!

LUKYN, *gazing up at the ceiling.* My first visit to the Hôtel des Princes was
in the year—the year—let me think.

CHARLOTTE, *whispering to* AGATHA. Isn't he going to help me?

LUKYN. Was it in '55?

AGATHA, *quickly passing her plate over to* CHARLOTTE. I'm not hungry.

CHARLOTTE. You're a dear.

LUKYN, *emphatically.* It was in '55. I'm forgetful again—pardon me. *He
hands plate of oysters to* CHARLOTTE, *and is surprised to find her eating vigor-
ously.* Why, I thought I—— *To* AGATHA. My dear madam, a thousand
apologies. *He helps her and then himself.* Pah! they're cold—icy—you
could skate on 'em. There's a dish of something else over there.

He goes to the sideboard; VALE'S *hand is again stretched forth with the other
covered dish.*

VALE. I say, Lukyn.

LUKYN, *taking the dish.* Thanks, old fellow. *He returns to the table and lifts
the cover.* Soles—they look tempting. If there are only some lemons!
Surely they are not so brutal as to have forgotten the lemons. Where
are they? *He returns to the sideboard.* Where are they? *In an undertone to*
VALE. Have you seen any lemons?

AGATHA. Pray, think less of us, Colonel Lukyn. Let me take care of you.
LUKYN *returns to table and sits in his chair.*

LUKYN. You're very kind. I wish you would let me ring for some lemons.
VALE'S *hand comes as before from behind the curtain to the sideboard, finds the
dish of lemons and holds it out at arm's length.*

VALE, *in a whisper.* Lemons.

AGATHA *is helping* LUKYN, *when suddenly* CHARLOTTE, *with her fork in the
air, leans back openmouthed, staring wildly at* VALE'S *arm extended with the dish.*

CHARLOTTE, *in terror.* Agatha! Agatha!

AGATHA. Charlotte, what's the matter, Charley?

CHARLOTTE. Agatha!

AGATHA. You're ill, Charlotte! Surely you are not choking?

CHARLOTTE. Look, look!

Pointing to the curtains, they both scream.

LUKYN. Don't be alarmed—I——

CHARLOTTE ⎱ *together.* ⎰ What's that?
AGATHA ⎰ ⎱ Who's that?

LUKYN. I can explain. Don't condemn till you've heard. I—I—— Damn it, sir, put those lemons down.

CHARLOTTE. He calls him "sir," it must be a man.

LUKYN. It is a man. I am not in a position to deny that.

AGATHA. Really, Colonel Lukyn!

LUKYN. It is my friend. He—he—he's merely waiting for his supper.

AGATHA. Your friend. *To* CHARLOTTE. Come home, dear.

LUKYN. Do, do hear me! To avoid the embarrassment of your encountering a stranger, he retreated to the balcony.

AGATHA. To the balcony? You have shamefully compromised two trusting women, Colonel Lukyn.

LUKYN. I would have laid down my life rather than have done so. I did lay down my friend's life.

AGATHA. He has overheard every confidential word I have spoken to you.

LUKYN. Hear his explanation. Why the devil don't you corroborate me, sir?

VALE, *from behind the curtain.* Certainly, I assure you I heard next to nothing.

CHARLOTTE, *grasping* AGATHA's *arm.* Oh, Agatha!

VALE. I didn't come in till I was exceedingly wet.

LUKYN, *to* AGATHA. You hear that?

VALE. And when I did come in——

CHARLOTTE, *hysterically.* Horace!

VALE. I beg your pardon.

CHARLOTTE. It's Horace, Captain Vale.

VALE, *coming from behind the curtain, looking terribly wet.* Charlotte—Miss Verrinder.

CHARLOTTE. What are you doing here? What a fright you look.

VALE. What am I doing here, Miss Verrinder? Really, Lukyn, your conduct calls for some little explanation.

LUKYN. My conduct, sir?

VALE. You make some paltry excuse to turn me out in the rain while you entertain a lady who you know has very recently broken my heart.

LUKYN. I didn't know anything of the kind.

VALE. I told you, Colonel Lukyn—this isn't the conduct of an officer and a gentleman.

LUKYN. Whose isn't, yours or mine?

VALE. Mine. I mean yours.

LUKYN. You are in the presence of ladies, sir; take off my hat.

VALE. I beg your pardon. I didn't know I had it on. *He throws hat away and the two men exchange angry words.*

CHARLOTTE. He's a very good-looking fellow, you don't see a man at his best when he's wet through.

AGATHA, *to* LUKYN. Colonel Lukyn, do you ever intend to send for a cab?

LUKYN. Certainly, madam.

VALE. One moment. I have some personal explanation to exchange with Miss Verrinder.

CHARLOTTE, *to* AGATHA. The slippers. *To* VALE. I am quite ready, Captain Vale.

VALE. Thank you. Colonel Lukyn, will you oblige me by stepping out on to that balcony.

LUKYN. Certainly not, sir.

VALE. You're afraid of the wet, Colonel Lukyn, you are no soldier.

LUKYN. You know better, sir. As a matter of fact, that balcony can't bear a man like me.

VALE. Which shows that inanimate objects have a great deal of common sense, sir.

LUKYN. You don't prove it in your own instance, Captain Vale.

VALE. That's a verbal quibble, sir.

They talk angrily.

AGATHA, *to* CHARLOTTE. It's frightfully late. Tell him to write to you.

CHARLOTTE. I must speak to him tonight, life is too short for letters.

AGATHA. Then he can telegraph.

CHARLOTTE. Too expensive.

AGATHA. Very well then, Lady Jenkins has a telephone. I'll take you there to tea tomorrow. If he loves you, tell him to ring up 1338091.

CHARLOTTE. You thoughtful angel.

LUKYN. Mrs. Posket—Miss Verrinder—ahem—we——

VALE. Colonel Lukyn and myself——

LUKYN. Captain Vale and I fear that we have been betrayed into a moment of——

VALE. Natural irritation.

LUKYN. Natural irritation, into the atrocious impropriety of differing——

VALE. Before ladies.

LUKYN. Charming ladies——

VALE. We beg your pardon—Lukyn!

LUKYN. Vale. *They grasp hands.* Mrs. Posket, I am now going out to hail a cab.

AGATHA. Pray do.

LUKYN. Miss Verrinder, the process will occupy five minutes.

VALE, *giving his hat to* LUKYN. Lukyn, I return your kindness—my hat.

LUKYN. Thank you, my boy.

LUKYN *puts on* VALE'S *hat, which is much too small for him. As he is going out, there is a knock at the door; he opens it;* BLOND *is outside.*

BLOND, *at door.* Colonel, it is ten minutes past the time of closing, may I ask you to dismiss your party?

LUKYN. Pooh! Isn't this a free country? *He goes out.*

BLOND. Yes, you are free to go home, Colonel. I shall get into trouble. *Following him out.*

CHARLOTTE, *to* AGATHA. I'll have the first word. Really, Captain Vale, I'm surprised at you.

VALE. There was a happy time, Miss Verrinder, when I might have been surprised at you.

CHARLOTTE. A few hours ago it was—"By Jove, all is over." Now I find you with a bosom friend enjoying deviled oysters.

VALE. I beg your pardon, I find you enjoying deviled oysters.

CHARLOTTE. Horace Vale. You forget you have forfeited the right to exercise any control over my diet.

VALE. One would think I had broken off our engagement.

CHARLOTTE. If you have not, who has? I have your letter saying all is over between us. That letter will be stamped tomorrow at Somerset House. I know how to protect myself.

VALE. Charlotte, can you explain your conduct with Gordon Bristow?

CHARLOTTE. I could if I chose; a young lady can explain anything.

VALE. But he is showing your gift to our fellows all over the place.

CHARLOTTE. It was a debt of honour. He laid me a box of gloves to a pair of slippers about "Forked Lightning" for the Regimental Cup, and "Forked Lightning" went tender at the heel. I couldn't come to you with debts hanging over me. *Crying.* I'm too conscientious.

VALE. By Jove, I've been a brute.

CHARLOTTE. Y-y-yes.

VALE. Can you forget I ever wrote that letter.

CHARLOTTE. That must be a question of time. *She lays her head on his left shoulder and then removes it.* How damp you are. *She puts her handkerchief upon his shoulder, and replaces her head. She moves his arm gradually up and arranges it round her shoulder.* If you went on, anyhow, every time I discharged an obligation, we should be most unhappy.

VALE. I promise you I won't mention Bristow's slippers again. By Jove, I won't—there.

CHARLOTTE. Very well then, if you do that, I'll give you my word I won't pay any more debts before our marriage.

VALE. My darling!

CHARLOTTE, *about to embrace him, but remembering that he is wet.* No—no—you are too damp.

ISIDORE, *outside.* I beg your pardon, it is a quarter of an hour over our time.

AGATHA *has been sitting on the sofa; suddenly she starts, listening intently.*

POSKET, *outside.* I know—I know. I'm going directly I can get the boy away.

AGATHA, *to herself.* Æneas!

CIS, *outside.* All right, Guv, you finish your bottle.

AGATHA. My boy.

ISIDORE, *outside.* Gentlemen, come—come.

AGATHA, *to herself.* Miserable deceiver. This then is the club, and the wretched man conspires to drag my boy down to his own awful level. What shall I do? I daren't make myself known here. I know, I'll hurry home, and if I reach there before Æneas, which I shall do, I'll sit up for him.

LUKYN *returns.*

Is the cab at the door?

LUKYN. It is.

AGATHA. Charlotte. Charlotte. *Drawing her veil down.*

CHARLOTTE. I'm ready, dear. *To* VALE. Married sisters are always a little thoughtless.

VALE, *offering his arm.* Permit me.

LUKYN, *offering his arm to* AGATHA. My dear madam.

They are all four about to leave, when BLOND *enters hurriedly.*

BLOND, *holding up his hand for silence.* Hush! Hush!

LUKYN. What's the matter?

BLOND. The police!

ALL, *in a whisper.* The police!

BLOND, *quietly.* The police are downstairs at the door. I told you so.

CHARLOTTE, *clinging to* VALE. Oh, dear! Oh, dear!

AGATHA. Gracious powers!

BLOND. Keep quiet, please. They may be satisfied with Madame Blond's assurances. I must put you in darkness, they can see the light here if they go round to the back. *Blows out candles, and turns down the lights.*

AGATHA } Oh!
CHARLOTTE

BLOND, *angrily.* Keep quiet, please! My licence is once marked already. Colonel Lukyn, thank you for this. *He goes out.*

AGATHA, *whimpering.* Miserable men! What have you done? Are you criminals?

CHARLOTTE. You haven't deserted or anything on my account, have you, Horace?

LUKYN. Hush! Don't be alarmed. Our time has passed so agreeably that we have overstepped the prescribed hour for closing the hotel. That's all.

AGATHA. What can they do to us?

LUKYN. At the worst, take our names and addresses, and summon us for being here during prohibited hours.

AGATHA. Oh!

CHARLOTTE, *to* VALE. Horace, can't you speak?

VALE. By Jove, I very much regret this.

ISIDORE *enters.*

LUKYN. Well, well?

ISIDORE. I beg your pardon, the police have come in.

LUKYN. The devil! *To* AGATHA. My dear lady, don't faint at such a moment.

BLOND *enters quickly, carrying a rug.*

BLOND. They are going over the house! Hide!

AGATHA
CHARLOTTE } *together.* Oh!

There is a general commotion.

BLOND. They have put a man at the back. Keep away from the window. *They are all bustling and everybody is talking in whispers;* LUKYN *places* AGATHA *under the table, where she is concealed by the cover; he gets behind the overcoats hanging from the pegs;* VALE *and* CHARLOTTE *crouch down behind sofa.*

Thank you very much. I am going to put Isidore to bed on the sofa. That will explain the light which has just gone out.

ISIDORE *quietly places himself upon the sofa,* BLOND *covering him with the rug.*

Thank you very much. *He goes out.*

AGATHA, *in a stifled voice.* Charley! Charley!

CHARLOTTE. Yes.

AGATHA. Where are you?

CHARLOTTE. Here.

AGATHA. Oh, where is Captain Vale?

CHARLOTTE. I think he's near me.

VALE. By Jove, Charlotte, I am!

AGATHA. Colonel Lukyn.

LUKYN, *from behind the coats.* Here, madam!

AGATHA. Don't leave us.

LUKYN. Madam, I am a soldier.

CHARLOTTE, *to* VALE. Oh, Horace, at such a moment what a comfort we must be to each other.

VALE. My dear Charlotte, it's incalculable.

ISIDORE *gently raises himself and looks over the back of sofa.*

CHARLOTTE, *in terror.* What's that?

ISIDORE, *softly.* I beg your pardon.

BLOND *enters quietly, followed by* CIS *and* POSKET *on tiptoe,* POSKET *holding on to* CIS.

BLOND. This way, be quick. Excuse me, the police are just entering the room in which these gentlemen were having supper. One of them is anxious not to be asked any questions. Please to hide him and his friend somewhere. They are both very nice gentlemen.

He goes out, leaving CIS *and* POSKET.

POSKET. Cis, Cis. Advise me, my boy, advise me.

CIS. It's all right, Guv, it's all right. Get behind something.

AGATHA, *peeping from under the tablecloth.* Æneas, and my child.

POSKET *and* CIS *wander about, looking for hiding places.*

VALE, *to* CIS. Go away.

CIS. Oh!

LUKYN, *to* POSKET, *who is fumbling at the coats.* No, no.

BLOND, *popping his head in.* The police—coming.

CIS *disappears behind the window curtain.* POSKET *dives under the table.*

AGATHA. Oh!

POSKET, *to* AGATHA, *in a whisper.* I beg your pardon. I think I am addressing a lady. I am entirely the victim of circumstances. Accept my apologies for this apparent intrusion. *No answer.* Madam, I applaud your reticence, though any statement made under the present circumstances would not be used against you. Where is that boy? Oh! Madam, it may be acute nervousness on your part, but you are certainly pinching my arm.

There is the sound of heavy feet outside; then MESSITER, *a gruff matter-of-fact Inspector of Police, enters, followed by* HARRIS, *a constable, and* ACHILLE BLOND.

BLOND. You need not trouble yourself—take my word for it.

MESSITER. No trouble, Mr. Blond, thank you. *Sniffing.* This is where the light was.

BLOND. Perhaps. My servant, Isidore, sleeps here, he has only just gone to bed.

MESSITER. Oh! *Taking a bull's-eye lantern from* HARRIS, *and throwing the light on* ISIDORE *who is apparently sleeping soundly.* Dead tired, I suppose?

BLOND. I suppose so.

MESSITER, *slightly turning down the covering.* He sleeps in his clothes?

BLOND. Oh yes.

MESSITER. Always?

BLOND. Always—it is the rule of the Hotel.

MESSITER. Oh—why's that?

BLOND. To be ready for the morning.

MESSITER. All right—all right. *Throwing the rug and blanket aside.* Isidore, go downstairs and give your full name and particulars to Sergeant Jarvis.

ISIDORE, *rising instantly.* Yes, sir—very good.

BLOND, *to* ISIDORE. Why do you wake up so soon? Devil take you!

ISIDORE. I beg your pardon. *He goes out.*

MESSITER. What is underneath that window, Mr. Blond?

BLOND. The skylight over the kitchen—devil take it!

MESSITER. Thank you—*you* can go down to the sergeant now, Mr. Blond.

BLOND. With pleasure—devil take me! *He goes out.*

MESSITER. Now then, Harris.

HARRIS. Yes, sir?

MESSITER. Keep perfectly still and hold your breath as long as you can.

HARRIS. Hold my breath, sir?

MESSITER. Yes—I want to hear how many people are breathing in this room. Are you ready?

HARRIS. Yes, sir.

MESSITER. Go!

> HARRIS *stands still, tightly compressing his lips;* MESSITER *quickly examines his face by the light of the lantern, then walks round the room, listening, and nodding his head with satisfaction as he passes the various hiding places.* HARRIS *writhes in agony; in the end he gives it up and breathes heavily.*

Harris!

HARRIS, *exhausted.* Yes, sir!

MESSITER. You're breathing.

HARRIS. Oh lor', yes, sir!

MESSITER. You'll report yourself tonight!

HARRIS. I held on till I nearly went off, sir.

MESSITER, *giving him the bull's-eye.* Don't argue, but light up; there are half a dozen people concealed in this room.

> *There is a cry from the women.* CHARLOTTE *and* VALE *rise.* LUKYN *steps from behind the coats.*

I thought so.

As MESSITER *turns,* AGATHA *and* POSKET *rise,* CIS *comes quickly, catches hold of* POSKET *and drags him across to the window.*

CIS, *to* POSKET. Come on, Guv. Come on!

They disappear through the curtain as HARRIS *turns up the lights. Then there is a cry and the sound of a crash.*

AGATHA. They're killed.

MESSITER, *looking through the window.* No, they're not; they've gone into the kitchen and the balcony with 'em. Look sharp, Harris.

HARRIS *goes out quickly.*

LUKYN, *to* MESSITER. I shall report you for this, sir.

MESSITER, *taking out his notebook.* Very sorry, sir; it's my duty.

LUKYN. Duty, sir! Coming your confounded detective tricks on ladies and gentlemen? How dare you make ladies and gentlemen suspend their breathing till they nearly have apoplexy? Do you know I'm a short-necked man, sir?

MESSITER. I didn't want you to leave off breathing, sir. I wanted you to breathe louder. Your name and address, sir.

LUKYN. Gur-r-r-h!

MESSITER. Army gentleman, sir?

LUKYN. How do you know that?

MESSITER. Short style of speaking, sir. Army gentlemen run a bit brusquish when on in years.

LUKYN. Oh! Alexander Lukyn—Colonel—Her Majesty's Cheshire Light Infantry, late Forty-first Foot, Third Battalion—Bengal—Retired.

MESSITER, *writing.* Hotel or Club, Colonel?

LUKYN. Neither. 19a Cork Street—lodgings.

MESSITER, *writing.* Very nice part, Colonel. Thank you.

LUKYN. Bah!

MESSITER. Other gentleman?

VALE, *with languid hauteur.* Horace, Edmund, Cholmeley, Clive, Napier, Vale. Captain—Shropshire Fusiliers—Stark's Hotel, Conduit Street.

MESSITER, *writing.* Retired, sir?

VALE. No, confound you—active!

MESSITER. Thank you, Captain. Ahem! Beg pardon. The—the ladies.

CHARLOTTE *clings to* VALE, AGATHA *to* LUKYN.

CHARLOTTE }
AGATHA   } No—no! No—no!

LUKYN, *to* AGATHA. All right—all right—trust to me! *To* MESSITER. Well, sir?

MESSITER. Names and addresses, please.

LUKYN. Officer—my good fellow—tell me now—er—um—at the present moment— What are you most in want of?

MESSITER. These two ladies' names and addresses, please. Be quick, Colonel. *Pointing to* AGATHA. That lady first.

LUKYN. Christian names—er—ah—er—Alice Emmeline.

MESSITER, *writing*. Alice Emmeline. Surname?

LUKYN. Er—um—Fitzgerald—101 Wilton Street, Piccadilly.

MESSITER. Single lady?

LUKYN. Quite.

MESSITER. Very good, sir.

AGATHA, *to* LUKYN, *tearfully*. Oh, thank you, such a nice address too.

MESSITER, *to* VALE. Now, Captain, please—that lady.

VALE, *who has been reassuring* CHARLOTTE. Haw! ah! this lady is—ah—um— the other lady's sister.

MESSITER. Single lady, sir?

VALE. Certainly.

MESSITER, *writing*. Christian name, Captain?

VALE. Ah—um—Harriet.

MESSITER, *writing*. Surname.

VALE. Er—Macnamara.

MESSITER, *with a grim smile*. Quite so. Lives with her sister, of course, sir?

VALE. Of course.

MESSITER. Where at, sir?

VALE. Albert Mansions, Victoria Street.

CHARLOTTE, *to* VALE. Oh, thank you; I always fancied that spot.

MESSITER. Very much obliged, gentlemen.

LUKYN, *who has listened to* VALE's *answers in helpless horror*. By George, well out of it!

CHARLOTTE *totters across to* AGATHA, *who embraces her*.

LUKYN, *taking down the overcoats and throwing one to* VALE. Vale, your coat.

HARRIS *enters*.

HARRIS, *to* MESSITER. Very sorry, sir; the two other gentlemen got clean off, through the back scullery door—old hands to all appearance.

MESSITER *stamps his foot, with an exclamation*.

AGATHA, *to herself*. My boy—saved!

LUKYN, *to* HARRIS, *who stands before the door*. Constable, get out of the way.

MESSITER, *sharply*. Harris!

HARRIS, *without moving*. Yes, sir.

MESSITER. You will leave the hotel with these ladies, and not lose sight of them till you've ascertained what their names *are*, and where they *do* live.

LUKYN *and* VALE. What!

AGATHA *and* CHARLOTTE. Oh!

MESSITER. Your own fault, gentlemen; it's my duty.

LUKYN. And it is *my* duty to save these helpless women from the protecting laws of my confounded country! Vale!

VALE, *putting his coat on the sofa.* Active!

LUKYN, *to* HARRIS. Let these ladies pass!

He takes HARRIS *by the collar and flings him over to* VALE, *who throws him toward the ladies, who push him away.* MESSITER *puts a whistle to his mouth and blows, there is an immediate answer from without.*

LUKYN. More of your fellows outside.

MESSITER. Yes, sir, at your service. Very sorry, gentlemen, but you and your party are in my custody.

LUKYN *and* VALE. What?

AGATHA *and* CHARLOTTE. Oh!

MESSITER. For assaulting this man in the execution of his duty.

LUKYN. You'll dare to lock us up all night?

MESSITER. It's one o'clock now, Colonel—you'll come on first thing in the morning.

LUKYN. Come on. At what Court?

MESSITER. Mulberry Street.

AGATHA. Ah! The Magistrate?

MESSITER. Mr. Posket, mum.

AGATHA *sinks into a chair,* CHARLOTTE *at her feet;* LUKYN, *overcome, falls on* VALE'S *shoulders.*

ACT THREE

SCENE 1

The first scene is the Magistrate's Room at Mulberry Street Police Court, with a doorway covered by curtains leading directly into the Court and a door opening into a passage. It is the morning after the events of the last Act.

POLICE-SERGEANT LUGG, *a middle-aged man with a slight country dialect, enters with* The Times *newspaper, and proceeds to cut it and glance at its contents while he hums a song.* MR. WORMINGTON, *an elderly, trim, and precise man, enters.*

WORMINGTON. Good morning, Lugg.

LUGG. Morning, Mr. Wormington.

WORMINGTON. Mr. Posket not arrived yet?

LUGG. Not yet, sir. Hullo! *Reading*. "Raid on a West-end Hotel. At a early hour this morning——"

WORMINGTON. Yes, I've read that—a case of assault upon the police.

LUGG. Why, these must be the folks who've been so precious rampageous all night.

WORMINGTON. Very likely.

LUGG. Yes, sir, protestin' and protestin' till they protested everybody's sleep away. Nice-looking women, too, though as I tell Mrs. Lugg, nowadays there's no tellin' who's the lady and who isn't. Who's got this job, sir?

WORMINGTON. Inspector Messiter.

LUGG. Messiter! That's luck; why, he's the worst elocutionist in the force, sir.* *As he arranges the newspaper upon the table, he catches sight of* WORMING-TON's *necktie, which is bright red*. Well, I—excuse me, Mr. Wormington, but all the years I've had the honour of knowin' you, sir, I've never seen you wear a necktie with, so to speak, a dash of colour in it.

WORMINGTON. Well, Lugg, no, that's true, but today is an exceptional occasion with me. It is, in fact, the twenty-fifth anniversary of my marriage, and I thought it due to Mrs. Wormington to vary, in some slight degree, the somberness of my attire. I confess I am a little uneasy in case Mr. Posket should consider it at all disrespectful to the Court.

LUGG. Not he, sir.

WORMINGTON. I don't know. Mr. Posket is punctiliousness itself in dress, and his cravat's invariably black. However, it is not every man who has a silver wedding day.

LUGG. It's not every one as wants one, sir.

WORMINGTON *goes out; at the same moment* POSKET *enters quickly and leans on his chair as if exhausted. His appearance is extremely wretched; he is still in evening dress, but his clothes are muddy and his linen soiled and crumpled, while across the bridge of his nose he has a small strip of black plaster.*

POSKET, *faintly*. Good morning, Lugg.

LUGG. Good morning to you sir. Regretting the liberty I'm taking, sir— I've seen you look more strong and hearty.

POSKET. I am fairly well, thank you, Lugg. *Sitting*. My night was rather— rather disturbed.

---

* *A city magistrate, censuring a constable for the indistinctness of his utterances in the witness box, suggested that the police should be instructed in a method of delivering evidence articulately.*

LUGG *crosses at back of table.*

Lugg?

LUGG. Sir?

POSKET. Have any inquiries been made about me, this morning, any
messenger from Mrs. Posket, for instance, to know how I am?

LUGG. No, sir.

POSKET. Oh! My child, my stepson, young Mr. Farringdon, has not called,
has he?

LUGG. No, sir.

POSKET, *to himself.* Where can that boy be? *To* LUGG. Thank you, that's all.

LUGG, *who has been eyeing* POSKET *with astonishment, goes to the door and then
touches the bridge of his nose.* Nasty cut while shavin', sir. *Goes out.*

POSKET. Where can that boy have got to? If I could only remember how,
when, and where we parted! I think it was at Kilburn. Let me think—
first, the kitchen. *Putting his hand to his side as if severely bruised.* Oh! Cis
was all right, because I fell underneath; I felt it was my duty to do so.
Then what occurred? A dark room, redolent of onions and cabbages
and paraffin oil, and Cis dragging me over the stone floor, saying,
"We're in the scullery, Guv, let's try and find the tradesmen's door."
Next, the night air—oh, how refreshing! "Cis, my boy, we will both
learn a lesson from tonight—never deceive." Where are we? In Argyle
Street. "Look out, Guv, they're after us." Then—then as Cis remarked
when we were getting over the railings of Portman Square—then the
fun began. We over into the Square—they after us. Over again, into
Baker Street. Down Baker Street, curious recollections while running,
of my first visit, as a happy child, to Madame Tussaud's, and wondering
whether her removal had affected my fortunes. "Come on, Guv—you're
getting blown." Where are we? Park Road. What am I doing? Getting
up out of puddle. St. John's Wood. The cricket ground. "I say, Guv,
what a run this would be at Lord's, wouldn't it? and no fear of being
run out either; more fear of being run in." "What road is this, Cis?"
Maida Vale. Good gracious! A pious aunt of mine once lived in
Hamilton Terrace; she never thought I should come to this. "Guv?"
"Yes, my boy." "Let's get this kindhearted coffee-stall keeper to hide
us." We apply. "Will you assist two unfortunate gentlemen." "No,
blowed if I will." "Why not?" "Cos I'm agoin' to join in the chase
after you." Ah! Off again, along Maida Vale! On, on, heaven knows
how or where, till at last, no sound of pursuit, no Cis, no breath, and
the early Kilburn busses starting to Town. Then I came back again,
and not much too soon for the Court. *Going up to the washstand and*

looking into the little mirror, with a low groan. Oh, how shockingly awful I look, and how stiff and sore I feel! *Taking off his coat and hanging it on a peg, then washing his hands.* What a weak, double-faced creature to be a magistrate! I really ought to get some member of Parliament to ask a question about me in the House. Where's the soap? I shall put five pounds and costs into the poor's box tomorrow. But I deserve a most severe caution. Ah, perhaps I shall get that from Agatha. *He takes off his white tie, rolls it up and crams it into his pocket.* When Wormington arrives I will borrow some money, and send out for a black cravat. All my pocket money is in my overcoat at the Hôtel des Princes. If the police seize it there is some consolation in knowing that that money will never be returned to me.

There is a knock at the door.

Come in!

LUGG, *entering.* Your servant, Mr. Wyke, wants to see you, sir.

POSKET. Bring him in.

LUGG *goes out.*

Wyke! From Agatha! From Agatha!

WYKE, *entering.* Ahem! Good morning, sir.

POSKET. Good morning, Wyke. Ahem! Is Master Farringdon quite well?

WYKE. He hadn't arrived home when I left, sir.

POSKET. Oh! Where is that boy? *To* WYKE. How is your mistress this morning, Wyke?

WYKE. Very well, I hope, sir; *she* ain't come home yet, either.

POSKET. Not returned—nor Miss Verrinder?

WYKE. No, sir—neither of them.

POSKET, *to himself.* Lady Jenkins is worse; they are still nursing her! Good women, true women!

WYKE, *to himself.* That's eased his deceivin' old mind.

POSKET, *to himself.* Now if the servants don't betray me and Cis returns safely, the worst is over. To what a depth I have fallen when I rejoice at Lady Jenkins's indisposition!

WYKE. Cook thought you ought to know that the mistress hadn't come home, sir.

POSKET. Certainly. Take a cab at once to Campden Hill and bring me back word how poor Lady Jenkins is. Tell Mrs. Posket I will come on the moment the Court rises.

WYKE. Yes, sir.

POSKET. And, Wyke, it is not at all necessary that Mrs. Posket should know of my absence with Master Farringdon, from home last night.

Mrs. Posket's present anxieties are more than sufficient. Inform Cook, and Popham, and the other servants that I shall recognize their discretion in the same spirit I have already displayed towards you.

WYKE, *with sarcasm.* Thank you, sir. I will. *He produces from his waistcoat pocket a small packet of money done up in newspaper, which he throws down upon the table.* Meanwhile, sir, I thought you would like to count up the little present of money you gave me last night, and in case you thought you'd been over liberal sir, you might halve the amount. It isn't no good spoiling of us all, sir.

LUGG *enters.*

POSKET. You are an excellent servant, Wyke; I am very pleased. I will see you when you return from Lady Jenkins's. Be quick.

WYKE. Yes, sir. *To himself.* He won't give me twopence again in a hurry. *He goes out;* LUGG *is about to follow.*

POSKET. Oh, Lugg, I want you to go to the nearest hosier's and purchase me a neat cravat.

LUGG, *looking inquisitively at* POSKET. A necktie, sir?

POSKET. Yes. *Turning up his coat collar to shield himself from* LUGG'S *gaze.* A necktie—a necktie.

LUGG. What sort of a kind of one, sir?

POSKET. Oh, one like Mr. Wormington's.

LUGG. One like he's wearing this morning, sir?

POSKET. Of course, of course, of course.

LUGG, *to himself.* Fancy him being jealous of Mr. Wormington, now. Very good, sir—what price, sir?

POSKET. The best. *To himself.* There now, I've no money. *Seeing the packet on the table.* Oh, pay for it with this, Lugg.

LUGG. Yes, sir.

POSKET. And keep the change for your trouble.

LUGG. Thank you, sir, thank you, sir—very much obliged to you, sir. *To himself.* That's like a liberal gentleman.

LUGG *goes out as* WORMINGTON *enters through the curtains with the charge-sheet in his hand.* WORMINGTON, *on seeing* POSKET, *uneasily tucks his pocket handkerchief in his collar so as to hide his necktie.*

WORMINGTON. Hm! Good morning.

POSKET. Good morning, Wormington.

WORMINGTON. The charge-sheet.

POSKET. Sit down.

WORMINGTON *puts on his spectacles.* POSKET *also attempts to put on his spectacles, but hurts the bridge of his nose, winces, and desists.*

To himself. My nose is extremely painful. *To* WORMINGTON. You have a bad cold, I am afraid, Wormington—bronchial!

WORMINGTON. Ahem! Well—ah—the fact is—you may have noticed how very chilly the nights are.

POSKET. Very, very.

WORMINGTON. The only way to maintain the circulation is to run as fast as one can.

POSKET. To run—as fast as one can—yes—quite so.

WORMINGTON, *to himself, looking at* POSKET's *shirt front.* How very extraordinary—he is wearing no cravat whatever!

POSKET, *buttoning up his coat to avoid* WORMINGTON's *gaze.* Anything important this morning!

WORMINGTON. Nothing particular after the first charge, a serious business arising out of the raid on the Hôtel des Princes.

POSKET, *starting.* Hôtel des Princes?

WORMINGTON. Inspector Messiter found six persons supping there at one o'clock this morning. Two contrived to escape.

POSKET. Dear me—I am surprised—I mean, did they?

WORMINGTON. But they left their overcoats behind them, and it is believed they will be traced.

POSKET. Oh, do you—do you think it is worth while? The police have a great deal to occupy them just now.

WORMINGTON. But surely if the police see their way to capture anybody we had better raise no obstacle.

POSKET. No—no—quite so—never struck me.

WORMINGTON, *referring to charge-sheet.* The remaining four it was found necessary to take into custody.

POSKET. Good gracious! What a good job the other two didn't wait. I beg your pardon—I mean—you say we have four?

WORMINGTON. Yes, on the charge of obstructing the police. The first assault occurred in the supper room—the second in the taxi on the way to the station. There were five persons in the cab at the time—the two women, the two men, and the Inspector.

POSKET. Dear me, it must have been a very complicated assault. Who are the unfortunate people?

WORMINGTON. The men are of some position: *Reading.* "Alexander Lukyn, Colonel"——

POSKET. Lukyn! I—I—know Colonel Lukyn; we are old schoolfellows.

WORMINGTON. Very sad! The other is—*reading*—"Horace, etc. etc., Vale—Captain—Shropshire Fusiliers."

POSKET. And the ladies?

WORMINGTON. Call themselves "Alice Emmeline Fitzgerald and Harriet Macnamara."

POSKET, *to himself.* Which is the lady which was under the table with me?

WORMINGTON. They are not recognized by the police at present, but they furnish incorrect addresses and their demeanour is generally violent and unsatisfactory.

POSKET, *to himself.* Who pinched me—Alice or Harriet?

WORMINGTON. I mention this case because it seems to be one calling for most stringent measures.

POSKET. Wouldn't a fine, and a severe warning from the bench, to the two persons who have got away——

WORMINGTON. I think not. Consider, Mr. Posket, not only defying the licensing laws, but obstructing the police!

POSKET. That's true—it is hard, when the police are doing anything, that they should be obstructed.

LUGG *enters.*

LUGG, *attempting to conceal some annoyance.* Your necktie, sir.

POSKET. S-ssh!

WORMINGTON, *to himself.* Then he *came* without one—dear me!

LUGG, *clapping down a paper parcel on the table.* As near like Mr. Wormington's as possible—brighter if anything.

POSKET, *opening the parcel and finding a very common, gaudy neckerchief.* Good gracious! What a horrible affair!

LUGG. According to my information, sir—like Mr. Wormington's.

POSKET. Mr. Wormington would never be seen in such an abominable colour.

WORMINGTON. Well—really—I— *Removing the handkerchief from his throat.* I am extremely sorry.

POSKET. My dear Wormington!

WORMINGTON. I happen to be wearing something similar—the first time for five-and-twenty years.

POSKET. Oh, I beg your pardon. *To himself.* Everything seems against me.

LUGG. One-and-nine it come to, sir. *Producing the paper packet of money and laying it upon the table.* And I brought back all the money you gave me, thinking you'd like to look over it quietly. Really, sir, I never showed up smaller in any shop, in all my life!

POSKET. Upon my word. First one and then another! What *is* wrong with the money. *Opens the packet.* Twopence! *To himself.* That man Wyke will tell all to Agatha! Oh, everything is against me.

LUGG *has opened the door, taken a card from someone outside, and handed it to* WORMINGTON.

WORMINGTON. From cell No. 3. *Handing the card to* POSKET.

POSKET, *reading.* "Dear Posket, for the love of goodness see me before the sitting of the Court. Alexander Lukyn." Poor dear Lukyn! What on earth shall I do?

WORMINGTON. Such a course would be most unusual.

POSKET. Everything is unusual. Your cravat is unusual. This prisoner is invited to dine at my house today—that's peculiar. He is my wife's first husband's only child's godfather; that's a little out of the ordinary.

WORMINGTON. The charge is so serious!

POSKET. But I am a man as well as a magistrate. Advise me, Wormington, advise me!

WORMINGTON. Well—you can apply to yourself for permission to grant Colonel Lukyn's request.

POSKET, *hastily scribbling on* LUKYN'S *card.* I do—I do—and after much conflicting argument I consent to see Colonel Lukyn here, immediately. *Handing the card to* WORMINGTON *who passes it to* LUGG, *who then goes out.* Don't leave me, Wormington—you must stand by me to see that I remain calm, firm, and judicial. *He hastily puts on the red necktie in an untidy manner.* Poor Lukyn, I must sink the friend in the magistrate and in dealing with his errors apply the scourge to myself. *To* WORMINGTON. Wormington, tap me on the shoulder when I am inclined to be more than usually unusual.

WORMINGTON *stands behind him, and* LUGG *enters with* LUKYN. LUKYN'S *dress clothes are much soiled and disordered, and he, too, has a small strip of plaster upon the bridge of his nose. There is a constrained pause,* LUKYN *and* POSKET *both cough.*

LUKYN, *to himself.* Poor Posket!

POSKET, *to himself.* Poor Lukyn!

LUKYN, *to himself.* I suppose he has been sitting up for his wife all night, poor devil! *To* POSKET. Ahem! How are you, Posket?

WORMINGTON *touches* POSKET'S *shoulder.*

POSKET. I regret to see you in this terrible position, Colonel Lukyn.

LUKYN. By George, old fellow, I regret to find myself in it. *Sitting and taking up newspaper.* I suppose they've got us in "The Times," confound 'em! *While* LUKYN *is reading the paper,* POSKET *and* WORMINGTON *hold a hurried consultation respecting* LUKYN'S *behaviour.*

POSKET. Hm! *To* LUGG. Sergeant, I think Colonel Lukyn may be accommodated with a chair.

LUGG. He's in it, sir.

LUKYN, *rising and putting down paper.* Beg your pardon, forgot where I was.
I suppose everything must be formal in this confounded place?

POSKET. I am afraid, Colonel Lukyn, it will be necessary even here to
preserve strictly our unfortunate relative positions. LUKYN *bows.* Sit
down. LUKYN *sits again.* POSKET *takes up the charge-sheet.* Colonel Lukyn!
In addressing you now, I am speaking, not as a man, but as an instrument of the Law. As a man I may, or may not, be a weak, vicious,
despicable creature.

LUKYN. Certainly—of course.

POSKET. But as a magistrate I am bound to say you fill me with pain and
astonishment.

LUKYN. Quite right—every man to his trade; go on, Posket.

POSKET, *turning his chair to face* LUKYN. Alexander Lukyn—when I look at
you—when I look at you—— *He attempts to put on his spectacles.* Ah—my
nose. *To* LUKYN. I say, when I look at you, Alexander Lukyn, I confront a most mournful spectacle. A military officer, trained in the ways
of discipline and smartness, now, in consequence of his own misdoings,
lamentably bruised and battered, shamefully disfigured by plaster, with
his apparel soiled and damaged—all terrible evidence of a conflict with
that power of which I am the representative.

LUKYN, *turning his chair to face* POSKET. Well, Posket, if it comes to that,
when I look at you, when I look at you—— *He attempts to fix his glass in
his eye.* Confound my nose! *To* POSKET. When I look at you, *you* are not
a very imposing object, this morning.

POSKET. Lukyn!

LUKYN. You look quite as shaky as I do—and you're not quite innocent
of court plaster.

POSKET. Lukyn! Really!

LUKYN. And as for our attire, we neither of us look as if we had slipped
out of a bandbox.

POSKET. Don't, Lukyn, don't! Pray respect my legal status!

WORMINGTON *leads* POSKET, *who has risen, back to his seat.*

Thank you, Wormington. Alexander Lukyn, I have spoken. It remains
for you to state your motive in seeking this painful interview.

LUKYN. Certainly! Hm! You know, of course, that I am not alone in this
affair?

POSKET, *referring to charge-sheet.* Three persons appear to be charged with
you.

LUKYN. Yes. Two others got away. Cowards! If ever I find them, I'll destroy them!

POSKET. Lukyn!

LUKYN. I will. Another job for you, Posket.

POSKET, *with dignity*. I beg your pardon, in the event of such a deplorable occurrence, I should not occupy my present position. Go on, sir.

LUKYN. Horace Vale and I are prepared to stand the brunt of our misdeeds. But, Posket, there are ladies in the case.

POSKET. In the annals of the Mulberry Street Police Court such a circumstance is not unprecedented.

LUKYN. Two helpless, forlorn ladies.

POSKET, *referring to charge-sheet*. Alice Emmeline Fitzgerald and Harriet Macnamara. Oh, Lukyn, Lukyn!

LUKYN. Pooh! I ask no favour for myself or Vale, but I come to you, Posket, to beg you to use your power to release these two ladies without a moment's delay.

WORMINGTON *touches* POSKET'S *shoulder*.

POSKET. Upon my word, Lukyn! Do you think I am to be undermined!

LUKYN. Undermine the devil, sir! Don't talk to me! Let these ladies go, I say! Don't bring them into Court, don't see their faces—don't hear their voices—if you do, you'll regret it!

POSKET. Colonel Lukyn!

LUKYN, *leaning across the table and gripping* POSKET *by the shoulder*. Posket, do you know that one of these ladies is a married lady?

POSKET. Of course I don't, sir. I blush to hear it.

LUKYN. And do you know that from the moment this married lady steps into your confounded Court, the happiness, the contentment of a doting husband, become a confounded wreck and ruin.

POSKET. Then, sir, let it be my harrowing task to open the eyes of this foolish doting man to the treachery, the perfidy, which nestles upon his very hearthrug!

LUKYN. Oh, lor'! Be careful, Posket! By George, be careful!

POSKET. Alexander Lukyn, you are my friend. Amongst the personal property taken from you when you entered these precincts may have been found a memorandum of an engagement to dine at my house tonight at seven o'clock. But, Lukyn, I solemnly prepare you, you stand in danger of being late for dinner! I go further—I am not sure—after this morning's proceedings, that Mrs. Posket will be ready to receive you.

LUKYN. I'm confoundedly certain she *won't!*

POSKET. Therefore, Lukyn, as an English husband and father, it will be my duty to teach you and your disreputable companions—*referring to charge-sheet*—Alice Emmeline Fitzgerald and Harriet Macnamara, some rudimentary notions of propriety and decorum.

LUKYN. Confound you, Posket—listen!

POSKET. I am listening, sir, to the guiding voice of Mrs. Posket—that newly made wife still blushing from the embarrassment of her second marriage, and that voice says, "Strike for the sanctity of hearth and home, for the credit of the wives of England—no mercy!"

WORMINGTON. It is time to go into Court, sir. The charge against Colonel Lukyn is first on the list.

LUKYN. Posket, I'll give you one last chance! If I write upon a scrap of paper the real names of these two unfortunate ladies, will you shut yourself up for a moment, away from observation, and read these names before you go into Court?

POSKET. Certainly not, Colonel Lukyn! I cannot be influenced by private information in dealing with an offence which is, in my opinion, as black as—as my cravat! Ahem!

WORMINGTON *and* POSKET *look at each other's necktie and turn up their collars hastily.*

LUKYN, *to himself.* There's no help for it. *To* POSKET. Then, Posket, you must have the plain truth where you stand, by George! The two ladies who are my companions in this affair are——

POSKET, *quickly.* Sergeant! Colonel Lukyn will now join his party.

LUGG *steps up to* LUKYN.

LUKYN. What, sir? What?

POSKET. Lukyn, I think we both have engagements—will you excuse me?

LUKYN. Posket! You've gone too far! If you went down on your knees, which you appear to have been recently doing, and begged the names of these two ladies, you shouldn't have 'em! No, sir, by George, you shouldn't.

POSKET. Good morning, Colonel Lukyn.

LUKYN. You've lectured me, pooh-poohed me, snubbed me—a soldier, sir—a soldier! But when I think of your dinner party tonight, with my empty chair, like Banquo, by George, sir—and the chief dish composed of a well-browned, well-basted, family skeleton, served up under the best silver cover, I pity you, Posket! Good morning! *He marches out with* LUGG.

POSKET. Ah! Thank goodness that ordeal is passed. Now, Wormington,

I think I am ready to face the duties of the day! Shall we go into Court?

WORMINGTON. Certainly, sir.

WORMINGTON gathers up paper from the table. POSKET *with a shaking hand pours out water from carafe and drinks.*

POSKET. My breakfast. *To* WORMINGTON. I hope I defended the sanctity of the Englishman's hearth, Wormington?

WORMINGTON. You did, indeed. As a married man, I thank you.

POSKET. Give me your arm, Wormington? I am not very well this morning and this interview with Colonel Lukyn has shaken me. I think your coat collar is turned up, Wormington.

WORMINGTON. So is yours I fancy, sir.

POSKET. Ahem!

They turn their collars down; POSKET *takes* WORMINGTON'S *arm. They are going towards the curtains when* WYKE *enters hurriedly at the door.*

WYKE. Excuse me, sir.

WORMINGTON. Hush! hush! Mr. Posket is just going into Court.

WYKE. Lady Jenkins has sent me back to tell you that she hasn't seen the Missis for the last week or more.

POSKET. Mrs. Posket went to Campden Hill with Miss Verrinder last night!

WYKE. They haven't arrived there, sir.

POSKET. Haven't arrived!

WYKE. No, sir—and even a slow four-wheeler won't account for that.

POSKET. Wormington! there's something wrong! Mrs. Posket quitted a fairly happy home last night and has not been seen or heard of since!

WORMINGTON. Pray don't be anxious, sir, the Court is waiting.

POSKET. But I am anxious! Tell Sergeant Lugg to look over the Accident-Book, this morning's Hospital Returns, List of Missing children, Suspicious Pledges, People left chargeable to the Parish, Lost Dogs, Attend to your Window Fastenings——! I—I—Wormington, Mrs. Posket and I disagreed last night!

WORMINGTON. Don't think of it, sir! you should hear me and Mrs. Wormington! Pray do come into Court.

POSKET. Court! I'm totally unfit for business! totally unfit for business!

WORMINGTON hurries off through the curtains. LUGG *enters, almost breathless.*

LUGG. We've got charge one in the Dock—all four of 'em. *Seeing* WYKE. Hallo! you back again.

WYKE. Yes—seems so.

They stand facing each other, dabbing their foreheads with their handkerchiefs. Phew! you seem warm.

LUGG. Phew! you don't seem so cool.

WYKE. I've been lookin' after two ladies.

LUGG. So have I.

WYKE. I haven't found 'em.

LUGG. If I'd known, I'd 'a been pleased to lend you our two.

From the other side of the curtains there is the sound of a shriek from AGATHA *and* CHARLOTTE.

WYKE. Lor'! what's that!

LUGG. That *is* our two. Don't notice them—they're hystericals. They're mild now to what they have been. I say, old fellow—is your gov'nor all right in his head?

WYKE. I suppose so—why?

LUGG. I've a partickler reason for asking. Does he ever tell you to buy him anything and keep the change?

WYKE. What dy're mean?

LUGG. Well, does he ever come down handsome for your extry exertion, do you ever get any tips?

WYKE. Rather. What do you think he made me a present of last night?

LUGG. Don't know.

WYKE. Twopence—to buy a new umbrella.

LUGG. Well, I'm blessed! And he gave me the same sum to get him a silk necktie. It's my opinion he's got a softening of the brain.

Another shriek from the two women, a cry from POSKET, *and then a hubbub are heard.*

Running up to the curtains and looking through. Hallo! what's wrong! Here! I told you so—he's broken out. He's broken out.

WYKE. Who's broken out?

LUGG. The lunatic. Keep back, I'm wanted. *He goes through the curtains.*

WYKE. Look at the Guv'nor waving his arms and going on anyhow at the prisoners! Prisoners! Gracious goodness—it's the Missis!

Amid a confused sound of voices, POSKET *is brought in, through the curtains, by* WORMINGTON. LUGG *follows.*

POSKET. Wormington! Wormington! the two ladies! the two ladies! I know them!

WORMINGTON. It's all right, sir, it's all right—don't be upset, sir!

POSKET. I'm not well, what shall I do?

WORMINGTON. Nothing further, sir. What you have done is quite in form.

POSKET. What I *have* done?

WORMINGTON. Yes, sir—you did precisely what I suggested—took the words from me. They pleaded guilty.

POSKET. Guilty!

WORMINGTON. Yes, sir—and you sentenced them.

POSKET. Sentenced them! The ladies!

WORMINGTON. Yes, sir. You've given them seven days, without the option of a fine.

POSKET *collapses into* WORMINGTON'S *arms.*

SCENE 2

The scene changes to POSKET'S *drawing-room, as in the First Act.* BEATIE *enters timidly, dressed in simple walking-costume.*

BEATIE. How dreadfully early. Eleven o'clock, and I'm not supposed to come till four. I wonder why I want to instruct Cis all day. I'm not nearly so enthusiastic about the two little girls I teach in Russell Square.
POPHAM *enters. Her eyes are red as if from crying.*

POPHAM, *drawing back on seeing* BEATIE. That music person again. I beg your pardon—I ain't got no instructions to prepare no drawing-room for no lessons till four o'clock.

BEATIE. I wish to see Mrs. Posket.

POPHAM. She hasn't come home.

BEATIE. Oh, then—er—um—Master Farringdon will do.

POPHAM, *in tears.* He haven't come home either!

BEATIE. Oh, where is he?

POPHAM. No one knows! His wicked old stepfather took him out late last night and hasn't returned him. Such a night as it was, too, and him still wearing his summer undervests.

BEATIE. Mr. Posket?

POPHAM. Mr. Posket—no, my Cis!

BEATIE. How dare you speak of Master Farringdon in that familiar way!

POPHAM. How dare I? Because me and him formed an attachment before ever you darkened our doors. *Taking a folded printed paper from her pocket.* You may put down the iron 'eel too heavy, Miss Tomlinson. I refer you to Bow Bells—"First Love is Best Love, or, The Earl's Choice." *As* POPHAM *offers the paper,* CIS *enters, looking very pale, worn-out, and disheveled.*

POPHAM ⎱ Oh!
BEATIE ⎰

CIS, *staggering to a chair.* Where's the Mater?

POPHAM. Not home yet.

CIS. Thank jiminy!

BEATIE. He's ill!

POPHAM. Oh!

    BEATIE, *assisted by* POPHAM, *quickly wheels the large armchair forward. They catch hold of* CIS *and place him in it; he submits limply.*

BEATIE, *taking* CIS's *hand.* What is the matter, Cis dear? Tell Beatie.

POPHAM, *taking his other hand.* Well, I'm sure! Who's given you raisins and ketchup from the store cupboard! Come back to Emma!

    CIS, *with his eyes closed, gives a murmur.*

BEATIE. He's whispering!

    They both bob their heads down to listen.

POPHAM. He says his head's a-whirling.

BEATIE. Put him on the sofa.

    They take off his boots, loosen his necktie, and dab his forehead with water out of a flower vase.

CIS. I—I—I wish you two girls would leave off.

BEATIE. He's speaking again. He hasn't had any breakfast! He's hungry!

POPHAM. Hungry! I thought he looked thin! Wait a minute, dear! Emma Popham knows what her boy fancies! *She runs out of the room.*

CIS. Oh, Beatie, hold my head while I ask you something.

BEATIE. Yes, darling!

CIS. No lady would marry a gentleman who had been a convict, would she?

BEATIE. No: certainly not!

CIS. I thought not! Well, Beatie, I've been run after by a policeman.

BEATIE, *leaving him.* Oh!

CIS. Not caught, you know, only run after; and, walking home from Hendon this morning, I came to the conclusion that I ought to settle down in life. Beatie—could I write out a paper promising to marry you when I'm one-and-twenty?

BEATIE. Don't be a silly boy—of course you could.

CIS. Then, I shall; and when I feel inclined to have a spree, I shall think of that paper and say, "Cis Farringdon, if you ever get locked up, you'll lose the most beautiful girl in the world."

BEATIE. And so you will.

CIS, *going to the writing-table.* I'd better write it now, before my head gets well again.

    He writes, she bends over him.

BEATIE. You simple, foolish Cis! If your head is so queer, shall I tell you what to say?

    POPHAM *enters carrying a tray with breakfast dishes.*

The Magistrate

POPHAM, *to herself.* He won't think so much of *her* now. His breakfast is my triumph. *To* CIS. Coffee, bacon, and a teacake.

BEATIE. Hush! Master Farringdon is writing something very important.

POPHAM, *going to window.* That's a cab at our door.

CIS. It must be the Mater—I'm off! *He picks up his boots and goes out quickly.*

BEATIE, *following him with the paper and inkstand.* Cis! Cis! You haven't finished the promise! You haven't finished the promise!

LUGG, *heard outside.* All right, sir—I've got you—I've got you.

POPHAM *opens door.*

POPHAM. The Master and a policeman!

LUGG *enters, supporting* POSKET, *who sinks into an armchair with a groan.*

Oh, what's the matter?

LUGG. All right, my good girl, you run downstairs and fetch a drop of brandy and water.

POPHAM *hurries out.*

POSKET. Oh!

LUGG. Now, don't take on, sir. It's what might happen to any married gentleman. Now, you're all right now, sir. And I'll hurry back to the Court to see whether they've sent for Mr. Bullamy.

POSKET. My wife! My wife!

LUGG. Oh, come now, sir, what *is* seven days! Why, many a married gentleman in your position, sir, would have been glad to have made it fourteen.

POSKET. Go away—leave me.

LUGG. Certainly, sir.

POPHAM *re-enters with a small tumbler of brandy and water; he takes it from her and drinks it.*

It's not wanted. I'm thankful to say he's better.

POPHAM, *to* LUGG. If you please, cook presents her compliments, and she would be glad of the pleasure of you downstairs, before leavin'.

They go out.

POSKET. Agatha and Lukyn! Agatha and Lukyn supping together at the Hôtel des Princes, while I was at home and asleep—while I ought to have been at home and asleep! It's awful!

CIS, *looking in at the door and entering.* Hallo, Guv!

POSKET, *starting up.* Cis!

CIS. Where did you fetch, Guv?

POSKET. Where did I fetch! You wretched boy! I fetched Kilburn, and I'll fetch you a sound whipping when I recover my composure.

CIS. What for?

POSKET. For leading me astray, sir. Yours is the first bad companionship I have ever formed! Evil communication with you, sir, has corrupted me! *Taking* CIS *by the collar and shaking him.* Why did you abandon me at Kilburn?

CIS. Because you were quite done, and I branched off to draw the crowd away from you after me.

POSKET. Did you, Cis, did you? *Putting his hand on* CIS's *shoulder.* My boy— my boy! Oh, Cis, we're in such trouble!

CIS. You weren't caught, Guv.

POSKET. No—but do you know who the ladies are who were supping at the Hôtel des Princes?

CIS. No—do you?

POSKET. Do I? They were your mother and Aunt Charlotte.

CIS. The Mater and Aunt Charlotte! Ha, ha, ha! *Laughing and dancing with delight.* Ha! ha! Oh, I say, Guv, what a lark!

POSKET. A lark! They were taken to the police station!

CIS, *changing his tone.* My mother?

POSKET. They were examined by the magistrate and sentenced.

CIS. Sentenced?

POSKET. To seven days' imprisonment.

CIS. Oh! *He puts on his hat fiercely.*

POSKET. What are you going to do?

CIS. Get my mother out first, and then break every bone in that magistrate's body.

POSKET. Cis! Cis! he's an unhappy wretch and he did his duty.

CIS. His duty! To send another magistrate's wife to prison! Guv, I'm only a boy, but I know what professional etiquette is! Come along! Which is the police station?

POSKET. Mulberry Street.

CIS. Who's the magistrate?

POSKET. I am!

CIS. You! *Seizing* POSKET *by the collar and shaking him.* You dare to lock up my mother! Come with me and get her out!

He is dragging POSKET *towards the door, when* BULLAMY *enters breathlessly.*

BULLAMY. My dear Posket!

CIS, *seizing* BULLAMY, *and dragging him with* POSKET *to the door.* Come with me to get my mother out.

BULLAMY. Leave me alone, sir! She *is* out! I managed it.

POSKET ⎱
CIS   ⎰ How?

BULLAMY. Wormington sent to me when you were taken ill. When I arrived at the Court, he had discovered, from your man-servant, Mrs. Posket's awful position.

CIS. You leave my mother alone! Go on!

BULLAMY. Said I to myself, "This won't do, I must extricate these people somehow!" *To* POSKET. I'm not so damned conscientious as you are, Posket.

CIS. Bravo! Go on!

BULLAMY, *producing his jujube-box.* The first thing I did was to take a jujube.

CIS, *snatching the jujube-box from him.* Will you make haste?

BULLAMY. Then said I to Wormington, "Posket was *non compos mentis* when he heard this case—I'm going to reopen the matter!"

CIS. Hurrah!

BULLAMY. And I did! And what do you think I found out from the proprietor of the hotel?

POSKET ⎫
CIS ⎭ What?

BULLAMY. That this young scamp, Mr. Cecil Farringdon, hires a room at the Hôtel des Princes.

CIS. I know that.

BULLAMY. And that Mr. Farringdon was there last night with some low stockbroker of the name of Skinner.

CIS. Go on—go on! *Offering him the jujube-box.* Take a jujube!

BULLAMY, *taking a jujube.* Now the law, which seems to me quite perfect, allows a man who rents a little apartment at an inn to eat and drink with his friends all night long.

CIS. Well?

BULLAMY. So said I from the bench, "These ladies and gentlemen appear to be friends or relatives of a certain lodger in the Hôtel des Princes."

CIS. So they are!

BULLAMY. "They were all discovered in one room."

POSKET. So we were—I mean, so they were!

BULLAMY. "And I shall adjourn the case for a week to give Mr. Farringdon an opportunity of claiming these people as his guests."

CIS. Three cheers for Bullamy.

BULLAMY. So I censured the police for their interference and released the ladies on their own recognizances.

POSKET, *taking* BULLAMY's *hand.* And the men?

BULLAMY. Well, unfortunately, Wormington took upon himself to despatch the men to the House of Correction before I arrived.

POSKET. I'm glad of it! They are dissolute villains! I'm glad of it.

POPHAM, *entering*. Oh, sir! Here's the Missis and Miss Verrinder! In such a plight!

CIS. The Mater! Guv, you explain! *Hurries out.*

> POSKET *rapidly retires into the window recess.* AGATHA *and* CHARLOTTE *enter, pale, red-eyed, and agitated.* POPHAM *goes out.*

AGATHA
CHARLOTTE } *falling onto* BULLAMY'S *shoulders.* O—o—h—h!

BULLAMY. My dear ladies!

AGATHA. Preserver!

CHARLOTTE. Friend!

AGATHA. How is my boy?

BULLAMY. Never better.

AGATHA. And the man who condemned his wife and sister-in-law to the miseries of a jail!

BULLAMY. Ahem! Posket—oh—he——

AGATHA. Is he well enough to be told what that wife thinks of him?

BULLAMY. It might cause a relapse!

AGATHA. It is my duty to risk that.

CHARLOTTE, *raising the covers of the dishes on the table.* Food!

AGATHA. Ah!

> AGATHA *and* CHARLOTTE *begin to devour a teacake voraciously.*

POSKET, *advancing, with an attempt at dignity.* Agatha Posket.

AGATHA, *rising, with her mouth full, and a piece of teacake in her hand.* Sir!

> CHARLOTTE *takes the tray and everything on it from the table and goes toward the door.*

BULLAMY, *going to the door.* There's going to be an explanation.

CHARLOTTE, *at door.* There's going to be an explanation.

> CHARLOTTE *and* BULLAMY *go out, quietly.*

POSKET. How dare you look me in the face, madam.

AGATHA. How dare you look at anybody in any position, sir? You send your wife to prison for pushing a mere policeman.

POSKET. I didn't know what I was doing.

AGATHA. Not when you requested two ladies to raise their veils and show their faces in the dock? We shouldn't have been discovered but for that.

POSKET. It was my duty.

AGATHA. Duty! You don't go to the police court again alone! I guess now, Æneas Posket, why you clung to a single life so long. *You liked it!*

POSKET. I wish I had.

AGATHA. Why didn't you marry till you were fifty?

POSKET. Perhaps I hadn't met a widow, madam.

AGATHA. Paltry excuse. You reveled in a dissolute bachelorhood!

POSKET. Hah! Whist every evening!

AGATHA. You can't play whist *alone*. You're an expert at hiding too!

POSKET. If I were I should thrash your boy!

AGATHA. When you wished to conceal yourself last night, you selected a table with a lady under it.

POSKET. Ah, did you pinch me, or did Charlotte?

AGATHA. I did; Charlotte's a single girl.

POSKET. I fancy, madam, you found my conduct under that table perfectly respectful?

AGATHA. I don't know—I was too agitated to notice.

POSKET. Evasion—you're like all the women.

AGATHA. Profligate! You oughtn't to know that!

POSKET. No wife of mine sups, unknown to me, with dissolute military men; we will have a judicial separation, Mrs. Posket.

AGATHA. Certainly—I suppose you'll manage that at your police court too?

POSKET. I shall send for my solicitor at once.

AGATHA. Æneas! Mr. Posket! Whatever happens you shall not have the custody of my boy.

POSKET. Your boy! *I* take charge of *him?* Agatha Posket, he has been my evil genius! He has made me a punter at an atrocious game, called "Fireworks"—he has tortured my mind with abstruse speculations concerning "Sillikin" and "Butterscotch" for the St. Leger—he has caused me to cower before servants, and to fly before the police!

AGATHA. He! My Cis?

CIS *enters, having changed his clothes.*

CIS, *breezily.* Hallo, Mater—got back?

AGATHA. You wicked boy! You dare to have apartments at the Hôtel des Princes!

POSKET. Yes—and it was to put a stop to that which induced me to go to Meek Street last night.

CIS. Don't be angry, Mater! I've got you out of your difficulties.

POSKET. But you got me into mine!

CIS. Well, I know I did—one can't be always doing the right thing! It isn't Guv's fault—there!

POSKET. Swear it!

AGATHA. No, he doesn't know the nature of an oath! I believe him! Æneas, I see now, this is all the result of a lack of candour on my part. Tell me, have you ever particularly observed this child?

POSKET. Oh!

AGATHA. Has it ever struck you he is a little forward?

POSKET. Sometimes.

AGATHA. You are wrong; he is awfully backward. *Taking* MR. POSKET'S *hand.* Æneas; men always think they are marrying angels, and women would be angels if they never had to grow old. That warps their dispositions. I have deceived you, Æneas.

POSKET. Ah! Lukyn!

AGATHA. No—no—you don't understand! Lukyn was my boy's godfather in 1866.

POSKET. 1866?

CIS. 1886.

CIS } *together, reckoning rapidly upon their fingers.* 1886.
POSKET }

AGATHA. S-s-s-h! Don't count! Cis, go away! *To* POSKET. When you proposed to me in the Pantheon at Spa, you particularly remarked, "Mrs. Farringdon, I love you for yourself *alone.*"

POSKET. I know I did.

AGATHA. Those were terrible words to address to a widow with a son of nineteen.

CIS *and* POSKET *again reckon rapidly upon their fingers.*

Don't count, Æneas, don't count! those words tempted me. I glanced at my face in a neighbouring mirror and I said, "Æneas is fifty—why should I—a mere woman, compete with him on the question of age? He has already the advantage—I will be generous—I will add to it!" I led you to believe I had been married only fifteen years ago, I deceived you and my boy as to his real age, and I told you I was but one-and-thirty.

POSKET. It wasn't the truth!

AGATHA. Ah! I merely lacked woman's commonest fault, exaggeration.

POSKET. But—Lukyn?

AGATHA. Knows the real facts. I went to him last night to beg him not to disturb an arrangement which had brought happiness to all parties. Look! In place of a wayward, troublesome child, I now present you with a youth old enough to be a joy, comfort, and support!

CIS. Oh, I say, Mater, this is a frightful sell for a fellow.

AGATHA. Go to your room, sir!

CIS. I always thought there was something wrong with me. Blessed if I'm not behind the age! *Goes out.*

AGATHA. Forgive me, Æneas. Look at my bonnet! A night in Mulberry Street without even a powder puff is an awful expiation.

POSKET. Agatha! How do I know Cis won't be five-and-twenty to-morrow?

AGATHA. No—no—you know the worst, and as long as I live, I'll never deceive you again—except in little things.

LUKYN *and* VALE *enter.*

LUKYN, *boiling with rage.* By George, Posket!

POSKET. My dear Lukyn!

LUKYN. Do you know I am a confounded jailbird, sir?

POSKET. An accident!

LUKYN. And do you know what has happened to me in jail—a soldier, sir—an officer?

POSKET. No!

LUKYN. I have been washed by the authorities.

POSKET. Lukyn, no!

CHARLOTTE *has entered, and she rushes across to* VALE.

CHARLOTTE. Horace! Horace! Not you, too?

VALE. By Jove, Charlotte, I would have died first.

BULLAMY *enters quickly.*

BULLAMY. Mr. Posket, I shall choke, sir! Inspector Messiter is downstairs and says that Isidore the waiter swears that you are the man who escaped from Meek Street last night.

LUKYN. What?

BULLAMY. This is a public scandal, sir!

LUKYN. Your game is up, sir!

BULLAMY. You have brought a stain upon a spotless police court!

LUKYN. And lectured me upon propriety and decorum.

POSKET. Gentlemen, gentlemen, when you have heard my story you will pity me.

LUKYN
BULLAMY } *laughing ironically.* Ha! ha!

POSKET. You will find your old friend a Man, a Martyr, and a Magistrate!

CIS *enters, pulling* BEATIE *after him.*

CIS. Come on, Beatie! Guv—Mater! here's news! Beatie and I have made up our minds to be married.

AGATHA. Oh!

POPHAM *enters with champagne and glasses.*

POSKET. What's this?

CIS. Bollinger—'seventy-four—extra dry—to drink our health and happiness.

CHARLOTTE. Champagne! It may save my life!

AGATHA. Miss Tomlinson, go home!

POSKET. Stop! Cis Farringdon, my dear boy, you are but nineteen at present, but you were only fourteen yesterday, so you are a growing lad; on the day you marry and start for Canada, I will give you a thousand pounds!

POPHAM, *putting her apron to her eyes*. Oh!

CIS, *embracing* BEATIE. Hurrah! We'll be married directly.

AGATHA. He's an infant! I forbid it!

POSKET. I am his legal guardian. Gentlemen, bear witness! I solemnly consent to that little wretch's marriage!

AGATHA *sinks into chair*.

Anatol

by ARTHUR SCHNITZLER

English version by Harley Granville-Barker

Anatol

by ARTHUR SCHNITZLER

English version by Harley Granville-Barker

CHARACTERS

MAX
ANATOL
HILDA
GABRIELLE
BIANCA
EMILY
MIMI
WAITER
ELSA
FRANZ
LONA

EINLEITUNG

ANATOL has a famous introductory poem by "Loris," namely, Hugo von Hofmannsthal. Since it can be read in the original by anyone who knows a little German, and since no one has yet succeeded in making poetry of it in English, it is printed here in the original.

E.B.

Hohe Gitter, Taxushecken,
Wappen, nimmermehr vergoldet,
Sphinxe, durch das Dickicht schimmernd . . .
. . . Knarrend öffnen sich die Tore.—
Mit verschlafenen Kaskaden
Und verschlafenen Tritonen,
Rokoko, verstaubt und lieblich
Seht . . . das Wien des Canaletto,
Wien von Siebzehnhundertsechzig . . .
. . . Grüne, braune, stille Teiche,
Glatt und marmorweiss umrandet,
In dem Spiegelbild der Nixen
Spielen Gold- und Silberfische . . .
Auf dem glattgeschor'nen Rasen
Liegen zierlich gleiche Schatten
Schlanker Oleanderstämme;
Zweige wölben sich zur kuppel,
Zweige neigen sich zur Nische
Für die steifen Liebespaare
Heroinen und Heroen . . .
Drei Delphine giessen murmelnd
Fluten in ein Muschelbecken . . .
Duftige Kastanienblüten
Gleiten, schwirren leuchtend nieder
Und ertrinken in dem Becken . . .
. . . Hinter einer Taxusmauer
Tönen Geigen, Klarinetten . . .
Und sie scheinen den graziösen

Amoretten zu entströmen,
Die rings auf der Rampe sitzen
Fiedelnd oder Blumen windend,
Selbst von Blumen bunt umgeben,
Die aus Marmorvasen strömen:
Goldlack und Jasmin und Flieder . . .
. . . Auf der Rampe, zwischen ihnen
Sitzen auch kokette Frauen,
Violette Monsignori . . .
Und im Gras, zu ihren Füssen,
Und auf Polstern, auf den Stufen:
Cavaliere und Abbati . . .
And're heben and're Frauen
Aus den parfümierten Sänften . . .
. . . Durch die Zweige brechen Lichter,
Flimmernd auf den blonden Köpfchen;
Scheinen auf den bunten Polstern,
Gleiten über Kies und Rasen,
Gleiten über das Gerüste,
Das wir flüchtig aufgeschlagen.
Wein und Winde klettert aufwärts
Und umhüllt die lichten Balken.
Und dazwischen, farbenüppig
Flattert Teppich and Tapete,
Schäferszenen, keck gewoben,
Zierlich von Watteau entworfen . . .
Eine Laube statt der Bühne,
Sommersonne statt der Lampen,
Also spielen wir Theater,
Spielen uns're eig'nen Stücke,
Frühgereist und zart und traurig,
Die Komödie uns'rer Seele,
Uns'res Fühlens Heut und Gestern,
Böser Dinge hübsche Formel,
Glatte Worte, bunte Bilder,
Halbes, heimliches Empfinden,
Agonien, Episoden . . .
Manche hören zu, nicht alle . . .
Manche träumen, manche lachen,
Manche essen Eis . . . und manche

Sprechen sehr galante Dinge . . .
. . . Nelken wiegen sich im Winde,
Hochgestielte, weisse Nelken,
Wie ein Schwarm von weissen Faltern . . .
Und ein Bologneserhündchen
Bellt verwundert einen Pfau an . . .

Herbst 1892   LORIS

I

ASK NO QUESTIONS AND YOU'LL HEAR NO STORIES

ANATOL, *an idle young bachelor, lives in a charming flat in Vienna. That he has taste, besides means to indulge it, may be seen by his rooms, the furniture he buys, the pictures he hangs on the walls. And if such things indicate character, one would judge, first by the material comfort of the place and then by the impatience for new ideas which his sense of what is beautiful to live with seems to show, that though a hedonist, he is skeptical of even that easy faith. Towards dusk one afternoon he comes home bringing with him his friend* MAX. *They reach the sitting room, talking . . .*

MAX. Well, Anatol, I envy you.

ANATOL. My dear Max!

MAX. Perfectly astonishing. I've always said it was all tricks. But he went off to sleep under my very eyes . . . and then he danced when you told him he was a ballet dancer and cried when you said his sweetheart was dead . . . and he sentenced that criminal very soundly when you'd made him a judge.

ANATOL. Didn't he?

MAX. It's wizardry!

ANATOL. We can all be wizards to some extent.

MAX. Perfectly uncanny.

ANATOL. Not more so than much else in life . . . not more uncanny than lots we've been finding out the last hundred years. If you'd suddenly proved to one of our ancestors that the world went round, he'd have turned giddy.

MAX. But this seems supernatural.

ANATOL. So must anything strange. What would a man think if he'd never seen a sunrise before, or watched the spring arrive . . . the trees and the flowers . . . and then felt himself falling in love.

MAX. Mesmerism . . .

ANATOL. Hypnotism.

MAX. Yes . . . I'll take care no one ever does it to me.

ANATOL. Where's the harm? I tell you to go to sleep. You settle down comfortably . . . off you go . . .

MAX. Then you tell me I'm a chimney sweep, and up the chimney I go and get all over soot.

ANATOL. But, you know, it has great scientific possibilities. We're hardly on the threshold of them yet . . . worse luck.

MAX. Why worse luck?

ANATOL. I could make what I liked of the world for that fellow an hour ago. Can I shift it a jot from what it damnably is for myself?

MAX. Can't you?

ANATOL. Haven't I tried? I've stared and stared at this ring of mine, saying Sleep . . . and then wake with this little wretch that's driving you mad gone clean from your mind.

MAX. Still the same little wretch?

ANATOL. Of course. I'm damned wretched.

MAX. And still suspecting her?

ANATOL. Not a bit of it. I know perfectly well that she's untrue to me. She puts her arms round my neck and kisses me, and we're happy. But all the time . . . as sure as she's standing there . . . I know that she's . . .

MAX. Oh, nonsense!

ANATOL. Is it!

MAX. Then how do you know?

ANATOL. When I feel a thing as I feel this . . . it must be true.

MAX. That's unarguable, anyhow.

ANATOL. Besides, girls of this sort always are unfaithful. It comes naturally to them . . . it's a sort of instinct. Just as I have two or three books that I read at a time, they must keep two or three men hanging around.

MAX. But doesn't she love you?

ANATOL. What difference does that make?

MAX. Who's the other man?

ANATOL. How do I know? Some one has seen her in the shop. Some one has made eyes at her in the train going home.

MAX. Rubbish!

ANATOL. Why? All she wants is to have a good time without thinking about it. I ask her if she loves me. She says Yes . . . and it's perfectly true. Then . . . Am I the only man she loves? She says Yes again . . . and that's true, too, for the time being. For the time being she's forgotten the other fellow. Besides . . . what else can a woman say? She can't tell you. . . . No, my darling, the very moment your back is turned . . . ! Still . . . I wish I knew for certain.

MAX. My dear Anatol, if she really loves you . . .

ANATOL. Oh, innocent! I ask you what has that to do with it?

MAX. A great deal, I should hope.

ANATOL. Then why am I not true to her? I really love her, don't I?

MAX. You're a man.

ANATOL. Thank you . . . it only needed that! Of course . . . we are

men and women are different. Some! If their mammas lock them up
or if they're little fishes. Otherwise, my dear Max, women and men are
very much alike . . . especially women. And if I swear to one of them
that she's the only woman I love, is that lying to her . . . just because
the night before I've been saying the same thing to another?

MAX. Well . . . speak for yourself.

ANATOL. Cold-blooded, correct gentleman! I'm afraid dear Hilda's rather
less like you than she is like me. Perhaps she isn't . . . but perhaps
she is. I'd give a lot to know. I might go on my knees and swear I'd
forgiven her already . . . but she'd lie to me just the same. Haven't
I been begged with tears a dozen times . . . for God's sake to tell
them if I'm true. They won't say an angry word if I'm not . . . only
tell them. Then I've lied . . . calmly and cheerfully. And quite right
too. Why should I make poor women wretched? They've believed in
me and been happy.

MAX. Very well, then . . .

ANATOL. But I don't believe in her and I'm not happy. Oh . . . if some
one could invent a way to make these dear damnable little creatures
speak the truth!

MAX. What about your hypnotism?

ANATOL. My . . . ?

MAX. Put her to sleep and draw it like a tooth.

ANATOL. I could.

MAX. What an opportunity.

ANATOL. Isn't it?

MAX. Does she love you . . . or who else is it? Where's she just been . . .
where's she going? What's his name . . . ?

ANATOL. Oh, if I knew that!

MAX. But you've only to ask her . . .

ANATOL. And she must answer.

MAX. You lucky fellow!

ANATOL. Yes . . . I am. It'll be my own fault if I worry any more, won't
it? She's under my thumb now, isn't she?

MAX. I say . . . I'm curious to know.

ANATOL. Why . . . d'you think she's not straight?

MAX. Oh . . . may nobody think it but you?

ANATOL. No, nobody may. When you've just found your wife in another
man's arms and an old friend meets you and says Poor fellow, I'm
afraid Madame isn't all that she should be . . . d'you clasp his hand
gratefully and tell him he's quite right? No . . . you knock him down.

MAX. Yes . . . the principal task of friendship is to foster one's friends' illusions.

ANATOL, *hearing something.* Tsch!

MAX. What?

ANATOL. How well I know the sound of her!

MAX. I don't . . .

ANATOL. In the hall. Here she is. Well . . . Hilda? *He opens the door to find her coming in.*

HILDA, *a personable young woman, enters.* Dearest! Oh . . . somebody with you.

ANATOL. Only Max.

HILDA. How are you? All in the dark!

ANATOL. I like the gloaming.

HILDA. Romantic darling.

ANATOL. Dearest.

HILDA. But don't let's have any more of it. You don't mind, do you? *She turns up the lights and then takes off her hat and things, and makes herself quite at home.*

ANATOL, *under his breath.* Isn't she . . . ? *Praise fails him.*

MAX, *with a shade of irony.* She is!

HILDA. Had a nice long talk?

ANATOL. Half an hour.

HILDA. What about?

ANATOL. All sorts of things.

MAX. Hypnotism.

HILDA. You're all going mad about that.

ANATOL. Yes . . .

HILDA. Anatol, why don't you hypnotize me some time?

ANATOL, *staggered at the sudden opportunity.* D'you mean it?

HILDA. Rather! Awfully jolly if you'd do it, darling.

ANATOL. Much obliged.

HILDA. Not any strange person messing about of course.

ANATOL. Very well . . . I'll hypnotize you.

HILDA. When?

ANATOL. Now.

HILDA. Will you? Oh, how nice! What do I do?

ANATOL. Sit in that chair and go to sleep.

HILDA. That all?

He settles her on a chair, and, taking another, settles himself opposite. MAX *is discreet in the background.*

ANATOL. You must look at me . . . straight at me. And then I stroke your forehead . . . and then over your eyes . . . like this.

HILDA. What else?

ANATOL. Let yourself go.

HILDA, *sitting limply with her eyes shut.* When you stroke me like that . . . it makes me feel funny all over.

ANATOL. Don't talk . . . go to sleep. You are rather sleepy.

HILDA. No, I'm not.

ANATOL. Just a little.

HILDA, *in tune with him.* Yes . . . just a little.

ANATOL. Oh . . . it's so hard to keep awake. Don't try. Why . . . you can't lift up your hand.

HILDA, *tonelessly.* No . . . I can't.

ANATOL, *making wider passes, and his voice is wonderfully soothing.* You are so sleepy . . . so sleepy . . . so very sleepy. Well, then . . . sleep, dear child, sleep . . . sleep. You can't open your eyes now.
It seems as if she made the most helpless effort.

ANATOL. You can't . . . because you're asleep. Keep sleeping . . .

MAX, *really excited.* Is she . . . ?

ANATOL. S-sh! *Then as before.* Sleeping . . . sleeping . . . fast asleep.
He stands silently for a minute looking down at HILDA *as she sleeps. Then he turns to* MAX *and says in his ordinary tones.*

ANATOL. All right now.

MAX. Is she really asleep?

ANATOL. Look at her. Let her be for a minute.
For a minute they both watch her.

ANATOL. Hilda, answer me when I ask you. What's your name?
Her mouth opens and the word is slowly formed.

HILDA. Hilda.

ANATOL. Hilda . . . we're walking along a road . . . out in the country.

HILDA. Yes . . . isn't it pretty? That's a tall tree. There's a bird singing . . .

ANATOL. Hilda . . . you're going to tell me the truth. Do you understand?

HILDA, *slowly again.* I am going to tell you the truth.

ANATOL. Answer me all I ask you quite truthfully . . . but when you wake up you will have forgotten. Do you understand?

HILDA. Yes.

ANATOL. Then sleep . . . soundly.
He turns to MAX *and they look at each other triumphantly, but hesitant.*

ANATOL. How shall we begin?

MAX, *after a moment.* How old is she?

ANATOL. She's nineteen. Hilda . . . how old are you?

HILDA. Twenty-five.

MAX. Oh! *And he dissolves into silent guffaws.*

ANATOL. Tsch! That's odd. But . . . *He brightens* . . . but there you are.

MAX. She never thought she'd be such a success.

ANATOL. Well . . . one more martyr to science. Let's try again. Hilda, do you love me? Hilda dear . . . do you love me?

HILDA. Yes.

ANATOL. There . . . that's the truth.

MAX. And now for the all-important question . . . is she true to you?

ANATOL, *striking the correct attitude for this.* Yes. Hilda, are you . . . ? *He frowns.* No . . . that won't do.

MAX. Why not?

ANATOL. I can't put it that way.

MAX. It's a simple question.

ANATOL. Not at all. Are you true to me! It may mean anything.

MAX. How?

ANATOL. She might look back over her whole life. You don't suppose she never fell in love till she met me, do you?

MAX. Well . . . I should like to hear about it.

ANATOL. Would you, indeed! Prying into schoolgirl secrets! How was the poor child to know that one day she'd meet me?

MAX. Of course she didn't.

ANATOL. Very well, then.

MAX. So why shouldn't she tell us?

ANATOL. I don't like putting it that way, and I shan't.

MAX. What about . . . Hilda, since you've known me have you been true to me?

ANATOL. Ah, that's different. *He faces the sleeper again.* Hilda . . . since you've known me have you been . . . *Again he frowns and stops.* And it's rather worse.

MAX. Worse?

ANATOL. Think how all love affairs begin. We met quite casually. How could we tell we should one day be all in all to each other?

MAX. Of course you couldn't.

ANATOL. Very well, then. Suppose when she first knew me she had some idle fancy still to shake free of . . . am I to blame her for that?

MAX. You make better excuses than ever she could.

ANATOL. Is it fair to take such an advantage of the girl?

MAX, *with a twisty smile*. You're a good fellow, Anatol. Try this. Hilda . . . since you've loved me, have you been true to me?

ANATOL. Yes . . . that's better.

MAX. Right.

Once more ANATOL *fixes his love with a gesture. But he suddenly drops it.*

ANATOL. No, it won't do . . . it won't do.

MAX. Well, really!

ANATOL. Think a minute. She's sitting in a train. A man opposite . . . good-looking fellow . . . slides his foot against hers. She looks up.

MAX. Well?

ANATOL. Think of the extraordinary subtlety of mind that has been engendered in her by this hypnotic trance. In her present unconscious state the remembrance of looking up not displeased might well be recalled as an act of infidelity.

MAX. Oh, come!

ANATOL. That's perfectly sound. And the more so because she already knows my views on such a point . . . which are a little exaggerated. I've often warned her not to go looking at men.

MAX. What has she said to that?

ANATOL. Oh . . . asked me to imagine her doing such a thing!

MAX. Which you were imagining quite well ten minutes ago.

ANATOL. Suppose she was kissed under the mistletoe last Christmas . . .

MAX. No . . . really!

ANATOL. She may have been.

MAX. All this means is, that you won't ask her the question.

ANATOL. Not at all. I will ask her the question. But . . .

MAX. Anatol, it won't do. Ask a woman if she's true to you and she doesn't think of men treading on her foot or kissing her under the mistletoe. Besides, if the answer's not clear, we can make her go into details.

ANATOL. I see. You've made up your mind I shall ask her, have you?

MAX. Dash it, no! It's you want to find things out . . . not I.

ANATOL. Yes. There's another thing to think of.

MAX. What now?

ANATOL. What about her sub-responsible self?

MAX. What the devil's that?

ANATOL. Under the stimulus of certain extraordinary circumstances, I quite believe that one is not a fully independent agent.

MAX. Would you put that into English?

ANATOL. Well . . . imagine some room . . . softly curtained . . . dimly lit . . . glowing with warmth and colour.

MAX. Right . . . I've imagined it.

ANATOL. There she sits . . . she and some other man.

MAX. But what's she doing there at all?

ANATOL. That's not the point for the moment. She is there, we'll suppose. Supper . . . a glass of wine . . . cigarettes . . . silence. And then a whispered word or two . . . ! Oh, my dear Max, colder women than she haven't stood prim against such temptation.

MAX. I should say that if you're in love with some one, you've no business to find yourself in a room like that with somebody else.

ANATOL. But I know how things will happen.

MAX. Anatol, it won't do. Here's your riddle with its answer ready. It's to be solved with a word. One question to find out if she's yours alone. One more to find out who shares her with you . . . and how big is the share. You won't ask them. You suffer agonies. What wouldn't you give to know . . . just to be sure. Well, here's the book open . . . and you won't even turn the page. Why? Because you might find written there that a woman you're in love with is no better than you swear all women are. You don't want the truth . . . you want to keep your illusions. Wake her up . . . and tomorrow be content with the glorious thought that you could have found out . . . only you wouldn't.

ANATOL. I . . . I . . .

MAX. You've been talking nonsense. It hasn't taken me in if it has you.

ANATOL. I will ask her.

MAX. Will you?

ANATOL. Yes . . . but not in front of you.

MAX. Why not?

ANATOL. If I'm to know the worst, I'll hear it privately. Being hurt is only half as bad as being pitied for it. I don't want your kind face to be telling me just how hard the knock is. You'll know just the same, because if she's . . . if she has been . . . then we've seen the last of her. But you won't be there at the awful moment. D'you mind?

MAX. Shall I wait in your bedroom?

ANATOL. Yes. It won't take a moment.

MAX *retires, and* ANATOL *faces the sleeping girl, who is half-smiling in her sleep. He braces himself for the effort, then speaks sternly, judicially.*

ANATOL. Hilda . . . do you . . . ? *He fails, then makes a further effort.* Hilda . . . are you . . . ? *He fails again and turns distractedly away.*

Then for the third time. Hilda . . . have you . . . ? *He begins to sweat with the emotion of it.*

ANATOL. Oh, Lord! Hilda . . . Hilda . . .

And then, with one qualm as to whether MAX *can overhear, he throws himself on his knees beside the girl.*

Oh . . . wake up, my darling, and give me a kiss.

With a couple of waves he can release her, and she sits up quite brightly.

HILDA. Have I been like that long? Where's Max?

ANATOL. Max!

MAX, *coming out of the bedroom, mischievously watchful.* Here.

ANATOL. Yes . . . a sound sleep. You've been saying things.

HILDA. Anything I shouldn't?

MAX. He's been asking you questions.

HILDA. What sort?

ANATOL. All sorts.

HILDA. And I answered them?

ANATOL, *with a look at* MAX. Every one.

HILDA. Oh, tell me . . . !

ANATOL. Aha! . . . we'll try again tomorrow.

HILDA. No, we won't. You asking me what you like . . . and now I can't remember any of it. I may have said the most awful things.

ANATOL. You said you loved me.

HILDA. Did I?

MAX. Who'd have thought it!

HILDA. I can say that better when I'm awake.

ANATOL. Sweetheart!

MAX. Good afternoon!

ANATOL. Going?

MAX. I must.

ANATOL. You can find your way out?

HILDA. Ta-ta.

MAX, *beckoning to* ANATOL, *who follows him to the door.* Perhaps you've made a scientific discovery besides. That women tell lies just as well when they're asleep. But so long as you're happy . . . what's the odds?

He departs, leaving the couple locked in a fond embrace.

II

A CHRISTMAS PRESENT

It is Christmas Eve, about five o'clock. In a bystreet, that links up two others busy with shops, a builder's scaffold has formed a little arcade. Beneath this, and just beside a big arc lamp that sheds its whiteness down, ANATOL, *hurrying along with umbrella up, meets* GABRIELLE.

ANATOL, *stopping.* Oh! How do you do?

GABRIELLE. Why, it's you!

ANATOL. What are you doing? All those parcels . . . and no umbrella!

GABRIELLE. I'm trying to find a cab.

ANATOL. But it's raining.

GABRIELLE. That's the reason. I've been buying presents.

ANATOL. Let me carry some of them . . . please.

GABRIELLE. It doesn't matter.

ANATOL. I insist. *He captures one.* But hadn't you better wait here in shelter? We shall find a cab just as quickly.

GABRIELLE. You really mustn't trouble.

ANATOL. Let me be a little attentive for once in a way.

GABRIELLE. I'll wait here a minute to see if one passes. Or I'll be grateful for the umbrella. *He tries for another parcel.* No, I can manage that, thanks. It's not at all heavy. *But she surrenders it.* Oh, very well then!

ANATOL. Won't you believe that I like being polite?

GABRIELLE. As one only notices it when it's raining, and I haven't an umbrella . . .

ANATOL. And it's Christmas Eve, and dark too . . . ! Warm weather for Christmas, isn't it?

GABRIELLE. Very. *They take their stand looking out for a cab to pass.* Marvelous to see you at all.

ANATOL. I've not been to call once this year . . . is that what you mean?

GABRIELLE, *with much indifference.* Oh, haven't you?

ANATOL. The fact is I've not been anywhere much. How is your husband . . . and how are the dear children?

GABRIELLE. Why ask that? You don't in the least want to know.

ANATOL. You read me like a book.

GABRIELLE. It's such very large print.

ANATOL. I wish you knew more of it . . . by heart.

GABRIELLE, *with a toss of her head.* Don't say things like that.

ANATOL. They just spring from me.

GABRIELLE. Give me my parcels. I'll walk on.

ANATOL. Oh, don't be angry . . . I'll be as prim and proper as you please.

GABRIELLE. There's a cab. No, it's full. Oh, dear, shall I have to wait long? *He is standing mum.* Do say something.

ANATOL. I'm longing to . . . but the censorship is so strict.

GABRIELLE. You can tell me your news, can't you? It's ages since we met. What are you doing now?

ANATOL. As usual . . . nothing.

GABRIELLE. Nothing?

ANATOL. Rather less than nothing.

GABRIELLE. Isn't that a pity?

ANATOL. Why say that . . . when you don't in the least care?

GABRIELLE. You shouldn't take that for granted.

ANATOL. If I'm wasting my life, whose fault is it? Whose, would you mind telling me?

GABRIELLE. I'd better go on. Give me my parcels.

ANATOL, *mischievously.* I didn't imply it was any one's fault in particular. I just wanted your valuable opinion.

GABRIELLE, *with a touch of feeling.* You idler!

ANATOL. Don't despise idlers. They're the last word in civilisation. But I'm not idling tonight. I'm as busy as you are.

GABRIELLE. What with?

ANATOL. I'm out to buy Christmas presents, too.

GABRIELLE. Are you?

ANATOL. If I could find anything worth buying. I've been looking at the shops for weeks. They haven't a notion amongst 'em.

GABRIELLE. That's what the good customer has to supply. But, bless me! an idle person like you ought to be thinking out his presents all the summer.

ANATOL. How could I? How can I tell in the summer who I may be making up to at Christmas? And the shops will be shut in an hour or two, and I'm still empty-handed!

GABRIELLE. Could I help?

ANATOL. Oh, you are a darling! What's my best shop?

GABRIELLE. Well, you must know that. We'll take the cab there when we find it.

ANATOL. Thank you for passing the Darling . . . it's my favorite word.

GABRIELLE. I ignored it.

ANATOL. Very well . . . I'm prim and proper again.

GABRIELLE. Where shall we go when the cab comes? What sort of a present? Who's it for?

ANATOL. Now . . . how shall I tell you?

GABRIELLE. It's for a woman, of course.

ANATOL. Didn't I say you could read me like a book?

GABRIELLE. What sort of a woman?

ANATOL. There, again! How do you women sort yourselves out?

GABRIELLE. Is it a woman I know?

ANATOL. Not at all.

GABRIELLE. Not . . . a woman I should call on?

ANATOL. Never.

GABRIELLE. No . . . I thought as much.

ANATOL. Don't sneer.

GABRIELLE. You have extraordinary tastes. What's she like . . . pretty-pretty?

ANATOL. Pretty.

GABRIELLE. A man is a marvelous creature. Good breeding, good manners, are nothing to you!

ANATOL. Oh, a great deal . . . when they'll condescend to us. But if they won't . . .

GABRIELLE. Don't be silly again. No, you prefer a cheap and easy conquest!

ANATOL. I go where I'm appreciated.

GABRIELLE. Can she read you like a book?

ANATOL. God forbid. But she admires the binding, and takes the rest on trust. While you despise the contents . . . as if you really knew them!

GABRIELLE. I really don't know what you mean. I can tell you of an excellent shop; I passed it just now. Cases of scent in the window. One with three sorts . . . Patchouli, Jockey Club, Cherry Blossom. I'm sure that's the very thing.

ANATOL. You're unkind.

GABRIELLE. Well, there was another shop next door . . . with brooches and suchlike. One with six Parisian diamonds in it . . . six. Oh, so sparkling! Or a bracelet with charms hung round; or a long bead necklace . . . quite savage! That's the sort of thing these ladies like, isn't it?

ANATOL. I'm afraid you know nothing about them.

GABRIELLE. Or I can tell you of a hat shop with a style of its own. Their bows are too large, and they put in a feather too many. These persons like to be conspicuous, don't they?

ANATOL. Not at all.

GABRIELLE. It's hard to be helpful. Make a suggestion yourself.

ANATOL. You're waiting to laugh at it.

GABRIELLE. I promise I won't. Let me know what she likes. Is she demure in sealskins?

ANATOL. I said you'd laugh.

GABRIELLE. I'm not laughing. Tell me about her.

ANATOL. I don't think I can.

GABRIELLE. Of course you can. How long have you known her?

ANATOL. Oh . . .

GABRIELLE. Well?

ANATOL. Ever so long.

GABRIELLE. Don't be so difficult. Tell me all about it.

ANATOL. There's nothing to tell.

GABRIELLE. What nonsense! Where did you meet her and what's she like? What's her name and her age? Is she tall or short and dark or fair?

ANATOL. It'll only bore you.

GABRIELLE. No it won't. I've always wanted to know about that sort of person . . . what they're really like.

ANATOL. You'll never know.

GABRIELLE. Why not?

ANATOL. As long as you fully believe that women you can't call on don't really exist at all.

GABRIELLE. But I want to learn better. And if no one dares tell me the truth . . .

ANATOL, *with a sudden break of tone.* Haven't you very virtuous ladies a feeling that this other sort of woman . . . somehow gets the better of you after all?

GABRIELLE. That's a delicate insult.

ANATOL. You wouldn't change places, of course, but . . . how dare she be so improperly happy?

GABRIELLE. Is it the only way then?

ANATOL. That's feminine fellow feeling, I'm told . . . and therefore all that's charming and charitable.

GABRIELLE. You've learnt to be very sarcastic since we last met.

ANATOL, *seriously, almost passionately.* Shall I tell you how? Once I used to believe that a good woman so-called was an honest woman. I've taken a few knockdown blows with my teeth shut . . .

GABRIELLE. Please don't be heroic . . . that's far worse!

ANATOL. Straight blows. I can take a No when it's honestly meant and said without flinching. But when the eyes say Perhaps and the smile says Wait a little, and what the No means is Yes Yes Yes . . . if only I dared! Then . . .

GABRIELLE, *biting her lips.* I think I won't wait for this cab to come by . . .

ANATOL. Then you've your choice between feeling a fool and becoming a cynic.

GABRIELLE. . . . unless you mean to go on telling me about . . . about your new friend.

ANATOL, *back to his bantering humor.* You simply must know, must you?

GABRIELLE. Certainly I must. How did you first meet?

ANATOL. How does one meet people? In the streets, at the seaside, in an omnibus, sharing an umbrella!

GABRIELLE. Never mind how one meets people. How did you meet her . . . the Her we're finding a Christmas present for? I'm sure she's like nobody else.

ANATOL. She's just as like every other girl of her sort as you are like every other woman of yours.

GABRIELLE, *for the first time really annoyed.* Am I indeed!

ANATOL. Oh, don't be offended. Or as I'm like every other man of mine. Are there a dozen different patterns of any of us altogether?

GABRIELLE. What's yours?

ANATOL. I, madam, am a Toy Philosopher.

GABRIELLE. And mine?

ANATOL. You are a Married Lady.

GABRIELLE. And what's she?

ANATOL. She? She is just a Dear Little Girl.

GABRIELLE. Then let's hear all about your Dear Little Girl.

ANATOL. It's not that she's so pretty, or so smart . . . and certainly not that she's so clever.

GABRIELLE. Never mind what she's not.

ANATOL. She's as sweet as a wild flower, and as elusive as a fairy tale . . . and she knows what love means.

GABRIELLE. No doubt. These Dear Little Girls have every chance to learn.

ANATOL. Quite so, but you'll never learn what she's really like. For when you were a dear little girl . . . of another sort . . . you knew nothing at all. And now you're a married lady you think you're so worldly wise.

GABRIELLE. Not at all. I'm quite openmouthed for your fairy tale. What sort of a castle does the princess live in?

ANATOL. Can you imagine a fairy princess in anything but the smartest of drawing rooms?

GABRIELLE, *a little tartly*. Thank you, I can.

ANATOL. Because this one lives in a little room . . . with a cheap and nasty wallpaper. With a few Christmas numbers hanging about and a white shaded lamp on her table. You can see the sun set from the window over the roofs and through the chimneys. And in the spring you can almost smell the flowers in a garden across the way.

GABRIELLE. It must be a sign of great happiness . . . looking forward to the spring.

ANATOL. Yes, even I feel happy now and then . . . sitting with her at that window.

GABRIELLE, *giving a little shiver*. It is getting late. Shall we walk on? You must buy her something. Something to hang on the nasty wallpaper and hide it a little.

ANATOL. She thinks it so pretty.

GABRIELLE. Why don't you refurnish the room to your taste?

ANATOL. Why should I?

GABRIELLE. With a Persian carpet, and . . .

ANATOL. No, no, no . . . She knows what she likes.
   There falls a little silence. But no cab passes.

GABRIELLE. Is she waiting for you now?

ANATOL. Sure to be.

GABRIELLE. What will she say when you come?

ANATOL. Oh . . . the right thing.

GABRIELLE. She knows your step on the stairs, doesn't she?

ANATOL. I expect so.

GABRIELLE. And goes to the door?

ANATOL. Yes.

GABRIELLE. And puts her arms round your neck, and says . . . What does she say?

ANATOL. The right thing.

GABRIELLE. What's that?

ANATOL. It's just . . . the right thing to say.

GABRIELLE. What was it yesterday?

ANATOL. It sounds nothing repeated. I suppose it's the way that she says it.

GABRIELLE. I'll imagine that. Tell me the words.

ANATOL. It is good to have you back again.

GABRIELLE. It is good . . . what?

ANATOL. To have you back again.

GABRIELLE. That's very beautiful.

ANATOL. You see . . . she means it.

GABRIELLE. And she lives there alone? You can always be with her?

ANATOL. She's quite alone. She has no father or mother.

GABRIELLE. And you . . . are all the world to her?

ANATOL, *the cynic in him shrugs his shoulders.* I hope so. For the moment. *There is another silence.*

GABRIELLE. I'm afraid I'm getting cold standing still . . . and all the cabs seem to be full.

ANATOL. I'm so sorry. I shouldn't have kept you. Let me see you home.

GABRIELLE. Yes . . . they'll all be fidgeting. But what about your present?

ANATOL. Never mind, I shall find something.

GABRIELLE. Will you? But I wanted to help you buy it.

ANATOL. No, no, you mustn't trouble.

GABRIELLE. I wish I could be there when you give it to her. I wish I could see that little room and that . . . lucky little girl. There's a cab empty. Call it, please.

ANATOL, *waving to the cab.* Taxi!

GABRIELLE. Thank you. *As the cab turns and she moves towards it.* May I send her something?

ANATOL. You?

GABRIELLE. Take her these flowers. Will you give her a message as well?

ANATOL. It's really most awfully good of you.

GABRIELLE. But you will take them to her, and promise to give her the message?

ANATOL. Certainly.

GABRIELLE. Promise.

ANATOL, *who has opened the cab door.* I promise. Why shouldn't I?

GABRIELLE. This is it . . .

ANATOL. Yes?

GABRIELLE. These flowers, dear little girl, are from . . . some one who might have been as happy as you . . . if she hadn't been quite such a coward! *Gets in without his help.* Tell him where to drive. *He does so, and goes his way.*

III

AN EPISODE

MAX'S *rooms are comfortable, if commonplace. The writing table he is sitting at is clumsy, but it's within reach of a cheerful fire. By the lamp on it he is reading a letter.*

MAX. We're back again for three months . . . you'll have seen it in the
papers. Old friends first . . . I'm coming along . . . Your affection-
ate Bibi. Nice little Bianca! I shall certainly stay in.
There's a knock at the door.
MAX. Already! No, this can't be . . . Come in.
ANATOL *walks in, carrying an enormous parcel. He looks most gloomy.*
ANATOL. How are you?
MAX. What on earth have you got there?
ANATOL. This is my past.
MAX. Your what?
ANATOL, *depositing the parcel on the table.* I have brought you my dead and
buried past. I want you to take care of it for me.
MAX. Why?
ANATOL, *with great solemnity.* May I sit down?
MAX, *as solemn as he.* You may.
ANATOL *takes off his hat and coat and settles himself in the most comfortable chair.*
ANATOL. May I smoke?
MAX. Try one of these.
ANATOL, *lighting a cigar and unbending a trifle.* I rather like these.
MAX, *pointing to the parcel.* Well?
ANATOL. I really cannot live with my past any longer. I'm going for a
holiday.
MAX. Ah!
ANATOL. I wish to begin a new life . . . even if I don't go on with it.
And this is naturally very much in the way.
MAX. In love again?
ANATOL. Out of love this time. So you might look after this rubbish for me.
MAX. Better burn it if it's rubbish.
ANATOL. I can't do that.
MAX. Why not?
ANATOL. This is how I'm true to them . . . to all the women I've ever
loved . . . I never forget a single one. I have only to turn over these
letters, and dead flowers, and locks of hair . . . You'll have to let me
come here and turn them over occasionally . . . and back they come
to me . . . I'm in love with them all again.
MAX. This is to be a sort of Usual place at half-past three and don't be
late . . . is it?
ANATOL. I've often wished there really were some Abracadabra which
would call them back out of the utter nothingness.

MAX. But a variegated sort of nothingness.

ANATOL. If I knew of a word . . .

MAX. Let's think of one. What about . . . My Only Love.

ANATOL. Yes . . . My Only Love! And then they'd all come. One from
a little suburban villa . . . one from her crowded drawing room . . .
one from her dressing room at the theatre . . .

MAX. Several from their dressing rooms at the theatre.

ANATOL. Several. One from a shop . . .

MAX. One from the arms of your successor!

ANATOL. One from the grave. One from here . . . one from there. Here
they all are!

MAX. Would you mind not speaking the word? I somehow don't think
they'd be pleasant company. I dare say they're not in love with you
still . . . but I'm pretty sure they're still jealous of each other.

ANATOL. Wise man! Let the phantoms rest.

MAX. And where am I to put this mausoleum?

ANATOL. I'd better undo it.

*He unwraps the parcel which is made up of a dozen or so other little parcels,
neatly tied up and ticketed.*

MAX, *gazing with delight.* Hullo!

ANATOL. Yes . . . I'm a methodical man.

MAX. Is it done alphabetically?

ANATOL. No, there's a label for each . . . like the motto in a cracker.
A verse or a phrase will recall the whole affair to me. No names!
Susan and Jane suggest nothing.

MAX. May I look?

ANATOL. I wonder if I can still fix them all. I can't have looked at some
of them for years.

ANATOL leans back in his chair, smoking. MAX *settles himself enjoyably to the
Past. He takes up the first packet and reads the motto.*

MAX.

"I loved her. When she left me I thought I should have killed her;
My kisses on your neck remain, and nothing else, Matilda."

But that's a name . . . what a name! Matilda!

ANATOL. It wasn't her real name, but I'd written "killed her," and there
aren't many rhymes to that. I always did kiss her on the neck, though.

MAX. Who was she?

ANATOL. It doesn't matter. I held her in my arms once. That's all there
is to her.

MAX, *putting the packet aside.* Stand down, Matilda. She does up small, anyhow.

ANATOL. One lock of hair.

MAX. No letters?

ANATOL. Letters from Matilda! That would have inked her fingers. Don't you sometimes wish women weren't taught to write? Exit Matilda.

MAX, *reading another label.* "Women are alike in one thing . . . they turn impudent if you catch them out in a lie."

ANATOL. They do.

MAX. Who was it? She's very heavy.

ANATOL. Lies eight pages long. Oh . . . put it away.

MAX. Was she so very impudent?

ANATOL. When I found her out. Throw her away.

MAX. Impudent little liar!

ANATOL. No . . . you mustn't insult her. I have held her in my arms. She is sacred.

MAX. How stupid of me! Who's next? *A third packet.*
"When sad, my child, and sick of earth,
My thoughts to your Young Man fly far,
And then I laugh for all I'm worth;
Oh, dear, how funny some things are!"

ANATOL. So they were!

MAX. What's inside?

ANATOL. A photograph. She and the Young Man.

MAX. Did you know him, too?

ANATOL. That's what was so funny. He really was quite an exceptional fool.

MAX. Hush! She has held him in her arms . . . he is sacred.

ANATOL. You shut up.

MAX. Stand down, my child, with your exceptionally foolish and mirth-provoking young man. *A fourth package.* What's this?

ANATOL. What?

MAX. "A box on the ears."

ANATOL. Oh . . . ! Oh, yes . . . yes . . . yes!

MAX. Was that how it ended?

ANATOL. No, how it began.

MAX. Ah! *A fifth label.* "How hard it is to grow a flower, but it's so easy to pick it." What does that mean?

ANATOL. Some other fellow grew the flower . . . I came along and picked it.

MAX. Oh! *A sixth label.* "She always carried her curling tongs."

ANATOL. Do you know she always did. Then it didn't matter what happened. I tell you . . . she was damn pretty. There's a bit of her veil left, isn't there?

MAX. It feels like that. *A seventh label.* "How did I lose you?" How did you lose her?

ANATOL. That's the point . . . I never knew. One fine day she just wasn't. Don't you know how you leave your umbrella somewhere . . . don't think of it till days later . . . no idea where you put it down.

MAX. Fare thee well, my lost umbrella! *An eighth label.* What's this one? "Sweet and dear you were to me . . ."

ANATOL, *catching him up.* "Girl with roughened finger tips. Past all . . ."

MAX. Oh . . . that was Hilda.

ANATOL. You remember Hilda?

MAX. What became of her?

ANATOL. She married a milkman.

MAX. Did she now?

ANATOL. That's what happens. I love a girl . . . I'm all the world to her . . . and then she marries a milkman. A dear child. I hope it's been good for trade.

MAX, *putting* HILDA *aside.* Milko! *The ninth package.* And what's "Episode"? Nothing inside but a little dust.

ANATOL, *leaning across and taking the little envelope from him.* Dust! It was once a rosebud.

MAX. What does "Episode" mean?

ANATOL. That's what it was . . . an episode . . . a couple of hours' romance. Pathetic, isn't it? Nothing left of its sweetness but dust!

MAX. Most pathetic. But one might call them all a little episodic.

ANATOL. Not with such dreadful truth. Of course, they all were . . . and I knew they were at the time. I had a fine idea of myself in those days. I used to catch myself thinking . . . Poor child, poor child!

MAX. Poor . . . ?

ANATOL. When I was very young indeed I saw myself as one of the world's great heroes of romance. These women, I thought . . . I pluck them, crush the sweetness from them . . . it's the law of nature . . . then I throw them aside as I pass on. I know now that I'm more of a fool than a hero . . . and I'm getting most unpleasantly used to knowing it.

MAX. What was "Episode"?

ANATOL. I caught her . . . then I threw her aside . . . crushed her under my heel.

MAX. Did you really?

ANATOL. But I tell you . . . they were the few most wonderful moments I ever passed. Not that you'd ever understand.

MAX. Why not?

ANATOL. Because it sounds nothing at all . . . unless you can feel it as I felt it.

MAX. I'll try.

ANATOL. I sat at the piano in that room of mine one evening. We'd been in love with each other just two hours. D'you remember a lamp I had and the curious glowing light it gave. Think of that lamp . . . it's most important.

MAX. I've thought of it.

ANATOL. I sat at the piano. She sat at my feet . . . I remember I couldn't reach the pedals. Her head in my lap . . . her hair loose . . . and the glowing light making such shadows in it! I let one hand wander on the keys . . . the other was pressed against her lips.

MAX. What else?

ANATOL. Isn't that like you? Nothing else! We'd loved each other for only an hour or two. It was our first solitude . . . it was to be our last. She said it would be. But I knew that she loved me madly . . . the very air was shimmering with it. Would you have noticed that? Do you wonder I felt a demigod and only thought . . . Oh, you poor, poor child! What was it to me? An episode. I should hardly cease to feel her kisses on my hand before she'd begin to slip into the shadows of memory. But she'd never forget . . . never be able to forget. Some women can . . . but not she. She lay there at my feet pouring out her soul in love. I knew that I was the whole world to her . . . and always would be . . . one is so certain of these things sometimes. While to me . . . she and her love were just an episode.

MAX. Who was the lady?

ANATOL. You knew her . . . we met her at supper once.

MAX. Did we? Sounds too romantic a person for any supper I ever went to.

ANATOL. Not a bit. You'll laugh when I tell you. She belonged to a . . .

MAX. Theatre?

ANATOL. No . . . a circus.

MAX. Not Bianca?

ANATOL. Yes . . . Bianca. I never told you I met her again after that night.

MAX. D'you mean to say that Bibi was in love with you?

ANATOL. She was. I met her in the street . . . it seems they went off to Russia the next morning.

MAX. And a good job for your romance they did.

ANATOL. Of course! Because it's somebody you knew the whole thing becomes commonplace. Oh, Max . . . why don't you learn how to be in love?

MAX. Teach me.

ANATOL. Learn to tune yourself up to the supreme moments.

MAX. With a little piano playing and a glowing light upon her shimmering hair?

ANATOL. Well . . . that's how I get wonders out of life. You saw no more in that girl than you could in that lamp of mine. A bit of glass, wasn't it . . . with a light behind? What a way to walk through the world . . . eyes open and imagination shut! Do you wonder you find nothing in it? You swallow life whole, Max . . . I taste it.

MAX. You've only to fall in love to make the universe all you want it to be!

ANATOL. That's how it's done.

MAX. How many glowing lamps would it take to work Bianca up to that pitch?

ANATOL. I know what she felt when I kissed her.

MAX. I know better.

ANATOL. Do you?

MAX. Because I've never kissed her . . . and never needed to imagine her anything but the pretty, harmless, worthless little baggage she is.

ANATOL. Oh!

MAX. Whatever else you want to find in her you must put there first.

ANATOL. It wasn't so then . . . it wasn't. Oh . . . I know all about the girl. She'd kissed men before, and she has kissed them since.

MAX. With just the same kisses that she kissed you.

ANATOL. No. I wish I hadn't told you.

MAX. Never mind. You felt all you felt and all she ought to have felt as well.

ANATOL. Have you ever seen much of her?

MAX. Quite a lot.

ANATOL. Have you?

MAX. Don't distress yourself. She's a witty little devil, and we always liked a chat.

ANATOL. A friendly chat?

MAX. Not a bit more.

ANATOL. Then I swear to you, Max . . . that girl loved me to distraction.

MAX. Quite so. Let's get on with the others. *He takes a tenth packet.* "Could I but tell the meaning of your smile, you green-eyed . . ."

ANATOL. I say . . . d'you know that circus is back again?

MAX. Yes . . . she's still with it.

ANATOL. Sure?

MAX. Quite. I shall see her this evening . . . she's coming to call.

ANATOL. Well! Why on earth didn't you tell me that before?

MAX. What's it to do with you? Your past is dead . . . look at it.

ANATOL. But . . .

MAX. Besides . . . yesterday's romance warmed up. Don't risk that.

ANATOL. I wonder if I could feel the same for her again.

MAX. There are other dangers. You take great care of this Episode of yours. Don't let it catch cold.

ANATOL. But I mustn't miss a chance of seeing her.

MAX. She's wiser than you! Has she ever sent you even a postcard? But perhaps she forgot all about you.

ANATOL. Max . . . why not believe me when I tell you . . . ?

MAX. Well?

ANATOL. That hour we spent together was one of those things that never fade.

A knock at the door of the flat.

MAX. Here she is!

ANATOL. What!

MAX. You go into my bedroom and then slip out.

ANATOL. Certainly not.

MAX. You'd much better.

ANATOL. I shall not.

MAX. Stand there then, where she won't see you at once.

ANATOL. But why . . . ?

Still, he stands in the shadow, and MAX *goes to the door to welcome* BIANCA.

BIANCA. Max! How are you? I'm back.

MAX. How are you, Bibi? Nice of you to come.

BIANCA. First visit.

MAX. Honored.

BIANCA. How's everybody? Suppers at Sacher's again now?

MAX. But you must turn up. Sometimes you didn't.

BIANCA. I did.

MAX. Not when you'd something better to do.

BIANCA. But you weren't jealous. I wish they'd all take lessons from you. Why can't a man be fond of one without making himself a nuisance? Oh . . . who's that? Making one jump! *She has discovered* ANATOL, *who comes forward, silent, expectant. She stares at him.*

MAX. An old friend, Bibi.

BIANCA. Oh . . .

MAX. Quite a surprise.

ANATOL *comes nearer.* BIANCA *is desperately puzzled, and doesn't recall him in the least. She is most polite.*

BIANCA. Of course . . . we've met . . .

ANATOL. Bianca.

BIANCA. Yes . . . to be sure.

ANATOL, *seizing her hand quite passionately.* Bianca.

BIANCA. But . . . I'm so stupid . . . where was it?

MAX. Try hard to remember.

BIANCA. Of course . . . in Petersburg.

ANATOL. No . . . it wasn't in Petersburg. *He drops her hand, takes his hat and coat, and goes.*

BIANCA. Oh . . .

The flat door slams.

MAX. He's gone.

BIANCA. But . . . I'm so sorry . . . what's wrong . . . ?

MAX. Don't you really remember him?

BIANCA. Yes . . . quite well. But I can't place him for the life of me.

MAX. Anatol, Bibi . . . Anatol.

BIANCA, *her brow wrinkling in puzzlement.* Anatol . . . Anatol?

MAX. Anatol . . . at the piano . . . and a lamp casting shadows on your shimmering hair. Here . . . not in Petersburg . . . three years ago.

BIANCA, *light breaking.* Well . . . of course . . . Anatol! How stupid of me. Oh, do call him back. Anatol! *Makes for the door.*

MAX. No . . . he's gone.

BIANCA, *looking from the window.* There he goes.

MAX, *behind her.* Yes . . . there he goes.

BIANCA, *calling.* Anatol!

MAX. No use . . . he can't hear.

BIANCA. You will apologize to him, won't you? I've hurt his feelings. Such a nice fellow.

MAX. You're quite sure you remember him?

BIANCA. Why, yes! But, you know, there is some one in Petersburg as like him as two peas.

MAX. I'll tell him so.

BIANCA. Besides . . . when you haven't given a man a thought for three years . . . and there he suddenly is plumped in front of you! One can't remember everybody.

MAX, *grimly smiling.* Let's shut the window . . . it's gone chilly.

BIANCA. I shall run against him somehow.

MAX. No doubt. *He picks up and holds out to her the little envelope marked "Episode."* D'you know what this is?

BIANCA. What?

MAX. The rosebud you were wearing that evening . . . the evening, Bibi . . .

BIANCA. Has he kept it?

MAX. As you see.

BIANCA. D'you mean he was in love with me?

MAX. Passionately . . . unfathomably . . . and for ever and a day. But so he was with all these others.

BIANCA, *surveying the table.* All that lot!

MAX. We've been sorting you out.

BIANCA. Sorting us . . . ?

MAX. Sorting you.

BIANCA. Oh, indeed! Where do I go?

MAX. Here. *He gravely drops "Episode" in the fire.*

BIANCA. Well!

MAX. All the revenge I can give him you see. But don't be cross . . . I want to hear your news.

BIANCA. I don't think I feel like it now.

MAX. Bibi . . . don't quarrel with me. Let's hear about the fellow in Petersburg, who's as like him as two peas.

BIANCA. Don't be absurd.

MAX. Or anything else you like. I'll tell you how to begin. *He settles her in a big armchair, and settles himself in another beside her.* Once upon a time there was a big, big city . . .

BIANCA. . . . and into the city came a big, big circus . . .

MAX. . . . and in the circus there was a tiny, tiny girl . . .

BIANCA. . . . who jumped through a big, big hoop.

MAX. Now we're getting on. And in a box every evening . . .

BIANCA. Yes . . . in a box every evening there sat a very good-looking man . . .

MAX. Quite so . . . and then?

They settle to their friendly chat.

IV

KEEPSAKES

EMILY'S *sitting room is quite prettily furnished, and looks over some gardens, where the trees are just now breaking into leaf. It is late in the afternoon. Alone in the room and at the writing desk sits* ANATOL. *He is feverishly searching the drawers.*

EMILY, *coming in and finding him.* What are you doing at my desk . . . rummaging about? Anatol!

ANATOL, *hardly looking up.* I have a perfect right to. And it's as well I did.

EMILY. What have you found . . . except your own letters?

ANATOL. My letters! What do you call these? *He shows her two tiny objects in his outstretched palm.*

EMILY. What?

ANATOL. These two stones. This one's a ruby . . . and this other dark one. I've never seen them before. I didn't give them to you.

EMILY *turns away, and for a moment doesn't answer.*

EMILY, *very quietly.* No . . . I had quite forgotten them.

ANATOL, *still brutally, sneeringly angry.* Had you! They were hidden away safe enough in the bottom of that drawer. Come on . . . you'd better confess. Don't lie. Oh, all you women do! Won't you? Don't pretend to be indignant. Yes, of course . . . sulk when you're found out. I want to know what else there is. Where have you hidden your other treasures? *He returns to his ransacking.*

EMILY. I haven't any others.

ANATOL. Haven't you!

EMILY, *quite passive.* You needn't look. I swear I haven't.

ANATOL. Well then . . . what about these?

EMILY. I suppose I was wrong. I shouldn't have . . .

ANATOL, *leaving the desk and facing her.* You suppose! Now Emily . . . tomorrow we were to be married. I thought we'd got rid of the past . . . utterly. Didn't I bring you everything I had that could remind me of mine . . . letters, keepsakes, everything . . . and didn't we burn them? And your rings and bracelets and earrings! Haven't we got rid of them too . . . all of them? Given them away . . . thrown them into the river . . . out of the window . . . anywhere? And you swore

to me that you had done with it all . . . wiped everything out!
You said that now you knew you'd never really been in love with any
one before. And I believed you! I suppose we always do believe women
when the lies are pleasant ones . . . from their first lie to their last
. . . because we want to.

EMILY. Shall I swear it again?

ANATOL. What's the good? I've done with you . . . done with you.
Oh, you were very clever about it! To see you standing there in front of
the fire watching those letters and things burn . . . poking them down
so that nothing should escape . . . wouldn't one have thought you
were only thankful to be rid of every speck of your past? You sobbed
in my arms that day by the river when we threw that bracelet into the
water! Tears of repentance? All a sham! Now I'll tell you . . . I
didn't trust you in spite of them. I came here to find out for myself
. . . and I have found out. *She is sitting silent, her head turned away.*
Say something. Defend yourself.

EMILY. No . . . you've made up your mind to have done with me.

ANATOL. But I want to know about these two things. Why keep just these
two?

EMILY. You don't love me any more.

ANATOL. Emily . . . I want to know the truth.

EMILY. What's the good if you don't love me any more?

ANATOL. Tell me the truth. Perhaps . . .

EMILY. Well?

ANATOL. Perhaps you can make things seem a bit better. I don't want
to think badly of you, Emily.

EMILY, *turning a little towards him.* D'you forgive me?

ANATOL. Tell me the truth.

EMILY. If I do . . . will you forgive me?
He doesn't answer for a moment.

ANATOL, *his voice half-hardening again.* This ruby! What about it . . . why
have you kept it?

EMILY. Will you be patient?

ANATOL. Yes . . . yes. Go on.

EMILY, *speaking quite tonelessly, her head bent.* It came out of a locket. It fell
out.

ANATOL. Who gave you the locket?

EMILY. Oh . . . that wasn't it. It was because of . . . the day I was
wearing it.

ANATOL. But who gave it you?

EMILY. What does it matter? My mother, I think. Oh, Anatol . . . if I were the bad lot you think me, I could easily say I kept the stone because my mother gave it me. You'd believe that. I kept it because I didn't want ever to forget that day I nearly lost it.

ANATOL. Go on.

EMILY. I am so glad to be telling you. But listen now. You'd laugh at my being jealous of the first woman you were ever in love with, wouldn't you?

ANATOL. What's that to do with it?

EMILY. But I dare say you're still in love with the memory of her. It's the sort of old unhappiness one never wants quite to lose, isn't it? The day I dropped that ruby means a lot to me, because it was the day I had my first glimpse of . . . everything that you and I can mean to each other now, if we will. Oh . . . if I'd never had to learn how to love . . . d'you think I could love you as I do? Anatol . . . if we'd met then . . . before we knew what love meant . . . should we have given each other a thought? Don't shake your head. You once said that to me yourself.

ANATOL. I did.

EMILY. You told me not to be so sorry that things were . . . as they were . . . because if we hadn't both learnt by experience, we could never love each other as we do.

ANATOL, *bitterly*. Yes . . . that's all the consolation one has in loving a woman who . . . *He swallows the insult.* Oh, never mind!

EMILY, *with dignity*. I'm telling you the truth about this. I kept it to remind me of the day that . . .

ANATOL. Say the words!

EMILY. You like to humiliate me. It was the very first time that . . . I was just a silly girl. What was I . . . sixteen?

ANATOL. He was twenty . . . and tall and dark . . . I'm sure.

EMILY, *quite simply*. D'you know I don't remember, dear. I remember the wood we were in, and the wind shaking the trees. It was in the spring. Yes . . . and the sun shone through the branches and made the primroses look so bright.

ANATOL, *pacing the room with a sudden excess of fury*. And you were stolen from me before I ever knew you! Don't you hate him . . . the very thought of him?

EMILY. Perhaps he gave me to you, Anatol. *That brings him to a stand.* No . . . whatever happens I don't hate the thought of him . . . I won't pretend I ever did. Don't you know I love you as I have never loved any one? And no one has ever loved you as I love you. But in spite of that . . . and even though when you kissed me first you made me forget every one else . . . all I'd ever gone through . . . wiped it out utterly . . . you can't make me forget, and you can't make me regret the moments that made me a woman.

ANATOL. You love me, do you?

EMILY. I hardly remember what he looked like . . . or anything he said.

ANATOL. Only that he kissed you . . . held you close to him . . . turned your ignorance into knowledge and your innocence into guilt. And you're grateful for that . . . grateful! Good God . . . can't you see what this means to me . . . stirring up again all this horrible past when I'd almost forgotten that there ever was or could be any other man in the world for you but me.

EMILY, *speaking with a certain cold sadness.* Yes . . . you don't understand. I think you were right. We'd better part.

ANATOL, *not quite prepared for this.* What else d'you expect of me?

EMILY, *emotional for the first time.* I envy a woman who can lie. It's a costly business telling the truth. But there's one thing I'd like to know. Why you have always begged me to be quite straight with you. How many times have you said that there was nothing you couldn't forgive me except a lie. So I confessed everything to you . . . and never cared how bad I made myself out. I told you that the only good thing about me was my love for you. Any other woman would have made excuses . . . I didn't. I let you know that I was vain and wanton . . . that I'd wasted and sold myself . . . that I wasn't worth your loving. I told you that before I'd let you come near me. I hid away from you, didn't I? It was just because I loved you so. You found me and you cried for me. But I still said No. I didn't want to drag you down . . . although your love meant more to me than anything else had ever meant in the world. I've never loved any one but you. In spite of everything you took me. I was so glad and so afraid! But why have you given me back bit by bit all the beauty and self-respect that the others had robbed me of . . . why have you made me innocent again by being great enough to be able to forgive . . . if now . . . ?

ANATOL, *echoing her as she pauses.* Now?

EMILY. If now you're done with me only because I am just like all the others?

ANATOL. No, no, dear . . . you're not, you're not.

EMILY. What do you want me to do then? Shall I throw it away? *Fingering the little ruby disdainfully.*

ANATOL, *passionately self-reproachful.* What is there great about me? I'm worse than human. Yes . . . throw it away. You dropped it, did you, among the primroses . . . and it glittered in the sun . . . *They sit there silently.*

ANATOL. It's dark . . . let's go out.

EMILY. It'll be so cold.

ANATOL. No . . . you can feel Spring's in the air.

EMILY. Very well, darling.

ANATOL, *his eye lighting on the other stone he had found.* But what about this one?

EMILY. That?

ANATOL. Yes, the black stone . . . what about that?

EMILY, *taking it up with care.* Don't you know what it is?

ANATOL. It looks like a . . .

EMILY. It's a black diamond! *Her eyes glitter as she holds it.*

ANATOL. What?

EMILY. They're very scarce.

ANATOL, *hardly articulate.* Why . . . have you kept it?

EMILY. It's worth a hundred pounds!

ANATOL. Ah! *He snatches the stone from her and throws it into the fire.*

EMILY, *shrieking out savagely.* What are you doing? *Throws herself on her knees and snatching up the tongs does her best to rescue it. He watches her grimly for a little; the firelight makes ugly shadows on her face.*

ANATOL, *quietly.* That was your price, was it? *He leaves her.*

V

A FAREWELL SUPPER

In a private room at Sacher's restaurant one evening, about suppertime. MAX *is comfortable upon a sofa with a cigarette.* ANATOL *stands by the door discussing the menu with the waiter.*

MAX. Haven't you done?

ANATOL. Just. *To the waiter.* Don't forget now. *The waiter disappears.* ANATOL *paces the room, nervously.*

MAX. Suppose she doesn't turn up after all.

ANATOL. It's only ten. She couldn't be here yet.

MAX. The ballet must be over long ago.

ANATOL. Give her time to take her paint off and dress. Shall I go over and wait for her?

MAX. Don't spoil the girl.

ANATOL, *mirthlessly laughing.* Spoil her . . . spoil her!

MAX. I know . . . you behave like a brute to her. Well . . . that's one way of spoiling a woman.

ANATOL. No doubt. *Suddenly stopping before his friend.* But, my dear Max . . . when I tell you . . . oh, Lord!

MAX. Well?

ANATOL. . . . What a critical evening this is!

MAX. Critical! Have you asked her to marry you?

ANATOL. Worse than that.

MAX, *sitting up very straight.* You've married her? Well!

ANATOL. What a Philistine you are. When will you learn that there are spiritual crises besides which such commonplace matters as . . .

MAX, *subsiding again.* We know! If you've only got one of those on I wouldn't worry her with it.

ANATOL, *grimly.* Wouldn't you? What makes this evening critical, my friend, is that it's to be the last.

MAX, *sitting up again.* What?

ANATOL. Yes . . . our farewell supper.

MAX. What am I doing at it?

ANATOL. You are to be the undertaker . . . to our dead love.

MAX. Thank you! I shall have a pleasant evening.

ANATOL. All the week I've been putting it off.

MAX. You should be hungry enough for it by this time.

ANATOL. Oh, we've had supper every night. But I've never known how to begin . . . the right words to use. I tell you . . . it's nervous work.

MAX. If you expect me to prompt you . . .

ANATOL. I expect you to stand by me. Smooth things down . . . keep her quiet . . . explain.

MAX. Then suppose you explain first.

ANATOL, *considering for half a second.* She bores me.

MAX. I see! And there's another she . . . who doesn't?

ANATOL. Yes.

MAX, *with fullest comprehension.* Ah!

ANATOL, *quite rapturously.* And what another!

MAX. Please describe her.

ANATOL. She makes me feel as I've never felt before. She . . . I can't describe her.

MAX. No . . . one never can till it's all over.

ANATOL. She's a little girl that . . . well, she's an andante of a girl.

MAX. Not out of the ballet again?

ANATOL. No, no! She's like a waltz . . . simple, alluring, dreamy. Yes, that's what she's like. Don't you know . . . ? No, of course you don't! And how can I explain? When I'm with her I find I grow simple too. If I take her a bunch of violets . . . the tears come into her eyes.

MAX. Try her with some diamonds.

ANATOL. I knew you wouldn't understand in the least. I should no more think of bringing her to a place like this . . . ! Those little eighteen-penny places suit her. You know . . . Soup or Fish: Entree: Sweets or Cheese. We've been to one every night this week.

MAX. You said you'd had supper with Mimi.

ANATOL. So I have. Two suppers every night this week! One with the girl I want to win, and the other with the girl I want to lose. And I haven't done either yet.

MAX. Suppose you take Mimi to the Soup or Fish, and bring the little Andante girl here. That might do it.

ANATOL. That shows you don't understand. Such a child! If you'd seen her face when I ordered a one and tenpenny bottle of wine.

MAX. Tears in her eyes?

ANATOL. She wouldn't let me.

MAX. What have you been drinking?

ANATOL. Shilling claret before ten. After ten, champagne. Such is life.

MAX. Your life!

ANATOL. But I've had enough of it. To a man with my nice sense of honour . . . my nice sense of honour, Max.

MAX. I heard.

ANATOL. If I go on like this much longer I shall lose my self-respect.

MAX. So shall I if I have much more to do with you.

ANATOL. How can I play-act at love if I don't feel it?

MAX. No doubt it's better acting when you do.

ANATOL. I remember telling Mimi in so many words . . . when we first met . . . when we swore that nothing should part us . . . My dear, I said, whichever first discovers that the thing is wearing thin must tell the other one straight out.

MAX. Besides swearing that nothing should part you. Good!

ANATOL. If I've said that once I've said it fifty times. We are perfectly free, and when the time comes we'll go each our own way without any fuss. Only remember, I said, what I can't stand is deceit.

MAX. Then I'm sure supper ought to go off very well.

ANATOL. Yes . . . but when it comes to the point . . . somehow I can't tell her. She'll cry. I know she'll cry, and I can't bear that. Suppose she cries and I fall in love with her again . . . then it won't be fair to the other one.

MAX. And the one thing you can't stand is deceit.

ANATOL. It'll be easier with you here. There's an honest, unromantic air about you that would dry any tears.

MAX. Happy to oblige. And how shall I start? Tell her she's better off without you. How can I?

ANATOL. Something of that sort. Tell her she won't be losing so much.

MAX. Yes . . .

ANATOL. There are hundreds of better-looking men . . . men better off.

MAX. Handsomer, richer . . . and cleverer.

ANATOL, *half-humorously*. I shouldn't exaggerate.

At this point the waiter shows in MIMI, *a lovely lady*.

WAITER. This way, Madame.

MIMI, *not in the best of tempers*. Oh . . . so here you are!

ANATOL, *cheerfully*. Here we are. *He takes off her wrap with much tenderness.* Let me.

MIMI. You're a nice one, aren't you? I looked up and down . . .

ANATOL. A good thing you hadn't far to come.

MIMI. If you say you'll be there for me you ought. Hullo, Max. Come on . . . let's feed.

A knock at the door.

MIMI. Come in! What's he knocking for?

The waiter enters.

ANATOL, *to the waiter*. Bring supper.

MIMI, *sitting at the table and, cat-like, fusses her appearance*. You weren't in front.

ANATOL, *with careful candor*. No . . . I had to . . .

MIMI. You didn't miss much. It was precious dull.

MAX. What was on before the ballet?

MIMI. I don't know. I go straight to the dressing room and then I go on the stage. I don't bother about anything else. Anatol . . . I've a bit of news for you.

ANATOL, *his brow wrinkling a little*. Have you, my dear? Important?

MIMI. M'yes: . . . may surprise you a bit . . . p'raps.

The supper arrives . . . oysters first.

ANATOL. Well . . . I've some for you, too.

MIMI. Wait a second. It's no concern of his. *Nodding her head towards the well-mannered, unconscious waiter.*

ANATOL. You needn't wait . . . we'll ring.

The waiter departs. Supper has begun.

ANATOL. Well?

MIMI, *between her oysters*. I think p'raps it will surprise you, Anatol . . . though I don't see why it should. P'raps it won't . . . and it oughtn't to.

MAX. They've raised your salary!

ANATOL, *watching her*. Tsch.

MIMI, *ignoring this levity*. No . . . why should it? I say . . . are these Ostend or Whitstable?

ANATOL. Ostend . . . Ostend.

MIMI. I do like oysters. They're the only things you can go on eating and eating . . .

MAX, *who is doing his full share*. And eating and eating and eating.

MIMI. That's what I always say.

ANATOL. Well . . . what's this news?

MIMI. D'you remember something you once said?

ANATOL. Which of the hundreds?

MIMI. Oh, I remember your saying it . . . Mimi, the one thing I can't bear is deceit!

ANATOL, *really taken aback*. What!

MIMI. Always tell me the whole truth before it's too late.

ANATOL. Yes, I meant . . .

MIMI, *roguish for a moment*. I say . . . suppose it was!

ANATOL. What d'you mean?

MIMI. Oh, it's all right . . . it isn't. Though it might be tomorrow.

ANATOL, *hot and cold*. Will you please explain what you mean?

MAX, *unheeded*. What's this?

MIMI, *meeting a fierce eye*. You eat your oysters, Anatol, or I won't.

ANATOL. Damn the oysters!

MIMI. You go on with them.

ANATOL. You go on with what you were saying. I don't like these jokes.

MIMI. Now didn't we agree that when it came to the point we weren't to make any fuss but . . . ! Well . . . it has come.

ANATOL, *bereft of breath*. D'you mean . . . ?

MIMI. Yes, I do. This is the last time we have supper together.

ANATOL. Oh! Why . . . would you mind telling me?

MIMI. All is over between us.

ANATOL. Is it!

MAX, *unable to be silent longer*. Admirable!

MIMI, *a little haughty*. Nothing admirable about it. It's true.

ANATOL, *with trembling calm*. My dear Mimi . . . please let me understand. Someone has asked you to marry him?

MIMI. Oh . . . I wouldn't throw you over for that.

ANATOL. Throw me over!

MIMI, *with her last oyster.* It's no use, Anatol. I'm in love . . . head over ears.

MAX *goes into such a fit of laughter that choking follows, and he has to be patted on the back.* ANATOL *does the friendly office, somewhat distractedly.*

MIMI, *very haughty indeed.* There's nothing to laugh at, Max.

MAX. Oh . . . oh . . . oh!

ANATOL. Never mind him. Now . . . will you please tell me . . . ?

MIMI. I am telling you. I'm in love with somebody else and I'm telling you straight out like you told me.

ANATOL. Yes, but damn it . . . who?

MIMI. Now, my dear . . . don't lose your temper.

ANATOL. I want to know.

MIMI. Ring the bell, Max, I'm so hungry.

MAX *recovering, does so.*

ANATOL. Hungry . . . at such a moment! Hungry!

MAX, *on way back to his chair, saying in* ANATOL's *ear.* Ah . . . but it'll be the first supper she's had tonight.

The waiter arrives.

ANATOL, *turning on him savagely.* And what do you want?

WAITER, *perfectly polite.* You rang, sir?

MAX. Bring the next thing.

While the plates are cleared ANATOL *fumes, but* MIMI *makes casual conversation.*

MIMI. Berthe Hoflich is going to Russia . . . it's settled.

MAX. Letting her go without any fuss?

MIMI. Oh . . . not more than a bit.

ANATOL. Where's the wine? Are you asleep tonight?

WAITER. Beg pardon, sir . . . the wine. *He points it out under* ANATOL's *nose.*

ANATOL. No, no . . . the champagne.

The waiter goes out for that and for the next course.

ANATOL. Now then . . . will you please explain?

MIMI. Never take a man at his word! How many times have you told me . . . when we feel it's coming to an end, say so and end it calmly and quietly?

ANATOL, *with less and less pretense of self-control.* For the last time . . .

MIMI. He calls this quietly!

ANATOL. My dear girl . . . doesn't it occur to you that I have some right to know who . . . ?

MIMI *hasn't let her appetite be disturbed; and at this moment she is relishing the wine, her eyes closed.*

MIMI. Ah!

ANATOL. Oh, drink it up . . . drink it up!

MIMI. Where's the hurry?

ANATOL, *really rather rudely.* You generally get it down quick enough.

MIMI, *still sipping.* Ah . . . but it's good-bye to claret, too, Anatol. It may be for years, it may be forever.

ANATOL, *puzzled.* Oh . . . why?

MIMI, *with fine resignation.* No more claret for me . . . no more oysters . . . no more champagne! *At this moment the waiter begins to hand the next course.* And no more filets aux truffes! All done with now.

MAX. Oh . . . what a sentimental tummy! Have some?

MIMI, *with gusto.* I will.

MAX. You've no appetite, Anatol.

The waiter having served them disappears once more.

ANATOL. Well, now . . . who's the lucky fellow?

MIMI, *serene and enjoying her filet aux truffes.* If I told you you wouldn't be any the wiser.

ANATOL. But what sort of a chap? How did you come across him? What does he look like?

MIMI, *seraphic.* He's a perfect picture of a man.

ANATOL. Oh, that's enough, of course.

MIMI. It's got to be. *She starts again her chant of self-sacrifice.* No more oysters . . . !

ANATOL. Yes . . . you said that.

MIMI. No more champagne!

ANATOL. Damn it . . . is that his only excuse for existence . . . not being able to stand you oysters and champagne?

MAX. He couldn't live by that.

MIMI. What's the odds as long as I love him! I'm going to try throwing myself away for once . . . I've never felt like this about any one before.

MAX, *with a twinkle.* Anatol could have given you an eighteenpenny supper, you know.

ANATOL. Is he a clerk? Is he a chimney sweep? Is he a candlestick maker?

MIMI. Don't you insult him.

MAX. Tell us.

MIMI. He's an Artist.

ANATOL. Music-hall artist?

MIMI, *with dignity*. He's a fellow artist of mine.

ANATOL. Oh . . . an old friend? You've been seeing a lot of him? Now then . . . how long have you been deceiving me?

MIMI. Should I be telling you if I had? I'm taking you at your word and speaking out before it's too late.

ANATOL. How long have you been in love with him? You've been thinking things . . . haven't you?

MIMI. Well . . . I couldn't help that.

ANATOL, *his temper rising fast*. Oh!

MAX. Anatol!

ANATOL. Do I know the fellow?

MIMI. I don't suppose you've ever noticed him. He's in the chorus. He'll come to the front.

ANATOL. When did this affair start?

MIMI. Tonight.

ANATOL. That's not true.

MIMI. It is. Tonight I knew it was my fate.

ANATOL. Your fate! Max . . . her fate!

MIMI. Yes . . . my fate. Why not?

ANATOL. Now . . . I want the whole story. I've a right to it. You still belong to me, remember. How long has this been going on . . . how did it begin? When had he the impudence . . . ?

MAX. Yes . . . I think you ought to tell us that.

MIMI, *impatient for the first time*. Oh . . . this is all the thanks I get for doing the straight thing. Suppose I'd gone on like Florrie with von Glehn. He hasn't found out yet about her and Hubert.

ANATOL. He will.

MIMI. Well, he may. And then again he mayn't. But you wouldn't have. I know a thing or two more than you do. *For proper emphasis she pours out another glass of wine.*

ANATOL. Haven't you had enough?

MIMI. What . . . when it's the last I shall get?

MAX, *with a nod*. For a week or so.

MIMI, *with a wink*. Don't you think it. I'm going to stick to Carl. I love him for himself alone. He won't badger and bully me, the dear!

ANATOL. You and he have been carrying on under my nose for . . . how long? Tonight indeed!

MIMI. Don't believe it if you don't want to.

MAX. Mimi . . . tell the truth. You two won't part friends unless you do.

ANATOL, *recovering some complacency*. And then I've a bit of news for you.

MIMI. Well . . . it began like this . . .

Once more the waiter, with the champagne this time. MIMI *stops very discreetly.*

ANATOL. Oh, never mind him.

She goes ahead, but in whispers, till the waiter departs, which he does very soon.

MIMI. A fortnight ago he gave me a rose. Oh, so shy he was! I laughed . . . I couldn't help it.

ANATOL. Why didn't you tell me?

MIMI. Start telling you those sort of things! I should never have done.

ANATOL. Well?

MIMI. And he hung round at rehearsals. It made me cross at first . . . and then it didn't.

ANATOL, *viciously.* No, I'm sure it didn't.

MIMI. Then we began to have little chats. And then I began to take such a fancy to him.

ANATOL. What did you chat about?

MIMI, *trying the champagne now.* Oh . . . things. He got expelled from school. Then he went into business, and that wasn't any good. Then he thought perhaps he could act.

ANATOL. And never a word to me!

MIMI. And then we found out we used to live close to each other as children. Just fancy!

ANATOL. Most touching!

MIMI, *simply.* Wasn't it?

ANATOL. Well?

The champagne has an instant effect. She becomes a little vague and distant.

MIMI. That's all. It's my fate. You can't struggle against your fate, can you? Can't . . . struggle . . . against . . . *She stops suddenly.*

ANATOL, *waiting for a minute.* But I've not been told what happened tonight.

MIMI. What happened . . . *Her eyes close.*

MAX, *with fine effect.* Hush . . . she sleeps.

ANATOL. Well, wake her up. Take that wine away from her. I want to know what happened tonight. Mimi . . . Mimi!

MIMI, *waking up.* Tonight? He told me he loved me.

ANATOL. What did you say?

MIMI. I said I was awfully glad. And I mustn't play the silly fool with him, must I? So it's good-bye to you.

ANATOL. It's him you're considering, not me.

MIMI, *with friendly candor.* I don't think I ever really liked you, Anatol.

ANATOL. Thank you. I'm happy to say that leaves me cold.

MIMI. Don't be nasty.

ANATOL. Would you be surprised to hear that I hope to get on very well without you for the future?

MIMI. Really?

ANATOL, *throwing his belated bomb.* I am in love, too.

MIMI, *indifferently skeptical.* Think of that!

ANATOL. And have been for some time. Ask Max. I was telling him when you came in.

MIMI, *smiling at this in the most irritating way.* Yes . . . I'm sure you were.

ANATOL, *piling it up.* She's younger and rather prettier than you.

MIMI. I'm sure she is.

ANATOL. And I'd throw six hundred and seventy of your sort into the sea for her. MIMI, *not in the least impressed or distressed, laughs aloud.* You needn't laugh. Ask Max.

MIMI. If I were you I should have invented all that a little earlier.

ANATOL, *aghast.* But it's true. I haven't cared that much about you since . . . ! You've been boring me till I could only stay in the room with you by sitting and thinking of her. I've had to shut my eyes tight and think it was her I was kissing.

MIMI, *as comfortable as ever.* Ditto to that, my dear.

ANATOL, *taking a nasty turn.* Well . . . that's not all. Say ditto to this if you can.

MIMI, *noticing the change in his tone, puts down her wineglass, and looks squarely at him.* To what?

ANATOL. I could have told you all you've been telling me months ago. And weeks ago I could have told you a good deal more.

MIMI. D'you mean . . . ?

ANATOL. Yes, I do. I have behaved very badly to you . . . dear Mimi.

MIMI, *getting up, outraged.* Oh . . . you cad!

ANATOL, *grateful for the abuse.* And only just in time, too . . . it seems! You wanted to get there first, did you? Well . . . thank God, I have no illusions!

MIMI *has gone to collect her things: her hat, her cloak. She puts them on, not waiting a moment.*

MIMI. Oh . . . it only shows!

ANATOL. Doesn't it! Shows what?

MIMI. What a brute a man can be!

ANATOL. A brute . . . am I?

MIMI. Yes, a brute . . . a tactless brute. *For a moment she gives him undivided attention.* After all . . . I never told you *that.*

ANATOL. What!

MAX. Oh, never mind!

ANATOL. Never told me what? That you and he . . .

MIMI, *with most righteous indignation.* And I never would have told it to you. Only a man could be so . . . unpleasant!

ANATOL *twitches with rage and amazement. But the timely calm waiter saves the situation with yet another course.*

WAITER. I beg pardon.

ANATOL. Oh, go to . . . ! *He swallows the word, and recovers a little.*

MIMI. Ices! *Pleased as a child, she goes back to her chair to begin on hers.*

ANATOL, *deeply shocked.* Can you eat ices at a moment like this?

MAX, *starting on his too.* Yes, of course she can. It's good-bye to them forever.

MIMI, *between the spoonfuls.* No more ices . . . no more claret . . . no more champagne . . . no more oysters! *Gets up to go.* And thank goodness . . . no more Anatol. *On her way to the door she notices the cigars on the sideboard. She helps herself to a handful. Then turns with the sweetest of smiles.* Not for me. They're for him! *She departs.*

MAX. I said it'd go off all right.

ANATOL *is speechless.*

VI

DYING PANGS

One spring afternoon it is growing dusk in ANATOL'S *room, though through the open window the broad expanse of sky still shines clear and blue.* ANATOL *and* MAX *come in from a walk.*

MAX. I didn't mean to come up with you.

ANATOL. But don't go.

MAX. I shall be in the way.

ANATOL. I'm not sure she'll come. Three times out of four she won't.

MAX. I couldn't stand that.

ANATOL. She has excellent excuses. I dare say they're sometimes true.

MAX. Three times out of four.

ANATOL. Hardly that! Max, never, never be the lover of a married woman. There's nothing deadlier.

MAX. Except being her husband.

ANATOL. I've been in this mess . . . how long? Two years? More. It was two years last Easter that . . .

MAX. What's gone wrong?

ANATOL, *who has taken off neither coat nor hat and still carries his stick in his hand, flings himself into a chair by the window.*

ANATOL. I'm weary of it. I wish . . . oh, I don't know what I wish.

MAX. Go abroad for a bit.

ANATOL. What's the good?

MAX. Wouldn't that bring it to an end quicker?

ANATOL. It might.

MAX. I've seen you through this sort of thing before. And the last time, how long did it take you to make up your mind to have done with that silly girl who had never been worth worrying about at all?

ANATOL. D'you think things are dead between us now?

MAX. That wouldn't matter . . . death doesn't hurt. But dying pangs do.

ANATOL. Job's comforter! You're quite right though.

MAX. Talk it over if you like . . . that helps sometimes. Not to bother over the whys and wherefores, but just to diagnose the case.

ANATOL. You'd like a cheerful ten minutes, would you?

MAX. Well . . . if you knew what a face you've been carrying round and round the park with you this afternoon.

ANATOL. She said she'd be there.

MAX. You weren't sorry she wasn't. You couldn't have looked as glad to see her as you did a couple of years ago.

ANATOL, *jumping up.* It's true. But why . . . why? Have I got to go through it again . . . this cooling . . . cooling . . . growing cold? It's a perfect nightmare.

MAX. Run away then . . . go abroad. Or else make up your mind to tell her the truth.

ANATOL. What is the truth?

MAX. That you're tired of her.

ANATOL. Tell a woman that sort of truth only because you're weary of telling lies! A pleasant job.

MAX. No doubt you'd both of you do anything rather than face the brutal facts. But why?

ANATOL. Because we still don't thoroughly believe in the brutal facts . . . that's why. Even in this dull, dying autumn of our passion, there come to us days of spring . . . brighter than any we've ever known. You never so much want to be happy with a woman as when you know that you're ceasing to care for her. And when the happy moments come, we don't look too closely at them either. We only feel so ashamed . . . we mutely apologise for having doubted ourselves and each other. Love's like a candle flame . . . it flickers highest when it's going out.

MAX. And the end's in sight often much sooner than we think. You can date the death of some love affairs from the very first kiss. But a man may be on his deathbed and swear he's never better.

ANATOL. Not I, worse luck. In love affairs, my friend, I have always been a valetudinarian. Very likely I knew that I wasn't so ill as I thought . . . I felt so much the worse for that. I've sometimes fancied I have a sort of evil eye . . . turned inwards . . . to wither my own happiness.

MAX. A most rare and distinguished deformity.

ANATOL. You're welcome to it for me. Lord . . . how I've envied lucky, careless devils, who can be supremely happy in the passing moment. I've never valued a thing when I had it.

MAX. Often they don't know they're happy.

ANATOL. But they needn't feel guilty afterwards.

MAX. Guilty?

ANATOL. She and I knew well enough, didn't we, that though we might swear to love each other till death and after, yet the end of it all was never so very far off? Then why didn't we make the most of our time? For we never did. We're guilty of lost opportunity.

MAX. Oh, my dear Anatol . . . these dragged-out affairs are very bad for you. You're too quick-witted for them.

ANATOL. Am I?

MAX. Haunted by the past and afraid of the future . . . why, your one chance of happiness is to keep the present, at least, clear and clean and forgetful. Be a little stupid about it if you must.

ANATOL. Yes . . . yes.

MAX. But you jumble past, present, and future together till I don't think you know which you're living in. All you think of today is your yesterday's remorse for the sins that you mean to commit tomorrow.

ANATOL. And that's not half the nonsense it sounds.

MAX. Thank you. But we must all talk our share of platitudes too . . . so here goes for mine. Anatol, pull yourself together . . . be a man.

ANATOL. Max . . . you can't keep a straight face as you say it. Besides, I don't think I want to pull myself together. What a lot one loses by being a Man! There are a dozen ways of being an interesting invalid, and a fellow can choose his own. But there's only one way of being in rude health . . . and that's such a dull one. No, thanks.

MAX. Vanity!

ANATOL. Now for a platitude about vanity.

MAX. No. My only concern is that you won't go abroad.

ANATOL. I may. But it must be at a moment's notice. I hate planning things. I particularly hate packing, and looking up trains, and ordering a cab, and . . .

MAX. I'll do all that for you.

Suddenly, as if in response to some instinct, ANATOL *turns to the window and looks out.*

MAX. What is it?

ANATOL. Nothing.

MAX. I beg your pardon. I forgot. I'm off.

ANATOL. Max . . . at this moment I feel more in love with her than ever.

MAX. You probably are more in love with her than ever . . . at this moment.

ANATOL. Then don't order the cab.

MAX. But the boat train doesn't leave for an hour and a half. I could send your luggage on after.

ANATOL. Thank you so much.

MAX. Now I must make a good exit . . . with an epigram.

ANATOL. Please.

MAX. Woman is a riddle . . .

ANATOL. Oh, really!

MAX. Wait, that's only half of it. Woman is a riddle . . . says a man. What a riddle would Man be for women . . . if they'd only brains enough to want to guess it.

ANATOL. Bravo.

MAX *bows to his applause and departs.* ANATOL *is more restless than ever. He paces the room. He goes to the window, where he can now hear some violinist practicing in the room above. He lights a cigarette and sits down to wait as patiently as may be. But he hears a sound in the hall. He jumps up and goes to the door as it opens to admit* ELSA. *She comes in a little furtively. She is dressed as a smart rich woman should be, but she is rather heavily veiled.*

ANATOL. At last!

ELSA. Yes . . . I'm late.

He quite tenderly puts up the veil to kiss her. After that she takes it off, her hat too.

ELSA. I couldn't come before.

ANATOL. You might have let me know. Waiting does get on one's nerves. But you can stop a bit.

ELSA. Not long, darling. You see, my husband . . .

He breaks away from her almost rudely.

ELSA. My dear . . . can I help that?

ANATOL. No, you can't. There it is . . . we may as well face it. Come to me. *He is by the window and tries to draw her to him.*

ELSA, *hanging back.* No, no . . . some one might see me.

ANATOL. It's too dark . . . and the curtain hides us. *She slips into his arms.* I wish you hadn't to go so soon. I've not seen you for two days. Then you only stayed ten minutes.

ELSA. Do you love me so?

ANATOL. Do I not? What aren't you to me? If I could have you here always . . .

ELSA. I'm glad.

ANATOL. Sit by me. *He draws her close beside him.* Where's your hand? *He holds it and kisses it.* That's the old man upstairs playing. Plays well, doesn't he?

They sit together there in the twilight, listening.

ELSA. Dear one!

ANATOL. Think if we were in Italy now . . . in Venice!

ELSA. I've not been to Venice since I was there for my honeymoon.

ANATOL, *shriveling.* Need you have said that?

ELSA, *with a gush of remorse.* Darling . . . but I've never loved any one but you. No . . . not . . . not my husband.

ANATOL, *in some agony.* Please do try and forget that you're married . . . just for thirty seconds. Can't you obliterate everything for a moment but ourselves?

She apparently does, and there is silence. A clock strikes.

ELSA, *looking round quickly.* What's that?

ANATOL. Elsa . . . never mind. Forget everything but me.

ELSA, *turning back to him all the more tenderly.* Haven't I forgotten everything but you . . . for you?

ANATOL. Oh . . . my dear . . . my dear! *He kisses her hand and there is silence again.*

ELSA, *tentatively, almost tremulously.* Anatol . . .

ANATOL. Yes, darling.

She makes a half-serious little face at him as a sign that she really must be off. He won't understand.

ANATOL. What is it?

ELSA. I simply must go.

ANATOL. Must?

ELSA. Must.

ANATOL, *getting up, and going away from her.* Very well.

ELSA. Oh . . . you are difficult.

ANATOL. Difficult! I sometimes think you want to drive me mad.

ELSA. And this is the thanks I get!

ANATOL. Thanks! What do you expect thanks for? Don't I give you as
   much love as I get? Is it worth less to you than yours is to me? Why
   thanks?

ELSA. Don't you owe me just a little gratitude for the sacrifice I've made
   for you?

ANATOL. I don't want sacrifices. If it was a sacrifice . . . then you didn't
   love me.

ELSA. Not love you! I'm an unfaithful wife for your sake . . . and you
   say I don't love you.

ANATOL. I didn't say so, Elsa.

ELSA. Oh . . . when I've done . . . what I've done.

ANATOL. What you've done! I'll tell you all that you've done. Seven years
   back you were a pretty gawky girl, weren't you? Your people got you
   married . . . because that's the thing to do with pretty, gawky girls.
   Then you went on a honeymoon in Venice . . . you liked that well
   enough.

ELSA, *indignantly.* I didn't.

ANATOL. Oh, yes, you did! You were in love . . . more or less.

ELSA. I wasn't.

ANATOL. He was, then. I'm sure he petted you nicely . . . anyhow, you
   were his little wife. Then back to Vienna . . . and after a bit to boredom. Because you'd grown a pretty woman by now . . . and, really,
   he's a precious fool. So you learned to flirt . . . harmlessly enough,
   no doubt! You tell me I'm the only man you've ever really loved.
   I can't prove it . . . but let's say that's so. It flatters me to believe it.

ELSA. You call me a flirt.

ANATOL. I do. Did you never indulge in that sensual hypocrisy?

ELSA. Oh . . . you're unjust!

ANATOL. Am I? Then real temptation came. You played with it . . . you
   were longing for a romance. For you grew prettier than ever . . .
   and your husband more of a fool. He was getting fat too . . . and
   ugly. So at last your conscience yielded. You coolly looked round for
   a lover, and chanced to hit upon me.

ELSA. Chanced to hit upon . . .

ANATOL. Yes . . . if it hadn't been me it would have been the next man.
   You thought you were unhappily married . . . or at least not happily
   married enough. You wanted to be . . . one calls it loved. Of course,

it was just a flirtation between us at first . . . we skated quite skillfully over thin ice. Till one fine day . . . what was it . . . ? one of your friends looking happier than usual . . . the sight of some merry little baggage in a box at the theatre. Well, and why shouldn't I? . . . said you. And you took the plunge. Leaving out fine phrases . . . that's the story of this little adventure.

ELSA, *not looking at him, her voice full of shame and reproach.* Oh . . . Anatol, Anatol!

ANATOL. Well?

ELSA. You don't mean it.

ANATOL. I do.

ELSA. That's what you think of me.

ANATOL. I'm afraid so.

ELSA. Then I'd better go.

ANATOL. I'm not keeping you.

ELSA, *going to the door, where she lingers.* You want me to.

ANATOL. My dear! Two minutes ago it was you that were in such a hurry.

ELSA, *looking up in some relief.* Darling . . . you know I can't help that. My husb . . .

ANATOL, *suddenly flashing round on her.* Elsa.

ELSA. Yes.

ANATOL. You do love me? Say so.

ELSA, *tears in her eyes.* Do I? Good heavens! . . . what better proofs can I give?

ANATOL. Shall I tell you?

ELSA. I love you with all my heart.

ANATOL. Then don't go. Don't go back home. Come away somewhere with me. Let me have you all to myself.

ELSA. Anatol!

ANATOL. Isn't that obviously the thing to do? How can you go back to him . . . loving me with all your heart? How could I ever have let you? We've been taking it all as a matter of course. But don't you see that it can't go on . . . it's impossible. Elsa, dear, come away with me . . . you must. We'll go wherever you like. To Sicily? Very well . . . further than. I'll go as far as you like, Elsa!

ELSA, *blankly.* My dear Anatol!

ANATOL. No one to take you from me ever again. Far away, dear . . . we two . . . belonging to each other.

ELSA. Go right away?

ANATOL. Yes . . . anywhere.

ELSA. But . . . my dear Anatol . . .

ANATOL. Well?

ELSA, *with a sort of puzzled blandness.* Where's the need?

ANATOL. Where's the . . . !

ELSA. Why go away . . . when we can see each other here almost as often as we want?

ANATOL, *taking a long look at her and then smiling queerly.* Yes . . . almost. True . . . there is no need.

ELSA. You didn't mean it, did you?

ANATOL. Did I? *He turns away from her.*

ELSA, *following him prettily.* Are you still angry?

The clock chimes again.

ANATOL, *turning back with the utmost politeness.* I'm sure you must go.

ELSA, *a little flustered.* Oh dear! . . . I didn't know it was so late. Till tomorrow. I can come at six.

ANATOL, *helping her with her things.* Please do.

ELSA. Not going to kiss me?

ANATOL. Of course! *He kisses her.*

ELSA, *encouragingly.* Things'll look brighter tomorrow.

ANATOL. Good-bye.

He takes her to the door, where she stops and looks up, all sweetness and charm.

ELSA. Kiss me again.

He looks at her hard for a minute, then very deliberately does so, and she slips away.

ANATOL, *turning back and savagely exclaiming.* She asked for that kiss. And it makes her another cheap woman at last . . . *To himself in the glass.* And you're a fool . . . a fool!

VII

THE WEDDING MORNING

Note. In Vienna a man's clothes for a wedding are what we should call evening dress. It also appears that on such occasions, to every bridesmaid there is a grooms-man, whose business it is to provide her with a bouquet.

It is a brilliant winter morning; the lately risen sun shines straight into ANATOL'S *room.* ANATOL *stands beside his bedroom door, which is slightly open. He is listening. After a moment he closes the door very softly and comes back into the room. He looks nervous and rather puzzled. He sits down on not the most comfortable chair with a fretful sigh. Then he gets up to ring the bell. Then he sits down again. His costume is a strange mixture of early morning and overnight:*

a dressing jacket and dress trousers, slippers, and a scarf round the neck; but he looks bathed and shaved, and his hair is brushed. FRANZ, *his man, answers the bell, and, not seeing him, is going into the bedroom.* ANATOL *jumps up and stops him, more by gestures than with his voice, which he hardly raises above a whisper.*

ANATOL. Here, where are you going? I didn't see you.

FRANZ. Did you ring, sir?

ANATOL. Yes . . . bring some breakfast.

FRANZ. Very good, sir. *Going for it.*

ANATOL. Quietly, you idiot. Don't make such a noise. FRANZ *is quiet, and apparently comprehending. When he is well out of the room,* ANATOL *makes for the bedroom door again, and again listens.* Still asleep!

FRANZ, *coming back with the light breakfast, which he puts on a table by the fire.* Two cups, sir?

ANATOL, *with a look at him.* Yes. *Hears a bell ring, and he jumps.* There's some one at the door. At this time in the morning! FRANZ *goes out again as quietly.* ANATOL *looks around, out of the window, at the bedroom door, then doubtfully at the teacups.* I don't feel in the least like getting married. MAX *arrives in the best of spirits;* FRANZ *behind, looking as if he ought to have stopped him.*

MAX. My dear fellow!

ANATOL. Tsch! . . . don't talk so loud. Get another cup, Franz.

MAX, *at the table.* Two cups here already.

ANATOL. Get another cup, Franz, and then get out.

FRANZ *obeys with discretion.*

ANATOL, *fretfully.* What are you doing here at eight o'clock in the morning?

MAX. Nearly ten!

ANATOL. Well . . . what are you doing here at ten o'clock in the morning?

MAX. It's my wretched memory.

ANATOL. Don't talk so loud!

MAX. I say . . . you're very jumpy. What's the matter?

ANATOL. Yes . . . I am very jumpy.

MAX. But not Today.

ANATOL. Oh . . . what is it you want?

MAX. You know your cousin Alma's to be my bridesmaid at the wedding. About her bouquet. . . .

ANATOL, *with rather sulky indifference.* What about it?

MAX. I forgot to order it and I forgot to ask her what color she's wearing. What do you think . . . white or red or blue or green?

ANATOL. Certainly not green!

MAX. Are you sure?

ANATOL. You know she never wears green.

MAX. How do I know?

ANATOL. Don't shout! It's nothing to be excited about.

MAX, *a little exasperated*. Do you know what color she will be wearing at your wedding this morning?

ANATOL. Yes . . . red or blue.

MAX. Which?

ANATOL. What does it matter?

MAX. Damn it . . . for the bouquet.

ANATOL. You order two . . . you can wear the other in your hair.

MAX. That's a silly joke.

ANATOL, *his head on his hand*. I'll be making a sillier in an hour or two.

MAX. You're a cheerful bridegroom . . . I must say!

ANATOL. Well . . . I've been very much upset.

MAX. Anatol . . . you're hiding something.

ANATOL, *with great candor*. Not at all.

From the bedroom comes a female voice, loud and clear.

THE VOICE. Anatol!

In the silence that follows MAX *looks at* ANATOL *in something more than surprise.*

ANATOL, *casually*. Excuse me a minute.

He goes and gingerly opens the bedroom door. A pretty pair of arms appears and rests upon his shoulders. In answer to the embrace, for a moment his head disappears. He shuts the door then and returns to his scandalized friend.

MAX. Well really, Anatol!

ANATOL. Let me explain.

MAX. If this is how you begin your married life . . . !

ANATOL. Don't be an ass.

MAX. I'm not a moral man myself . . . but hang it all!

ANATOL. Will you let me explain?

MAX, *looking at his watch*. Hurry up then . . . your wedding's at half-past twelve.

ANATOL. So it is! *He sits silent for a moment.* Last night I was at my father-in-law's . . . my future father-in-law's.

MAX. I know that. I was there.

ANATOL. So you were . . . I forgot. You were all there. You were all very lively. There was lots of champagne. A lot of you drank my health . . . and Sophia's health.

MAX. I drank your health . . . and her health . . . and wished you both happiness.

ANATOL. So you did. Happiness! Thank you very much.

MAX. You thanked me last night.

ANATOL. They kept it up till past twelve.

MAX. I know. I kept it up.

ANATOL. They kept it up till really . . . I thought I was happy.

MAX. Well . . . that's enough about that.

ANATOL. That fellow Sophia was in love with as a girl . . . !

MAX. Young Ralmen?

ANATOL. Silly young ass . . . writes verses! Sort of fellow who seems to be everybody's first love and nobody's last.

MAX. Hadn't you better come to the point?

ANATOL. I didn't mind his being there . . . it rather amused me. We broke up about half-past twelve, didn't we? I gave Sophia a kiss . . . and she gave me a kiss. No . . . she gave me an icicle. My teeth just chattered with it as I went downstairs.

MAX. Well?

ANATOL. There were three or four of them still on the doorstep . . . and they wished me happiness all over again. And Uncle Edward was quite drunk and would insist on kissing me. And Professor Lippmann sang a comic song . . . in the street. Then Sophia's first love turned up his coat collar and went off . . . on the tiles. And then somebody . . . I forget who that was . . . said of course I'd spent the night under Sophia's window. Damn nonsense . . . it was snowing! And after a bit they'd all tailed off . . . and there I was alone.

MAX, *to express some sympathy.* T-t-t!

ANATOL. Alone, in the cold and the snow! Great big flakes . . . perfectly beastly.

MAX. So what did you do?

ANATOL. So . . . I thought I'd go to the ball at the Opera.

MAX. Oho!

ANATOL. And why not?

MAX. Now I'm afraid I understand.

ANATOL. Not at all! There I stood in the cold and the snow . . . !

MAX. Teeth still chattering.

ANATOL. It was beastly cold. And it suddenly came over me . . . made me perfectly wretched . . . that I wasn't going to be a free man any more. Never more a jolly bachelor! Never to go home again without

some one asking where you've been. I'd had my last night out. I'd
been in love for the last time.

MAX. Get on.

ANATOL. They were in full swing at the Opera. I watched for a bit. Oh
. . . that swish of a silk petticoat! And don't a girl's eyes shine through
a mask? It makes her neck look so white. Then I just plunged into it
all. I wanted to breathe in the sound and the scent of it . . . to bathe
in them.

MAX, *consulting his watch again.* Time's getting on. What happened then?

ANATOL. Was I drunk with champagne at papa-in-law's?

MAX. Not a bit.

ANATOL. I got drunk with that dancing . . . mad drunk. It was my
Opera ball . . . given on purpose to say good-bye to poor bachelor
me! I say . . . you remember Katinka?

MAX. Green-eyed Katinka!

ANATOL. Tsch!

MAX, *pointing to the bedroom.* Is that Katinka?

ANATOL. No, it just isn't Katinka. Green-eyes was there, though! And a
pretty, dark girl called . . . no, never you mind about her. Do you
remember the tiger-lily girl that Theodore . . . ? Lisa! I didn't see
Theodore . . . but we didn't look far for him. I could tell them all
through their masks. I knew their voices . . . I knew their ankles.
One girl I wasn't sure about. And whether I was running after her or
she after me . . . ? But something in the way she swung her shoulders
. . . ! And we met and we dodged, and at last she caught me by the
arm . . . and then I knew her right enough.

MAX. An old friend?

ANATOL. Can't you guess? When did I get engaged? It's not more than
two or three months ago. That meant the usual lie . . . Going away
for a bit . . . back soon.

MAX, *pointing again.* Lona?

ANATOL. Tsch!

MAX. What . . . not even Lona?

ANATOL. Lona right enough . . . don't fetch her in yet. We went and
sat under a palm. Back again . . . she said. Yes . . . I said. When?
. . . she said. Not till last night. Why haven't you written . . . where
on earth have you been? Off the map . . . I said . . . but I'm back
again, and I love you still. And don't I love you still? . . . she said.
And the waiter brought the champagne. We were very happy.

MAX. Well . . . I'm blessed.

ANATOL. Then we got into a cab . . . just as we used to. She put her head on my shoulder. Never to part she said . . . and went to sleep. We didn't get back till seven. She's still asleep . . . was, when you came. *He sits contemplating the world generally with puzzled distress.*

MAX, *jumping up.* Anatol . . . come to your senses.

ANATOL. Never to part! And I've got to be married at half-past twelve!

MAX. Yes . . . to somebody else.

ANATOL. Isn't that just like life? It's always somebody else one gets married to.

MAX. You ought to change . . . you've not much time.

ANATOL. I suppose I'd better. *He studies the bedroom door doubtfully, and then turns to his friend.* You know . . . looked at in a certain light this is pathetic.

MAX. It's perfectly disgraceful.

ANATOL. Yes . . . it is disgraceful. But it's very pathetic, too.

MAX. Never mind that . . . you hurry up.

At this moment the door opens and LONA *first puts her head round it and then comes in. A handsome shrew. She is still in her fancy ball dress; the domino thrown over it making an excellent morning wrap.*

LONA. Oh . . . it's only Max.

MAX. Only Max.

LONA. Why didn't you tell me? . . . I'd have come in before. How's Max . . . and what do you think of this ruffian?

MAX, *feelingly.* I think that's just what he is.

LONA. I've been crying my eyes out for him for months. And all the time he's been . . . where have you been?

ANATOL, *with picturesque vagueness.* Over there.

LONA. Didn't he write to you either? But now I've got him safe, he doesn't get away again. Never to part, darling! Give me a kiss.

ANATOL. No . . . really . . .

LONA. Max doesn't mind. *Taking his chin between finger and thumb, she secures her kiss.* What a face! Look pleasant. Let's all have breakfast and be happy. *She settles herself most domestically at the little table and begins to pour out tea.*

ANATOL, *looking on miserably.* Certainly.

MAX. Lona, I'm afraid I can't stop . . . thanks very much. *Glancing at the wretched* ANATOL. And I really don't see . . .

LONA. What don't you see?

MAX. Anatol ought . . .

LONA. What ought Anatol?

MAX. Anatol, it's high time that you . . . that you . . .

LONA. High time for what?

MAX. He ought to dress.

LONA, *surveying him in his queer costume without any disapproval.* What's the hurry? We'll stop at home today.

ANATOL. My dear . . . I am afraid I can't.

LONA. You can if you try.

ANATOL. I'm asked out.

LONA. You send a message and say you can't go.

MAX. He must go.

ANATOL, *with desperate inspiration.* I am asked to a wedding.

LONA. Oh . . . that don't matter.

ANATOL. But it does matter. I'm . . . what you might call the best man.

LONA. Is your bridesmaid in love with you?

MAX, *who has followed these efforts encouragingly.* We won't go into that.

LONA. Because I am . . . so he'd much better stop at home with me.

ANATOL. My dear child, I must go.

MAX. He really must.

ANATOL. For a couple of hours.

LONA. Sit down, both of you. How many lumps, Max?

MAX, *thinking it tactful to obey.* Three.

LONA, *to* ANATOL, *with a fond smile.* How many lumps, darling?

ANATOL. I ought to be gone now.

LONA, *with loving severity.* How many lumps?

ANATOL, *sitting down helplessly.* You know I always take two.

LONA. Cream or lemon?

ANATOL. You know I take lemon.

LONA. Lemon and two lumps of sugar. Those are his principles.

MAX. I say . . . I must be off.

ANATOL. No . . . no . . . no.

LONA. Drink your tea first, Max.

The two drink their tea, unhappily.

ANATOL. My dear child . . . I simply must go and change.

LONA. Good goodness! . . . what time is this silly wedding?

MAX. Half-past twelve.

LONA. Are you asked, too?

MAX. Yes.

LONA. Who's the man?

ANATOL. No one you know.

LONA. But who? Not a secret, is it?

ANATOL. The whole thing's a deadly secret.

LONA. With a best man and bridesmaids? Nonsense.

ANATOL, *explicit.* You see . . . his people . . .

LONA. You're both dear boys . . . but you are telling lies.

MAX, *with dignity.* I beg your pardon.

LONA. God knows what it's all about, but it doesn't matter. You go where you like, Max . . . Anatol stops with me.

ANATOL, *becoming desperate.* I tell you I can't. The man's my best friend. I must get him married.

LONA, *prettily to* MAX. Shall I let him go?

MAX. Dear Lona . . . I think you'd better.

The tension is a trifle relieved.

LONA. Where's it to be?

ANATOL, *very uneasily.* What do you want to know that for?

LONA. I'd like to go and look on.

ANATOL. You mustn't do that.

LONA. I must have a look at your bridesmaid, Anatol. Best men marry bridesmaids, don't they? I can't have you getting married . . . so make up your mind to that.

MAX. What would you do if he did?

LONA, *with perfect simplicity.* Forbid the banns.

ANATOL. Would you now?

LONA. Or I might make a scene at the church.

MAX. That's commonplace . . . I shouldn't do that.

LONA. No . . . one ought to invent something new.

MAX. Such as . . . ?

LONA. Turning up at the wedding . . . dressed like a bride too! That'd be striking.

MAX, *drily.* Very! I must go.

His decisive getting up encourages ANATOL.

ANATOL. Look here, Lona . . . I simply must change. I shall be late!

In comes FRANZ *with a bouquet swathed in its tissue paper.*

FRANZ. The flowers, sir.

LONA. What flowers?

FRANZ. The flowers, sir.

ANATOL *takes them silently, and* FRANZ *departs.*

LONA. Still got Franz, have you? You said you were going to get rid of him.

MAX. And I almost think you'd better, Anatol.

LONA. Let's see.

MAX. It's the bouquet for his bridesmaid.

LONA *detaches one wrap of the paper.* Orange blossoms!

LONA. It's a bride's bouquet!

ANATOL, *with great readiness.* Well, I say . . . if they haven't sent the wrong one! Franz . . . Franz! *He carries it off.*

MAX. And the wretched bridegroom has got his!

ANATOL, *serenely returning.* I've sent Franz back with it.

MAX. And I really must go. *He kisses* LONA's *hand and is off.*

ANATOL, *catching him half through the door.* What the devil shall I do?

MAX. Confess.

ANATOL. How can I?

MAX. I'll come back soon.

ANATOL. Do . . . for goodness' sake.

MAX. But what color will your cousin be in?

ANATOL. Blue . . . or red.

MAX. Damn!

ANATOL *most unwillingly shuts the door on him, for no sooner has he than* LONA *is round his neck.*

LONA. Thank goodness he's gone . . . darling.

ANATOL. Darling!

LONA. Be nicer than that!

ANATOL. I said Darling.

LONA. Must you go to this silly wedding?

ANATOL. I'm afraid I must.

LONA. Shall I drive with you to the church?

ANATOL. Better not. I'll see you in the evening. You've to go to the theatre.

LONA. I'll send and say I'm ill.

ANATOL. I wouldn't. I'll come and fetch you. Now I must dress. Lord . . . look at the time! Franz! Franz! FRANZ *is there.* Have you put out my things?

FRANZ. Your wedding things, sir?

ANATOL, *very steadily.* Yes . . . the things in which I always go to weddings.

FRANZ. I will see to it, sir.

ANATOL. After the theatre then . . . that's settled.

LONA. And I thought we'd have such a jolly day.

ANATOL. Don't be childish. Jolly days have to give way to more important matters.

LONA, *round his neck again.* I love you dreadfully. I don't know what's more important than that.

ANATOL, *as he removes her*. Then you'll have to learn.

FRANZ, *passing through from the bedroom*. Everything's ready, sir.

ANATOL. Thank you. You've a lot to learn yet.

Into the bedroom he goes, and his talk—or rather his shouting—from there is muffled by the changing of vest and shirt, and punctuated by the tying of ties and slipping in of studs and the brushing of hair. LONA, *left alone, twists discontentedly about the room.*

LONA. Are you really going to change?

ANATOL. I couldn't go to a wedding like this, could I?

LONA. Must you go?

ANATOL. Don't let's begin it all over again.

LONA. I shall see you this evening?

ANATOL. After the theatre.

LONA. Don't be late.

ANATOL, *blandly*. Late! Why should I be late?

LONA. You kept me waiting an hour once.

ANATOL. Did I? I dare say I did.

LONA, *still on the prowl*. Anatol . . . you've got a new picture.

ANATOL. Yes . . . do you like it?

LONA. What do I know about pictures?

ANATOL. It's quite a good one.

LONA. Did you bring it back with you?

ANATOL, *puzzled*. Bring it back!

LONA. From where you went away to.

ANATOL. Of course . . . from where I went away to! No . . . it was a present.

Silence for a moment. A shade of half-angry cunning falls on LONA'S *face.*

LONA. Anatol.

ANATOL. What is it?

LONA. Where did you go?

ANATOL. I told you.

LONA. You didn't.

ANATOL. I did . . . last night.

LONA. I've forgotten.

ANATOL. I went to Bohemia.

LONA. Why Bohemia?

ANATOL. Why not?

LONA. Were you shooting?

ANATOL. Yes . . . rabbits.

LONA. For three months?

ANATOL. Every day. *It sounds as if he were rearing slightly under this spur of cross-examination.*

LONA. Why didn't you come and say good-bye to me before you went?

ANATOL. I just thought I wouldn't.

LONA. Tried to give me the slip, didn't you?

ANATOL, *ironically bland.* No . . . no . . . no . . . no . . . no . . .

LONA. You did try once.

ANATOL. I tried.

LONA, *sharply.* What's that?

ANATOL. I said I tried. I tried hard . . . but it didn't come off.

LONA. I should think not . . . and it's not likely to.

ANATOL. Ha ha!

LONA. What did you say?

ANATOL. I said Ha ha.

LONA. It isn't funny. Glad enough to come back to me that time . . . weren't you?

ANATOL. That time.

LONA. So you are this time. Just a little bit in love with me . . . aren't you?

ANATOL. Worse luck.

LONA. What?

ANATOL. Worse luck.

LONA. Yes . . . shout it from the next room. You dare say that to my face?

ANATOL, *still brushing his hair, puts his head round the door.* Worse luck!

LONA *makes for him, but he disappears and the door closes.*

LONA, *calling through the door.* What do you mean by that, Anatol?

ANATOL. Things can't go on like this for ever.

LONA. What?

ANATOL. They can't go on for ever.

LONA. Can't they? Ha ha!

ANATOL. What?

LONA, *with some violence, tugging the door open.* I said Ha ha.

ANATOL. Shut the door . . . shut the door. *He slams it to.*

LONA. No, my darling . . . you don't get rid of me in a hurry.

ANATOL. Think not?

LONA. I'm sure not.

ANATOL. Quite sure?

LONA. Quite . . . quite . . . quite sure.

ANATOL. You can't hang round my neck for ever.

LONA. We'll see about that.

ANATOL. Don't you be silly.

LONA. Do you see me giving you up?

ANATOL. When you can't help it.

LONA. When will that be?

ANATOL. When I get married.

LONA, *eyes flashing now, beginning to drum the door with her fingers.* And when will that be . . . my precious?

ANATOL, *unkindly mimicking.* Soon . . . my precious.

LONA. How soon? *The drumming grows louder.*

ANATOL. Don't bang on the door. This time next year I may be quite an old married man.

LONA. Fool!

ANATOL. Suppose I get married in a month or two?

LONA. Some one simply waiting to marry you?

ANATOL. There is . . . at this very moment.

LONA. In a month or two?

ANATOL. Or even less.

LONA *laughs with great derision.*

ANATOL. You needn't laugh. I'll be married in a week.

LONA *still laughs.*

ANATOL. You needn't laugh, Lona!

LONA *tumbles herself on the sofa, she is laughing so much.* ANATOL *walks in, sprucely dressed: coated, hatted, and gloved for his wedding; very self-possessed now.*

ANATOL. I said you need not laugh.

LONA. When are you going to be married?

ANATOL. At half-past twelve.

LONA, *stopping very short in her laughter.* What?

ANATOL. At half-past twelve, my dear.

LONA. Anatol, don't be silly.

ANATOL. I am perfectly serious. I am going to be married at half-past twelve to-day.

LONA, *taking it in and her breath is leaving her.* Are you . . . ?

ANATOL. Franz!

FRANZ, *at the door.* Sir?

ANATOL. Bring those flowers.

LONA. Anatol . . . !

FRANZ *brings in the orange blossoms which were not sent back.* LONA *understands now. She makes a grab at them.* FRANZ *is too quick for her, gives them to* ANATOL, *and departs again, suppressing a grin.*

LONA. It's true?

ANATOL, *coolly*. Quite.

> *But* LONA *is not to be conquered with coolness now. It seems that she is endowed with the very rare faculty of losing her temper. She suddenly makes for* ANATOL *and the bouquet with such complete abandonment of the conventions of civilization that, with no manly dignity at all, he bolts from her.*

ANATOL. What are you up to?

LONA. You beast . . . you beast.

> *The bouquet seems most to excite her and it's that she's after.* ANATOL, *other methods of defending it failing, jumps on a chair at last and holds it above his head, at which moment* MAX *arrives back dressed for the wedding too and with his bouquet: pink roses.*

ANATOL. Here . . . Max . . . help!

> MAX *incautiously comes near. Pink roses are better than nothing to* LONA, *and with one snatch she has them from him and with half a dozen pulls she has them in pieces and under her stamping feet.*

MAX, *in agony*. Lona . . . don't do it! It's my bouquet! *Surveys the wreckage.* Well . . . now what shall I do?

> *The lady having sated her natural lust for the destruction of something—anything; bursts into violent tears, and abandons herself to the sofa.*

ANATOL, *still standing on the chair*. Oh . . . she has been riling me! Now start crying, of course. I told you not to laugh! Said I daren't run away from her . . . said I daren't get married. So now I shall . . . just to spite her. *He gets off the chair.*

LONA, *in another fit of fury*. Sneak! Liar!

> ANATOL *gets on chair again. Again* LONA *tumbles down exhausted.*

MAX, *collecting the remnants of the roses*. I say . . . look at my flowers.

LONA. I thought it was his. I don't care. You're as bad as he is!

ANATOL. Do be reasonable.

LONA, *flinging her wrongs to heaven*. Reasonable! When you treat me like this! But you wait! I'll show you! You'll see!

> *She jumps up and makes for the door. By good luck* MAX *is in the way.*

ANATOL. Where are you going?

LONA. You'll soon see. You let me go!

MAX, *his back to the door and holding tight to the handle*. Lona . . . what are you up to?

LONA. You let me go! You let me go!

ANATOL. Be reasonable.

LONA. You won't . . . won't you!

> *She then proceeds to wreck the room. The teapot goes into the fire and the teacups*

out of the window. The table goes over and so do the chairs. A cigar box smashes the new picture and cushions fly around. MAX *and* ANATOL *do nothing. Her work accomplished, the lady has violent hysterics.*

ANATOL, *the tumult subsiding a little.* Oh . . . I say! Why get married when you can have all the comforts of home without it?

And they gaze at LONA *awhile.*

ANATOL. She's getting quieter.

MAX. But we must go. And look at my flowers!

FRANZ, *coming in.* The carriage is at the door, sir. *Goes out again.*

ANATOL. The carriage! What am I to do?

He sits beside the sobbing LONA *and takes her hand.* MAX *sits on the other side, and takes her other hand.*

MAX. Lona! *Over the top of her head to* ANATOL. Go along . . . I'll put it right somehow.

ANATOL. I really must. Poor girl . . . I can't . . . *Obviously melting towards the sobbing* LONA.

MAX. You go along.

ANATOL. Are you sure you can manage her?

MAX. Yes . . . I'll follow you. Watch me when I get there. I'll wink if it's all right.

ANATOL. I don't like it . . . poor child. She might . . .

MAX, *envisaging new complications.* Will you go?

ANATOL. I'd better!

He gets to the door. His heart melts again. He comes back and kisses the top of her head. Then he goes to his wedding. MAX, *left alone with her, perseveringly strokes the hand he holds. She sobs on.*

MAX. Ahum!

LONA, *looking up.* Where's he gone?

MAX, *securing the other hand.* Now . . . Lona!

LONA, *jumping up.* Where's he gone?

MAX. You'd never catch him.

LONA. Yes, I will.

MAX. Lona . . . you don't want to make a scandal.

LONA. Yes, I do. Where is the wedding?

MAX. Never mind.

LONA, *trying to pull away.* I'm going there!

MAX. No, you're not. What good would it do?

LONA. To be treated like this!

MAX. Doesn't it always happen?

LONA. Be quiet with your beastly philosophy.

MAX. If you weren't in such a temper you'd see that you'd only get laughed at for your pains.

LONA, *viciously.* On the wrong side of their mouths!

MAX. Think now . . . there are lots of good fish in the sea.

LONA. That shows how much you know about me.

MAX. Suppose he were dead or gone abroad? Suppose you'd really lost him . . . and no help for it.

LONA. What d'you mean by that?

MAX. It's not so much you that he's treating badly . . . Suppose he leaves her some day . . . ! Wait and see.

She has calmed a little to the influence of his smooth voice.

LONA, *her face lighting up with the wildest triumphant happiness.* Oh . . . if I thought he would!

MAX, *letting her go.* That's nice of you.

LONA. Let me just get a bit of my own back!

MAX. Hell knows no fury like a woman scorned.

LONA. No, it doesn't . . . does it?

MAX. That is heroic of you. And while you're waiting, can't you avenge your whole sex on every man you meet?

LONA. I will. *She is restored to sanity and self-respect.*

MAX, *looking at his watch rather anxiously.* Now I've just time to take you home in a cab. *He adds half to himself.* If I don't . . . catastrophe for sure! *He offers her his arm.* Say good-bye to this happy home.

LONA. Not good-bye.

MAX. Till you come back a goddess of vengeance . . . though you're really a rather silly woman. Not but what that answers the purpose as a rule.

LONA. For the present. . . .

Most dramatically, with flashing eyes and curling lip she goes off with him, leaving the wrecked room.

Dr. Knock

A Comedy in Three Acts

by JULES ROMAINS

English version by Harley Granville-Barker

CHARACTERS

DOCTOR KNOCK

DOCTOR PARPALAID

MOUSQUET

BERNARD

THE TOWN CRIER

A COUNTRY FELLOW

ANOTHER COUNTRY FELLOW

SCIPIO

JEAN

MADAME PARPALAID

MADAME RÉMY

A FARMER'S WIFE

MADAME PONS

A NURSE

ACT ONE

The scene is in and around a motorcar; a very old motorcar, built certainly not later than 1902. We have almost forgotten these strange vehicles, with their Dutch-oven shaped bonnets and enormous bastioned bodies, in which the reckless travellers were perched. During the act this antediluvian monster moves and its surroundings change. But we first see it standing outside a small railway station in one of the mountainous districts of France. From the station come the rather more than middle-aged DR. PARPALAID *and his wife. They are followed by* DR. KNOCK; *and he, in turn, is followed by* DR. PARPALAID's *servant, an old country man-of-all-work, who is carrying* KNOCK's *luggage, and who is to drive the car.*

PARPALAID. And have we all your luggage, my dear sir?

KNOCK. We have, Dr. Parpalaid.

PARPALAID. Jean will take it in front with him . . . and we can make ourselves quite comfortable . . . yes, the three of us . . . at the back. So roomy . . . and the seats you let down . . . perfect arm chairs. These modern cars . . . one might as well be in a canoe.

KNOCK, *to* JEAN, *who is piling the things in.* Please be careful of that box. It has appliances in it . . . they're breakable.

MADAME PARPALAID, *to her husband.* Ah . . . I've never been sorry we said No to all the offers we've had for this car.

KNOCK *now surveys the vehicle with some slight surprise.*

PARPALAID. You have, as one may say, the convenience of a car with the comfort of a barouche.

KNOCK. True . . . true!

By this time the front seat is well choked with the bags.

PARPALAID. Notice, for instance, how the luggage fits in . . . not the least in the driver's way. It's a pity you've no more. You'd see what she can do when she's put to it.

KNOCK. Is it far to St. Maurice?

PARPALAID. Six miles. Just the right distance from the railway, I suggest to you, for the keeping a practice together. Patients don't play you the trick of going to see doctors in the county town.

KNOCK. No omnibus?

PARPALAID. An old shandrydan. Use it once and you'll walk ever after.

MADAME PARPALAID. No . . . one can't do without a car here. . . .

PARPALAID. In our profession.

To this KNOCK *makes no response.*

JEAN, *to* PARPALAID. Shall I start her up?

PARPALAID. Yes . . . yes! I should start starting her up.

MADAME PARPALAID. We pass through a most charming piece of country . . . which Zoraide Fleuriot has described in one of her stories . . . one of her finest stories . . . though I fear the name of it now escapes me. *As she gets in she says to her husband.* You'll sit sideways. Doctor Knock by me . . . then he can see the view better.

PARPALAID. Not that a car like this won't take three on the back seat with the utmost ease. Still . . . you do want room to turn in to see a view. *To* JEAN. All well? Is the petrol flowing nicely . . . into both cylinders? Have you wiped the spark plugs? It's always as well to, after a six or seven-mile run. And wrap up the carburetor . . . an old handkerchief is better than this rag. *He comes round to the back of the car again.* Yes . . . all's well . . . all's well. *He gets in.* I'll sit here . . . excuse me, my dear sir. Really it is a movable armchair!

MADAME PARPALAID. The road climbs all the way to St. Maurice. Walking, with one's bags to carry, it would be a terrible business. But in a car . . . how delightful!

PARPALAID, *expanding.* Once upon a time, my dear sir . . . once upon a time, I used to woo the Muse. And I wrote a sonnet . . . a fourteen-line sonnet . . . to these same wonders of Nature that we are about to show you. For the life of me, though, I can't remember it now. "Ye valleys deep, where happy labouring swains . . ."

While they sit thus JEAN *is desperately cranking, cranking. . . .*

MADAME PARPALAID. Albert, for these last two or three years you will begin it "Ye valleys deep." But surely it was always "Ye valleys green."

PARPALAID. You're right . . . you're right. "Ye valleys green. . . ."

The engine fires.

PARPALAID. Aha! D'you hear? She's going to start. Just a turn or two more of the handle . . . to vaporize sufficient gas and . . . aha! one! . . . another! . . . we're off!!

JEAN *gets in. There is a rattling of gears. The car throbs away. The scene slowly changes as the road winds up among the hills. The travellers sit in silence for a few moments; then* PARPALAID *leans forward and taps* KNOCK *encouragingly on the knee.*

PARPALAID. Well, well! The King is dead . . . long live the King! Yes, my dear sir . . . from this moment. And I congratulate you. Yes, from this very moment, my practice is yours. And, if on the road we meet a patient who happens to recognize me in spite of the speed we're travelling . . . stops me and asks my advice . . . my answer will be: "No, my good friend, no . . . here is your doctor now. As for me, . . . *The motor starts exploding spasmodically.* I don't open my mouth again unless you should do me the honor to call me into consultation. *More explosions.* But you've had great luck, may I tell you, in happening on a man who meant to tempt fortune himself once again.

MADAME PARPALAID. Yes . . . he has always promised himself that when he did retire it should be from a town practice.

PARPALAID. Singing my swan song where the world may hear it! Folly . . . folly! Paris was my heart's desire . . . Lyon will have to do.

MADAME PARPALAID. And when he might have gone on quietly making a fortune here!

KNOCK *looks at each of them in turn, gives a glance at the view and seems thoughtful.*

PARPALAID. But it's not for you, my very dear sir, to make fun of me. For it's thanks to this little weakness of mine that I sell you my practice here for a song.

KNOCK. Would you call it that?

PARPALAID. Oh . . . you'll see.

KNOCK. Well . . . I didn't do much bargaining, did I?

PARPALAID. You did not . . . and I liked you the better for it. And I liked . . . I liked your settling it all by letter. Here we are meeting for the first time with our agreements signed and sealed in our pockets. Most sporting! Quite . . . quite American! But I say again . . . you're in luck. A settled connection . . . and all to yourself.

MADAME PARPALAID. Not another doctor near.

PARPALAID. A chemist who sticks to his own job.

MADAME PARPALAID. And a town that you can't spend money in if you try.

PARPALAID. No costly amusements.

MADAME PARPALAID. Why, in six months' time you'll have saved what the practice has cost you . . . twice over.

PARPALAID. And you've only to pay it in quarterly instalments. Well, well . . . if it hadn't been for my wife's rheumatism, I doubt if I'd have said Yes after all.

KNOCK. Oh . . . you suffer, Madame, from rheumatism.

MADAME PARPALAID. I'm sorry to say it.

PARPALAID. The healthiest of climates. But it just doesn't suit her.

KNOCK. Is there much rheumatism about?

PARPALAID. Is there . . . ? My dear sir! Isn't there!

KNOCK. That's very interesting.

PARPALAID. Oh . . . if you're interested in rheumatism . . . !

KNOCK. In treating it.

PARPALAID. Ah . . . no, there's nothing in that. People here will no more come to you for their rheumatism than you'd go to the parish priest and ask him to provide a little fine weather.

KNOCK. Very tiresome of them.

MADAME PARPALAID. But isn't this a wonderful view? We might be in Switzerland!

The car has begun to make most ominous noises.

JEAN, *speaking over his shoulder to the Doctor.* Something's gone wrong again . . . yes, there's something wrong. I'll have to 'tend to that carburetor.

PARPALAID. Must you? Right! I was just thinking . . . let's stop here a minute or two.

MADAME PARPALAID. Why?

PARPALAID. And get a good look at the mountains.

MADAME PARPALAID. You see them better higher up. *But the car has stopped and* MADAME PARPALAID *understands.*

PARPALAID. Then we'll stop higher up as well. For, after all, there's nothing to stop us . . . stopping whenever we want to. We're not road hogs, thank heaven! Do notice, my dear sir . . . how easily and accurately the car stops. Perfect control over pace . . . most important in a hilly country. Aha! . . . we shall make a motorist of you . . . and sooner than you think. But beware of trying up-to-date rubbish! It's the stuff your car's made of which tells.

So now they get out of the car and stroll about a bit.

KNOCK. If rheumatism goes for nothing I suppose pneumonias may be worth a bit . . . and pleurisies?

PARPALAID. Jean . . . as we have stopped give a look to your carburetor. Pleurisy, you were saying, my dear doctor . . . and pneumonia. Well, neither is common. The air here . . . you can feel it . . . is bracing, very bracing. If you're a weakly child you die in your first six months . . . before the doctor has time to do much for you. If you survive your first six months . . . well, you take a lot of killing! Apoplexies . . . bad hearts . . . oh, yes. People who are certain there's nothing the matter with them and fall down dead when they're fifty.

KNOCK. But you've not made your fortune, I take it, by writing out death certificates.

PARPALAID. Ha, ha! No . . . good! . . . no, certainly not. Well, there's always the influenza. Not the common influenza, of course. They rather like a touch of that. They think a good septic cold once a year keeps them from catching all sorts of other things. No, but the big epidemics . . . the world-wide epidemics.

KNOCK. If I've to wait for a world-wide epidemic!

PARPALAID. I've seen two. One in 89–90 . . . one in 1918.

MADAME PARPALAID. And in 1918 our death rate was really high . . . oh, higher than in some of the very biggest towns. You compared the figures, didn't you?

PARPALAID. Oh, yes, we were ahead . . . we were well ahead.

KNOCK. And they sent for you then?

PARPALAID. Usually when it was too late.

MADAME PARPALAID. But at Michaelmas the books . . . I keep them . . . looked very well indeed.

KNOCK. I beg your pardon.

MADAME PARPALAID. The people here pay at Michaelmas.

KNOCK. At Michaelmas!

PARPALAID. Twenty-ninth of September.

KNOCK. And to-day's October the third. What a good time to choose for parting with the practice. But . . . if they come to your dispensary they pay on the nail?

PARPALAID. No, at Michaelmas. That's the custom.

KNOCK. But if they come just once . . . and you're never going to see them again?

PARPALAID. They pay at Michaelmas.

MADAME PARPALAID. Not till Michaelmas.

KNOCK *looks first at the Doctor, then at* MADAME PARPALAID. *A silence falls.* JEAN *is now lying on his back beneath the car.*

MADAME PARPALAID. Most of them, of course, only do come once.

KNOCK. Really?

MADAME PARPALAID. Yes.

DOCTOR PARPALAID *begins to look rather vaguely about him.*

KNOCK. But what about the regular patients?

MADAME PARPALAID. Regular patients?

KNOCK. Those that you'll see two or three times a week . . . well, two or three times a month?

MADAME PARPALAID. My dear . . . d'you hear that? Patients who come calling like the butcher and the baker! Oh, my dear Doctor Knock, when you've had a little more experience . . . !

PARPALAID, *laying his hand ever so kindly on* KNOCK's *arm*. No, but believe me . . . you'll find this the very best type of practice. For it leaves you so free.

KNOCK. Evidently!

PARPALAID. Let me explain. Patients . . . if you don't know from one day to another whether they'll get well or not . . . why, when they do, it upsets all your calculations. And you feel the loss of them. But when every visit's unexpected . . . every visit is a gain. And you're master of your time.

KNOCK. I see. What I really should have brought with me is a fishing rod. No doubt I can buy one. Well, the situation is now . . . crystal clear. My dear Doctor Parpalaid, you have sold me . . . for some four thousand francs, which I still owe you . . . a practice which I may liken to your motorcar here. At nineteen francs it would not be dear . . . at twenty-five it would. Come, I'll be reckless . . . I'll give you thirty for it.

PARPALAID. Thirty francs . . . for my Panhard. I wouldn't sell it for six thousand.

KNOCK, *much dashed!* I feared not. I can't have it?

PARPALAID. I'll consider any reasonable offer.

KNOCK. It's a pity. I'm a bit of a carpenter. The body would make a good wardrobe. But keep it, my dear doctor, with my blessing. And I'd say the same for your practice if I still could.

PARPALAID. Now as to that, my good sir . . . you are mistaken.

KNOCK. Don't apologize. I'm not grumbling. I've been done. I've only myself to blame.

MADAME PARPALAID. Done! My dear, you really cannot let yourself be spoken to like that.

PARPALAID. No . . . I merely wish to convince our friend that he is mistaken.

KNOCK. And pay you every quarter and wait for a year for the patients to pay me . . . how's that to be managed? But you're not to worry about me. I detest being in debt. Still, after all, one might have worse things to put up with . . . lumbago . . . why, a trick of biting one's tongue is more painful.

MADAME PARPALAID. What? You don't intend to pay us? But you've agreed to.

KNOCK. My dear madam, I shall be most anxious to pay you. But lying awake at night won't bring Michaelmas any nearer, will it?

PARPALAID. But you've money of your own?

KNOCK. Not a penny. I live on what I earn. At least, the sooner I can begin to the better. And what really vexes me is that I had . . . and I have . . . a new and original idea for improving this practice. But one can't improve what doesn't exist. However . . . there are more ways than one, perhaps. . . .

PARPALAID. Certainly. You mustn't sit down under a little disappointment, which, believe me, my dear sir, only springs from your inexperience. A doctor's calling can be made a most lucrative one . . . in time . . . all in good time. You're young . . . you're young.

KNOCK. I'm forty.

PARPALAID. Still . . . this is your first practice.

KNOCK. Not quite.

PARPALAID. But you told me you took your degree only last year.

KNOCK. That is so. And my essay entitled "The common misuse of the word Cure in Medicine" had an honorable mention. It began with a quotation . . . as I think . . . from the works of Claude Bernard; "Do you tell me you feel well, Sir? That only means you don't know you're ill."

PARPALAID. Then we're agreed . . .

KNOCK. Upon that?

PARPALAID. . . . . your experience still lies ahead of you.

KNOCK. Not at all. I began practising twenty years ago.

PARPALAID. Without a degree? And where, may I ask?

KNOCK. Not hidden away, sir, in any little provincial hole. My first practice may be said to have extended over some four thousand miles.

PARPALAID. I don't in the least understand you.

KNOCK. It's quite simple. I took my University degree with honors in Ancient History . . . and a year later I was earning my living selling shirts at the Bon Marché.

PARPALAID. In Paris?

KNOCK. Ah, no! Only at Marseilles. Even so, I lost the situation. Then, walking one day near the harbor I saw stuck up: "Wanted at once upon a ship bound for India, a surgeon . . . partly qualified." What would you have done?

PARPALAID. I? Nothing!

KNOCK. Yes . . . but there are doctors who, like poets, are born, not made. I went in. I detest pretense. I said: "Gentlemen, how easy for

me to tell you I am a doctor! I am not a doctor, I have not even failed,
gentlemen, to pass my examinations, for I have not tried." They
thanked me for my candor. Nevertheless, I told them, out of mere
respect for the profession I should insist upon being addressed as Doctor
on board. They thought that most desirable. I took ten minutes more
telling them how and why I had overcome the temptation not to
apply for this post of Doctor as I wasn't a doctor . . . till it only left
two, I found, for settling my pay. They were in a hurry. But two minutes
sufficed.

PARPALAID. And you were totally ignorant of . . . !

KNOCK. Ah, now we come to it. From my earliest childhood, from the
moment I could read, the advertisements of patent medicines in the
papers had a strange fascination for me . . . and more, even more, the
"Directions for Use" wrapped round the bottles of pills and powders
my father and mother used to buy. When I was nine I knew by heart
the whole long history of Mr. Fellows and his Syrup of Hypophosphites.
And at this moment I could repeat to you a letter . . . an admirable
letter . . . written in 1892 by Mrs. Ephraim B. Studding of Monkville,
Pa., to Dr. Williams, whose Pink Pills for Pale People had, after years
of suffering, completely cured her of . . . ! Shall I?

PARPALAID. No . . . no, thank you.

KNOCK. Literature like this gave me the professional touch. And, better,
it showed me what the true aim of the doctor . . . what the true end
of all medical knowledge should be . . . which recognized teaching
nowadays, sir, loses and buries in mere scientific rubbish-heaps. By the
time I was twelve I was a doctor at heart . . . qualified by instinct,
fully qualified. And it is on this training that my present methods of
practice are built.

PARPALAID. And would you be so kind as to tell me what they are?

KNOCK. No . . . I don't advertise. After all, it's the results that count.
You are handing me over today . . . by your own admission . . . a
practice without patients.

PARPALAID. I admit nothing of the sort.

KNOCK. Come back in a year . . . and see what you'll see! And the less
I start with . . . thanks to you! . . . the greater the credit.

JEAN. Sir . . . st! . . . sir. DOCTOR PARPALAID *goes over to him.* I'm afraid
I'll have to take that carburetor down.

PARPALAID. Very well . . . very well! If we're going on with our talk he
may as well give his carburetor its usual monthly cleaning, I tell him.

MADAME PARPALAID, *to* KNOCK. But what did you do on that ship?

KNOCK. I spent two days, Madame, and two sleepless nights making my plans. The six months' trial I gave them showed me how well they worked. And that, after all, is how hospitals are run. By trial and error.

MADAME PARPALAID. Had you many people to look after?

KNOCK. The crew and seven passengers . . . not very first-class passengers. Thirty-five all told.

MADAME PARPALAID. And enough, too.

PARPALAID. How many died?

KNOCK. None. I do not approve of patients dying. I am a firm believer in the checking of the death rate.

PARPALAID. As we all are, I trust.

KNOCK. Are you? I shouldn't have thought it. No, whatever the difficulties, whatever the temptation, leave nothing untried by which these sufferers may be preserved to us.

MADAME PARPALAID. I do think there is something in that.

PARPALAID. And how many patients had you on board?

KNOCK. Thirty-five.

PARPALAID. What . . . the whole crew . . . and all the passengers?

KNOCK. The whole crew . . . and all the passengers.

MADAME PARPALAID. But how did the ship manage?

KNOCK. Oh . . . everyone took it in turns.

Silence falls for a moment.

PARPALAID. But tell me . . . you are really a doctor now? Because here one has to be. It'd mean a lot of trouble. If you're not, better say so at once.

KNOCK. I am now really and truly and most professionally a doctor. When I'd proved to myself that my methods were the right methods there was only one thing I wanted . . . a chance to apply them on dry land . . . and broadcast, broadcast! And naturally I knew that taking a degree was a needful formality.

MADAME PARPALAID. But you told us that you only quite recently . . .

KNOCK. Yes, I couldn't go straight ahead. I had my living to earn. I traded for some years in monkey nuts.

MADAME PARPALAID. Monkey nuts.

KNOCK. Otherwise called peanuts, groundnuts, hognuts . . . properly called *Arachis hypogaea*. No . . . I didn't go round with a barrow. I organised a depot where the costermongers could buy them. And if I'd stuck to it ten years I'd have been a millionaire. But it bored me. Ah, my dear madam . . . there are few callings in which boredom does not lurk . . . as I've found to my cost. Yes, I think medicine, politics, high finance, and the Church are the only ones I've not tried.

MADAME PARPALAID. And these medical methods you speak of . . . do you mean to try them here?

KNOCK. If I felt I couldn't, I should . . . as the homely phrase has it . . . cut my sticks, and you'd never see me again. Naturally, I'd prefer a good town practice. . . .

MADAME PARPALAID, *to* PARPALAID. As you're going to Lyon yourself, my dear, you might as well ask Doctor Knock what these methods are. No harm done.

PARPALAID. Doctor Knock doesn't seem very anxious to tell me.

KNOCK. Here's an offer. Instead of paying you for the practice . . . God knows when! . . . in money, I'll pay you in kind right away. Work with me for a week and I'll show you how I do it.

PARPALAID. Well, really! It's likelier that in a week's time you'll be writing to ask me how I did it.

KNOCK. Oh, I won't wait till then. There are one or two things you might tell me here and now.

PARPALAID. Ask away.

KNOCK. Has St. Maurice a crier?

PARPALAID. Do you mean a town crier?

KNOCK. I mean a town crier.

PARPALAID. Yes. He cries the lost dogs . . . and if anyone has missed their purse . . . or a sale of old furniture . . . and he does odd jobs for the Mayor.

KNOCK. Good. What's the population?

PARPALAID. Three thousand five hundred, perhaps . . . six thousand if you count the two villages beyond.

KNOCK. And in the whole district?

PARPALAID. More than double.

KNOCK. Poor people mostly?

MADAME PARPALAID. Not at all. Many of them well off . . . and some of them quite well off. There are some very big farms . . . and lots of them own land.

PARPALAID. But stingy . . . stingy!

KNOCK. Manufactures?

PARPALAID. No.

KNOCK. Much trade?

MADAME PARPALAID. There are shops enough.

KNOCK. Are the shopkeepers keen?

PARPALAID. What on? Oh, on selling things! No. They make a little extra by it . . . and it passes the time.

MADAME PARPALAID. And while the wife keeps the shop, the husband can go about a bit.

PARPALAID. Or the other way on.

MADAME PARPALAID. Not so often the other way on. But, after all, where have the women to go? The men have fishing, and rabbits to shoot . . . and they play skittles . . . and in winter there's the café.

KNOCK. Are the women religious?

DOCTOR PARPALAID *laughs.*

KNOCK. It's a most important question, I assure you.

MADAME PARPALAID. They go to Church.

KNOCK. But do they think about God a lot?

MADAME PARPALAID. Oh, dear me, no!

KNOCK. Good. And how about vice?

PARPALAID. Vice! What sort of vice?

KNOCK. Drug-taking, fornication, blasphemies, political aberrations?

PARPALAID. I fail to see any connection whatever between . . . ! Drug-taking . . . no, hardly any. Politics . . . the usual thing.

KNOCK. No one who'd go to the stake for the Single Tax or the Capital Levy . . . or send you there?

PARPALAID. Thank goodness, no.

KNOCK. Much adultery?

PARPALAID. What!

KNOCK. Would you say that conjugal infidelity was more epidemic or endemic . . . and in which category does it prevail?

PARPALAID. You really do ask the most amazing questions! Here, as elsewhere, there may be a few husbands whose wives are no better than they should be. But not more than elsewhere.

MADAME PARPALAID. Less. What chance have they? The way people spy on you!

KNOCK. Good. Nothing else to tell me? No queer religions, superstitions, Orders of Druids, and such-like?

MADAME PARPALAID. I did know some ladies very taken up with spiritualism.

KNOCK. Aha!

MADAME PARPALAID. They used to meet at the Notary's . . . in her drawing room . . . and do table-rapping.

KNOCK. Horrid habit! Most degrading!

MADAME PARPALAID. But that's over.

KNOCK. So much the better. And no old herb women . . . no white witches?

JEAN, *at intervals, is now cranking at the car. At each failure to make any effect upon it, he stops for breath and mops his forehead.*

PARPALAID. Once upon a time may be. But that's all done with.

KNOCK. Then the reign of medical science can begin. *Showing some signs of excitement, rubbing his hands, pacing up and down.* Would it, my dear sir, be too cruel to ask this venerable vehicle to make one more effort to carry us to our destination? I can't tell you how anxious I am to get there.

MADAME PARPALAID. This is very sudden.

KNOCK. Can't we make a move?

PARPALAID. But what's the attraction . . . now?

KNOCK, *takes a turn or two without answering.* My good Doctor Parpalaid . . . I am strongly convinced that at St. Maurice you have made a mess of a most magnificent opportunity. You should be leaving with your pockets full of gold . . . you should be bulging behind and before with bank notes and bonds. And you, my dear madam, with three rows of pearls round your neck, rolling off in a two-hundred-thousand-franc limousine . . . and not in this Noah's Ark.

MADAME PARPALAID. Are you joking, Dr. Knock?

KNOCK. It is not a matter for joking, Madame.

MADAME PARPALAID. But how dreadful! Alfred . . . do you hear?

PARPALAID. My dear! Dr. Knock . . . He will forgive my saying so . . . is something of a visionary. And such rushing to extremes may denote, I think, incipient paranoia. A minute ago the practice wasn't worth twopence. Now it's a gold mine.

MADAME PARPALAID, *her mind not upon* DR. KNOCK *at all.* But, you know, you never would listen to reason. And haven't I said again and again we could have done so much better at St. Maurice if only we'd set about it the right way?

PARPALAID. Very well, very well! I shall be back three months hence for my first instalment . . . and then we'll see.

KNOCK. Then you shall see. Can't we get along now?

PARPALAID, *to* JEAN. Are you ready?

JEAN, *in his ear.* Oh, I'm ready enough. But how we're ever going to start her up again . . .

PARPALAID. Why ever not?

JEAN. It'll take a bit of doing. . . .

PARPALAID. We must give a push behind. . . .

JEAN. Maybe!

PARPALAID. We've twenty yards on the flat. I'll drive . . . and you push.

JEAN. Me?

PARPALAID. And when she's well started . . . just jump on. Now, my dear, get in. Get in, my dear Doctor. I'll drive a little now. And Jean . . . who's a perfect Hercules . . . is just going to show us how the car can be set in motion without any cranking at all. A sort of self-starter . . . though in place of electricity we have the human muscle. Though that again stands for a sort of electricity or magnetism, does it not? Now! Now, then! DR. PARPALAID *sits to the steering wheel. And* JEAN *wedges himself behind the car and begins to push.*

ACT TWO

DOCTOR PARPALAID's *old consulting room, which* KNOCK *has already begun to re-equip with up-to-date medical apparatus; its steel and enamel shining against the furniture. On the walls hang some charts and discreet anatomical diagrams. In particular there is a blackboard. At the back, through curtained glass doors, the waiting room with its benches, empty at present, can be seen. In the middle of the room is a table at which* KNOCK *himself is busy writing. The* TOWN CRIER *has just come in and stands cap in hand.*

KNOCK, *looking up.* Oh, yes . . . you're the Town Crier.

THE CRIER. Yes, Mr. Knock.

KNOCK. Doctor Knock.

THE CRIER. Doctor Knock.

KNOCK. When I speak to you, please answer "Yes, Doctor," or "No, Doctor." And when you talk of me say "The Doctor did this," or "The Doctor said so and so." It's a thing I'm particular about. How did you all speak of Doctor Parpalaid?

THE CRIER. Oh . . . all right. Not much in him . . . but he was a good sort.

KNOCK. That's not what I asked you. Didn't you call him "Doctor"?

THE CRIER. Well . . . we did and we didn't.

KNOCK. But there wasn't much in him, you thought.

THE CRIER. I didn't. Some did.

KNOCK. Why?

THE CRIER. Why . . . you'd come here to see him . . . and nine times out of ten he'd say, "Be off with you," he'd say . . . "there's nothing wrong with you . . . you'll be all right tomorrow," he'd say.

KNOCK. Really.

THE CRIER. And half the time he'd not be listening to what you told him. "Yes, yes, yes . . ." that's all you'd get out of him. And then he'd start talking of his motorcar.

KNOCK. Which wasn't what you came for?

THE CRIER. Or he'd tell you to take some twopenny remedy. Drink a glass of hot water first thing in the morning . . . or a cup o' camomile when you went to bed. Now, when a man pays eight francs for his doctor he does like his physic to cost something. No, I'm not such a fool, am I, that I can't drink a glass of water . . . if I'd happen to want it.

KNOCK. Well . . . I'm sorry to hear all that. But I wanted to ask you something. What did you charge Dr. Parpalaid when he employed you professionally?

THE CRIER, *grimly*. He never did.

KNOCK. What . . . in all the thirty years he was here?

THE CRIER. Not once.

KNOCK. Oh, you must have forgotten. Well . . . what do you charge?

THE CRIER. Three francs for a half round . . . and five francs for the whole round. You may call that dear. But it takes doing . . . to do it well. And if ever you want a round cried, Mr. . . .

KNOCK. Doctor!

THE CRIER. Doctor! . . . if the extra two francs is not a great matter to you . . . it's worth it for the whole round.

KNOCK. What's the difference?

THE CRIER. With the half round I cry you five times. In front of the Town Hall, in front of the Post Office, in front of the Hôtel Dauphin, at Gallows' Gate and at the corner of the Market. But with the whole round I cry you eleven times. I cry you in front of the . . .

KNOCK. Good. I'll take the whole round. Are you free this morning?

THE CRIER. This minute.

KNOCK. Very good. Here's what I want you to cry. *He hands him the document he has been writing.*

THE CRIER, *surveying it*. Handwritings of all sorts, as you may say, aren't much mystery to me. But you might read it me through just once.

KNOCK, *reading*. Dr. Knock, who has now taken over Dr. Parpalaid's practice, presents his compliments to the inhabitants of St. Maurice, and begs to inform them that in the public interest, and with the hope of checking the alarming increase of those diseases which for the last few years have been spreading through this once healthy district . . .

THE CRIER. That's true . . . so they have.

KNOCK. . . . he will give from nine-thirty to eleven-thirty every Monday morning free consultation and advice to the aforesaid inhabitants of St. Maurice. To strangers the charge will be eight francs as usual.

THE CRIER, *much impressed, taking the paper.* That's a great scheme. They'll think a lot of that. "In the public interest." But of course it is. Have you forgotten, though, that it's Monday today? If I cry that now they'll all be at you before you can turn round.

KNOCK. D'you think so?

THE CRIER. And Monday's market day, what's more . . . ah, you hadn't thought of that. Why, half the countryside's here on a Monday. When they've heard me cry this . . . you won't have room for them.

KNOCK. I'll manage.

THE CRIER. But there's another thing. It's market days when the patients do come. Market days were when Parpalaid had his . . . when he had any. So if you're going to see them free, gratis . . .

KNOCK. My good man, what I want you to grasp is this. The health of the people must be watched over. Nothing is more important. If I wanted to make money I should be in Paris . . . or New York.

THE CRIER. Ah, you put your finger on it, you do! We don't take care of ourselves as we ought. We don't go easy as we ought . . . we're always working. And the worse we feel the harder we go. Beasts of burden we might be.

KNOCK. You're a man that thinks for himself, I see.

THE CRIER. I do. I've not had the education of some. But there is some I can teach a thing or so to for all that. You ask the Mayor. Why, one day, Mr. Knock . . .

KNOCK. Dr. Knock.

THE CRIER. . . . Dr. Knock. Why, one day, Doctor, the Prefect himself was at our Town Hall here . . . and ask any of the gentlemen present if it's not true . . . ask the Deputy Mayor . . . ask the Town Clerk. And there was I, as it might be now . . .

KNOCK. And the Prefect saw at a glance the sort of a man you were . . . and that here was a Town Crier that knew a thing or two more than many a man that wasn't a Town Crier knew . . . for all they might think themselves more knowing than any Town Crier in the country. And who was it had no answer to make to that? The Mayor.

THE CRIER, *highly delighted*. That's true . . . every word! Why, you might have been there.

KNOCK. I wasn't.

THE CRIER. Then someone must have told you.

KNOCK *smiles a diplomatic denial*.

THE CRIER. Then you've been talking to the Prefect.

KNOCK *makes a noncommittal gesture*.

KNOCK. Well . . . I rely on you. And don't waste time about it, will you?

THE CRIER. No . . . no. *Then with some little diffidence*. But if I don't come back till I've done . . . why, I'll be too late. So d'you think, p'raps, you'd be so kind as to see me now?

KNOCK. What? Well, well, well . . . we must be quick about it. I've appointments with Monsieur Bernard, the schoolmaster, and with Monsieur Mousquet, the chemist . . . and I must get through with them before the patients begin. What's wrong with you?

THE CRIER. I must think. I know! When I've had my dinner I'll sometimes get a sort of a feeling . . . yes, a kind of a feeling here. *He plants a finger somewhere about the middle of his person*. A sort of a tickling . . . or a scratcheling.

KNOCK, *putting on an air of the greatest concentration*. Wait. Let's be clear about this. Does it scratch . . . or does it tickle?

THE CRIER. Scratch. Well . . . sometimes it tickles too.

KNOCK. Show me the exact spot.

THE CRIER. There.

KNOCK. There? Or there?

THE CRIER. There. Well . . . it might be there. Between the two.

KNOCK. Quite so . . . between the two. I wonder if it's not a thought to the left . . . where my finger is now.

THE CRIER. I believe it may be.

KNOCK. Hurt you when I press . . . so?

THE CRIER. Yes . . . it sort of hurts.

KNOCK. Ah! Now do you feel that tickling, as you call it, more than usual when you've been eating venison?

THE CRIER. I don't ever eat venison. But if I did . . . I believe I would.

KNOCK. Ah! Ah! That's most important. How old are you?

THE CRIER. Fifty-one. Fifty-two next year.

KNOCK. Nearer fifty-two than fifty-one?

THE CRIER. Yes . . . I am. *Apprehension is growing on him. His eyes are rounder, his jaw is loosening a little*.

KNOCK, *kindly but severe*. Well, my friend . . . well . . . well! You can

work today as usual. Go to bed early. Tomorrow . . . stop in bed,
I'll come and see you. I shan't charge you anything. But don't go telling
people that now.

THE CRIER. Thank you, Doctor . . . thank you . . . very kind. But . . .
is it something serious that's wrong?

KNOCK. No . . . no . . . we won't call it serious . . . yet. We're taking
it in time . . . just in time. Do you smoke?

THE CRIER. I chew.

KNOCK. Stop it. Do you drink?

THE CRIER. The usual.

KNOCK. Not a drop. Are you married?

THE CRIER. Yes.

KNOCK. Forget it.

THE CRIER, *wiping the sweat from his brow.* Can I eat anything?

KNOCK. Well, as you'll be working today you can take a little soup. Tomorrow we'll see what we can really cut you off. Till then . . . do as
I've told you.

THE CRIER. Doctor . . . you don't p'raps think I'd better go to bed at
once, do you? I don't feel at all well.

KNOCK. No, no! Not on any account. In a case like yours one must never,
never be in bed between sunrise and sunset. You go your rounds as if
nothing had happened . . . and wait till tonight.

Distracted, but docile, THE CRIER *departs. In the waiting room stands* MONSIEUR
BERNARD, *the schoolmaster. He is a meek and rather nervous man.* KNOCK
ushers him into the consulting room and they bow ceremoniously.

KNOCK. Good morning, Monsieur Bernard, good morning. I hope this is
not an inconvenient time for you?

BERNARD. No, Doctor, no. I've a minute or two. My assistant is there.
It's the play interval.

KNOCK. But I was very anxious for a talk with you. We have so many
mutual interests . . . and such important ones . . . and I am not the
man, believe me, to wish to weaken the excellent understanding that
existed between you and my predecessor.

BERNARD. The understanding . . . ?

KNOCK. Nor am I the sort, you'll find, that wants it all his own way . . .
upsets things for the sake of upsetting them. No. It's your advice I need
to begin with.

BERNARD. I'm afraid I don't quite see . . .

KNOCK. Let us leave things for the moment as they are . . . and later
improve them if we can.

BERNARD. But . . .

KNOCK. Over sending things to the local papers . . . over lectures, even in our talks together . . . I'll take my cue from you . . . I'll fit my time to yours.

BERNARD. I fear I don't in the least understand what you are talking about.

KNOCK. I only want to assure you that as far as I am concerned our association from the very beginning shall be a fruitful one.

BERNARD, *utterly, hopelessly fogged.* I'm afraid I'm very stupid.

KNOCK. My dear sir . . . your association with Dr. Parpalaid was naturally a very close one. . . .

BERNARD. I used to meet him sometimes at the Café. We played billiards now and then.

KNOCK. No, no, no, no . . . not that sort of association.

BERNARD. I don't know of any other.

KNOCK. But, my dear sir . . . however did you set about teaching people here the laws of health . . . setting up the right standards of household hygiene . . . of . . . good heavens! . . . the hundred and one things a doctor and a schoolmaster can only do if they do them together?

BERNARD. We didn't set about them at all.

KNOCK. You preferred each to work at it your own way.

BERNARD. No, not our own way . . . nor any way. We never gave the matter a thought . . . either of us. Nor has anyone else in the place that I've ever known of.

KNOCK, *staring at him; amazed, quite overcome.* If I had not heard that from your own lips I'd never have believed it.
A painful silence falls.

BERNARD, *apologetically.* I'm sorry to disappoint you. But it wasn't quite my place to begin such a thing . . . even if I'd ever thought of it . . . even if the school work left me time.

KNOCK. No, no! You waited for the call. It never came.

BERNARD. Oh . . . whenever I've been asked to do anything I've been only too anxious. . . .

KNOCK. Monsieur Bernard, I am sure of it.
Another silence falls.

KNOCK, *indignation overwhelming him.* Good God! To think of those wretched people left to their own devices . . . hygienically . . . prophylactically!

BERNARD. They certainly are.

KNOCK. I'll wager they drink the water here, and give never a thought to the billions of bacteria in each mouthful.

BERNARD. No, I'm sure they don't.

KNOCK. Do you suppose they even know what a microbe is?

BERNARD. I doubt it. Some of them have heard the word. But I expect they think it's a sort of fly.

KNOCK. Terrible! Terrible! Well, my dear Monsieur Bernard . . . it'll naturally take a little time now to destroy this Fools' Paradise. But we must do our best . . . you and I. We must do our best.

BERNARD. Oh, I'm quite willing. I only fear I shan't be of much help.

KNOCK. Monsieur Bernard . . . somebody who knows you very well tells me you have one serious fault. You're too modest. You are the only person apparently who is not aware of the moral authority you wield . . . and what a quite extraordinary personal influence you have. Forgive a mere stranger for putting it so bluntly. But I'm told that nothing of any importance gets done in this town without you.

BERNARD, *his face wreathing into timid smiles.* Oh, my dear Doctor . . . !

KNOCK. But it's so! Now, I can treat my patients . . . true! But the disease itself . . . who'll help fight that and eradicate that if you don't? Who but you can tell these poor ignorant people of the dangers that besiege them every minute of the day . . . can teach them at least that it's no use waiting till they're dead to call in the doctor?

BERNARD. They are very careless. I don't deny that.

KNOCK. Well . . . let's begin at the beginning. I have here the material for several popular lectures . . . very full notes, good pictures . . . and I've a magic-lantern. You, of course, are an accomplished speaker. But, for a start . . . here's one all written out . . . most interesting, quite entertaining . . . on typhoid fever. The various unexpected forms it takes. The many media by which it may invade the system . . . water, bread, milk, shellfish, vegetables of all sorts, watercress, dust, contagious breath, etc., etc. How it may be breeding in you for weeks and months and you'll never know it . . . till, one day . . . Pfth! The complications that come with it and after it. And all embellished with the most excellent pictures . . . the bacilli well magnified, specimens of secreta, sections of a diseased gland, of an intestinal perforation. All in colors . . . pink, red, yellow, green . . . you know.

BERNARD, *showing signs of a most pathetic discomfort.* Really . . . I'm afraid . . . I'm of a rather nervous nature. And if I were to start studying all this . . . d'you know, I shouldn't sleep at night.

KNOCK. But that's what I want . . . that's the idea. Or rather, that's the very sort of shock that I want you to give them all. Oh, you'll get used to it. But they mustn't sleep at night. That's what is wrong. They sleep and they sleep . . . lulled in their false security. And when they wake, it's too late. Disease has them by the throat.

BERNARD. But my own health is already by no means what it should be.

My father and mother never thought I'd live to grow up. Of course, I know . . . the microbes on the slides . . . are not real microbes. But all the same . . .

KNOCK, *buoyantly.* And if that one doesn't appeal to everybody . . . here's another: "The Germ Carrier." No one need be frightened by this. But it makes it as plain as day, proves by instance upon instance, that a man can go about looking the picture of health, clean tongue, eye bright, appetite excellent, and be carrying in every nook and cranny of his system trillions of germs . . . poisonous enough to infect a whole county. I have a right to suspect any man I see of being a germ carrier. You now! What is there to prove to me that you are not?

BERNARD. I . . . me!

KNOCK. Show me the man who'll leave that lecture and crack jokes about it.

BERNARD. Doctor . . . do you really think . . . that I am a germ carrier?

KNOCK. No, not necessarily . . . not you in particular. I merely make an example of you.

MONSIEUR BERNARD *is dumfounded.*

KNOCK, *glancing toward the waiting room, where* MOUSQUET, *the chemist, has now established himself.* Ah, there's Monsieur Mousquet. Well, we'll meet again soon. And thank you . . . thank you for being so ready to help me. I was sure you would be . . . I was sure of it.

And MONSIEUR BERNARD *finds himself outside, while* MONSIEUR MOUSQUET *takes his place. A foxy and rather a tart little man.*

KNOCK. Sit down, my dear Monsieur Mousquet . . . pray sit down. I found time yesterday just to give one glance round your . . . establishment. Well . . . one glance showed me how excellently it is equipped . . . and how admirably you manage it. Everything spick and span and up to date. All that a chemist's shop should be.

MOUSQUET. Doctor, you're too kind.

KNOCK. No, no . . . these things concern me very closely. A physician, I always say, who has not a first-class pharmaceutical chemist to depend on is like a general fighting a battle without guns.

MOUSQUET. I'm glad you give my profession its due.

KNOCK. Still . . . such a high standard of service as you provide must bring its own reward as well. You can't make less than twenty-five thousand francs a year.

MOUSQUET. Profit? My dear Doctor . . . I wish I made half.

KNOCK. Come, come, Monsieur Mousquet . . . I'm not the income-tax collector. As between friends . . . between colleagues.

MOUSQUET. No reason whatever, Doctor, I shouldn't tell you the truth . . .

and this is the truth, I'm sorry to say. It takes me all my time to make ten thousand.

KNOCK. But that's monstrous. Oh . . . I'd have said twenty-five thousand at the very least. You've no competitors?

MOUSQUET. Not one . . . for ten miles or more.

KNOCK. Enemies?

MOUSQUET. Not that I know of.

KNOCK, *his voice dropping confidentially.* And there's never been any little accident? Oh, these things will happen. One's in a hurry . . . the laudanum's where the castor oil ought to be . . . it's done in a moment . . . and the patient's got the bottle!

MOUSQUET. Never . . . never, never. No, believe me . . . not the slightest mistake made . . . these twenty years.

KNOCK. Then . . . we needn't look further perhaps! . . . was my predecessor not quite up to his work?

MOUSQUET. Well . . . that depends on how you look at it.

KNOCK. Come . . . between ourselves.

MOUSQUET. Dr. Parpalaid was a most worthy man. Personally, we couldn't have got on better . . .

KNOCK. But if you'd bound up his prescriptions at the year's end they wouldn't have made a very big book I suppose?

MOUSQUET. You've hit it.

KNOCK. Then I ask myself . . . putting together all I've heard about him so far . . . did he really believe in the science of medicine?

MOUSQUET. I did my best . . . I always did the right thing by him. If customers had anything out of the way the matter with them I'd send them on to him. Did I ever see them again? No.

KNOCK. I really cannot tell you how it distresses me to hear things like this. My dear Monsieur Mousquet . . . our calling, yours and mine, ranks second to none in the world. How shameful to let it sink bit by bit from that high place of prosperity and influence to which our predecessors have raised it! It's a sort of treason.

MOUSQUET. Yes, it is. And setting the money question aside, does it seem right, sir, I ask you, for me to be thought less of than the ironmonger and the grocer? And I assure you that Madame Mousquet can no more afford the hats and stockings that the ironmonger's wife here shows herself off in, Sundays and weekdays both, than . . .

KNOCK. Don't talk of it . . . don't talk of it. You might as well be telling me that the Prime Minister's mother had to take in washing.

MOUSQUET. I wish Madame Mousquet could hear you say so.

KNOCK. We are not here, you and I, to be treated like that in a place like this.

MOUSQUET. We ought not to be.

KNOCK. For, to begin with, every single soul in the place is, ipso facto, a potential patient.

MOUSQUET. That's asking a good deal.

KNOCK. Every single one of them.

MOUSQUET. Yes, I suppose there's nobody that at some time or another doesn't have to look to us . . .

KNOCK. It should be all the time.

MOUSQUET. But he has to fall ill.

KNOCK. "Fall ill!" That is a phrase, Monsieur Mousquet, that modern science has made meaningless. Health is a mere word . . . and a word we'd do far better to take out of the dictionary. I only see around me people suffering more or less acutely from diseases more or less serious, which more or less rapidly get the better of them. Of course, if you go telling them they're quite well they're glad enough to believe it. But you tell them what is not true. And your only excuse for doing it is if you have so many patients on your hands already that you can't attend to any more.

MOUSQUET. That seems a very sound theory.

KNOCK. It is simply the modern scientific view of the matter. Think it over. Why . . . we compel every citizen to defend his country. On the very same principle we should force him . . . whether he likes it or not . . . to fight against disease.

MOUSQUET. You're a man of ideas, Doctor . . . I can see that. And people who haven't any may say what they like . . . it's ideas that count.

KNOCK *gets up:* MOUSQUET, *too, to take his leave.*

KNOCK. Listen to me. I may be too sanguine. I daresay there are disappointments in store for me. But if, this time next year, you haven't made that twenty-five thousand francs profit you deserve . . . and if Madame Mousquet hasn't the dresses and hats and silk stockings she simply owes it to her position to have . . . I give you leave to come here and kick me down my own stairs.

MOUSQUET. My dear Doctor . . . if I weren't grateful to you for what you say, I'd be a fool . . . and I'd be a scoundrel if I didn't help you in every possible way.

KNOCK. I rely on you. And you may on me.

They part on the best terms with each other and with themselves. Patients have gathered in the waiting room by now.

KNOCK, *going out among them and speaking to some unseen attendant.* My patients. A dozen of them already. Well . . . if any more come you'd better warn them that after eleven-thirty I really can see no more . . . at least I can't see them gratuitously. Are you the first, Madame?

Enter a farmer's wife, middle-aged, in black, and of a very operculous countenance and habit of body. She carries her morning's purchases, a basketful, besides a new saucepan and one other more mysteriously shaped package, and is reluctant to let them go.

KNOCK. You do belong to the district?

FARMER'S WIFE. I do.

KNOCK. To St. Maurice?

FARMER'S WIFE. The big farm on the road to Luchere.

KNOCK. Is it your own?

FARMER'S WIFE. Mine and my husband's.

KNOCK. A farm like that now . . . means a lot of work.

FARMER'S WIFE. It does. Eighteen cows, the bull, the fat stock. There's a mare in foal . . . we've goats and a dozen pigs . . . and then there's the poultry.

KNOCK. And no one to help you?

FARMER'S WIFE. Why, of course! Three men . . . and a girl in the house. And more for the hay and the harvest.

KNOCK. Dear me . . . dear me. But it doesn't leave you much time to look after yourself.

FARMER'S WIFE. No, indeed.

KNOCK. And you feel ill?

FARMER'S WIFE. No, I don't. But I get blown.

KNOCK. Blown? Blown! Show me your tongue. H'm. Not much appetite?

FARMER'S WIFE. No.

KNOCK. What do you eat mostly?

FARMER'S WIFE. Meat.

The examination proceeds with the usual formalities.

KNOCK. Bend over. Breathe. Breathe. Cough. Cough again. Did you ever fall off a ladder when you were young?

FARMER'S WIFE. I don't remember.

KNOCK, *still tapping and listening; now giving her a good sharp punch in the small of the back.* Ever feel a pain here . . . at night . . . when you're getting into bed . . . a sort of a cramp?

FARMER'S WIFE. Yes . . . sometimes.

KNOCK. Now, try and remember. It might have been quite a big ladder.

FARMER'S WIFE. It would have been.

KNOCK. Nine feet high, say . . . and placed against a wall. And you fell backwards . . . plump! That's where you caught it . . . on the left one . . . luckily.

FARMER'S WIFE. Was it?

KNOCK. Did you never see Dr. Parpalaid about this?

FARMER'S WIFE. No.

KNOCK. Why not?

FARMER'S WIFE. He never saw you for nothing.

KNOCK *finishes his examination, makes her sit down, sits opposite her, turns his shining spectacles full on her. There is a pause.*

KNOCK. Do you realize what's wrong with you?

FARMER'S WIFE. No.

KNOCK. That's as well, perhaps. Now! You want to be cured . . . or you don't want to be cured.

FARMER'S WIFE. I do.

KNOCK. Let me warn you at once that it will be a very long and a very costly business.

FARMER'S WIFE. Oh! My gracious! Why will it?

KNOCK. Because a trouble that has been going on forty years can't be cured in five minutes.

FARMER'S WIFE. Forty years!

KNOCK. Ever since you fell off that ladder.

FARMER'S WIFE. What's it going to cost me?

KNOCK. What's a yearling calf worth now?

FARMER'S WIFE. That depends on the size and the market rate. A good one . . . oh, four or five hundred francs.

KNOCK. And a pig for killing?

FARMER'S WIFE. Oh . . . a thousand, or more.

KNOCK. Well . . . it'll cost you two pigs and a calf and a half.

FARMER'S WIFE. What . . . what? Three thousand francs! Mother Mary . . . what a thing to happen to me!

KNOCK. Would you sooner try Lourdes? I say nothing against it.

FARMER'S WIFE. That costs a lot too . . . and it's never sure. But how can I have got all that the matter with me?

KNOCK, *with a most obliging air, takes a piece of chalk and goes to the blackboard, upon which he sketches in a masterly fashion.*

KNOCK. I can show you in a minute on the blackboard. Here's your spinal cord . . . in section . . . very roughly, of course. This is your Turck's facellum . . . and this is your Clarke's column. Can you follow? Well, when you fell off that ladder your Turck and your Clarke slipped . . . side-slipped . . . like that. *He demonstrates with the chalk.* Oh . . . a fiftieth of an inch. That's not much, is it? No, you're quite right. But look at them. What a position! The result is a constant and severe strain upon the multipolaries.

FARMER'S WIFE. Think of that now . . . oh, think of that!

KNOCK. Don't imagine you're going to die of it today or tomorrow. We can take our time.

FARMER'S WIFE. And all through falling off that ladder!

KNOCK. It might . . . it might even be better to let the thing alone. Money's hard to get . . . heaven knows. And when one's old . . . a few years of life, more or less! There's little pleasure in them anyhow.

FARMER'S WIFE. Couldn't you . . . somehow . . . manage to . . . do it a little cheaper? Though I'd want it done properly, mark you, all the same.

KNOCK. I'll tell you what I can do . . . I can keep you under observation for a little. That'll cost next to nothing. Then, at the end of a week, say . . . you'll know yourself how you're feeling . . . worse or better. And then you can make up your mind.

FARMER'S WIFE. That's right! That's right!

KNOCK. Good. Now go back home. Did you drive here?

FARMER'S WIFE. I walked.

KNOCK, *sitting at his table and as he talks writing out his directions.* Find someone to drive you back. Go to bed when you get there. Is there a room you can be left alone in . . . quite alone? Have the shutters pulled to and the blinds down . . . so that the light won't trouble you. And say you're not to be talked to by anyone . . . not by anyone. Now . . . you'll eat no solids for a week. A glass of Vichy water every two hours. And . . . if you can't do without . . . half a biscuit, not more, soaked in milk . . . warm milk . . . morning and night. And I'd rather you went without the biscuit . . . if you could. Well . . . that won't cost you much, will it? Then, at the end of the week, we'll see how you are. If you feel quite yourself again . . . spry and ready for anything . . . we shall know that things are less serious than we have reason to suppose . . . and no one will be more pleased than I. But if, on the other hand, you're rather weak, rather run down . . . head swimming a little . . . wanting to stay in bed . . . then we mustn't delay any longer . . . for a course of treatment will most undoubtedly be indicated. So that's understood.

FARMER'S WIFE. I suppose so.

KNOCK. I've written it all down . . . and I'll be round to see you soon. *He takes her to the door, and most considerately out into the waiting room. To the invisible attendant.* Mariette . . . help this lady very carefully down the stairs, please. And get her a cab if you can. Now, Madame . . . *This last is to a lady who has at once detached herself from the now gathering crowd of waiting patients. She is a lady of sixty, dressed rather flowingly in violet. She carries a crutch-handled stick, which seems to lend her an almost royal dignity.* KNOCK *bows her into the consulting room. She begins at once and most categorically, and she is a lady of rapid speech.*

THE LADY. Yes, Doctor . . . you may well be surprised to see me.

KNOCK. A little surprised.

THE LADY. When a Madame Pons, that is . . . a Mademoiselle Lempoumas that was . . . comes with all the rest for free treatment . . . somewhat astonishing!

KNOCK. But the greater compliment . . . and I am conscious of it.

MADAME PONS. A pretty upshot, isn't it, of this ghastly state of things . . . a lot of riffraff, a crew of pork butchers, rolling in their carriages and giving champagne suppers to light ladies . . . while a Demoiselle Lempoumas, whose family dates from the thirteenth century and once owned half the countryside, who is related to everyone of any consequence for miles round, comes to stand in line with the paupers of St. Maurice. Not quite as it should be, I think, Doctor.

KNOCK. By no means, Madame.

MADAME PONS. Well, well . . . I won't pretend my income's what it was . . . or that I still keep my six servants . . . or the four horses in the stable . . . or that things are as they were while my uncle was alive. Only last year I had to sell a three-hundred-acre estate . . . La Michouille . . . which my grandmother left me. Michouille . . . the word's Græco-Latin originally . . . our parish priest says . . . comes from Mycodium . . . and means mushroom-hating. And it's quite true that not a single mushroom has ever been found on the place . . . it really is as if the soil did hate them. And what with taxes and repairs it was bringing in next to nothing. Ever since my husband died the tenants . . . needless to say . . . have taken advantage of me . . . worrying, day in and day out, to have something done for them here, or to be left off paying something there . . . till I was weary of the

whole thing . . . weary, weary, weary! So don't you agree, Doctor,
that, taking everything into account, I was right to get rid of it?

KNOCK, *who has listened with the greatest attention.* Yes, Madame, I do . . .
more especially if you were fond of mushrooms . . . and if you invested
the money it brought you to advantage.

MADAME PONS. Ah . . . but that's the sore spot! Day and night I ask
myself . . . have I done the right thing? And I doubt it . . . I gravely
doubt it. I took advice from this idiot of a local lawyer . . . oh, but
he's the best of men! I really don't believe, though, that he has as much
business sense as his wife's drawing-room table . . . which did rap out
an answer or two when the spirits had hold of it. I bought oil shares.
Doctor . . . what do you think of oil?

KNOCK. One of the most useful of minerals. As an investment . . . specu-
lative rather . . . apt to rise a little and then fall a lot for no very
apparent reason.

MADAME PONS. You make me go cold all over. I believe I bought them
when they were . . . right up. Fifty thousand francs' worth. Wasn't it
rather foolish to put all that into oil . . . when one hasn't overmuch
to spare?

KNOCK. I should think it somewhat unwise to put more than ten per cent
of one's capital into oil.

MADAME PONS. Ah, well! But as long as it's not more than ten per cent . . .
why, that's what you'd call not altogether unwise.

KNOCK. By no means.

MADAME PONS. Thank you so much. That relieves my mind . . . it does
indeed. You don't know what a worry the managing of my few little
pennies is to me. I often tell myself I'd be the better for some other
troubles . . . to drive that one away. For we're poor creatures, my
dear Doctor. What's the saying? "Life's a choice of Evils." Well, a
change of any sort does one good, I suppose. And I'm thankful enough,
I'm sure, not to be bothered by tenants and leases and the like. And
I'm too old for adventures . . . of any sort. *The implication is faintly
coquettish.* And I don't want to fly round the world. And you're wondering perhaps what I have come for . . . and whatever did induce me to
stand in line for a free visit to the doctor?

KNOCK. Whatever your reasons, Madame, I am sure they were good ones.

MADAME PONS. I wanted to set them all a good example. When I heard
what you were doing I said . . . Now, that's magnificent, that's most
public-spirited. But I know the people here so well . . . oh, so well!
And I thought to myself . . . No, this is something new . . . and

they'll none of them go near him . . . and that's all the thanks he'll get. But then I said to myself . . . if they see that a Madame Pons, a Mademoiselle Lempoumas that was, is not ashamed to pay a free visit to the doctor . . . why, nor will they be. For the least thing I do is remarked upon . . . quite naturally.

KNOCK. A most praiseworthy step to take, Madame . . . and I thank you for it.

MADAME PONS, *rising to take her leave.* Well, then, my dear Doctor, I am most happy to have made your acquaintance. I am at home every afternoon. And a few friends come in. A select little circle . . . a little pleasant talk round a tea table which my great-great-grandmother sat at in her day. And there will always be a cup on it for you.

KNOCK *bows his thanks.*

MADAME PONS, *goes towards the door, then turning as if at a casual afterthought.* But I have been very, very worried . . . first by my tenants and now by these investments. There are whole nights, I do assure you, when I simply cannot sleep. It's most exhausting. I suppose you don't know, Doctor, do you, of any really good cure for sleeplessness?

KNOCK. Have you suffered from insomnia long?

MADAME PONS. Longer than I care to remember.

KNOCK. Did you consult Dr. Parpalaid about it?

MADAME PONS. Often.

KNOCK. What had he to say?

MADAME PONS. He told me to buy a good Blue Book, or a volume of law reports . . . and to read six pages every night in bed. Oh, he never took the matter seriously at all.

KNOCK. He may have been wrong. I have known cases of insomnia which proved to be of the very gravest import.

MADAME PONS. Really?

KNOCK. Insomnia, for instance, which was due to some organic disease of the intra-cerebral circulation, that change in the arterial walls which we call atheroma. Your cerebral arteries, Madame, the arteries that feed the brain may . . . it is possible . . . be as hard and brittle as pipestems.

MADAME PONS. Pipestems!

KNOCK. A common comparison.

MADAME PONS. Heavens! Would smoking bring that on? I do smoke a little.

KNOCK. We should have to take that into account. Then again . . . insomnia may come from a constant sapping of the grey matter of the brain by nerves that are diseased.

MADAME PONS. But how dreadful! Would you please explain that, Doctor?

KNOCK. Certainly. Try and picture to yourself a sort of crab . . . or a kind of octopus . . . or a very large spider . . . which nibbles at you . . . and sucks at you . . . and little by little drains away all the inside of your head.

MADAME PONS, *going off into hysterics.* Oh! Aha! Oho! How terrible! How horrible! Yes, that's what's the matter. I know it! I knew it! Oh, Doctor, Doctor, I'd rather die at once . . . I'd sooner you killed me. I'm going to faint . . . No, I'm not. But the pain's coming on. Hadn't you better give me a little morphia . . . hadn't you? Doctor . . . what can you do for me? I cannot face it . . . I simply cannot face it . . . I simply cannot face it. But I'd rather know . . . I'd sooner be told straight out. Is it absolutely fatal?

KNOCK. No.

MADAME PONS. Can it be cured?

KNOCK. In time.

MADAME PONS. You're not deceiving me? I'd rather know the worst. I'll be brave.

KNOCK. If you're ready to go through with the treatment steadily and patiently.

MADAME PONS. Which is it you can cure . . . the thing that's like a pipe-stem, or the spider? It's the spider I've got . . . I know!

KNOCK. Either can be cured. Not that I'd dare say that to an ordinary patient . . . who'd have neither the time nor the means for it. But with you, of course . . . !

MADAME PONS. Oh, I'll be a perfect patient, Doctor . . . I'll be most biddable. There's nothing I won't do . . . nothing I won't suffer . . . as long as it's not too painful.

KNOCK. There'll be nothing painful about it. Radium . . . or strictly speaking radioactivity, is the curative agent employed. The only thing is that one must persevere with the cure . . . for two or three years if need be. And one must have a conscientious medical man at hand who will control the modus operandi with the utmost care, and calculate the radioactive applications with the greatest nicety . . . and, in fact, see you nearly every day.

MADAME PONS. Oh . . . I'll persevere. But it's you, Doctor . . . you won't want to give me all that attention.

KNOCK. I'll want to . . . of course I'll want to. There's nothing I'd like better. But can I? That's the trouble. Do you live far away?

MADAME PONS. No . . . in the next street.

KNOCK. Well, well . . . then I can try to run round every morning . . .
I'll do my very best to. Not on Sundays, though. And not on Mondays
. . . because I must be here.

MADAME PONS. But two days running . . . won't that be too long to go?
No treatment at all from Saturday to Tuesday?

KNOCK. Yes . . . well! We must try leaving you very careful directions.
And I shall run in when I can . . . if not Sunday morning . . . Monday afternoon.

MADAME PONS. Oh . . . please, please! But oughtn't I to do something
at once?

KNOCK. Go straight home . . . and stay in your own room. I'll call tomorrow morning and examine you . . . thoroughly.

MADAME PONS. But won't you give me something to take . . . in case . . . ?

KNOCK. Ah . . . yes. Do you pass the chemist's? Ask Monsieur Mousquet
if he'll be good enough to make that up as soon as possible. *And, having
written* MONSIEUR MOUSQUET *his first prescription, he bows* MADAME PONS *to
the door.*

The waiting room is now full, and KNOCK *looks around him with some severity.*

KNOCK. Mariette . . . Mariette! What are all these people waiting for?
The free visits finish at half-past eleven. Don't they know that?

MARIETTE'S VOICE. I've told them. But they say they'd rather stay.

KNOCK. Who's first then?

Two countrymen come forward together. They are the picture of health. KNOCK
*surveys them. They stand there in sheepish mischief, struggling with ill-suppressed
giggles, encouraging each other with a nudge and a wink. The crowd must be in
on the joke, too, by the look of it, by the chuckling which turns, as* KNOCK *stands
there, to an apologetic cough or so. But he takes no notice.*

KNOCK. Well . . . which of you?

FIRST COUNTRYMAN. Both of us.

KNOCK. You don't want to see me together.

FIRST COUNTRYMAN. Both together.

This last remark has a great success in the waiting room.

KNOCK. I don't see patients two at a time. Settle it between you. Besides,
you weren't here just now, were you? There are others before you.

FIRST COUNTRYMAN. They've give us their turn. You ask them. They've
give it us.

SECOND COUNTRYMAN. Give it us both . . . him and me . . . we're sort
of twins.

The waiting room is enjoying it thoroughly. KNOCK *pauses. But suddenly he
makes up his mind, ushers them in and shuts the door sharply. The interview*

which follows resolves itself more into action than talk. KNOCK's *phrases are very curt indeed, and he goes about his business in an almost military way. For the first few moments the pseudo-patients enjoy their joke greatly; then, somehow, it begins to pall.*

KNOCK. Come in. *To the first.* Undress. *To the second.* You . . . sit there.

FIRST COUNTRYMAN. Altogether?

KNOCK. Take your shirt off. That'll do.

KNOCK *then "goes over" him pretty completely. Tongue, teeth, eyes, eyelids. Then he takes an illuminated laryngoscope and flashes it, first, to his alarm, in the fellow's face and next, to his great discomfort, into the depths of his throat. Then he points to the examination couch.*

KNOCK. Lie down there. Put your knees down.

And then an even worse ordeal begins, soundings, tappings, and pinchings of the most expert and scientific sort. KNOCK's *face is gravity itself, and his patient's comes to match it. So does the companion's. The silence is broken but once by the Doctor's short "Put your arm up." Then it settles heavily till the examination ends.*

KNOCK. That'll do. Dress yourself.

Silence again while he does so. KNOCK *is in an attitude of scientific detachment. He gives a glance at his fingernails. He takes a paper from his table and puts it down again. Heaven knows what he is thinking of.*

KNOCK, *suddenly.* Father alive?

FIRST COUNTRYMAN. Dead.

KNOCK. Die suddenly?

FIRST COUNTRYMAN. Yes.

KNOCK. Thought so. Wasn't an old man?

FIRST COUNTRYMAN. Forty-nine.

KNOCK. So much!

Another silence. This little exchange has spread a deep discomfort through the room. Then KNOCK *takes up a sheaf of large colored anatomical designs which he shows, one by one. They are of the chief organs of the human body, and they show, above, man as he should be; below, and very luridly, man as he is when he drinks a very great deal more than is good for him.*

KNOCK. I'm going to show you what your inside is like. That represents the kidneys of a healthy man. Your kidneys! Liver of a healthy man. Your liver! Heart of a healthy man. Your heart! No . . . your heart's worse than that.

The depression deepens as the Doctor quietly puts the pictures away.

FIRST COUNTRYMAN, *meekly.* Perhaps I oughtn't to drink quite so much, Doctor?

KNOCK. It won't make any difference.

FIRST COUNTRYMAN. Isn't there anything I can take for it?

KNOCK. Hardly worth while. *To the other.* Now . . . you!

FIRST COUNTRYMAN. I'd be very glad to come back again . . . and pay, Doctor.

KNOCK. Quite useless. *His eye is now upon the other fellow, who is cowering on his chair.*

SECOND COUNTRYMAN. There's nothing the matter with me, Doctor.

KNOCK, *tremendously.* How do you know?

SECOND COUNTRYMAN. I feel quite well . . . I do indeed.

KNOCK. Then what did you come here for?

SECOND COUNTRYMAN. He asked me . . .

KNOCK. Because he wasn't big enough to come all alone? Undress!

SECOND COUNTRYMAN. No, Doctor, please . . . no, no . . . not today! I'll come back . . . some other time, Doctor . . . some other time. . . . *He opens the door and flies. So does his fellow. The waiting room, it would seem, has been joyfully expectant of the re-emergence of the two protagonists of the joke. But at the sight of them the chuckling stops, an awed hush falls, and* KNOCK *watches them depart in silence, through a silent crowd. Then, left alone, he rubs his hands. It is a favorite gesture of his.*

ACT THREE

We are in the front hall of St. Maurice's one hotel. It is just what one would expect to find in a small French town—at least, it was once. But a curious change has come over it. It has undergone much scrubbing and all dust-collecting super-fluities of furnishing are removed. Certainly there still hang on the walls a few cheery advertisements of liqueurs, a motoring map with a tire company's name, an effigy superscribed. But, outnumbering and subduing these, we find placards which in harsher, firmer tones tell us of vaccination, of inoculation, of notifiable disease. We are even told to wipe our feet when we come in. In fact, the whole place looks less hotel than hospital; we can almost smell the antiseptic.

It is winter time, for through a window we can see the valley in deep snow. From her kitchen regions comes Madame Rémy, the landlady. Through the front door comes Scipio, the hotel factotum, luggage laden.

MADAME RÉMY. The omnibus come, Scipio?

SCIPIO. Yes'm.

MADAME RÉMY. They said the road was blocked by the snow.

SCIPIO. No . . . it's only a quarter-hour late.

MADAME RÉMY. Whose luggage?

SCIPIO. Lady from Livron . . . come for a consultation.

MADAME RÉMY. But she's not due till this evening.

SCIPIO. Wrong. Lady from St. Marcellin this evening.

MADAME RÉMY. Whose bag's this?

SCIPIO. Old Parp's.

MADAME RÉMY. Monsieur Parpalaid? No!

SCIPIO. Yes. Outside there now.

MADAME RÉMY. But whatever's he turned up for?

SCIPIO. Come for a consultation . . . likely.

MADAME RÉMY, *turning to the board on which are the numbered hooks and keys.* But I've only got 9 and 14 free. And I was keeping 9 for the lady from St. Marcellin. And the lady from Livron must have 14. Why didn't you tell him there wasn't a room left?

SCIPIO. I thought there'd be 14. I'd had no orders about old Parp. How was I to know?

MADAME RÉMY. It's most annoying.

SCIPIO. You'll manage somehow. Now I've got my patients.

MADAME RÉMY. Nothing of the sort, Scipio. You'll stay here and tell Monsieur Parpalaid that there are no rooms left. I can't.

SCIPIO. Well, I can't. The Doctor's due in five minutes and I've only just time to get my white coat on. *He's looking at his notebook now.* And I've No. 5 to see to. Sputum from 2. Temperature charts, 13, 4, 12, 17, 18 . . . and that's not all. And I'm not going to get into trouble with him.

MADAME RÉMY. Can't you even carry the lady's luggage up for her?

SCIPIO. Where's the nurse? What's she doing? Polishing her fingernails? *He vanishes. And* MADAME RÉMY, *sighting* PARPALAID *it would seem, vanishes also.* DOCTOR PARPALAID *appears, as from his journey, all wrapped up. There is something strange about the place, though it puzzles him to say what.*

PARPALAID. Nobody! Madame Rémy! Scipio! Whatever have they been doing to this hotel? Scipio. . . .

At this moment a most immaculate nurse passes through the hall, carrying some shining, nickel-plated piece of apparatus.

NURSE, *seeing a stranger and pausing benignly.* Can I do anything for you?

PARPALAID. I . . . I want Madame Rémy.

NURSE. May I ask what for?

PARPALAID. I want her to show me my room.

NURSE. No . . . there I can't help you, I fear. You're one of the patients that's expected?

PARPALAID. Patients! I'm not a patient. I'm a doctor.

NURSE. Oh . . . the new assistant. Well . . . that's a good thing.

PARPALAID. But . . . surely you know me.

NURSE. I'm sorry. No.

PARPALAID. I'm Dr. Parpalaid. I was the doctor here up to three months ago. Ah . . . you don't belong here?

NURSE. Certainly, I belong here. But I never heard of any doctor but Dr. Knock. If you'll excuse me. Madame Rémy will come in a moment, I'm sure. I must finish sterilizing my pillowcases. *She passes on, efficient and immaculate.*

PARPALAID. Something very odd has happened to this hotel.

MADAME RÉMY, *peeping round a door.* Oh, dear, he's still there. *She makes up her mind to it and comes out.* And how do you do, Monsieur Parpalaid? You've not come to stay with me at any rate?

PARPALAID. Yes, I have. Well . . . how are things?

MADAME RÉMY. Things are quite well, thank you. I've no rooms free.

PARPALAID. It's not the fair today?

MADAME RÉMY. Oh, no.

PARPALAID. Why are you full then? What's happened? Who are all these people?

MADAME RÉMY. Patients.

PARPALAID. Patients?

MADAME RÉMY. Taking treatment.

PARPALAID. But what do they stop here for?

MADAME RÉMY. There's nowhere else to stop. But I'm sure they've nothing to complain of . . . though it'll be much better when our new wing's built. But they're well looked after. And as far as hygiene goes . . . oh, we're very, very strict.

PARPALAID. But wherever do they come from?

MADAME RÉMY. The patients? Lately, from all over the place. To begin with, it was people passing through . . .

PARPALAID. I don't understand one bit.

MADAME RÉMY. . . . on business. And they'd hear all the talk about Dr. Knock . . . and of course they'd want to consult him. They mightn't know what was wrong with them . . . but they'd feel there was something. And great good luck for them it was that they did happen to come here . . . or they'd have been dead now, some of them.

PARPALAID. Why would they?

MADAME RÉMY. The way they were going on and never giving a thought to it . . . eating things and drinking things, and doing everything they shouldn't!

PARPALAID. And they come and stay here?

MADAME RÉMY. Why, yes. As soon as ever they've seen the Doctor, to bed they go for treatment. But now it's different. People come more on purpose . . . and we haven't room to put them. But when our new building's ready . . .

PARPALAID. This is amazing.

MADAME RÉMY, *complacently, reflectively.* Yes, I suppose it does seem that to you. And if you led the life the Doctor does, you'd be calling out, I tell you!

PARPALAID. What sort of a life?

MADAME RÉMY. He's just a galley slave. The minute he's up he's out to see someone. He's here by ten . . . five minutes more and you'll see him. Then there'll be people waiting for him at home. Then more visits to pay . . . for miles round. Of course, he's got his new car now. That saves time. Sixty miles an hour he can do with it . . . and he does. But often and often he has to sit and lunch in it . . . off a sandwich.

PARPALAID. Oh! Ah! Yes . . . it's like that at Lyon with me.

MADAME RÉMY. Is it now? You took things a bit quieter here. You've not gone back in your billiards, I hope?

PARPALAID. People certainly don't seem to have been so ill in my time.

MADAME RÉMY, *with some severity.* Oh, it's not that, Monsieur Parpalaid. People didn't know then how to look after themselves . . . which is quite a different thing. There may be some as think we countryfolk are no better than heathen savages . . . and that it's no matter what becomes of us. Get along anyhow . . . and if anything goes wrong with you, die like a dog! And that proper medicines and proper treatment and apparatus and what's up to date is only for city people. Not at all, Monsieur Parpalaid. We're as important as anyone, I hope. And though we may like to make our savings we can spend them too if need be. You're behind the times in your notions of people here, let me tell you, if you think there's no one that wouldn't let his eye drop out or his leg drop off sooner than spend three francs at the chemist's. No . . . things have changed, thank God!

PARPALAID, *tartly.* Oh, if people that are well would rather be ill . . . a pity to stop them! It's an ill wind that blows the doctor no good.

MADAME RÉMY, *really roused.* I beg your pardon. That's a thing no one can say of Dr. Knock. Didn't he begin by seeing people free? And that never

happened here before. If you go to see him and you can afford to pay
. . . you pay. And why not, I'd like to know? But he never takes one
penny from the poor. Why, he'll go half across the country . . . ten
francs' worth of petrol it'll cost him . . . and he'll stop his great fine
car in front of some little shanty to see some poor old creature who
hasn't even a spare bit of bread and cheese to offer him. And no one
need try insinuating that he makes out people are ill when they're not.
Look at me. Since he has been coming here every day he has examined
me ten times . . . ten times. And each time he has taken the same
trouble. He has tapped me and he has listened to me all over . . . and
used all his instruments . . . a whole twenty minutes I'll be with him.
And each time he says: No, I'm not to worry; that all I need do is to
eat well and drink all I want. And he has never charged me one penny!
And the same with Monsieur Bernard, the schoolmaster . . . who got
it into his head somehow that he was a germ carrier . . . and got in
such a state about it! Well, the Doctor has had every sort of sample of
him taken and sent to Paris to be analyzed . . . twice! Here's Monsieur
Mousquet. He has to help take a blood in No. 15. You talk to him.
Here, give me your bag, I'll have to squeeze you in somehow . . . for
the sake of old times.

This paean of praise having quite restored her good temper, MADAME RÉMY *goes
off with the bag and* MONSIEUR MOUSQUET *arrives. Whatever the effect of the
three months on* MADAME MOUSQUET'S *wardrobe, on his it has been considerable
—upon the man himself too. Discreetly prosperous, sleek, self-confident and ready
to patronize, we should hardly know* MONSIEUR MOUSQUET.

MOUSQUET. The Doctor not here yet? Dr. Parpalaid! I thought it was a
ghost. Well . . . you are a stranger. How long since we saw you?

PARPALAID. Three months . . . why, it's not three months. . . .

MOUSQUET. Isn't it? No . . . well, how amazing . . . I suppose it isn't.
Doing well at Lyon?

PARPALAID. Thank you. Very well.

MOUSQUET. That's right . . . that's right! I suppose you found a nice little
practice . . . all ready made.

PARPALAID. I have increased it considerably already. Madame Mousquet
is well, I hope?

MOUSQUET. Much better.

PARPALAID. Was anything the matter with her?

MOUSQUET. You don't remember? No. The headaches she was always complaining of. Anyhow, you thought nothing of them. Well . . . Dr.

Knock diagnosed a serious lack of pituitary secretion and prescribed the appropriate endocrine with remarkable success.

PARPALAID. So now she's all right?

MOUSQUET. Yes. Well . . . she doesn't get those headaches any longer. When she gets one now it's from overwork . . . and that's to be expected. For we really are so pressed. I'm looking for a fully qualified assistant. You don't know of a reliable man?

PARPALAID. I'll think. . . .

MOUSQUET. I tell you! I tell you . . . we don't lead the quiet life we did. There's many a night . . . if you'll believe me . . . that I don't get to bed till half-past eleven. And then I won't have finished making up prescriptions.

PARPALAID. Quite a gold mine!

MOUSQUET. Oh, certainly. I do five times the business I did . . . and one mustn't grumble at that. But that's not the only thing. I'm proud of my profession, Dr. Parpalaid . . . and it does me good to feel that I'm benefiting my fellow creatures. Some of us are like that, you know. Here's the Doctor!

KNOCK, *arriving at last; grave, self-contained, authoritative.* Good morning, gentlemen. Ah, Dr. Parpalaid! I was just thinking of you. Have you had a good journey?

PARPALAID. Quite, thank you.

KNOCK. Did you come in your car?

PARPALAID. By train.

KNOCK. Just as well. Let me see . . . we've some business together. That instalment. . . .

PARPALAID. Well, as I am here. . . .

MOUSQUET. You'd like to be alone, gentlemen. *To* KNOCK. I'll be in No. 15. MOUSQUET *goes his way.*

PARPALAID. Well . . . you can't say now that you've been taken in.

KNOCK. No fault of yours, my dear friend, if I've not been.

PARPALAID. Come, I sold you my practice . . . and it has proved pretty well worth having.

KNOCK. Oh, you could have stayed on. I don't think we'd have been in each other's way. Has Mousquet told you of the sort of start we've made?

PARPALAID. I've been hearing about it.

KNOCK, *opening the little portfolio which he brought with him, and taking from it various charts which he handles with a pleasing dexterity.* I keep very careful

records. Shall I show you one or two . . . just for your own eye? You
won't have forgotten our talk three months ago. First . . . patients
seen . . . curve showing weekly totals. Datum line . . . average of
patients seen in your time. I forget it . . . but I call it five.

PARPALAID. Five . . . a week! You may call it double.

KNOCK. Right . . . we'll make it double. Now . . . patients seen weekly
by me . . . and I'm leaving out those I see free on Mondays. Mid-
October . . . 37. End of October . . . 90. End of November . . .
128. End of December . . . not added up yet. But it'll be over 150.
But I'll have to drop "Patients Seen" . . . it takes too much time.
Here's "Regular Treatments." For after all . . . seeing people casually
. . . that's all very well . . . but it's like picking blackberries off a
hedge. But "Regular Treatment" . . . ah, that's gardening!

PARPALAID, *with his nose in the charts.* You don't mind my asking . . . are
these totals accurate?

KNOCK. Strictly.

PARPALAID. D'you mean to tell me that in one week . . . here in this
town . . . one hundred and fifty persons feel ill enough to come knocking at your door to ask advice . . . and pay for it? Without anyone
making them?

KNOCK. Well, the police don't bring them.

PARPALAID. Incomprehensible!

KNOCK. Now do let me show you "Regular Treatments." Patients under-
going a course of regular treatment at home. Datum line . . . end of
September, when you left . . . none! PARPALAID *protests, but in vain.*
End of October . . . 32. End of November . . . 121. End of December . . . well, it'll be between 245 and 250.

PARPALAID. You're making fun of me.

KNOCK. But what is there extraordinary in that? We have 2853 households
in the district and 1502 incomes of over 12,000 francs.

PARPALAID. Incomes! But what's that got to do with . . . ?

KNOCK. You cannot, of course, expect a family to set anyone aside for
regular and constant treatment unless their income is at least 12,000
francs. That would be unreasonable. No . . . these things must be
properly regulated. I sift people into four categories. To begin with . . .
for families of twelve to twenty thousand francs' income I provide a
simple treatment . . . the very simplest . . . involving, say, one visit
a week and fifty francs' worth of medicine in the course of a month.
And so on till we reach the first category and full treatment . . . for

incomes of 50,000 francs and over . . . which will include four visits a week at least and about 300 francs a month spent on such things as X-rays, radium, massage, analyses . . . and the usual drugs.

PARPALAID. But how do you know what your patients' incomes are?

KNOCK *now makes his preparations for work. His coat comes off. His sleeves go up, and he turns to the little lavabo which always hangs in these inn halls, and begins a most elaborate, almost ritual, washing of his hands.*

KNOCK. Well, I don't ask the tax collector. He mightn't tell me . . . and what he told me wouldn't interest me either. Odd, isn't it? By my count there are 1502 people hereabouts with more than 12,000 francs a year. He makes it only 17. The richest man he knows of has 20,000 francs a year. I could find him one with five times that. So much for bureaucracy!

PARPALAID. But how do you get to know?

KNOCK, *allowing himself a smile.* Never mind. It takes some doing. I spent all October on it. And now I've to keep it up-to-date. *With a soapy finger, he points to a map on the table which* PARPALAID *then unfolds.* Do look at that . . . pretty, isn't it?

PARPALAID. Is it a map . . . oh, yes, of the district. What are all those red dots?

KNOCK. That map is my Survey of the advance of medical science. Each red dot shows a regular patient. A month ago that . . . there . . . looked like a great grey smudge . . . a bad lot . . . the Chabrières blot.

PARPALAID. The . . . ?

KNOCK. You know the place. For these last three weeks I've given great attention to it. Well . . . it's still there . . . but it's pinker than it was. You can see from here!

Silence for a moment.

PARPALAID. My dear sir . . . my very dear sir . . . you could knock me down with a feather. No . . . there's no doubt about this . . . everything goes to confirm it. You are a remarkable man. Some of us wouldn't own that to you . . . but we'd think it all the same . . . we'd not be doctors if we didn't. But may I ask you one very blunt question?

KNOCK. Please.

PARPALAID. If I had your talent and could do what you're doing if I wanted to . . .

KNOCK. Well?

PARPALAID. Could I be doing it now . . . with a clear conscience?

KNOCK. That's for you to say, I should think.

PARPALAID. Mind, I'm not laying down the law. It's a nice point, no doubt.

KNOCK. Make it a little plainer then.

PARPALAID. You may say I'm pernickety . . . that I'm splitting hairs. But isn't all this perhaps done just a little more for the benefit of the doctor than the patient?

KNOCK. Dr. Parpalaid . . . I think you forget there is a higher cause to be served than either.

PARPALAID. What now?

KNOCK. The cause of medical science. And I make it mine.

PARPALAID. I see. I see. I see.

And from now on it almost seems as if the cold winter atmosphere gave way to the even colder, stronger light of Science itself, in which, as is well known, the green and violet rays prevail.

KNOCK. Here in this town live some thousands of people . . . a featureless, meaningless mass of humanity. What is my task? To rescue and resolve each one of them into a scientific individuality, into a medical existence of his own. I put a man to bed. I watch. I wait. Something will come of it. He can't deceive me. Tubercle, neurasthenia, arteriosclerosis . . . it doesn't matter much what as long as it is something. There's nothing irritates me more than the wretched being who is always "pretty well, thank you."

PARPALAID. But you can't put a whole town to bed.

KNOCK. Why not? That remains to be seen. I've known five in a family all ill at once, all in bed at once . . . and they got along excellently. You're like the people who said the War wouldn't last six weeks because no one could afford it. What's wrong is that we doctors are all too timid. I believe I'm the only man amongst you that would put a whole town to bed . . . and keep it in bed till I found out what was really the matter with it. Though I grant you a certain number of healthy people, so-called, must be kept to look after the unhealthy ones. Or rather, let us think of them as a sort of reserve ready to be called up for treatment when there's time to attend to them. But we cannot have people boasting about their health. That won't do. Overlook it occasionally . . . yes. Some of them it's a little hard to disabuse. But when it comes to their strutting around and turning one to ridicule . . . no, no, then I get annoyed. As Monsieur Raffalens here has found out.

PARPALAID. What . . . our local Hercules . . . that can lift his mother-in-law up with one hand!

KNOCK. Can he. Well . . . he defied me for close on three months. But it wouldn't do.

PARPALAID. What has happened?

KNOCK. He's in bed. His bragging was becoming very mischievous . . . it was sapping the whole town's scientific enthusiasm.

PARPALAID. I seem to see one other difficulty though.

KNOCK. Name it.

PARPALAID. Your mind is on medical science . . . nothing else. But there are other interests in the world . . . political, social, intellectual. If you had your way everywhere people might begin to lose hold of them . . . and they have their uses surely.

KNOCK. They are no concern of mine. I am a doctor.

PARPALAID. True. And when railways or bridges are building they don't ask our advice about that.

KNOCK. Not they! *He beckons the other to the window.* Come here, Dr. Parpalaid. Look. Oh . . . you'll have glanced out often enough between the strokes of those good games of billiards you used to play. Over there Mont Aligre marks us off from the rest of the world. We can see Mesclat and Trébures on the left . . . if it weren't for the way the town rises up just in front of us I believe we could see every village in the valley. But all you ever saw was the scenery. You've a taste for scenery, as I remember. A rough countryside, barely scratched by civilization! But I show it you today teeming, pullulating beneath the life-giving touch of the noble science of medicine. The first time I stood here looking out . . . the morning after I came . . . I wasn't overconfident, I can tell you. It didn't seem to make much odds whether I stood here or not. The whole place turned its back on me. But now . . . like an organist at his keyboard . . . I pull a stop, I touch a note . . . and from far off the sounds respond! In two hundred and fifty of those houses . . . we can't see them all for the distance and the trees . . . there are two hundred and fifty rooms, and in each one at this very moment somebody is testifying to the might of medical science. Upon two hundred and fifty beds those prostrate forms bear witness to life's meaning . . . and through me they are all made one with the great cause I serve. And at night it's more wonderful still. For the lights are lit . . . and they're of my lighting. People with nothing the matter with them go to sleep in the dark . . . blotted out of existence. But the sick man has his night light or his lamp. Yes, then everything untouched by the healing art fades away and is forgotten. The villages vanish . . . and those lights as I look at them are like a starlit sky in which I reign almighty. And, remember, when those men and women wake their thoughts turn first to me and my prescriptions. In a minute or two now you'll hear the clock strike ten. At ten o'clock my patients, every one, take their temperatures for the second time. Picture it, my dear Parpalaid! Two hundred and fifty clinical thermometers lifted in unison and gently placed and held beneath two hundred and fifty silent tongues!* *He stands wrapt in an austere ecstasy.*

PARPALAID, *overwhelmed, by a somewhat different emotion.* My dear friend . . . my excellent colleague . . . I've something to suggest to you.

KNOCK. What?

PARPALAID. A little country town's no use to a man like you. You need a city to work in.

KNOCK. That's where you'll find me . . . some day.

PARPALAID. But think. You're now at the very height of your powers. A few years' time . . . it won't be the same. Oh, believe me . . . I know it.

KNOCK. Well?

PARPALAID. Why wait, then?

KNOCK. Do you know of another practice?

PARPALAID. Mine. I'll give it up to you. How better can I show the deep admiration I have for you?

KNOCK. Oh! And what'll you do?

PARPALAID. I . . . will settle down here again.

KNOCK. Ah!

PARPALAID. And what's more, I'll make you a present of those few thousand francs you still owe me . . . as you may remember.

KNOCK. Yes. Quite. You know, you're not quite such a fool as they say you are.

PARPALAID. I beg your pardon.

KNOCK. You're not much good at anything yourself. But you know how to make money out of other people. You have the merchant's mind.

PARPALAID. I beg to assure you that . . .

KNOCK. A bit of a psychologist, too. As soon as I'm making money I cease

* A distinctly Anglo-Saxon rendering of the original French: "Songez que, dans quelques instants, il va sonner dix heures, que pour tous mes malades, dix heures, c'est la deuxième prise de température rectale, et que, dans quelques instants, deux cent cinquante thermomètres vont pénétrer à la fois . . ." [E.B.]

to care for it, you think. Quite right! Conquering Lyon in the cause of Medicine, I'd forget my curves and my charts here. Yes, I should! Don't worry . . . I don't mean to grow old at St. Maurice. But I'm in no hurry.

MONSIEUR MOUSQUET *crosses the hall on his way out.*

KNOCK. Come here, my dear fellow. D'you know what Dr. Parpalaid is suggesting? That we change practices. I'm to go to Lyon. He'll come back here.

MOUSQUET, *aghast.* You're not serious?

KNOCK. Quite. It's a firm offer.

MOUSQUET. Of all the . . . ! Well, of course, you say No.

PARPALAID. Why should he say No, pray?

MOUSQUET. Because if a man offers you an old gunmetal watch in exchange for a good gold one and you're not quite a lunatic . . . you do say No. Have you asked him to swap motorcars too?

PARPALAID. Will you please understand that at Lyon I have a first-rate practice . . . taken over from Dr. Merlu . . . a man of great reputation.

MOUSQUET. But that's three months ago. And things run down hill quicker than you can push them up again. However, it's no great matter, my dear Doctor . . . for the people in St. Maurice simply won't hear of it.

PARPALAID. What's it to do with them? Who's asking their opinion, I'd like to know?

MOUSQUET. They'll give it you all the same. I won't say it'll mean rioting . . . we don't do things that way. But you'll find yourself sitting in the train for Lyon with the carriage door locked before you know where you are. Well, if you don't believe me. . . .

At this moment MADAME RÉMY *is passing from kitchen to dining room carrying a pile of plates.*

MOUSQUET. Madame Rémy, I've a piece of good news for you. Dr. Knock is leaving us and Dr. Parpalaid is coming back.

The plates are just saved from destruction.

MADAME RÉMY. What! Oh, no . . . oh, dear me, no . . . nothing of the sort. I can assure you you'll do no such thing. You'll have to fly off by night in a flying machine. They'll take the tires off your motorcar to stop you. And as for you, Monsieur Parpalaid . . . if that's what you're here for I'm sorry to tell you I haven't a room to spare . . . and January or no January, snow or no snow, you'll have to sleep in the street.

PARPALAID. And this . . . this is how you treat a man that has given twenty-five years of his life to you! Very well! If St. Maurice prefers quackery let me earn an honest living in Lyon . . . and a very good living, too. And if I thought for one moment of taking up my old work here again . . . because of my poor wife's health . . . a town life doesn't at all suit her . . . ! Dr. Knock, we will settle our business at once, if you please. I leave this evening.

KNOCK, *benevolently authoritative.* No, no, my dear friend . . . you won't treat us like that. Madame Rémy was so taken by surprise . . . and nothing of the sort's going to happen, Madame Rémy . . . that she nearly dropped her plates . . . and she didn't think what she was saying. But now the crockery's safe . . . look at her. Kindness itself as she always is! And full of gratitude to you, my dear Doctor . . . as who in St. Maurice is not? . . . for your twenty-five years of self-effacement in its service.

MADAME RÉMY. I've never said but what Monsieur Parpalaid wasn't always a very nice gentleman. And no doubt he did as well as another while we didn't need any doctoring in particular. But not when there was real illness about. No use telling me that any doctor calling himself a doctor would have let people die like that of the influenza.

PARPALAID. Calling himself a . . . ! What perfect nonsense! Do you really suppose, my good woman, that any doctor, whatever he calls himself, can fight an epidemic. As well tell the village policeman to go and arrest an earthquake. You wait for the next . . . and see if Dr. Knock pulls you through it any better than I did.

MADAME RÉMY. Monsieur Parpalaid, there may be things I can't argue over with you . . . such as motorcars . . . for I know nothing about them. But I do begin to know something about being ill. And let me tell you, it's a town that has all its sickly people in bed to start with can best stand an epidemic when it does come. Being taken by surprise is what you've to guard against. Monsieur Bernard put that very well in his lecture last Thursday: "Carry an umbrella . . . and then let it rain."

MOUSQUET. Take my advice, Doctor . . . don't let yourself in for scientific discussion here. We're all experts now. We've all got our own ideas. The first man you meet in the street will take you on.

KNOCK. But let us not lose ourselves in these academic disputes. Madame Rémy and Dr. Parpalaid may differ profoundly . . . as they do . . . in medical theory . . . personally they can remain on the best possible terms. You've got a room for the Doctor, haven't you?

MADAME RÉMY. No. I haven't. You know well enough we can scarcely cram the patients in. If he were a patient . . . I'd get him in somehow . . . whether I could or not! . . . it'd be my duty.

KNOCK. Very well, then. Suppose I tell you that Dr. Parpalaid is not fit to travel again this afternoon . . . and that, speaking as a medical man, I consider he should take a day's rest before he leaves.

MADAME RÉMY. Oh . . . that's another matter. But he . . . he didn't come here to see you professionally, did he?

KNOCK. That, Madame Rémy, professional etiquette would quite forbid me to tell you.

PARPALAID. What's all this? I leave this afternoon . . . and there's an end of it.

KNOCK. No, my dear Parpalaid, you do not. Twenty-four hours' complete rest is indicated. I deprecate your travelling today . . . and, if need be, I shall forbid it.

MADAME RÉMY. Oh, well, of course, Doctor, I didn't know that. Monsieur Parpalaid shall have a room . . . by all means. Are we to take his temperature?

KNOCK. I'll let you know later.

MADAME RÉMY *departs, all smiles.*

MOUSQUET, *tactfully going.* I'll leave you to talk. I've broken my hypodermic. I must go and get another.

The two are alone. DR. PARPALAID *sits looking up at* KNOCK. KNOCK's *gleaming spectacles are turned full upon him.*

PARPALAID. I say . . . you weren't serious then, were you? Still, thanks all the same. I really didn't fancy another eight hours' journey tonight. I'm not so young as I was. You do keep it up very well. The way you said that to me just now! If I didn't know the ropes myself . . . ! Your manner . . . the way you look at one . . . as if you saw right inside one. Oh . . . very well done indeed!

KNOCK. It is interesting. For really, I do it almost unconsciously. The minute I set eyes on a man I begin to diagnose his case . . . whether I mean to or not. So much so that lately, d'you know, I've had to stop looking at myself in the glass.

PARPALAID. But . . . you don't mean that you can really diagnose, do you . . . ?

KNOCK. Certainly! I tell you that whether I try to or not . . . as soon as I see a man I find myself making note of every little sign and symptom . . . skin, eyes, hair, breathing, beard . . . PARPALAID's *at the moment* . . . all sorts of things. And the bit of my brain which puts all this together, which completes the diagnosis . . . works apparently quite automatically. I must take care. That sort of thing makes for insanity.

PARPALAID. But . . . forgive me . . . I don't want to make too much of it . . . but I've a reason for asking. When you said I needed a day's rest . . . were you in fun . . . or were you . . . ? Because it does fit in with . . . something that has been a little on my mind lately. I have been noticing one or two trifling things about myself which have . . . well, I mustn't say worried me, but . . . ! So that . . . just for the interest of it . . . I should rather like to know if my own observations . . . fit in, so to speak, with this automatic diagnosis of yours. *Finishes with a little nervous laugh.*

KNOCK, *his spectacles seeming to gleam more brightly than ever.* My dear sir . . . for the moment we'll let that be. Ten o'clock. I must begin my rounds. But you'll lunch with me, please. And as to the state of your health . . . and whatever may need to be done about it . . . we can go into that in my consulting room . . . this afternoon . . . at our leisure.

PARPALAID *is left to think it over. For the clock chimes and strikes, and* KNOCK *goes his way. Then* SCIPIO, *the* NURSE, *and* MADAME RÉMY, *spotless, capped and gloved, and bearing various instruments of medical ritual, pass in a sort of procession through the hall.*

Saint Joan of the Stockyards

by BERTOLT BRECHT

English version by Frank Jones

CHARACTERS

PIERPONT MAULER ⎫
CRIDLE
LENNOX   ⎬ *Meat Kings*
GRAHAM
SLIFT   ⎭

JOAN DARK   ⎫
MARTHA   ⎬ *Black Straw Hats*
MAJOR PAULUS SNYDER
JACKSON   ⎭

MULBERRY, *a landlord*

MRS. LUCKERNIDDLE, *a worker's wife*

GLOOMB, *a worker*

MRS. SWINGURN, *a worker's wife*

A WAITER

AN OLD MAN

A BROKER

AN APPRENTICE

2 DETECTIVES

5 LABOR LEADERS

2 POLICEMEN

And, as groups: WHOLESALERS, STOCKBREEDERS, SMALL SPECULATORS, WORKERS, NEWSBOYS, PASSERS-BY, JOURNALISTS, VOICES, MUSICIANS, SOLDIERS, POOR FOLK

I

THE MEAT KING PIERPONT MAULER GETS A LETTER FROM HIS FRIENDS IN NEW YORK

SCENE: *Chicago stockyards.*

MAULER, *reading a letter.* "As we can plainly see, dear Pierpont, the stock market has been badly constipated for some little time. Also tariff walls to the south of us are resisting all our attacks. In view of this it seems advisable, dear Pierpont, to let the packing business go." I have this hint today from my dear friends in New York. Here comes my partner. *Hides letter.*

CRIDLE. Well, my dear Pierpont! Why so gloomy?

MAULER. Remember, Cridle, how some days ago—
We were walking through the stockyards, it was evening—
We stood beside our brand-new packing machine.
Remember, Cridle, the ox that took the blow,
Standing there blond, huge, dumbly gazing up
Toward Heaven: I felt the stroke was meant for me.
Oh, Cridle! Oh, our business is bloody.

CRIDLE. So—the old weakness, Pierpont!
Almost incredible: you, giant of packers,
Lord of the stockyards, quaking at the kill,
Fainting with pain, all for a fair-haired ox!
Don't tell a soul of this but me, I beg you.

MAULER. O loyal Cridle!
I oughtn't to have visited the stockyards!
Since I went into this business—that's seven
Years—I'd avoided them; and now—oh, Cridle,
I cannot bear it any longer! I'm giving up today.
You take this bloody business, with my share!
I'll let you have it cheap: you above all,
For no one else belongs to it like you.

CRIDLE. How cheap?

MAULER. No long palaver can be held
On such things by old friends like you and me.
Let's say ten million.

CRIDLE. That would not be expensive but for Lennox,

Who fights with us for every case of meat
And ruins our market with his cut-throat prices
And will break us all if he does not go broke.
Before he falls, and only you can fell him,
I shall not take your offer. Until then
Your cunning brain must be in constant practice.

MAULER. No, Cridle! That poor ox's outcry
Will nevermore go mute within me. Therefore
This Lennox must fall fast, for I myself
Have willed to be a decent man henceforth
And not a butcher. Cridle, come with me,
And I will tell you what to do to make
Lennox fall fast. But then you must
Relieve me of this business, which hurts me.

CRIDLE. If Lennox falls.

Exeunt.

II

THE COLLAPSE OF THE GREAT PACKING PLANTS

SCENE: *In front of the Lennox Plant.*

THE WORKERS. We are 70,000 workers in Lennox's packing plant and we
Cannot live a day longer on such low wages.
Yesterday our pay was slashed again
and today the notice is up once more:
ANYONE NOT SATISFIED
WITH OUR WAGES CAN GO.
All right then, let's all go and
shit on the wages that get skinnier every day.

A silence.

THE WORKERS. For a long time now this work has made us sick
the factory our hell and nothing
but cold Chicago's terrors could
keep us here. But now
by twelve hours' work a man can't even

earn a stale loaf and
the cheapest pair of pants. Now
a man might just as well go off and
die like a beast.
A silence.

THE WORKERS. What do they take us for? Do they think
we are going to stand here like steers, ready
for anything? Are we
their chumps? Better lie and rot!
Let's go right now.
A silence.

THE WORKERS. It must be six o'clock by now!
Why don't you open up, you sweatshop bosses? Here
are your steers, you butchers, open up!
They knock.
Maybe they've forgotten us?
Laughter.

THE WORKERS. Open the gates! We
want to get into your
dirt-holes and lousy kitchens
to cook stuffed meat
for the eaters who possess.
A silence.
We demand at least
our former wages, even though they were too low, at least
a ten-hour day and at least——

A MAN, *crossing stage.* What are you waiting for? Don't you know
that Lennox has shut down?
NEWSBOYS *run across stage.*

THE NEWSBOYS. Meat king Lennox forced to shut down his plants!
70,000 workers without food or shelter! M. L. Lennox a victim of
bitter competitive struggle with Pierpont Mauler, well-known meat
baron and philanthropist.

THE WORKERS. Alas!
Hell itself
shuts its gate in our faces!
We are doomed. Bloody Mauler grips
our exploiter by the throat and
we are the ones who choke!

P. MAULER

SCENE: *A street.*

THE NEWSBOYS. Chicago Tribune, noon edition! P. Mauler, meat baron and philanthropist, to attend opening of the P. Mauler Hospitals, largest and most expensive in the world! P. MAULER *passes, with two men.*

A PASSER-BY, *to another.* That's P. Mauler. Who are the men walking with him?

THE OTHER. Detectives. They guard him so that he won't be knocked down.

TO COMFORT THE MISERY OF THE STOCKYARDS, THE BLACK STRAW HATS LEAVE THEIR MISSION-HOUSE. JOAN'S FIRST DESCENT INTO THE DEPTHS

SCENE: *In front of a Black Straw Hats Mission.*

JOAN, *at the head of the Black Straw Hat shock troop.*
In gloomy times of bloody confusion
ordered disorder
planful wilfulness
dehumanized humanity
when there is no end to the unrest in our cities:
Into such a world, a world like a slaughter-house—
summoned by rumors of threatening deeds of violence
to prevent the brute strength of the short-sighted people
from shattering its own tools and
trampling its own bread-basket to pieces—
we wish to reintroduce
God.
A figure of little glory,
almost of ill repute,
no longer admitted
to the sphere of actual life:
But, for the humblest, the one salvation!
Therefore we have decided
to beat the drum for Him
that He may gain a foothold in the regions of misery
and His voice may ring out clearly among the abattoirs.
To the Black Straw Hats.
And this undertaking of ours is surely

the last of its kind. A last attempt
to set Him upright again in a crumbling world, and that
by means of the lowest.
They march on, drums beating.

FROM DAWN TO DARK THE BLACK STRAW HATS WORKED IN THE STOCKYARDS,
BUT WHEN EVENING CAME THEY HAD ACCOMPLISHED JUST ABOUT NOTHING

SCENE: *In front of the Lennox Plant.*

A WORKER. They say there's another spell of dirty dealing going on at
the livestock market. Till it's over we'll have to bide our time, I guess,
and profiteer in coal-smoke.

A WORKER. Lights are on in the offices. They're counting up the profits.
THE BLACK STRAW HATS *arrive. They put up a sign: Room for a Night,
20 cents; With Coffee, 30 cents; Hot dogs, 15 cents.*

THE BLACK STRAW HATS, *singing.*
Attention, your attention!
We see you, man that's falling
we hear your cry for help
we see you, woman calling.
Halt the autos, stop the traffic!
Courage, sinking people, we're coming, look our way!
You who are going under,
see us, oh, see us, brother, before you say you're beat!
We bring you something to eat,
we are still aware
that you are standing out there.
Don't say it can't be helped, for things are changing
the injustice of this world cannot remain
if all the people come and join us marching
and leave their cares behind and help with might and main.
We'll bring up tanks and cannon too
and airplanes there shall be
and battleships over the sea
all to conquer a plate of soup, brother, just for you.
For you, yes, you, poor folk,
are an army vast and grand,
so even in times like these
we've all got to lend you a hand!
Forward march! Eyes right! Rifles ready to fire!

Courage, you sinking people, we're coming, look our way!

During the singing the BLACK STRAW HATS *have been distributing their leaflet,* "*The Battle Cry,*" *spoons, plates and soup. The* WORKERS *say* "*Thank you*" *and listen to Joan's speech.*

JOAN. We are the Soldiers of the Lord. On account of our hats we are also called the Black Straw Hats. We march with drums and flags wherever unrest prevails and acts of violence threaten, to remind men of the Lord whom they have all forgotten, and to bring back their souls to Him. We call ourselves soldiers because we are an army and when we are on the march we have to fight crime and misery, those forces that want to drag us down. SHE *begins to ladle out the soup herself.* That's it, just eat some hot soup and then everything will look real different, but please give a little thought to Him who bestows it upon you. And when you think that way you will see that this is really the complete solution: Strive upward, not downward. Work for a good position up above, not here below. Want to be the first man up, not the first man down. Surely you realize now what sort of trust you can place in the fortunes of this world. None at all. Misfortune comes like the rain, that nobody makes, and still it comes. Tell me, where does all your misfortune come from?

AN EATER. From Lennox & Co.

JOAN. Maybe Mr. Lennox has more worries right now than you have. After all, what are you losing? His losses run into millions!

A WORKER. There's not much fat floating in this soup, but it contains plenty of wholesome water and there's no lack of warmth.

ANOTHER WORKER. Shut up, revellers! Listen to the heavenly text, or they'll take away your soup!

JOAN. Quiet! Tell me, dear friends, why are you poor?

WORKER. Aw, *you* tell *us.*

JOAN. All right, I will tell you: it is not because you aren't blest with worldly goods—that is not for all of us—but because you have no sense of higher things. That is why you are poor. These low pleasures for which you work so hard, a bite to eat, nice homes, the movies, they are just coarse sensual enjoyments, but God's word is a far finer, more inward, more exquisite pleasure, maybe you can't think of anything sweeter than whipped cream, but God's word, I tell you, is still sweeter, honestly it is, oh, how sweet God's word is! It's like milk and honey, and in it you dwell as in a palace of gold and alabaster. O ye of little faith, the birds of the air have no *Help Wanted* ads and the lilies of the field have no jobs, and yet He feeds them, because they sing

His praises. You all want to get to the top, but what kind of top, and how do you propose to get there? And so it's we Straw Hats who ask you, quite practically: What does a man need to rise?

WORKER. A starched collar.

JOAN. No, not a starched collar. Maybe you need a starched collar to get ahead on earth, but in God's eyes you need much more than that around you, a quite different sort of splendor, but before Him you don't even have a rubber collar on, because you have utterly neglected your entire inner natures. But how are you going to get to the top— whatever, in your ignorance, you call the top—by brute force? As if force ever caused anything but destruction! You believe that if you rear up on your hind legs there'll be heaven on earth. But I say to you: that way not paradise but chaos is created.

WORKER *enters, running.* A place was just vacated!
It pays, and it's calling you over
to Plant Number Five!
It looks like a urinal on the outside.
Run!

THREE WORKERS *put down full plates of soup and run.*

JOAN. Hey, you, where are you off to? Talk to you about God, *that* you don't want to hear, eh?

A BLACK STRAW HAT GIRL. The soup's all gone.

THE WORKERS. The soup's all gone,
fatless it was and scant,
but better than nothing.

ALL *turn away and stand up.*

JOAN. Oh, keep your seats, no harm's done, the grand soup of heaven never gives out, you know.

THE WORKERS. When will you finally
open your roachy cellars,
you butchers of men?

Groups form.

A MAN. How am I to pay for my little house now, the cute damp thing with twelve of us in it? Seventeen
installments I've paid and now the last is due:
They'll throw us onto the street and never again
will we see the trampled ground with the yellowish grass
and never breathe again
the accustomed pestilent air.

A SECOND MAN, *in a circle.* Here we stand with hands like shovels

and necks like trucks wanting to sell
our hands and necks
and no one will buy them.

THE WORKERS. And our work-tool, a giant pile
of steam hammers and cranes,
barred in behind walls!

JOAN. What's up? Now they're simply leaving! Finished eating, have you?
Hope you enjoyed it? Thanks. Why have you listened till now?

A WORKER. For the soup.

JOAN. We're moving on. Sing!

THE BLACK STRAW HATS, *singing.* Go straight to the thick of the fight
where there's the toughest work to do.
Sing with all your might! It may still be night,
but already the morning is coming in might!
Soon the Lord Jesus will come to you, too.

A VOICE FROM THE REAR. There's still work to be had at Mauler's!
Exeunt WORKERS, *all but a few women.*

JOAN, *gloomily.* Pack up the instruments. Did you see how they hurried
away as soon as the soup was gone?
This thing gets no higher up
than the rim of a dish. It believes
in nothing that it does not
hold in its hand—if it believes in hands.
Living from minute to minute, uncertainly,
they can no longer raise themselves
from the lowest ground. Only hunger
is a match for them. They are touched
by no song, no word
penetrates their depths.
To the bystanders.
We Black Straw Hats feel as though we were expected to satisfy a
hungry continent with our spoons.
The WORKERS *return. Shouting in distance.*

THE WORKERS, *in front.* What's that yelling? A huge stream of people from
the packing houses!

A VOICE, *in back.* Mauler and Cridle are shutting down too!
The Mauler works are locking us out!

THE RETURNING WORKERS. Running for jobs, we met halfway
a stream of desperate men
who had lost their jobs and

asked us for jobs.

THE WORKERS, *in front.* Alas! From over there, too, a troop of men!
You can't see the end of it! Mauler
has shut down too! What's to become of us?

THE BLACK STRAW HATS, *to* JOAN. Come along with us now. We're freezing
and wet and we have to eat.

JOAN. But now I want to know who's to blame for all this.

THE BLACK STRAW HATS. Stop! Don't get mixed up in that! They're sure
to give you an earful. Their minds are stuffed
with low ideas! They're lazybones!
Gluttonous, shirkers, from birth onward
void of all higher impulse!

JOAN. No, I want to know. *To the* WORKERS. Tell me now: why are you
running around here without any work?

THE WORKERS. Bloody Mauler's locked in battle
with stingy Lennox; so we go hungry.

JOAN. Where does Mauler live?

THE WORKERS. Over there where livestock is bought and sold,
in a big building, the livestock market.

JOAN. There I will go, for
I have to know this.

MARTHA, *one of the Black Straw Hats.*
Don't get mixed up in that! Ask many questions
and you'll get lots of answers.

JOAN. No, I want to see this Mauler, who causes such misery.

THE BLACK STRAW HATS. Then, Joan, we take a dark view of your further
fate.
Do not mingle in the quarrels of this world!
He who meddles in a quarrel becomes its victim!
His purity swiftly perishes. Soon
his small warmth perishes in the cold
that reigns over everything. Goodness abandons him
who flees the protective hearth.
Striving downward
from level to level toward the answer you never will get,
you will disappear in dirt!
For only dirt is stuffed into the mouths
of those who ask without caution.

JOAN. I want to know.

Exeunt BLACK STRAW HATS.

III

PIERPONT MAULER FEELS A BREATH
FROM ANOTHER WORLD

SCENE: *In front of the livestock market. Lower level,* JOAN *and* MARTHA *waiting; upper level, the meat packers* LENNOX *and* GRAHAM, *conversing.* LENNOX *is white as chalk.*

GRAHAM. How you have felt the blows of brutal Mauler,
My good friend Lennox! There's no hindering
The rise of this monstrosity: to him
Nature is goods, even the air's for sale.
What we have inside our stomachs he resells to us.
He can squeeze rent from ruined houses, money
From rotten meat; throw stones at him,
He's sure to turn the stones to money; so
Unruly is his money-lust, so natural
To him this lack of nature that he himself
Cannot deny its driving force within him
For I tell you: himself, he's soft, does not love money,
Cannot bear squalor, cannot sleep at night.
Therefore you must approach him as though you could hardly speak,
And say: "Oh, Mauler, look at me and take
Your hand off my throat—think of your old age—"
That will frighten him, for sure. Maybe he'll cry . . .
JOAN, *to* MARTHA. Only you, Martha, have followed me this far.
All the others left me with warnings
as if I were bound for the end of the world.
Strange warning from their lips.
I thank you, Martha.
MARTHA. I warned you too, Joan.
JOAN. And went with me.
MARTHA. But will you really recognize him, Joan?
JOAN. I shall know him!
CRIDLE, *coming out of building.*
Well, Lennox, now the underbidding's over.
You're finished now and I'll close up and wait
Until the market recovers. I'll clean my yards
And give the knives a thorough oiling and order some

Of those new packing machines that give a fellow
A chance to save a tidy sum in wages.
LENNOX. Damnable times!
Waste lies the market, flooded out by goods.
Trade, that was once so flourishing, lies fallow.
Scuffling over a market that's long been costive,
You wrecked your own prices by underbidding one another: thus
Do buffaloes, fighting for grass, trample to shreds the grass they
fight for.
MAULER *comes out, with his broker,* SLIFT, *among a crowd of* PACKERS, TWO
DETECTIVES *behind him.*
THE MEAT PACKERS. Now everything's a matter of holding out!
MAULER. Lennox is down. *To* LENNOX. Admit it, you are out.
And now I ask you, Cridle, to take over
The packing plant as stated in our contract,
Presuming Lennox finished.
CRIDLE. Agreed, Lennox is out. But also finished
Are good times on the market; therefore, Mauler,
You must come down from ten million for your stock!
MAULER. What? The price stands
Here in the contract! Here, Lennox, see if this
Is not a contract, with a price right on it!
CRIDLE. Yes, but a contract made in better times!
Are bad times also mentioned in the contract?
What can I do alone with a stockyard now
When not a soul will buy a can of meat?
Now I know why you couldn't bear to watch
More oxen dying: it was because their flesh
Cannot be sold!
MAULER. No, it's my heart
That swells, affected by the creature's shrieks!
GRAHAM. Oh, mighty Mauler, now I realize
The greatness of your actions: even your heart
Sees far ahead!
LENNOX. Mauler, I wanted to talk with you . . . again . . .
GRAHAM. Straight to his heart, Lennox! Straight to his heart!
It's a sensitive garbage pit!
He hits MAULER *in the pit of the stomach.*
MAULER. Ouch!
GRAHAM. You see, he has a heart!

MAULER. Well, Freddy, now I'll make a settlement with Cridle
So he can't buy a single can from you,
Because you hit me.

GRAHAM. You can't do that, Pierpy! That's mixing
Personal matters with business.

CRIDLE. O.K., Pierpy, with pleasure. Just as you please.

GRAHAM. I have two thousand workers, Mauler!

CRIDLE. Send them to the movies! But really, Pierpy, our agreement isn't
valid. *Figuring in a notebook.* When we contracted for your withdrawal
from the business, the shares—of which you hold one-third, as I do—
stood at 390. You gave them to me for 320; that was cheap. Today
it's expensive, for now they're down to 100; with the market blocked
the way it is, if I'm going to pay your price I'll have to throw the shares
onto the market. If I do that they'll go down to 70, and what can I
use to pay you then? Then I'll be done for.

MAULER. If that's your situation, Cridle, I must certainly
Get my money out of you right away,
Before you're done for.
I tell you, Cridle, I am so afraid
I'm all of a sweat, the most I can let you have
Is six days! What am I saying? Five days
If that's your situation.

LENNOX. Mauler, look at me.

MAULER. Lennox, you tell me if the contract says anything about bad
times.

LENNOX. No.
Exit.

MAULER, *watching him go.* Some worry seems to be oppressing him,
And I, on business bent (would I were not!)
Did not perceive it! Oh, repulsive business!
Cridle, it sickens me.
Exit CRIDLE. *Meanwhile* JOAN *has called one of the* DETECTIVES *over to her
and said something to him.*

THE DETECTIVE. Mr. Mauler, there are some persons here who want to
talk to you.

MAULER. Unmannerly lot, eh? With an envious look, eh?
And violent, no doubt? I
cannot see anyone.

THE DETECTIVE. They're a pair from the Black Straw Hat Organization.

MAULER. What kind of an organization is that?

THE DETECTIVE. They have many branches and are numerous and respected among the lower classes, where they are called the Good Lord's
Soldiers.

MAULER. I've heard of them. Curious name:
the Good Lord's Soldiers . . . but
what do they want of me?

THE DETECTIVE. They say they have something to discuss with you.
During this the market uproar has resumed: Steers 43, Hogs 55, Heifers 59, etc.

MAULER. All right, tell them I will see them.
But tell them also they may say nothing that I
do not ask about first. Nor must they break out
into tears or songs, especially sentimental ones.
And tell them it would be most profitable to them
for me to get the impression
that they are well-meaning people, with nothing to their discredit,
who want nothing from me that I do not have.
Another thing: do not tell them I am Mauler.

THE DETECTIVE, *going over to* JOAN. He consents to see you, but
you must ask no questions, only answer
when he asks you.

JOAN, *walking up to* MAULER. You are Mauler!

MAULER. No, I'm not. *Points to* SLIFT. That's him.

JOAN, *pointing to* MAULER. You are Mauler.

MAULER. No, he is.

JOAN. You are.

MAULER. How do you know me?

JOAN. Because you have the bloodiest face.

SLIFT *laughs.*

MAULER. You laugh, Slift?

Meanwhile GRAHAM *has hurried off.*

MAULER, *to* JOAN. How much do you earn in a day?

JOAN. Twenty cents, but food and clothing are supplied.

MAULER. Thin clothes, Slift, and thin soup too, I guess!
Yes, those clothes are probably thin and the soup not rich.

JOAN. Mauler, why do you lock the workers out?

MAULER, *to* SLIFT. The fact that they work without pay
is remarkable, isn't it? I never heard
of such a thing before—a person working
for nothing and none the worse. And in their eyes
I see no fear

of bridge-arches or misery.
To JOAN.
Extraordinary folk, you Black Straw Hats.
I shall not ask you what particularly
You want of me. I know the fool mob calls me
Mauler the Bloody, saying it was I
Who ruined Lennox or caused unpleasantness
For Cridle—who, between ourselves, is one
Of little merit. I can say to you:
Those are just business matters, and they won't
be interesting to you. But there's something else, on which
I would like to hear your views. I am thinking of giving up
this bloodstained business, as soon as possible; once for all.
For recently,—this *will* interest you,—I saw
a steer die and it upset me so
that I want to get rid of everything, and have even sold
my interest in the plant, worth twelve million dollars. I gave it to that
    man
for ten. Don't you feel
that this is right, and to your liking?
SLIFT. He saw the steer die and made up his mind
to butcher wealthy Cridle
instead of the poor steer.
Was that right?
The PACKERS *laugh.*
MAULER. Go on, laugh. Your laughter's nothing to me. I'll see you crying
    some day.
JOAN. Mr. Mauler, why have you shut down the stockyards?
    This I must know.
MAULER. Was it not an extraordinary act to take my hand
out of a mighty concern, simply because it is bloody?
Say this is right, and to your liking.
All right then, don't say it, I know, I admit, some people
did poorly out of it, they lost their jobs,
I know. Unhappily, that was unavoidable.
A bad lot anyway, a tough mob, better not go near them, but tell me:
my act in withdrawing my hand from the business,
surely that is right?
JOAN. I don't know whether you ask in earnest.

MAULER. That's because my damned voice is used to faking,
and for that reason too I know: you
do not like me. Say nothing.
To the others.
I seem to feel a breath from another world wafted toward me.
HE *takes everybody's money from them and gives it to* JOAN.
Out with your money, you cattle butchers, give it here!
HE *takes it out of their pockets, gives it to* JOAN.
Take it to give to the poor folk, Joan!
But be assured that I feel no obligation in any way
and sleep extremely well. Why am I helping here? Perhaps
just because I like your face, because it is so unknowing, although
you have lived for twenty years.
MARTHA, *to* JOAN. I don't believe in his sincerity.
Forgive me, Joan, for going away now too:
it seems to me you also
should really drop all this!
Exit MARTHA.
JOAN. Mr. Mauler, you know this is only a drop in the bucket. Can you
not give them real help?
MAULER. Tell the world I warmly commend your activities and
wish there were more like you. But
you mustn't take this thing about the poor this way.
They are wicked people. Human beings do not affect me:
they are not guiltless, and they're butchers themselves. However, let's
drop the matter.
JOAN. Mr. Mauler, they are saying in the stockyards that you are to
blame for their misery.
MAULER. On oxen I have pity; man is evil.
Mankind's not ripe for what you have in mind:
Before the world can change, humanity
Must change its nature.
Wait just one more moment.
In a low tone, to SLIFT.
Give her more money away from here, when she's alone.
Say "for the poor folk," so that she can take it
without blushing, but then see what she buys for herself.
If that's no help—I'd rather it were not—
then take her with you

to the stockyards and show her
those poor of hers, how wicked and gross they are, full of treachery
   and cowardice
and how they themselves are to blame.
Maybe that will help.
To JOAN.
Here is Sullivan Slift, my broker; he will show you something.
To SLIFT.
I tell you, it's almost intolerable in my eyes
that there should be people like this girl, owning nothing
but a black hat and twenty cents a day, and fearless.
Exit MAULER.

SLIFT. I would not care to know what you want to know;
   Still, if you wish to know it, come here tomorrow.

JOAN, *watching* MAULER *go.* That's not a wicked man, he is the first
   to be started out of the tanglewoods of meanness by our drums and
     to hear the call.

SLIFT, *departing.* I give you fair warning: do not take up with those people
   down in the yards, they're a lowdown lot, really
   the scum of the earth.

JOAN. I want to see it.

IV

THE BROKER SULLIVAN SLIFT SHOWS JOAN DARK
THE WICKEDNESS OF THE POOR: JOAN'S SECOND
DESCENT INTO THE DEPTHS

SCENE: *The stockyards district.*

SLIFT. Now, Joan, I will show you
   the wickedness of those
   for whom you feel pity and
   how out of place the feeling is.

THEY *are walking alongside a factory wall inscribed "Mauler and Cridle,
Meat Packing Company." The name Cridle has been painted out in crosswise
strokes.* TWO MEN *come through a small gate.* SLIFT *and* JOAN *hear their
conversation.*

FOREMAN, *to a young apprentice.* Four days ago a man named Luckerniddle fell into our boiler, we couldn't stop the machinery in time so he got caught in the bacon-maker, a horrible thing to happen, this is his coat and this is his cap, take them and get rid of them, all they do is take up a hook in the cloakroom and make a bad impression. It's a good plan to burn them, right away would be best. I entrust the things to you because I know you're a reliable man. I'd lose my job if the stuff were found anywhere. Of course as soon as the plant opens again you can have Luckerniddle's job.

THE APPRENTICE. You can count on me, Mr. Smith. *The* FOREMAN *goes back in through the gate.* Too bad about the fellow that has to go out into the world as bacon, but I feel bad about his coat too, it's still in good shape. Old Man Bacon has his can to wear now and won't need this any more, but I could use it very well. Shit, I'll take it. *Puts it on and wraps his own coat and cap in newspaper.*

JOAN. I feel sick.

SLIFT. That's the world as it is. *Stopping the young man.* Wherever did you get that coat and cap? Didn't they belong to Luckerniddle, the man that had the accident?

YOUNG WORKER. Please don't let it get around, sir. I'll take the things off right away. I'm pretty nearly down and out. That extra twenty cents you get in the fertilizer-cellars fooled me into working at the bone-grinding machine last year. There I got it bad in the lungs, and a troublesome eye inflammation too. Since then my working capacity has gone down and since February I've only been employed twice.

SLIFT. Keep the things on. And come to Canteen No. 7 at noon today. You'll get a free lunch and a dollar there if you tell Luckerniddle's wife where your cap and coat came from.

YOUNG WORKER. But, sir, isn't that sort of raw?

SLIFT. Well, if you don't need the money . . . !

YOUNG WORKER. You can rely on me, sir.

JOAN *and* SLIFT *walk on.*

MRS. LUCKERNIDDLE, *sitting in front of the factory gate, lamenting.*
You in there, what are you doing with my husband?
Four days ago he went to work, he said:
"Warm up some soup for me tonight!" And to this
day he hasn't got back! What have you done with him
you butchers! Four days I have been standing here
in the cold, nights too, waiting, but nobody tells me

anything, and my husband doesn't come out! But I tell
you, I'm going to stand right here until I get to see him!
You'll rue the day if you've done him any harm!

SLIFT, *walking up to the woman.* Your husband has left town, Mrs. Luckerniddle.

MRS. LUCKERNIDDLE. Oh, don't give me that again.

SLIFT, I'll tell you something, Mrs. Luckerniddle, he is out of town and
it's very embarrassing to the factory to have you sitting around here
talking foolishness. So we'll make you an offer which could not be required of us by law. If you give up your search for your husband, you
may eat dinner in our canteen every noon for three weeks, free.

MRS. LUCKERNIDDLE. I want to know what's become of my husband.

SLIFT. We're telling you, he's gone to Frisco.

MRS. LUCKERNIDDLE. He has not gone to Frisco, he's had some accident
because of you and you're trying to hide it.

SLIFT. If that's what you think, Mrs. Luckerniddle, you cannot accept
any meals from the factory, but you will have to bring suit against
the factory. But think it over thoroughly. I shall be at your disposal
in the canteen tomorrow. SLIFT *goes back to* JOAN.

MRS. LUCKERNIDDLE. I must have my husband back. I have nobody but
him to support me.

JOAN. She will never come.
Twenty dinners may mean much
to one who is hungry, but
there is more for him.

JOAN *and* SLIFT *walk on.* THEY *stop in front of a factory canteen and see*
TWO MEN *looking in through a window.*

GLOOMB. There sits the overseer who's to blame for my getting my hand
in the tin-cutting machine—stuffing his belly full. We must see to it
that this is the last time the swine gorges at our expense. You'd better
give me your club, mine will probably splinter right off.

SLIFT. Stay here. I want to talk to him. And if he approaches you, say
you're looking for work. Then you'll see what kind of people these are.
Going up to GLOOMB. Before you get carried away into doing something—
that's the way it looks to me—I'd like to make you a profitable proposi-
tion.

GLOOMB. I have no time right now, sir.

SLIFT. That's too bad, because there would have been something in it
for you.

GLOOMB. Make it short. We cannot afford to let that swine go. He's got to get his reward today for that inhuman system he plays overseer to.

SLIFT. I have a suggestion to make for your own benefit. I am an inspector in the factory. Much inconvenience has been caused by your place remaining vacant. Most people think it too dangerous, just because you have made all this to-do about your fingers. Now it would be just fine if we had someone to fill that post again. If you, for example, could find somebody for it, we would be ready to take you on again right away,—in fact, to give you an easier and better paid job than you've had up to now. Perhaps even a foreman's position. You seem a clever man to me. And the one who has it now happens to have got himself disliked lately. You understand. You would also have to take charge of tempo, of course, and above all, as I say, find somebody for that place at the tin-cutting machine, which, I admit, is not safe at all. Over there, for instance, there's a girl looking for work.

GLOOMB. Can a man rely on what you say?

SLIFT. Yes.

GLOOMB. That one over there? She looks weak. It's no job for anyone who tires easily. *To the others.* I've thought it over, we'll do the job tomorrow night. Night's a better time for that kind of fun. So long. *Goes over to* JOAN. Looking for a job?

JOAN. Yes.

GLOOMB. Eyesight good?

JOAN. No. Last year I worked at a bone-grinding machine in the fertilizer cellars. I got it bad in the lungs there and a troublesome eye inflammation too. Since then my work-capacity has gone down badly. I've been out of a job since February. Is this a good place?

GLOOMB. The place is good. It's work that even weaker people, like yourself, can do.

JOAN. Are you sure there's no other place to be had? I've heard that working at that machine is dangerous for people who tire easily. Their hands get unsteady and then they grab at the blades.

GLOOMB. That isn't true at all. You'll be surprised to see how pleasant the work is. You'll fan your brow and ask yourself how people could ever tell such silly stories about that machine.

SLIFT *laughs and draws* JOAN *away.*

JOAN. Now I'm almost afraid to go on—what will I see next!

THEY *go into the canteen and see* MRS. LUCKERNIDDLE, *who is talking to the* WAITER.

MRS. LUCKERNIDDLE, *figuring.* Twenty dinners . . . then I could . . . then I'd go and then I'd have . . . SHE *sits down at a table.*

WAITER. If you're not eating you'll have to leave.

MRS. LUCKERNIDDLE. I'm waiting for somebody who was going to come in here today or tomorrow. What's for dinner today?

WAITER. Peas.

JOAN. There she sits.

I thought she was firmly resolved, and feared

that still she might come tomorrow, and now she has run here faster than we

and is here already, waiting for us.

SLIFT. Go and take her the food yourself—maybe she'll think again.

JOAN fetches a plate of food and brings it to MRS. LUCKERNIDDLE.

JOAN. Here so soon?

MRS. LUCKERNIDDLE. It's because I've had nothing to eat for two days.

JOAN. You didn't know we were coming in today, did you?

MRS. LUCKERNIDDLE. That's right.

JOAN. On the way over here I heard someone say that something happened to your husband in the factory and the factory is responsible.

MRS. LUCKERNIDDLE. Oh, so you've reconsidered your offer? So I don't get my twenty meals?

JOAN. But you got along with your husband very well, didn't you? People told me you have nobody except him.

MRS. LUCKERNIDDLE. Well, I've had nothing to eat for two days.

JOAN. Won't you wait till tomorrow? If you give up your husband now, no one will ask after him any more.

MRS. LUCKERNIDDLE *is silent.*

Don't take it.

MRS. LUCKERNIDDLE *snatches the food from her hands and begins to eat greedily.*

MRS. LUCKERNIDDLE. He's gone to Frisco.

JOAN. And basements and storerooms are full of meat

that cannot be sold and is going rotten

because no one will take it away.

The WORKER *with the cap and coat enters, rear.*

WORKER. Good morning, is this where I eat?

SLIFT. Just take a seat beside that woman over there.

The MAN *sits down.*

That's a good-looking cap you have there.

The WORKER *hides it.*

Where did you get it?

WORKER. Bought it.

SLIFT. Well, where did you buy it?

WORKER. Not in any store.

SLIFT. Then where did you get it?

WORKER. I got it off a man that fell into a boiling vat.

MRS. LUCKERNIDDLE *feels sick.* SHE *gets up and goes out. On the way out* SHE *says to the* WAITER.

MRS. LUCKERNIDDLE. Leave the plate where it is. I'm coming back. I'm coming here for dinner every day. Just ask that gentleman.

Exit.

SLIFT. For three whole weeks she will come and feed, without looking up, like an animal. Have you seen, Joan, that their wickedness is beyond measure?

JOAN. But what mastery you have
over their wickedness! How you thrive on it!
Do you not see that it rains on their wickedness?
Certainly she would have liked
to be true to her husband, as others are,
and to ask after the man who supported her
for some time longer, as is proper.
But the price was too high: it amounted to twenty meals.
And would that young man on whom
any scoundrel can rely
have shown the coat to the dead man's wife
if things had gone as he would like?
But the price appeared too high to him.
And why would the man with only one arm
have failed to warn me? if the price
of so small a scruple were not so high for him?
Why, instead, did he sell his wrath, which is righteous, but too dear?
If their wickedness is beyond measure, then
so is their poverty. Not the wickedness of the poor
have you shown me, but
the poverty of the poor.
Now that you have shown me the wickedness of the poor
I will show you the suffering of the wicked poor.
Demoralization: premature rumor!
Be refuted by their stricken faces!

V

JOAN INTRODUCES THE POOR TO THE
LIVESTOCK EXCHANGE

SCENE: *The Livestock Exchange.*

THE PACKERS. We have canned meat for sale!
  Wholesalers, buy canned meat!
  Fresh, juicy canned meat!
  Mauler and Cridle's bacon!
  Graham's sirloins, soft as butter!
  Wilde's Kentucky lard, a bargain!
THE WHOLESALERS. And silence fell upon the waters and
  bankruptcy among the wholesalers!
THE PACKERS. Due to tremendous technical advances
  engineers' hard work and entrepreneurs' farsightedness
  we have now succeeded
  in lowering prices for
  Mauler and Cridle's bacon
  Graham's sirloins, soft as butter
  Wilde's Kentucky lard, a bargain
  BY ONE-THIRD!
  Wholesalers, buy canned meat!
  Seize your opportunity!
THE WHOLESALERS. And silence fell upon the mountaintops
  and hotel kitchens covered their heads
  and stores looked away in horror
  and middlemen turned pale!
  We wholesalers vomit if we so much as
  see a can of meat. This country's stomach
  has eaten too much meat from cans
  and is fighting back.
SLIFT. What news from your friends in New York?
MAULER. Theories. If they had their way
  the meat ring would be lying in the gutter
  and stay there for weeks till there wasn't a peep left in it
  and I'd have all that meat around my neck!
  Madness!
SLIFT. I'd have to laugh if those men in New York really had

tariffs lowered now, opened up the South
and started a bull-market—just supposing!—and we
were to miss the bus!

MAULER. What if they did? Would you be brazen enough
to hack your pound of flesh from such misery
as these men's here, with eyes like lynxes'
watching for action? I couldn't be that brazen.

WHOLESALERS. Here we stand, wholesalers with mountains of cans
and cellars full of frozen steers
wanting to sell the steers in cans
and no one will buy them!
And our customers, the kitchens and stores,
are stuffed to the ceiling with frozen meat!
Screaming for buyers and eaters!
No more buying for us!

PACKERS. Here we stand, packers with slaughterhouses and packing space
and stables full of steers; day and night the machines
run on under steam; brine, tubs and boiling vats
wanting to turn the lowing ravenous herds
into canned meat and nobody wants canned meat.
We're ruined.

STOCKBREEDERS. And what about us, the stockbreeders?
Who'll buy livestock now? In our stables stand
steers and hogs eating expensive corn
and they ride to town in trains and while they ride
they eat and eat and at stations
they wait in rent-devouring boxcars, forever eating.

MAULER. And now the knives motion them back,
Death, giving livestock the cold shoulder,
closes his shop.

PACKERS, *shouting at* MAULER, *who is reading a newspaper.*
Traitorous Mauler, nest-befouler!
Do you think we don't know who's selling livestock here—
oh so secretly—and knocking the bottom out of prices?
You've been offering meat for days and days!

MAULER. Insolent butchers, cry in your mothers' laps
because the hunted creature's outcry ceases!
Go home and say that one of all your number
could not hear oxen bellow any longer
and would rather hear your bellow than their bellow!

I want my money and quiet for my conscience!

A BROKER, *bellowing from the Exchange entrance, rear.*

Terrific drop in stock exchange quotations!

Colossal sales of stocks. Cridle, formerly Mauler,

whirl the whole meat ring's rates down with them

into the abyss.

Uproar arises among the meat-packers. THEY *rush at* CRIDLE, *who is white as chalk.*

PACKERS. What's the meaning of this, Cridle? Look us in the eye!

Dumping stocks, with the market the way it is?

BROKERS. At 115!

PACKERS. Are your brains made of dung?

It's not yourself alone you're ruining!

You big shit! You criminal!

CRIDLE, *pointing to* MAULER. There's your man!

GRAHAM, *standing in front of* CRIDLE.

This isn't Cridle's doing, someone else

is fishing these waters and we're supposed to be the fish!

There are people who want to take care of the meat-ring, now,

and do a final job! Defend yourself, Mauler!

PACKERS, *to* MAULER. The story is, Mauler, that you're squeezing your money

out of Cridle, who, we hear, is groggy already, and Cridle

himself says nothing and points to you.

MAULER. If I leave my money in this Cridle's hands an hour longer—

a man who's confessed to me personally that he's lazy—who among you

would still take me seriously as a businessman? And I want nothing

so much as for *you* to take me seriously.

CRIDLE, *to the bystanders.* Just four weeks ago I made a contract with Mauler. He wanted to sell me his shares—one-third of the total—for ten million dollars. From that time on, as I've just found out, he has been secretly selling quantities of livestock, cheap, to make a still worse mess of prices that are sagging already. He could ask for his money whenever he wanted to. I intended to pay him by disposing of part of his shares on the market—they were high then—and reinvesting part. Then the drop came. Today Mauler's shares are worth not ten but three million. The whole plant is worth ten million instead of thirty. That's exactly the ten million I owe Mauler, and that's what he wants overnight.

PACKERS. If you're doing this, making things hard for Cridle,
  whose in-laws we are not, then you're well aware
  that this concerns us too. You're stripping
  all business bare: the fault is yours
  if our cans of meat are as cheap as sand,
  because you ruined Lennox with cheap cans!
MAULER. You shouldn't have gone and slaughtered so many cattle,
  you raving butchers! Now I want my money;
  though you should all go begging, I must have
  my money! I have other plans.
STOCKBREEDERS. Lennox smashed! And Cridle groggy! And Mauler
  pulls all his money out!
SMALL SPECULATORS. Oh, as for us, the little speculators,
  nobody cares. They scream when they see
  the colossus topple, but don't see where it falls,
  whom it strikes down. Mauler! Our money!
PACKERS. Eighty thousand cans at 50, but fast!
WHOLESALERS. Not a single one!
  Silence.
  The drumming of the BLACK STRAW HATS *and* JOAN'S VOICE *are heard.*
JOAN. Pierpont Mauler! Where is Mauler?
MAULER. What's that drumming? Who
  is calling my name?
  Here, where every man
  shows his bare chops all smeared with blood!
  The BLACK STRAW HATS *march in.* THEY *sing their war-chant.*
BLACK STRAW HATS, *singing.* Attention, pay attention!
  There is a man who's falling!
  There is a cry for help!
  There is a woman calling!
  Halt the autos, stop all traffic!
  Men falling all around us and no one looks their way!
  Is there no sight in your eye?
  Say hello to your brother, not just any guy!
  Get up from where you've dined—
  Is there no thought in your mind
  for the starving folk nearby?
  I hear you say: it will always be the same,
  the injustice of the world will still remain.
  But we say this to you: You've got to march

and leave your cares and help with might and main
and bring up tanks and cannon too
and airplanes there shall be
and battleships over the sea
to conquer a plate of soup, poor brother, just for you.
You've all got to lend us a hand
and it must be today
for the army of the good
is not a vast array.
Forward march! Eyes right! Rifles ready to fire!
Men falling all around us and no one looks their way!
Meanwhile the Exchange battle has continued. But laughter, prompted by
exclamations, is spreading toward the front of the scene.

PACKERS. Eighty thousand cans at half price, but fast!

WHOLESALERS. Not a single one!

PACKERS. Then we're finished, Mauler!

JOAN. Where is Mauler?

MAULER. Don't go, Slift! Graham, Meyers,
stay there in front of me.
I don't want to be seen here.

STOCKBREEDERS. Not a steer to be sold in Chicago any more
This day spells ruin for all of Illinois
With mounting prices you prodded us on into raising steers
and here we stand with steers
and no one will buy them.
Mauler, you dog, you are to blame for this disaster.

MAULER. Enough of business. Graham! My hat. I've got to go.
A hundred dollars for my hat.

CRIDLE. Oh, damn you to hell.
Exit CRIDLE.

JOAN. Now, you stay here, Mr. Mauler, and listen to what I have to say
to you. It is something you all may hear. Quiet! Yes, indeed, you
hardly think it right for us Black Straw Hats to turn up like this in the
dark hidden places where you do your business! I've been told about
the kind of things you do here, how you make meat more and more
expensive by your carryings-on and subtle trickery. But if you ever
supposed you could keep it all concealed, then you're on the wrong
track, now and on the Day of Judgment, for then it will be revealed,
and how will you look then, when our Lord and Savior has you walk
up in a row and asks with His big eyes, "Well, where are my steers?

What have you done with them? Did you make them available to the
people at prices within their reach? What has become of them, then?"
And when you stand there embarrassed, groping for excuses, the way
you do in your newspapers, which don't always stick to the truth, then
the steers will bellow at your backs in all the barns where you keep
them tucked away to make prices go sky-high, and by their bellowing
they will bear witness against you before Almighty God!
Laughter.

STOCKBREEDERS. We stockbreeders see nothing funny in that!
Dependent on weather, summer and winter, we stand
considerably nearer the Lord of old.

JOAN. And now an example. If a man builds a dam against the unreasonable water, and a thousand people help him with the labor of their
hands, and he gets a million for it, but the dam breaks as soon as
the water rises and everybody working on it and many more are
drowned—what kind of man is he who builds a dam like that? You
may call him a businessman or a rascal, depending on your views, but
we tell you he's a numskull. And all you men who make bread dear
and life a hell for human beings, so that they all become devils, you
are numskulls, wretched, stingy numskulls and nothing else!

WHOLESALERS, *shouting.* Because of your irresponsible
juggling with prices and filthy lust for profit
you're bringing on your own ruin!
Numskulls!

PACKERS, *shouting back.* Numskulls yourselves!
Nothing can be done about crises!
Unshakable above our heads
stands economic law, the not-to-be-known.
Terrible is the cyclic recurrence
of natural catastrophes!

STOCKBREEDERS. Nothing to be done about your hold on our throats?
That's wickedness, barefaced lying wickedness!

JOAN. And why does this wickedness exist in the world? Well, how could
it be otherwise? Naturally, if a man has to smash his neighbor's head
for a ham sandwich so that he can satisfy his elementary needs, brother
striving with brother for the bare necessities of life, how can the sense
of higher things help being stifled in the human heart? Why not think
of helping your neighbor simply as serving a customer? Then you'll
understand the New Testament in a flash, and see how fundamentally
modern it is, even today. Service! Why, what does service mean if

not charity—in the true meaning of the word, that is! Gentlemen,
I keep hearing that the poor haven't enough morals, and it's true, too.
Immorality makes its nest down there in the slums, with revolution
itself for company. I simply ask you: Where are they to get morals
from, if they have nothing else? Where can they get anything without
stealing it? Gentlemen, there is such a thing as moral purchasing-power.
Raise moral purchasing-power, and there's your morality. And I
mean by purchasing-power a very simple and natural thing,—that is,
money, wages. And this brings me back to the practical point: if you
go on like this you'll end by eating your own meat, because the people
outside haven't got any purchasing power.

STOCKBREEDERS, *reproachfully*. Here we stand with steers
  And nobody can afford them.

JOAN. But you sit here, you great and mighty men, thinking that no one
  will ever catch on to your tricks, and refusing to know anything about
  the misery in the world outside. Well then, just take a look at them,
  the people whom your treatment has brought to this condition, the
  people you will not admit to be your brothers! Come out now, you
  weary and heavy-laden, into the light of day. Don't be ashamed! JOAN
  shows to the Exchange crowd the poor people she has brought along with her.

MAULER, *shouting*. Take them away! HE *faints.*

A VOICE, *rear*. Pierpont Mauler has fainted!

THE POOR PEOPLE. He's the one to blame for everything!

  The PACKERS *attend to* MAULER.

PACKERS. Water for Pierpont Mauler!
  A doctor for Mauler!

JOAN. If you, Mauler, showed me the wickedness
  of the poor, now I show you
  the poverty of the poor, for they live far away from you
  and that puts beyond their reach goods they cannot do without—
  the people out of sight, whom you
  hold down in poverty like this, so weakened and so urgently
  in need of unobtainable food and warmth that they
  can be just as far away from any claim
  to higher things than the lowest gluttony, the beastliest habits.

  MAULER *comes to.*

MAULER. Are they still here? I implore you, send them away.

PACKERS. The Black Straw Hats? You want them sent away?

MAULER. No, those others, behind them.

SLIFT. He won't open his eyes before they get out.

GRAHAM. Can't bring yourself to look at them, eh? But it was you
who brought them to this state.
Shutting your eyes won't rid you of them,
far from it.
MAULER. I beseech you, send them away! I'll buy!
Listen, all of you: Pierpont Mauler's buying!
So that these people may get work and go.
Eight weeks' production in cans of meat—
I'll buy it!
PACKERS. He's bought! Mauler has bought!
MAULER. At today's prices!
GRAHAM, *holding him up.* And what about back stocks?
MAULER, *lying on the floor.* I'll buy 'em.
GRAHAM. At 50?
MAULER. At 50!
GRAHAM. He's bought! You heard it, he has bought!
BROKERS, *shouting through megaphones, rear.* Pierpont Mauler keeps the meat
market going. According to contract, he's taking over the meat-ring's
entire stock, at 50, as of today, besides two months' production, starting
today, also at 50. The meat-ring will deliver at least 800,000 cwt. of
canned meat to Pierpont Mauler on November 15.
MAULER. But now, my friends, I beg you, take me away.
MAULER *is carried out.*
JOAN. That's fine, now have yourself carried out!
We work at our mission jobs like plough-horses
and this is the kind of thing you do up here!
You had your man tell me I shouldn't say a thing.
Who are you, I'd like to know,
to try to muzzle the Lord in His goodness? You shouldn't even
muzzle the ox that's yoked to the thresher!
And speak I will.
To the poor people.
You'll have work again on Monday.
POOR PEOPLE. We've never seen such people anywhere. But we'd prefer
them to the two that were standing beside him. They have a far worse
look than he does.
JOAN. Now sing, as a farewell song, *Who Ever Feels the Lack of Bread.*
BLACK STRAW HATS, *singing.* Who ever feels the lack of bread
Once he's given the Lord his bond?
A man will never be in need if he stays within God's grace.

For how shall snow fall on him there?
And how shall hunger find that place?

WHOLESALERS. The fellow's sick in his head. This country's stomach
has eaten too much meat from cans and it's fighting back.
And he has meat put into cans
that no one will buy. Cross out his name!

STOCKBREEDERS. Come on, up with those prices, you lousy butchers!
Until you double livestock prices
not an ounce will be delivered, for you need it.

PACKERS. Keep your filth to yourselves! We will not buy.
For the contract which you saw agreed on here
is a mere scrap of paper. The man who made it
was not in his right mind. He couldn't raise
a cent from Frisco to New York
for that kind of business.
Exeunt PACKERS.

JOAN. Well, anyone who is really interested in God's word and what He
says and not just in what the ticker tape says, and there must be some
people here that are respectable and conduct their business in a God-
fearing way, we have nothing against that,—well, he's welcome to
visit our Divine Service Sunday afternoon in Lincoln Street at 2 p.m.
Music from three o'clock, no entrance charge.

SLIFT, *to the* STOCKBREEDERS. What Pierpont Mauler promises he fulfills.
Breathe freely now! The market's getting well!
You who give bread and you to whom it's given,
At last the doldrums have been overcome!
They menaced confidence, and even concord.
You who give work, and you to whom it's given,
You're moving in and opening wide the gates!
Sensible counsel, sensibly adopted,
Has got the upper hand of foolishness.
The gates are opening! The chimney's smoking!
It's work you've both been needing all the time.

STOCKBREEDERS, *placing* JOAN *up on the steps.*
Your speech and presence made a great impression
on us stockbreeders and many a man
was deeply moved, for we
have terrible sufferings too.

JOAN. You know, I have my eye
on Mauler, he has woken up, and you,

if there's something you need to help you out,
then come with me, that he may aid you also,
for from now on he shall not rest
till everyone is helped.
For he's in a position to help: so
let's go after him.

Exeunt JOAN *and* BLACK STRAW HATS, *followed by the* STOCKBREEDERS.

VI

THE CRICKET CAUGHT

SCENE: *The City. The broker Sullivan Slift's house, a small one with two entrances.*

MAULER, *inside the house, talking to* SLIFT. Lock the door, turn on all the lights
  there are,—then take a good look at my face, Slift, and see if it's true
  that anybody could tell by it.
SLIFT. Tell what by it?
MAULER. My business!
SLIFT. A butcher's? Mauler, why did you fall down when she talked?
MAULER. What did she say? I did not hear it,
  for behind her there stood such people with such ghastly faces
  of misery—misery that comes
  before a wrath that will sweep us all away—
  that I saw nothing more. Slift,
  I will tell you what I really think
  about this business of ours.
  It can't go on this way, nothing but buying and selling
  and one man coldly stripping off another's skin:
  there are too many people howling with pain
  and they are on the increase.
  That which falls into our bloody cellars
  is past all consolation:
  when they get hold of us they'll slap us against the pavement
  like rotten fish. All of us here,
  we're not going to die in our beds. Before
  we get that far they will stand us up against walls
  by the herd, and cleanse the world of us and
  our hangers-on.

SLIFT. They have upset you! *Aside.* I'll fix him a rare steak. His old weakness has come over him again. Maybe he'll come to his senses after
enjoying some raw meat. HE *goes and broils* MAULER *a steak on a gas stove.*
MAULER. I often ask myself why
I'm moved by that fool talk, worlds away,
the cheap, flat chitter-chatter they study up . . .
Of course, it's because they do it for nothing, eighteen hours a day and
in rain and hunger.
SLIFT. In cities which are burning down below
and freezing up on top, there are always people
who'll talk of this and that—details that aren't
in perfect order.
MAULER. But what is it they're saying? In these cities, incessantly
on fire, in the downward rush
of howling humanity,
surging towards hell without respite
for years on end, if I hear a voice like that—
foolish, of course, but quite unlike a beast's—
I feel as if I'd been cracked on the backbone with a stick
like a leaping fish.
But even this has only been evasion until now, Slift,
for what I fear is something other than God.
SLIFT. What is it?
MAULER. Not what is above me
but what is below me! What stands in the stockyards and cannot
last through the night and will still—I know—
rise up in the morning.
SLIFT. Won't you eat a little meat, my dear Pierpont? Think, now you
can do it with a clear conscience again, for from this day onward you
won't have anything to do with cattle-slaughtering.
MAULER. Do you think I should? Perhaps I could.
I ought to be able to eat now, oughtn't I?
SLIFT. Have a bite to eat and think over your situation. It's not very satis-
factory. Do you realize that today you bought up everything there is
in cans?
Mauler, I see you engrossed in the contemplation of your noble nature,
allow me to give you a concise account of your situation, the external,
the unimportant one.
The main point is that you've taken 300,000 cwt. of stocks away from
the meat-ring. You'll have to get rid of these in the next few weeks

on a market that can't swallow one more can even today. You've paid
50 for them, but the price will go down at least to 30. On November 15,
when the price is 30 or 25, the meat-ring will deliver 800,000 cwt.
to you at 50.

MAULER. Slift! I'm done for!
I'm finished. I've gone and bought up meat.
Oh, Slift, what have I done!
Slift, I've loaded myself with all the meat in the world.
Like Atlas, cans by the hundredweight on my shoulders,
I stumble straight down to the bridge-arches. Only this morning
many men were about to fall and I
went to see them fall and laugh at them
and tell them not a soul
would be fool enough to buy meat in cans now
and while I stand there I hear my own voice saying:
I'll buy it all.
Slift, I've gone and bought meat, I'm done for.

SLIFT. Well, what do you hear from your friends in New York?

MAULER. That I ought to buy meat.

SLIFT. You ought to do what?

MAULER. Buy meat.

SLIFT. Then why are you yammering because you have bought it?

MAULER. Yes, they told me I ought to buy meat.

SLIFT. But you have bought meat!

MAULER. Yes, that is so, I did buy meat, but I bought it
not because of the letter that said I should
(that's all wrong anyhow, green-table theory)
not from any low motives, but because
that person gave me such a shock, I swear
I barely riffled through the letter, it only came this morning.
Here it is. "Dear Pierpont——

SLIFT, *reads on.*—today we are able to inform you that our money is
beginning to bear fruit. Many congressmen are going to vote against
tariffs, so it seems advisable to buy meat, dear Pierpont. We shall
write you again tomorrow."

MAULER. This bribery, too, is something
that shouldn't happen. How easily a war
might start from a thing like that, and thousands bleed
for filthy lucre. Oh, my dear Slift, I feel
that nothing good can come of news like this.

SLIFT. That would depend on who had written the letters.
  Bribing, abolishing tariffs, making wars—
  not everybody can do that. Are these people all right?
MAULER. They're solvent.
SLIFT. But who are they?
  MAULER *smiles.*
  Then prices might go even higher still?
  Then we'd be sitting pretty after all.
  That might be a prospect if it wasn't for the farmers—
  by offering all their meat, only too eagerly,
  they'd bring prices crashing down again. No, Mauler,
  I don't understand that letter.
MAULER. Think of it this way: a man has committed theft
  and is caught by a man.
  Now if he doesn't knock the other man down
  he's done for; if he does, he's out of the woods.
  The letter (which is wrong) demands (so as to be right)
  a misdeed like that.
SLIFT. What misdeed?
MAULER. The kind I could never commit. For from now on
  I wish to live in peace. If they want to profit
  by their misdeeds—and they will profit—
  they need only buy up meat wherever they see it,
  beat into the stockbreeders' heads the fact
  that there's too much meat around and mention
  the flattering of Lennox and take
  their meat away from them. This above all:
  take the stockbreeders' meat from them . . . but then
  they'll be duped all over again . . . no, I'll have nothing
  to do with that.
SLIFT. You shouldn't have bought meat, Pierpont.
MAULER. Yes, it's a bad business, Slift.
  I'm not going to buy so much as a hat or a shoe
  until I get out of this mess, and I'll be happy
  if I have a hundred dollars when I do.
  Sound of drums. JOAN *approaches, with the* STOCKBREEDERS.
JOAN. We'll lure him out of his building the way you catch a cricket.
  You stand over there, because if he hears us singing he'll try to get
  out the other way, to avoid meeting me again: I'm a person he doesn't
  care to see. SHE *laughs.* And so are the people who are with me.

The STOCKBREEDERS *take up a position in front of door, right.*

JOAN, *in front of door, left.* Please come out, Mr. Mauler, I must talk to you about the terrible condition of the stockbreeders of Illinois. I also have several workers with me—they want to ask you when you're going to reopen your factory.

MAULER. Slift, where's the other exit? I don't want to run into her again, still less the people she has with her. I'm not opening any factories now, either.

SLIFT. Come out this way.

They go through the interior to door, right.

STOCKBREEDERS, *in front of door, left.* Come on out, Mauler, our troubles are all your fault, and we are more than 10,000 Illinois stockbreeders who don't know whether they're coming or going. So buy our livestock from us!

MAULER. Shut the door, Slift! I'm not buying.

With the whole world's canned meat around my neck,
Now should I buy the cattle on the dog-star?
It's as if a man should go to Atlas when
He can barely drag the world along, and say:
"They need another carrier on Saturn."
Who's going to buy the livestock back from me?

SLIFT. The Grahams, most likely—they need it!

JOAN, *in front of door, left.* We're not leaving this place until the stockbreeders get some help.

MAULER. Most likely the Grahams, yes, they need livestock. Slift, go out and tell them to let me have two minutes to think things over.

SLIFT *goes.*

SLIFT, *to the* STOCKBREEDERS. Pierpont Mauler wishes to give careful consideration to your request. He asks for two minutes' thinking time.

SLIFT *re-enters the house.*

MAULER. I'm not buying. HE *starts figuring.* Slift, I'm buying. Slift, bring me anything that looks like a hog or a steer, I'll buy it, whatever smells of lard, I'll buy it, bring every speck of fat, I'm the buyer for it, and at today's price too, at 50.

SLIFT. Not a hat will you buy, Mauler, but
all the cattle in Illinois.

MAULER. Yes, I'll still buy that. Now it's decided, Slift.
Take A.

HE *draws on A on a closet door.*

A man does something wrong, let that be A,

he did it because his feelings overcame him,
and now he goes on to do B, and B's wrong too
and now the sum of A and B is right.
Ask the stockbreeders in, they're very nice people,
badly in need and decently clothed and not
the sort of folk that scare you when you see them.

SLIFT, *stepping out in front of the house; to the* STOCKBREEDERS. To save Illinois and avert ruin from its farmers and stockbreeders, Pierpont Mauler has decided to buy up all the livestock on the market.

STOCKBREEDERS. Long live Pierpont Mauler! He's saved the livestock trade!

THEY *enter the house.*

JOAN, *calling after them.* Tell Mr. Mauler that we, the Black Straw Hats, thank him for this in the name of the Lord. *To the workers.* If the people who buy cattle and the people who sell cattle are satisfied, then there'll be bread once more for you too.

VII

THE EXPULSION OF THE MONEY-CHANGERS
FROM THE TEMPLE

SCENE: *The Black Straw Hats' Mission. The* BLACK STRAW HATS, *sitting at a long table, are counting out from their tin boxes the widows' and orphans' mites they have collected.*

BLACK STRAW HATS, *singing.* Gather the pennies of widows and orphans
  with song!
Great is the need
They have no roof or bread
But Almighty God
Won't let them go hungry long.

PAULUS SNYDER, *Major of the Black Straw Hats, getting up.* Very little, very little. *To some poor folk in the background, among them* MRS. LUCKERNIDDLE *and* GLOOMB. You here again? Don't you ever leave this place? There's work at the stockyards again, you know!

MRS. LUCKERNIDDLE. Where? The yards are shut down.

GLOOMB. We were told they would open up again, but they haven't.

SNYDER. Well, don't go too near the cash-box. HE *motions them still further back.*

MULBERRY, *the landlord, enters.*

MULBERRY. Say, what about my rent?

SNYDER. My dear Black Straw Hats, my dear Mulberry, my honored listeners! As to this troublesome problem of financing our operations—anything that's good speaks for itself, and needs propaganda more than anything—hitherto we have aimed our appeals at the poor, indeed the poorest, on the assumption that they, being most in need of God's help, were the people most likely to have a bit left over for Him, and that their sheer numbers would produce the desired effect. To our regret, it has been borne in upon us that these very classes manifest an attitude of reserve toward God that is quite beyond explanation. Of course, this may be due to the fact that they have nothing. Therefore, I, Paulus Snyder, have issued an invitation in your name to Chicago's wealthy and prosperous citizens, to help us launch a major offensive next Sunday against the unbelief and materialism of the city of Chicago, primarily among the lower orders. Out of the proceeds we shall also pay our dear landlord, Mr. Mulberry, the rent he is so kindly deferring for us.

MULBERRY. It would certainly be very welcome, but please don't worry about it.

Exit.

SNYDER. Well, now go happily about your work and be sure to clean the front steps.

Exeunt BLACK STRAW HATS.

SNYDER. Tell me, are the locked-out workers in the stockyards still standing there patiently, or have they begun to talk like rebels?

MRS. LUCKERNIDDLE. They've been squawking pretty loud since yesterday, because they know the factories are getting orders.

GLOOMB. Many are saying already that they won't get any more work at all if they don't use force.

SNYDER, *to himself.* A good sign. The meat kings will be more likely to come and listen to our appeal if they're driven in by stones. *To the* POOR PEOPLE. Couldn't you split our wood, at least?

POOR PEOPLE. There isn't any more, Major.

Enter the packers CRIDLE, GRAHAM, SLIFT, MEYERS.

MEYERS. You know, Graham, I keep asking myself where that livestock can be hiding out.

GRAHAM. That's what I'm asking too, where can that livestock be hiding out?

SLIFT. So am I.

GRAHAM. Oh, you too? And I guess Mauler is too, eh?

SLIFT. I guess he is.

MEYERS. Somewhere some swine is buying everything up.
Someone who knows quite well that we're committed
by contract to deliver meat in cans
and so need livestock.

SLIFT. Who can it be?

GRAHAM, *hitting him in the stomach.*
You cur, you!
Don't play any tricks on us there, and tell Pierpy not to either!
That's a vital spot!

SLIFT, *to* SNYDER. What do you want of us?

GRAHAM, *hitting him again.* What do you think they want, Slift?
SLIFT, *with exaggerated mockery, makes the gesture of handing out money.*
You said it, Slift!

MEYERS, *to* SNYDER. Fire away.

THEY *sit down on the prayer benches.*

SNYDER, *in the pulpit.* We Black Straw Hats have heard that 50,000 men are standing around in the stockyards without work. And that some are beginning to grumble and say: "We'll have to help ourselves." Aren't your names beginning to be called as the ones to blame for 50,000 men being out of work and standing idly in front of the factories? They'll end by taking the factories away from you and saying: "We'll act the way the Bolsheviks did and take the factories into our own hands so that everybody can work and eat." For the story is getting around that unhappiness doesn't just come like the rain but is made by certain persons who get profit out of it. But we Black Straw Hats try to tell them that unhappiness does come down like the rain, no one knows where from, and that they are destined to suffering and there's a reward for it shining at the end of the road.

PACKERS. Why mention rewards?

SNYDER. The reward we speak of is paid out after death.

PACKERS. How much will it cost?

SNYDER. $800 a month, because we need hot soup and loud music. We also want to promise them that the rich will be punished—when they're dead, of course. *The* PACKERS *laugh noisily.* All that for a mere eight hundred a month!

GRAHAM. You don't need that much, man. Five hundred.

SNYDER. Well, we could get along with seven hundred and fifty, but then——

MEYERS. Seven hundred and fifty. That's better. Let's make it five hundred.

GRAHAM. You do need five hundred, certainly. *To the others.* They've got to get that.

MEYERS. Out with it, Slift, you fellows have that livestock.

SLIFT. Mauler and I have not bought one cent's worth of livestock, as true as I'm sitting here. The Lord's my witness.

MEYERS, *to* SNYDER. Five hundred dollars, eh? That's a lot of money. Who's going to pay it?

SLIFT. Yes, you'll have to find someone who will give it to you.

SNYDER. Yes, yes.

MEYERS. That won't be easy.

GRAHAM. Come on, Slift, cough it up, Pierpy has the livestock.

SLIFT, *laughing.* A bunch of crooks, Mr. Snyder.

ALL *laugh except* SNYDER.

GRAHAM, *to* MEYERS. The man has no sense of humor. Don't like him.

SLIFT. The main point is, man, where do you stand? On this side of the barricades, or the other?

SNYDER. The Black Straw Hats stand above the battle, Mr. Slift. This side. *Enter* JOAN.

SLIFT. Why, here's our sainted Joan of the Livestock Exchange!

THE FOUR, *shouting at* JOAN. We're not satisfied with you, can't you tell Mauler something from us? You're supposed to have some influence with him. They say he eats out of your hand. Well, the market is so short of livestock that we have to keep an eye on him. They say you can bring him round to doing whatever you want. Have him get that livestock out. Listen, if you'll do this for us we're willing to pay the Black Straw Hats' rent for the next four years.

JOAN *has seen the poor people and is shocked.*

JOAN. Why, what are you doing here?

MRS. LUCKERNIDDLE, *coming forward.*

The twenty dinners are all eaten now.

Please don't get angry because I'm here again.

It's a sight I would be glad enough to spare you.

That's the awful thing about hunger: no sooner

is it satisfied than back it comes again.

GLOOMB, *coming forward.* I know you, it was you I tried to talk

into working on that slicer that tore my arm off.

I could do worse things than that today.

JOAN. Why aren't you working? I did get work for you.

MRS. LUCKERNIDDLE. Where? The stockyards are closed.

GLOOMB. We were told they would open up again, but they haven't.

JOAN, *to the* PACKERS. So they're still waiting, are they?

The PACKERS *say nothing.*

And I thought they had been provided for!
It's been snowing on them now for seven days
and the very snow that kills them cuts them off
from every human eye. How easily
I forgot what everyone likes to forget for the peace of his mind!
If one man says things are all right again, no one looks into them.
To the PACKERS.
But surely Mauler bought meat from you? He did it at my
request! And now you still refuse to open up your factories?

CRIDLE, GRAHAM, MEYERS. That's quite right, we wanted to open up.

SLIFT. But first of all you wanted to leap at the farmers' throats!

CRIDLE, GRAHAM, MEYERS. How are we to do any slaughtering when
there's no livestock?

SLIFT. When Mauler and I bought meat from you we took it for granted
you would start employment going again so that the workers would
be able to buy meat. Now who will eat the meat we got from you?
For whom did we buy meat if consumers can't pay for it?

JOAN. Look, if you people have control of all the equipment your em-
ployees use in your all-powerful factories and plants, then the least
you could do would be to let them in, if they're kept out it's all up
with them, because there is a sort of exploitation about the whole
thing, and if a poor human creature is tormented till the blood comes,
and can think of no way out but to take a club and bash his tormentor's
head in, then it scares the daylights out of you, I've noticed that, and
then you think religion's fine and it's supposed to pour oil on the
troubled waters, but the Lord has His pride too, and He won't pitch
in and clean your pigsties for you all over again. And I run around
from Gog to Magog, thinking: "If I help you people on top, the people
under you will also be helped. It's all one in a way, and the same strings
pull it," but I was a prize fool there. If a man wants to help folks that
are poor it seems he'd better help them get away from you. Is there
no respect left in you for anything that wears a human face? Some
day, maybe, you won't rate as human beings either, but as wild animals that will simply have to be slaughtered in the interest of public
order and safety! And still you have the confidence to enter the house

of God, just because you own that filthy Mammon, everybody knows where you got it and how, it wasn't come by honestly. But this time, by God, you've come to the wrong people, we'll have to drive you out, that's all, yes, drive you out with a stick. Come on, don't stand there looking so stupid, I know human beings shouldn't be treated like steers, but you aren't human beings, get out of here, and fast, or I'll lay violent hands on you, don't hold me back, I know what I'm doing, it's high time I found out.

JOAN *drives them out, using as a stick a flag held upside down. The* BLACK STRAW HATS *appear in the doorways.*

Get out! Are you trying to turn the house of God into a stable? Another Livestock Exchange? Get out! There's nothing for you here. We don't want to see such faces here. You're unworthy and I'm showing you the door. For all your money!

THE FOUR. Very well. But forty months' rent goes with us—simply, modestly, irretrievably. We need every cent of it anyway: we're facing times as terrible as the livestock market has ever seen. *Exeunt.*

SNYDER, *running after them.* Please stay, gentlemen! Don't go, she has no authority at all! A crazy female! She'll be fired! She'll do whatever you want her to do.

JOAN, *to the* BLACK STRAW HATS. Well, that certainly wasn't very smart at a time like this, what with the rent and all. But we can't think about that now. *To* LUCKERNIDDLE *and* GLOOMB. Sit down back there, I'll bring you some soup.

SNYDER, *returning.* Go on, make the poor your guests
and regale them with rainwater and fine speeches
when there's really no pity for them up above,
nothing but snow!
You followed your very first impulses,
utterly without humility! It is so much easier
simply to drive the unclean out with arrogance.
You're squeamish about the bread we have to eat,
much too curious how it's made, and still
you want to eat it! Now, woman above the world,
get out in the rain and face the snowstorm in righteousness!

JOAN. Does that mean I'm to take off my uniform?

SNYDER. Take off your uniform and pack your bags! Get out of this house and take along the riff-raff you brought us. Nothing but riff-raff and scum followed you in here. Now you'll be in that class yourself. Go and get your things.

JOAN *goes out and comes back dressed like a country servant, carrying a little suitcase.*

JOAN. I'll go find rich man Mauler, he is not
without fear or good will, and ask his help.
I won't put on this coat or black straw hat
ever again or come back to this dear house
of songs and awakenings till
I bring in rich man Mauler as one of us,
converted from the ground up.
What if their money has eaten away
their ears and human faces like a cancer
making them sit apart but loftily
beyond the reach of any cry for help!
Poor cripples!
There must be *one* just man among them!
Exit.

SNYDER. Poor simpleton!
You're blind to this: set up in huge formations
the givers and the takers of work
confront one another:
warring fronts: irreconcilable.
Run to and fro between them, little peacemaker, little mediator—
be useful to neither and go to your doom.

MULBERRY, *entering.* Have you the money now?

SNYDER. God will still be able to pay for the definitely scanty shelter
He has found on earth, I said scanty, Mr. Mulberry.

MULBERRY. Yes, pay, that's the ticket, that's the problem! You said the
right word then, Snyder! If the Lord in His goodness pays, good. But
if He doesn't pay, not so good. If the Lord in His goodness doesn't
pay His rent, He'll have to get out, and what's more, He'll have to go
on Saturday night, eh, Snyder?
Exit.

VIII

PIERPONT MAULER'S SPEECH ON THE INDISPENSABILITY OF CAPITALISM AND RELIGION

SCENE: *Mauler's office.*

MAULER. Well, Slift, today's the day
when our good friend Graham and all his crew
who wanted to wait for the lowest livestock prices
will have to buy the meat they owe us.
SLIFT. It will cost them more, because anything
the Chicago market can show in the way of lowing cattle
is ours now.
Every hog they owe us
they'll have to buy from us, and that's expensive.
MAULER. Now, Slift, let loose all your wholesalers!
Let them torment the livestock market with demands
for everything that looks like hogs and cattle
and so make prices go up and up.
SLIFT. What news of your Joan? There's a rumor
around the Livestock Exchange that you slept with her.
I did my best to scotch it. She hasn't been heard of
since that day she threw us all out of the temple:
it's as though black roaring Chicago had swallowed her up.
MAULER. I liked her action very much,
throwing you all out like that. Yes, that girl's afraid of nothing.
And if I'd been along on that occasion
she'd have thrown me out with the rest and that's
what I like about her and that house of hers,
the fact that people like me are impossible there.
Force the price up to 8o, Slift. That will make those Grahams
rather like mud you stick your foot into
merely to see its shape again.
I won't let an ounce of meat go by:
this time I'll rip their skins off for good and all,
in accordance with my nature.
SLIFT. I'm overjoyed that you've shaken off
your weakness of the past few days. And now
I'll go and watch them buy up livestock.

MAULER. It's high time this damn town had its skin ripped off
and those fellows were taught a thing or two
about the meat market: what if they do yell "Crime!"
Enter JOAN, *carrying a suitcase.*

JOAN. Good morning, Mr. Mauler. You're a hard man to find. I'll just
leave my things over there for the time being. You see, I'm not with
the Black Straw Hats any more. We had an argument. So I thought,
Well, I'll go look for Mr. Mauler. Having no more of that wearing
mission work to do, I can pay more attention to the individual. So,
to begin with, I'm going to occupy myself with you a little, that is,
if you'll let me. You know, I've noticed that you are much more
approachable than many other people. That's a fine old mohair sofa
you have there, but why do you have a sheet on it? —and it isn't made
up properly, either. So you sleep in your office? I thought surely you
would have one of those great big palaces. MAULER *says nothing.* But
you're quite right, Mr. Mauler, to be a good manager in little things
too, being a meat king. I don't know why, but when I see you I always
think of the story about the Lord when He visited Adam in the Garden
of Eden and called out, "Adam, where are you?" Do you remember?
Laughs. Adam is standing behind a bush with his arms up to the elbows
in a doe, and he hears the voice of God just like that, with blood all
over him. And so he acts as if he wasn't there. But God doesn't give
up, and calls out again, "Adam, where are you?" And then Adam says,
faintly and blushing crimson: "This is the time you pick to visit me,
right after I've killed a doe. Oh, don't say a word, I know I shouldn't
have done it." But your conscience is clear, Mr. Mauler, I hope.

MAULER. So you're not with the Black Straw Hats any more?

JOAN. No, Mr. Mauler, and I don't belong there either.

MAULER. Then what have you been living on?

JOAN *says nothing.*

I see. Nothing. How long ago did you leave the Black Straw Hats?

JOAN. Eight days ago.

MAULER, *turns away and weeps.*
So greatly changed, and in a mere eight days!
Where has she been? To whom has she been talking? What was it
that drew those lines around her mouth?
The city she has come from
is a thing I do not know.
HE *brings her food on a tray.*

I see you very much changed. Here's something to eat, if you like.
I'm not hungry myself.

JOAN, *looking at the food.* Mr. Mauler, after we drove the rich people out
of our house——

MAULER. Which amused me very much, and seemed the right thing to
do——

JOAN. The landlord, who lives on the rent we pay, gave us notice to get
out next Sunday.

MAULER. Indeed! So the Black Straw Hats are poorly off financially?

JOAN. Yes, and that's why I thought I'd go and see Mr. Mauler. SHE
begins to eat hungrily.

MAULER. Don't you fret. I'll go into the market and get you the money
you need. Yes, I'll do that, I'll get hold of it whatever it costs me, even
if I have to slice it right out of the city's skin. I'll do it for you. Money's
expensive, of course, but I'll produce it. That will be to your liking.

JOAN. Yes, Mr. Mauler.

MAULER. So you go and tell them: "The money is on the way. It will be
there by Saturday. Mauler will get hold of it. He just left for the livestock market to dig it up." That matter of the fifty thousand didn't go
so well, not exactly as I wanted it. I was unable to get them work immediately. But for you I'll make an exception, and your Black Straw
Hats shall be spared, I'll get the money for you. Run and tell them.

JOAN. Yes, Mr. Mauler!

MAULER. There, I've put it in writing. Take it.
I too am sorry that the men are waiting for work
in the stockyards and not very good work at that.
Fifty thousand men
standing around in the stockyards, not even leaving at night.
JOAN *stops eating.*
But that's the way this business goes:
it's to be or not to be—a question whether
I am to be the best man in my class or go
the dark and dreary way to the stockyards myself.
Also, the scum is filling up the yards again
and making trouble.
And now—I'll tell you the simple truth—I would have liked
to hear you say that what I do is right
and my business is natural: so
tell me for sure that it was on your advice

I ordered meat from the meat-ring and from
the stockbreeders too, thus doing good; then,
because I know well that you are poor and right now
they're trying to take away the very roof over your heads,
I'll give you something in return, as token
of my goodwill.
JOAN. So the workers are still waiting in front of the abattoirs?
MAULER. Why are you set against money? and yet look
so very different when you haven't any?
What do you think about money? Tell me,
I want to know; and don't get wrong ideas,
the way a fool will think of money as
something to be doubted. Consider the reality,
the plain truth, not pleasant maybe, but still
true for all that: everything is unsteady and the human race
is exposed to luck, you might say, to the state of the weather,
but money's a means of making some improvement—even if only
for certain people—apart from that, what a structure!
Built up from time immemorial, over and over again
because it keeps collapsing, but still tremendous: demanding sacrifice,
very hard to set up, continually set up
with many a groan, but still inescapably
wresting the possible from a reluctant planet,
however much or little that may be; and accordingly defended
at all times by the best. Just think, if I—
who have much against it, and sleep badly—
were to desert it, I would be like a fly
ceasing to hold back a landslide. There and then
I would become a nothing and it would keep on going over me.
For otherwise everything would have to be overturned
and the architect's design fundamentally altered
to suit an utterly different, incredible, new valuation of man,
which you people don't want any more than we do, for it would
    take effect
with neither us nor God, who would have no function left
and be dismissed accordingly. Therefore you really ought to
collaborate with us, and even if you don't sacrifice
what we don't want of you anyhow, still sanction the sacrifices:
in a word, you really ought
to set God up once more—

the only salvation—and
beat the drum for Him so that He may
gain a foothold in the regions of misery and His
voice may ring out among the abattoirs.
That would suffice.
Holding out the note to her.
Take what you get, but know the reason
before you take it! Here's the voucher, this is four years' rent.

JOAN. Mr. Mauler, I don't understand what you have been saying
and do not wish to either.
Rising.
I know I should be overjoyed to hear
that God is going to be helped, only
I belong to those for whom
this does not mean real help. And to whom
nothing is offered.

MAULER. If you take the money to the Black Straw Hats you can also
stay in their house again: this living
on nothing is not good for you. Believe me,
they're out for money, and so they should be.

JOAN. If the Black Straw Hats
accept your money they are welcome to it,
but I will take my stand among the people waiting in the stockyards,
until the factories open up again, and
eat nothing but what they eat and if
they are offered snow, then snow,
and the work they do I will do also, for I have no money either
and no other way to get it—honorably, anyhow—
and if there is no more work, then let there be none
for me either, and
you, who live on poverty and
cannot bear to see the poor and judge
something you do not know and make arrangements
so as not to see what sits there being judged,
abandoned in the abattoirs, disregarded,
if you want to see me again
come to the stockyards.
Exit.

MAULER. Tonight then, Mauler,
get up every hour and look out of the window

to see if it's snowing, and if it is
it will be snowing on the girl you know.

IX

JOAN'S THIRD DESCENT INTO THE DEPTHS: THE SNOWFALL

SCENE: *Stockyards district.*

JOAN. Listen to the dream I had one night
a week ago.
Before me in a little field, too small
to hold the shade of a middle-sized tree, hemmed in
by enormous houses, I saw a bunch
of people: I could not make out how many, but
there were far more of them than all the sparrows
that could find room in such a tiny place—
a very thick bunch indeed, so that
the field began to buckle and rise in the middle
and the bunch was suspended on its edge, holding fast
a moment, quivering: then, stirred
by the intervention of a word,—uttered somewhere or other,
meaning nothing vital,—it began to flow.
Then I saw processions, streets, familiar ones, Chicago! you!
I saw you marching, then I saw myself:
I, silent, saw myself striding at your head
with warlike step and bloodstains on my brow
and shouting words that sounded militant
in a tongue I did not know; and while many processions
moved in many directions all at once
I strode in front of many processions in manifold shapes:
young and old, sobbing and cursing,
finally beside myself! Virtue and terror!
Changing whatever my foot touched,
causing measureless destruction, visibly influencing
the courses of the stars, but also changing utterly
the neighborhood streets familiar to us all—
so the procession moved, and I along with it,
veiled by snow from any hostile attack,
transparent with hunger, no target,

not to be hit anywhere, not being settled anywhere;
not to be touched by any trouble, being accustomed
to all. And so it marches, abandoning the position
which cannot be held: exchanging it for any other one.
That was my dream.
Today I see its meaning:
before tomorrow morning we
will start out from these yards
and reach their city, Chicago, in the gray of dawn,
displaying the full range of our wretchedness in public places,
appealing to whatever resembles a human being.
What will come after, I do not know.

SCENE: *Livestock Exchange.*

MAULER, *to the* PACKERS.
  My friends in New York have written me to say
  that the tariff in the south
  was repealed today.
PACKERS. This is awful, the tariff law gone and here we are
  without any meat to sell! It's been sold already
  at a low price and now we are asked to buy meat when it's going up!
STOCKBREEDERS. This is awful, the tariff law gone and here we are
  without any livestock to sell! It's already been sold
  at a lower price!
SMALL SPECULATORS. Awful! Eternally inscrutable
  are the eternal laws
  of human economy!
  Without warning
  the volcano erupts and lays the country waste!
  Without an invitation
  the profitable island rises from the barren seas!
  No one is told, no one is in the picture! But the last in line
  is bitten by the dogs!
MAULER. Well, seeing that livestock is being demanded
  in cans at an acceptable price
  I now request you to hand over quickly
  the canned meat I am supposed to get from you
  according to contract.
GRAHAM. At the old price?

MAULER. As the contract specified, Graham.
   800,000 hundredweight, if I remember correctly
   a moment when I was not myself.
PACKERS. How can we take livestock now, with prices rising?
   Someone has made a corner in it,
   nobody knows who—
   release us from the contract, Mauler!
MAULER. Unfortunately I must have those cans. But there is
   still livestock enough, a bit expensive, granted, but
   livestock enough. Buy it up!
PACKERS. Buy livestock now? The hell with it!

   SCENE: *A little tavern in the stockyards district. Men and women workers,*
   JOAN *among them.—A group of Black Straw Hats enter.* JOAN *rises and makes*
   frantic gestures at them during what follows.

JACKSON, *after a hurried song.*
   Brother, why won't you eat the bread that Jesus gives?
   See how happy and glad are we.
   It's because we have found the Lord Jesus, Lord of all our lives.
   Hurry, come to Him heartily!
   Hallelujah!
   One of the Black Straw Hat girls talks to the workers, making side remarks
   to her comrades.
BLACK STRAW HAT. (It's no use, is it?) Brothers and sisters, I too used to
   stand sadly by the wayside, just as you are, and the old Adam in me
   cared for nothing but meat and drink, but then I found my Lord Jesus,
   and then it was so light and glad inside me, but now (They aren't
   listening at all!) if I just think real hard about my Lord Jesus, who
   redeemed us all by His suffering in spite of our many wicked deeds,
   then I stop feeling hungry and thirsty, except for our Lord Jesus' word.
   (No use.) Where the Lord Jesus is, there is not violence, but peace,
   not hate but love. (It's quite hopeless!)
BLACK STRAW HATS. Hallelujah!
   JACKSON *passes the box around. Nothing is put into it.*
   Hallelujah!
JOAN. If only they wouldn't stay here in the cold
   making all that nuisance and talking, talking!
   Really, now I can hardly bear
   to hear the words

that once were dear and pleasant to me! If only a voice,
some remnant inside them, would say:
There's snow and wind here, be quiet here!

A WOMAN. Oh, let them be. They have to do this to get a bit of warmth
and food. I wish I was in their shoes.

MRS. LUCKERNIDDLE. That was nice music!

GLOOMB. Nice and short.

MRS. LUCKERNIDDLE. But they really are good people.

GLOOMB. Good and brief, short and sweet.

WOMAN WORKER. Why don't they give us a real talk, and convert us?

GLOOMB, *making a gesture of paying out money.* Can you keep the pot boiling,
Mrs. Swingurn?

WOMAN WORKER. The music is very pretty but I was expecting them to
give us a plate of soup, maybe, seeing they had brought a pot along.

WORKER, *surprised at her.* No kidding, you thought that?

JOAN. Are there no people here with any enterprise?

A WORKER. Yes, the Communists.

JOAN. Aren't they people who incite to crime?

THE WORKER. No.

SCENE: *Livestock Exchange.*

PACKERS. We're buying livestock! Yearlings!
Feeders! Calves! Steers! Hogs!
Offers, please!

STOCKBREEDERS. There isn't any! We've sold whatever was saleable.

PACKERS. Isn't any? The depots are bursting with cattle.

STOCKBREEDERS. Sold.

PACKERS. To whom?
Enter MAULER.
Milling around him.
Not a steer to be found in Chicago!
You'll have to give us more time, Mauler.

MAULER. You'll deliver your meat as agreed.
Going over to SLIFT.
Squeeze 'em dry.

A STOCKBREEDER. 800 Kentucky steers at 400.

PACKERS. Impossible. 400! Are you crazy?

SLIFT. I'll take them. At 400.

STOCKBREEDERS. 800 steers sold to Sullivan Slift for 400.

PACKERS. It's Mauler! What did we say? He's the one!
You crooked hound! He makes us deliver canned meat
and buys up livestock! So we have to buy from him
the meat we need to fill his cans!
You filthy butcher! Here, take *our* flesh, hack yourself off a slice!

MAULER. If you're a dumb ox you shouldn't be surprised when people's appetites grow with looking at you.

GRAHAM, *makes as if to attack* MAULER. He's got it coming, I'll settle his hash!

MAULER. All right, Graham, now I demand your cans.
You can stuff yourself into one of them.
I'll teach you the meat business, you
traders! From now on I get paid, and well paid,
for every hoof, every calf from here to Illinois*
and so I'll offer 500 steers at 56 to start with.
Dead silence.
And now, in view of the weak demand, seeing nobody here needs livestock,
I want 60! And don't forget my cans, either!

SCENE: *Another part of the stockyards. Placards are inscribed: Solidarity with Locked-out Stockyard Workers! All out for General Strike! In front of a shed two men from the union local are speaking to a group of workers. Enter* JOAN.

JOAN. Are these the people who lead the movement of the unemployed? I can help them. I've learned to speak in streets and meeting-halls, I have no fear of hecklers and I think I can explain a good thing well. Because, as I see it, something's got to be done right away. I have some suggestions to make, too.

A LABOR LEADER. Listen, all. So far the meat gang hasn't shown the least inclination to open up its factories. At first it seemed that the exploiter Pierpont Mauler was all out for a reopening because he wants from the meat gang huge quantities of meat that they owe him by contract. Then it became clear that the meat they need for packing is in Mauler's own hands and he won't even consider letting it go. Now we know that if things are left up to the meat gang we workers will never all get back into the slaughterhouses, and never at the old wages. With things in this pass we've got to realize that nothing can help us but the use of force. The city utilities have promised to join the general

* *Sic.*—F.J.

strike by tomorrow morning at the latest. Now this news must be spread
in all parts of the stockyards; if it isn't, there's a danger that the masses
will be excited by some rumor or other and leave the yards, and then
be forced to yield to the meat gang's terms. So these letters, stating
that the gas, water and electric workers are going to help us by going
on strike, must be handed out to delegates who will be awaiting our
password in different parts of the stockyards at ten o'clock tonight.
Stick that under your vest, Jack, and wait for the delegates in front of
Mother Schmitt's canteen.

A WORKER *takes the letter and leaves.*

SECOND WORKER. Give me the one for the Graham works, I know them.

LEADER. 26th Street, corner Michigan Park.

WORKER *takes letter and leaves.*

13th Street by the Westinghouse Building. *To* JOAN. Well, and who may
you be?

JOAN. I was fired from the job I had.

LEADER. What job?

JOAN. Selling magazines.

LEADER. Who were you working for?

JOAN. I'm a peddler.

A WORKER. Maybe she's a spy.

THE OTHER LEADER. Who can tell what she will do with the letter we give
her?

FIRST LEADER. Nobody.

To JOAN.

A net with a torn mesh
is of no use:
the fish swim through at that spot
as though there were no net.
Suddenly all its meshes
are useless.

JOAN. I used to sell papers on 44th Street. I'm no spy. I'm for your cause
heart and soul.

SECOND LEADER. Our cause? Why, isn't it your cause?

JOAN. It certainly isn't in the public interest for the factory owners to
leave all those people sitting in the streets just like that. Why, it makes
you think the poverty of the poor is useful to the rich! You might say
poverty is all their doing! *The* WORKERS *laugh uproariously.* It's inhuman, that's what it is! I even have people like Mauler in mind when
I say that. *Renewed laughter.* Why do you laugh? I don't think you have

any right to be malicious and to believe without proof that a man like Mauler can be inhuman.

SECOND LEADER. Not without proof! You can give the letter to her, all right.

FIRST LEADER. Go to gate 3 at the Graham plant. When you see three workers come up and look around them, ask if they are from the Cridle plant. This letter is for them.

SCENE: *Livestock Exchange.*

SMALL SPECULATORS. Quotations going down! The packing plants in peril!
What will become of us, the stockholders?
The man with small savings who gave his last cent
for the middle class, which is weakened anyway?
A man like Graham ought to be
torn to shreds before he makes waste paper
out of the note with our share marked on it, the one
we earned from his bloody cellars.
Buy that livestock, buy it at any price!
Throughout this scene the names of firms suspending payment are being called out. "Suspending payment: Meyer & Co.," etc.

PACKERS. We can do no more, the price is over 70.

WHOLESALERS. Mow 'em down, they won't buy, the high-hats.

PACKERS. 2000 steers demanded at 70.

SLIFT, *to* MAULER, *beside a column.* Shove 'em up.

MAULER. I see that you have not stood by your part
of the contract I drew up with you that day
in the wish to create employment. And now I hear
they're still standing around out there in the yards. But
you're going to regret it: out with the canned meat
which I have bought!

GRAHAM. There's nothing we can do: meat has completely
vanished from the market!
I'll take 500 steers at 75.

SMALL SPECULATORS. Buy them, you greedy hounds!
They won't buy! They'd rather hand over
the packing plants.

MAULER. We shouldn't push it up any higher, Slift.
They're powerless now.
They are meant to bleed, but they mustn't perish;

if they go out we're goners too.

SLIFT. There's life in them yet, put it up a notch.

500 steers at 77.

SMALL SPECULATORS. Did you hear that? Why

didn't they buy at 75? Now

it's gone to 77 and still climbing.

PACKERS. We get 50 from Mauler for the cans and can't pay Mauler 80
for the livestock.

MAULER, *to a group of men.* Where are the people I sent to the stockyards?

A MAN. There's one.

MAULER. Well, let's have it.

The FIRST DETECTIVE *reports.*

FIRST DETECTIVE. Those crowds, Mr. Mauler, you can't see the end of
them. If you called the name of Joan, ten or maybe a hundred would
answer. The mob sits there and waits, without a face or a name. Besides, nobody can hear just one man's voice and there are far too many
people running around asking after relatives they've lost. Serious unrest
prevails in the sections where the unions are at work.

MAULER. Who's at work? The unions? And the police let them agitate?
Damn it all! Go and call the police right away, mention my name,
ask them what we're paying taxes for. Insist that the troublemakers
get their heads cracked, speak plainly to them.

Exit FIRST DETECTIVE.

GRAHAM. Oh, give us a thousand at 77, Mauler;

if it knocks us out, it's the end of us.

SLIFT. 500 to Graham at 77. All the rest at 80.

MAULER, *returning.* Slift, this business no longer entertains me.

It might take us too far.

Go up to 80, then let it go at 80.

I'll hand it over and let them go.

Enough's enough. The town needs a breathing-spell.

And I have other worries.

Slift, this throat-squeezing isn't as much fun

as I thought it would be.

Seeing the SECOND DETECTIVE.

Did you find her?

SECOND DETECTIVE. No, I saw no woman in a Black Straw Hat uniform.
There are a hundred thousand people standing around in the stock-
yards; besides, it's dark and that biting wind drowns your voice.
Also, the police are clearing the yards and shots are being fired already.

MAULER. Shots? At whom? Oh, yes, of course.
It seems strange—you can't hear a thing in this place.
So she's not to be found, and shots are being fired?
Go to the phone-booth, look for Jim and tell him
not to call, or people will say again
that we demanded the shooting.
Exit SECOND DETECTIVE.

MEYERS. 1500 at 80!

SLIFT. Not more than 500 at 80!

MEYERS. 500 at 80, you cutthroat!

MAULER, *returning to the column*. Slift, I feel unwell. Let up, will you?

SLIFT. I wouldn't think of it. There's life in them yet. And if you start
to weaken, Mauler, I'll shove them up higher.

MAULER. Slift, I need a breath of air. You carry on
the business. I can't. Carry it on
the way I would. I'd rather give it all away
than have more things happen because of me!
Go no higher than 85! But manage it
the way I would. You know me.
Exit.

SLIFT. 500 steers at 90!

SMALL SPECULATORS. We heard that Mauler was willing
to sell at 85. Slift has no authority.

SLIFT. That's a lie! I'll teach you
to sell meat in cans and then
not have any meat!
5000 steers for 95!
Pandemonium.

SCENE: *Stockyards. Many people waiting,* JOAN *among them.*

PEOPLE. Why are you sitting here?

JOAN. I have to deliver a letter. Three men are supposed to come by here.
A group of REPORTERS *comes up, led by a* MAN.

MAN, *pointing to* JOAN. That's the one. *To* JOAN. These people are reporters.

REPORTERS. Hello, are you Joan Dark, the Black Straw Hat?

JOAN. No.

REPORTERS. We have heard from Mauler's office that you've sworn not
to leave the stockyards before the plants open up. We have it, you can

read it here, in big front-page headlines. JOAN *turns away.* Our Lady
of the Stockyards Avers God Solidly Behind Stockyard Workers.

JOAN. I said no such thing.

REPORTERS. We can assure you, Miss Dark, that public opinion is on your
side. All Chicago sympathizes with you, except a few unscrupulous
speculators. Your Black Straw Hats will reap terrific success from all
this.

JOAN. I'm not with the Black Straw Hats any more.

REPORTERS. That can't be. For us, you belong to the Black Straw Hats.
But we don't want to disturb you, we'll keep well in the background.

JOAN. I would like you to go away.

THEY *sit down some distance off.*

WORKERS, *in the stockyards, rear.*

Before our need is at its worst
they will not open the factories.
When misery has mounted
they will open up.
But they must answer us.
Do not go before they answer.

COUNTER-CHORUS, *also rear.* Wrong! Let misery mount,
they will not open up,
not before profits mount.
If you wait for the answer
you will get the answer:
out of cannon and machine guns
they will answer you.
And we advise you to wait
for this answer: do not go.

JOAN. I see this system and on the surface
it has long been familiar to me, but not
in its inner meaning! Some, a few, sit up above
and many down below and the ones on top
shout down: "Come on up, then we'll all
be on top," but if you look closely you'll see
something hidden between the ones on top and the ones below
that looks like a path but is not a path—
it's a plank and now you can see it quite clearly,
it is a seesaw, this whole racket
is a seesaw, with two ends that depend

on one another, and those on top
sit up there only because the others sit below,
and only as long as they sit below;
they'd no longer be on top if the others came up,
leaving their place, so that of course
they want the others to sit down there
for all eternity and never come up.
Besides, there have to be more below than above
or else the seesaw wouldn't hold. A seesaw, that's what it is.
The REPORTERS *get up and move upstage, having received some news.*

A WORKER, *to* JOAN. Say, what have you to do with those fellows?

JOAN. Nothing.

WORKER. But you were talking to them.

JOAN. They took me for someone else.

OLD MAN, *to* JOAN. You sure look frozen. Like a swig of whisky? JOAN *drinks.*
Stop! Stop! That's no mean shot you took!

A WOMAN. Scandalous!

JOAN. Did you say something?

WOMAN. I said, scandalous! Guzzling all the old man's whisky!

JOAN. Shut your trap, you silly old thing. Hey, where's my shawl? They've gone and swiped it again. That's the last straw! Going and stealing my shawl, on top of everything else! Now who's got my shawl? Give it here pronto.
SHE *grabs a sack off the head of the woman standing next to her. The* WOMAN *resists.*
Oh, so it's you. No lies! Gimme that sack.

THE WOMAN. Help, she's killing me!

A MAN. Shut up!
Someone throws her a rag.

JOAN. For all you people care, I might be sitting around in this
draft nekkid.
It wasn't as cold as this in my dream.
When I came to this place with brave plans,
fortified by dreams, I still never dreamed
that it could be so cold here. Now the only thing I miss
of all I have is my nice warm shawl.
You may well be hungry, you have nothing to eat,
but they're waiting for me with a bowl of soup.
You may well freeze
but I can go into the warm hall any time,

pick up the flag and beat the drum
and speak about HIM who lives in the clouds. After all,
what did you leave? What I left
was no mere occupation, it was a calling,
a noble habit, but a decent job as well
and daily bread and a roof and a livelihood.
Yes, it seems almost like a play,
something undignified, for me to stay in this place
without extremely pressing need. And yet
I may not go, and still—
I'll be frank about it—fear tightens round my throat
at the thought of this not eating, not sleeping, not knowing where
  you are,
habitual hunger, helpless cold and—
worst of all—wanting to get away.
WORKERS. Stay here! Whatever happens,
do not break ranks!
Only if you stand together
can you help each other!
Realize that you have been betrayed
by all your public sponsors
and your unions, which are bought.
Listen to no one, believe nothing
but test every proposal
that leads to genuine change. And above all learn:
It will only work out by force
and only if you do it yourselves.
The REPORTERS *return.*
REPORTERS. Hey there, gal, you've had sensational success: we've just
found out that the millionaire Pierpont Mauler, who has vast quantities
of livestock in his hands now, is releasing it to the abattoirs in spite
of rising prices. This being so, work will be resumed in the yards
tomorrow.
JOAN. Oh, what good news! The ice has thawed in their hearts. At least
the one just man among them
has not failed us. Appealed to as a man,
he has answered as a man.
There *is* kindness in the world.
Machine guns rat-a-tat in the distance.
What's that noise?

REPORTER. Those are army machine guns. The army has orders to clear the stockyards because the agitators who are inciting to violence will have to be silenced now that the slaughterhouses are to be reopened.

A WORKER. You just take it easy and stay here. The stockyards are so big it'll take the army hours to get this far.

JOAN. How many people are there in them now, anyway?

REPORTER. There must be a hundred thousand.

JOAN. So many?

Oh, what an unknown school, an unlawful space
filled up with snow, where hunger is teacher and unpreventably
need speaks about necessity.
A hundred thousand pupils, what are you learning?

WORKERS, *rear*. If you stay together
they will cut you to pieces.
We advise you to stay together!
If you fight
their tanks will grind you to pulp.
We advise you to fight!
This battle will be lost
and maybe the next
will also be lost.
But you are learning to fight
and realizing
that it will only work out by force
and only if you do it yourselves.

JOAN. Stop: no more lessons
so coldly learned!
Do not use force
to fight disorder and confusion.
Certainly the temptation is tremendous!
Another night like this, another wordless
oppression like this, and nobody
will be able to keep quiet. And certainly
you have already stood together
on many a night in many a year and learned
to think coldly and terribly.
Certainly acts of violence and weakness
are matching one another in the dark
and unsettled business is piling up.
But the meal that's cooking here—who
will be the ones to eat it?

I'm leaving. What's done by force cannot be good. I don't belong with them. If hunger and the tread of misery had taught me violence as a child, I would belong to them and ask no questions. But as it is, I must leave.

SHE *remains seated.*

REPORTERS. Our advice to you is, leave the stockyards right now. You made a big hit, but that's over and done with.

Exeunt. Shouting, rear, spreading forward. The WORKERS *rise.*

A WORKER. They're bringing the men from the local. *The two* LEADERS *of the workers are brought forward, handcuffed.*

A WORKER, *to his handcuffed leader.* Never mind, William, it isn't evening every day.

ANOTHER, *shouting after the group.* Bloodhounds!

WORKERS. If they think they're stopping anything that way, they're on the wrong track. Our men have taken care of everything.

In a vision JOAN *sees herself as a criminal, outside the familiar world.*

JOAN. The men who gave me the letter! Why are they
handcuffed? What is in the letter?
I could do nothing
that would have to be done by force and
would provoke force. A person like that would stand
against his fellow man, full of malice
and beyond the range of any settlement
that human beings usually make.
Not belonging, he would lose his way
in a world no longer familiar to him. The stars
would hurtle past his head breaking
the ancient rules. Words
would change meaning for him. Innocence
would abandon one who was constantly persecuted.
He can look at nothing without suspicion.
I could not be like that. So I'm leaving.
For three days Joan was seen
in Packingtown, in the stockyards swamps
going down, downward from level to level
to clear the mud away, to manifest
to the lowest. Three days walking
down the slope, growing weaker on the third
and finally swallowed by the swamp. Say:
"It was too cold."

SHE *gets up and goes. Snow begins to fall.*

A WORKER. I thought right away that she'd take off when the real snow
came.

THREE WORKERS *come by, look around for someone, fail to find him, and leave.
As it grows dark, a writing appears:*

The snow is starting to fall,
Will anyone stay at all?
They'll stay today as they've stayed before—
Stony ground and folk that are poor.

PIERPONT MAULER CROSSES THE BOUNDARY OF POVERTY

SCENE: *A Chicago street corner.*

MAULER, *to one of the detectives.*

No further, let's turn back now, what do you say?
Admit it: you laughed. I said, "Let's turn back now,"
and you laughed. They're shooting again.
Seems to be some resistance, eh? But this is what
I wanted to impress upon you: think nothing of it
if I turned back a couple of times
as we came nearer the stockyards. Thinking
is nothing. I'm not paying you to think.
I probably have my reasons. I'm known down there.
Now you are thinking again. Seems I've taken
a couple of nitwits along. Anyway,
let's turn back. I hope the person I was looking for
has listened to the voice of sense and left that place
where hell appears to be breaking loose.
A NEWSBOY *goes by.*
Aha! the papers! let's see how the livestock market is going!
HE *reads, and turns pale.*
Well, something's happened here that changes things:
it's printed here, black on white, that livestock
is down to 30 and not a slice is being sold,
that's what it says here, black on white, the packers
are ruined and have left the livestock market.
And it also says that Mauler and Slift, his friend,
are the worst hit of all. That's what it says and it means
that things have reached a point that certainly was not striven for,
but is greeted with sighs of relief. I can help them no further—
I freely offered

all my livestock for the use of any man that wanted it
and nobody took it and so I am free now
and without pretensions and hereby
I dismiss you in order to cross
the boundary of poverty, for I no longer require your services.
Henceforth nobody will want to knock me down.

THE TWO DETECTIVES. Then we may go.

MAULER. You may indeed, and so may I, wherever I want.
Even to the stockyards.
And as for the thing made of sweat and money
which we have erected in these cities:
it already seems as though a man
had made a building, the largest in the world and
the most expensive and practical, but—
by an oversight, and because it was cheap—he used dog-shit
as its material, so that it would have been very difficult
to live in and in the end his only glory was
that he had made the biggest stink in the world.
And anyone who gets out of a building like that
should be a cheerful man.

A DETECTIVE, *departing.* So, he's finished.

MAULER. Bad luck may crush the man of humble size;
Me it must waft to spiritual skies.

SCENE: *A No-Man's-Land in the Stockyards.* JOAN, *hurrying towards the city, overhears two passing workers.*

FIRST WORKER. First they let the rumor leak out that work would start up again, full blast, in the stockyards; but now that a part of the workers have left the yards to come back early tomorrow morning, they're suddenly saying that the slaughterhouses won't be opened at all, because Mauler has ruined them.

SECOND WORKER. The Communists were right. The masses shouldn't have broken ranks. All the more so because the Chicago utilities had all called a general strike for tomorrow.

FIRST WORKER. We didn't know that.

SECOND WORKER. That's bad. Some of the messengers must have failed us. A lot of people would have stayed put if they'd known about it. Even in the teeth of the cops' violence.

Wandering to and fro, JOAN *hears voices.*

A VOICE. He who does not arrive
  can plead no excuse. The fallen man
  is not excused by the stone.
  Let not even the one who does arrive
  bore us with reports of difficulties
  but deliver in silence
  himself or what is entrusted to him.
  JOAN *has stood still and now runs in another direction.*
A VOICE, JOAN *stands still.* We gave you orders
  our situation was critical
  we did not know who you were
  you might execute our orders and you might
  also betray us.
  Did you execute them?
  JOAN *runs farther and is halted by another voice.*
A VOICE. Where men are waiting, someone must arrive!
  Looking around for an escape from the voices, JOAN *hears voices on all sides.*
VOICES. The net with a torn mesh
  is of no use:
  the fish swim through it at that point
  as though there were no net.
  Suddenly all its meshes
  are useless.
  JOAN *falls to her knees.*
JOAN. Oh, truth, shining light! Darkened by a snowstorm in an evil hour!
  Lost to sight from that moment! Oh, how violent are snowstorms!
  Oh, weakness of the flesh! What would you let live, hunger?
  Whatever outlasts you, frost of the night!
  I must turn back!
  SHE *runs back.*

X

PIERPONT MAULER HUMBLES HIMSELF AND IS EXALTED

SCENE: *The Black Straw Hats' Mission.*

MARTHA, *to another Black Straw Hat.* Three days ago a messenger from
  Pierpont Mauler, the meat king, came to tell us that he wishes to pay
  our rent and join us in a big campaign for the poor.

MULBERRY. Mr. Snyder, it's Saturday evening. I'm asking you to pay your rent, which is very low, or get out of my building.

SNYDER. Mr. Mulberry, we expect Mr. Pierpont Mauler any minute now and he has promised us his support.

MULBERRY. Dick, old man, Albert, old man, put the furniture out in the street.

TWO MEN *begin to move the furniture out.*

BLACK STRAW HATS. Oh! They're taking the prayer bench!
Their greedy grasp even threatens
pipe organ and pulpit.
And louder still we cry:
Please, rich Mr. Mauler, come
and save us with your money!

SNYDER. Seven days now the masses have been standing
in rusting stockyards, cut off from work at last.
Freed from every kind of shelter they stand
under rain and snow again, sensing above them
the zenith of an unknown decision.
Oh, dear Mr. Mulberry, give us hot soup now
and a little music and they'll be ours. In my head I see
the Kingdom of Heaven ready and waiting.
Just give us a band and some decent soup,
really nourishing, and God will see to things
and all of Bolshevism, too,
will be out of its misery.

BLACK STRAW HATS. The dams of faith have burst
in this Chicago of ours
and the slimy flood of materialism surges
menacingly round the last of its houses.
Look, it's tottering, look, it's sinking!
Never mind—keep going—rich man Mauler's on the way!
He's started out already with all his money!

A BLACK STRAW HAT. Where can we put the public now, Major?
Enter THREE POOR PEOPLE, MAULER *among them.*

SNYDER, *shouting at them.* Soup, that's all you want! No soup here! Just the Word of God! We'll get rid of them straight off when they hear that.

MAULER. Here are three men coming to their God.

SNYDER. Sit down over there and keep quiet.

The THREE *sit down. A* MAN *enters.*

MAN. Is Pierpont Mauler here?

SNYDER. No, but we're expecting him.

MAN. The packers want to speak to him and the stockbreeders are screaming for him.

Exit.

MAULER, *facing audience.* I hear they're looking for a man named Mauler.
I knew him: a numskull. Now they're searching
high and low, in heaven and in hell,
for that man Mauler who was dumber all his life
than a dirty drink-sodden tramp.

Rises and goes over to BLACK STRAW HATS.

I knew a man who once was asked
for a hundred dollars. And he had about ten million.
And he came along without the hundred but threw
the ten million away
and gave himself.

HE *takes two of the* BLACK STRAW HATS *and kneels with them on the prayer
bench.*

I wish to confess my sins.
No one who ever knelt here, friends,
was as humble as I am.

BLACK STRAW HATS. Don't lose confidence,
Don't be souls of little faith!
He's sure to come—already he's approaching
with all his money.

A BLACK STRAW HAT. Is he here yet?

MAULER. A hymn, I pray you! For my heart
feels heavy and light at once.

TWO MUSICIANS. One piece, but no more.

THEY *intone a hymn. The* BLACK STRAW HATS *join in abstractedly, eyes on the
door.*

SNYDER, *bent over the account books.*
I won't tell how this comes out.
Quiet!
Bring me the housekeeping record and the unpaid bills. I've got to
that stage.

MAULER. I accuse myself of exploitation,
misuse of power, expropriation of everybody
in the name of property. For seven days I held
the city of Chicago by the throat
until it perished.

A BLACK STRAW HAT. That's Mauler!

MAULER. But at the same time I plead that on the seventh day
  I rid myself of everything, so that now
  I stand before you without possessions.
  Not guiltless, but repentant.

SNYDER. Are you Mauler?

MAULER. Yes; and torn to pieces by remorse.

SNYDER, *with a loud cry.* And without any money? *To the* BLACK STRAW HATS.
  Pack up the stuff, I hereby suspend all payments.

MUSICIANS. If that's the man you were waiting for
  to get the cash to pay us with
  then we can go. Good night.
  Exeunt.

CHORUS OF BLACK STRAW HATS, *gazing after the departing musicians.*
  We were awaiting with prayers
  the wealthy Mauler, but into our house
  came the man converted.
  His heart
  he brought to us, but not his money.
  Therefore our hearts are moved, but
  our faces are long.
  Confusedly the BLACK STRAW HATS *sing their last hymns as they sit on their last chairs and benches.*

BLACK STRAW HATS. By the waters of Lake Michigan
  we sit down and weep.
  Take the proverbs off the walls
  shove the songbooks into the cloth that wraps the defeated flag
  for we can pay our bills no more
  and against us rush the snowstorms
  of approaching winter.
  Then they sing "Go Into the Thick of the Fight." MAULER *joins in, looking over a Black Straw Hat's shoulder.*

SNYDER. Quiet! Everybody out now—*to* MAULER—especially you!
  Where is the forty months' rent from the unconverted
  whom Joan expelled? Look what she's driven in instead! Oh, Joan,
  give me my forty months' rent again!

MAULER. I see you would like to build your house
  in my shade. Well, for you a man
  is what can help you; likewise, for me
  a man was only plunder. But even
  if man were only what is helped,

there would be no difference. Then you'd need drowning men,
for then it would be your business
to be straws for them to clutch at. So all remains
within the mighty orbit of wares, like that of the stars.
Such teaching, Snyder, leaves many souls embittered.
But I can see that as I am
I'm the wrong man for you.

MAULER *makes to go, but the meat kings stop him at the door;* THEY *are all white as chalk.*

PACKERS. Forgive us, noble Mauler, for seeking you out,
disturbing you amid the involved emotions
of your colossal head.
For we are ruined. Chaos is around us
and over us the zenith of an unknown intention.
What are you planning for us, Mauler?
What will your next step be? We're sensitive
to the blows you rain on our necks.

Enter the STOCKBREEDERS *in great commotion, equally pale.*

STOCKBREEDERS. Damnable Mauler, is this where you've sneaked off to?
You pay for our livestock, instead of getting converted!
Your money, not your soul! You would not need
to lighten your conscience in a place like this
if you hadn't lightened our pockets! Pay for our livestock!

GRAHAM, *stepping forward.* Permit us, Mauler, to give a brief account
of the seven-hour battle which began this morning and ended
by plunging us all into the abyss.

MAULER. Oh, everlasting slaughter! Nowadays
things are no different from prehistoric times
when they bloodied each other's heads with iron bars!

GRAHAM. Remember, Mauler, by our contract to deliver
meat to you, you forced us to buy meat
in these of all times, and it had to be
from you, as only you had meat to sell.
Well, when you went away at noon, that Slift
pulled the rope even tighter around our necks.
With harsh cries he kept on raising prices
until they stood at 95. But then
a halt was called by the ancient National Bank.
Bleating with responsibility, the old crone dumped
Canadian yearlings on the chaotic market, and prices stood quivering.
But Slift—that madman!—scarcely had he seen

the handful of widely-travelled steers but he grabbed them at 95,
as a drunkard who's already swilled an oceanful
and still feels thirsty greedily laps up one
tiny drop more. The old crone shuddered at the sight.
But some people leaped to the beldame's side to hold her up—
Loew and Levi, Wallox and Brigham, the most reputable firms—
and offered all their possessions down to the last eraser,
as pledges that they would bring forth the last remaining steer
from the Argentine and Canada within three days—they even promised
to get hold of unborn ones, ruthlessly,
anything that was steerlike, calfly, hoggish!
Slift yells: "Three days? No! Today, today!"
and shoves the prices higher. And in floods of tears
the banks threw themselves into the death-struggle,
because they had to deliver the goods and therefore buy.
Sobbing, Levi himself punched one of Slift's brokers
in the belly, and Brigham tore his beard out
screaming: NINETY-SIX! At that point
an elephant might have wandered in
and been crushed underfoot like a berry.
Even the pageboys, seized with despair, bit one another
without saying a word, as horses in olden times
would bite each others' flanks among their fighting riders!
Unsalaried clerks, famous for lack of interest in business,
were heard gnashing their teeth that day.
And still we bought and bought; we had to buy.
Then Slift said: ONE HUNDRED! You could have heard a pin drop.
And as quietly as that the banks collapsed,
like trampled sponges—formerly strong and firm,
now suspending payment like respiration. Softly
old Levi spoke, and all of us heard him: "Now
take over the packing plants yourselves, we can no longer
fulfil our contracts," and so,
packer after packer, they sullenly laid
the shut-down, useless packing plants at your feet,—
yours and Slift's—, and went away;
and the agents and salesmen snapped their brief cases shut.
And at that moment, with a sigh as of liberation—
since no more contracts compelled its purchase—
livestock settled into the bottomless pit.
For unto prices it was given

to fall from quotation to quotation
as water hurtles from crag to crag
deep down into the infinite. They didn't stop before 30.
And so, Mauler, your contract became invalid.
Instead of gripping our throats you have strangled us.
What does it profit a man to grip the throat of a corpse?

MAULER. So, Slift, that was how you managed the fight
I left on your hands!

SLIFT. Tear my head off.

MAULER. What good is your head?
I'll take your hat, that's worth five cents!
What is to become
of all that cattle no one has to buy?

THE STOCKBREEDERS. Without becoming excited
We request you to tell us
whether, when and with what
you wish to pay
for the bought but unpaid-for cattle.

MAULER. At once. With this hat and this boot.
Here is my hat for ten million, here
my first shoe for five. I need the other.
Are you satisfied?

THE STOCKBREEDERS. Alas, when moons ago
we led the frisky calf
and clean young steers,
carefully fattened, by ropes to the station in far-off Missouri
the family yelled after us
and even after the rolling trains,
with voices broken by toil they yelled:
"Don't drink the money away, fellows, and
let's hope prices will rise!"
What'll we do now? How
can we go home? What
shall we tell them
showing the empty ropes
and empty pockets?
How can we go home in such a state, Mauler?

MAN WHO WAS THERE BEFORE, *enters.*

MAN. Is Mauler here? There's a letter from New York for him.

MAULER. I *was* the Mauler to whom such letters were addressed. *Opens it,*
reads it aside. "Recently, dear Pierpont, we wrote to tell you to buy

meat. Today, however, we advise you to arrive at a settlement with
the stockbreeders and limit the quantity of livestock, so as to give
prices a chance to recover. To this end we shall gladly be of service
to you. More tomorrow, dear Pierpont.—Your friends in New York."
No, no, that won't work.

GRAHAM. What won't work?

MAULER. I have friends in New York who claim to know a way out. It
doesn't seem feasible to me. Judge for yourselves. *Gives them the letter.*
How completely different
everything seems now. Give up the chase, my friends.
Your property is gone: you must grasp that, it is lost.
But not because we are no longer blest with earthly
goods—not everyone can be that—
only because we have no feeling for higher things.
That's why we're poor!

MEYERS. Who are these friends of yours in New York?

MAULER. Horgan and Blackwell. Sell. . . .

GRAHAM. Would that be Wall Street?

Whispering spreads through the gathering.

MAULER. The inward man, so cruelly crushed within us. . . .

PACKERS AND STOCKBREEDERS. Noble Mauler, consent to bring yourself
to descend to us from your lofty
meditations! Think of the chaos
that would swoop on everything, and take up—
since you are needed, Mauler—
the burden of responsibility again!

MAULER. I don't like to do it.
And I won't do it alone, for the grumbling in the stockyards
and the rat-tat-tat of machine-guns
still resound in my ears. It would only work
if it were sanctioned in a very grand style
and conceived as vital
to the public good.
Then it might work.
To SNYDER. Are there many Bible shops like this one?

SNYDER. Yes.

MAULER. How are they doing?

SNYDER. Badly.

MAULER. Doing badly, but there are many of them.
If we promoted the cause of the Black Straw Hats
in a really big way,—if you were equipped

with lots of soup and music
and suitable Bible quotations, even with shelter
in great emergencies,—would you then speak
on our behalf, saying everywhere that we are good people?
Planning good things in bad times? For only
by taking extremest measures—measures that might seem harsh
because they affect some people, quite a few really,
in short: most people, nearly everybody—
can we preserve this system now, the system
of buying and selling which is here to stay
and also has its seamy side.

SNYDER. For nearly everybody. I understand. We would.

MAULER, *to the* PACKERS. I have merged your packing plants
as one ring and am taking over
half of the stocks.

PACKERS. A great mind!

MAULER, *to the* STOCKBREEDERS.
My dear friends, listen!

THEY *whisper.*
The difficulty which oppressed us is lifting.
Misery, hunger, excesses, violence
have one cause only and the cause is clear:
there was too much meat. The meat market was
all stuffed up this year and so the price of livestock
sank to nothing. Now, to maintain it,
we, packers and stockbreeders, have formed a united front
to set some limits to this unbridled breeding:
to restrict the livestock coming into market
and eliminate excess from the current supply. This means
burning one-third of the livestock total.

ALL. Simple solution!

SNYDER, *announcing his presence.*
Might it not be possible—if all that cattle
is so worthless that it can be burned—
just to give it to the many standing out there
who could make such good use of it?

MAULER, *smiling.* My dear Snyder, you have not grasped
the root of the situation. The many
standing out there—*they are the buyers!*
To the others.
It's hardly credible.

ALL *smile for a long time.*
They may seem low, superfluous,
indeed, burdensome sometimes, but it cannot elude
profounder insight that *they* are the buyers!
Likewise—there are very many who do not understand this—it is essential
to lock out a third of the workers.
It is also work that has clogged our market and therefore
it must be limited.

ALL. The only way out!

MAULER. And wages lowered!

ALL. Columbus' egg!

MAULER. All this is being done so that
in gloomy times of bloody confusion
dehumanized humanity
when there is no end to the unrest in our cities
(for Chicago is again upset by talk of a general strike)
the brute strength of the short-sighted people
may not shatter its own tools and trample its own bread-baskets underfoot,
but peace and order may return. That is why we are willing
to facilitate by generous contributions
the work by which you Black Straw Hats encourage order.
It's true that there ought to be people among you again
like that girl Joan, who inspires confidence
by her mere appearance.

A BROKER, *rushing in.* Glad tidings! The threatened strike has been suppressed. They've jailed the criminals who impiously troubled peace and order.

SLIFT. Breathe freely now! The market's getting well!
Again the doldrums have been overcome.
The difficult task has once again been done
and once again a plan is finely spun
and the world resumes the way we like it run.
Organ.

MAULER. And now, open wide your gates
unto the weary and heavy laden and fill the pot with soup.
Tune up some music and we will sit
upon your benches, in the very front row,
to be converted.

SNYDER. Open the doors!

The doors are flung wide open.

BLACK STRAW HATS, *singing, eyes on the door.*

Spread the net far out: they're bound to come!
They've just abandoned the last redoubt!
God's driving cold on them!
God's driving rain on them!
So they're bound to come! Spread the net far out!
Welcome! Welcome! Welcome!
Welcome to our humble home!

Bolt everything tight so that none will escape!
They're on their way down to us all right!
If they've no work to do
if they're deaf and blind too
not one will escape! So bolt everything tight!
Welcome! Welcome! Welcome!
Welcome to our humble home!

Whatever may come, gather everything in!
Hat and head and shoe and leg and scamp and scum!
Its hat has gone sky-high
so it comes right in to cry!
Gather everything in, whatever may come!
Welcome! Welcome! Welcome!
Welcome to our humble home!

Here we stand! Watch them coming down!
Watch their misery drive them like animals to our hand!
Look, they're bound to come down!
Look, they're coming down!
They can't get away from this spot: here we stand!
Welcome! Welcome! Welcome!
Welcome to our humble home!

SCENE: *Stockyards. Environs of Graham's Warehouse. The yards are almost empty. Only a few groups of workers are still passing by.*

JOAN, *coming up to ask.*

Did three men go by here asking for a letter?
Shouting from rear, spreading toward front. Then enter FIVE MEN *escorted by* SOLDIERS: *the two from the union local and the three from the power stations. Suddenly one of the union men stands still and speaks to the soldiers.*

MAN. If you're taking us to jail now, there's something you ought to know. We did what we did because we are for you.

SOLDIER. Keep moving, if you're for us.

MAN. Wait a little!

SOLDIER. Getting scared, eh?

MAN. Yes, that too, but that's not what I'm talking about. I just want you to stand still a little so I can tell you why you have arrested us, because you don't know.

SOLDIERS, *laughing*. O.K., tell us why we arrested you.

MAN. Without property yourselves, you help men of property because you don't yet see any possibility of helping men without property.

SOLDIER. That's fine. Now let's move on.

MAN. Wait, I haven't finished the sentence: on the other hand, the working people in this town are starting to help the people without work. So the possibility is coming nearer. Now worry about that.

SOLDIER. I guess you want us to let you go, eh?

MAN. Didn't you understand me? We just want you to know that your time's coming soon too.

SOLDIERS. Can we go on now?

MAN. Yes, we can go on now.

> THEY *move on.*
>
> JOAN *stays where she is, watching the arrested men go. Then* SHE *hears two people talking beside her.*

FIRST MAN. Who are those people?

SECOND MAN. Not one of them
cared only for himself.
They ran without rest
to get bread for strangers.

FIRST MAN. Why without rest?

SECOND MAN. The unjust man may cross the street in the open, but the just man hides.

FIRST MAN. What's being done to them?

SECOND MAN. Although they work for low wages and are useful to many men
not one of them lives out the years of his life,
eats his bread, dies contented
or is honorably buried, but
they end before their time,
struck down and trampled on and heaped with shame.

FIRST MAN. Why don't we ever hear about them?

SECOND MAN. If you read in the papers that certain criminals have been shot or thrown into prison, they're the ones.

FIRST MAN. Will it always be like that?

SECOND MAN. No.

As JOAN *turns to go, she is accosted by the* REPORTERS.

REPORTERS. Isn't this Our Lady of the Stockyards? Hi there! Things have gone wrong! The general strike was a flop. The stockyards are opening up again, but only for two-thirds of the personnel and only at two-thirds' pay. But meat prices are going up.

JOAN. Have the workers accepted this?

REPORTERS. Sure. Only a part of them knew the strike was being planned, and the cops drove that part out of the yards by force.

JOAN *falls to the ground.*

XI

DEATH AND CANONIZATION OF ST. JOAN OF THE STOCKYARDS

SCENE: *The Black Straw Hats' House is now richly furnished and decorated. Its doors are flung wide open; in ordered groups, the Black Straw Hats with new flags, packers, stockbreeders and wholesalers stand waiting for the Gloombs and Luckerniddles.*

SNYDER.

Thus our task meets happy ending:
God's foothold has been found again.
For the highest good contending,
We have faced the depths of pain.

Both our mounting and descending
Show what we can mean to you:
Lo, at last the happy ending!
Look, at last we've put it through!

Enter a group of poor people, with JOAN *at their head, supported by* TWO POLICEMEN.

POLICEMEN. Here's a homeless woman we picked up in the stockyards in a sick condition. Her last permanent residence was here, she says.

JOAN *holds her letter high as though still anxious to deliver it.*

JOAN. The man who has perished will never
take my letter from me.
Small enough service to a good cause, the only service
demanded of me my whole life long!—
and I did not perform it.

While the poor people sit down on the benches to get their soup, SLIFT *consults with the packers and* SNYDER.

SLIFT. It's our own Joan. Why, her coming is like an answer to our prayers. Let's cover her with glory; by her philanthropic work in the stockyards, her championship of the poor, and even her speeches against us, she helped us over some really difficult weeks. She shall be our St. Joan of the Stockyards! We will cultivate her as a saint and refuse her no jot of respect. The fact that she is shown under our auspices will prove that we hold humaneness in high regard.

MAULER.
May the pure and childlike soul
Ever figure on our roll;
May our humble choir delight
In her singing clear and glad;
May she damn whatever's bad
And defend our every right.

SNYDER. Rise, Joan of the stockyards,
champion of the poor,
comforter of the lowest depths!

JOAN. What a wind in the depths! What is that shrieking
the snow is trying to hush?
Eat your soup, you!
Don't spill your last bit of warmth, you
ragamuffins! If only I had lived
as tranquilly as a cow,
and yet delivered the letter that was entrusted to me!

BLACK STRAW HATS, *going up to her.*
Sudden daylight makes her ache
After nights of stupefaction!
Only human was your action!
Only human your mistake!

JOAN, *while the girls dress her in the Black Straw Hat uniform again.*
The noise of transport is starting again, you can hear it.
Another chance to stop it—wasted.
Again the world runs
its ancient course unaltered.
When it was possible to change it
I did not come; when it was necessary
that I, little person, should help,
I stayed on the sidelines.

MAULER.
Alas, that man cannot abide
In his distress the earthly bond,

But with swift and haughty stride
Rushes past the everyday
Which he thinks will turn him gray
Past his target and beyond
Into worlds outside his ken,
Endless worlds too high for men.

JOAN. I spoke in every market place
and my dreams were numberless but
I did harm to the injured
and was useful to those who harmed them.

BLACK STRAW HATS.
Alas! All effort, sages write,
Achieves but piecework, void of soul,
If matter make not spirit whole.

PACKERS.
And ever 'tis a glorious sight
When soul and business unite!

JOAN. One thing I have learned and I know it in your stead,
dying myself:
How can I say it—there's something inside you
and it won't come out! *What* do you know in your wisdom
that has no consequences?
I, for instance, did nothing.
Oh, let nothing be counted good, however helpful it may seem,
and nothing considered honorable except that
which will change this world once for all: that's what it needs.
Like an answer to their prayers I came to the oppressors!
Oh, goodness without consequences! Intentions in the dark!
I have changed nothing.
Vanishing fruitless from this world
I say to you:
Take care that when you leave the world
you were not only good but are leaving
a good world!

GRAHAM. We'll have to see to it that her speeches only get through if
they are reasonable. We mustn't forget that she has been in the stockyards.

JOAN. For there is a gulf between top and bottom, wider
than between Mount Himalaya and the sea
and what goes on above
is not found out below

or what happens below, above
and there are two languages, above and below
and two standards for measuring
and that which wears a human face
no longer knows itself.

PACKERS AND STOCKBREEDERS, *very loud, so as to shout* JOAN *down.*

Top and bottom must apply
For the building to be high
That's why everyone must stay
In the place where they belong
Day after day
Man must do what suits his stature
For if he forgets his nature
All our harmonies go wrong.
Underdogs have weight below,
The right man's right when up you go.
Woe to him who'd rouse that host—
Indispensable but
Demanding, not
To be done without
And aware of that—
Elements of the nethermost!

JOAN. But those who are down below are kept below
so that the ones above may stay up there
and the lowness of those above is measureless
and even if they improve that would be
no help, because the system they have made
is unique; exploitation
and disorder, bestial and therefore
incomprehensible.

BLACK STRAW HATS, *to* JOAN. Be a good girl! Hold your tongue!

PACKERS.

Those who float in boundless spaces
Cannot rise to higher places,
For to climb you need a rung,
And to reach for things aloft
You must make a downward tread!

MAULER.

Action, alas, may break a head!

BLACK STRAW HATS.

Conscious of the bloody shoe,

PACKERS.

Do not try to pull it off!

For you'll need it e'er anew.

BLACK STRAW HATS.

Keep conduct high and spirit young.

But do not forget to rue it!

PACKERS.

Do anything!

BLACK STRAW HATS.

But always do it

With a twinge of conscience, for—

Being given to contemplation

And to self-vituperation—

Your conscience will be sore!

Men of trade, be informed:

You cannot afford

To forget the splendid

Quite indispensable

Word of the Lord

Which is never ended

And ever transformed!

JOAN. Therefore, anyone down here who says there is a God

when none can be seen,

a God who can be invisible and yet help them,

should have his head knocked on the pavement

until he croaks.

SLIFT. Listen, people, you've got to say something to shut that girl up.

You must speak—anything you like, but loud!

SNYDER. Joan Dark, twenty-five years old, stricken by pulmonary inflammation in the stockyards of Chicago, in the service of God: a fighter and a sacrifice!

JOAN. And the ones that tell them they may be raised in spirit

and still be stuck in the mud, they should have their heads

knocked on the pavement. No!

Only force helps where force rules,

and only men help where men are.

ALL *sing the first verse of the chorale in order to stop* JOAN'S *speeches from being heard.*

ALL.

Fill the full man's plate! Hosanna!

Greatness to the great! Hosanna!

To him that hath shall be given! Hosanna!
Give him city and state! Hosanna!
To the victor a sign from Heaven! Hosanna!

During these declamations loudspeakers begin to announce terrible news:
POUND CRASHES! BANK OF ENGLAND CLOSES FOR FIRST TIME IN 300 YEARS!
EIGHT MILLION UNEMPLOYED IN U.S.A.! FIVE YEAR PLAN A SUCCESS!
BRAZIL POURS A YEAR'S COFFEE HARVEST INTO OCEAN! SIX MILLION
UNEMPLOYED IN GERMANY! THREE THOUSAND BANKS COLLAPSE IN U.S.A.!
EXCHANGES AND BANKS CLOSED DOWN BY GOVERNMENT IN GERMANY!
BATTLE BETWEEN POLICE AND UNEMPLOYED OUTSIDE FORD FACTORY IN
DETROIT! MATCH TRUST, BIGGEST IN EUROPE CRASHES! FIVE YEAR PLAN
IN FOUR YEARS!

*Under the impression of this news those not engaged in declamation scream abuse
at one another, as:* "You slaughtered too much livestock, you rotten
butchers!" "You should have raised more stock, you lousy stockbreeders!" "You crazy money-grubbers, you should have employed more
labor and handed out more pay-checks! Who else will eat our meat?"
"It's the middleman that makes meat expensive!" "It's the grain
racket that raises livestock prices!" "The railroads' freight rates are
strangling us!" "The banks' interest rates are ruining us!" "Who can
pay those rents for stables and silos?" "Why don't you start plowing
under?" "We did, but you aren't!" "The guilt is yours and yours
alone!" "Things won't improve until you're hanged!" "You should
have been in jail years ago!" "How come you're still at large?"

ALL, *sing second and third verses of chorale.* JOAN *is now inaudible.*
Pity the well-to-do! Hosanna!
Set them in Thy path! Hosanna!
Vouchsafe Thy grace, Hosanna!
And Thy help to him that hath! Hosanna!
Have mercy on the few! Hosanna!

ALL, JOAN'S *talk is noticeably stopping.*
Aid Thy class, which in turn aids Thee, Hosanna!
with generous hand! Hosanna!
Stamp out hatred now! Hosanna!
Laugh with the laugher, allow, Hosanna!
his misdeeds a happy end! Hosanna!

During this verse the girls have been trying to pour some soup down JOAN'S
*throat. Twice she has pushed the plate back; the third time she seizes it, holds
it high and then tips the contents out. Then she collapses and is now lying in
the girls' arms, mortally wounded, with no sign of life.* SNYDER *and* MAULER
step towards her.

MAULER. Give her the flag!

The flag is presented to her. It drops from her hands.

SNYDER. Joan Dark, twenty-five years of age, dead of pulmonary inflammation in the stockyards in the service of God, a fighter and a sacrifice!

MAULER.

Something pure
Without a flaw,
Uncorrupted, helpful, whole—
It thrills us common folk to awe!
Rouses in our breast a newer,
Better soul!

ALL *stand in speechless emotion for a long time. At a sign from* SNYDER, *all the flags are gently lowered over* JOAN *until she is entirely covered by them. A rosy glow illumines the picture.*

THE PACKERS AND STOCKBREEDERS.

Since the age of sticks and stones
Man has suffered storm and stress
In that toward the higher zones
His ardent longings ever press:
He sees the stars upon their thrones,
Senses a thousand ways to heaven,
Yet downward by the flesh is driven:
This is his shame and dire distress.

MAULER.

A twofold something cuts and tears
My sorely troubled inward state
Like a jagged, deep-thrust knife:
I'm drawn to what is truly great,
Free from self and the profit rate,
And yet impelled to business life
All unawares!

ALL.

O man, two souls have made their home
Within thy breast!
Seek not a choice of one alone,
To live with both is best.
Stay in strife and stormy weather!
Let them battle one another!
Keep the high and keep the lowly,
Keep the coarse and keep the holy,
Keep them both together!

Intimate Relations

(LES PARENTS TERRIBLES)

A Play in Three Acts

by JEAN COCTEAU

English version by Charles Frank

CHARACTERS

YVONNE. *Yvonne confesses somewhere in the play that she is forty-five years old. She is not very tall and has the kind of face that makes her look eighteen one day and a hundred the next. She can be full of charm or full of poison, and she never mixes the two. It would be hard to say whether Yvonne has been or still is beautiful. It depends entirely on whatever impression she wishes to make on the person she happens to deal with at the time.*

LEONIE. *Leonie (or Leo, as everybody calls her) is Yvonne's elder sister. She is supposed to be forty-seven. However, the two ladies do not look like sisters at all. Leo is tall, exceedingly well groomed, and highly attractive. Everything about her is shiny and resplendent. She is the representative of "order" as against Yvonne's, Michael's and George's preference for "disorder."*

MADELEINE. *Madeleine is twenty-five. Her hair is a natural golden blonde. She is not perhaps of a classical beauty, but she is extremely attractive. In fact, she is irresistible. She is not tall, and she is very simply but delightfully dressed.*

GEORGE. *George is a well preserved, middle-aged man. He may be a little older than his wife, Yvonne, but not much. He is of medium height, not terribly tall, and he has never had the looks of the proverbial film star, but he has a good face and a kind face and is altogether a most likeable fellow.*

MICHAEL. *Michael, Yvonne's and George's son, is twenty-two. He is a little taller than his father, very good-looking, very charming, and in many ways young for his age. He is, however, not quite as young any more as his mother likes to think.*

SCENES

The time is today.
The place is Paris.

———————

ACT ONE   Yvonne's Bedroom
ACT TWO   Madeleine's Apartment
ACT THREE   Yvonne's Bedroom

NOTE: Both sets must be built solidly enough to allow for the doors to be slammed ad lib.

Yvonne's room represents the world of disorder, Madeleine's the world of order.

ACT ONE

SCENE: *Yvonne's bedroom.*

TIME: *Today.*

The door to LEO'S *room is on the left in the wings.*

Downstage left, there is an armchair and a dressing table.

Upstage left, there is a door leading to the rest of the flat.

Upstage right, another door leading to the bathroom which appears to be white and brightly lit.

The door to the hall is in the wings on the right. Upstage right, with the foot towards the center, a very big and very untidy bed. Dressing gowns, scarfs, towels, etc., are scattered over it. By the end of the bed a chair.

Upstage, center, a large cupboard, large double doors below, small double doors above. One wing of the upper double doors has the awkward habit of opening slowly at the most unexpected moments, and frequently during the action, LEO *automatically tries to shut it, only for it to open a few seconds later.*

Near the bed, a small table with a lamp. The chandelier in the center of the room is not alight. More dressing gowns lie about untidily.

The windows are felt to be at the side of the auditorium. An unpleasant half light comes from them, that of the block of flats opposite.

The lighting in the room is dim.

As the curtain rises, GEORGE, *dressed in an ordinary flannel suit, runs from the bathroom to* LEO'S *door and knocking on it frantically, he calls:*

GEORGE. Leo! Leo! Quick—where are you?

LEO'S VOICE. What is it? Michael?

GEORGE. No! Never mind Michael! Hurry up!

LEO, *fastening a very smart dressing gown.* What's the matter?

GEORGE. It's Yvonne. She's poisoned herself.

LEO, *flabbergasted.* Poisoned herself?

GEORGE. With her insulin. She must have taken much too much.

LEO. Where is she?

GEORGE. There—in the bathroom.

　　YVONNE *opens the bathroom door already ajar and enters. She is wearing a somewhat dilapidated bathrobe. She is deadly pale and can hardly stand on her feet.*

LEO. Yvonne—what have you done? *Crosses over to her and supports her.* Yvonne! YVONNE *shakes her head.* Tell me—what have you done?

YVONNE, *almost inaudibly*. Sugar . . .

GEORGE. I'll get the doctor. It's Sunday. He'll be out!

LEO. Don't lose your head. Fetch the sugar. *She helps* YVONNE *to lie down on her bed*. Don't you know yet that if you don't eat after taking insulin, you must take sugar?

GEORGE. Good Heavens, of course! *He rushes into the bathroom and comes back stirring the sugar in a glass of water*.

LEO, *taking it and making* YVONNE *drink it*. Drink it up . . . come on, try . . . make an effort . . . surely you don't want to die before you've seen Michael again!

YVONNE *braces herself up and drinks*.

GEORGE. I'm stupid! If you hadn't been here, Leo, I should just have let her die . . .

LEO, *to* YVONNE. How do you feel?

YVONNE, *very faintly*. It's working. I'm better. Please forgive me.

GEORGE. I can still hear the doctor say: "No ordinary household sugar; get some cane sugar." Why didn't I think of it? The glass is always prepared in the bathroom.

YVONNE, *her voice is a little clearer*. It was my fault.

LEO. One never knows where one is with a crazy creature like you.

YVONNE, *sitting up and smiling*. I was a touch crazier than usual.

GEORGE. Exactly! That's what muddled me up.

YVONNE. Leo, at any rate, is not crazy. Still, I had no intention of springing this pleasant little surprise on Michael.

GEORGE. I wish he was as considerate.

LEO *arranges the pillows behind her back*.

YVONNE. Well, this is what happened. It was five o'clock, time for my injection. Just when I'd finished and should have taken the sugar, I thought I heard the lift stop at our floor. I ran to the hall to see if it was Michael. On the way back to the bathroom, I almost fainted. George turned up by a miracle.

GEORGE. It *was* a miracle!

LEO. Nonsense, you were working up in the clouds as usual and you heard five o'clock strike down here on earth, and walked along here automatically to see if Yvonne had remembered her injection. It wasn't a miracle at all.

YVONNE, *to* GEORGE. Never mind her. Without you . . .

GEORGE. And without Leo . . .

YVONNE. If you two hadn't been here, both of you, I would have caused

you a lot of unnecessary suffering and only because I'm feeling a bit
hurt myself.

GEORGE. You *have* been caused a lot of unnecessary suffering! Michael did
not come home last night! Damn it all, he knows you! He can guess
the state you must be in. Your nerves are all to pieces or you wouldn't
have forgotten your sugar. It's outrageous.

YVONNE. If only nothing has happened to him. Do you think it has, and
they daren't ring us up?

GEORGE. If something had happened, we'd have heard. No, no! It's
in-cre*dd*ible*!

YVONNE. But where can he be? Where is he?

LEO. Don't excite yourself after this shock. Don't excite her, George. Why
don't you go back to your work? We'll call you if we need you.

YVONNE. Yes, you go back and try to work.

GEORGE, *mumbling as he goes*. I can't seem to get my figures right. I put
them down and I add them up, but they're always wrong and I keep
starting all over again . . .

LEO *listens at the door to make sure* GEORGE *has gone*.

YVONNE. Leo, where did that child spend the night? He must know I'm
going mad here with worry! Why doesn't he ring me up? Surely he
could 'phone . . .

LEO. That depends. Certain . . . honest . . . slightly awkward boys . . .
like Michael, are not much good at lying on the telephone.

YVONNE. Why should Mick lie to me?

LEO. Well, it must be one of two things. Either he daren't come home or
else he feels so happy wherever he is that he's forgotten. At any rate, he
is hiding something.

YVONNE. You can't teach me anything about Mick. "Forgotten to come
home"—it's ridiculous. Perhaps he's in some terrible danger; perhaps
he *can't* 'phone!

LEO. One can always telephone. Michael can but won't. *She picks up a
stray silk stocking and puts it away.*

YVONNE. You're so calm and composed. You must know something.

LEO. Yes, but there's no point in my telling you, you wouldn't believe it,
you'd only say "It's in-cre*dd*ible!" And it *is* incredible the way you've
all started to use that word lately.

* *Note:* This word is to be pronounced in this fashion and is for reasons of this
particular pronunciation spelled with double "dd" except when pronounced in the
ordinary way.

YVONNE. Nonsense, it's one of Michael's expressions.

LEO, *softly*. Maybe. It's rather funny how a word sometimes sneaks into a family and gets itself adopted. Where does it come from, I wonder? I'd very much like to know.

YVONNE, *laughing*. Well, and why shouldn't a bunch of lunatics and gypsies like us, a family that lives in a caravan. . . .

LEO, *interrupting*. You're trying to be funny because I once said this flat was like a gypsy caravan. Well, so it is, and I repeat it. And I also repeat that you're a bunch of lunatics.

YVONNE. The house is a caravan. Agreed. We're all lunatics. Agreed. And whose fault is it?

LEO, *exasperated*. That's it: dig up grandfather again!

YVONNE, *unperturbed*. Grandfather who collected semicolons. He counted the semicolons in Victor Hugo. He said: "I make it 37,000 semicolons in 'Les Miserables'." And then he started all over again in case he'd made a mistake. Only in those days they wouldn't call him crazy, they would say, "He had a mania." Nowadays with a bit of good will, you can call anybody crazy.

LEO. So you admit you're lunatics. I see.

YVONNE. And you're a lunatic, too, in your own way.

LEO. Possibly. I certainly have a mania for order and you for disorder. You know very well why uncle left his money to me. He knew I should have to keep you all.

YVONNE. Leonie . . . !

LEO. Don't get excited. I'm not complaining. Nobody admired George more than I. And I am only too glad that thanks to this legacy, he can carry on with his research.

YVONNE. Well, that you of all people should take this research business seriously—it beats me! Now George, now there's a typical lunatic for you! Perfecting the underwater rifle! Between you and me, it's ridiculous, and at his age, too.

LEO. George is a child. He likes pottering about but he *is* an inventor. You're being unfair.

YVONNE. The electronic underwater submachine gun! The one thing that was missing in our caravan! We've already got the fortuneteller, that's me telling the cards in my old dressing gown. Then there's you, the lion tamer; you'd be terrific as a lion tamer. And Mick . . . Mick . . .

LEO. The Eighth Wonder of the World!

YVONNE. Don't be nasty . . .

LEO. I am not being nasty, but I've been watching you, Yvonne, since yesterday. There are two kinds of people in this world: the children and the grownups. I, alas, belong to the grownups; you, George, Mick . . . you belong to the children, who never stop being children, who would commit crimes . . .

YVONNE, *stopping her*. Sh! . . . Listen! *Silence*. No, I thought I heard a taxi. You were talking of crimes. I think you were calling us criminals just now . . .

LEO. Why can't you listen to me properly . . . I am talking of crimes that people commit simply because they don't know what they're doing. There's no such thing as simple souls. Any country priest will tell you that. Even in the tiniest village there exist instincts of murder, incest, and theft such as you won't find in the big cities. No, I wasn't calling you criminals. On the contrary! The background of real criminals is sometimes preferable to the twilight which you enjoy so much and which I detest!

YVONNE. Mick must have had too much to drink. He is not used to it. He has stayed with a friend. Perhaps he's asleep. Perhaps he's ashamed. It's unforgivable of him to make me go through that awful night and this endless day, but I must say I can't call it criminal.

LEO, *approaching* YVONNE's *bed*. Tell me, Yvonne, are you pulling my leg?

YVONNE. I beg your pardon . . .

LEO, *taking her by the chin*. No, you're not. I thought you were putting on an act. I was wrong. You're just blind.

YVONNE, *brushing* LEO's *hand away*. Explain yourself, will you!

LEO, *taking a step back*. Michael has spent the night with a woman.

YVONNE. Michael??

LEO. Yes, Michael.

YVONNE. You must be out of your mind. Mick is a child. You said so yourself just now. . . .

LEO. Oh, Heavens, he's no longer a child the way you're thinking. He is a man.

YVONNE *looks at her amazed*.

Well, he's twenty-two!

YVONNE. Well . . .

LEO. You're fantastic . . . you're reaping what you've been sowing, but you don't see it.

YVONNE. What have I been "sowing"? And what am I "reaping"?

LEO. You've been sowing dirty washing, cigarette ends, and the Lord knows what, and you're reaping this: Michael is suffocating in your Caravan and he has gone to get some fresh air.

YVONNE. And you're suggesting that he's gone to get this fresh air in the company of women, of prostitutes?

LEO. Ah, now we're back at the old clichés! D'you want to know why Michael did not telephone? So as not to hear at the other end: "Come home at once, your father wishes to speak to you," or some such middle-class rubbish. Now I ask you, what does it mean: a family of the upper middle class? It means a well-to-do family with everything in perfect order and with domestic servants. Here, there's no money, no order, and no servants. No maid stays longer than four days. I've had to make do with a daily who doesn't come on Sundays. But the old principles and the old slogans are still going strong!

YVONNE. What's the matter with you, Leo . . . ? You're getting so excited. . . .

LEO. I'm not getting excited, but there are moments when you go too far! D'you know why there's a mountain of dirty washing piling up right in the middle of Michael's room? D'you know why the dust on George's desk is so thick that he could write his figures in it with his finger? Why the bath has been blocked for a week and hasn't been seen to yet?

YVONNE, *surprised*. Is the bath blocked?

LEO, *exasperated*. Oh! Because sometimes it gives me a kind of morbid satisfaction watching you sink and sink and drown, till my mania for order gets the better of me and I have to come to your rescue.

YVONNE. Hm. And according to you, our Caravan has driven Michael to find himself a better home . . . with some woman or other.

LEO. He isn't the only one.

YVONNE. You mean George . . .

LEO. I mean George.

YVONNE. Are you accusing George of being unfaithful to me?

LEO. I'm not accusing anyone. I don't indulge in gossip.

YVONNE. Have you found out that George is deceiving me?

LEO. Well, you're deceiving him, aren't you?

YVONNE. I . . . deceiving George . . . with whom?

LEO. Ever since Michael was born you've been unfaithful to George. You stopped looking after George, and you only cared for Michael. You adored him . . . you were crazy about him. And the more he grew up, the crazier you got about him . . . And George was left alone. And you are surprised that he should have looked elsewhere for a little affection.

YVONNE. All right . . . suppose all this nonsense is true, that George who

is only interested in his so-called inventions has an affair, and that
Michael who tells me everything and who calls me his best friend . . .
has spent the night with a woman—why didn't you tell me before?

LEO. I couldn't believe you were blind. I thought: it's impossible. Yvonne
is making the best of it. She is shutting her eyes to it . . .

YVONNE, *very strained*. George . . . in a way . . . I could understand
. . . After twenty years of married life one's love changes . . . There
is a kind of relationship which would make certain things . . . very
embarrassing . . . almost indecent . . . in fact, quite impossible.

LEO. You are a strange woman, Yvonne . . .

YVONNE. Not at all . . . but I must appear strange to you, there's such
a world between us. Just think: you've always been beautiful, elegant,
well-groomed and well-permed—and I came into the world with
chronic hay fever, my hair in a constant mess, and my dressing gowns
riddled with cigarette holes. And if I use powder and rouge I look like
a tart.

LEO. You are forty-five and I am forty-seven.

YVONNE. You look much younger than I do.

LEO. All the same, George chose you. He was engaged to me. Suddenly
he decided you were the one he wanted, you're the one he was going to
marry.

YVONNE. You couldn't have wanted him very much. You almost threw
us together.

LEO. That's my business. I was afraid that with me everything came from
here—*she taps her head*—with you it was all there—*she taps her heart*—or
thereabouts. I didn't know you wanted a son so desperately—and of
course, spoilt children like you always get what they want—and I
didn't think that you'd be so crazy about him that you'd drop George
altogether.

YVONNE, *sarcastically*. George could always have gone to you for comfort.

LEO. So you would have liked me to sleep with George to get him out of
your way . . . no, thank you, I prefer to remain an old maid.

YVONNE, *wearily*. Oh, really . . .

LEO, *equally ironically*. Besides, he wouldn't have wanted me, anyway, it's
youth he's after!

YVONNE. Well, well, well!

LEO. You needn't believe it, but it doesn't alter the fact, Yvonne. There
are certain things even an old maid notices. There's a phantom, a
female phantom, a very young one, flitting about the house.

YVONNE. It's in-cre*dd*ible!

LEO. There's that word again! George brought it here, Michael caught it and then you . . . like measles.

YVONNE. Is that so! And I suppose Michael, too, is unfaithful to me, I mean is lying to me . . .

LEO. You were right the first time; there's no need to take it back: he's *been* unfaithful to you, he is *being* unfaithful to you.

YVONNE. I can't imagine it. It's impossible. I don't want to, I cannot imagine it.

LEO. You don't seem to mind the idea of George deceiving you. But Michael, that's another story . . .

YVONNE. It's a lie! Michael and I have always been friends, he can tell me everything.

LEO. No mother is a friend to her son. Soon enough he finds out that the "friend" is a bit of a spy and the spy nothing but a jealous woman.

YVONNE. Mick doesn't see me as a woman.

LEO. That's where you're so wrong. You just refuse to see Michael as a man! To you he is still the little Michael you used to carry to bed and who was allowed to play in your bedroom while you were dressing. In Michael's eyes you have become a woman. And you're very silly not to try and be a little more glamorous. He has watched you and judged you, and he's left the Caravan.

YVONNE. And where would the poor boy find the time to devote himself to this mysterious woman?

LEO. Time is elastic. With a little ingenuity one can be in one place and pretend to be in another.

YVONNE. What are you talking about? I've seen the drawings he brings back from Art School.

LEO. D'you find Mick very gifted for drawing?

YVONNE. He is gifted for all sorts of things.

LEO. Exactly! He knows a bit of everything and nothing properly. Maybe if he really went to the Art School, his drawings would look a little different.

YVONNE. I stopped him from going to life classes.

LEO. How could you make yourself so ridiculous!

YVONNE. He was only eighteen . . .

LEO. You have the most peculiar ideas about age and sex.

YVONNE. Michael *is* working hard.

LEO. Not a bit of it. Besides, you don't want him to. You're not a bit keen that he should work.

YVONNE. Well, that's a new one!

LEO. Yvonne, you've always prevented Michael from taking a job!

YVONNE. If you can call them that.

LEO. He was offered a number of jobs, and he could have earned his living.

YVONNE. I made inquiries every time. They were such stupid jobs. He would have had to mix with a lot of film people and car people—awful people! George always found him the most ridiculous jobs!

LEO. One of them was very good. But he would have had to go abroad. You wouldn't even let him go to the interview.

YVONNE. It was Michael who didn't want to go.

LEO. Have you ever encouraged him? Did you ever let him meet boys and girls of his own age? Ever thought of him getting married?

YVONNE, *horrified.* Mick . . . getting married?

LEO. Why not? Lots of young men get married at twenty-three or twenty-four . . .

YVONNE. But Mick is a baby!

LEO. And if he weren't a baby any longer?

YVONNE. I should be the first to find him a wife.

LEO. Yes . . . some stupid, ugly girl who would let you go on playing first fiddle and dominating your son.

YVONNE. You're quite wrong. Michael is completely free. That is, as far as is good for such an unsophisticated boy . . . who's so much sought after.

LEO. Well, I warn you, don't try to lock him up. If he finds out . . . he may not like it.

YVONNE. I didn't know you were such a psychologist. *Without a break.* Oh, dear, someone's ringing at the door!

The door bell rings.

Oh, you go, Leo, go quickly! I haven't the strength.

LEO *exits by the door on the right. She is barely gone when* YVONNE *snatches the handbag that* LEO *has left on the bed. She opens it, looks at herself in the mirror, powders her nose, puts on lipstick and tidies her hair. The door opens. She has just time to throw back the bag where it was. Enter* LEO *and* GEORGE. GEORGE *puts on the light.*

YVONNE, *turning away.* Who put the light on?

GEORGE. I did. I'll turn it off. I thought . . . it's so dark in your room.

YVONNE. I like it dark . . . Who was it?

GEORGE. Someone for the doctor upstairs. I told him the doctor was out. He always goes shooting on Sundays. *Silence.* Any news?

YVONNE. No.

GEORGE. The specialist's gone shooting, too. If you're ill on a Sunday, you can just die. *Silence.*

YVONNE. How silly of me . . . of course, Michael's got the keys.

GEORGE. It is absolutely intolerable that the keys of the flat should be dragged about all over the place!

YVONNE. He might easily have lost them.

GEORGE, *very angrily and full of authority.* And one day one wakes up and finds oneself murdered. He's got to return them at once.

LEO. It's a great pity one can't make a gramophone record of your conversation.

They're all grouped in the foreground. While they are talking, MICHAEL *enters through the door on the right without being heard. He looks very cheerful, like a boy who has just made a wonderful joke.*

YVONNE. What time is it?

MICHAEL. Six o'clock.

They all jump, even YVONNE *who stands near her bed.*

It's all right, it isn't my ghost, it's me.

GEORGE. Michael—how could you have frightened your mother like this! Look at her! How did you get here?

MICHAEL, *while* LEO *helps* YVONNE *back to bed.* Through the door. I ran up four at the time . . . let me get my breath back . . . Sophie! What's the matter with you?

GEORGE. First of all, I find it impossible at your age that you should persist in calling your mother "Sophie."

YVONNE. That's been an old joke between us ever since I read him the forty-nine instalments of "Sophie, The Problem Child."

GEORGE. Your mother is not at all well, Michael!

MICHAEL, *tenderly.* Sophie—did *I* get you into such a state? *He approaches to kiss his mother.*

YVONNE, *pushing him away.* Don't . . .

MICHAEL. Cheer up, all of you; I didn't commit a crime.

GEORGE. You very nearly did, my boy. Your mother almost died of anxiety. She lost her head over her injection. Luckily your aunt and I didn't lose ours!

MICHAEL. I was so looking forward to seeing you all . . . to being back in the Caravan . . . I wanted to kiss Mummy . . . I am terribly sorry . . .

GEORGE. And so you should be! Where have you been?

MICHAEL. Give me a chance. I've an awful lot to tell you.

LEO, *to* GEORGE. You see . . .

MICHAEL. Aunt Leo's the only one who hasn't lost her head. As usual.

LEO. We had every reason for losing our heads, Michael. I'm not joking. Today I sympathize entirely with your mother's attitude.

MICHAEL. What have I done?

GEORGE. You didn't come home last night! You've spent the night out! And you didn't let us know when to expect you back!

MICHAEL. I am twenty-two, Dad . . . I've never done it before. I mean, really . . .

YVONNE. Where've you been? Your father's been asking you where you've been.

MICHAEL. Listen, children . . . oh, sorry . . . listen, Dad, listen, Aunt Leo, don't spoil it all . . . I wanted to . . .

YVONNE. You wanted to . . . you wanted to . . . your father gives the orders here. Besides, he wishes to speak to you. Follow him into his study.

LEO, *copying them.* In-cred*d*ible!

MICHAEL. No, Sophie. First of all, Dad hasn't got a study; he's got a very untidy room. And then I'd like to speak to you, to you alone, first.

GEORGE. My dear boy, I don't know if you visualize——

MICHAEL. I can't visualize a thing, it's pitch dark in here. *He switches on the table lamp.*

YVONNE. Since Michael finds it easier to talk to me first . . . would you mind . . . ?

LEO, *ironically.* Of course—!

YVONNE. If Mick has something on his mind, it's only natural he should confide in his mother. George, go back to your work. Leo, take him with you.

MICHAEL, *to* GEORGE *and* LEO. Don't be angry with me, I'll tell you every-thing. I can hardly wait.

YVONNE. It's nothing serious; is it, Mick?

MICHAEL. N . . . o, yes and no.

YVONNE. George, you embarrass him.

MICHAEL. That's right, Dad embarrasses me. And you, Aunt Leo, you're too clever.

YVONNE. And I'm his best friend. You see, Leo, I told you so.

LEO. Well, good luck. Come along, George. Let's get out of the con-fessional. *She turns back towards* YVONNE. Don't you want the light switched off? You scolded George for turning it on.

YVONNE. That was the chandelier; the lamp doesn't worry me.

GEORGE, *before leaving.* I still want to talk to you, my boy; I haven't finished with you yet.

They exit.

MICHAEL. All right, Dad. *He shuts the door. Turning towards* YVONNE, MICHAEL *puts his finger to his lips. He then winks at her and tiptoes back to the door, jerking it open.* LEO, *who had had her ear against it, tumbles into the room.*

LEO, *shrugging.* Very funny . . . *Dignified exit.*

MICHAEL, *leaping across the room like a small boy and onto his mother's bed.* Sophie, my darling Sophie, you're not angry with me, are you . . . *He grabs her and kisses her forcibly while she is struggling to free herself.*

YVONNE. Can't you ever give me a kiss without knocking me about . . . stop pulling my hair . . . MICHAEL *continues.* Not in the ear, Michael! I hate that . . . Michael . . .

MICHAEL. I didn't do it on purpose.

YVONNE. I should hope not——

MICHAEL, *leaning back and in a tone of phony surprise.* Oh, I say!

YVONNE. What—?

MICHAEL. Oh, but Sophie, you've got lipstick on!

YVONNE. What, me?

MICHAEL. Yes, you! *And* make-up. Nice goings-on! Is it for anyone in particular? It's in-cred*d*ible! Make-up . . . real make-up. . . .

YVONNE. I was as white as a sheet, I didn't want to frighten your father.

MICHAEL. Don't wipe it off, it looks nice on you . . .

YVONNE. As if you ever noticed me . . .

MICHAEL. Sophie! You're actually making a scene! As if I didn't know you by heart. . . .

YVONNE. You may know me by heart but you never so much as look at me; you ignore me.

MICHAEL. Far from it, madame. I am looking at you out of the corner of my eye, and I was even thinking that you were rather neglecting yourself lately.

YVONNE. Really—!

MICHAEL. Yes. Now, if you'd only let me do your hair for you and make you up . . .

YVONNE, *drily.* That would be charming.

MICHAEL. Stop sulking, Sophie; you're still angry with me.

YVONNE. I never sulk. No, Mick, I'm not angry with you. I'd just like to know what's going on.

MICHAEL. Patience—and you shall know everything.

YVONNE. I'm listening.

MICHAEL. Don't look so solemn, darling, please don't look so solemn!

YVONNE. Michael!

MICHAEL. Promise me not to put on the family act, the Caravan act! Promise me not to scream and that you'll let me explain to the end. Promise?

YVONNE. I don't promise anything.

MICHAEL. You see—!

YVONNE. Other people are making much too much fuss of you. But when I tell you things as they are . . .

MICHAEL. Sophie—I am going in to Dad. I'll tell him to take off his goggles and listen to me . . .

YVONNE, *interrupting.* Don't you make fun of your father's work.

MICHAEL. You're always making fun of the electronic underwater sub-machine gun . . .

YVONNE. That's different. It's bad enough that I let you call me Sophie . . . except in public . . .

MICHAEL. We're never *in* public.

YVONNE. Very well, then, you may call me Sophie, but you've been having things much too much your own way, and I haven't been able to put a stop to your untidiness. Your room is a pigsty . . . don't interrupt me . . . a pigsty, that's what it is! Nothing but dirty washing.

MICHAEL. Aunt Leo looks after the laundry . . . besides, you've told me hundreds of times you liked my things lying about, that you hated cupboards and moth balls and . . .

YVONNE. I never said anything of the sort!

MICHAEL. I beg your pardon! Oh, darling. . . .

YVONNE. Years and years ago I said I liked to find little children's things lying about. It was perfectly natural. But one day I noticed that these little things were men's socks, men's shirts, men's pants. I then asked you to keep your things out of my room.

MICHAEL. Mummy——

YVONNE. You remember now, don't you! It upset me enough at the time.

MICHAEL. You wouldn't tuck me in any more . . . we had a fight.

YVONNE. Mick! I carried you to bed till you were eleven. After that you got much too heavy. You were hanging round my neck. Then you put your little bare feet on my slippers, you held on to my shoulders and we marched together to your bed. One evening you made fun of me because I was tucking you in, and I told you to go to bed on your own in the future.

MICHAEL. Sophie! Let me come up on your bed.

YVONNE. No, Michael!

MICHAEL. I'm taking off my shoes. *He throws his shoes off, snuggles up against* YVONNE *and puts his head against her shoulder.* Now listen: I don't want you to look at me . . . this is lovely, stay like that, don't move . . . we'll look straight ahead at the window opposite . . . all right?

YVONNE. I don't like these preparations.

MICHAEL. You promised you'd be very, very nice.

YVONNE. I promised nothing at all.

MICHAEL. You're awful.

YVONNE. Don't try to humor me. If you have something to tell me, tell me now. The longer you put it off, the harder it'll be. Are you in debt?

MICHAEL. Don't be ridiculous.

YVONNE. Michael!

MICHAEL. Please—!

YVONNE. All right, Mick. Go on. I'm listening.

MICHAEL *begins, rather quickly. He is a little embarrassed; while he talks, without looking at his mother,* YVONNE'S *face becomes distorted with pain and anger to the point of almost becoming frightening.*

MICHAEL. Sophie . . . I am so wonderfully happy . . . I wanted to make quite sure everything was all right before letting you know. Because I couldn't be happy if you weren't happy with me. You understand that, don't you? YVONNE *nods briefly.* Well, here it is: at the school, I met a girl . . .

YVONNE, *trying to control herself and to speak casually.* It isn't a mixed school . . .

MICHAEL, *putting his hand over* YVONNE'S *mouth.* Will you listen to me, please? I'm not talking of the drawing classes, I'm talking of the shorthand-typing class. Dad had told me that he had a secretary's job in mind for me and that shorthand was essential. I tried it but when you talked me out of the job I gave up the course. I only went there three times. And the last time I went she was there, too. It was a miracle. She is a young girl or rather a young lady, she is three years older than I. There is an old chap of fifty who is interested in her. She's like a daughter to him. He's a widower and he had lost a daughter who apparently looked just like her. Anyway, she told me her whole story. It was awfully sad. We met again. I cut the drawing classes. I prepared my sketches in advance . . . jugs and tulips and things . . . I shouldn't have dreamt of going on with it if she hadn't made up her mind to drop the old bloke and to start from scratch. I'm so in love with her, and she loves me, and you'll love her, too, and now she is free, and our Caravan has got the right spirit, and tomorrow please let me take you to her, you and Dad and Leo. Tonight she'll explain it all to the old boy. He thought she had a sister from the country staying with her, and he didn't come to see her any more. They hardly ever met any longer. There is no point in being jealous at all. It would have been far worse if she'd been a married woman, because I should hate anything that wasn't . . . well, you know . . . above board.

YVONNE, *making a superhuman effort to talk*. And this person . . . helped you . . . I mean, you've never got a penny. She must have been helping you . . .

MICHAEL. One can't keep a thing from you; she did help me a bit for meals, cigarettes, taxis . . . *Silence*. Oh, I'm happy, I'm so happy . . . Are you happy, Mummy?

YVONNE *swings round at him. He is horrified by her expression.*

YVONNE. Happy?

MICHAEL *recoils*.

So that's my reward!! That's why I brought you into the world, that's why I've been looking after you night and day, making a fool of myself for you all these years . . . that's why I neglected my poor George, so that an old woman should take you away, should steal you from us and get you involved in her revolting machinations.

MICHAEL. Mother!

YVONNE. Revolting, I say; and you take money from her! I suppose you know what that's called!

MICHAEL. What are you talking about? Madeleine is young, and . . .

YVONNE. So that's her name!

MICHAEL. I never meant to keep it dark . . .

YVONNE. And you thought all you had to do was to put your arms round me and to flatter me. It's no use flattering *me*, my boy! To think that my son is being kept by the lover of a peroxided old woman.

MICHAEL. Madeleine is blonde; you're right there. But not peroxided, and I tell you again she is twenty-five. Will you please listen to me!! And there's no other man but me!

YVONNE, *pointing her finger at him*. Ah, now you admit it!

MICHAEL. What do you mean I admit it? For an hour I've been telling you everything in detail!

YVONNE, *jumping up and putting her hands in front of her face*. I'm going mad!

MICHAEL. Don't excite yourself, go back to bed.

YVONNE, *marching up and down*. Back to bed! Ever since last night I've been lying on that bed like a corpse. I should *not* have taken the sugar. It would all be over by now. I needn't be dying of shame.

MICHAEL. You talk of suicide because I'm in love with a girl?

YVONNE. To die of shame is worse than suicide. Don't try to be clever with me. If you were in love with a young girl . . . if you had come to me with a nice decent romance worthy of you and of us, I should probably have listened to you without getting angry. Instead of which you daren't look me in the face and you come out with a disgusting story.

MICHAEL. I forbid you——

YVONNE. What?

MICHAEL, *on an adorable impulse*. Kiss me, darling . . .

YVONNE, *pushing him away*. You've got lipstick all over your face.

MICHAEL. It's your own!

YVONNE. I'm afraid I couldn't bring myself to kiss you . . . now.

MICHAEL. Sophie, that's not true! *He starts to balance himself on a stool.*

YVONNE. Your father and I will take the necessary steps to have you locked up, to prevent you from seeing that woman, to protect you against yourself. Stop it, Michael, you won't be satisfied until you've broken that stool!

MICHAEL. You're a mother all right, Sophie, a real mother. I thought you were my friend. How often did you tell me——

YVONNE, *interrupting*. I am your mother. Your best friend would do exactly as I do. *Pause.* How long has this been going on?

MICHAEL. Three months.

YVONNE. Three months of lies . . . of shameful lies . . .

MICHAEL. I didn't lie to you, Mother, I just said nothing.

YVONNE. Three months of lies, of plots, of false affections!

MICHAEL. I didn't want to upset you.

YVONNE. Thanks very much. Don't worry about me. I can look after myself. It's you who are in trouble.

MICHAEL. Me?

YVONNE. Yes, you . . . you poor little fool, fallen into the clutches of a woman older than yourself, a woman who's bound to lie about her age . . .

MICHAEL. You only have to look at Madeleine. . . .

YVONNE. God forbid. Your Aunt Leonie makes out she is thirty. You don't know women.

MICHAEL. I'm beginning to get an idea.

YVONNE. Don't be impertinent!

MICHAEL. Really, Sophie, why should I want to go elsewhere for what I've got at home, and better than anyone else? Why should I try and find a woman of your age?

YVONNE, *jumping up*. Now you're insulting me!

MICHAEL, *stupefied*. What?!

YVONNE. I may look like an old woman, but I only look it! You'll do as I say!!

MICHAEL. I think we've said enough. We'll only hurt each other more.

YVONNE, *furious*. Oh, no, oh, no! That would be too easy! I'll say what I like! It's my turn, now! As long as I live, you'll never marry that bitch!

MICHAEL, *as if hit in the face*. Take that back . . .

He gets hold of her arms, she makes an effort to free herself, but she slips and falls to her knees.

Terrified. Get up, Mother! Mummy!

He tries to lift her up, but she neither lets go of him, nor does she attempt to get up.

YVONNE, *more furious than ever*. I'll show you . . . I'll tell everyone what you're doing to me . . .

Muffled knocks are heard from below.

MICHAEL. There! The neighbors have heard us! They're knocking on the wall! *He tears her hands from his jacket that she is clutching.*

YVONNE, *giving a little sound of pain*. You've hurt me, you beast! You've twisted my arm! You want to kill me! Look at your eyes!

MICHAEL. And you, look at yours!

YVONNE, *pulling herself up until she stands on her feet, but she doesn't let go of him*. You want to kill me . . . that's what it is . . . you want to kill me . . .

MICHAEL. You're raving mad—!

YVONNE. Just you wait . . . I'll stop you from going out . . . I'll have you locked up . . . I'll call the police . . . *Suddenly she lets go of him and tries to rush towards the window, i.e., the public*. I'll open the window . . . I'll call out the whole street . . .

MICHAEL, *putting his hand over her mouth and trying to stop her*. Aunt Leo . . . Aunt Leo . . . Dad . . . quickly . . .

LEO, *rushing in and putting her arms round* YVONNE. Yvonne, control yourself!

YVONNE. Go to hell!

GEORGE *appears in the door*. MICHAEL *stands aside, stupefied*.

LEO. George, get a glass of water . . . Lie down on your bed, Yvonne.

YVONNE. Leave me alone . . .

LEO. The neighbors are knocking . . .

YVONNE. The neighbors be damned, who cares?

GEORGE, *reappearing with a glass of water which he holds awkwardly in his hand.* Well, I do. I've had just about enough trouble with our neighbors because of the noise we're making. We'll probably be given notice . . .

YVONNE. Notice . . . or no notice . . . what does it matter now! Your son is a scoundrel! He has insulted me, he has hit me!

MICHAEL. That's not true, Dad——

GEORGE, *drinking up the glass of water which* YVONNE *has pushed away.* Come to my room.

MICHAEL, *to* YVONNE. I shall talk to Dad. Certain things should only be discussed among men! *He picks up his shoes and exits behind his father and bangs the door.*

YVONNE, *choking.* Leo, Leo . . . listen to him . . .

LEO. Yes, banging the doors again for a change.

YVONNE. Leo . . . you were listening at the door . . . you must have heard him . . .

LEO. I couldn't help hearing, but I didn't get everything.

YVONNE. You were right, Leo. He is in love. With a typist or something like that. He would leave us all for her. He looked at me in the most horrible way. He doesn't love me any more.

LEO. That doesn't follow at all.

YVONNE. Yes, it does, Leo. What you give to one you take from another. You can't help it.

LEO. A boy of Michael's age must live his own life, and you mothers had better shut your eyes to certain things. It may not be easy for a boy to get a woman out of his system.

YVONNE, *interrupting.* And what about us mothers? Didn't we carry them in our system? But those are things you can't possibly imagine.

LEO, *coldly.* Possibly not. But sometimes you just have to make a special effort to control yourself.

YVONNE. You can talk. Could you do it if you had to?

LEO. I've had to.

YVONNE. It all depends on the circumstances.

LEO. The circumstances were bad enough. You all live in the clouds, of course, but your selfishness, yours, Yvonne, in particular, surpasses everything.

YVONNE. My selfishness?

LEO. What exactly do you think I've been doing in this house for twenty-three years? I've been going through hell. I loved George and I still do and I shall probably love him till I die. *She silences* YVONNE *with a gesture*. When he broke off our engagement without the slightest reason, out of the blue, and decided it was you he wanted to marry, *and* went as far as to ask *me* for my advice, I pretended to take the blow lightly. To try and talk him out of it would have made me unhappy. To send you away would have meant losing him. And like the fool I was I sacrificed myself. Yes, it may seem unbelievable to you, but I was young, in love, an idealist and a fool. I thought you two had more in common, that you'd be a better wife, a better mother. That was twenty-three years ago. What have I been in this house since? I ask you! A maid!

YVONNE. Leo, you hate me . . .

LEO. No . . . I did hate you, though . . . not when he broke it off . . . the idea of my sacrifice thrilled me and kept me going. I began to hate you after Michael was born. I hated you because you loved Michael too much and you neglected George. At times, I've been unfair to Michael, because I blamed him for it all. It's odd . . . I might have hated you if your marriage had been a success. No, I can't analyse my feelings towards you. You're not really bad, Yvonne, one just can't hold you responsible. You do people harm without realizing it. You don't notice a thing. Not a single thing.

YVONNE. I see.

LEO. No, you don't. You trail around from room to room, from mess to mess, with your eyes shut. Long ago I noticed that George was up to something. And I was furious with you for not seeing it and trying to stop him. I felt all along he was getting involved and I felt it was getting him nowhere. And now that Michael's been trying to do the same thing, I felt I had to talk to you and warn you.

YVONNE, *scathingly*. Not to save the family, I bet. You were glad! For me to lose Michael made up for your loss of George!

LEO, *furious*. That's typical of you, Yvonne!

YVONNE. I don't know what you mean.

LEO, *exploding*. Yes, I'm glad if Michael takes money from that woman! Maybe that'll teach you not to let a man go out without enough money to buy himself a lollipop. I'm glad if Michael marries a tart! If your bloody Caravan turns over in the ditch it can stay there and rot! I shan't lift a finger to get you out of it. Poor George . . . twenty-three years . . . and life is long, my girl, long . . . long . . . *She feels that* GEORGE *is entering behind her back and without transition she carries on in a very feminine voice*. . . . and the jacket is short, and if you take it off, you're in evening dress and you can go anywhere in it.

YVONNE, *at first bewildered, sees* GEORGE.

GEORGE. You can talk about clothes. You're lucky.

YVONNE. What's the matter with you? You look ill . . .

GEORGE. I've been listening to Michael . . .

YVONNE. Well——?

GEORGE. Well . . . he's sorry if he's hurt your arm . . . he's sorry if he's upset you . . . he'd like to see you . . .

YVONNE. Is that all he's sorry about?

GEORGE. Yvonne . . . the boy's unhappy . . . don't ask him to apologize or some such nonsense . . . It's rather serious . . . I shall stay with Leo . . . I'd like you to stay with Michael for a bit.

YVONNE, *stubbornly.* No.

GEORGE. Please, Yvonne . . . you'd help him and you'd help me. I can't do any more.

YVONNE. I hope he didn't manage to twiddle you round his little finger . . .

GEORGE. Listen, Yvonne, I tell you again: this is serious! The boy is in love, very much in love . . . there's no getting away from that . . . Don't bother him, don't question him . . . he's sitting on a pile of dirty washing; just sit down beside him and hold his hand.

LEO. George is right.

YVONNE, *going over to the door.* I'll go, on one condition . . .

GEORGE, *smiling sadly.* Go . . . unconditionally . . . *He kisses her and pushes her out through the door at the back on the left.*

LEO. George, something's happened . . . what is it?

GEORGE. I'll tell you quickly, Leo; they may be back any minute.

LEO. You frighten me——

GEORGE. Wait till I tell you. I've just been hit over the head with a sledge hammer.

LEO. Is it about Michael?

GEORGE. It's Michael all right. I tell you there hasn't been a better farce in years.

LEO. Go on, George . . . *Silence.* George! *She shakes him.* George!

GEORGE, *coming to.* Oh, yes. I'd forgotten where I was. I'm sorry. Leo, I've been a fool and I'm paying dearly for it. Six months ago I needed a shorthand-typist. I was given an address and I found a young woman of twenty-five, unhappy, good-looking, simple, perfect. I was feeling very lonely at home. You're always running about. Yvonne thinks of nothing but Michael. Michael thinks of nothing but . . . anyway . . . I took on a false name, I said I was a widower, that I had a daughter who died, who looked just like her . . .

LEO. My poor George . . . who can blame you . . . you wanted some
   air . . . here—one can't breathe.

GEORGE. And so I went on inventing; I invented so much I didn't even
   tell her about my inventions. She told me she loved me . . . that
   young men bored her and so on and so forth. After three months her
   attitude changed. A sister from the country came up to stay with her.
   Some married sister, very severe, very narrow-minded. I borrowed
   quite a nice sum of money from you . . .

LEO. Just as I thought . . .

GEORGE. You're the only person I can talk to. Anyway—with the money
   that was supposed to help me with my work, I took some horrible base-
   ment flat. But she hardly ever came. Every time there was another
   excuse, and I was getting into a terrible state. You can guess the rest.
   The sister was a young man she'd fallen in love with. And the young
   man was Michael. He just told me so himself.

LEO. Does he suspect anything?

GEORGE. Not a thing. He's in Seventh Heaven. He thought I was shocked
   for the same reason as his mother.

LEO. What did he want?

GEORGE. He's just informed me that Madeleine—we might as well call
   her by her name—that Madeleine was making arrangements to see me
   tonight. The idea was . . . how shall I put it . . . ?

LEO. To give you your notice . . .

GEORGE. Yes, and to confess everything, it seems. Confess everything to
   Mr. X., so that they can be free and proper and worthy of each other.
   It'll kill me, Leo, I am crazy about her.

LEO. I don't know if this is a tragedy or a farce; but it certainly is a
   masterpiece.

GEORGE, *grimly*. It's a rotten masterpiece. How can such a coincidence
   happen in an enormous city like Paris . . . ?

LEO. I thought you didn't believe in coincidence. You people who are
   always so fond of "miracles," here's a good one for you. How did you
   feel facing Michael?

GEORGE. Terrible—terrible. I'm not angry with him. It's not his fault.

LEO. What're you going to do?

GEORGE. I wish you'd tell me. I shan't go and see her tonight, of course.

LEO. Now I know why there was such a false sense of order about the
   Caravan lately. When one of you was in, the other was out. My poor
   George . . .

GEORGE. What I've had to swallow! Michael kept referring to "the old bloke." He admitted that Madeleine used to help him out.

LEO. With your money . . .

GEORGE. No, with yours.

LEO. Now that is rather funny. It's just as well that our money should finally land in your son's pocket. And in all fairness that'll teach you not to let a boy of his age run around without a penny.

GEORGE, *rather hurt.* I know I'm ridiculous . . . but I'm very unhappy.

LEO, *taking his hand.* George, darling . . . I'm going to help you.

GEORGE. How, Leo?

LEO. You must hit and you must hit hard and you must make this marriage impossible. Michael wants the whole Caravan to visit this woman tomorrow. All right, we shall go.

GEORGE. Are you mad?

LEO. On the contrary.

GEORGE. Yvonne will never agree.

LEO. She will.

GEORGE. Can you imagine the scene . . . *I* walk in . . .

LEO. The girl will bite off her tongue rather than give herself away.

GEORGE. But when she sees me, she might faint or scream or something . . .

LEO. Leave that to me. You go and let her have it.

GEORGE. She has asked for it, Leo.

LEO. Break with her first, and then, if she refuses to give up Michael, threaten her. Threaten her that you'll tell *Michael everything!*

GEORGE, *taken aback.* You're a devil . . .

LEO. I am very fond of you, George. I want to protect your home.

GEORGE. Yes, but Yvonne . . . She will never, never in her life will she . . .

LEO. Sh! She's coming——

GEORGE. What big ears you have, grandmother . . .

LEO. The better to keep you from being eaten, my child!

The door at the back opens. YVONNE *appears.*

GEORGE. Well——?

YVONNE. We didn't say a word. After a while he looked as if he wanted to be left alone. So I came out. I'm finished. I don't know what I'm doing. I'd like to sleep, but I don't think I could. What's going to happen? You can see Michael isn't himself. He is under a bad influence.

LEO. Well, we'd better get to know this bad influence.

GEORGE. I know it only too well.

LEO, *giving* GEORGE *a warning glance.* I mean, we must be very careful. We mustn't get Michael's back up.

YVONNE. No, no—we must make a clean break.

LEO. D'you think you can stop these children from seeing each other?

YVONNE. What children?

LEO. Good Heavens, Yvonne—Michael and his girl.

YVONNE. But Leo, how can you talk of a "girl"? There's a woman who goes to bed with anybody . . . a woman Heaven knows how old she is . . . a little hypocrite who Mick believes is a Saint.

LEO. All the more reason to make him see her as she really is.

YVONNE. I am counting on George to show some character for once and strike while the iron is hot.

GEORGE. That's a good old cliché.

YVONNE. Besides, even if that woman really does want to leave her . . . protector . . . even suppose she *were* set on marrying Mick, it would be your duty to stop him taking on such an absurd responsibility. Mick can't just make her drop this old man and then leave her in the lurch.

LEO. Now at last you're talking sense.

YVONNE. And how did he expect to keep her?

GEORGE. He told me he was fed up doing nothing: he's made up his mind to get a job.

YVONNE. And to live on our money, or rather his aunt's.

LEO. You know what little money I have is yours.

YVONNE. Yes, but not that woman's. I'm not dreaming now, I see it all quite clearly: George must go and settle it. Leo . . . tell him, it's up to him.

GEORGE. That's easily said . . .

YVONNE. All you've got to do is to be firm and to *forbid* her . . .

LEO. D'you think it's any good giving orders to people in love?

YVONNE. Mick doesn't love this girl. He thinks he does. It's his first romance. He imagines he's found the ideal love, the love that lives forever.

LEO. Even if he only imagines it, it's just as real to him.

YVONNE. Nonsense! He'll start writing poems, he'll paint pictures, he'll go for endless walks, he'll get over it that way. I know my Mick.

LEO. Shall we say: you used to——

YVONNE. You really *are* in-cred*d*ible, both of you! I've been watching this boy for twenty-two years. And you say that any Miss What-you-may-call-her can just come and change him through and through in three months.

GEORGE. Not in three months, Yvonne, in three minutes. That is love.

YVONNE. My goodness . . . if I were a man, if I had to talk to her, I'd know what to say.

LEO. Well, that's just what Michael wants you to do . . .

YVONNE. Perhaps he expects me to obey his orders!

GEORGE. Who's talking of orders? Why do you dramatize everything? Yvonne—!

YVONNE. Just a minute . . . If I'm not mistaken . . . you're presuming you and George . . .

GEORGE. I'm not presuming anything——

YVONNE. All right, all right! You consider it feasible that I should accompany George to see this . . . this woman, with Leo bringing up the rear?

GEORGE. It's a reconnaissance, a simple reconnaissance . . . in enemy territory.

YVONNE. The Caravan in full marching order paying their respects on New Year's Eve . . .

LEO, *loudly*. I'm afraid you don't understand at all, Yvonne: can you face the prospect of living with a Michael who doesn't tell you anything any more, who tries to avoid you or who tells you lies from morning till night? Can you bear the thought of having to live without Michael . . . of Michael leaving the house altogether?

YVONNE. Please, don't . . .

LEO. You silly little idiot . . . do you know what would happen? You'd go and humiliate yourself again and again . . . you'd run after him, you'd go down on your knees to him . . . you'd go and beg that woman to . . .

YVONNE. Don't . . . don't . . . please, Leo, don't!!!

LEO. Darling, now wouldn't it be so much simpler to use a little cunning to win Michael back. One day he'll thank you for it.

YVONNE. I couldn't deceive Mick like that. It would only make matters worse afterwards.

LEO. You'd be deceiving him for his own good! Of course, you can always agree to this marriage if you find the girl is—all right.

GEORGE. Believe me, Yvonne, at first this idea gives you a shock. It gave *me* a shock. But eventually you realize that Leo's suggestion isn't as mad as it sounds.

YVONNE, *pacing up and down*. No, I won't! I'm always giving way, I'm sick of it, and I won't go near that woman! I won't!

LEO, *walking up towards* YVONNE *and making her stop*. And another thing,

Yvonne, the most important point of all: if someone had left me who was very dear to me, I just couldn't bear not knowing where he'd gone. Don't you want to know what that creature is like? What her place is like? The place where they both hurt you so much! When something that belongs to you has been stolen, don't you try and imagine where you may find it again?

YVONNE, *between her teeth.* In the hands of that thief . . .

LEO, *at her most formidable.* Then go to that thief, Yvonne. Go and get back what is yours. Go with George. And I . . . I shan't let you go alone.

YVONNE *sits down on the edge of her bed, her hand in front of her eyes. Only by this gesture, by her silence, does she at last accept.*

GEORGE. I admire you, Yvonne. You are always stronger than one would expect.

YVONNE. Or weaker.

LEO. It takes courage, for you to leave your dark room and go out into the sun.

YVONNE. If that's what you call the sun, give me the night any day.

LEO. Be very, very careful how you break the news to Michael, he may smell a rat.

GEORGE. Leo, you go and fetch him . . . tell him you've got a surprise, you've got good news for him.

LEO. Leave it to me . . . *She exits by the door at the back.*

YVONNE. What a nightmare . . .

GEORGE. You're telling me . . .

YVONNE. If I go to see this person . . . I'll hide myself somewhere with Leonie while you talk to her.

GEORGE, *grimly.* I promise you I'll talk to her alone.

YVONNE. Don't make me talk to her, George, I'd lose my temper . . . I'm not used to this type of woman.

GEORGE. Neither am I . . . At my age it's not easy to get used to things . . . *The door at the back opens.* LEO *pushes* MICHAEL *into the room. His clothes and his hair are in disorder. He appears to be on the defensive.*

LEO. Go on——

GEORGE. Come in, Michael.

MICHAEL. What is it?

GEORGE. Your mother will tell you.

MICHAEL *advances into the room.* LEO *shuts the door.* YVONNE *begins to speak with an effort, looking down.*

YVONNE. Mick, I'm afraid I've been unkind and I didn't appreciate your frankness. I am sorry. Your father is very kind. We talked it over. Mick, darling, we wouldn't want to hurt you for the world, you know that . . . on the contrary . . . I only want what is best for you and I hate being unfair. What you asked us to do is almost impossible . . .

MICHAEL. But——

GEORGE. Let your mother finish.

YVONNE. Anyway . . . this almost impossible step you asked us to take . . . we have decided to . . . to . . . we shall go and see your friend.

MICHAEL, *jumping towards his mother.* Mummy, Dad . . . is that true?

GEORGE. Yes, Michael. You may announce our visit for tomorrow.

MICHAEL. I can't believe it . . . How can I ever thank you . . . Mummy . . . *He tries to kiss* YVONNE.

YVONNE, *turning her face away.* Don't thank us, thank your Aunt.

MICHAEL. You, Aunt Leo! *He runs towards* LEO, *picks her up and swings her round and round.*

LEO, *screaming.* You're choking me . . . stop it . . . Mick . . . stop it . . . I'd nothing to do with it . . . Mick . . . stop it . . . please . . . don't thank me, thank the Caravan!

CURTAIN

ACT TWO

SCENE: MADELEINE'S *apartment.*

A large well-lit room.

Downstage left a spiral staircase leading to the attic above.

Upstage left, the entrance door.

Downstage right, the door to the bathroom.

Downstage centre, a large divan and a small table.

On all walls, especially in the back wall, but wherever possible, book-shelves full of books.

The room is kept scrupulously tidy.

MADELEINE *sits on the divan while* MICHAEL *is heard singing rather loudly in the adjoining bathroom. Suddenly there is the noise of a glass falling and breaking. The singing stops and* MICHAEL *appears holding the pieces of the glass, in shirt and trousers but without socks and shoes.*

MADELEINE. Oh, darling . . . it's in-cre*dd*ible!

MICHAEL. D'you know that everybody at home says, "it's in-cre*dd*ible"?

I sometimes think we said it before I met you and that you got it from
me. Mother'd be mad if she knew she's copying you.

MADELEINE. I don't see what's so peculiar about my way of pronouncing
this word. I say it like everyone else.

MICHAEL, *tenderly.* You say it like no one else and without rhyme or reason.
It's a habit that you've passed on to me and I've passed on to all the
others, to Mother and Father and to Aunt Leo. Now they all say:
"it's in-cre*dd*ible!"

MADELEINE. Michael——

MICHAEL. Yes——

MADELEINE. Did you remember to pull the plug out?

MICHAEL. No . . . *He runs into the bathroom.*

MADELEINE. Well, hurry up. Your mother would never believe that you
had to have your bath *here*, because yours is blocked.

MICHAEL. It's all Aunt Leo's fault. The bath is her department. Usually
she's order personified. You two'll get on like a house on fire.

MADELEINE, *proudly. My* bath works.

MICHAEL. *We* wash in the basin, when Leo decides to let us down. But
she's much too fond of her comfort; she can't keep it up.

MADELEINE. May I dry your hair?

MICHAEL. It would never have occurred to me that my having a bath here
would annoy Mother; and it would, you know! You're like Aunt Leo,
you're a great diplomatist.

MADELEINE. You seem to have studied your Aunt pretty closely.

MICHAEL. Only because we all live on top of each other. Usually I'm not
very observant.

MADELEINE. What I like about you is that you're so clean.

MICHAEL. That's a good one.

MADELEINE. You're not really dirty. You're dirty like a child. Children's
knees aren't really dirty.

MICHAEL. Childish and ignorant, that's me.

MADELEINE. And what about me?

MICHAEL. Oh, you . . . you're my learned friend: you read the classics!

MADELEINE. I don't read them, I only bind them.

MICHAEL. You're too clever for me. One of these days you'll make a living
out of this bookbinding of yours. You'll have to keep me.

MADELEINE. You're going to work, my darling. You might even help me,
and one day we'll open a shop.

MICHAEL. And we'll make a fortune. And then—when we've got our own
house . . .

MADELEINE. A "flat," Michael. Why do you always say "a house"? It's so frightfully grand!

MICHAEL. At home, we always say "house"; this house, our house, my house. . . .

MADELEINE, *laughing*. It's in-credd*i*ble!

MICHAEL. But that's how it is. Now listen: when we've got our own house, if you won't let me be untidy, I'll drag you over to the Caravan, and lock you up and force you to share my room with me and my dirty washing and my ties in the flowerpot.

MADELEINE, *vastly superior*. Within five minutes, my dear, your room would be in perfect order.

MICHAEL. You're the devil. If this was our house, your whole bookbinding studio would be down here in the sitting room; or the sitting room would be all over your studio. Things keep following me like cats. How *do* you do it?

MADELEINE. I have a feeling for order. You either have it or you don't.

MICHAEL, *finding his socks underneath* MADELEINE. Look where I find my socks. I'm sure I took 'em off in the bathroom.

MADELEINE. You took them off in the sitting room.

MICHAEL, *putting on his socks*. There's no such thing as a sitting room at our place. Every drama takes place in Mother's bedroom, the scene of the crime . . . When the rows get too noisy, the neighbors knock on the wall, and the truce, the peace treaties, and the stormy silences take place in a kind of phantom dining room, a waiting room, an empty hole with a big, ugly, awkward table which keeps on falling to pieces, and which the charwoman keeps screwing together again.

MADELEINE. And does your father put up with—?

MICHAEL. Oh, Dad . . . Dad thinks he's a great inventor . . . *Smiling*. Actually, he's about ten years younger than I am . . .

MADELEINE. And your mother?

MICHAEL. When I was little, I wanted to marry Mummy. And when Dad told me "You're too young," I said: "Then I'll wait till I'm ten years older than Mummy."

MADELEINE, *very moved*. Oh, my darling . . . *She kisses him.*

MICHAEL. I am sorry to keep on about my family. You see, I didn't want to talk too much about them until I'd told *them* everything . . . I'm not very clever, you know . . . so I just shut up about them altogether. I'm making up for it now.

MADELEINE. It was very sweet of you, and I do understand.

MICHAEL. When I told them . . . Sophie was wonderful, and Dad and Aunt Leo, too. But it started with a scene all right.

MADELEINE, *frightened.* A scene——

MICHAEL. Mother wanted to call the police, to have me arrested.

MADELEINE, *stupefied.* The police? Whatever for?

MICHAEL. Oh, that's Mother's style . . . it goes with her room.

MADELEINE. It's—

MICHAEL ⎫
⎬ —in-cre*dd*ible!
MADELEINE ⎭

MADELEINE, *laughing.* And whose fault was the scene, Michael?

MICHAEL. It was my fault. No, it was your fault. I just couldn't resist spending a night with you. And in the morning . . . in the morning I . . .

MADELEINE, *imitating him and taking his foot off some piece of furniture.* And in the morning you had the jitters.

MICHAEL. Quite.

MADELEINE. I told you a hundred times to go and ring up.

MICHAEL. Don't put your foot in it, my love—although I grant you: it's an adorable foot—don't tell Sophie that you told me to telephone.

MADELEINE. Look who's talking! You can't walk a step without putting your foot in it.

MICHAEL. Quite.

MADELEINE. And that's another thing I love about you, my stupid darling: you're incapable of telling lies.

MICHAEL. It's just too complicated, that's all.

MADELEINE. I hate lies. I realise you have to shut up sometimes or re-arrange things a bit not to hurt people's feelings. But lying . . . just for the sake of lying . . . I am not a particularly moral person myself . . . but I always feel that telling a lie is apt to set off some mechanism or other outside our control which upsets and ruins everything in the end. *During this* MICHAEL *has finished lacing up his left shoe; he now commences to search for the other one.*

MICHAEL. Hm. Where's my other shoe?

MADELEINE. Look for it.

MICHAEL. This *is* incredible; I saw it a minute ago . . .

MADELEINE. Keep looking.

MICHAEL, *on all fours.* You know where it is, don't you?

MADELEINE. I can just see it from here. It's staring you in the face.

MICHAEL, *walking away from the table on which the shoe lies.* Getting hot?

MADELEINE. You're freezing.

MICHAEL. And then you tell me to hurry up.

MADELEINE. Diplomatist! Here you are! *She picks up the shoe on one lace and lets it swing in front of* MICHAEL'S *eyes.*

MICHAEL. That's the end. Mother would have fished it out of my bed.

MADELEINE. What an adorable woman your mother must be. And what a pity I'm scared to death.

MICHAEL, *putting on the other shoe.* Mummy thinks she's ugly, but she's much more beautiful than if she were beautiful, if you know what I mean. She'll be done up in all her war paint. I bet you Aunt Leo insists on Mummy making up and getting the moth balls out of the furs.

MADELEINE. I'm scared . . . I'm scared . . .

MICHAEL. It's they who're scared! Aunt Leo will break the ice, she is very strong!

MADELEINE. Do you always go everywhere in a gang?

MICHAEL. Mother never goes out at all. Dad goes out, pottering. Aunt Leo goes out shopping. And I go out because I love you.

MADELEINE, *taking his hands.* Do you, Michael?

MICHAEL. Have a look. *He turns round and round on the spot.* I'm all set, nice and clean and ready to ask your hand in marriage. Oh!

MADELEINE, *alarmed.* What's the matter?

MICHAEL. I wanted to have my hair cut.

MADELEINE. You can't. It's Monday. They're shut on Mondays.

MICHAEL. How do you manage to know everything?

MADELEINE. Everyone knows they're shut on Mondays!

MICHAEL. No . . . *He kisses her.* How do you know it's Monday? I only know when it's Sunday because our char doesn't come on Sunday and I have to help in the kitchen.

MADELEINE. You can tell it's Sunday by other things. People are freer. There's disorder in the air . . . a sad kind of disorder.

MICHAEL. You with your order and your disorder!

MADELEINE. What are your people expecting to find here?

MICHAEL. They're expecting the worst. They expect to find a peroxided old woman.

MADELEINE. I *am* an old woman. I am three years older than you.

MICHAEL. I have a presentiment that this old woman will give them the surprise of their lives!

MADELEINE. Touch wood . . .

MICHAEL, *taking her in his arms.* Madeleine, darling, you would conquer anybody. No, there's only one thing that worries me a little.

MADELEINE. What's that?

MICHAEL. I so much wanted this other business to be over and done with.

MADELEINE. He's put it off till tomorrow. Tomorrow everything will be in order.

MICHAEL. You seem to be glad he put it off.

MADELEINE. In a way, yes. When George rang up I didn't insist, I didn't have the courage.

MICHAEL. Dad's name is George.

MADELEINE. You can imagine what my talk with the first George is going to be like. But it doesn't worry me half as much as meeting your George.

MICHAEL. Anyway, you don't love the man.

MADELEINE. I do, Michael.

MICHAEL. You love him?!

MADELEINE. It isn't as simple as all that, Michael. I only love you. But I love George, in a way.

MICHAEL. Well, I'll be——

MADELEINE, *interrupting*. If I did not love him . . . in a way . . . I shouldn't love you. Because I should never have known you. I should be dead. I told you what I was going to do just before I met him.

MICHAEL, *a little snootily*. You're certainly grateful to him, anyway . . .

MADELEINE, *quite seriously*. No, Michael, it's more than that.

MICHAEL. Now I don't understand anything any more . . .

MADELEINE. But you must, my darling. A number of men offered me what George offered me. I refused. If I nearly accepted his offer, it was because I loved him . . . in a way.

MICHAEL. Oh, well, you didn't know *me* then.

MADELEINE. You horrible little egoist! *She kisses him.* No, I didn't love him all that much; I was waiting for something different. And when I met you, I'd found it. Still, I was sufficiently in love with him to hide it, to delay things, even to accept his help. In fact, I love him enough to be ill at the thought of having to fire this news at him point blank.

MICHAEL. It's in-cred*d*ible!

MADELEINE. Listen, Michael, be fair! Try and put yourself in his place. He's a widower. He's lost his daughter. I look just like her, it seems. You're asking me to sign his death warrant. He's convinced I would never lie to him. I'm everything to him!

MICHAEL, *exasperated*. But take him, take him after all, there's still time! I'll cancel the family! No problem at all . . .

MADELEINE. Don't be absurd. Did I say I wouldn't do it? When you are in love . . . as I am with you . . . you can do anything . . . however difficult . . . and I mean that. So that is all settled.

MICHAEL, *after a moment's pause.* I'm sorry, we shouldn't have talked about it.

MADELEINE. I never mentioned you to him. He knows nothing about you. I thought it was better that way.

MICHAEL. Look . . . if Mother . . . if I had to choose . . . I wouldn't hesitate a moment . . .

MADELEINE. Yes, you would. And you'd be right. And that's one of the reasons why I love you. But it isn't a fair comparison, Michael. Your mother has your father and your aunt.

MICHAEL. No. She has only me.

MADELEINE. Then—she must hate me very much.

MICHAEL. No one could hate you! Mother will love you as soon as she understands that you and I are one and the same person.

MADELEINE. You shouldn't have told her about the other man.

MICHAEL. I don't have to hide anything from Sophie. She's my friend.

MADELEINE. Then why didn't you tell her about us at once?

MICHAEL. Because I was embarrassed about the other chap. Our family is full of prejudices . . . of conventional nonsense . . . and there are always scenes. I wanted them to see you free with nothing to hide between us at all. When I did tell them, I told them our whole story from A to Z.

MADELEINE. You were right. Absolutely. Once you begin you must tell everything.

MICHAEL. I'm glad you agree. If you think that it'll help you tomorrow.

MADELEINE. Let's not talk about it any more. Just think that I was as fond of George as I shall be of your father.

MICHAEL. But——

MADELEINE. Sh—! *She stops him with a gentle kiss.*

MICHAEL. Are you angry with me?

MADELEINE. I'd be angry if you weren't jealous.

MICHAEL. They're awfully sweet, really they are. I mean this visit proves it, doesn't it?

MADELEINE. This visit terrifies me. It's all too simple. You told me your mother wouldn't hear of it. Next minute she has changed her mind completely. It terrifies me.

MICHAEL. First they get mad and shout and bang the doors, then Aunt Leo calms them down. Sophie is like that. Impulsive. She says: "No, young

man, never!" Then she locks herself in and I sulk. Then she comes
back, gives me a kiss and says: "All right, Mick." And I give *her* a kiss
and that's that.

MADELEINE. I can't understand it.

MICHAEL. I'm telling you: Aunt Leo is the guardian angel of the Caravan.
She is very beautiful, very elegant, and very outspoken. She criticizes
our disorder all the time, but if it came to the point, she couldn't do
without it.

The door bell rings. They both jump.

MADELEINE. They're here! I'm off! I'm going upstairs!

MICHAEL. Don't leave me!

MADELEINE. You come and fetch me!

MICHAEL. Madeleine, please!

MADELEINE. Yes, yes—it's much better like that.

She climbs up the little staircase rapidly, while MICHAEL *leaves the stage to open
the door.*

MICHAEL, *off stage.* Oh, it's you, Aunt Leo . . . you're alone?!

LEO *enters through the back stage door, followed by* MICHAEL.

MICHAEL. Has anything been changed? Are they coming?

LEO. Don't worry. They're coming. I arranged to get here well ahead
of the others.

MICHAEL. That's very good of you.

LEO, *looking round.* I say: what order!

MICHAEL. That's me. You can see that. That's me all over.

LEO. I wonder. Oh, what a gorgeous view—that's what your mother
ought to have, spending all day in her room, instead of that ugly
building opposite.

MICHAEL. Don't run down the Caravan. I look out on the courtyard—I
like it.

LEO. Where's your friend?

MICHAEL. Upstairs. She's got a bookbinding studio upstairs. *He begins to
climb up.*

LEO. Can't you call her?

MICHAEL. No, you can't hear a thing up there.

LEO. That's a bit of luck.

MICHAEL. Why?

LEO. Your father is in a very good mood. He must talk to your friend
alone. It would be no good your mother being here and interfering all
the time. I'll take her up there; and when we come down, everything
will be over.

MICHAEL. Angel! *He gives her a kiss.* I'll bring her to you.

He runs upstairs four at the time. He bangs the studio door behind him. LEO *goes to the bathroom, opens the door, looks, grunts surprised approval of what she sees and shuts the door again. She now proceeds upstage and begins to look at the titles of the books.*

MADELEINE, *pushed forward by* MICHAEL, *appears at the top of the staircase. She comes down slowly with* MICHAEL *holding her by the shoulders.*

MICHAEL, *to* MADELEINE. I tell you she's alone. You're not going to be afraid of Aunt Leo . . . she's the advance guard.

MADELEINE *smiles timidly at* LEO; LEO *stretches out her hand;* MADELEINE *takes it gladly; they shake hands.*

LEO. How do you do?

MADELEINE. How do you do? *It is almost a whisper.*

LEO. You are very beautiful, my dear.

MADELEINE. Oh . . . thank you . . . Michael was right. . . .

MICHAEL. I told her that you were cross-eyed, hunchbacked, and lame.

MADELEINE. He always talks about how beautiful, how elegant you are. Won't you sit down?

LEO, *sitting on the divan.* He didn't mention my "order" by any chance? I can see I'm not the only one to appreciate it.

MADELEINE. I'm afraid disorder terrifies me.

LEO. I shall congratulate you if you can do anything in that line with Michael.

MADELEINE. He's making progress.

MICHAEL. Yes. I now leave my shoes on the sitting room table instead of Mother's bed. I was sure you'd be impressed by her order. Tell me, are you?

LEO, *smiling.* Very—!

MICHAEL. You see, Madeleine, Aunt Leo is very impressed. What's the matter with Mother and Dad? Where are they?

LEO. I said I was going to meet them here. Your mother didn't like it, but I hate arriving anywhere in a gang. I said I had some shopping to do. I don't mind telling you I wanted to get here first and prepare the ground.

MICHAEL. Aunt Leo thinks of everything.

MADELEINE. I can certainly see that.

LEO. Well, now we're partners in crime. *Pointing at the staircase.* Your studio is just what we need. I was afraid you'd only have one room.

MADELEINE. It's an old attic, in fact the whole thing is just two attics converted.

LEO. And you're sure one can't hear from the attic what goes on down here?

MADELEINE. Quite sure.

LEO. That's most important. They won't be here for a few minutes. So let's make quite sure: upstairs, you two, lock yourself in, I'll shout something down here.

MICHAEL. What?

LEO. Oh—anything!

MADELEINE and MICHAEL run upstairs giggling like schoolchildren. MICHAEL bangs the door to the attic. LEO picks out a book from the library; it is Alfred de Musset's 'Lorenzaccio,' opens it at random and begins to yell. While she recites, MICHAEL and MADELEINE reopen the attic door and, creeping forward on their hands and knees, listen to LEO in extreme silence.

LEO. 'Help! Help! They're killing me! They're cutting my throat! Oh death, death, death! Stamp your foot . . . this way, archers . . . Lorenzo, the Devil! Thou art a wretch, a cur! I'll bleed you, swine! His heart . . . go for his heart! There, my men! Tear his guts! Now wilt thou cry, now stamp thy foot, now try and kill me if thou canst! Let's cut him into pieces, friends, and throw them to the winds . . .'

MICHAEL. Bravo!

LEO. Michael! You weren't in the attic!

MICHAEL. I was, but I couldn't hear a thing, and I wanted to hear you scream.

LEO. You ought to be used to that at home.

MICHAEL. Ah, but I wanted to listen to you *here* . . . you were terrific, Aunt Leo, you'd make a wonderful actress!

MADELEINE. You were grand!

LEO. Your mother can be quite a good actress, too, when she wants to be. Between ourselves, I believe our grandmother was a singer, and she had to give it up when she married grandpapa. But of course, these things are never mentioned in the family.

The door bell rings.

LEO. Here they are. *To* MADELEINE. Upstairs, quickly! Remember: I haven't seen you. I don't know you. I've only just come. *To* MICHAEL, *while* MADELEINE *goes upstairs.* And you, Michael, you refused to show me your friend. Go on . . . remember . . . your mother first . . . *The door bell rings again.* MICHAEL *runs to open the door. The voices of* GEORGE, YVONNE *and* MICHAEL *are heard in the hall.*

GEORGE'S VOICE. I thought we'd come to the wrong floor.

YVONNE'S VOICE. No maid?

MICHAEL'S VOICE. No, same as at home. *He enters ahead of* GEORGE *and* YVONNE. Aunt Leo, did *you* hear them ring?

GEORGE *and* YVONNE *enter*.

YVONNE, *suspiciously*. Is Leo here?

LEO. I just got here. I rang three times. We nearly met at the door.

YVONNE. Have you been here long?

LEO. I tell you I just got here. Didn't I, Michael?

MICHAEL. Aunt Leo thought she was late and would find you here.

YVONNE. You're . . . alone?

MICHAEL. Madeleine's upstairs. She's got a bookbinding studio upstairs.

LEO, *to* GEORGE. Michael wouldn't dream of showing her to me before showing her to Yvonne . . . *Quickly turning to* YVONNE. . . . and to George . . .

MICHAEL. Upstairs you don't hear the bell, you don't hear a thing. She's been hiding up there for half an hour.

YVONNE, *raising her eyebrows*. Hiding?

MICHAEL. Well . . . she's afraid of the family.

YVONNE, *coldly*. We're not monsters.

MICHAEL. It's only natural that Madeleine should be a bit nervous.

LEO. I see her point.

YVONNE, *looking around*. What luxury!

MICHAEL, *modestly*. It's quite neat . . .

YVONNE. That never used to be your strong point.

MICHAEL. Give me a chance. I don't come here very often. If I lived here or came more often, it wouldn't stay like that for long.

LEO. I wonder.

YVONNE, *almost snapping at* LEO. Why do you say that?

GEORGE, *cutting in quickly*. Michael—don't you think you should announce our arrival?

MICHAEL. Yes, of course . . . Oh Dad, don't be so stiff, and you, Sophie, sit down . . . sit down both of you . . . try to look natural. Aunt Leo, make them comfortable, do the honors. Poor Madeleine is very nervous. If you aren't going to help her, she'll stand there like a poker and you'll think she's putting it on.

GEORGE. I wonder, my boy, if you realize the seriousness of this visit? It wouldn't appear so.

LEO. He's only trying to break the ice.

MICHAEL, *meaning it*. I'm going to cry in a minute.

YVONNE. Now please, Leo, George is rather concerned about all this. It's at times like these that we become fathers, mothers, and sons; one can't treat these things lightly.

LEO, *drily*. In that case, try not to become conventional fathers and mothers, just because the situation is somewhat unconventional. I think Michael is very brave and very sweet. Go and fetch the child.

YVONNE, *between her teeth*. If you can call her that.

MICHAEL, *at the foot of the staircase*. Now listen: this means my whole life to me. For the last time, I ask you to help Madeleine and not to cold-shoulder her.

YVONNE. We didn't come here with that intention.

MICHAEL. Mother, darling, Dad, Leo—don't be angry with me . . . I'm in a bit of a state . . .

LEO. We're not angry with you. We're all putting on an act because we all feel frightfully self-conscious. We'll get over it. Go on!

MICHAEL, *running upstairs*. All right!

YVONNE, *to* GEORGE. You look even worse than I do . . .

GEORGE. Sit down, Yvonne. I'll just stand over here behind Leo.

They form a group. LEO *sits on the left nearest to the staircase,* YVONNE *by her side.* GEORGE *stands behind the sofa, i.e., behind* YVONNE.

MICHAEL, *walking down backwards, talking over his shoulder*. Smile, please!

MADELEINE *comes downstairs without looking.* YVONNE *rises and advances towards* MADELEINE. GEORGE *stays where he is, still covered by* LEO.

This is my mother.

MADELEINE. How do you do?

YVONNE. You're charming, my dear. You look very young. May I ask how old you are?

MADELEINE. I am twenty-five. I am so glad to . . . *At this instant she discovers* GEORGE. *Her voice fails her. She takes a few steps in his direction.* Oh, God . . . What are you doing here? *She turns towards the ladies, her face quite drawn.* Excuse me, this gentleman . . .

MICHAEL, *coming forward laughingly*. This gentleman is my father. Dad, this is Madeleine.

MADELEINE, *trying not to draw back, but she cannot help herself altogether*. Your father . . . !

MICHAEL. Nobody ever believes Dad is old enough to be my father. If we went out together they'd think we were brothers.

LEO. Introduce me.

MICHAEL. I don't know what I'm doing . . . Madeleine . . . *He takes her by the hand.* Darling, how cold you are! Feel her hand, Leo!

LEO *takes* MADELEINE'S *hand. She makes a superhuman effort not to faint.*

LEO. Her hands are like ice. LEO *smiles at* MADELEINE. Are we as bad as that?

MICHAEL. Shake hands with Aunt Leo!

MADELEINE, *has no voice left.* How do you do . . .

LEO. I'm Michael's aunt, and now that you've met us, I trust there is nothing to frighten you any longer.

MICHAEL. Well, that's the lot. You've met the family. You see, there was nothing to it.

MADELEINE *drops onto the divan but she gets hold of herself at once and she manages to sit up.*

MICHAEL. Darling . . . are you all right?

MADELEINE. Yes, Michael . . . I'm all right.

YVONNE. I believe Michael wants to show us how nicely the attic has been arranged. No, please don't bother to get up. MADELEINE *tries to get up.* No, really, Miss . . . my sister will come up, too. Come on, Michael . . .

MICHAEL. But . . .

YVONNE. Lead the way. Leo and I will follow you.

GEORGE, *making a move.* I could perhaps . . .

YVONNE. No, I think you'd better stay.

MICHAEL. We've got the tea ready upstairs . . . and three cups. And sugar. And some T. T. milk.* We know how to entertain!

YVONNE *walks over to the staircase and is about to climb up.* LEO *follows her.* MICHAEL *kisses* MADELEINE *quickly on the shoulder and moves to follow* LEO.

MADELEINE, *quickly rising to her feet.* Are you leaving me alone!

MICHAEL. Not alone . . . with Dad!

MADELEINE. No . . . please . . . don't leave me . . . listen, Michael . . .

YVONNE. Michael!

MADELEINE. Please, ladies . . . let me show you the way . . . I must pour out the tea . . .

YVONNE. We'll manage. Michael will help us. I shall be curious to see if there are still three cups left when we've finished.

MICHAEL. As a matter of fact, there were six. I've only broken three.

MADELEINE *makes a move to follow* MICHAEL *towards the staircase.*

GEORGE, *speaking to* MADELEINE *without moving from where he stands.* Please stay. I promised Michael to have a talk with you and, since my wife is much more nervous than I am, to speak to you alone. It is nice of Michael to say that I look so young; but don't be afraid. I'm an old man really, compared with you two.

* Tuberculin tested. A British translation of the French "concentrée."

YVONNE, *from the top of the stairs*. Hurry up, and let us know when you've finished.

MADELEINE. No, please! Couldn't your sister please stay with us? A woman would . . .

YVONNE, *interrupting*. My dear child . . . would you mind if we had our tea now? I am against women getting mixed up with certain problems. You've heard yourself what Michael said about his father. You will be talking to a friend of Michael's, a very good friend, easy to get on with, much more easy than *I* should be.

MICHAEL. They don't wish us any harm, Madeleine, on the contrary . . . Use your charm, make Dad fall for you in a big way . . . but don't run off together, you two . . . Would you like me to bring you down a cup of tea?

LEO. She'll have her tea afterwards. LEO *pushes* YVONNE *through the attic door and exits herself, followed by* MICHAEL.

MICHAEL, *popping his head out again*. Make her smile, Dad! Be good! *He blows* MADELEINE *a kiss and bangs the door.*

GEORGE. Well, this is it.

MADELEINE, *burying her face in her hands*. This is monstrous——

GEORGE. Exactly. It's monstrous. It's unbelievable, but it's true. It's a masterpiece. *He walks up to the bookshelves and taps the backs of books.* All these gentlemen here who have written masterpieces, have written them around little monstrosities such as this. That's why they're so interesting and so popular! There is, however, one little difference: I'm not the hero of a tragedy. I'm the hero of a comedy. A blind man makes them weep, a deaf man makes them laugh. My part makes them laugh. Just think of it: a man deceived by a woman, that's funny already. A man of my age deceived in favour of a young man, that's funnier still. But if that young man is the old boy's son, that is the farce to end all farces. We're classical figures, you and I! Aren't you proud of yourself? I should be if I were you.

MADELEINE. George——

GEORGE. I hope they can't hear us from the studio.

MADELEINE. You know they can't.

GEORGE. You're right. That was a stupid question. The first couple of times your "sister" came, I was locked in up there. I imagine that was Michael? *She nods.* Admirable. But you didn't mind my taking a furnished flat. Only you hardly ever came. Why did you bother to continue with me? And why did you lie to me? I suppose you had to live. Did you help Michael out?

MADELEINE. Michael was even poorer than I was. I paid for his cigarettes, or for a meal once in a while.

GEORGE. So after all it was quite respectable as it was I who paid for my own son.

MADELEINE. I'm making enough with my bookbinding to look after myself.

GEORGE. I prefer to think that it was I who paid. I thought the slightest lie makes you ill. So why did you lie to me?

MADELEINE. It's no use, you wouldn't believe me.

GEORGE. You . . . of all people . . . a liar!

MADELEINE. And you, why did *you* lie to me? What confidence you had in me! You were very careful, weren't you?

GEORGE. I was very unhappy. My home wasn't a home at all. I was all alone. I made up my mind to give myself another chance. I invented a story. And when I was with you, I was happy. I forgot everything, even my inventions, even Michael. Not once did I allow my other life to interfere with ours—so you can imagine what I felt when Michael told me the truth yesterday.

MADELEINE. You should have told me your real name.

GEORGE. You would have met Michael just the same.

MADELEINE. I would have avoided him.

GEORGE. Oh, nonsense! The only difference would have been, you would have broken it off with me three months ago. But why didn't you tell me? I suppose you liked the arrangement: an old man, a young man——

MADELEINE. George, I beg you . . . don't say such filthy things! I lied to you because I loved you, because I love you still. . . .

GEORGE. You're in-cred*d*ible!

MADELEINE. Yes, George, I am very, very fond of you.

GEORGE. Oh, sure, sure . . .

MADELEINE. Please, let me finish. I am sorry if I couldn't give you all you wanted from me. You told me that you had lost a daughter. You were kind. You weren't like all the others. I was in an awful state when you met me. I was pretty well through with everything. I met you and I clung to you with all my heart . . .

GEORGE. All I want to know is: did you love me? Because I did. I was crazy about you. I asked you a thousand times, "Do you love me?" and you always said: "Yes, George, I love you." That's true, isn't it?

MADELEINE. George, there are certain reservations which one can guess even if you don't put them into so many words. I often told you: "I love you a lot," but every time you'd lose your temper and then you'd beg me and worry me and insist on an answer; so in the end I gave in and said: "Yes, George, I love you."

GEORGE. You shouldn't have said it!

MADELEINE. These last months . . . what a nightmare! I did everything to open your eyes. You didn't want to see anything.

GEORGE. It was too late! If you had told me in time, "I don't love you, but I shall try, you must wait . . ." But you let me sink in up to the neck, you let me love you more and more, until I was caught for good. And you let it drag on and you kept putting me off till what *you* call love, dropped on you from the sky. And then, since I was in the way . . .

MADELEINE. You're quite wrong. I couldn't bring myself to hurt you. That was the reason. The idea of breaking with you was torture to me. I said so to Michael.

GEORGE, *face to face with* MADELEINE. Do you love Michael?

MADELEINE. Are you asking for yourself or for him?

GEORGE. I am asking as his father.

MADELEINE. He is my whole life. I can't imagine myself without him. Unhappiness makes one very humble. I had given up hope for love. I mean, greater love than yours and mine. It had to be Michael to make me realise that love is something very different . . .

GEORGE. And does Michael love you?

MADELEINE. I think . . . today . . . proves it. But if he knew, if he ever found out the truth . . .

GEORGE. There is no question of him finding out.

MADELEINE, *immensely relieved.* You really will put Michael's happiness before anything else? Oh, George, all my life I shall be grateful to you.

GEORGE. So you imagine that I am going to give you Michael, do you?

MADELEINE. . . . D'you want to take Michael away from me?

GEORGE. At once.

MADELEINE. No—! *It is hardly more than a sound.*

GEORGE. What did you expect? That I would give in, that I would throw Michael into your arms and watch you together for the rest of my life?

MADELEINE. You're mad! He is your son! You are talking of your son's happiness, of Michael's happiness!

GEORGE. What sort of happiness would that be, do you think, with an unfaithful woman? Since you have deceived me, how do I know that you're not going to deceive him? How do I know that you haven't even done so already?

MADELEINE, *rushing at him, tearing him by the shoulders.* George . . . George! You don't mean that! Tell me you don't mean that!

GEORGE. No, I don't. To tell you the truth, I don't.

MADELEINE, *smiling through her agony.* I knew it. *She tries to take his hand.*

GEORGE, *turning away from her.* But, my dear Madeleine . . . since this third person does not exist . . . and we know that he doesn't . . . we'll have to invent him.

MADELEINE. Invent him . . . ?

GEORGE. We must invent a young man of your age. A bit older than Michael, a man who fascinates you completely . . . a man you can never give up. On the other hand, you're ashamed of him, and you are only going to marry Michael to ensure your social position and so make the best of both worlds.

MADELEINE. You're not serious, George——

GEORGE. I've never been more serious in my life.

MADELEINE. What you're suggesting is horrifying, it's ghastly.

GEORGE. It's got to be done, Madeleine, or I'll tell Michael the truth.

MADELEINE. You wouldn't tell your son, your wife——

GEORGE. Don't—don't concern yourself about my wife. I have decided to tell her everything, whatever happens. I owe it to her.

MADELEINE. She'll—she'll tell Michael!

GEORGE. She will if you force her to, if you don't leave Michael alone.

MADELEINE. So this is what I've dragged him into. How right I was to be afraid. He was so innocent, so trusting. Suppose I lie to him . . . suppose I tell him this appalling story, he'll never believe me! Michael knows me.

GEORGE. Didn't you tell him again and again how much you hated lying? You can never lie—to him. "Michael knows you."

MADELEINE. If you can bring yourself to do this, don't think I'll ever see you again.

GEORGE. See you again . . . ? No. I'm cured. And I intend to cure Michael.

MADELEINE. Of loving me?

GEORGE, *icily.* I shall cure him of a project of marriage which circumstances render inadmissible.

MICHAEL, *opening the attic door and speaking from the top of the staircase.* Have you finished? Can we come down?

GEORGE. Not yet. We're talking like old friends.

MICHAEL. Well done! . . . Madeleine, I've broken a cup. Get us out of here soon! *He exits, banging the attic door.*

MADELEINE. Sometimes—when people you love are away, you don't realize they're still alive. A minute ago, when I was talking to you it was

nothing but words. I have just heard Michael's voice. He is alive . . .
I'm not going to "leave him alone," as you said. I'll keep him.

GEORGE. I've thought it over, too, Madeleine. You're free. And I'll tell
him the truth. Michael will know who the other man was. I shall lose
him, but we'll lose him together.

MADELEINE. That's blackmail . . . it's wicked . . .

GEORGE. You leave me no alternative. *He turns away from her towards the
staircase.*

MADELEINE, *running after him.* George . . . George . . . listen to me, believe me . . .

GEORGE. D'you really think I am so naïve . . . ?

MADELEINE. Yes, naïve and kind. You're everything I used to love. Everything I worship in Michael. Haven't I been punished enough by your
coming here today? I might have given everything away.

GEORGE. I knew that you'd control yourself, if you really loved Michael.

MADELEINE. Ah, you see . . . you know I love him.

GEORGE. This marriage is absurd. I want quite another sort of life for
Michael. For one thing, he must marry in his own class.

MADELEINE. I am the daughter and the granddaughter of a workman.
I'll change Michael. He'll work. He's changing already. If you make
him unhappy now, you'll regret it for the rest of your life.

GEORGE. He won't be unhappy for long.

MADELEINE. That's where you're wrong! Michael is a child. Children
remember pain! And you, George, you're a child, too. Someone has
broken your toy. Because that's all I was—I'm not important to you,
George. But to Michael, I mean a lot. Michael needs me. How can you
compare our adventure, built on entirely false foundations, a false name
and address, even, how can you compare that with the adventure of a
boy who gives himself body and soul?

GEORGE. His mother would never agree.

MADELEINE. So you're both against me! But his Aunt Leonie, perhaps
she——

GEORGE, *interrupting.* She loved me when she was a girl. She's still got some
affection for me. Perhaps she's still in love with me, I don't know. She'd
hate you if I were to be made to look ridiculous because of you.

MADELEINE. She'll see me love Michael and Michael love me, and if we
have children . . .

GEORGE. Children! Bring children into the world out of a sordid mess like
this—!

MADELEINE. Please, George, don't take it like that, be fair!

GEORGE. We want Michael back. We must invent this third person. Make up your mind to tell this lie or else I shall tell them the truth.

MADELEINE. You're mad!

GEORGE. I am a father who is saving his son from falling into a trap he fell into himself.

MADELEINE. You're lying! You're not a father! You're a man who's been turned down and who is trying to get his own back!

GEORGE. I forbid you . . .

MADELEINE, *going for him*. Yes, you liar, you liar! *He pushes her back*. I don't mind you knocking me about, I prefer it even, but don't tell me it's because of your son! You don't give a damn whether he's happy or unhappy, you're jealous!

GEORGE. For the last time! Which story is it to be?

MADELEINE. The truth!

GEORGE. All right. I hope you realise the implications of the truth?

MADELEINE. No . . . no . . . don't . . . don't tell him . . . I was mad . . . If he doesn't know . . . there is still hope . . . even if he leaves me . . . there must be a chance . . . but if he knows, I've lost everything.

GEORGE. You see, I was right.

MADELEINE. I shall never have the strength.

GEORGE. I'll help you.

MADELEINE, *her eyes shut, in a whisper*. This is in-cre*dd*ible . . .

GEORGE. Don't you think it was "in-cre*dd*ible" for me yesterday, when Michael told me that he loved you, that you were his mistress, referring to me as "the old bloke"?

MADELEINE, *in tears for the first time*. He was so proud of you, of your youth . . .

GEORGE, *through his teeth*. *You* were my youth . . .

MADELEINE. Be generous, George! It's his turn to live!

GEORGE, *icily*. May I repeat this is not a personal question. All I am trying to do is to save my son's future and to guide it in the right direction.

MADELEINE. You're lying . . . you're lying . . . you're cold and hard and inhuman, all of you . . . only Michael is human . . . and you're going to destroy him . . .

GEORGE. Have you made up your mind? *Silence*. Do I tell them the truth?

MADELEINE, *with an outcry*. No!

GEORGE. You'll do as you're told?

MADELEINE. Yes.

GEORGE. You swear it?

MADELEINE. Yes.

GEORGE. Swear it on Michael.

MADELEINE. Yes.

GEORGE. "I swear it . . ."

MADELEINE. I swear it . . . on Michael. I once tried to kill myself. I've no need to try again. I'll just die.

GEORGE. Thank you for not blackmailing me with suicide. You'll live. You'll work. And you'll forget Michael.

MADELEINE, *very quietly.* Never.

GEORGE. I see. GEORGE *begins to climb up the staircase. He opens the attic door and calls.* All right. *Without waiting for them, he climbs down and moves over to the far side of the divan where* MADELEINE *first saw him.* YVONNE *appears first, followed by* LEO *and* MICHAEL.

MICHAEL. Is it animal, vegetable, or mineral?

GEORGE. Michael—I'm afraid you're going to be hurt.

MICHAEL. Hurt? *He turns towards* MADELEINE *and sees the state she is in.* Madeleine! What's the matter, darling?

GEORGE. I've had a long and very interesting talk with your friend.

MICHAEL. Madeleine can't have told you anything I haven't told you already.

GEORGE. She couldn't bear to hurt you, but talking to me she summoned up her courage. Apparently there is somebody else.

MICHAEL. No one is more sorry than Madeleine about that. Tomorrow everything will be in order; isn't that so, Madeleine?

GEORGE. Forgive me if I do the talking; I promised her I'd do that. She is quite prepared to sacrifice the man you're thinking of . . . That leaves the other one.

MICHAEL. Which other one?

GEORGE. As far as you knew, there were two of you. There are three.

MICHAEL. Three . . . ? What are you talking about?

GEORGE. Look here, Michael, you are young, very young. You don't know women, and you don't know much about life. This young woman is in love——

MICHAEL. With me!

GEORGE. She may be in love with you. I don't wish to dispute that. I don't wish to discuss it either. But she is utterly dependent, she's a slave if you like, of another man—a man of her own age, a man she never let you meet because she's ashamed of him. She only wants to marry you to insure her social position.

MICHAEL. That's a lie, an invention; I know Madeleine! Madeleine! Tell them it isn't true! *Silence.* I know Madeleine's life from A to Z. You're lying!

YVONNE. Michael!

MICHAEL. Madeleine! Help me! Tell them they're lying! Tell them to go to hell!

GEORGE. I realize this is a great blow to you, but . . . has it ever occurred to you that you saw very little of this young woman, you only saw her in the day, her nights were free . . .

MICHAEL. But who, who?

GEORGE. She says you don't know him. She was hoping for a miracle. She's tried everything. That fellow has a hold over her. It's an old story.

MICHAEL. If that's true! *He rushes at* MADELEINE. Tell me, you . . .

YVONNE. Michael! You're losing your head! You can't hit a woman . . .

MICHAEL. Can't I!! *He raises his hand but face to face with* MADELEINE, *he falls on his knees and buries his face in her lap.* MADELEINE *is clinging helplessly to a bookshelf, her body shaking with sobs.* Madeleine, forgive me . . . I know they're lying . . . I know they only want to know if I love you . . . tell me you forgive me . . . I beg you . . . I was forgetting last night . . . as if you could deceive me! As if our marriage could be a plot!

GEORGE. I didn't say that. I said she couldn't give up this other man.

MICHAEL. But I don't understand . . . everything was wonderful, and I didn't know . . . I swallowed it all . . . Who is he? Tell me? Who is he?

GEORGE. She says you don't know him . . . you can't possibly know him.

MICHAEL, *rushing over to his mother.* You were right in everything you said. And I wouldn't believe you!

YVONNE. My love, mothers always know. They seem foolish, unbearable spoilsports—but they know. Come! You've still got your old mother. There . . . there . . .

MICHAEL, *freeing himself and turning back to* MADELEINE. Once more, Madeleine, answer me! It's a lie, isn't it, it's a nightmare, wake me up, shake me . . . Madeleine!

YVONNE. Michael—try to keep calm!

MICHAEL. Calm! I kept saying to myself: Daddy is discovering how wonderful Madeleine is, he'll help to convince Mother. Aunt Leo is already on our side. And I find a woman who confesses her past, a hypocrite, an abomination . . .

MADELEINE, *without a voice.* Michael——

MICHAEL. And she dares open her mouth! She dares to speak to me!

YVONNE. Michael, don't! This lady could have gone on with the game if she'd wanted to, she could have bamboozled your father, entered our home under false pretenses. Instead—she has been decent enough to warn us in time. *To* MADELEINE. May I thank you on our behalf. If at any time . . .

MADELEINE. Enough!! I can't stand any more! I can't stand it! *She turns to the staircase, stumbles up the stairs and into the attic, banging the door behind her.*

MICHAEL. Madeleine!

GEORGE. Michael!

YVONNE. Michael, my boy——

MICHAEL. Take me away, I want to go home . . . no! I'll stay here. *He sits down on the divan.* I want to know it all!

GEORGE. What for?

MICHAEL. You're right. I don't want to know anything. I want to go home. I want my room . . .

YVONNE. No one will disturb you. *I'll* look after you.

MICHAEL. I should never have left the Caravan.

YVONNE. You needed this experience.

MICHAEL. I could have done without it, thank you. How wise you are, never to go out. People are vile.

YVONNE. Not all of them, Michael——

MICHAEL. All of them! *He looks around.* What order, eh, Leo! Not a chance of getting the visits mixed up, no forgotten umbrellas or shirts or hats or cigarette ends . . . but every modern convenience.

MADELEINE *appears on the top step. She can hardly stand on her feet.*

MADELEINE, *imploring.* Will you please go . . .

MICHAEL. Number three is getting impatient. Don't go. *I'm* taking my time now. And this woman has dared to tell me she was in love with me. She loves us all! A mighty big heart. There's room in it for everybody. Bitch!

MADELEINE *trips up on one of the steps. For a moment it looks as if she has fainted.* LEO *rushes over to her, as she comes to, guides her gently towards the divan which* MICHAEL *vacates contemptuously.*

YVONNE. Mick, my boy . . .

MICHAEL. Never mind, Leo. Leave her alone. Let her faint. It's an act.

YVONNE. Don't be hard. She needn't have told us anything.

GEORGE *slips out into the hall.*

MICHAEL. If Dad hadn't found her out, she'd have taken me in completely. Deeper and deeper into the muck. It's good to know there are some people left who care for you, who don't know anything about plots and frame-ups. Come on. I want to get out of here. Where is Dad?

LEO, *drily.* Gone. He doesn't like scenes.

MICHAEL. His inventions don't get him into lovely little surprises like this.

YVONNE. Darling—you're trembling . . .

MICHAEL. I'm *not* trembling!

YVONNE. Yes, you are . . . here, come home with me . . . we'll go down together.

MICHAEL *exits.*

Following him. Leo . . . we can't leave this child all alone in such a state.

LEO. Take Michael home . . . I'll stay here for a minute.

YVONNE. Thank you, Leo.

YVONNE *exits. The door of the flat is heard to close.*

MADELEINE. Michael . . . Michael . . . darling . . . please don't go . . . please!!

LEO. There . . . there . . . pull yourself together . . . Try and lie down a bit . . . ?

MADELEINE. Oh, please . . . please . . . oh, God . . . I can't, I can't . . .

LEO. Listen to me, my dear . . . try and listen to me.

MADELEINE. I can't . . . I can't . . . you've no idea . . .

LEO. Yes, I have . . . I've guessed.

MADELEINE. What . . . ?

LEO. That the "old bloke" and Michael's father are one and the same person.

MADELEINE. Oh, my God—How could you possibly know?

LEO. Well, my dear child, not to notice you'd have to be blind, as blind as my sister and Michael. The truth hit you in the eye. I tell you, it could only have escaped people like Michael and Yvonne.

MADELEINE. It would have killed me . . . if Michael had found out.

LEO. And this third person, this Number Three . . . he is a myth? I mean to say, he doesn't exist, does he?

MADELEINE. Oh, no . . . he does *not* exist . . . and Michael didn't even try to find out, he didn't doubt it at all; he swallowed this grotesque story without a moment's thought, otherwise he must have known it was a lie.

LEO. That was a bit of luck. If he'd been capable of thinking clearly, he might have suddenly discovered the truth . . . So George bullied you, threatened to give the show away . . .

MADELEINE. Yes, he did.

LEO. He would have done it, too.

MADELEINE. I'd have put up with anything rather than that—even losing Michael . . .

LEO. Funny . . . I thought George would give in to his son and implore *you* to keep quiet.

MADELEINE. He tortured me . . . he threatened me all the time . . . He wanted to 'cure' Michael, he said . . . he had it all prepared . . . this lie . . . he had it all worked out . . .

LEO, *grimly*. Damn it all—there are limits. *She takes* MADELEINE'S *hands*.

MADELEINE. Thank you . . . thank you . . . I never hoped . . .

LEO. Sh—don't talk about it. I like you very much. You've made quite a conquest of me. I had no more confidence in Michael's choice of women than in George's. I didn't come here as your ally, still less as your accomplice. Now I should like to be both. I am coming over to your side.

MADELEINE. Oh, what's the good . . . it's all over . . . Perhaps he's right . . . perhaps I don't belong to your class . . .

LEO. What class? Don't be silly. Now listen to me . . . Madeleine . . . *She shakes her.* Listen to me, Madeleine: tomorrow at five o'clock, you'll come to the Caravan . . .

MADELEINE. . . . the Caravan . . .

LEO. To us. To George.

MADELEINE. Who? Me?

LEO. Yes, you.

MADELEINE. They'll throw me out.

LEO. No, they won't.

MADELEINE. I can't believe it . . .

LEO, *putting lipstick on, and talking with the grimaces of a woman thus occupied.* You know, there are moments when love revolts me. There are others when it stirs me to the depths of my being and gets the better of me. Who knows what goes on inside us? That's Greek, I suppose. Don't try to understand me, I'm a pedantic kind of person.

MADELEINE. George will give away everything!

LEO. George will shut up. Leave that to me.

MADELEINE. He swore he would——

LEO. He was jealous. Tomorrow he'll be the noble father who protects his son.

MADELEINE. He was a brute.

LEO, *wincing slightly*. No, my dear. George isn't a brute. George is a child, he doesn't know what he's doing. He might easily break somebody's heart without realizing it at all.

MADELEINE. You're very kind . . .

LEO. No, I'm not. I hate disorder, that's all. I am disgusted by the mess that George has left behind him. It must be sorted out, washed, dried and ironed. Come tomorrow!

MADELEINE. But——

LEO. No buts. At five o'clock. It's an order. Swear it on Michael.

MADELEINE, *with the first faint suggestion of a smile.* . . . on Michael . . .

LEO. I swear . . .

MADELEINE. I swear.

LEO. On Michael. . . .

MADELEINE. On Michael.

LEO. Splendid. Now try and get some sleep. I want you to look your very best tomorrow. Don't you get your eyes red. Here's the address. *She gives it to* MADELEINE.

MADELEINE. After this nightmare——

LEO, *getting up.* That's all over and done with. I've adopted you. From now on you're under my very special protection. All right, child?

MADELEINE. Aunt Leo. . . .

LEO. That's what I wanted to hear. *She walks toward the door.* Don't move, I can find my way out.

MADELEINE. Please let me say how——

LEO. No, dear, don't! As far as I'm concerned, all these thanks and thank-yous and thank you so much . . . *She shrugs her shoulders significantly and shuts the door behind her, the curtain coming down already over her last words.*

CURTAIN

ACT THREE

SCENE: YVONNE'S *bedroom. The same as in Act One.*
To start with, the stage is in considerable darkness, but it becomes gradually lighter as if the eye was getting used to the dark.
The usual state of disorder.

LEO, *to* GEORGE *who enters through the door upstage left.* Still the same?

GEORGE. Still the same. I can't bear to stay in my own room. I'm in a bad way myself, and I'm afraid I shall soon be behaving like Michael.

LEO. I can't bear it in my room either. I can hear Mick groaning and banging on the floor. I can't say I am in hysterics like the rest of you, I just feel I am at the other end of the world, far away from something that is about to happen, and I feel it's going to happen to Yvonne. Now if *I* go off the rails, that *will* be the end.

GEORGE. There's no air in this place.

LEO. Is Yvonne with Michael?

GEORGE. Yes. Impossible to get a word out of him. I never thought him capable of suffering like this. It's beastly. And I've got to control myself, when *I* feel I can hardly bear it another minute.

LEO. It's the first time he's been in love, the first time he's really suffered.

GEORGE, *a little bitter.* Well, of course, if you manage to control yourself, you don't get any sympathy.

LEO. No one in the world, George, could understand you better and be more sorry for you than I am. But I simply refuse to compare your feelings, however tough it may be for you, to what this boy is going through. He's had no idea what it means to be unhappy, and now from one day to another——

GEORGE. He's got Yvonne . . .

LEO. No really, George . . .

GEORGE. I mean it! He has Yvonne. He doesn't say anything to her, but he snuggles up against her. It's instinctive. And Yvonne is triumphant. She's "found him again." She's found her son again. That's all she can say. And there was I, pouring out my heart to her, making a special effort to tell her everything, making a fool of myself, and she didn't even notice. She didn't show any surprise at all. She only thinks of Michael, of the danger that he might hear something, and she keeps asking me to be careful of what I am saying. As far as I was concerned, she just looked vaguely into the distance and said: "That is your punishment, my poor George . . . that is your punishment." That is the wife I "find" again, that "finds" me again and helps me to get over it . . .

LEO, *sarcastically.* That this story wouldn't upset her unduly was to be expected, I suppose. That father and son, each in turn, meet the same girl, without knowing it, and play hide-and-seek with each other, is probably an everyday occurrence in Yvonne's world. And as far as your punishment is concerned, she is perhaps not altogether wrong.

GEORGE. Well, I like that! Punishment indeed! Punishment for what?

LEO. George, I stayed behind with the girl after you'd all gone. I talked to her, and she talked to me, that is, as far as she was able to, considering the state she was in.

GEORGE. Well?

LEO. George, what you did was inhuman!

GEORGE. Say that again . . .

LEO. George, what you did was inhuman!

GEORGE. How d'you mean what *I* did? Leo, what *you* did! It was you who told me what to do, who invented the whole plot!

LEO. I advise you never to say that again, never as long as you live to say anything which sounds like it!

GEORGE. It's in-cre*dd*ible!

LEO. You and your "incredible"! I've heard that girl say it herself and she didn't say it at all as I expected. What I heard and saw there, wasn't distorted by the haze of this Caravan. I made a mistake, I admit it. Your whole story didn't look very genuine to me at the time, in fact I thought it was rather cockeyed. And perhaps you won't be very much surprised if I confess that I had precious little confidence in yours and Michael's taste as far as the choice of a wife was concerned. I pictured your young woman as a tart, a little gold digger, leading you around by the nose! I was wrong. I regret it.

GEORGE. Madeleine's taken you in, too.

LEO. No, my dear George, no. She hasn't taken me in. She wouldn't know how. She is a child, an unhappy child.

GEORGE. Oh, superb! This young lady deceives me with Michael, she deceives Michael with . . .

LEO. You aren't going to believe in a ghost you invented yourself!

GEORGE. That *we* invented, that *you* invented.

LEO. George!

GEORGE. All right, all right . . . that *I* invented. But, dearest Leo, perhaps neither of us invented anything: a woman who is capable of——

LEO, *interrupting*. Look, you're not going to believe this atrocity now, just because it suits you!

GEORGE. Superb! Superb! Now she's being canonized! Madeleine is a Saint!

LEO. She is young and she loves Michael and she is quite fond of you . . . poor George. That's your share of the bargain. It suddenly occurred to me how we went to this child—yes I say that on purpose—we went there with our old habits, our selfishness, our manias, all set to wipe out youth and order . . . the future, in fact.

GEORGE. So that's how she's got you—with her order!

LEO. George, will you get into your head that there's no question of getting or not getting me. The point is to put right the wrong that I have done . . .

GEORGE. Ah!

LEO. I'm so confused I don't know any more what I'm saying. What I mean is that we must make good the wrong that *you* have done, that *we* have done, that poor Yvonne has done without realizing it. And we must do it at any cost!

GEORGE. Go back on yesterday? Not on your life! Never!

LEO. I am sorry, but I must make you understand. Yvonne must pay for this, and so must you.

GEORGE. And you? What about you? Here you are setting yourself up as a judge and making everybody pay! Where's your share in this beastly affair? Are you sacrificing yourself the least little bit?

LEO. That happened long ago.

GEORGE. What d'you mean "that happened long ago"?

LEO. I mean: how do you know I haven't had my share and bought the right to call on you for yours?

GEORGE. What share, what sacrifice are you talking about, I'd like to know.

LEO. I was very much in love with you, George. Who knows, perhaps I still am. I believed I was sacrificing myself for the sake of your happiness. Well, I was wrong. But this time, I am not wrong. It is inconceivable that you should sacrifice Michael and that poor girl just like that, so that you can all carry on as if nothing had happened. It's contemptible.

GEORGE, *trying to take her hand.* Leo . . .

LEO. No, please . . . let's have no sentimentalities, no thank-yous. I can do without them. We must make Yvonne see this, George. We must bring Madeleine here. It is essential. She must come here.

GEORGE. Bring her here? But my poor Leo, even supposing for a moment that I'd put up with the torture of having these lovers here, Yvonne would never agree to it, she'd shout, she'd scream, she's "found him again," she's "found her Mick again" . . . you try and take him away from her.

LEO. She's found a wreck. She'll soon realize that.

GEORGE. She'd rather hang on to him dead than see him go off alive with someone else.

LEO. If that's true, you must act. I know you, you won't tolerate anything so inhuman and unspeakable.

GEORGE. But—what shall we tell Michael?

LEO. That's easy. We shall tell him that Madeleine's been wonderful— by the way, that's not saying too much—that she invented this third person to set Michael free, to return him to the bosom of his family. You'll see, he'll only love her all the more. She deserves it.

GEORGE. I didn't know you had such a big heart . . .

LEO. My heart was no use to anybody. It's the first time it serves some purpose. I love Michael. He's your son.

GEORGE, *slightly cynical.* And Yvonne? Do you love her too, Leo? Do your plans include her happiness, too?

LEO, *coolly.* Don't search too deeply into the heart, George. That's a thing one mustn't do. You might find a bit of everything. Don't search too deeply into my heart, nor into yours.

Silence.

GEORGE. If we do this, it's a complete contradiction of everything we did yesterday.

LEO. I like contradicting myself! It's my only luxury, my own private disorder, do let me keep it. Oh, let's stop pretending, George, you know as well as I do, this family of ours is a wreck, its days are gone. It's only a shadow of that blind, idiotic force that goes crushing every dream, every hope, every chance of happiness, with its "narrow path" and its "inflexible middle class morality." I don't want to preach, George, but let's seize our opportunity, let's salvage something out of the wreck. Let's choose our own path, by all means, but don't let's prevent the others from choosing theirs . . .

GEORGE, *lowering his head.* Leo—I believe you're right.

LEO, *kindly, as if talking to a good little boy.* George—I love you.

On this last word, the door opens and YVONNE *enters. She is dressed in her bathrobe of Act I, and her hair is disheveled.*

GEORGE. We were waiting for you here. We were hoping he'd relax being alone with you. Leo could hear him right through the door.

YVONNE. It's hell.

LEO. Did he speak to you?

YVONNE. No. He held my hand so tightly, he nearly crushed it. I wanted to stroke his hair. I stupidly asked him if he was thirsty. He said: "Go away." I waited at the door hoping he would call me back. He said again: "Go away." It's hell. I can't stand any more. I can't!

GEORGE. Shall *I* go to him?

YVONNE. If he sends *me* away, it means he doesn't want anybody. He doesn't want to be pitied, to be touched, he doesn't want anybody to see him . . .

GEORGE. He's had a terrible shock.

YVONNE. If that woman wasn't a prostitute, I'd send for her, I'd give her to him. That's what I've come to.

LEO. That's easy to say now.

YVONNE. No, Leo . . . that's not easy to say. For me to say it, I must be pretty well finished.

LEO. You'd give her to him . . . ?

YVONNE. Anything . . . yes . . . I can't go on like this any more.

LEO. Well, Yvonne, that's what I've been wanting to hear you say. I didn't want to say it first, nor did I want George to make you say it. Go on, tell her, George!

YVONNE. More words!

GEORGE. No, Yvonne. I don't know if you consider my confession to you nothing but words, but what I have to tell you is much more serious that that.

YVONNE. What can be more serious than the state we're in now?

GEORGE. The fact that the state we're in, is the direct result of a crime, and that I happen to be the criminal.

YVONNE. You?

GEORGE. Yvonne—Madeleine is innocent. The mysterious stranger does not exist.

YVONNE. I'm afraid I don't understand . . .

GEORGE, *handing over to* LEO. Leo . . .

LEO. As you know, I stayed alone with her yesterday . . .

YVONNE. And she's fooled you? My innocent sister! And George, the victim, has become the criminal.

GEORGE. Let me do it, Leo. I'd like to get the whole thing off my chest. This is it, Yvonne: I forced that poor girl to lie. I invented the whole miserable story. I made the most of Michael being ready to believe anything and of Madeleine being terrified that he'd find out the truth.

YVONNE. You did that?

GEORGE. I did that. I swear it.

YVONNE. George, you might have killed Michael!

GEORGE. What I did is not much better. That's why I said "crime." I might have killed Madeleine walking in on her like that. And after I got her into the state which you took for nerves, I took advantage of the tête-à-tête that you insisted on and completely finished her off. Nice going, eh! My best invention, the only one that really worked. And I was proud of it. Until Leo came and rubbed my nose in it.

LEO. George . . . no! I want to be fair. If it hadn't been for me——

GEORGE. If it hadn't been for you, I'd have gone on with it. No, Leo, I want to take the responsibility and I want to take it alone. It is almost as if the Caravan—exercises a kind of charm . . . *He turns to* YVONNE *and kisses her.* . . . Yvonne's charm . . . and makes us all deaf and blind. We were just talking about it before you came in. That's why when you said you'd give her to him it took such a weight off our minds. I admit I was afraid I'd have to fight you for it.

YVONNE. George, you're indulging in a positive orgy of self-humiliation. Leo is much too clearheaded, she knows what I mean. Take care, this time it's you who are daydreaming! And I, the notorious sleepwalker and fortuneteller of this Caravan, I am the one who sees clearly for a change. What's done is done. Neither Michael nor this young woman are dead. They're going through a crisis, like yourself, like all of us. The wise thing to do is to say: "nothing has happened that we were afraid would happen" and make the most of our luck.

GEORGE. Our luck! What luck? Are you aware of the words you're using?

YVONNE. I'm using the words that come to me most naturally. I'm a mother who loves her son, and I'm not a bit sublime. I agree you did wrong, perhaps, possibly, yes, but on the whole we've been lucky, yes, lucky, to get out of it safe and sound.

GEORGE. Five minutes ago, you said with a dying voice: "It's hell, I can't stand any more, I'm finished!"

YVONNE. Exactly! It's because I can't stand any more, because I'm finished that I've got just about enough strength to say stop before you restart something which is finished and done with. I repeat, I, the village idiot, that we've been very lucky in this unfortunate business, that we must make the most of our luck and let sleeping dogs lie.

LEO. But, Yvonne, what is this luck you're talking about?

YVONNE. Well . . . for instance . . . it was a bit of luck that the old bloke in question happened to be George.

GEORGE. Thanks very much.

YVONNE. Because if it had been someone else . . . I know you, George . . . you'd have gone all sentimental and given in.

GEORGE. Sentimental? I was trying to get my own back in the lowest possible way, pretending to myself that I was doing you a service, that I was carrying out your instructions . . .

LEO. My dear Yvonne, your point is lost on George; I'm afraid you two misunderstand each other.

GEORGE. I don't misunderstand, I don't understand at all.

LEO. You see? *To* GEORGE. This is what Yvonne has in mind, if I'm not mistaken: she thinks it's a bit of luck, in spite of what has been done to Madeleine, that Michael now feels this marriage is impossible.

YVONNE. But . . .

LEO. Just a second—and George, on the other hand, is trying to prove to you that there is now no reason to stop it.

YVONNE. To stop what?

GEORGE. To stop Michael and Madeleine's love.

YVONNE. What was that you said?

GEORGE. I am saying, that we very nearly killed these children out of selfishness and that it is high time to bring them back to life, that's what I'm saying.

YVONNE. You are saying this . . . you!

GEORGE. Yvonne, this is the moment to tell the truth and nothing but the truth: I never had anything from Madeleine; yes I did, I want to be fair, she was very fond of me, but I pretended there was more to it than that, and I kept on pretending, I just refused to appreciate her frankness. I forced her to drag this wretched lie around when all she did was to ask me to face up to the truth. However, all this would only be serious now, if by some misfortune Michael should hear of it . . .

YVONNE. That would be terrible!

GEORGE. At least, we agree on that.

LEO. And you're going to agree on the rest as well.

YVONNE. George, do you honestly think, you and Leo, have you considered calmly and dispassionately, this person could bear our name, could fit into our class?

GEORGE. Your grandfather collected semicolons, her grandfather was a bookbinder; my dear Yvonne, I can see there a certain . . .

YVONNE. I'm not joking; I'm asking you . . .

GEORGE. Well, don't ask me to consider seriously anything so absurd! Classes! Families! To listen to you, one might think we were the issue of Jupiter's thigh! I am a second-rate inventor, a failure. You are a sick woman who lives in the dark. Leo has remained an old maid because . . . because she wants to be with us when we need her help. And it's in the name of all this, of all this tradition of incompetence and failure, that you would refuse Michael some air, some space, and a chance to make a success of his life. No, Yvonne, I won't have it.

LEO. Bravo, George!

YVONNE. Ah, of course! George is a god! He's infallible!

LEO. I admire him.

YVONNE. Why don't you say you're in love with him.

GEORGE. Yvonne!

YVONNE. Go on! Get married! The lot of you! I'll go away . . . you can take my place . . . no trouble at all . . .

LEO. Are you going mad?

YVONNE, *full of contrition suddenly.* Yes, Leo, I *am* going mad; don't be angry with me.

LEO. I'm not angry with you.

YVONNE. Thank you. I'm sorry.

LEO. Let's cut out the thank-yous and the apologies, shall we? Listen to me, Yvonne: if I had really wanted George, I wouldn't have let you take him. It's far too late to start that up again. There's only one way to salvage our wreck and that is to save Michael, to listen to George, to tell Michael the good news and bring him back to life.

YVONNE. Is that what you call life?

GEORGE. Don't pretend you could go on enduring Michael in his present state. So what are you waiting for, Yvonne? *Pause.*

YVONNE. Anyway, this girl is much too young.

LEO. I beg your pardon . . .

GEORGE. She's three years older than Michael. Yesterday you said she was too old.

YVONNE. She is too young . . . compared with me.

GEORGE. Well, I'm damned!

YVONNE. You're asking the impossible.

GEORGE. We asked Madeleine to do the impossible, and she did it.

YVONNE. I've found Mick again, I can't let him go.

GEORGE. You won't find Michael again until you give him Madeleine. The Michael you think you have found no longer exists. If you let him go on thinking that Madeleine is deceiving him—which is abominable and which I will not stand—something inside him would doubt and go on living with her. You wouldn't benefit by the criminal thing you've done.

LEO. If I understand you rightly: your ideal would be to have an invalid son, so that he could never leave the house.

YVONNE, *broken, bursting into tears.* It's too much . . . it's too much for me!

GEORGE. Nothing is too much when you love somebody. You love Michael. Think of seeing him grateful and happy, instead of having him bitter and ill.

LEO. Or he'll probably marry some dreadful girl, which will be much worse.

GEORGE, *putting his arm round her shoulder.* Yvonne—show you've got a heart! YVONNE *breaks away from* GEORGE *and jumps on her bed where she hops about on her knees and points her hand accusingly at* GEORGE.

YVONNE. Leave me alone! Come off your pedestals, both of you! You aren't any better than me! Lies, nothing but lies everywhere! *To* GEORGE. You, try and get out of this one: Yesterday, when we got to that woman's flat, I remember perfectly—you went so far as to put on an act about the wrong floor, you pretended you didn't know her floor! You were trying to fool me, and you nearly did it. You dared to take me to your mistress!

GEORGE. You know very well . . .

YVONNE. Yes! To your mistress!

GEORGE. Shut up, Yvonne! You're losing your head; d'you want the boy to hear you?

YVONNE. I know what to tell him!

GEORGE, *very quietly.* Yvonne—it isn't very often that we can make up for what we have done . . . we can save ourselves and two other people . . . Darling, say you agree!

YVONNE. Again we'd have to summon the boy . . . make our way back to that woman . . . humiliate ourselves . . .

GEORGE. For Heaven's sake! Nobody's going to "summon" Michael and tell him to "follow his father into the study"; all you have to do is to run to his room, give him a kiss, and you'll work a miracle.

LEO. As regards Madeleine, at my own risk and peril, I've been taking care of that.

YVONNE, *going straight for* LEO. What business is that of yours? What have you done?

LEO. My duty. I talked to her, listened to her, I consoled her. I even telephoned her.

YVONNE, *stressing every syllable.* You telephoned her?

LEO. To come here. *She quickly goes to her room.*

YVONNE. So that's what you two have been plotting!

GEORGE. That's what Leo's been plotting without my knowledge and for which I'm very grateful to her.

YVONNE. You want to force my hand.

GEORGE. We want to save you, and us, and Michael.

YVONNE. So she gets what she's been after; she'll be in possession here.

GEORGE. Please don't talk like that; it's so bad.

YVONNE. You've all become Saints.

GEORGE. Yvonne!

YVONNE. Give me time. Don't rush me!

GEORGE. I thought you might realize the effort I have to make myself.

YVONNE. Poor old boy . . .

GEORGE. Poor old girl . . . we're not old, Yvonne, neither of us, and yet . . .

YVONNE. And yet one day one finds the children are growing up and want to take over from us.

GEORGE. That's in the order of things.

YVONNE, *with a tired smile.* I'm afraid order isn't my strong point.

GEORGE. It isn't mine, either. *He takes her hand.* Your hand is like ice.

YVONNE, *listless.* Oh that——

LEO, *re-entering, full of spirits.* Let's get ready for the party. Let's light the candles. That's the spirit! Mind we keep it up.

GEORGE. I am not much good at parties or surprises.

YVONNE. Oh, I don't know; I think you're doing fine.

LEO. Now then, now then, stop arguing.

GEORGE. Well, what do we do now?

LEO. It's quite simple. Yvonne, the good news must come from you, he must owe it to you.

YVONNE. But . . .

LEO. No buts.

YVONNE. But I'm not actually in favor of this . . .

LEO. You mustn't show it.

YVONNE. It'll look all wrong. Besides, I'm freezing cold. Look at me! Listen! My teeth are chattering.

LEO. It's your nerves.

YVONNE. One of these days I'll die and you'll say it's my nerves. My knees are wobbly.

LEO. Make an effort. It's got to be done.

GEORGE. Yes, it's got to be done, Yvonne. Think of the present you're going to put in his stocking.

YVONNE. If I can find one of them!

A door slams.

LEO. A door bang! That's Michael. That makes things much easier. You see? A "miracle"!

YVONNE. What are you doing to me . . .

GEORGE, *listening.* What's *he* doing? Where's he going?

LEO. What if he's going out?

GEORGE. He'd slam the other door.

LEO. That's right.

YVONNE, *very quietly, in a very clear voice.* He hasn't eaten anything since yesterday. He's at the sideboard. Now . . . he's coming to my door. He listens . . . he puts his hand on the door knob . . .

The door knob begins to turn.

The door's opening . . .

The door opens slowly.

I'm afraid . . . as if it wasn't Michael . . . as if it was something . . . something awful . . . Leo, George . . . what's happening to me? *She clings to* LEO *and* GEORGE *as if in terror of something invisible; suddenly she calls out.* Mick!

MICHAEL *enters, leaving the door open. He looks washed out, his eyes red and half-closed.*

MICHAEL. It's me, Sophie . . .

YVONNE. Well, come in . . . and shut the doors!

MICHAEL. What d'you mean the "doors"? All right, I'll shut the door. I'm going out again, anyway. I was looking for the sugar.

YVONNE. Well, you know where to find it.

MICHAEL. Yes, I know. Are you alone?

YVONNE. My poor darling, can't you see your aunt and your father?

MICHAEL. Oh! I'm sorry, Leo—sorry, Dad. I can't see a thing. Am I disturbing you? *He vanishes for a moment into the bathroom and re-emerges almost immediately munching some sugar.*

LEO. You're not disturbing us at all. As a matter of fact, your mother was just about to go and fetch you.

MICHAEL. I wanted to talk to you, Mother. Since I'd only have to repeat it all afterwards to Leo and Dad, I'll tell you all now. First of all, Sophie, I want to apologize for telling you to go away. I was sick of myself . . . I didn't want to . . . Well, you understand.

YVONNE, *melting away.* I understand perfectly, my poor Mick.

MICHAEL. Don't pity me!

GEORGE. What did you want to tell us, Michael?

MICHAEL, *eating his sugar, a little embarrassed.* Well . . . I can't go on like this . . . so I thought . . . Dad, you remember that job in Algiers, you said to me at the time, if I'd make up my mind . . .

YVONNE. You want to leave me?

MICHAEL. My mind's made up.

YVONNE. Mick!

MICHAEL. Oh, Sophie, I'm no good to anybody these days, and worse still, I'm beginning to get you all down . . .

YVONNE. You're mad!

MICHAEL. I'm going mad here in Paris. I can't stay here . . . I want to go far away and to go quickly. I'll get a job. I know a bit of everything and nothing properly. Suicide disgusts me. I must have a complete change . . .

YVONNE. What about me? What about all of us?

MICHAEL. Oh! Sophie!

YVONNE. Give me your hand . . . listen to me, Mick. Listen to me. Look at me. What if you didn't have to go?

GEORGE. What if we had some good news for you, for example?

MICHAEL. There's no such thing as good news any more, as far as I'm concerned.

LEO. That depends. What if the motive for your . . . departure was no longer valid?

YVONNE. What if your reasons for leaving us were no longer true?

MICHAEL. It's no use, Sophie. I'm going back to my room. Dad . . .

GEORGE. No, Michael, don't go back to your room and don't ask me to see what I can do about this job.

MICHAEL. You promised me . . .

GEORGE. Mick, I want to tell you some news, some very, very good news. Madeleine . . .

MICHAEL, *furiously.* Don't speak to me any more about that person! Never again! Just you leave that alone, d'you hear! Don't you see I can't take any more? So why don't you shut up!

LEO. Michael—listen to what your father has to say!

MICHAEL, *still more furiously.* Stop it, will you! Leave it alone! I forbid you to mention that person, d'you hear!

GEORGE. I'm sorry, I must speak to you about her. GEORGE *stops* MICHAEL *from leaving.*

MICHAEL. I'm not going to listen to you! I've had enough! *He kicks* YVONNE's *bed.*

GEORGE. Would you mind not kicking your mother's bed; she is ill. And stop shouting!

MICHAEL, *stubbornly.* What do you want?

GEORGE. Your aunt stayed behind yesterday, after we'd left.

MICHAEL. You're trying to trick me into staying in Paris by inventing lies. You're trying to stop me from making up my mind. You needn't bother; my mind is made up.

YVONNE, *in an outcry.* You're not going!

MICHAEL, *pointing at his mother.* You see!

GEORGE. You're not going because it would be criminal to go.

MICHAEL. Why criminal?

GEORGE. Because if your family doesn't count any longer, there is someone else to whom you should apologize and whom you ought to ask for permission to go, first.

MICHAEL, *with an ugly laugh, to* GEORGE. I see . . . how silly of me . . .

I've got it now: The lady had plenty of courage when *you* were talking
to her, but she lost it all when she was up against Leo. She realized she'd
found her match, so she turned on the charm.

LEO. I'm not easily taken in.

MICHAEL. I shall never believe anything again!

GEORGE. Well, you'd be wrong! Yvonne . . .

YVONNE. Do believe it, Mick! Do believe it!

MICHAEL. Don't torture me . . .

GEORGE. No one wants to torture you . . . not only is Madeleine innocent, but she's behaved admirably.

MICHAEL. In what way, for heaven's sake?

GEORGE. Michael—I'm afraid I owe you an apology. Yesterday, our
attitude was too much for Madeleine. She felt she wouldn't be able to
hold out against us. So she lied to me. I felt it but I turned a deaf
ear. Mick, *she invented the whole story* to set you free, to help us to get rid
of her.

MICHAEL. If that's true, would you have waited so long to tell me? Mother
would never have let me . . .

LEO, *interrupting.* Your mother didn't know before. We needed proof.
Actually, it was my fault, the delay. I was plotting something . . . I
was preparing a surprise for you.

MICHAEL. Mummy, you—you tell me.

YVONNE. I've already told you.

MICHAEL, *now fully convinced.* But then we must go to her, we must 'phone,
we must try and find her at once! She might have done something
frightful . . . Dad . . . Leo . . . quickly . . . where is she?

LEO, *pointing to the door.* Here.

YVONNE, *sitting bolt upright.* Here?

LEO. She's been waiting in my room since five o'clock.

At these words, MICHAEL *stands quite still as if rooted to the spot. He does not
see that* LEO *has opened the door and that* MADELEINE *appears in the opening.
He is covering his eyes with one hand while reaching out with the other as if he
wanted to hold on to something.* LEO'S *surprise has been a little too much for him.
While* YVONNE, LEO *and* GEORGE *are saying something,* MADELEINE, *who
has only eyes for* MICHAEL, *is rushing up to him. She takes his arm that is
searching for support and puts it around herself. She is holding him in her arms.
All her love, all her tenderness are in this gesture. She does not speak.*

YVONNE. Mick! Mick! Is he ill?

MADELEINE *does not speak. She tries but she can't. So she holds him closer still.*
MICHAEL *opens his eyes, as she gently pulls his hand from his face. He looks at*

MADELEINE *and as he looks, he slowly sinks to his knees. When he speaks, it is hardly more than a whisper.*

MICHAEL. Madeleine . . . my darling . . . forgive me, please . . .

MADELEINE, *kneeling down beside him, and smiling through her tears.* Michael, my love . . . will you forgive me . . . I've hurt you so much . . .

MICHAEL. No, Madeleine, it was me . . . I've been such a fool . . .

LEO. If I were you, children, I'd leave the explanations alone and start all over again.

During this, YVONNE *is making several brave attempts to join the group. She even manages to smile bravely at* MICHAEL's *happiness—but no one seems to notice her, and her expression changes to that of a child, lost and alone.*

GEORGE. Leo is right.

MICHAEL, *jumping to his feet and helping* MADELEINE *up.* Leo is terrific.

GEORGE. Leo most certainly is.

MADELEINE. I still can't believe this is true, this is really happening. . . .

MICHAEL. Nor can I. And I wanted to run away and take a job in Algiers!

MADELEINE. In Algiers?

GEORGE, *grinning.* Yes! While you were waiting in Leo's room, Michael came to us, with a face like an undertaker and sucking a piece of sugar at the same time, and said that he'd decided to live in Algiers.

YVONNE *tries once more to join the others. But no one sees her. All eyes are on* MICHAEL *and* MADELEINE.

LEO. When are you leaving, Michael?

MICHAEL. All right, I've asked for it.

GEORGE. He wouldn't listen to any of us, he just wouldn't!

MICHAEL. Dad—!

LEO. Shut up, George . . .

GEORGE. All right, all right. I shan't say another word.

MADELEINE. How kind you all are . . .

On this YVONNE, *who has slowly walked over to the bathroom, turns away from them all, and shuts the bathroom door behind her.*

MICHAEL, *taking* MADELEINE's *hand into his own.* You're cold?

MADELEINE. I suddenly turned cold when I saw you standing there like that. I couldn't help it. I think the shock was a bit too much. But it's all right now, I'm fine. I couldn't see anything at all, when I came in, except you.

GEORGE. You didn't see anything because nobody can see a thing in here. My wife detests strong light. Never turn on the top light whatever you do.

LEO, *whispering to* MICHAEL. Michael, your mother . . .

MICHAEL, *looking around.* Where's she got to?

MADELEINE. Perhaps that's my fault . . .

GEORGE. No, no, no! She was here a second ago.

LEO, *to* MICHAEL. You should have made a little more fuss over her!

MICHAEL. I thought she was here! Sophie!

GEORGE. Yvonne!

YVONNE, *from the bathroom*. I'm not lost. I'm here. I'm doing my injection.

MADELEINE, *calling to* YVONNE. Can I be of any help?

YVONNE. No, thanks. I'm used to being alone.

LEO. Yvonne can't bear people to help her. It's one of her manias.
    They all speak very hush-hush.

MADELEINE. Perhaps in time she'll let me . . .

MICHAEL. That would be a major victory.

LEO, *to* MADELEINE. Yvonne is very sensitive. Michael only had eyes for you, which is very natural, but . . . be careful, children.

MADELEINE. Exactly. I was afraid she'd gone because of me.

GEORGE. Of course not. Leo, don't make Yvonne out to be such a monster.

LEO. I'm not. I'm only warning Michael. In Madeleine's interest. He mustn't make Yvonne jealous.

GEORGE. That's right, frighten her now . . .

MICHAEL. No, Dad—Madeleine is very sensible.

MADELEINE. I'm not frightened, Michael, but I'm afraid . . .

GEORGE, *interrupting*. Sh—!
    The bathroom door opens. YVONNE, *standing in the shadow, leans against the door frame. She speaks in a strange voice.*

YVONNE. You see, my dear, how much I am loved? I've only to go out of the room for a second, and they're lost without me. I wasn't lost. I have to look after myself. *She goes to her bed and drops on to it.* Without insulin I'd be dead.

LEO, *whispering to* MICHAEL. Go and give her a kiss.

MICHAEL, *trying to pull* MADELEINE *with him*. Come with me.

MADELEINE, *pushing him*. No, no . . . go on . . .

GEORGE, *to* YVONNE. You're not ill, are you?

YVONNE, *with an effort*. N-no . . .

MICHAEL, *letting go of* MADELEINE *and coming to* YVONNE's *bed*. Sophie, are you happy?

YVONNE. Very. MICHAEL *tries to kiss her*. Don't be so rough! *To* MADELEINE. You'll be lucky, my dear, if Mick doesn't pull your hair out every time he kisses you.

LEO, *as if struck by an inspiration*. Michael, you ought to go and show Madeleine your famous room.

MICHAEL. I daren't!

MADELEINE. Michael! Are you refusing to show me your room?

MICHAEL. You'll start tidying up!

MADELEINE. Oh!

GEORGE. I'll come with you . . . I'll show you my electronic underwater submachine gun.

MICHAEL. We'll do her the honors of the Caravan. Forward march! *He opens the door and turns round again.* Sophie, we shall leave you with the representative of order. . . . Leo, try and stop Mummy from running us down behind our backs.

YVONNE. Mick! Don't go! Stay with me!

GEORGE, *rushing to her.* What's the matter? Yvonne! YVONNE *falls back.* Yvonne!

YVONNE. I'm so afraid. . . .

GEORGE. Afraid of what?

YVONNE. I'm so afraid . . . I'm horribly afraid . . . don't go . . . don't go! George, Mick, Mick! I'm so horribly afraid!

LEO. That's not the insulin . . . she has taken something else! *She rushes into the bathroom and returns almost immediately, shouting.* I knew it! *Turning to* YVONNE. What have you done? How could you! Yvonne!

YVONNE. My head's spinning . . . George, I've done a mad thing, a ghastly thing . . . I've . . .

MICHAEL. Mummy—tell me!

YVONNE. I can't . . . help me . . . save me, Mick . . . forgive me! I saw you all together, over there, in the corner . . . I thought I was in your way . . . I thought I was a nuisance to you. . . .

MICHAEL. Oh, Mummy!

GEORGE. Oh, my God!

YVONNE. I lost my head. I wanted to die. But I don't want to die any more. I want to live. I want to be with you. I want to see you both happy. Madeleine, I love you. I *will* love you. I promise! Try and do something. I want to live. I'm so afraid. Help me, please!

MADELEINE. Michael, don't just stand there!

GEORGE, *cutting in.* Run to the doctor upstairs.

MADELEINE, *to* MICHAEL, *who is in a daze.* Go on, darling, hurry!

GEORGE. I'll ring the specialist at the hospital!

MADELEINE *pushes* MICHAEL *gently. He runs off through the door upstage right. A door slams.*

Right through to the end of the Act, there is an incessant slamming of doors.

LEO, *to* GEORGE. Go and ring up. I'll stay here.

GEORGE *exits through the door.*

Feeling YVONNE's *pulse.* Her pulse is very weak, regular but weak. I knew something was going to happen. I felt it all the time.

MADELEINE, *slowly walking away from the bed,* LEO *following her.* This is all my fault. I ought not to be here. I ought to go.

LEO. Go where?

MADELEINE. I ought to leave Michael.

LEO. Don't be silly. Stay where you are. It's an order. Besides, Michael is going to need you. *As if suddenly struck by it.* Just as George is going to need me.

There is a moment's silence.

YVONNE, *her voice, weak but edgy.* I can hear you, Leo.

LEO. What can you hear?

YVONNE. I've heard you. You'd forgotten I could hear you.

LEO. Hear what?

YVONNE. Don't pretend you don't know. You want to get rid of me . . .

LEO, *interrupting.* Yvonne—!

YVONNE. I've poisoned myself, and I'll poison you, Leo! *To* MADELEINE. And I'll poison you! I saw you over there, in the corner . . . I saw you all. You wanted to put me on the scrap heap . . . that's what you wanted . . . you wanted . . . . You—Mick! Mick!

LEO, *very loudly.* George—!

GEORGE, *rushing in from the left.* The specialist's in the country, they're sending someone else.

LEO. George, Yvonne is delirious. . . .

YVONNE. No, Leo, I'm not delirious. They want to get rid of me. I see it all now. I'll—tell—ev'-ry-thing.

GEORGE, *kissing* YVONNE *on the lips, genuinely distressed.* Quiet, Yvonne, quiet please!

YVONNE. How many years . . . is it . . . since you . . . kissed me . . . on the lips . . . ? Are you only kissing them now to shut my mouth?

GEORGE, *trying to quieten her by caressing her.* There . . . there . . . there. . . .

YVONNE. I'll poison . . . your . . . lives . . . I'll tell Mick . . . every-thing . . .

MICHAEL, *rushing in.* No one at home, no answer!

YVONNE. Michael, listen to me . . . listen to me, Michael . . . I don't want . . . I want you . . . I want you to know. . . .

LEO, *as loudly as she can, while* YVONNE *is trying to speak.* Michael, your mother is delirious. Ring up the hospital again. Madeleine, my dear, go and help him, will you? He'll never find the number. Go on, hurry, there's not much time!

She pushes MICHAEL *and* MADELEINE *out of the room through the door upstage left, while* YVONNE *desperately tries to make herself heard.* LEO *returns to the foot of* YVONNE's *bed.* YVONNE *is now madly angry.*

YVONNE, *during the above.* Don't go, stay here . . . Mick, Mick . . . they're deceiving you . . . they're cheating you . . . they're sending you—away—under false—pretenses . . . you liars—I won't let you—get away with it. . . .

LEO. Yvonne—!

YVONNE, *lifting herself up with all the strength at her command.* It's you—it's you—it's all your doing. . . . You wanted me to die . . . you wanted to be alone with George. . . .

GEORGE. This is ghastly!

YVONNE. Yes! This is ghastly! And I—I . . . *She falls back.*

GEORGE. If only that doctor would come. Send Michael in a taxi!

LEO. He'd be bound to miss him.

GEORGE. But what shall we do?

LEO. Wait.

YVONNE, *opening her eyes.* Mick, are you there? Where are you?

GEORGE. He is here, he is coming.

YVONNE, *her voice sweet and charming.* I'll be good—I didn't mean to be un-kind. I saw you all . . . over there in the corner . . . I was so alone . . . everybody had forgotten me. I wanted to do you all a good turn . . . My head . . . George, pull up my pillow a bit . . . thank you. Is that you, Leo? And Madeleine? I'm going to love you, Madeleine . . . I want to live. I want to go on living with you . . . I want my Mick. . . .

LEO. You'll see how happy your Mick's going to be. Just try and stay quiet for a little. The doctor's on his way. We're looking after you.

YVONNE, *having a relapse.* You again! Always you! You and George! Have them arrested! I want to give evidence! Look—they're frightened to death. Don't touch me! Keep away from me! There they are! Come in! Come in! Michael! Michael! Help me! Michael! Michael! Michael! Michael! Michael! Michael! Michael! Michael! *Screams.* Michael! Michael! Michael! Michael! Michael! Michael! Mick, Mick, Mick . . . Mick . . . Mick . . . Mick! *Suddenly she is still and rigid.*

GEORGE *and* LEO, *during* YVONNE's *outburst.* Yvonne, I beg you, lie down! Don't do this! You're killing yourself! You're exhausting yourself com-pletely! Listen to me, listen to us! Try and help us!

LEO *is picking up one of* YVONNE's *pillows that has fallen to the floor while* YVONNE *has been having this attack. She now is about to put it again under*

YVONNE'S *head, but as she is lifting it,* YVONNE *ceases to shout.* LEO *puts her head down again slowly and drops the pillow. She looks at* GEORGE.

GEORGE. It's not possible. . . . GEORGE *sinks down and buries his face in the sheets of* YVONNE'S *bed.*

MICHAEL, *rushing in with* MADELEINE. Can't get any information at all, don't know if the doctor's on his way or what . . . I'll go down and see if he's coming.

LEO. It's no use, Michael.

There is a sudden silence.

Your mother is dead.

MICHAEL. What . . . *He is dazed for a moment, then he walks towards the bed.*

GEORGE, *raising his head.* My poor Mick . . .

Slowly, LEO *moves away from the bed.*

LEO, *very bitter.* Look at you! You'd give anything to bring her back to life, but you'd go on torturing her just the same.

MICHAEL, *furious.* You hated her!

LEO. Perhaps. And I loved her.

MICHAEL, *going for her.* You . . .

GEORGE. Michael, are you forgetting your mother!

MICHAEL, *stamping his foot.* Mother, mother! Sophie isn't my mother. She's my friend, the best friend I've ever had! *He rushes to the bed.* Tell them, Mummy, didn't you tell me a thousand times . . . *He tears* YVONNE'S *body into his arms and covers her face with kisses.*

MADELEINE, *rushing towards him and trying to pull him away.* Michael, you're mad . . .

The door bell rings.

MICHAEL, *utterly bewildered.* Oh God, I'd forgotten! I'll always forget . . . I'll never be able to realize it . . . never . . .

LEO *has crossed over to open the door.*

MICHAEL *looks like a little boy that is going to cry any minute.*

MADELEINE *holds him in her arms.*

MADELEINE. Michael . . . my darling . . . my love . . .

LEO, *slowly coming back.* It was the charwoman. I told her there is nothing for her to do, that everything is in order.

CURTAIN

Cecile, *or* The School for Fathers

by JEAN ANOUILH

English version by Luce and Arthur Klein

CHARACTERS

MONSIEUR ORLAS
CECILE, *his daughter*
ARAMINTHE, *governess of* CECILE
THE CHEVALIER
MONSIEUR DAMIENS, *father of* ARAMINTHE
VALETS *and* BODYGUARDS

A garden framed by boxed orange trees. The house is on the left, a small Chinese Pavilion on the right.

MONSIEUR ORLAS *is seated in the pavilion and* ARAMINTHE *is standing beside him. Costumes are either Louis XVth or perhaps Louis XVIth of the bourgeois class. In either case they are as false as possible.*

MONSIEUR ORLAS. Araminthe, I am very disturbed. I have always thought you were too young and much too charming to take care of my daughter.

ARAMINTHE. If you remember, Monsieur, there were four candidates for the position of governess. The three others were old and uglier than sin. Why then did you choose me, Monsieur?

MONSIEUR ORLAS. Precisely because you were young and beautiful. And yet sometimes I fear that I chose you only for my own sake. I could not bear the thought of dining with an old hag at my table. Still I believe I have been a bad father. I ought to have confided Cecile to an old dragon of a woman and to have borne it stoically. I ought to have taken my meals apart or else read the newspapers while eating.

ARAMINTHE. Among other things, Monsieur, you insisted that I teach Mademoiselle Cecile that nothing was more rude than to read while eating.

MONSIEUR ORLAS. I have been a fool! In the first place you are the same age.

ARAMINTHE. Mademoiselle Cecile is seventeen years old and I will soon be twenty-three.

MONSIEUR ORLAS. It is the same thing.

ARAMINTHE. Allow me to contradict you, Monsieur. I feel I have learned very many things in five years. And particularly to be suspicious of men.

MONSIEUR ORLAS, *suddenly.* Why do you say that to me?

ARAMINTHE. So that you will not be troubled by what seems to upset you. I am very capable of protecting Mademoiselle Cecile whose youth and inexperience could so easily be deceived by lovely words. You should at least give me credit, Monsieur, for not being deceived myself.

MONSIEUR ORLAS. I wonder why you insist on being so disagreeable with me, Araminthe?

ARAMINTHE. Have I said anything disagreeable?

MONSIEUR ORLAS. "You should at least give me credit, Monsieur, for not being deceived myself." Just what do you mean by that? That I try to deceive you? The rhetoric of young girls has always sounded Greek to me! It is true I have paid you several compliments! So what? You are no longer a child, Araminthe. You are twenty-three years old. I am a man for whom love has always been the chief interest, and although the father of Cecile I am still capable of loving. Thank God for that! Do you suppose it is easy to live in the same house with so ravishing a creature as yourself? To have you opposite me at table each day, to have you smile at me while Cecile is dreaming of heaven knows only what! . . . And then in the evening to have all three of us climb the stairs together to our respective rooms. And yours only next door to mine! I am a fool! I should have chosen a hag!

ARAMINTHE. You still have time.

MONSIEUR ORLAS. Yes, there is always time to make myself unhappy needlessly. I do not speak only of the grief Cecile would feel. You know how attached she is to you. But my entire existence would be saddened. I would gulp my meals to shorten the torture, and I would develop ulcers . . . You know what that does to one's temper. Besides I could never bear to know you were living in another home where you would be the prey to men's desires. You are a child, Araminthe. Do not forget you are only twenty-three! What do you know of life, my dear? Here you live with a well-bred gentleman who respects you. Imagine yourself governess of the baron's daughter who I know has suggested it. And on my life I wager two days would not pass before he came and knocked at your chamber door!

ARAMINTHE. Render unto Caesar the things which are Caesar's, Monsieur. You waited an entire week before you did it yourself!

MONSIEUR ORLAS. I am a well-bred man. Besides you did not open the door.

ARAMINTHE. As I would not open it for the baron were I to lose your confidence and find myself at his home.

MONSIEUR ORLAS. All the same you do not mean to compare me with this old fogy, this graybeard?

ARAMINTHE. I thought I heard you say you studied together and except for a year or so were the same age.

MONSIEUR ORLAS. Yes, but he looks it! I don't! Anyway that has no importance. Still if I had not paid you some attention one way or another you would have been the first to feel offended. I have come to know the contradictions in a woman's heart. *He rises thoughtfully.* I do not mind telling you, Araminthe, that I am very upset by this young chevalier. He comes here much too much.

ARAMINTHE. He loves your daughter and your daughter loves him.

MONSIEUR ORLAS. What do they know at their age? In the first place he doesn't have a sou! His father is in straitened circumstances besides which he already supports two older sons. And even if he made nuns out of his three daughters he still could not give the boy a sou! If his great-uncle died in time he might perhaps become a Knight of Malta. But that is all he can expect. Therefore from every point of view the marriage is an impossibility for him. I will not permit them to see each other!

ARAMINTHE. Then they will do so behind your back.

MONSIEUR ORLAS. Thunder and blazes, Mademoiselle, are you here to tell me that! You are here to prevent it!

ARAMINTHE. It would be beyond my powers even if I wanted to. Their passion will overcome all obstacles. And besides, Monsieur, I would not want to. I cannot see anyone in love unhappy.

MONSIEUR ORLAS. So you would find the suffering of this silly fop unbearable if I prevent him from seeing Cecile? And yet I have been pining away at your door these six months past, and it does not trouble you in the least! Does it?

ARAMINTHE. If I had opened my door to you, Monsieur, do you believe you still could have entrusted Mademoiselle Cecile to me?

MONSIEUR ORLAS. Do not confuse the issue. I simply demand that you be very strict with Cecile who is still a child, and . . .

ARAMINTHE. We are the same age.

MONSIEUR ORLAS. The same age? Ridiculous! You are twenty-three and she is only seventeen. In five years a young lady has the time to learn to know the world, to judge the virtue of a man and the sincerity of a feeling. I do not understand you, Araminthe. After all, you must plainly see that I am madly in love with you.

ARAMINTHE. Indeed, I believe that one cannot help but see it, Monsieur. You are as indiscreet about it as possible. I must exercise every ingenuity so that Mademoiselle Cecile will not perceive it. And if you do not stop trying to touch my knee under the table, one of these days you will surely touch hers!

MONSIEUR ORLAS. A friendly caress from her father would not astonish this child. I kiss her a hundred times a day.

ARAMINTHE. If she happened to suspect that this friendly caress from her father was meant for another knee, I fear she would be offended, Monsieur. And more seriously than your frivolousness is able to imagine.

MONSIEUR ORLAS, *grumbling dreamily.* My frivolousness . . . my frivolousness . . . *He asks in another tone.* So according to you, Araminthe, I am a bad father? I shall never get over it.

ARAMINTHE. You have the desire to be the best father in the world, Monsieur. And I believe it is my duty to see that at least this one of your desires is fulfilled. I assure you that is why I put my knees under my chair in the most uncomfortable of positions. And I never hear your little knocks on my door at night.

MONSIEUR ORLAS, *approaching her with a lascivious look in his eye.* And if I should put Cecile in a convent—and I mean a very gay convent—or if I should send her to spend some time with her Aunt who is a canoness? She would have many young cousins there with whom to play . . .

ARAMINTHE. Would you want to cause her this grief by separating her from her young chevalier? And furthermore, if Mademoiselle Cecile is gone then my place will no longer be in this home. I take care of her, Monsieur, but she takes care of me as well. We could not do without each other midst all the dangers that surround us.

MONSIEUR ORLAS, *sighs.* Life is an abyss full of contradictions, Araminthe! I am going into my study and think of all that. I am unwilling to believe that there is no solution and that duty and happiness can not be reconciled.

ARAMINTHE. I believe that is what men have always been seeking, Monsieur, ever since they left their caves to try and live in society. They have only invented marriage to try and reconcile these two notions for a time.

MONSIEUR ORLAS. For a very short time, Araminthe. Believe a man who has gone through the venutre. Afterwards it is like these chemical tests our neighbor Monsieur de Voltaire enjoys making. At first the mixture is very effervescent; then happiness which is vaporous vanishes like smoke, and the pipette contains only the large gray stone of duty. *He asks thoughtfully.* Is the chevalier coming again today?

ARAMINTHE. Just as every afternoon.

MONSIEUR ORLAS. Do not leave them alone for a minute! These children caress and embrace each other as soon as your back is turned.

ARAMINTHE. One does that at their age.

MONSIEUR ORLAS, *a bit dryly.* One does it at mine and yet I do without. *He starts to go, changes his mind, then goes to her.* You are too cruel, Araminthe. Let me take you just once in my arms?

ARAMINTHE, *pushing him back firmly and with a smile.* No, Monsieur. Not even for the tiniest second.

MONSIEUR ORLAS, *feeling vexed, starts to leave.* Be merciless with them! See that their chairs do not even touch! And keep a close eye on the tablecloth if they should take tea! It is so easy to stretch your leg under it.

Listen, Araminthe, why not teach my daughter how to sit on a chair so that no knee could possibly touch hers?

ARAMINTHE, *smiling*. I think such a gymnastic exercise is less important for her than for me, Monsieur.

MONSIEUR ORLAS, *exits with a sigh*. I am indeed an unhappy man, Araminthe.

THE CHEVALIER, *entering*. Araminthe!

ARAMINTHE. Monsieur?

THE CHEVALIER. Do you think I have come too soon?

ARAMINTHE. You always come too soon, Monsieur le Chevalier. We have just finished eating.

THE CHEVALIER. And yet I have waited more than an hour in the street before coming in. Such time lost, Araminthe! I can see that you have never loved. Ah yes, Araminthe, when you will be my age . . .

ARAMINTHE. I am afraid that will never happen again, Monsieur.

THE CHEVALIER, *protesting*. What? To love and to be loved as beautiful as you are? *He takes her hands and kisses them.*

ARAMINTHE, *withdrawing her hands and laughing*. No, Monsieur. To be your age. It is an experience I underwent three years ago. I am told it happens only once.

THE CHEVALIER. I was twenty only three days ago, and I tell you, Araminthe, it is a terrible thing.

ARAMINTHE. You will accustom yourself to it, I assure you. And by the time you have done so it will not be terrible any longer.

THE CHEVALIER. Soon I will be old, Araminthe, and I have not yet even lived. You say you reached my age without loving. Does not your heart feel oppressed for having wasted your life?

ARAMINTHE. To be truthful with you, Monsieur le Chevalier, I still have hope.

THE CHEVALIER. And you are right. You are too pretty not to have hope. Do you know that if I was not in love with Cecile I would just die to kiss your hand. I trust you will forgive my speaking so informally. After all, you are like my sister.

ARAMINTHE, *withdrawing her hand*. Speak informally if it gives you pleasure, only I beg you to treat my hand with more formality.

THE CHEVALIER, *suddenly*. Do you know that I am desperate, Araminthe?

ARAMINTHE. Really! As much as yesterday?

THE CHEVALIER. Much more. I had it out with my father this morning and it was a stormy session. He forbade me to see Cecile again. He made me swear that I had entered this home for the last time.

ARAMINTHE. And you swore?

THE CHEVALIER. Yes. . . . with all kinds of mental reservations. But you see I was forced to do so.

ARAMINTHE. Your father has no heart.

THE CHEVALIER. I believe more particularly that he has no money. And Cecile's dowry is meager. (You know, Araminthe, that fathers are the most extraordinary creatures I know. My father already had the most explicit information from her father's notary as to the amount of her dowry before I had kissed Cecile even once!) He says that he wants only my happiness, and I think he does. But he has my two older brothers whom he must first set up. Nothing will be left for me. I can choose between two things: Either wait until my uncle dies and then become a Knight of Malta—which leaves Cecile out of the picture since the order insists on celibacy—or else marry a crock of gold which equally leaves Cecile out of it.

ARAMINTHE. And has he found it?

THE CHEVALIER. What?

ARAMINTHE. The "crock"?

THE CHEVALIER. Yes. And it is overflowing. But she is like a skeleton, ugly as a witch, and old on top of all that. She will soon be twenty-five years old.

ARAMINTHE. So in two years I shall be old! You are not very gracious, Monsieur le Chevalier.

THE CHEVALIER, *kissing her hands.* You do not understand. Naturally, if it concerns you, Araminthe, age would not count . . . *He stops.* No . . . no, you see, even if it did concern you, I still love Cecile . . . And yet I like to kiss your hands. You know so much about life, Araminthe, tell me, do you believe that everything always remains so entangled in one's heart?

ARAMINTHE. Always.

THE CHEVALIER. In any case, you won't leave us if I marry Cecile, will you? You are like her sister somehow, and I want to marry you as well— like a sister.

ARAMINTHE. You ask for Cecile's hand, but you also want my two hands from time to time, don't you? Monsieur le Chevalier gets on quite well for someone who was twenty years old only three days ago. But I am afraid you are not going to have either. How can you possibly marry Cecile since her dowry is too small and you have absolutely nothing!

THE CHEVALIER. Ah? I haven't told you yet. But I have come to a decision.

ARAMINTHE. Yes?

THE CHEVALIER. I am eloping with her this very night. To see her again

I am forced to do that since I swore never to set foot here any more. Naturally, I am taking you as well.

ARAMINTHE. I ought not to tell you but I believe Mademoiselle Cecile is crazy enough to follow you. However, I am here to dissuade her from it.

THE CHEVALIER. You would have the heart to prevent us from loving each other?

ARAMINTHE. To prevent you from doing something stupid? Why, of course. Have you even thought of the consequences of what you plan to do?

THE CHEVALIER. The consequences are quite simple. Thank heavens, Monsieur Rousseau has made it fashionable for fathers to be sympathetic. When Cecile and I are married, Araminthe, we will have to endure their scandalized reproofs—just for custom's sake—and then they will have nothing left to do but give us their blessing.

ARAMINTHE. Perhaps they will agree to give you their blessing since it costs nothing. But they certainly won't give you a sou.

THE CHEVALIER. Don't you think that if my father had my three sisters become nuns he could find it possible to do some little thing for me?

ARAMINTHE. I am not familiar with your father's state of affairs but I do believe you decide your sisters' vocations a bit too easily!

THE CHEVALIER. Bah! They are ugly, Araminthe. They will never find a more indulgent husband than Jesus Christ. And then their eternal life would be assured. Everything passes so quickly here below! Look at yourself! You just said three years have hardly gone by since you were twenty and you are already disillusioned. We help them avoid I don't know how many opportunities for feeling bitter and how many temptations to sin in condemning them to heaven! And then, I love Cecile so much!

ARAMINTHE, *putting her finger on his chest.* This nice little heart, all brand new, which beats so violently for everything seems to me, Monsieur le Chevalier, to be a pretty little stone.

THE CHEVALIER. Do not deceive yourself. I am sensitive. I have often wept torrents of tears. But one cannot weep for the entire world. It is beyond human strength. One must choose.

ARAMINTHE. Never mind; leave your sisters. It is wicked to think as you do . . . And besides no good could come out of it. I am sure your father would not have the heart to sacrifice all three even if circumstances forced him to let you marry Cecile. You must weigh the consequences of your act. Are you willing to accept poverty?

THE CHEVALIER. What do you mean by that, Araminthe? All the same I would be able to have a new coat tailored from time to time, wouldn't I?

ARAMINTHE. Yes, I believe so. I am sure that no matter how poor Monsieur Orlas may be he would not let Cecile nor you go without ribbons. But you are a handsome man, Chevalier, and come from a very good family. Have you never dreamt of having a great fortune? Dreamt of life at court, festive occasions, the King's favor, and perhaps a famous regiment with you as commander?

THE CHEVALIER, *exclaiming miserably.* I have dreamt only of these things since I was fifteen! You know that very well! But I love Cecile. You are cruel, Araminthe. Why do you delight in putting salt on the wound?

ARAMINTHE. To see if I am able to give you my consent.

THE CHEVALIER. I would give everything in the world to lead my men on a horse and lead them to assault! The smell of gunpowder, the swords glimmering in the sun, death! . . . Ah! what a wonderful life!

ARAMINTHE. Well, my little horseman, you cannot take Cecile with you on your horse. You cannot lead an assault well when a woman you love rides with you. No, do not lower your head. Look at me. *She raises his head.*

THE CHEVALIER, *taking her hands and covering them with kisses.* Oh! your hands! yours hands! I adore your hands, Araminthe!

ARAMINTHE. You adore my hands, you adore to lead an assault, you adore Cecile, but at bottom I am afraid that you only adore yourself. I refuse to give my consent, Monsieur. You will not elope with my pupil.

THE CHEVALIER. You are not serious, Araminthe? I would kill myself.

ARAMINTHE. My little finger told me no.

THE CHEVALIER. And you believe it? Show me your finger and I will give it a piece of my mind! *He takes the little finger and kisses it.*

MONSIEUR ORLAS, *entering.* Chevalier!

THE CHEVALIER, *greeting him.* I kiss your hands, Monsieur.

MONSIEUR ORLAS. Mine as well? Does it seem perfectly natural to you, Monsieur le Chevalier, that I cannot open a single door in this house without finding you kissing somebody?

THE CHEVALIER. I was merely greeting Araminthe.

MONSIEUR ORLAS. And in a moment you will merely be greeting my daughter. Well, you are a young man who greets too much. I have a great many things to do in this house. In the future behave in such a manner that I can open any door with peace of mind.

THE CHEVALIER, *bowing gravely.* I promise to see to that, Monsieur.

MONSIEUR ORLAS *exits.* Have I spoken to him with sufficient respect? It seems to me that I have been perfect with him.

ARAMINTHE. Perfect. Only he has just caught you kissing the hands of a person he is courting, and you are going to elope with his daughter tonight.

THE CHEVALIER. What are you saying? Monsieur Orlas is courting you? I will not permit it!

ARAMINTHE. Really? And why not?

THE CHEVALIER. Have I not told you that you are my sister! I am going to find him at once and demand an explanation of his behavior. I tell you, Araminthe, that I will not allow anyone to bother you!

ARAMINTHE. How do you know that he bothers me? And as for demanding an explanation of his behavior, wait until tomorrow. He will have to demand an explanation from you then, and that way you can kill two birds with one stone.

THE CHEVALIER. It would be the height of absurdity to wait until tomorrow. He would clearly have the upper hand after what will take place tonight and I would be at a distinct disadvantage. I am going at once!

ARAMINTHE, *stopping him*. And if I should forbid you to go?

THE CHEVALIER. Ah, so you are flattered by his attentions! The attentions of a man almost forty who already has a foot in his grave? You appall me, Araminthe! . . . You do not know how to read your own heart. You cannot possibly love this old man!

ARAMINTHE. Who said that I loved him?

THE CHEVALIER. You love me, Araminthe. You love me like a brother because I love Cecile. But still, you love me.

ARAMINTHE. That is news to me!

CECILE, *entering, in a rage*. I have been waiting for you, Monsieur, at the appointed place for over an hour. I know you have been here a long time for I heard the front bell ring. And all this while you have been speaking to Araminthe!

THE CHEVALIER, *going to her*. Cecile, my love, I was simply arranging the final details with her for tonight. My father forced me to swear that I would never come here again. Things are coming to a point. Tonight I must elope with you.

CECILE. If you are in so little hurry, Monsieur, to see me when you come here, what will it be like when we are married and you can see me all the time? I must think this over again. I am not so sure I want to elope.

THE CHEVALIER, *trying to take her hands*. Cecile, my love!

CECILE. No, Monsieur. Tell these pretty words you say so well to others, Monsieur. Kiss their hands!

THE CHEVALIER. This is scandalous! Who dared tell you? Your father, was it not?

CECILE. I have not seen my father since lunch, and he told me nothing at all! But I know enough about men to have understood everything while I was waiting for you.

THE CHEVALIER. Who could have been wicked enough to have told you that, Cecile? It is true that I kissed Araminthe's hands, but I was only thanking her for helping our love . . .

CECILE. What are you saying, Monsieur? Do my ears deceive me? You kissed Araminthe's hands? No, it cannot be true . . .

THE CHEVALIER. But you have just said to me yourself that someone told you he had seen me!

CECILE. I told you that no one said anything to me, Monsieur! You took the responsibility of disclosing this deed yourself which at least is something in your favor. So then! You keep my esteem for this confession, as cruel as it may be, even if you have lost my love. Farewell, Monsieur. Keep the oath you made to your father. Never show your face here again. *She exits.*

THE CHEVALIER, *throwing himself at Araminthe's feet.* Araminthe, I perish before your eyes! Catch her! Tell her I love her! Tell her I don't love you! It is true your hands are like honey to my lips, but their sweetness is the fleeting pleasure of a moment. But as soon as Cecile leaves my side everything grows dark! Quickly, run after her and tell her I love only her, Araminthe, and I swear that I will always love you!

ARAMINTHE. All right, Monsieur. But now we do not have much time. I do not want to waste time pointing out your contradictions, and I am going to try and arrange your affairs. Have everything ready for to-night.

THE CHEVALIER. You agree then to my elopement?

ARAMINTHE. I will see when the moment comes if I can allow everything to take its course. At least, I agree to your making believe to elope. You are right. Perhaps it is a way to make your fathers come to some agreement.

THE CHEVALIER. Oh, thank you! I adore you, Araminthe! Let me kiss your hands!

ARAMINTHE. Monsieur, you are completely irresponsible.

THE CHEVALIER. Yes, it is true. I forgot. I shan't ask you any more. Or at least only after I have married Cecile, and will no longer risk losing her!

ARAMINTHE, *exits laughing.* You can be sure of it! Shrewd young man!

THE CHEVALIER, *alone.* Ah, how amusing life is! . . . I must go and warn my bodyguards. We may be forced to resort to violence tonight. I adore Cecile, I adore Araminthe, tonight I kidnap them both and only three days ago I was twenty years old! *He exits.*

The stage remains empty for a moment. Perhaps some soft music is heard. Then MONSIEUR ORLAS *and* CECILE *enter, returning from a walk.*

MONSIEUR ORLAS. Cecile, I must have a talk with you. I have wanted to for ever so long. Neither of us does so very much all during the day, and yet I simply haven't found the time. The problems in this house overwhelm me. You are very young, Cecile, and you will learn as you grow older that knowing how to live is quite a problem. "Ah, yes, Papa," you will tell me. "You merely have to get up in the morning and go to bed at night and with a little patience the day goes by . . . If only you enjoy the delicacies of a well-set table and have a friend or two come and chat with you during the afternoon, the trick is done! Then it is time to go back to bed and to forget everything!" But unfortunately the brain keeps ticking away.

CECILE. Yes, Papa.

MONSIEUR ORLAS. "Yes, Papa!" What kind of an answer is that? I don't want you to listen to me politely while you are thinking of something else, Cecile. I want you to make an effort to understand what I am saying to you. It is too easy to remain a child and think: "Fathers are stupid, and definitely narrow-minded. They live with the prejudices of their time. They know nothing of what is good. Listen to them respectfully since that is the custom. Yes, Papa. I promise indeed, Papa." . . . And then as soon as my back is turned you do whatever you like.

CECILE. No, Papa.

MONSIEUR ORLAS. "No, Papa!" It is the same thing. I demand a little less respect, Cecile, but instead a little gleam in your eye which proves to me you are listening. If I speak to you as a father and you listen as a young daughter, when we have finished you will make me a pretty curtsy and I will give you a little friendly pat on the cheek, but we won't have accomplished a thing! I would much prefer that you cast aside the privilege of your age and that you grant me for a brief moment the attention and consideration you would have for another child!

CECILE. You know that I always respectfully obey you in everything, Papa.

MONSIEUR ORLAS. Well! Now you are acting like a little fool. You know very well I do not ask you that. Still there is something in your glance that has betrayed you and I think you understand me. You are a lively little creature, cunning, with the wisdom of an old Chinese philosopher under your wild youthfulness. But century-old conventions have placed impenetrable barriers between us. Each of us thinks he must act the ready-made part just because I am your father and you are my daughter. Everything I want to tell you is already branded in your mind as banal, conventional, and boring. You are unjust, Cecile . . . Can't you imagine that I am not your father for a minute? And that I am a witty and charming man.

CECILE. Yes, Papa.

MONSIEUR ORLAS, *bitterly*. "Yes, Papa!" It is better if you do not answer at all! We will make headway more quickly. I want to confess something first, Cecile: I am just about as old as you! *He looks at her with satisfaction.* Well, at least I have managed to surprise you all the same! . . . But I see very well that you still do not trust me! You are thinking it is an unusual beginning. But let us be wary. All this will end as usual by lecturing. Everybody knows nothing else can come from a father's lips. Do you know what you look like this very moment, Cecile? Like a little prisoner being questioned by an enemy General Staff . . . However, you are grown-up and beautiful. In a year, in a month, who knows . . . perhaps even tomorrow you will have gone over to the other side. You as well: you will be a woman. Then we shall be able to understand each other, but perhaps it will be too late. I would have liked to find the way to your heart before.

CECILE. But my heart is yours, Papa.

MONSIEUR ORLAS. Like a little closed-up box whose key one has lost. I will never know what is inside.

CECILE, *after a moment*. I do not know what you mean, Monsieur.

MONSIEUR ORLAS. Ah, this time you did not say "Papa." We are making headway. Now I confess a second thing, Cecile: not only are we the same age, but you please me very much. We are lucky to have disentangled ourselves from conventions. I would never have tried to attract your attention had you been very ugly, bigoted, or stupid. But for the past ten minutes I have been making witty remarks to please you and I am not even sure that I have astonished you. It is really sad, Cecile. You will see when you are a bit older that there are not many interesting men in the world. You had one close at hand. It is a pity you paid no attention to him because he was your father.

CECILE, *after a pause*. You urge me too quickly, Monsieur. This is our first meeting. We must see each other again.

MONSIEUR ORLAS. Thank you, Cecile! You are a clever girl. Thank God,

I was not mistaken! And you are wisdom itself. Indeed, I have rushed things a bit. One must be a terribly young man to believe you can push matters of the heart. Well, we will take all the time that is necessary. You see there are certain things you know much more about than I do. Let me kiss your hand as I would a lady. I gather you have promised me another rendezvous. Shall we say this evening after dinner in the garden? We shall do as usual and seem to go to our rooms and then when everyone is asleep we will find each other here again, hmm? It is better if no one knows anything about our meetings.

CECILE, *stammering bewilderedly.* Did you say this evening, Monsieur?

MONSIEUR ORLAS. Yes. Does it seem too soon to you? Do you want more time to think over matters? CECILE *does not say a word.* Well, answer me! What is wrong with you?

CECILE, *suddenly.* Since you demand that we speak frankly, Monsieur . . . this evening I have a rendezvous.

MONSIEUR ORLAS, *slumping.* Have a rendezvous! After dinner? What do you mean? I cannot have heard correctly!

CECILE. Oh, but you have! I have a rendezvous. I cannot tell you more, Monsieur.

MONSIEUR ORLAS, *beside himself.* You cannot tell me more, Mademoiselle? Do you realize that you are making a fool of me right now? And that I will not stand for it! With whom do you have a rendezvous this evening? Hmm? Well, answer! CECILE *remains silent.* Cecile, I am your father and I demand a reply! Now you are going too far! "Monsieur, this evening I have a rendezvous!" To have the audacity even to say that in front of me, her own father and only seventeen! Do you think of making me the accomplice in your debauchery, wretched child? What becomes of the respect you owe me in every matter? Do you forget who I am and is it mandatory that I remind you? Ah, believe me, I regret my credulousness and my confidence: But from now on I will treat you as you deserve. Now go to your room, Mademoiselle. CECILE *starts to speak.* Not a word! I order you to stay there until you hear otherwise—and I assure you I shall do everything to prevent you from going out of your room tonight! Now go!

CECILE *curtsies and goes toward the house. She turns at the door and in a pitiful voice says simply.* You see how difficult it is, Monsieur. *She exits.*

MONSIEUR ORLAS. "You see how difficult it is, Monsieur!" And to her own father! Ah, nothing is sacred any longer! *To* ARAMINTHE, *who has just entered.* Araminthe, I am beside myself!

ARAMINTHE. What has happened, Monsieur?

MONSIEUR ORLAS. I decided to have a heart-to-heart talk with Cecile. I did everything I could to inspire her with confidence, to make her understand that it was not the father but a friend who spoke to her. I thought I was on the point of solving the mystery of this little Sphinx and making myself understood for once! I proposed that we meet in the garden at night so that the moon and the stars might add a bit of romantic atmosphere to our conversation. I told her to be frank with me and forget who I was. And do you know what reply she made?

ARAMINTHE, *laughing*. That she would be unable to because she had another rendezvous this evening?

MONSIEUR ORLAS, *jumping*. Thunder and blazes, Mademoiselle! Does everyone make a fool of me in this house! Did you know all about it?

ARAMINTHE. You wanted Cecile to speak to you as a friend, Monsieur. I think the confidence she showed you terribly moving. She simply told you the truth. It is true. She has a rendezvous tonight.

MONSIEUR ORLAS. My daughter has a rendezvous tonight! And her governess herself tells me so to my face! We are in an insane asylum. Would it be indiscreet, Mademoiselle, to inquire with whom my daughter has a rendezvous tonight?

ARAMINTHE. Yes, Monsieur. It would be most indiscreet. It is a secret between the two of us.

MONSIEUR ORLAS. A secret between the two of you! That is really incredible . . . I am deeply hurt, Araminthe. Cecile is only a little child with a child's brain. But I did hope that you at least would not make a fool of me. I am a very lonely man, Araminthe. I may seem gay, but most of the time I am sunk in despair. *You* all believe that I am working when I lock myself in my study, don't you? Working at God only knows what since I have never done anything in my life! The entire household goes about on tiptoe so as not to disturb me. But do you know what I actually do in this sanctuary of mine? I sit for hours in front of my desk and look at the wall opposite me.

ARAMINTHE. You should come and speak to us, Monsieur. Your daughter and I would be most happy to amuse you.

MONSIEUR ORLAS. I do not feel either of you trusts me. Something tells me that you always have some little secret which belongs only to you both. You giggle over your tapestries whispering Heaven only knows what in each other's ear. As soon as I come you stop! One would really think that I turn you into stone!

ARAMINTHE. It is the respect we both owe you, Monsieur, that makes us pause. You are the master, you have serious problems. We believe that you have no time for our silly chatter.

MONSIEUR ORLAS. You are wrong. I have nothing to think of, Araminthe, except my ennui. I have a modest income, but it takes care of itself. And I have never had the good fortune to take politics seriously as most men of my age. When I was twenty, I lived as flippantly as you and time slipped through my fingers. As I grew older, I believed I had to strike an attitude to give myself importance. Yet each day that goes by enchains me more and more to this ridiculous prison where I am my own jailer. Why don't you free me, Araminthe, by loving me? It would be a charitable act.

ARAMINTHE. I think the only reason one loves, Monsieur, is for his own pleasure. But you are still young and handsome. Why do you not take a mistress? That would keep you busy.

MONSIEUR ORLAS. A fine thing to come from your lips!

ARAMINTHE. I know at least two or three young and beautiful women in the town who would be delighted to become your mistress.

MONSIEUR ORLAS. I know them too. They do not appeal to me at all.

ARAMINTHE. Still if you need them to cure you?

MONSIEUR ORLAS. But love is not a medicine! Once pleasure passes, and it passes quickly—as you will learn one day, my child—I shan't have anything to tell them and I will simply die of boredom. I would rather sit in front of my wall. At least, I don't feel compelled to speak to myself.

ARAMINTHE. Do you believe, Monsieur, in all frankness, that you would have very much more to tell me if I left my door ajar to you? Once pleasure passes—and it passes quickly as you have just taught me—it would be exactly the same.

MONSIEUR ORLAS. With you?

ARAMINTHE. Yes, with me, Monsieur, for you do not love me as I want to be loved one day. You are bored: I am young and fresh and I live here at your home. There is no more mystery than that. You spoke to me of the baron a while ago. But tell me honestly what man finding himself in your position would not try—just for the sake of trying—to knock softly on my door while going to bed at night? You simply conform to the most banal order of things, and for my part I do the same by not opening it. You can be sure that when I know that I love and am loved—I will hear. I have a sharp ear and I will hear, however softly one knocks.

MONSIEUR ORLAS, *severely*. And if this young man who kissed your hand a while ago would softly knock, Mademoiselle, would you hear him? I was not born yesterday, Araminthe. Other women were already playing this little game with me while you were still a child. So don't try to fool me! It isn't worthy of you—nor of me. My eyes are finally opening, you little schemer. Cecile is only a pretext which explains your entire attitude. This young fellow comes here to see you!

ARAMINTHE. And if it were so, Monsieur? I am single. I am free. Who could find anything wrong in that?

MONSIEUR ORLAS. I could, Heaven knows!

ARAMINTHE. You could? And by what right?

MONSIEUR ORLAS. By right of . . . Don't ask me so many questions! Your father entrusted you to me, Araminthe. The sacredness of your honor is in my hands. I am not a suspicious man—perhaps I should be more so—but woe to the one who trifles with me when it comes to honor. It will be my duty to warn your father if ever you are mad enough to open your door to this little puppy! And you can be sure he will be warned.

ARAMINTHE. And who would have warned my father then, had I opened it to you, Monsieur?

MONSIEUR ORLAS, *slightly embarrassed*. Well, in such a case . . . Oh, stop joking, Araminthe! You are the only one who laughs at your jokes!

ARAMINTHE. Then stop living in a dream world, Monsieur! The little Chevalier comes here to see Cecile and not me! Everybody knows it, and you as well. I will even tell you a secret if you swear not to repeat it. But first you must swear. I do not trust you completely, Monsieur. It is true you are a gentleman but still you have two or three personalities and sometimes you are unable to tell one from the other.

MONSIEUR ORLAS. Enough, enough. I swear. But heaven alone knows if I understand you.

ARAMINTHE. Swear on what is most precious to you, and swear that you will never tell anyone. Well, go on and swear! And everything must be according to rules. So spit as well!

MONSIEUR ORLAS. Araminthe, you are making fun of me. But there, I swear. *He holds up his hand.* And I spit!

ARAMINTHE. Well, Monsieur, the Chevalier thinks so little of me that he is eloping with your daughter tonight.

MONSIEUR ORLAS, *at first astounded, bursts out laughing.* Ah! Ah! That is a good one! Whom do you take me for? The stock father in a comedy? You think that I am going to masquerade in a dark cloak and catch a cold in the garden just to see if I don't find a hidden ladder, hmm? You are talking to the wrong person, Mademoiselle.

ARAMINTHE. I believe it would be most prudent, Monsieur. If Cecile told
you she had a rendezvous tonight, it was not without reason.

MONSIEUR ORLAS. I will lock Cecile in her room, Mademoiselle, and save
that unfortunate child from playing I don't know what scandalous part
in this affair between you and your lover. And I shall sleep soundly
tonight, have no fears! After all, it is no business of mine if you have
decided to ruin yourself!

ARAMINTHE. And you are right! But if I were in your place, Monsieur,
I would still keep a watch to see if anyone were kidnapped tonight.

MONSIEUR ORLAS. That's right, laugh at me. Now I see that you never
loved me and never will love me. I am going to my study and think
of ways not to suffer any more. I am too old now to yield to despair.
Tomorrow I will tell you what I have decided. Adieu, Araminthe! I am
deeply wounded. *He takes a step and looks back.* Yet, Araminthe, I want
to tell you something. It is true I knocked at your door. But I never
really insisted. And although God knows how much I love making
love, I was almost happy that your door remained closed.

ARAMINTHE, *stammering, bewildered.* What do you mean, Monsieur?

MONSIEUR ORLAS, *continuing.* Yes, almost happy. You may already be the
mistress of this boy, and I am making myself ridiculous by speaking to
you as I do. I am not easily respectful, Araminthe. There is something
about a skirt floating around a supple waist that does away with the
sense of respect in my mind. And yet there are such strong contradictions
in one's heart, that I was almost happy in my bitterness to learn
how to respect you before your silent door. There it is. Ask that little
man tonight if he understands anything of this! *He exits.*

ARAMINTHE, *smiling happily to herself and whispering.* It only had to be said,
Monsieur . . . You went through so much trouble for nothing before!
. . . And now without even wanting to you have found the words
which unlock a girl's door . . . Poor little men! Poor little strutting
peacocks! They spread out their tails as conquerors almost as soon as
they are able to walk . . . And they could have such an easy victory
if they knew they only had to be a little wounded and sad . . . But
we are certainly not going to teach them that! . . . I have no fears
for this one! He will be in the garden as soon as night falls, with a dark,
concealing cloak, pistols at his side, and a taste for blood in his mouth.
He may catch a cold there, or he may find love . . . Or perhaps
even both. Well, we shall see! . . . I will tell you a secret: The playwright himself doesn't know! . . . *She exits after a small curtsy.*

The stage remains empty and night begins to fall while a mocking tune is being

*played. When night is fully established—quickly enough for this time of year—
a man appears wrapped in a dark cloak. He advances cautiously. He beckons to
someone and two men also in dark cloaks come from a black corner of the garden
and join him.*

THE MAN. Ssssh!

THE MEN. Ssssh!

*Still another figure in a dark cloak comes from the house, his face concealed in
the folds of his cloak. It is* MONSIEUR ORLAS. *The man who first appeared
motions his men to go away.* MONSIEUR ORLAS *and the other man cautiously
survey each other before approaching.*

MONSIEUR ORLAS, *in a low voice.* Monsieur Damiens?

MONSIEUR DAMIENS, *in the same voice.* Monsieur Orlas?

MONSIEUR ORLAS. Yes. It is I. *They greet each other.*

MONSIEUR DAMIENS. Many thanks, Monsieur, for warning me.

MONSIEUR ORLAS. Do not mention it, Monsieur. It was only my duty. I am
a father like yourself, Monsieur. *He motions to the two men who are waiting.*
Are these gentlemen with you?

MONSIEUR DAMIENS. Two bodyguards whom I thought worth while bringing. I thought that we might have to meet force with force.

MONSIEUR ORLAS. You did wisely, Monsieur. I myself am armed with
pistols. *He points to them under his cloak.*

MONSIEUR DAMIENS. How can I ever thank you, Monsieur?

MONSIEUR ORLAS. It is the most natural thing in the world, Monsieur.
You have entrusted Araminthe to my care. Her honor is as precious to
me as to you. But why are you trembling? Have no fear.

MONSIEUR DAMIENS. I am a father, Monsieur. And I will also tell you
without false shame that I am an old lawyer, Monsieur, and that I
have little experience when it comes to battles.

MONSIEUR ORLAS. I have no more taste for fighting than you, Monsieur.
But when my daughter's honor is concerned or your daughter's—you
see I place them both on the same level—I am ready to take up arms.
Besides, the law is on our side.

MONSIEUR DAMIENS. Yes, it is. Still I don't hide from you that I would
have preferred a good lawsuit. I would have crushed my opponent
with the situation I hold and such a flagrant offense as this! Alas! A
lawsuit would have been too slow. Lovers work more quickly than we
do, Monsieur. You are a father yourself. You know how difficult it is to
protect your daughter!

MONSIEUR ORLAS. You're telling me, Monsieur! I had fears for my own
daughter before seeing through their intrigue. These little young fellows

no longer have respect for anything. It seems to me when we were their age we had more respect for family honor.

MONSIEUR DAMIENS. Oh, I don't know! We have also had our day. I can tell you a hundred stories in which I have been a little imprudent. I was hot-blooded when I was twenty.

MONSIEUR ORLAS. Yes, they were still speaking about it when I was old enough to understand. You were really hot-blooded, Monsieur!

MONSIEUR DAMIENS. He! He! Yes, I suppose I was!

MONSIEUR ORLAS. Plenty of the ladies in this part of the country know a thing or two! They blushed every time your name was mentioned.

MONSIEUR DAMIENS. He! He! Yes, I suppose they did!

MONSIEUR ORLAS. I was still only a boy, Monsieur, when I dreamt of following in your footsteps!

MONSIEUR DAMIENS. He! He! Yes, I suppose you were! You flatter me, Monsieur. It is true that very few women treated me cruelly under the late King. But if I am not mistaken, Monsieur, I believe that you yourself have established some reputation in our little town, haven't you?

MONSIEUR ORLAS. Well! I suppose I have broken several hearts, but I was paid back in time. One has to make hay while the sun shines!

MONSIEUR DAMIENS. And we made it, Monsieur. But with good manners. We were not like these little young fellows . . .

MONSIEUR ORLAS. Who respect nothing, Monsieur!

MONSIEUR DAMIENS. We were satisfied with married women! After all, what is the difference between one cuckold more or less!

MONSIEUR ORLAS. Or even some servant, if need be! Or some wayward peasant! Hmm? But when it comes to young ladies of quality, Monsieur! . . .

MONSIEUR DAMIENS. Without caring for the father's honor! . . .

MONSIEUR ORLAS. We must be ruthless, Monsieur! Sssh! Be careful! Let us hide! I think I saw a shadow at the end of the path by the linden trees. It must be our adventurer.

MONSIEUR DAMIENS. Do you think he is the kind of man who draws his sword easily? These little Monsieurs of the Nobility believe that everything is permitted them!

MONSIEUR ORLAS. The law is on our side, Monsieur. And besides there are four of us with your bodyguards.

MONSIEUR DAMIENS. Yes. But we should take care not to be wounded. Let us hide far away. We will throw our men at him at the proper time.

MONSIEUR ORLAS. Do not be afraid. We will shame that boy before he even thinks of drawing his sword.

THE CHEVALIER *enters dressed in a dark cloak as well. He goes toward the house, gives a signal.* ARAMINTHE *appears at the window.*

THE CHEVALIER. Is it you, Araminthe?

ARAMINTHE. Yes, it is. *She appears at the door, wrapped in a cloak and goes to him.*

THE CHEVALIER. And where is Cecile?

ARAMINTHE. She is coming. But there is a little difficulty I shall tell you about directly. You must hide here for a while. *She leads him to the little Chinese pavilion and lets him in.* Do not make a sound until I return, and no matter what you hear, do not make a move. *She locks him inside.*

THE CHEVALIER, *in the pavilion.* Why do you lock the door?

ARAMINTHE. To be sure I will find you here at the proper time. Sssh! Not a word! Everything will be all right. *She returns to the house and gives a signal.*

CECILE, *appears, hidden under a mantle.* Is it you, Araminthe?

ARAMINTHE. Yes. You can come now. Everything is going as we expected. I am going in to get our things. Wait for me there.

CECILE. Where is the Chevalier? You know very well that I am afraid in the dark.

ARAMINTHE. One must not be afraid the night one elopes, Mademoiselle! . . . The Chevalier will join you in a minute. *She disappears into the house.*

MONSIEUR ORLAS, *hidden under his cape, walks around* CECILE, *who grows obviously worried and is not sure that she recognizes him.*

MONSIEUR ORLAS, *in a whisper.* Is it you?

CECILE, *in the same tone.* Yes, it is. Is it you?

MONSIEUR ORLAS. Yes. *To himself.* Aha, the bird is caught. I shall make believe I am the Chevalier.

CECILE. I am a little afraid.

MONSIEUR ORLAS. Do not be afraid of anything, my child. I am here.

CECILE. Are you sure at least that you love me? Because if you don't there still is time.

MONSIEUR ORLAS. Do not doubt it, my sweet. I am yours forever.

CECILE. How strangely you speak! I do not recognize your voice.

MONSIEUR ORLAS. It is because I speak low so that no one will hear us . . .

CECILE. As soon as she comes we'll run away quickly. Are your horses and bodyguards at the little gate?

MONSIEUR ORLAS. As arranged. *To himself.* The scoundrels! They planned to take my daughter as well.

CECILE. What are you saying?

MONSIEUR ORLAS. I said: "She is very nice but why bother to take that child?" Would we not be better off without her?

CECILE. I may be mad, Monsieur, but I shall not elope without my chaperon.

MONSIEUR ORLAS. What! This infant your chaperon? And what will her father say?

CECILE. And what will mine say? You must put up with some little unpleasantness when you elope.

MONSIEUR ORLAS, *to himself.* "Some little unpleasantness!" Ah, how they dare trifle with serious matters!

CECILE. What are you always muttering about? I cannot see your face.

MONSIEUR ORLAS. I was simply telling myself that she would get in our way, and that we would have been much better alone, my beloved.

CECILE. She is my sister, Monsieur. I cannot do anything without her. But you must swear to me that you will never kiss her hands again.

MONSIEUR ORLAS, *to himself.* Ha! Ha! Now it comes out!

CECILE. You elope with us both, but I am the one you are marrying!

MONSIEUR ORLAS. And do you doubt it, my love? *To himself.* I was right! The rascal intended to play with them both! *To* CECILE. My attentions towards her were only a convenient mask to hide my real feelings for you. Besides why speak of marriage at all? Is not love, love alone, enough for us?

CECILE. I love you, Monsieur, and it is indeed a sufficient reason to follow you. But must we not conform to law?

MONSIEUR ORLAS. What an ugly word in such a pretty mouth! What other law is there but the law of our hearts?

CECILE. But what about my father, Monsieur?

MONSIEUR ORLAS. What does that suspicious old man matter? We will travel, my love. We will be like those glamorous persons hated by weak-hearted ones who never dared give everything to love! We shall be lovers! Ah, lovers! Have you ever been able to hear that word without feeling disturbed? Have you, Araminthe?

CECILE, *draws back, murmuring.* Araminthe?

MONSIEUR ORLAS. Is it not better than a household with screaming children hanging on your apron strings, and servants with their pots and pans to order around? The drudge of daily life ruins the sense of love. But each morning will see our love blossom anew, ready to be defended and conquered anew. We will have frightful scenes, wound each other to the heart. Each of us will torment the other, and yet we won't ever be able to part. Each of us will be the slave and the tyrant of the other. Men, all men, will desire you at the sumptuous gatherings where we will spend our nights, and their desire will reveal you to yourself and you will make a game of torturing me. I will never know if you really love me nor what is concealed behind your smiles. And if one day you happen to be away from me for a single hour, anxiety will gnaw my heart away. Because you will always lie to me and you will always be an everlasting mystery to me . . . This is life, Araminthe! This is what it is to be a woman and to love!

CECILE, *who has recognized her father while he was speaking, has a little smile as she says.* Good Heavens, Monsieur, how mistaken you are! I have no desire ever to leave you—even for an hour. Nor have I any desire to lie to you. And how absurd to think I would torment you! Can't you see that the least little sadness in your eye makes me suffer so? I simply want to be yours and to know it will always be that way. You certainly are very young and you know nothing about women. Even the wildest among them, Monsieur, wish for nothing else.

MONSIEUR ORLAS. Have you not read the lives of famous mistresses? They only love themselves, my poor child. Men were clods of clay they molded according to their whims. Men were simply instruments of their own triumph like their splendid gowns and their luxurious jewels. Does it not tempt you to become one of these monstrous goddesses, and to ravage all the hearts about you?

CECILE. Not at all, Monsieur! Not in the least! How monotonous it must be to love only one's self. And do you believe that if any of those famous ladies had ever known real happiness with one man they would have had any desire to change? I never think of them, but if one day I should it would be to pity them for never having found love.

MONSIEUR ORLAS. Love! Love! What do you know about love at your age?

CECILE. Everything that cannot be taught, Monsieur. That is to say, almost everything.

MONSIEUR ORLAS, *drawing nearer to her.* Very well, then, I will teach you the rest . . .

CECILE, *drawing back.* Indeed, Monsieur, these are strange words coming from your mouth and they disturb me. Throw off your disguise now. You know that I recognized you in spite of the dark. What would your daughter who loves and respects you say if she knew that you speak this way to other girls at night?

MONSIEUR ORLAS, *at first surprised, taking off his disguise.* Very well! Off with my disguise! Araminthe! You have recognized me. I am the man who has desired you for so long a time. I wanted to prevent this ridiculous elopement, because I know better than you that you cannot love that little boy. And do not worry about Cecile. She is a child who doesn't know anything. Don't give her another thought. We shall put her in a convent or send her to her aunt's. And tonight you will follow no one but me. For I love you, Araminthe, you hear me, I love you, love you madly, and I cannot live without you any more!

CECILE, *in her true voice.* I have known for a long time that you love Araminthe, but if you love her as much as you say, why don't you marry her, Papa?

MONSIEUR ORLAS, *jumps and draws back, shouting.* Papa! Who are you then? Unfortunate child! How could you possibly make fun of your father in this way?

CECILE. Did I approach you, Monsieur? Did I take the initiative of beginning this strange conversation?

MONSIEUR ORLAS. Wretched little girl! Forget at once everything I said to you. Not a word of it was true.

CECILE, *softly.* But I have not heard a word, Monsieur.

MONSIEUR ORLAS. You must know that I recognized you myself and I only wanted to shame you.

CECILE. Then why all this comedy? It would have been so easy to tell Araminthe that you love her.

MONSIEUR ORLAS, *sternly.* Mademoiselle! It is your father's right to ask you questions and not yours! What were you doing in the garden so late at night, and in a traveling cloak as well? To whom did you think you were speaking before you recognized me?

ARAMINTHE, *appears smiling.* To the Chevalier, Monsieur, who loves her and wanted to elope with her this very night to marry her and make her happy. I warned you, remember?

MONSIEUR ORLAS. You dare show your face, Mademoiselle? You should know by now that there are laws in this country which protect a father's honor. It will rest with others to weigh your part in this escapade for I intend to notify the proper authority of all this! You were going to make yourself the accomplice of a villainous act, Mademoiselle! Let me tell you marriage is a sacred thing and it alone can sanctify love! You wanted my daughter to elope tonight, didn't you? You wanted to make her like one of those lost creatures who ruin themselves forever by placing love before duty, didn't you? Well, answer me!

ARAMINTHE. I was at the window, Monsieur, and I heard you when you thought you convinced me of the contrary a little while ago. You compromise yourself too much. You do better not to insist, and far better to leave your pistols alone. Your daughter and I have been able to keep our honor without you—and sometimes even in spite of you! Haven't we? Cecile has parried your wily thrusts as well as I could have done myself. Are you not willing to grant us a bit of respect and confidence now?

MONSIEUR ORLAS. Come into my arms, my charming girl! Cecile was right indeed. If I love you why not admit it and simply ask you to marry me! . . . I know now that you love me too.

CECILE. You may kiss her, Monsieur. I shan't look.

MONSIEUR ORLAS. Thank you, Cecile. But I shall do it with such tenderness that even you can be a witness.

MONSIEUR DAMIENS, *rushing in with his bodyguards.* Upon him, my brave men! We have him now! *They throw themselves on* MONSIEUR ORLAS. Caught in the very act, Monsieur! Kissing my daughter! And eloping! You will surely be condemned to the galleys! *He recognizes* MONSIEUR ORLAS. But what is this? A betrayal? To find you, Monsieur, kissing my daughter in the dark?

MONSIEUR ORLAS. I can explain everything, Monsieur. . . .

MONSIEUR DAMIENS. I thought you were a father, Monsieur, but you are only a vile seducer! Did you not swear a while ago with pistols in your hands that you would protect the honor of your ladies . . . or was I dreaming?

MONSIEUR ORLAS, *beginning to explain with embarrassment.* Love, Monsieur, is my only excuse. This feeling is stronger than anything and . . .

MONSIEUR DAMIENS. To whom do you think you are talking, Monsieur? I was not born yesterday! Do you bandy the most sacred things so lightly, Monsieur? Are you one of these thoughtless men who ruin ladies' reputations?

MONSIEUR ORLAS. No, Monsieur. But sometimes there are occasions where love . . .

MONSIEUR DAMIENS. Idle talk! Take care, Monsieur, you are speaking to a father! Love is a word they do not understand! I was greatly mistaken, Monsieur, to put so much confidence in you! You are nothing but a young puppy!

MONSIEUR ORLAS. But Monsieur . . .

MONSIEUR DAMIENS. Have respect for my age, Monsieur! I am old enough to be your father, Monsieur!

ARAMINTHE, *in the arms of* MONSIEUR ORLAS. Thank you, Papa, for this charming phrase! Now I know I can love him!

MONSIEUR DAMIENS. Love! Love! Don't any of you know any other word? Am I the only one too old to use it? I shall make you young people pay for it, and dearly too!

MONSIEUR ORLAS. You are unfair, Monsieur. You have known love yourself. You confessed as much a little while ago. There is in love a force which triumphs over everything and it is why . . . *He sees* CECILE *being kissed by* THE CHEVALIER *whom* CECILE *has freed with* ARAMINTHE'S *key.* One minute, Monsieur. Here is our young rascal! *He approaches them with indignation.* Monsieur! Am I dreaming? Do you dare kiss my daughter, in my own garden at night and before my very eyes?

THE CHEVALIER. I love her, Monsieur!

MONSIEUR ORLAS. A good excuse, Monsieur!

THE CHEVALIER. But you just said yourself, Monsieur, that love . . .

MONSIEUR ORLAS. It is too easy a word for you to use, young man. It has an entirely different meaning in my mouth! Yes, my young libertine, I know what dark designs you were contriving. But God be praised, I came in time. The law will take care of you! And do you know the price you will pay? Hmm? The galleys, Monsieur, the galleys! . . .

THE CHEVALIER. But, Monsieur, you would not have the heart to . . .

MONSIEUR ORLAS. You are speaking to a father, Monsieur, the protector of his daughter's honor. A father, do you hear? There is something in the majesty of the word "father" which should have made you pause!

MONSIEUR DAMIENS, *taking hold of him.* A fine thing for you to be saying! What about me, Monsieur? I am also a father, Monsieur! Do not try to change the issue by talking of your daughter's honor! I want you to account for my own daughter's honor, Monsieur!

MONSIEUR ORLAS. But since I tell you that I love her, Monsieur! . . .

THE CHEVALIER, *to* MONSIEUR ORLAS. But since I tell you that I love her! . . .

ARAMINTHE, *coming forward.* This little comedy is beginning to be too long. Don't you think we have all spoken enough? Papa, Monsieur Orlas is marrying me. *To* MONSIEUR ORLAS. The Chevalier, Monsieur, has the honor to ask for your daughter's hand. Don't you think we can set our dark cloaks aside and continue this discussion in another place than the garden? The night is cool, we risk catching a cold, and besides I have had a midnight table laid for us. *She claps her hands. Two footmen appear with candelabras. Other candles are lit inside the house.* If you only take the trouble to enter the house, you will find everything ready . . . I even had musicians come secretly, and had an enormous engagement cake made for dessert with our four names engraved in silver icing.

MONSIEUR ORLAS. Did you know then that everything would end this way, precious girl?

ARAMINTHE. I was in on the secret of this comedy, Monsieur. And there must always be a happy ending for this kind of play.

MONSIEUR ORLAS, *taking* MONSIEUR DAMIENS's *arm.* Come, Monsieur Damiens, let us go and dine! Everything ends this way in France. Everything! Weddings, christenings, duels, burials, swindlings, diplomatic affairs . . . everything is a pretext to a good dinner. Besides my cook is a genius! She would be reason enough, Monsieur, for your entering my family. . . . You may as well tell your bodyguards to go and have a drink in the kitchen. *To* THE CHEVALIER. Tell yours as well, Monsieur, who it seems are waiting at the little gate.

THE CHEVALIER. A thousand thanks, Monsieur! But it so happens that we have the same bodyguards!

MONSIEUR DAMIENS. What do you mean, "the same"! I shall have them hanged!

MONSIEUR ORLAS, *drawing him towards the house.* Forgive them, Monsieur. We only have two bodyguards in our little town and work is so scarce. *They go in a procession into the now illuminated house. One can hear music playing.* CECILE *remains behind, and appears to be sulking.*

THE CHEVALIER, *going to her.* Well, Cecile, here you stand sulking while happiness stares you in the face. What are you waiting for?

CECILE. I am making a very important decision, Monsieur.

THE CHEVALIER. I swear to you, my love, that I will never kiss Araminthe's hands any more. Never!

CECILE. I should hope so, Monsieur. But I have been thinking about everything my father has just told me . . . How really naïve I was . . . When all is said and done, Monsieur, I think that I will make you suffer. *She enters the house, the worried* CHEVALIER *following her. The music grows clear and brisk as the curtain falls.*

The Cretan Woman

(Based on the Hippolytus *of Euripides)*

by ROBINSON JEFFERS

PERSONS

CHORUS: *Three poor women of the country. Tattered clothes, colorful patches; flowers in hair, or bright ribbons.* SECOND WOMAN *carries a basket,* THIRD WOMAN *a primitive musical instrument, called here a zither.*

SELENE: PHAEDRA'S *waiting-woman; neither young nor old; demurely well dressed according to her station in life.*

PHAEDRA

THE GODDESS APHRODITE

HIPPOLYTUS

ALCYON *and* ANDROS, *friends of* HIPPOLYTUS

MESSENGER

THESEUS, *old, powerful, heroic in appearance*

ARMED ATTENDANTS *of* THESEUS

SCENE

In front of the house of THESEUS *at Troezene. Old masonry; big door, two or three stone steps up to it.*

Left foreground, stone altar of APHRODITE. *Wooded hills in the blue background.*

CHORUS—*the three poor* WOMEN—*enter from the right, along a curving path that goes near the altar before it reaches the house.*

FIRST WOMAN. We have never quite starved, thanks to some god or other: but my husband has had no work since New Year's.

SECOND WOMAN. Don't be troubled, darling. You are still young enough to attract a lover from time to time. Some kindly old gentleman . . .

FIRST WOMAN. How you talk!

SECOND WOMAN. A piece of fish or a pound of olives, if not a copper coin.

THIRD WOMAN. My husband has plenty of work, and well-paid too; but he drinks every penny. I don't think we could live without these handouts from the palace.

They are approaching the altar.

FIRST WOMAN. We have still a handful of meal in the bin . . . *She throws her hand to her heart, staring at the altar, and steps backward.* Oh—hush!

THIRD WOMAN, *staring and retreating.* I feel it too!

FIRST WOMAN. Something divine is here. There was such a dizziness at my heart suddenly . . .

THIRD WOMAN. I feel my eyes dazzle and my knees tremble.

SECOND WOMAN. Did you feel something? It is the great Goddess—Aphrodite—*her* altar.

FIRST WOMAN, *her hand at her throat.* Walk wide of it! She is angry.
There is a divine anger in this place: like the glaring eyes
Of a wild beast. Yet she is kind, we know . . .

SECOND WOMAN. What I felt—like an earthquake. Something has roused her.

They tiptoe at distance around the altar and approach the door of the house.

FIRST WOMAN, *speaking low.* I hope that all's well in this great house. The Goddess doesn't waste wrath on poor people.

THIRD WOMAN. I am still afraid. Terribly. I feel the power . . .

SECOND WOMAN. If this great house ever falls—I wish it no evil—I wish my boy had the looting of it.

FIRST WOMAN. The door is tight shut, and I dare not knock. Make a little music on that zither of yours, Cleone. But softly.

THIRD WOMAN *plucks the strings of her instrument; a low music is heard. The door opens partially;* SELENE *speaks through the opening.*

SELENE, *intensely whispers*. Go away. Be quiet.

FIRST WOMAN. Our children are hungry. Have you nothing for us today?

SELENE. Be off. Let my lady sleep.

FIRST WOMAN. Not even a spoiled cake or a stale crust?

SELENE, *slips through the doorway and stands on the threshold, closing the door carefully behind her*. Will you worry me to death? Be quiet, women.
My lady is ill; she never closed her eyes all night long,
And has just fallen asleep. She has been delirious, I think.
I have been beaten like a fluttering bird, all night and day,
In the storm of her mind.

FIRST WOMAN.   What is it, a fever?

SELENE.   And for three days she has
   not tasted food.
Oh, I am weary!

SECOND WOMAN. You mean there was food and she wouldn't eat it!

SELENE.   She is like someone possessed
By an angry god.

THE WOMEN, *startled, look significantly at each other, and back toward the altar.*
Oh!

FIRST WOMAN. What goddess?

SELENE.   A divine power—how could I know? There
   is a mystery . . .
In the delirium, in all the wild rush of her mind
There is something she avoids, something she hides. Like the mad
   waves of the sea, moulding but hiding
A sunken reef.

FIRST WOMAN. I will tell you. We felt the anger—we all felt it—of a—
   certain Divine Person
When we approached this house.

SELENE. What Person? FIRST WOMAN *shakes her head, finger to lips, afraid to speak.* I say what god, or what goddess? FIRST WOMAN *shakes her head;* SECOND WOMAN *points stealthily toward the altar.*

SELENE. There? Aphrodite? That's out. Or it has nothing to do with my
   lady Phaedra.
She is loving and good, and she neglects no divinity.
And faithful to her dear husband, my lord Theseus: almost *too* faithful
To be a woman. Oh, what a time I've had
Trying to make her eat, cooking things . . .

SECOND WOMAN, *hungrily*. What kind of things?

SELENE. Little Cretan cakes, for instance. Brown spice, golden honey, a
    whipped egg . . .

SECOND AND THIRD WOMEN.   Oh! Oh!

SELENE. I thought perhaps she was homesick for the dear island
    Where she was born. That's what they eat there.
    She poured the dish on the floor when it came in . . .

SECOND WOMAN.   Oh!

SELENE.   And the slaves had them.

        Worse than that:
    Once she called for raw meat, flesh with the blood, like a northern
        barbarian: she, royal-born,
    Of the most highly cultured family in Europe! and naturally
    Shrieked when the mere smell . . . *Listening.* Oh dear! Is she calling
        me?
    Is she awake?
    The door opens as she turns to it. PHAEDRA *stands in the doorway; a beautiful
    woman wound carelessly in a cloak, haggard but royal.* SELENE *steps back from her.*

SELENE. My lady!

    PHAEDRA *stands bewildered, gazing at the women and the scene. Her lips move,
    but without a voice. Finally she speaks aloud, slowly and clearly.*

PHAEDRA. I will not shame myself. I will not defile this house.

SELENE.   What are you saying?

PHAEDRA.   I *will* not.

    And you, be silent. You are my servant, I think. What's your name?
        Selene? My poor Selene.
    She gazes from one to other of the women.
    Who are all these women, Selene? So many and so very many and
        such proud faces?
    Are you the queens of the East that have come to comfort me?
    I will die sooner.

SELENE. You are ill, my lady. You are weak, trembling with fever: come
        back, dear,
    Into the house.

PHAEDRA, *stepping down from the doorway.* Not at all: I will walk in my
        lovely garden: up and down: and feel the warm sun . . . *She
        shudders violently.*
    They say death's bitter cold. Ah? You beautiful haughty queens,
    I shall soon know. SELENE *supports her as she moves forward.* THE WOMEN
        follow.

PHAEDRA, *to herself.* I'll tear it out of me. Tear. *Tear,* you know: like a barbed spearhead

Out of my bitter heart. *She shudders.* Bitter cold: bitter heart: my bitter longing. The bitter end.

What a queer word!

FIRST WOMAN. She is going straight toward the goddess.

SECOND WOMAN. The altar: see? Like a gray moth

To candle flame. Like a sleepwalker.

FIRST WOMAN. Let us go back to the great door, Cleone,

And see if we can get something.

They return to the door, but often looking back to see what happens. THIRD WOMAN *plays her zither. Presently the door half opens, the basket is passed through it. Meanwhile* PHAEDRA *moves helplessly toward the altar.*

SELENE, *trying to draw her aside.* This way, my lady: the path is better.

PHAEDRA. Let me alone, woman.

I will pray here: it seems to be a religious place. I cannot well re-member . . .

There are so many gods in so many places . . .

SELENE. Do not go near it!

She reaches out her arms in vain; PHAEDRA *blindly moves on. But suddenly jerks and stiffens, throwing her head back.*

PHAEDRA, *in a strangled voice.* This is the one! *Retreating.* The awful power

That has me in hand. The goddess of love and longing, cruel, cruel and beautiful. I may as well confess now.

The crime is not great if I will not yield.—It is my husband's son by that Amazon woman.

It is Hippolytus.

I have long loved his beauty: but now the goddess has thrown stark madness

Into my heart: *I want. I want* . . . I will never yield to it.

SELENE. You—are in love with— Hippolytus?

PHAEDRA. If you call it love!

This loathsomeness in me. This disease. This burning shame. *Dazed, looks around.* Why, where have my great queens of the East gone to? *Laughing.*

They thought I meant it! They thought I didn't know a beggar-woman From a great queen!

SELENE, *pointing*. They are at their trade yonder. *Thoughtfully*. Hippolytus . . .

Is not the kind of young man for any woman to love.

PHAEDRA.   What?

SELENE, *with slow emphasis*.   He does not care for
women.

PHAEDRA. I am glad of that. Why should he waste himself? Cold, proud
and pure. —I'm going in, Selene.

Oh, I am tired of the light. I have a cold edge in me

That thinks it is worse than evil; it is ridiculous. —Like all our miseries!
—Will you come?

—And of course you understand that this is secret; and we'll never,
never, speak of it again. I shall not live long.

SELENE. You are better for having told me, dear. You walk more firmly;
you have faced the truth . . .

PHAEDRA.   Be silent, will you!

I have not faced the truth but an idiot deception, a great false fire in
the fog

On a phantom coast. —If decency and common shame were out of
the question—For I love his father,

My husband Theseus. It is not even *possible* to love two men. I know
how my heart lighted up

When I came down the plank from the Cretan ship and saw him
—tall, fierce and tender, there waiting for me,

In the dirty-cluttered Athenian harbor among the sailors—like the
temple of a god

On a high rock. For I *love* him, you know! Theseus I love. I have
been fighting myself . . .

He is—not young—if any person he loves should betray him . . .
When anyone's very young he can slide

From one lust to another, nothing is mortal: but a fierce man of war
growing grizzle

Under the helmet: I know him: if anyone should betray him even in
thought,

He'd hate the world. —And when I look at . . . his son . . . my
eyes

Scald with the stupid tears. —Die . . . ah? No choice. *Quietly*. I am
going in to hide myself

From the great eye of the sun; I have only one god

To pray to now. Not Love, not Light, not Fortune. Death, tall and
silent,

Has a flower in his hand; its name is Forgetfulness.

Its name—we hope—is Peace. *They approach the door.* Why, look: here
are my gay-colored East-queens!

Have you had good fortune, majesties? SECOND WOMAN *hides the basket
behind her.* No: show me. *It is shown.* Poor women: it is not much.
May I take a crust from it?

I do not think I have eaten since dawn.

SELENE.　　　　　　　　　　　　　　　　My lady!

PHAEDRA.　　　　　　　　　　　　　　One little crumb. I
have been too proud in my lifetime:

That's a great sin. But now I will beg of beggars, a bit of bread to
eat. You are kind, women.

I am truly grateful. *She goes into the house;* SELENE *follows, weeping. The
stage is gradually growing darker.*

FIRST WOMAN.　　　　　　　　The goddess has unraveled her mind. As if she
were struck by sudden lightning

When she went near the altar.

SECOND WOMAN, *terrified.* The altar! Look!

THE WOMEN *cower and shield their eyes. The goddess* APHRODITE *has glided
from behind a flowering bush, and leans her hand on the altar, her spot of light
increasing. She is tall and very beautiful, marble white and marble-polished, but
perhaps pale gold hair. She has a spray of fruit-blossom in her hand, and plays
with it. She speaks as if she were alone, thinking aloud.*

APHRODITE. . . . So I have come down to this place,

And will work my will. I am not the least clever of the powers of heaven.

She smiles, fondling the blossom-spray. I am the goddess the Greeks call
Aphrodite; and the Romans will call me Venus; the Goddess of
Love. I make the orchard-trees

Flower, and bear their sweet fruit. I make the joyful birds to mate
in the branches. I make the man

Lean to the woman. I make the huge blue tides of the ocean follow
the moon; I make the multitude

Of the stars in the sky to love each other, and love the earth.

Without my saving power

They would fly apart into the horror of night. And even the atoms
of things, the hot whirling atoms,

Would split apart: the whole world would burst apart into smoking
dust, chaos and darkness; all life

Would gasp and perish. But love supports and preserves them: *my saving power.*

This is my altar,

Where men worship me. Sometimes I grant the prayers of those that worship me: but those who reject me

I will certainly punish. Not because I am angry: love is my nature: the man who rejects love

Will be certainly punished.

There is a young man here,

Hippolytus, the son of Theseus, who rejects love and disdains to worship me. Horses, hounds and keen hunting,

And the dear friendship of the young men, his comrades, are all he cares for.

Bitterly. A chaste young athlete. He boasts of it:

That he will never make love to a woman nor worship

The Queen of Love. *Pauses and smiles, admiring the blossom spray.* Well

. . . I shall have my will of him. The young man

Will be taken care of. It is not right—nor safe—to be insolent

To a great goddess.

I am a little sorry for the lady Phaedra, his old father's young wife,

Who must go down into shame and madness to make his ruin; and I am sorry for the old hero,

Theseus, his father: but to suffer is man's fate, and they have to bear it. We gods and goddesses

Must not be very scrupulous; we are forces of nature, vast and inflexible, and neither mercy

Nor fear can move us. Men and women are the pawns we play with; we work our games out on a wide chess board,

The great brown-and-green earth. *She pauses, lifts her head and smiles frankly at the audience.* You are gathered here

To see the game?

Watch, then. I have planted the agony of love in that woman's flesh, like a poisoned sword

In her beautiful body: and I shall watch unseen, from my altar here, the sudden accomplishment

Of my planned purpose. The day will be

Today. *This* day. Look: the dark night is passing;

The beautiful feet of dawn come over the mountain, **the pale bright feet sandaled with music,**

Driving the gentle stars, like a man frightening
A flock of birds.

*Light increases on the sky and background, and comes slowly downward onto the
stage. Pastoral music of flutes, increasing with the light. Meanwhile the spot
of light fades from the altar; the goddess vanishes. She leaves her blossom spray
on the altar.*

THE WOMEN, *who have been crouching by the door of the house, are seen clearly
again. They move like persons awaking from a night's sleep.*

FIRST WOMAN, *pushing back her hair.* I had a terrible dream.

SECOND WOMAN.   A dream? I too!

FIRST WOMAN. I dreamed that a strong flame burned on the stone . . .
    Furtively pointing.

The altar there . . . a white-hot column of fire,

Whirling and smoking: and little men and women were struggling
    in it,

Burning alive. Frightful . . .

SECOND WOMAN.   I dreamed that a great white cat—a snow-
    leopard—

With pitiless glaring eyes and fierce claws unsheathed

Crouched on the altar, ready to pounce . . . on me I thought . . .

Oh, how foolish it is to tell our dreams!

They bring bad luck.

THIRD WOMAN.   Not mine, dear. I too had a dream, a pleasant one.

I dreamed that a pure-white dove came down from heaven

And perched on the altar; she had a spray of white apple blossom

In her beak . . . Why, look, look! There it *is*!

Was my dream true?

FIRST WOMAN.   No doubt someone left it there in the evening.

The door opens, and THE WOMEN *move backward from it.* HIPPOLYTUS *stands
in the doorway, tall and young, dressed for hunting. He has a short heavy lance
in his hand. He moves forward on to the doorstep, his head held high, looking
at the distant country. Another young man, slender and rather effeminate, comes
from the door.*

HIPPOLYTUS. How beautiful the early light is; when the mist rises from the
    mountain and the lark sings high. Did you bring the heavy arrows,
    Alcyon?

ALCYON. Heavy and light, both quivers, for beasts and birds.

    My lord Hippolytus . . .

HIPPOLYTUS.   Come, come! We have no lords here.

I am Hippolytus: you are my dear friend Alcyon,
My young hunting companion.

ALCYON. I will remember, sir.

HIPPOLYTUS. And no sirs either. Indeed I think I am half a year
Younger than you are, Alcyon.

ALCYON. That's true.

*A third young man comes into the doorway. He is burly, somewhat older than the
others, heavy-shouldered and yawning.*

HIPPOLYTUS, *with a gesture.* Our studious friend,
Andros.

ALCYON. Studious, you call him?

HIPPOLYTUS. Of drinking-songs and merry music. Oh, he's a
student.
What got you up so early, Andros?

ANDROS. The cock crowing: the tall bird that hates sleep.
He rubs his eyes sleepily.
We'll eat him, I hope, this evening.

HIPPOLYTUS, *laying his arm affectionately around* ALCYON'S *shoulders.* What
shall we do with our day, Andros? Do we hunt again?
The country people say that a great wild boar
Rages in the wood yonder.

ANDROS. All right, all right: I'll risk anything.
I am still drunk . . . with sleep.

HIPPOLYTUS. Or shall we race
Our horses along the shore, where the careful waves
Comb the sand clean and smooth?

ANDROS. Just as you like. But what's happened to you?
Are you in love, Hippolytus? I never knew you
To lack decision.

HIPPOLYTUS. We'll hunt, then. *He smiles at* ALCYON, *turns back to* ANDROS.
I love my friends, Andros . . .
If they are brave and beautiful.

ANDROS. That's good. But pretty girls too,
And tenderly smiling women are worth considering. There is a kind
of an altar over there . . . *pointing* . . .
You ought to pray to.

HIPPOLYTUS. I? No. I will worship the great Goddess of Love
. . . At a great distance. *He makes a gay gesture of salutation.* All hail!
Hail, Aphrodite! —The truth is:

I am a little cold toward the divinities
That are worshipped at night, with grotesque antics; the Goddess of
  Witchcraft and the Goddess of Love . . .
Such a pair! Seriously, Andros:
The world is full of breeders: a couple in every bush: disgusting. As
  for me, I'll spend my passion
On wild boars and wild horses.

THIRD WOMAN.   I see the blossom spray
Move on the altar!

SECOND WOMAN. I see the glaring eyes . . .

FIRST WOMAN. I see the fire of her anger . . .

HIPPOLYTUS.   What are the women singing, Alcyon? *Pointing.*
Those poor patched women?

ALCYON.   Some uncomfortable old ballad, no doubt.
They are too far away: I can hear the voices
But not the words.

SELENE *comes around the corner of the house, wringing her hands.*

SELENE. I don't know what to do! I know well enough: I must obey my
  lady's will. But I'm terribly afraid . . .
*She approaches the young men from behind them. They are looking at the beggar
women.*

ANDROS. Those three? They come to the house every day with their little
  basket; they make a music
And beg for food.

ALCYON, *to* SELENE, *seeing her behind his shoulder.*   What is it?

SELENE.   I have a message for my lord Hippolytus.

HIPPOLYTUS, *turns and looks down at her; speaks impatiently.*
Well, What?

SELENE.   From my lady Phaedra . . .
It is private, sir.

HIPPOLYTUS.   Speak your message: these are my friends.

SELENE.   I should have said
Secret. She is dying, sir.

HIPPOLYTUS.   What!

SELENE.   I think so.

HIPPOLYTUS. I am sorry that she is ill. Will you go down to the stable, my
  friends? I'll see you presently,
Or send for you.

ALCYON, *to* ANDROS, *as they go off together.* Bad news comes suddenly!

ANDROS. The mornings are unlucky, boy. We ought to sleep longer.
Exeunt.

HIPPOLYTUS. I knew that your lady had been ill, Selene: I never
  thought . . .

SELENE. It was last night, sir.

She lay like one in a trance, perfectly motionless, drugged with her
  sorrow, not even breathing . . .

HIPPOLYTUS. What sorrow?

SELENE. I cannot tell you. *A pause.* Suddenly—it was near dawn—she
  started up

With a moan like a scream. She stood like a dim white pillar in the
  dark room, saying "I can't die

And I can't live. Why should I bear this pain forever in silence?"
  It was pitiful, sir.

HIPPOLYTUS. Certainly. But what can I do?

SELENE. She made me comb her bright
  hair, "to look well," she said,

"When I am cold. For I am the daughter of a great man, and the
  wife

Of a great man." And now for hours

She has walked back and forth, back and forth, moaning. This is the
  restless agony that comes when death

Is at the door.

PHAEDRA *comes into the doorway; pale, calm, self-possessed; clothed like a
  queen. They do not see her yet.*

SELENE. She spoke your name once or twice.

Your father is away from home, and in his absence

You are head of the house.

HIPPOLYTUS. My father will be back tomorrow, I
  believe.

PHAEDRA. I do not know

Whether I have to die. I shall soon know.

SELENE. Oh, my lady . . .

PHAEDRA. You may go in, Selene.

I shall not need you. SELENE *hesitates;* PHAEDRA *comes down and stands
  on the lowest step. Speaks imperiously.* Go in!

With the other servants.

SELENE, *wringing her hands, returns as she has come; but stops and stands
  watching by the house corner.*

HIPPOLYTUS. You have been ill, Phaedra.

PHAEDRA. I have been patient,
  Hippolytus.

I think we must bear our fates, and accept

What the gods send. They send sickness or health, evil or good, pas-
sionate longing
Or the power to resist it. We have to do
What the gods choose.

HIPPOLYTUS.   Not entirely, Phaedra.
We have to *suffer* what they choose: but we control our own wills
and acts
For good or evil.

PHAEDRA.   But if one becomes *insane*, Hippolytus? The gods send
madness too. Madness, you know.
And we have to submit. *Smiling suddenly*. What a bore these philosophies
are, my dear! Good and evil! We're not schoolchildren—
Though fairly young still.

HIPPOLYTUS.   I am very glad, Phaedra,
That you are not so ill as your woman said. She pretended
You had a dying message for me.

PHAEDRA.   Why. Yes. I have. I nearly
Forgot. And I am truly very near to death. It is not well with me . . .
pressing her hand between her breasts . . .
In here. *A pause*. I am your father's wife, Hippolytus: I love you
I love you very deeply.
It is my duty. — How high and angrily you turn away from me!
That haughty thrust of the chin. I've always noticed
This coldness in you: it grieved me.

HIPPOLYTUS.   You are quite wrong. I am not
demonstrative perhaps . . . I have affections
Like other men; or perhaps more than others—and I am very glad
that my father chose
So good and beautiful . . .

PHAEDRA.   Let us not speak any more of your father: this
concerns *me*. I only want you
To be kind to me—as I would be to you . . . *She breaks off*. I think
so much of my childhood lately,
In the high sacred island, in my father's palace,
Beautiful Crete: we used to play a game there called hide-'n'-seek:
there was room there: one of my sisters
Got lost in the endless echoing corridors, the famous Labyrinth: we
hunted her for hours, we could hear her crying
Pitifully, far off . . . Hunt *me*, Hippolytus!
You are a great hunter, it is your life,

Hunting wild beasts in the black woods: can't you hear me crying?
I am lost, I am lost, I am crying
Pitifully . . .

HIPPOLYTUS.   I am bound to honor you: I cannot understand you clearly.

PHAEDRA. You cannot understand?
No, you can't understand. You know the secret ways of the deer on the mountain; you know where the wolves run;
You know on what rock over what hidden water deep in wet woods the spotted lynx
Watches, and her wild topaz eyes
Burn like twin fires in the green twilight, flaming for blood:—but what a woman wants . . .
No, you can't understand. You think I have something monstrous hidden in my mind. It is not true.
Kindness I want. Only kindness: Is that a monster? Why do you hate me, Hippolytus?
All cold, all angry.

He turns sharply away from her and turns back.

HIPPOLYTUS.   You are mistaken in that, Phaedra. I have felt kindness . . . I will confess it:
In my manner I loved you. The way you moved, and your mind and soul. I have thanked God that my nature
Is not . . . *inclined* toward women: or I might have loved you
Beyond what's right. Oh, I could conquer it: we know how to rule ourselves, we have self-control; we are not leaves
Blown by the wind!
But it might have been painful.

PHAEDRA.   So I am to suffer all the pain,
And you go free! —The battle-captain of those grim warrior-women, the breastless Amazons,
Was your mother: your father conquered her with his sword and his spear, he clubbed her down and she hated him . . .
And he raped her. *You* were born of that horror: no wonder
You distrust love! —Listen to me. I am a civilized person, Hippolytus, in exile here
Among savages: the fierce little cutthroat tribes of Greece, feudists and killers. Lovers of tragedy! —We Cretans
Love light and laughter. We like things refined and brilliant; bright games, gay music, brave colors. We have girl-acrobats

Who ride wild bulls, diving over the horns, blithe on the snout of
death: *our* courage, that hates no person.
—I tell you, Hippolytus, there are two heads of civilization on earth:
Egypt and Crete: but holy Egypt
Is so old, so old, stone-stiff and pious
In the petrified desert: we Cretans
Can be passionate still. We have hot blood, we love beauty, we hate
bigotry,
We know that good and evil and virtue and sin—are words, tired
words: but *love* is more beautiful than sunrise
Or the heart of a rose: the love of man and woman can be more
beautiful than the great-throated nightingale
Her heartbreak song: when all the leaves of the trees hang still to
hear it, and the stars in hushed heaven
Hold their breath and lean lower. —Ours could be. *Our* love could be.
THE THREE WOMEN *have come near them to listen.*

HIPPOLYTUS.   I say keep your tongue carefully.
If you have evil thoughts do not speak them. *Pointing.* These peering
creatures have ears
Under their hair.

PHAEDRA, *staring with dazed eyes at the women.* There are people here?
Why—*who cares?*—not I. Listen, women:
I have put all my life on this little hope—and I think I am losing it—
I am no doubt a dead woman talking to you: Theseus will kill me
If this man will not—but I am not ashamed of this little hope, I will
not hide it, I will sing it aloud
From the tops of the houses . . .

HIPPOLYTUS.   Have you gone mad?

SELENE, *who has been watching, runs to her.*

FIRST WOMAN.   We are your friends, my lady.
What wrong is done you?

PHAEDRA, *to* HIPPOLYTUS, *ignoring the women.* Mad—if you like—more or
less— But not so mad as a rabid dog in the dog-days, in the white
of summer,
Slavering and snapping . . . And not so mad as my mother who
went insane with love of a black bull,
That snuffling horror:—I know well enough
All the shames of my race; the slaves used to whisper in the dark
arches . . . There is a goddess, Hippolytus,
A terrible one: she rides me . . .

SELENE, *catching her arm, terrified for her.* Hush! Hush!

PHAEDRA. Merciless, with quirt
and spur . . . She is like a leopard

That has leaped on a deer: the great hooked claws drag through the tender flesh: the young doe staggers

Under that weight of pain, sobbing and running— Forgive me: I do not want to seem pitiful—

She is called the Goddess of Love, that merciless one— I cannot help myself—forgive me . . . *Sobs, hiding her face from him.*

SELENE. My lady!
For God's sake, hush!

HIPPOLYTUS. Let her go on, woman. Let her speak it all out, all her stark madness:

And I shall be proved innocent. There are witnesses . . .

Now: and if the woman wants to destroy herself, let her do so.

My patience has reached an end.

PHAEDRA. *Be careful!* You are not perfectly sure of being proved innocent, Hippolytus.

A black thought crossed my mind—like a vulture

Across a window—but I'm not mean enough—

Oh, be at rest, fear nothing. I have degraded myself already

Beyond all bounds.

SELENE, *her arm around her.* Come into the house, dear. My darling . . . my precious . . . PHAEDRA *shakes her off.*

PHAEDRA. Keep off me, will you! *Raises her head proudly.* As I was saying, this goddess—

I was speaking of one of the powers of Heaven, I think? Some divine one . . . My mind goes black suddenly

From time to time . . . *She draws her hand over her eyes.* This goddess, the Cyprian, the sweetly smiling white Aphrodite—

She was born of the sea, and the sea's treachery

Is in her blood: she has broken my little boat—no more of that!— she has the sea's sucking whirlpool

In her white body: *all* women have: it wants . . . it wants . . . As for me:

I am a little mad, as you say. —You breed horses, Hippolytus?

HIPPOLYTUS, *turning from her.* Observe her, women.

And if you are called in witness, report it. She is clearly insane; not responsible; not to be blamed.

As if some raging alien spirit overpowered her: demon or goddess:

Outside her own pure heart. You know the taint in the blood—
curse, if you call it so—

On the royal family of rich Crete—

PHAEDRA.   This man so hates me

That he digs up my father and my mother and my ancestors! *To*
HIPPOLYTUS. You have a good lance there:

That boar-spear with the great metal head, your toy that you play
with: will you do me a kindness, fellow?

You say you are not unfriendly to me—Stick it into me! *She kneels,*
tears at the cloth on her breast.

Here! Here I say. Slake your hate and my love!

HIPPOLYTUS, *gravely, with pity.* You see her, women?

PHAEDRA, *still kneels, her body and head arched backward.* You'd better strike:
I am growing dangerous.

I am growing to be a poison . . . Oh, my dear, my dear, have pity
on me! I am not hateful yet.

My skin is white, I think, and my mind still clean, and my body
stainless: at least

It is not ugly: my women have sometimes called me beautiful. Slaves'
flattery: ah? Well, not much worse

Than a deer in the woods, or one of those wildcats

You hunt so avidly . . .

This arm seems round and smooth, and the throat's fair enough;
and the clear shoulders: I have no blemish I know of . . .

I am the humblest person alive, Hippolytus,

Here, praying to you.

HIPPOLYTUS, *relenting.* Let me say this, Phaedra,

And then be silent forever: it is true you are very beautiful; and I
could love you . . . in spite of nature . . .

But not of honor. That holds me.

PHAEDRA, *embraces his knees.* I am so thirsty for you, Hippolytus!

I am burning alive. Forget your father: forget your honor and mine,
what do they matter? Forget

Your impediment of nature. I have put life and death on this throw
of the dice: and degraded myself . . .

I am not insane. I have loved you a long while. I have degraded
myself . . .

Take this degraded body here kneeling to you. Do what you like:
love it or kill it. Oh . . .

Lift it up: love it! *She embraces his knees.*

HIPPOLYTUS.   Shameless: take your hands from me. Stand up,
will you! It is not my intention
    To be made publicly ridiculous. *To* SELENE. You there! Uncoil your
    madwoman: she wearies me.
    Nurse her into the house.
PHAEDRA, *standing up.* I do not need
    Anyone's help. And I am not a weeper, either. I've played my life
    and lost, and here's death—
    Without a tear. —Very well: go back then:
    And hunt your beasts. Ride with your laughing boys. Run your fleet
    horses. It is possible some pointed thing
    Will fly after you.
HIPPOLYTUS, *turning to go.* There is nothing so unclean as madness.
    Turning back to SELENE. Watch your mistress carefully:
    Not to do herself harm. *He goes toward the rear.*
PHAEDRA.   Me? Let him watch his own disaster!
ANDROS, *comes from the trees in the distance; stops at sight of* HIPPOLYTUS. Oh,
    are you coming?
    We waited long for you: horse, hound and man too. Is the lady really
    so ill?
HIPPOLYTUS, *shaking his head, joining him.* Very ill, very ill.
    Ask me no questions, Andros: the best is silence.
    I am sorry for her. —Are Alcyon and the others there?
ANDROS.   Fussing with dog-leashes. . . .
    They go out together.
    Meanwhile PHAEDRA *has fallen on the door steps, in spite of* SELENE *supporting
    her.* THE WOMEN *stand watching.*
FIRST WOMAN. This is the worst thing that can happen to a woman: when
    love meets contempt.
    PHAEDRA'S *body jerks as under a whiplash. She half raises herself.*
PHAEDRA.   Contempt. I know: contempt—
    Is for the fallen. Not alone I will fall.
SECOND WOMAN.   To give gold for sawdust, and
    love for light ashes—
    Is woman's fate. To give her dear fragrance for a dog-bite . . .
PHAEDRA, *sitting on the step.* He said: "Keep your hands off me."
    Looking at her hands. Rejected: you pale things: I will send rougher hands
    Than these poor lilies. *She relapses on the step, face down, sobbing.* Ah,
    darkness, darkness, darkness . . .
SELENE.   Hush, child. Oh, hush . . .

THIRD WOMAN. While the young man goes laughing with his companions.

PHAEDRA. He will not last long! —What are *you*? Spirits tormenting me?

There was a kind of hypocrisy about my passion before. I could see
through it more or less.

Now it's deep, thick . . . I have quite lost myself. *Looks down at herself.*
Feels herself with her hands. This thing: this pitiful flesh: is this Phaedra,

The daughter of the wise ruler of famous Crete?

Or a scorned whore? *Stroking her hand down her arm.* Oh, here's something. *She takes off her bracelet and flings it.* Break it in three pieces.

THE WOMEN *pick up the heavy bracelet, show it to each other.* Gold, gold. We
are rich!

A man running dashes onto the stage, speaks breathlessly.

MESSENGER. He sent me ahead. I ran faster than the horses.

I heard the wind of their breath blowing behind me.

Is all well here?

THE WOMEN *gape at him in frightened silence.* PHAEDRA *in her black meditation
ignores him.*

PHAEDRA, *her hands tearing at each other.* A refused whore! *She gathers herself;
stands up, cool and self-possessed.* What did you say? Certainly all is well
here. And my lord Theseus

Is well, I hope?

MESSENGER, *who did not see her at first.* Oh—Very well, Madame: but much
troubled

By the tone of the oracle.

PHAEDRA, *calmly.* The oracle—I remember. He went to consult it.

MESSENGER. And it answered . . .

PHAEDRA. You needn't tell me, Messenger. My lord will tell me.

MESSENGER. 　　　　　　　　　　　　　　It answered strangely.

It said that his house was burning, he must hasten home!

PHAEDRA, *easily.* Did it so? Very interesting.

But you can see there's no fire here: no sort of trouble.

Take the man into the house, Selene. Let him eat and drink.

MESSENGER. No, no. My thanks, Madam. I must race back

To say all's well. *He goes.*

PHAEDRA, *instantly dismissing him from her mind, relapsing into black meditation.*

A scorned importunate whore: refused

And despised: kneeling, hugging his thighs: let her be hanged.

　　　　—And how his young men will laugh!

Between the minstrel's song and the juggler's tricks,

Over the wine.

FIRST WOMAN.   Truly his house was burning, and the god knew it.
But that fire's out.
PHAEDRA.   Is it out? A worse burns then.
A deadlier fire.
SELENE.   No: on the kindly hearth:
The warm life of the house.
PHAEDRA.   From the hearth to the roof-beams
This red fire leaps.
SELENE.   No. No. No! Women: Will you hear me? I pray
you listen to me.
You are friendly to my dear mistress: you take her bounty: I think
you love her: promise me on oath, women,
Never to speak of what you have seen and heard here, neither to my
lord Theseus nor any other:
Your husbands, your children: not to any acquaintance: never to
whisper it. For gossip and scandalous tongues are worse
Than fire in the roof.
THE WOMEN.   I promise. Oh, I swear it.
SELENE.   My mistress is pure and good:
you know that.
Our silence will make her well. This wound will heal,
This black storm will blow over.
PHAEDRA.   Fool!
SECOND WOMAN.   Truly it will, Phaedra! For time,
that eats up our pleasures,
Also mends pain.
FIRST WOMAN.   A man crossing the mountain
Feels the cold like a knife
Severing his bones; he sees black abysses
Infinitely far down;
And here the jagged rock-heads, the death-white
Teeth of snow on the rock.
He shudders in the knife-keen wind.
It is death, he thinks.
PHAEDRA.   I do not *think:* I *know*
That death is here at hand: but not a clean death.
SECOND WOMAN. From the wide plain looking backward, from the rich
plain
The traveler: his mountain
Hangs like a hyacinth bell,

Purple on the pale sky:
The peaks of the rock are like a flower's petals
And the color joyful . . .

PHAEDRA. I am preparing a thing that will *not* be joyful.

FIRST WOMAN. Would God that I knew the joy
Of driving through pleasant valleys in a green land,
As Theseus does: the horses lean on the yoke,
They snort the storm of their breath:
On one side of the way is clear water welling
Cold under willows; behind me white dust
Floats in the sun like a flag;
On the other side of the way is perhaps a hill
Clothed with green vineyard,
The little wax-yellow flowers and the curling tendrils
Like a girl's hair: on high the temple of a god
Lifts honey-colored marble above green leaves.
Happy are the hours there . . .

PHAEDRA. The woman sees happiness.
But as for me, I see shame, I see corpses.

SECOND WOMAN. The girls and young men go up
Singing together, carrying the lamb and the golden corn,
The broad green leaves and the grape clusters,
To the beauty of the god in the blue-veiled autumn . . .

PHAEDRA. I say, be quiet! —How can I endure myself?
He knew me for what I am, and he did rightly
When he despised me. False to the bone. I think too much,
And lose myself among the pictures my mind makes. The core of
    me—the—what they call heart—
Hidden and I cannot find it. I feel my mind swooping, I feel the awful
    storms of brute instinct,
And between—nothing. —But this I know: I will not betray him.
I will not be false. —As for you, women, I pray you—when Theseus
    comes—
Be silent. Cover up my folly. Have mercy on me. Let my name be
    remembered
As one who was chaste and faithful, never looking aside from her one
    man, and died young,
For no particular reason . . .

SELENE, *frightened*. He is coming now my lady! Listen: they are here.

We must be ready, we must smile and be quiet: that's woman's happiness.

PHAEDRA.   Woman's . . . happiness!

SELENE. I pray you, my lady!

PHAEDRA. Let him come.

FIRST WOMAN, *to* PHAEDRA. Silence is God's best gift.

THESEUS, *with armed attendants, comes rapidly forward.*

SECOND WOMAN.   I will be silent . . .

SELENE. Lock up your lips, women!

THESEUS, *looking at the house; to his nearest attendant.* The house has no
   damage at all; nor the roof either.

No smoke; no wailing. What did that priestess mean? *Suspiciously.*

Why are you crowding the door, women?

They move aside, in silence. THESEUS *sees* PHAEDRA, *sitting on the step, staring
at him.* Is it well with you, Phaedra? *She stares at him, without moving.*

SELENE, *stammering with nervousness.* She has been a little ill. I brought her
   out for the sun . . .

It is no great disorder, my lord: your absence
Has made her sad.

THESEUS.   I galloped home at the full stretch of the horses,
   my charioteer

Whipping and shouting: for the oracle

Sang that my house was fired. What has happened?

SELENE.   .   Nothing, sir.

THESEUS. Why does she not speak then?

SELENE.   Nothing whatever, sir—

Except my lady's small illness.

PHAEDRA, *standing up, clear and bitter.* She lies, Theseus.

THESEUS.   What?

PHAEDRA.   Evil *has* happened.

The worst and shamefullest.

SELENE, *rapidly.*   She is full of fever, my lord: her mind wanders
   and boggles like a lost bird . . .

PHAEDRA. What a desperate liar! —But it is not her fault: I'll not let any
   servant of mine

Be whipped for *me.* I say the woman is an open liar; but trying to
   protect me

From your just wrath. My lord, a common sweating peasant weary
   at the plow

Would not endure it.

SELENE.   Her delirium of fever . . .

PHAEDRA.   Silent, you!
Pray to God in your heart.

THESEUS.   I am not a patient man. I hate the female herd,
that chatters like monkeys
And never speaks.

PHAEDRA.   Without chattering, my lord: nothing shrill, no outcry:
Coldly and clearly: —Your bed is defiled and your house broken.
If I should bear a child,
It will not be yours.

*THESEUS draws his short sword half way from the scabbard, and slams it back
again; staggering with rage.*

THESEUS.   Go on. Speak.

PHAEDRA.   This defiled body
Is waiting for you to scour it with sudden death.

THESEUS.   Go on. Speak more.

PHAEDRA.   Its
woman-weakness met violence
In the bed of shame.

THESEUS.   So you say. They all say that. —Who was the man?

PHAEDRA.   It is
true, my lord.
See on my throat the marks of his strangling hands.

THESEUS.   I do not see them.
Shouts. Who?

PHAEDRA.   A man well known to you.
Now give me death, Theseus.

THESEUS.   Presently perhaps. Who was it? *No answer.*
Who?

PHAEDRA. I will not tell you.

THESEUS.   White fool—
Will you drive me mad?

PHAEDRA.   No. *He* was mad, I think. *I* will be silent.
I will not drive you mad: you'd run stark raving
If I answered you.

THESEUS. You'll answer, you'll answer. You cheap toy—broken trinket—
mud-trampled rose-petal—
I have to kill a swine: *what* swine?

PHAEDRA. You have killed too many men, Theseus, famous for blood. Your hands stink of it.

I noticed that.

THESEUS, *shouting*. Who was it?

PHAEDRA. No matter how well you wash them, Theseus.
—I'd sent my woman away
Because her breathing made a noise in the night. I was alone,
Naked in bed, half asleep: the door moved on its well-oiled hinges, and that young man
Stood in the room.

THESEUS, *black with rage, controlling himself*. Patience. Patience.

PHAEDRA. I saw him
well: there was a night-lamp:
And he told me his name. He said that something deadly had happened, and he had to speak to me.
I knew him well, Theseus; I perfectly trusted him;
I let him come near the bed. When your wrath cools
I'll speak his name. It is one you trust. He held a knife at my throat—
And . . . did . . . his will. I was too weak and cowardly to cry to the slaves. I pled with him.
I wept and pled: saying, "Though my life and honor are nothing to you,
Will you dishonor your father Theseus, whose wife I am?"

THESEUS, *shouting*. Agh! —No. —What were you saying?
What did you say, Phaedra?

PHAEDRA. That my prayer was vain. He was like a beast, like a wild beast.
Coldly. That is his nature.

THESEUS, *drawing his sword*. You dirty leavings. —You say that my son Hippolytus—

PHAEDRA. I will not send the father against the son.
I never named him.

THESEUS. —took you by force? Raped you? Oh, lying fool—
Tell me something true once!

SELENE, *screams suddenly*. Ai! *Sobs*. Oh, oh . . .

PHAEDRA, *coldly watching her*. These women know it.
They will probably lie, to cover it.

THESEUS. Who caught you at it? Who?

That woman?

Indicating SELENE.

You'd not tell but for that.

PHAEDRA.   No one. They slept. But I being mad with grief
and my life is death—

I told them.

FIRST WOMAN. We saw her making lamentation, sir.

This morning. Weeping and crying.

THESEUS.   You repented—ah?

You tempted him, you perverted him, handled him, slavered on him—
And you repented. *Pause.* I don't believe it.

Somebody caught you at it: you wept for *that. Covering his eyes.*

—My own loved son.

FIRST WOMAN.   Oh, she is not to blame, sir, not to blame; guiltless.
It was her misfortune

But not her crime.

THESEUS.   Call it *misfortune* do you, foul-mouth?

You prim-tongued fool! Misfortune! God help me hold myself!

I want to go stabbing, stabbing, stabbing . . . *To his nearest* ATTENDANT.

Bring him in!

ATTENDANT. What, sir?

THESEUS. Bring him in. He is either hunting or about the place somewhere . . . PHAEDRA *smiles a little.*

THESEUS, *grimly self-controlled.* I will not enter my house

Until I've cleaned it.

ATTENDANT.   We'll find him, sir. *He and another go out.*

THESEUS.   Take men with you. Bind him
if he resists.

But wound him not.

ANOTHER ATTENDANT, *an old man.* Take heed, my lord, not to judge
rashly. We know

That all women are liars.

THESEUS.   Not to their own hurt.

OLD ATTENDANT.   Even to their own hurt, my lord.

And your son, we know, dislikes women . . .

THESEUS.   Therefore he did it.

Pure hatred. Pure evil.

PHAEDRA, *almost brightly.* How many people have you killed in all your
life, Theseus? Three hundred?

With your own hand?

That's what they call a hero. That's what they call a great man.
  Kill, kill, and kill:
They put up statues. But spare your son, Theseus,
Though he is vicious: a beast, an evil beast: you twisted his name out
  of me . . .

THESEUS, *ignores her; sheathes his sword; his eyes rove about the scene; fasten on*
THIRD WOMAN. You with the zither.
You patched thing. Make music.

THIRD WOMAN   Me, sir? It is vile music, sir, dog's music—
And we are broken with the woe of this house . . .

THESEUS, *both hands on his temples, his body tense and writhing.* Play!

PHAEDRA.   It will not heal your wound, Theseus.
Only blood heals . . . *your* wounds.

THESEUS.   It will pass the interval. You have half an hour,
  I believe, of life yet.
Before your breath stops.

PHAEDRA, *smiling.* But I *wish* to die, Theseus!

THIRD WOMAN *begins to play.*

SECOND WOMAN. I am terrified . . .
  She sings—or rather speaks, but with consciousness of the music. What is best
    for a man?
For our human half-darkness under the stars
Is full of evil; grief after grief comes in,
Like wolves leaping the fold-wall . . .

FIRST WOMAN. Silence is best.

SECOND WOMAN. Grief after grief,
Like waves flooding the sea-wall: but wealth could stop them.
A golden dyke: a rich man can buy security . . .

FIRST WOMAN. Then why do the great kings die by violence?

SECOND WOMAN. Pure love is best.
Let pure love be my heaven, and fair love my fortress . . .

FIRST WOMAN. But if you love someone, death comes and takes him.

THIRD WOMAN, *striking the zither strings with her hand, breaking off the music.*
Then death is best!

FIRST WOMAN.   Death is good in his time.
Silence is best.

THIRD WOMAN. An old old song, my lord. It doesn't make sense—
And I can't help it.

PHAEDRA.   See how you've calmed him, women! He has bitten his lips through, the beard's blood-lined,

Black-red on the grim gray. Why—it's the gnashing muzzle of a wild
  boar! Perhaps Hippolytus
Would like to hunt it! —I warned you, Theseus,
Music will never soothe: you didn't even hear them. What your
  wound wants for cure is somebody's blood.
Sword's joy: a turn of the wrist—
And the flashing red river.

THESEUS.   I have been thinking so. *He moves threateningly toward her.*
PHAEDRA.   The joy of stabbing . . .
He comes to her, hand on sword-hilt.—Me? No! Not me Theseus! *She
shrinks backward from him.*
Not me! You are grim, dearest, but you are just. All men have said
That you are just . . . *She kneels to him.*

THESEUS.   What a harlot's face you have!
PHAEDRA.   Now my life hangs on a hair—
  consider yet,
Would I—or any woman—willingly embroil myself with a young man
  well known
Averse from women? Think what you like of me—dearest, don't
  strike!—
I am not such a fool. Hippolytus is that sex—higher or lower, I know
  not, but strange—
That loves its own . . .

THESEUS.   I'll ask him when he comes. I see you have consid-
  ered him.
PHAEDRA. Not till you forced me to!
THESEUS. It doesn't matter. You'll not be alive when he comes. As you say:
  It will be a great pleasure. I know that my son Hippolytus
  Is pure and true.
PHAEDRA, *standing up.* Very well. I beg no more. How they'll laugh in
  Athens!
How they'll whisper it here: "That poor Cretan woman!
The son wronged her and the father killed her, though innocent.
  That's what she gets for marrying a deadly Greek!"
I have a strange horror of that gray blade, Theseus: but here's my
  throat. I am not a coward.
THESEUS, *sighing.* You have a few minutes yet: I'll hear him first. I am
  just, as you say.
I have lived with some honor and respect. I have led the people and
  been true to my friends, and done—they tell me—

Valiantly once or twice. I have been thought of as a man who could—
at least—
Guard his own gear . . . But old age comes, old age comes,
And flies defile us. —Presently you will hear such a slapping of flies
around here—but not Hippolytus,
Not for your weight in lies . . . Oh Phaedra, Phaedra!
This is a dream, not truth. You will wake up and say: "What was
I saying?
It was a dream." . . . I know you are not false—when I first saw
you—those wide-open shieldless eyes
Full of trust, brave little circles of tender sky—and the soft mouth
that knew not
Whether to laugh or weep, and did both at once—I loved you, Phaedra,
forever.
You were like a small child: a beautiful courageous child . . . *He
lifts his head to listen.* Are they coming now? Tell them it's over.
It was a dream. —But truly, if my son hurt you . . .
He shall not live.

HIPPOLYTUS *enters. He moves freely and with confidence. But the two guards,
walking slightly behind him on each side, look like jailers rather than attendants.*

PHAEDRA, *clearly and carefully.* Do you still despise me, Hippolytus?

HIPPOLYTUS, *ignoring her.*
You have come home, Father: I am glad of that.
But why in anger? —At least your honest idiots, the axemen here,
Seem to believe so . . . Apparently they are right for once. I see
the black
Vein on your brow . . .

THESEUS, *eyes him gravely in silence; turns to* PHAEDRA. Is this the man?

PHAEDRA.   No.

THESEUS. What do you mean—no? That you lied? *Trembling with anger
again.*
And now confess it? I will put the matter more plainly:
Is this the man who rode you last night?

HIPPOLYTUS.   Are you raving mad, Father!

THESEUS.   *Someone* is going to
die. Not you, perhaps.

PHAEDRA, *to* THESEUS. I have some nerves of decency still: though you
don't think so. I will not talk your sword
Into the belly of your son.

THESEUS, *his hand on the hilt.* Into your own then?

PHAEDRA, *calmly.* I am such a coward, Theseus. If I hadn't been a coward
   I'd have screamed and got help: but he was over me
   Like a wild beast. Don't strike, dear! It was he: yes: Hippolytus.
      Don't strike!

THESEUS. Do they say I am not a patient man?
   Fools! Cold as stone. *To* HIPPOLYTUS. Why were you not hunting today?

HIPPOLYTUS.   She lies, Father: that's clear enough:
   Either out of insanity or shaking terror. Shut her up: and tell me
      clearly what monstrous thing
   I am accused of.

THESEUS.   A crime. You are my son, God help me. A crime that
   only iron-in-the-guts
   Cures. —Why were you not hunting today?

HIPPOLYTUS.   Because I did not choose to. I was somewhat . . .
      dejected.
   I was at the stable: some of the young men went . . .

THESEUS.   Dejected?

HIPPOLYTUS.   Sad; tired;
      sorrowful . . .

THESEUS.   Oh! Your exertions
   In the night tired you? *Moaning with rage.* Oh, Oh . . . You . . .
      blond pillar of righteousness! Filth: filth: filth!
   God strike you dead!

HIPPOLYTUS.   God is more just, I hope,
   Than you are. This is blind nonsense. Have you ever known me
   To follow women? As for being . . . tired: a person whom I once
      loved and honored had done
   A shameful thing. It grieved me.

THESEUS.   What person?

HIPPOLYTUS.   I cannot tell you,
      Father: I am not a tale-bearer.
   The thing failed, and is finished.

PHAEDRA.   Do you think it is *finished*,
      Hippolytus? *Love* has an end: but deep hate has no floor,
   It falls forever. —I say that he had neither shame nor mercy, Theseus.
   He choked me with his claws while his body soiled me.
   You take it quietly. It is true you are growing old, Theseus.

THESEUS.   Shut your mouth.

PHAEDRA. It is right for a violent man to be very careful
   Before he acts.

HIPPOLYTUS, *to* PHAEDRA. I understand you now: clearly. There is not one
hair of difference between the extremes
Of love and hate. They are the same thing, one identical fury. —This
woman is insane, Father.
She is unspeakably false.

PHAEDRA, *quietly and sadly.* I loved you once, Hippolytus.

HIPPOLYTUS. Yes? *I will tell him.*

PHAEDRA. And you, pitiless,
Came in and robbed me! I pray you, Theseus, to kill me now. You
are a man of blood, as all know.
They say shame dies in the grave. But as for the young man, although
he is evil, and has earned sudden darkness:
He is your son, remember.

THESEUS, *scowling with doubt, looking from one to the other, like a tormented bull.*
The worse. But something holds my hand . . .

PHAEDRA. He was right, then. He said,
"My father is an old man and will hardly care."

THESEUS, *sword in hand.* Ah . . . *He takes a step toward* HIPPOLYTUS, *but
turns to look when* ALCYON *cries out.*

ALCYON *has entered in wild haste, cries loudly.* What are they doing to you,
Hippolytus?

HIPPOLYTUS. Nothing . . . A little matter
of life and death, my dear.
And honor, as they say—if anything like that is left in this foul pit.
You cannot help me. But wait, for these women may.

ALCYON, *struggling to come near him, but held back by the guards.* I'll serve
you with my life or my death: that much I know.

HIPPOLYTUS *smiles at him, then speaks to* THE WOMEN. Women: you were
here this morning, when . . . *pointing* . . . *she* there
Displayed her shame. I was sorry for it. But now you can bear true
witness. The woman made a shrill noise,
Pitiful and indecent . . . no more of that. Did she say at any time
she had suffered violence?
From me or anyone?
They stand silent, gaping at him.

THESEUS. Answer!

FIRST WOMAN, *after a moment.* Silence is best.

THESEUS. You gaudy dummies, who bribed you? *To* ATTENDANT. Bring
whips!

SECOND WOMAN, *to* HIPPOLYTUS. She begged you to kill her, sir.

HIPPOLYTUS. Did she accuse me of anything?

SECOND WOMAN.　　　　She said, "hard-hearted"—

PHAEDRA.　　　　　　　　　　　He had come to my bed like
　　a wild beast in rut:
　I said, *hard-hearted!* Tell him the truth, women, the truth at last:
　　that I said
　He had destroyed me—that I said he had come . . .

THESEUS.　　　　　　　　　　Silent! Let *them* talk.

PHAEDRA.　　　　　　　　　　　You then, Selene!
　　You know well
　Whether he had me or not, by force and violence,
　In the awful night.

SELENE.　　　　　And from that moment
　You have never ceased weeping. Oh, it was cruel! Oh, it was mon-
　　strous! I'd gladly cut out his eyes
　With my own hand.

THESEUS, *gravely, moving toward his son.* You have heard your death sung,
　　Hippolytus.

ALCYON, *screaming.* It is a lie! Stop! She lies. She'll say anything
　To please her mistress . . .

SECOND WOMAN.　　　　What the woman says is true, sir,
　God's frightful truth. Although I begged her to cover it up with
　　silence—there is no crime in silence . . .

FIRST WOMAN.　　　　　　　　It is all true.

ALCYON, *screaming.* Stop! Kill *her:* kill Phaedra: *she* is the one . . .
　Meanwhile THESEUS *has come slowly and fatally to* HIPPOLYTUS.

HIPPOLYTUS, *holding out his hand to ward off the sword; speaking quietly.* They're
　　making a fool of you, Father. —It is bitter to be killed innocent, by
　　women's lies.

THESEUS. You model of chastity!
　*He shifts his sword with skilled suddenness, drives it under the breastbone, from
　below upward.*

HIPPOLYTUS, *bending forward and falling.* Fool. Oh . . . *Shocked silence; then*
　　PHAEDRA'S *clear voice.*

PHAEDRA. Do you still despise me, Hippolytus?

HIPPOLYTUS, *struggling for breath.* Stand off . . . Give me room to die
　　in . . . *He raises head and shoulders from the ground: a gasping shout.* Yes!
　I despise you. *Turns painfully in silence; looks up at* THESEUS *and says
　　tenderly.* My poor father. *He dies.*

PHAEDRA, *like a bewildered child, quietly, her hand to her mouth.* But I love him, Theseus!

ALCYON, *struggling with a guard.* Let me pass. Let me pass, fellow. Let me at him.

THE GUARD. Watch out: he has a knife . . .

A yelp of pain. Ow!

ANOTHER GUARD, *behind* ALCYON, *brutal and unexcited.* Kill: huh? *He stabs him from behind;* ALCYON *drops silently.* Woman-boy, huh? Lie down. *No one gives attention to this by-play,* THESEUS *stands looking down at his son.*

PHAEDRA. But I'd have died for you, Hippolytus! Gladly have died for you. I fought myself—

I tried to save you . . .

He was your best, old man: and so you have killed him. The best youth in all Greece, beautiful Hippolytus,

Is slain for *me.* I lied, you understand: he was clear: he was pure as crystal: and any fool but you, Theseus,

Would have perceived it. I ran mad for love of him; I prayed to him, I pursued him, I hugged his knees—

Here, before these women, in the eyes of the morning—

And he refused me. He loved me perhaps a little: but he was pure And honorable: so I had you kill him.

It was you I hated, Theseus: an old gray manslayer; an old gray wolf, stinking of blood, destroyer

Of generations. For fifty years you have been killing the sons of men— *and now your own son.*

THESEUS, *looks vaguely up at her.* Pray you, be quiet . . . *He looks down again.*

PHAEDRA. You understand you have killed him, Theseus? Your son is dead: he will never rise again.

Your beautiful son. *You* killed him. Now *me,* I hope.

His face is contorted; he shudders; finally looks up.

THESEUS. You yap at me like a sick hound, and I cannot hear you.

PHAEDRA. I see that you understand though, Theseus. *A pause.*

Dull, and a man of blood, easy to fool . . . *A pause.*

Your lovely son. *A pause.* Hold all the agony you can. Stuff it into your heart. *Mine's* full. *A pause.* Still silent?

You will soon burst, Theseus. *A pause.* Perhaps you will kill yourself. *A pause.* Me first, you know.

THESEUS, *looks at her; rubs his eyes.* I have some blood in them . . .
Dull, and a man of blood . . . Some god came into me;
Some evil god. *He looks down again.*

PHAEDRA.　　　　How cowardly it is in men, to say
That a god did it! *You* did it. *A pause.* And *I* . . . deluded you. *A pause.*

Surely you can do it again? For me? *She comes near him, pulling open the clothing at her breast.* See: deep! *He gives her no attention.*

Not yet? —I am almost a little sorry for us. —I wish the long black ship that brought me here
Had split on the sharp reef in the raging storm. I wish my bones were churning unfleshed forever,
White in black water, out of the sun, wide-washed, far-apart, scattered; and slime-running seaweed—
Those cold black leaves—grew where my blood runs—where my heart beats—here in the ribs—here—
Where your red sword should rest soon. —You were so beautiful, Hippolytus, you were so beautiful!
I sought you as a brown moth seeks the bright flame: or as the young darkness
Loves the evening star: or a starved beast his prey. I was that beast. On my knees I hunted you.
You have died: who can live? *She has approached the steps, and now goes up into the doorway; gazes back at the body.* I loved you so.

THESEUS.　　　　The woman makes a great noise
And it means nothing.

PHAEDRA.　　　　　　　　Are you beginning at last to understand? Are you beginning
To *feel* now, Theseus?

THESEUS, *on one knee by the body; shakes his head in bewilderment.* I loved him . . .

PHAEDRA, *pityingly.* I know. I counted on it.
How wretched I should be if I alone wept! —Stay there and watch him for me, Selene,
And tell me all that he does: his groans, words, grief, outcries and so forth—
And whether he goes wild or not. Watch very carefully:
For he—my husband—is a great man, powerful and pitiable; the glory of Athens and Greece,

Famous into far Asia: And I have almost come to the Greek opinion: that there is nothing

Nobler than a great man in his mortal grief. Or . . . *She begins to weep* . . . a loved beautiful youth . . .

Suddenly slain. Oh . . . *She raises her head, speaks proudly.*

These are the agonies that men remember forever; imperishable jewels of the age; and their mighty spirits

In spite of God live on. As for me—me too perhaps they'll remember— to spit on.

I can't say that I care. As for you, Theseus— *She smiles brightly at him, speaks slowly and lovingly.*

Come soon, dear. What else can you do? Weep, and then come. *She stands a moment, gazing, and goes into the house.* THESEUS *ignores her, crawling beside his son's body. Violently trembling he touches the body; shakes his head stupidly. Touches it again.*

FIRST WOMAN. He will not dare to touch the face.

SECOND WOMAN. He has touched the face.

THIRD WOMAN. He never will dare to kiss it.

FIRST WOMAN.   When his mind comes back to him,
Suddenly he will give a great cry,
And spring at us with his sword . . .

SECOND WOMAN.   Do you think so!

THIRD WOMAN. And kill us all. *They, with* SELENE, *withdraw from him in terror, still watching. The guards have already stood back, drilled and impassive. The body of* ALCYON *is concealed behind them.* THESEUS *is alone with his dead son.*

FIRST WOMAN. He is gazing at him. He has touched his throat.

SECOND WOMAN. He is fondling the bright hair. He is fondling . . .

THIRD WOMAN. He kissed the face!

FIRST WOMAN. He is stroking the cheeks and the bright hair . . .

THESEUS, *leaping up.* Quick, you dogs! Help me!
I saw him breathe. The color is creeping back
Into his lips. Bring water and wine and a great linen bandage—
Oh! Did I hurt you?

You'll live, you'll live! *He half raises the body; lets it down again; kneels by it.*

FIRST WOMAN, *after a pause.* The man you have struck *never* lives, Theseus.

THESEUS.   O God of the Sea: *my* God,
My foster-father, God of the high and shining and leaping Sea: you promised me

You'd answer three prayers of mine, whatever they were. I pray you
  all three at once:
Make my son live! *Make my son live. Make my son live.*
FIRST WOMAN.   You would have to
  pray to the God of Death, Theseus,
Not to the Sea. He has no power in this matter.
SECOND WOMAN.   And as to Death: those gray
  stone lips
Have never answered a prayer. His ears are stone: men never pray
  to him. His cold gray hands implacably
Hold what they take.
A scream is heard from the house; running feet and voices.
CONFUSED CRIES IN THE HOUSE. Ai! Oh! Oh! Help me. Lift her higher,
  loose the cord! A knife, a knife!
THESEUS, *kneeling by the body, seems not to hear them.*
SECOND WOMAN. What new horror has happened!
SELENE, *screams,* My dearest! Ai! My baby! *She runs into the house.*
FIRST WOMAN, *pointing at* THESEUS. Look, women!
  He has kissed the wound!
A burst of lamentation—keening—is heard from the house.
SECOND WOMAN.   Listen: do you hear them?
FIRST WOMAN.   Someone has died in the house.
THIRD WOMAN. Death in the house: death here. *She strikes her zither and
  joins in the musical lamentation.*
SELENE *comes from the doorway, stands on the top step; cries loudly.* Theseus!
  Theseus!
My lady is dead. My lady Phaedra has died. She hanged herself.
She knotted the hard cord around her white throat . . . *Weeps, covering
  her face.* Oh, Oh, Oh . . .
THESEUS, *slowly stands up; shakes his head like a hurt bull.* Be silent, yelpers.
You howlers in the doorways— *Shouting* . . . be silent!
He looks all about the scene, except at his son's body.
I am not so stupid as you believe. I wish my mother had strangled me
In the night I was born! I wish the sun had gone blind that morning.
  I wish that Aethra my mother
Had pointed her breasts with poison before she suckled me, before
  I began to be a slayer of men
And a woman's fool. I say there is no pleasure in it; it is not delightful
To be old, mocked and a fool. I say that liars have swindled me out
  of reason, like a poor old peasant

Duped in the market; they have diddled him out of his land and his
    cows and his very teeth—and there they go laughing
And hang themselves. Why did she laugh like that? What did she
    mean? I will never draw sword again.
I wish it had turned in my hand and stabbed me, in my first fight:
    but now let it stick in the sheath, blackened
With dear dear blood. My enemies will come and mock me, old and
    disarmed: I shall say, "Where is my son
To speak to them between the tall stones? Where is my son Hippolytus
To take my part?" He will lie still, he will not come, he will not answer.
    There is a darkness:
And those who enter it have no voice any more; and their hands
    and feet
Will not move any more; and the dear flesh falls from the rotting
    bones, and the beauty is ugliness;
The brave cold eyes are humbled, the bodies stink. I wish I had died
    for them!
They were like two stars in heaven: when the high clouds break open,
    and a warm wind
Blows in the dark: but I was easily fooled . . .
And my hand leaped. They were nearly the same age; they were
    brave and beautiful. I should have helped her
In her deep trouble.
And all this noise was nothing—froth and a noise—a little noise in
    the night. The two I loved
Are gone: that's all. I stand
Between two gods; and my north is grief and my south is wailing
    and the children laugh at me.
She was in trouble and I did not help her. Indeed I never understood
    her; she was too beautiful for me.
Her mind moved like a bird.
And now I have to go down all alone in blood, having lived in it,
    alone to death,
Having loved deeply. As to—my dear, dear son . . .
He looks down at the body, gives an animal cry of pain, flings himself on the body.
The scene begins to darken.

FIRST WOMAN. A mighty man, like a beaten dog or a shot bird,
    Crawls in the dust.
The worst wounds that we suffer we inflict on ourselves.
SECOND WOMAN. Hippolytus was happy.

He had his youth, he did no evil, suddenly he died.
The pity of these things has broken my heart.
*The scene has darkened to deep twilight. Clear female laughter is heard from
the altar of* APHRODITE. *Light shines increasingly on the altar; the goddess
appears there. All gaze at her; except* THESEUS *by the body of his son.*
APHRODITE, *laughing.* We are not extremely sorry for the woes of men.
   We laugh in heaven.
We that walk on Olympus and the steep sky,
And under our feet the lightning barks like a dog:
What we desire, we do. *She smiles.* I am the power of Love.
She stands smiling and considering.
In future days men will become so powerful
That they seem to control the heavens and the earth,
They seem to understand the stars and all science—
Let them beware. Something is lurking hidden.
There is always a knife in the flowers. There is always a lion just
   beyond the firelight.
Her light dims out and she vanishes. The scene is all dark.

NOTES

LEONCE AND LENA

Georg Büchner submitted a draft of LEONCE AND LENA in a publisher's play contest in 1836 but continued to work on the play almost until his death (in the following year). There were, finally, two MS. versions, neither of which has survived. Scholars have made different dispositions of the available materials. The present translator, claiming no right to an opinion in this field, has simply followed one of the most authoritative editions, that published by Inselverlag: Georg Büchner's *Werke und Briefe* (Leipzig, 1949). A. H. J. Knight's *Georg Büchner* (Blackwell, England, 1951) contains an admirable 20-page section on the play. A previous English translation appeared in Geoffrey Dunlop's *The Plays of Georg Büchner* (1928, reprinted 1952). One of the plays Büchner has drawn on in this work that has often been considered chiefly a plagiarism is Musset's *Fantasio*, which appears in *From the Modern Repertoire*, Series One. Another is Clemens Brentano's *Ponce de Leon*. While Léonce is an accepted French form of the name Leo (Leon, Leontius, etc.), it has been suggested that Büchner arrived at it by putting Ponce and Leon together; at any rate, a joking literary allusion to Brentano may lurk in the name. *Leonce and Lena* was first performed in 1911 at the Residenzbühne in Vienna. Karl Walser's design for a later performance at the Lessing Theatre in Berlin is reproduced as Color Plate 3 in Oskar Fischel's *Das moderne Bühnenbild*. Peter Larkin's drawings were commissioned expressly for the present book.

A DOOR SHOULD BE EITHER OPEN OR SHUT

Alfred de Musset, who early in life made a reputation as a lyric poet of somewhat sentimental cast, turned to playwriting in earnest in the mid-1830s, by which time, though hardly more than twenty-five years old, he thought himself "too old to write." Most of his plays were published first in the *Revue des Deux Mondes* as pieces to be "seen from one's own armchair" and republished in book form as *Comédies et Proverbes*. Only a good while later did theatre managers discover that these "trifles" were thoroughly actable and moving. The proverb A DOOR SHOULD BE EITHER OPEN OR SHUT dates from 1845 and was first performed on April 7, 1848, in the midst of the revolution of that year. The drama historian Martin Lamm has the following to say of the French genre of "proverbs": "During the 18th century the *proverbe* was really a sort of game played on social occasions; familiar proverbs were acted, and the audience had to guess them, as in charades. The composition of such pieces soon took literary form, and the proverb which provided the theme of the play was printed at the head or the end of the play. Musset used this device solely to present psychological situations and scenes in dramatic form."

THÉRÈSE RAQUIN

THÉRÈSE RAQUIN, which laid the foundation of the theatre of naturalism, and led directly to such masterpieces of the genre as Strindberg's *Miss Julie*, was first performed at the Renaissance Theatre in Paris, July 11, 1873. The play has been staged in various English adaptations but it is doubtful whether any faithful rendering of the French original has previously been published. Zola's famous preface appears in Appendix A.

THE MAGISTRATE

There are artists who long to be recognized as serious but who are famous only for their light verse or their comic operas. Pinero's fate was the opposite. He is famous only for *The Second Mrs. Tanqueray;* William Archer's generation, in their enthusiasm for his problem plays, put his great farces in the shade. The present editor was led back to THE MAGISTRATE (1885) by the following remarks from James Agate's *Short View of the English Stage:* "In 1885 he [Pinero] inaugurated with *The Magistrate* that series of brilliant farces which are equal to the best of Labiche. . . . These little pieces show this playwright as a first-class man of the theatre and a *vaudevilliste* of genius." Another testimonial is to be found in Lord Alfred Douglas's book on Oscar Wilde: ". . . he [Wilde] considered *The Magistrate* to be the best of all modern comedies."

ANATOL

Schnitzler's first essay in drama, ANATOL (1893), has proved also his most popular. Granville-Barker prefixes the following note to his version, published in 1911: "It seems that in a faithful translation the peculiar charm of these dialogues will disappear. To recreate it exactly in English one must be another Schnitzler: which is absurd. This is the only excuse I can offer for my paraphrase."

Another version of the play, by Grace Isabel Colbron, was published by Boni & Liveright in the Modern Library in 1917. It is kept in print by Random House today in *Sixteen Famous European Plays* (Modern Library Giant).

DR. KNOCK

DR. KNOCK had its première at the Comédie des Champs Elysées on December 15, 1923, with Louis Jouvet in the title role. Granville-Barker's version was published in England in 1925 and produced in London in the following year with Dennis Eadie as Knock. Granville-Barker prefixes the following note to the first edition: "This version of *Knock* has been done for the theatre, for English actors to play to an English audience. I have had to provide, then, dialogue which could be spontaneously spoken and currently understood. So there are passages—not more than a dozen, I dare say—which have not been literally translated. Some would have called, so, for technical explanation, and there is no place for footnotes on the dramatic page. Some few phrases, harmless enough, would not sound to English ears as they do to French. It is a question of custom. And the translator must always try for an equivalent effect. I confess to a certain elaboration of the stage directions, but this is based upon Monsieur Louis Jouvet's admirable production in Paris. And I do not think my translation betrays any of Monsieur Romains' intentions. I hope not, at least, for I have tried to be most faithful to them." Monsieur Jouvet's own comments are to be found in Appendix B.

SAINT JOAN OF THE STOCKYARDS

SAINT JOAN OF THE STOCKYARDS, having been written in Germany shortly before Hitler came to power, was never performed. The first edition (Berlin, 1932) has an author's note to the following effect: "Experiment 13, *Saint Joan of the Stockyards*, is meant to portray the contemporary stage in the development of Faustian man. The piece originated in the play *Happy End* by Elisabeth Hauptmann. Beyond this, certain classical models and stylistic elements were used: the representation of given events received the form historically appropriate to it. Thus, the intention is to exhibit not only events but the manner of their subjection to the processes of literature and theatre." To which Frank Jones now adds: "*Saint Joan of the Stockyards* is written in four styles: prose, free verse, blank verse, and rhyming verse. This translation tries to reflect these styles as closely as possible. The parts in prose and blank verse proved easiest to handle. In the free verse parts, it was of course impossible to preserve exactly the rhythms of the original, as these depend largely on German word order; but I have tried to reproduce in each line the number of stressed syllables employed by Brecht. In the rhyming verse parts, it was not always feasible to combine literalness in rendering meaning with faithful reproduction of form. The latter, in view of the author's intentions as expressed in the above note, seemed more important." There is a sixty-page chapter on the play in Ernst Schumacher's *Die dramatischen Versuche Bertolt Brechts 1918–1933* (Rutten & Loening, Berlin, 1955). Further comments by Frank Jones are to be found in Appendix C.

INTIMATE RELATIONS

INTIMATE RELATIONS (*Les parents terribles*) had its première at the Théâtre des Ambassadeurs, November 14, 1938. The first English-language production seems to have been that of the Gate Theatre Club (London) two years later. This was a private performance. Public performances were banned in England by the Lord Chamberlain from 1938 to 1951. Mr. Frank's version had its première at the Arts Theatre, London, in March, 1951. Subsequently, Mr. Frank made a film out of his version, while Cocteau made a film of the French original; the latter was shown in America under the title *The Storm Within*. Jean Cocteau's two prefaces appear in an appendix to the present volume.

CECILE, OR THE SCHOOL FOR FATHERS

CECILE, OR THE SCHOOL FOR FATHERS appeared in the volume *Pièces Brillantes*, 1952. In 1953 there was a single private performance in honor of the approaching marriage of Catherine Anouilh, the author's daughter. The official première took place on October 29, 1954, at the Théâtre de la Comédie des Champs-Elysées, the other play on the bill being *Il est important d'être aimé*, a French adaptation of *The Importance of Being Earnest* by Jean Anouilh and Claude Vincent.

THE CRETAN WOMAN

THE CRETAN WOMAN was first published in *Hungerfield and Other Poems* in 1954, and successfully produced in the same year at the Provincetown Playhouse in New York City. Horace Gregory writes: "The quality of this [Aphrodite's] speech equals the speeches in the plays of the Greek dramatists, but it is also singularly modern poetry; the quality of its language is direct and unstrained—no irrelevant effort at meaning is forced into it: the poetic nature of the speech is *there*, and for its purpose cannot be said in any other way; it is evidence enough of the genius of the man who wrote it. *The Cretan Woman* is a far more successful play to read than Jeffers' *Medea;* for his *Medea* opens with a flood of emotional speeches that cannot be sustained throughout the first act, therefore the play is top-heavy, and his readers as well as his audiences are likely to be exhausted long before the final curtain falls. Jeffers' version of Euripides' *Hippolytus* reserves its strength for the last scene and agony of Theseus; and at this conclusion, one believes that Jeffers has lost none of the mastery that he acquired thirty years ago, rather he has set himself the further task of transforming his narrative genius into writing verse for the stage, or perhaps television." (*New World Writing*, 7th Mentor Selection, 1955.)

APPENDIX A: *Author's Preface to Thérèse Raquin*

It is always dangerous, in my opinion, to make a play from a novel. One of them will inevitably be inferior to the other and the result is often detrimental to both. The world of the theatre differs so widely from that of the novel that, in order to fit his intentions into another mold, the author finds himself forced to distort his intentions, to coarsen and disfigure them and in the process possibly to reveal diffuseness or omissions. It is the bed of Procrustes, the bed of torture, and the result is a mutilated monster. Then, too, an artist must show some consideration for the maidenly feelings of his beloved daughters, no matter whether they be ugly or beautiful and when he has projected them into the world he no longer has the right to subject them to the hazards of another birth.

In bringing *Thérèse Raquin* into the theatre, therefore, I am acting against my own creed. Indeed, I hesitated for a long time and if, at long last, I yielded it was because of a certain state of affairs which will at least serve as attenuating circumstances. To begin with, the critics were extremely severe to the novel when it appeared and they challenged me to make a play from it. They regarded the book as utter filth. They dragged it gaily through the gutter and declared that if such vileness were to be paraded on the stage, the hisses of the audience would extinguish the footlights. I am, by nature, extremely curious. I have no dislike of a good scrap and from that moment I promised myself a fine one. The provocation was there. It would have been childish to yield to this desire merely for the chance of giving the lie to the critics; I had a higher motive. It seemed to me that *Thérèse Raquin* offered a dramatic subject for a project of which I had often dreamed. In it I found a collection of people such as I had been seeking, characters who completely satisfied me, in short the components I required and all ready to be used. That decided me.

I certainly do not wish to boast about my play; it has great faults and no one can be severer to them than myself. If I were the critic the only thing that would be left standing would be its definite purpose of helping in the theatre the broad movement of truth and experimental knowledge which in the last century has been growing and spreading throughout the whole field of human intelligence. The impulse has been given by the new scientific methods. Because of them, naturalism has had an effect on criticism and history by submitting man and his works to an exact analysis, taking into account circumstances, environment and physical attributes. Then, too, art and literature have, in their turn, been influenced by this mighty current. Painting has become altogether realistic and our landscape school has killed the historical school. The novel, with its study of groups and individuals, with its flexible form, has gradually absorbed all the various branches of literature as classified by the rhetoricians of old and now covers their whole field. These are facts no one can deny. In the endless progression of new ideas to which mankind has given birth there is now revealed the newborn babe of truth. And that alone is the driving force of the century. Everything progresses and he who wants to go backwards or to escape will be smothered under the dust of all those who are marching forward. That is why I am absolutely convinced that we shall soon see the naturalist movement forced upon the theatre, bringing with it the power of reality, the new life of modern art.

Any innovation in the theatre is an extremely delicate matter and literary revolutions are slow to make themselves felt. The theatre will most probably be the last citadel which truth will have to besiege. The public in the mass do not like to have their customs interfered with and their judgments are as brutal as the death sentence. But there comes a time when the public themselves unconsciously become the accomplices of the innovators. That time is when, weary with the old ways and touched by the new inspiration, they feel the imperious need for freshness and originality.

It is possible that I may be mistaken but it seems to me that the public have now arrived at that point. Drama is at its last gasp; only a blood transfusion can save it. It is said that operetta and fairy plays have killed the drama. That is not true. It is dying a natural death; it is dying of magniloquence, of unreality, of platitudes. If comedy still manages to survive in the midst of this general collapse, it is because it has kept closer to real life and truth. I defy the romantics to put on a cloak and dagger drama; the medieval clanking of old iron, the secret doors, poisoned wines, and the rest of it would convince nobody. Melodrama, that middle-class offspring of the romantic drama, is even more dead and no one wants it any more. Its false sentimentality, its complications of stolen children, recovered documents, its brazen improbabilities, have all brought it into such scorn that any attempt to revive it would be met with laughter. The great works of 1830 will remain as struggles, as literary dates and as colossal attempts to overthrow the old classical traditions. But now it is all thrown overboard and the cloaks and the daggers have had their day. The time has come to produce plays of reality. To put the classical tradition in the place of the romantic would be refusing to profit by the liberty gained for us by our elders. There must no longer be a school, a formula or a high priest of any kind. There is only life, an immense field where each can study and create in his own way.

I am not merely making out an argument for my own cause. It is my profound conviction—and I insist on this point—that the experimental and scientific spirit of the age is going to reach the theatre and that it is from this direction only that that regeneration of our stage can come.

Let the critics look around and tell me any other source from which we can expect a reviving breath of life. The past, indeed, is dead. We must look to the future and the future is the human problem studied within the bounds of reality; it is the abandonment of all legendary tales; it is the living drama of characters and their environments, purged of all nursery tales, historical rag bags, magniloquence, trivialities, and conventional heroics. The rotten framework of the drama of yesterday has brought about its own downfall. There must be a clean sweep. The well-known tricks for introducing and unraveling a plot have been worked to death; what is needed now is a broad and simple portrayal of men and affairs —the kind of drama Molière might have written. Apart from certain conventions which are theatrically necessary, what is today called theatrical technique is nothing but a collection of meaningless little tricks, a sort of narrow tradition which brings the stage into contempt and a code of conventional language which no original mind would stoop to employ.

Furthermore, naturalism is already making its hesitant voice heard in the theatre. I do not want to mention any one work but among plays produced in recent years there are some which contain the germ of the movement of which I have been speaking. Leaving aside for the moment the younger writers I am speaking especially of certain plays by dramatic authors who have grown old in their profession and who are clever enough to have some idea of the literary transformation which is taking place. Either the drama will die or it will become modern and realistic.

It is under the influence of these ideas that I have made a play of *Thérèse Raquin*. As I have said here were a subject, characters, and an environment and I considered that these provided first-class elements for my project. I could make a purely human study free of all irrelevancies and going straight to the target. The action lies not in some story or other but in the inner conflicts of the characters. It was not a matter of portraying facts but of working out feelings and attitudes of mind. The ending became the mathematical solution of a set problem. So I followed the novel step by step. I made the one damp, dark room the setting for the play so that nothing should detract from its atmosphere and sense of fate. I chose ordinary, colorless, subsidiary characters to show the banality of everyday life behind the excruciating agonies of my chief protagonists. In constructing the play I have tried to stress the ordinary occupations of my characters so that they shall not appear to be "acting" but "living" before the public. I was, I confess, counting—and with some reason—on the poignancy of the drama to make the audience accept this absence of plot and this minute attention to detail. The attempt has succeeded and it has made me even happier for my future plays than for *Thérèse Raquin*, for I am publishing this with a vague regret—with a foolish desire to change whole scenes.

There has been stormy criticism and my play has been the subject of violent discussion. I do not complain and I am even grateful for it. I have had my reward in hearing praise of the novel from which it was taken—that novel which, when it appeared, was treated so harshly. Today the novel is good; it is the play that is worthless. It is to be hoped that I can write something else which will be condemned and then perhaps the play will be acclaimed. Now in the matter of criticism one must know how to read between the lines. How, for instance, would it be possible for those old champions of the 1830 drama to be kind to *Thérèse Raquin*? All very well if my haberdasher heroine were a queen and if my murderer wore an apricot-colored jerkin! At the end, too, Thérèse and Laurent should have drunk the poison from a golden cup filled with the wine of Syracuse! Down with this shop-parlor stuff! Down with these common people who permit themselves to be the center of a drama round their oilcloth-covered table! Even if they had discovered some merit in my work, the old romantics would certainly have denied it with the noble injustice of literary passion. Then there are the critics whose beliefs are opposed to mine. These have tried quite honestly to prove me mistaken in following a path which was not theirs. I have read them carefully and I will try to profit by the fair comments which especially struck me. Finally I have to thank those critics who were altogether sympathetic, those of my own age and with similar aspirations—for sad to relate, one rarely finds support among one's elders. We must grow up each with his own generation, impelled forward by those coming after us and finally emerging with the views and methods of our own time. And here is the final balance sheet of the criticism of *Thérèse Raquin*. Both Shakespeare and Paul de Kock have been mentioned; between these two there is room for me to dwell at ease.

It rests for me to express publicly all my gratitude to M. Hippolyte Hostein who has been so good as to give his whole artistic hospitality to my play. I found in him not merely a play producer but a friend, a colleague with a broad and original mind. But for him *Thérèse Raquin* would have remained long at the back of a drawer. To rescue it, it took an unhoped-for meeting with a manager who believed as I did in the necessity for reviving the drama by looking to the realities of the modern world. While an operetta was making one of his neighbors rich, it was magnificent to see M. Hippolyte Hostein in the height of summer, wanting to lose money with my drama. He has my eternal gratitude.

As for the artistes who interpreted the play, they achieved one of the most outstanding successes ever experienced in the theatre. It gave me the greatest joy both to see what I had imagined come to life so fully and also to have given them the opportunity of employing all their wonderful resources. Mme. Marie Laurent in very truth created the part of Mme. Raquin. I claim very little credit for it. It was she who discovered all that there was in that amazing character in Act IV, that towering figure of punishment, mute and relentless, those two living eyes fastened on the guilty pair, never ceasing to watch them even in the throes of death. Her simple good nature in Act I, her Mother's grief in Act II, the terrifying climax of Act III, in all she gave a magnificent performance and this part will remain as one of her most amazing creations. Mlle. Dica-Petit was a Thérèse such as I had never hoped to find. She showed herself possessed of unexpected talent. Even her admirers were surprised at her interpretation of this complex character, this type of passionate woman, a whole world in herself, who goes from frantic love to fierce hatred passing through moods of hypocrisy, disgust, and terror, all the shades of passion and of normal human feelings. The reality of her screams lifted her audience from their seats.—From now on, she is in the first rank of great creative actresses. Still another tremendous part to play is that of Laurent and M. Maurice Desrieux carried it off incomparably. He was in turn that great idle, cautious fellow who loves Thérèse "because she costs him nothing," then the lover whose mistress drives him so mad with love that she makes him a murderer, and then the poor creature refined by suffering and grown cowardly, his mind deranged to the point of hallucination who drifts towards a second crime which is to wipe out the first. Particular mention should be made of his ghastly stupefaction in Acts III and IV, his wild beast moans and all the signs of incipient madness hammering at a man's brain. And it was not only this terrible trio, the mother and the two murderers, who gave good performances. The production was such that the minor roles stood out as I never dared to hope. M. Grivot played the part of Camille, that sickly, spoilt, obstinate creature, with rare intelligence, bringing out the bourgeois miserliness and the sickly health remarkably well. M. Montrouge made an unforgettable type of comic reality of the old clerk Grivet, without ever overstepping the mark and with a tact and finesse just short of caricature, giving evidence of a really cultured mind for which I am infinitely grateful. M. Reykers really got into the skin of the retired police superintendent with the head, walk, and voice, even the mannerisms and the rough good humor of the profession. Finally, Mlle. Blanche Dunoyer was the roguish smile of this dark drama, the music of the sixteen-year-old alternating with the solo of Thérèse, and her telling of the Blue Prince story was exquisite.

I say what a captain should say to his men the day after the battle. My thanks to all these great artistes; it is to them alone I owe the victory.

EMILE ZOLA
(translated by Kathleen Boutall)

APPENDIX B: *Director's Preface to Dr. Knock*

One day, without a word of warning, for he isn't in the habit of talking about his work before it is finished, Jules Romains brought me the play. I read the manuscript standing up, and the author, standing just behind my shoulder, followed the reading and observed my responses.

When we arrived at the last line of the play we were thoroughly satisfied— Jules Romains with my enthusiasm, and I with the fresh perfection of this farce, in which comedy rises so often to lyricism. He listened to my innumerable questions with the astonished pleasure of an author who has just heard the characters he has described speaking for themselves and who sees them beginning to take on a life of their own by way of receding a little from him. A great many ideas and suggestions at once occurred to me. From time to time Jules Romains would reply to one of them—evasively, with a smiling and slightly ironical Why Not? I felt that he was embarrassed, grateful, flabbergasted. In the end he stopped me: "Look, your ideas are very interesting but I can't tell yet exactly how I'd like to see my play performed; I don't know, and I wouldn't know how to explain to you what I want. But during the rehearsals I'll tell you very readily what I don't want. So begin by casting the play, show me the actors you've chosen, and when they start rehearsing it'll be very easy. . . ."

The play was put on in six weeks; the work went smoothly. We felt sure of a literary success though not at all of a "commercial" run. We rather feared we wouldn't be able to keep the play going more than three weeks, much as I liked it and admired it.

Today I am reassured. I've been playing *Dr. Knock* for twenty-five years.*

By its plot and its characters, and because it is about medicine, *Dr. Knock* recalls certain works of Molière. But the two authors are not bound together by this picturesque analogy. What really links them is a transcendent vision that enables both Molière and Jules Romains to pass from the individual to the century, and to grasp a tendency of the times, one of the general aspects of our human condition.

If *Dr. Knock* is "about medicine," it is also true that medicine is a pretext. The work goes beyond the kind of representation in which the medical profession occasionally recognizes its own image or that of colleagues who are suspect. Rather, the parable of *Dr. Knock* illustrates the various threats that have swept over the world during the past half-century.

It is not charlatanism, confidence tricks, "public relations," gullibility, or the prestige of medicine, or the foolishness of patients, that is the real theme. A more important premise and a more essential perception dominate the work—and were no doubt its inspiration. We see how ideas take hold of minds and bodies, how, by an insidious kind of challenge, they gain the mastery over men and enslave them.

Dr. Knock bears witness. It reveals the insensate mechanisms that dominate the

* Written in 1948 for the program of a revival of the play. [E.B.]

world. It demonstrates and lays bare the manufacture of new needs. *Dr. Knock* depicts the founders of nostalgias, and their adherents, corporate and individual.

By an intuition which proved a revelation, Jules Romains placed the audience— his contemporaries—as it were on a balcony or watch-tower from which, clearly and suddenly, they see men against the panorama of a whole era.

The actor who plays this drama and presents the mysterious vocation of Knock or the naïve adventure of Parpalaid feels that he holds in his hands the secret of a true work of art.

If to be classical is to have authority and simplicity and to take the measure of man's scope itself, *Dr. Knock* is a great classical play.

LOUIS JOUVET
(translated by Eric Bentley)

APPENDIX C: *Translator's Preface to Saint Joan of the Stockyards*

Saint Joan of the Stockyards (*Die heilige Johanna der Schlachthöfe*) is perhaps Bertolt Brecht's most ambitious venture in verse drama. His two greatest successes in the theatre, *The Threepenny Opera* and *Rise and Fall of Mahagonny Town*, were significant as contributions to opera; *Saint Joan* he labels a *Schauspiel*, a drama. It is the thirteenth in his series of *Experiments* (*Versuche*) in stage and radio drama, poetry, fiction, and criticism, German publication of which was interrupted in 1933.* The following comments are by way of expatiation on his note to the play.

By 1932 Brecht had tried nearly everything in the theatre: naturalism with symbolic overtones, as in *Drums in the Night;* straight poetic drama, as in *Edward II*, adapted from Marlowe; satirical ballad opera, as in *The Threepenny Opera*, adapted from Gay; and "epic theatre," as in *The Mother*, adapted from Gorki. The range of his adaptation is also that of his experimentation and, in the proper sense, of his originality. His primary concern throughout has been with Left theatre, the Theatre of the People in a revolutionary sense. In seeking the type of drama most vitally demanded by our time Brecht thus mastered severally the styles synthesized in *Saint Joan:* prose naturalism, satirical and parodic use of traditional forms, and dramatic verse modeled on the rhythms of contemporary speech.

The stylistic backbone of *Saint Joan* is the free verse Brecht developed in his experiments of the late Twenties in didactic poetry for reading or recitation. This verse is strongly molded, often periodic, striding. Its Biblical foundations are as clear as those of Whitman's verse. In *Saint Joan* it is employed where the central emotional drives are most emphatic and sincere: in Joan's soliloquies, Mauler's sermon on capitalism, Slift's account of the market crash. Blank and rhymed verse enter when the tycoons' hypocrisy or the salvationists' naïveté subjects the motifs to extravagant transformations. The wildest of these satirical flights employ strict meter, as in Mauler's preposterous plaint about the slaughtered steer, and in the final chorus of Mammon's seraphs, a parody of apotheosis scenes such as the finale of Goethe's *Faust*. Rhyme in freer, cruder rhythms characterizes the Black Straw Hats' pep songs, folksy as the lyrics of *The Threepenny Opera*. When the scene shifts to the class struggle in the stockyards—the stark reality which underlies all these attitudes—the primary medium is prose: a prose of rapid, crackling phrases, bare and harsh as the verse is flexible and suggestive. This style is most strikingly employed in Scene 4, "Joan's Second Descent into the Depths," where the wretched Mrs. Luckerniddle utters her sadness in verse

---

* But continued after the Second World War. This sentence and the one above about Brecht's greatest successes betray the fact that Mr. Jones' preface, like his translation, was written some time ago. In fact, it was originally intended that New Directions should publish them in the wake of *Mother Courage*, which appeared in *New Directions in Prose and Poetry 1941*. Instead, fifteen years have passed, and Brecht has had his biggest theatrical success with *Mother Courage* which has been in the repertoire of the Berlin Ensemble nearly eight years as these words go to press (Summer, 1956). [E.B.]

and her overmastering hunger in prose, and Joan meditates in verse on the lesson she has learned about "the poverty of the poor." This collaboration of styles facilitates numerous dramatically effective transitions and contrasts. Especially striking is the first part of Scene 3, where Mauler begins in his best pompous blank verse, gradually breaks through it in disputing with his competitors, and resumes it when satisfied that he has ruined them.

Thus the play "exhibits not only events, but the manner of their subjection to the processes of literature and theatre." This complex procedure is no mere virtuoso exercise. Brecht's work has always been designed to deepen the spectator's understanding of a social issue and spur him to anger, constructive thought or even action. To this end he has always diversified his appeal. The ideal spectator of *Saint Joan* will be amused by the pompous speeches, roused by its grimly realistic scenes, instructed by the message expressed through the heroine's social education. Clearly the play owes much to Shaw's *Major Barbara;* but the difference is crucial. Shaw's salvationist heroine moves by free choice and argumentative persuasion to a different plane of Reforming Womanhood, an intellectual success—from her and Shaw's point of view—that may leave us cold. Brecht so portrays his heroine that one cannot fail to sympathize to some degree with her deeper predicament, her more tragic failure. His satiric theatre, more Aristophanic than Shavian, transcends both verbal dialectics and reformist sentimentalism.

There is no need here to analyze the dramatic structure of *Saint Joan.* Its rigorous simplicity will be clear to all perceptive readers. But a word may be said about its characterization. Joan and Mauler are among Brecht's most successful creations. In them he has solved the problem of making satire-types credible as human beings. Good satiric drama can be written with pure types, strands in an intellectual pattern: *Mahagonny* is an example. But the best satiric drama has characters on the level of Mauler—the Big Boss figure made at once convincingly human and satirically effective by his absurd emotions, his half-false, half-genuine crises of conscience. His palpable humanity makes genuinely dramatic the conflict between him and the equally credible Joan, whose saintliness, a trifle simple-minded, both nourishes and weakens her value to society.

The translation is less effective in the free verse parts than in those employing blank or rhymed verse. These forms have been preserved in every case but one, Slift's last speech in Scene 5, which rhymes in the original. Here rhymed translation, always difficult, seemed neither possible nor essential. As to the rest, I must beg that blame be at least divided between myself and German sentence-structure, cornerstone of Brecht's free verse, rock of anguish to his translators.

The characters' names call for a concluding comment. Mauler derives from *Maul,* "animal's mouth," and also a slang term for the human mouth. Strictly, therefore, it should be pronounced *mowler, ow* as in *howl;* but plain *mauler,* if preferred, has connotations equally relevant to the character. Joan's surname is a pun on (Jeanne) d'Arc. For the rest—Slift, Luckerniddle, Gloomb, *et al.*—this is not Dickens gone mad, but a foreigner having fun with our quirky nomenclature. Pierpy is hardly a likely nickname for Pierpont, and probably no one but the hero of *The Threepenny Novel* ("A Penny for the Poor") is called Fewkoombey. Such distortions may be taken to typify Brecht's approach to the workaday world—the distortion being in the approach or the world, dear reader, as you please.

FRANK JONES

APPENDIX D: *Author's two prefaces to Intimate Relations*

I. *(written with the play)*

In a modern play, the chief difficulty appears to be to create good theatre while painting a faithful portrait of an eternally drifting society. I have tried to write a drama which is at the same time a comedy, whose fundamentals would be those of a 'vaudeville' if the development of the major scenes and characters were not those of a drama. I was anxious to depict a family whose members were capable of contradicting themselves, of behaving paradoxically; but I was just as anxious to preserve the shape of the play which, in order to leave its mark, must appear to be hewn in one block.

It is much easier to achieve this aim if a leading character never abandons any particular vice or virtue he may possess, and if the lesser parts around him or her never change their line of conduct from start to finish. Therefore, the problem facing these three Acts was to portray people who did not keep on singing the same tune, who were not afraid to change their minds, their moods or their methods, and yet who presented quite naturally one organic whole.

The inevitable result of this method was that the parts had to be sacrificed to the play—thus being of use to it rather than using it for their own ends.

So we find that in the Second Act the mother stands aside to give preference to the young girl, whilst in Act One the young girl does not appear at all except through the image the others have conjured up of her, and that the father shows his real worth only in Act Three, having until then appeared to be egotistical, cruel, and weak.

Two rôles, representing Order and Disorder, form the motivation for this play: the boy, whose disorder is pure, and his aunt whose order is not. I have insisted, as I always do, on remaining a dispassionate observer from the outside, unwilling to defend this cause or that or in any way to take sides. The theatre should be the scene where deeds and thoughts are put into action, no matter whether they be good or bad. In France we are no longer compelled to moralize on the stage. The obstacle to overcome is to find the right style without affectation and with a maximum of simplicity.

Ought I to add that I have invented my characters and that I have not tried to copy anyone I may know? I have given them life by driving to their logical conclusion the chain-reactions of illogical events. I have been helped in this by the voices and inflections and little peculiarities of certain actors known and dear to me for some time.

II. *(written in the theatre)*

Here—without a doubt—is the most delicate and the most dangerous of all my creations. Maybe I should lock myself into a hotel room in Montargis and turn my back on the scandal caused by the production of my play. But how can I? I am the cause of the trouble and the scandal. A scandal only becomes scandalous indeed when it ceases to be spontaneous and wholesome, to become dogmatic, arrogant and, let us admit it, profitable for its instigators.

After the days of Antoine, the sets, the costumes and the gestures were all larger than life. We followed the fashion. The text had become but a means for clever direction. It was time to change the rules of the game.

To retreat into the past is impossible. But to join hands with it subtly can be tempting. I vividly remember the time when the 'Théâtre du Boulevard' reigned supreme. The director of a show was never mentioned. The newly-acquired simplicity of Lucien Guitry and Réjane was as theatrical as the over-acting of Drama's Holy Monsters: Sarah Bernhardt, Mounet-Sully, de Max. In those days, I dreamt of the theatre by way of certain titles of plays, through posters and programmes and the sight of my mother leaving for the theatre in a red velvet gown. I imagined a theatre of my own, and this theatre of my dreams soon took charge of my imagination.

I tried to write a play which was not meant to serve as a vehicle for a director but for some truly great actors. I have always liked the use of sets that play a part: a door allowing Fate to enter and to exit, a chair to accommodate Chance. I hate to overload a play with props and artificial aids. I got rid of them all. I wanted to write a play, naked in its essentials, a play that would allow neither the actors nor the public to get back their breath. I cut out the telephone, letters, servants, cigarettes—I even suppressed surnames. The result of it all was a comedy, a drama, a melodrama, a succession of scenes—each a little act of its own—in which five characters were moving "in camera" beyond good and evil, driven solely by the power of their feelings towards breaking-point.

JEAN COCTEAU
(translated by Charles Frank)

POSTSCRIPT. The following information about Thérèse Raquin came to hand when this book was already in page proof.

"Originally," Miss Boutall writes, "I was commissioned by the administrators of the Old Vic to translate the play, and they allowed me to keep the copyright. It was produced in London under the title of *Guilty* at the Lyric Theatre, Hammersmith, on April 18th, 1944 after a provincial tour. Flora Robson, playing Thérèse was the star and, at Tyrone Guthrie's request, I wrote up her scenes to some extent. . . . Mr. Guthrie, directing the play magnificently, created a convincing period French atmosphere, and his 'business' was superb. The mounting tension of the play was terrific, and the tragedy was thrown into relief by the use made of every ounce of the comedy between the two old men and by the treatment of the character of Camille. Mr. Guthrie stressed the man's naiveté with the result that his stupidity was endearing, and the lovers' crime so much the more horrible. He also changed the ending of the play, cutting out the lovers' deaths, and it was implied that they were to live out their cat-and-dog lives under the accusing eyes of Mme. Raquin. This feature was not altogether convincing; as such a tragedy on the stage seems to require a definite and not an implied ending."

In preparing her script for this anthology, Miss Boutall cancelled Mr. Guthrie's changes and restored her earlier, faithful rendering.